DIMENSIONS OF BLACK CONSERVATISM IN THE UNITED STATES

MADE IN AMERICA

EDITED BY GAYLE T. TATE
AND LEWIS A. RANDOLPH

palgrave

DIMENSIONS OF BLACK CONSERVATISM IN THE UNITED STATES
© Gayle T. Tate and Lewis A. Randolph, 2002

First published 2002 by PALGRAVE™
175 Fifth Avenue, New York, N.Y.10010 and
Houndmills, Basingstoke, Hampshire RG21 6XS.
Companies and representatives throughout the world.

PALGRAVE is the new global publishing imprint of St. Martin's Press LLC
Scholarly and Reference Division and Palgrave Publishers Ltd (formerly
Macmillan Press Ltd).

ISBN 0–312–23861–4 hardback
ISBN 0–312–29370–4 paperback

Library of Congress Cataloging-in-Publication Data
Dimensions of Black conservatism : made in America / edited by Gayle T. Tate and
Lewis A. Randolph.
    p. cm.
    Includes bibliographical references and index.
    ISBN 0–312–23861–4 (cloth)—ISBN 0–312–29370–4 (pbk.)
    1. African Americans—Politics and government. 2. Conservatism—United States.
3. African Americans—Civil rights. 4. African Americans—Social conditions.
5. African American politicians. 6. African American intellectuals. 7. United
States—Race relations—Political aspects. I. Tate, Gayle T. II. Randolph, Lewis A.

E185.D46 2001
320.52'089'96073—dc21

                                                                    2001044657

A catalogue record for this book is available from the British Library.

Design by Letra Libre, Inc.

First edition: May 2002
10 9 8 7 6 5 4 3 2 1

Printed in the United States of America.

In
Memory
of

Rhonda M. Williams
1957–2000

and to

Marietta L. Matthews, Adriane M. Livingston,
and Adah Ward Randolph

for their courage, wit, and wisdom

CONTENTS

PART IV
STRUGGLE, CLASS, AND IDEOLOGY

NOTES ON THE CONTRIBUTORS

JAMES JENNINGS is Professor of Political Science in the Department of Urban and Environmental Policy at Tufts University and a Research Associate with the William Monroe Trotter Institute at the University of Massachusetts in Boston. He has published numerous articles in such varied journals as *Review of Black Political Economy, Social Science Journal, National Political Science Review, Urban Affairs Review, PS (Political Science and Politics)*, and the *Annals of the American Academy of Political and Social Science*. He is the author, editor, or coeditor of *Puerto Rican Politics in Urban America* (1984); *The Politics of Empowerment: Transformation of Black Activism in Urban America* (1992); *Race, Politics, and Black Economic Development: Community Perspectives* (1992); *Blacks, Latinos, and Asians in Urban America: Status and Prospects for Activism* (1994); *Understanding the Nature of Poverty in Urban America* (1994); *Race and Politics in the United States: New Challenges and Responses* (1997); *An Introduction to Poverty: The Role of Race, Power, and Wealth* (1999); *A New Introduction to Poverty: The Role of Race, Power, and Politics* (1999); and *Racism: Essential Readings* (forthcoming).

RHETT S. JONES, Professor of History and Afro-American Studies at Brown University, is interested in the study of race in the Americas before the nineteenth century. Although he has written over thirty articles on eighteenth-century African American and Caribbean history, his recently published work focuses on African American/Native American relations. His recent articles include "Subverting the Master Narrative: Paradigms for the Study of Native American and African American Relations" (1999); "Indian/Black Relations in the Americas: Past Paradigms, Future Possibilities" (2001); and "Native American/ African American Relations: An Overview of the Scholarship" (2001). He chaired Brown University's Afro-American Studies Program for twelve years, and from 1991 to 1995 served as director of the University's Center for the Study of Race and Ethnicity in America.

MARCUS D. POHLMANN is Professor of Political Science and Chair of the Department of Political Science at Rhodes College in Memphis, Tennessee. His work has been published in the *Urban Affairs Review, Urban Affairs Quarterly, National Forum, Journal of Sociology and Social Welfare, Political Science Quarterly*, and *Journal of Urban Affairs*. He is the author of several books including *Political Power in the Industrial City* (1986); *Black Politics in Conservative America* (1990 and 1999); *Governing the Post Industrial City* (1993); *African American Political Thought: An Anthology* (Forthcoming); *Landmark Congressional Laws on Civil Rights* (Forthcoming); and *Pursuing Power:*

Black Political Thought in the Twentieth Century (Forthcoming). He is the co-author of *Racial Politics at the Crossroads: Memphis Elects Dr. W. W. Herrenton* (1996).

LEWIS A. RANDOLPH is an Associate Professor of Political Science at Ohio University at Athens. He has published in such disparate journals as *Proteus, the Western Journal of Black Studies*, the *Review of Black Political Economy*, and the *Journal of Black Studies*. He has co-authored *Rights for a Season: Race, Class and Gender in a Southern City, Richmond, Virginia* (with Gayle T. Tate) to be published in Spring 2003; and the forthcoming *What Ever Happened to Black Capitalism: The Rise and Fall of Richard M. Nixon's Plan for Black America* (with Robert E. Weems, Jr.).

SHERRI SMITH, former Assistant Professor of Communication Arts at the University of Alabama in Huntsville, currently works in NASA's Media Relations Office. Her research interests focus on diversity issues, specifically interracial and intraracial communication, and gender and communication. Actively involved in the Ala-Hunt chapter of the American Business Women's Association, Dr. Smith's other civic interests include prison education and mental health care reforms.

JAMES B. STEWART is a Professor of Labor Studies and Industrial Relations and African and African American Studies at Penn State University. He previously served as Vice Provost for Educational Equity and Director of the Black Studies Program. He has published over forty articles in economics and black studies professional journals. He is the author, co-author, editor, or co-editor of six monographs, including *Black Families: Interdisciplinary Perspectives; The Housing Status of Black Americans; Research on the African American Family: A Holistic Perspective; Blacks in Rural America; W. E. B. DuBois on Race and Culture: Philosophy, Politics, and Poetics;* and *African American and Post-Industrial Labor Markets.* He has served as editor of *The Review of Black Political Economy* and president of the National Economic Association and is currently President of the National Council for Black Studies.

GAYLE T. TATE is an Assistant Professor of Political Science in the Department of Africana Studies at Rutgers University. She has previously served as Chairperson of the Department of Africana Studies. Her published articles have appeared in the *Western Journal of Black Studies, Women & Politics*, the *National Political Science Review, Urban Affairs Annual Review, ABAFAZI, Third World in Perspective, Black Women's History at the Intersection of Knowledge and Power*, and the *Journal of Black Studies*. Her work has also appeared in several encyclopedias including *Black Women in America: An Historical Encyclopedia*. She was an associate editor for *Africana: An Introduction & Study*. She is the author of *Unknown Tongues: Black Women's Political Activism in the Antebellum Era, 1830–1860*, to be published in Fall 2002, and co-author of *Rights for a Season: Race, Class, and Gender in a Southern City, Richmond, Virginia* (with Lewis A. Randolph) to be published in Spring 2003.

ROSALYN TERBORG-PENN is Professor of History and the Coordinator of Graduate Programs in History at Morgan State University in Baltimore. She was one of the early pioneers in black women's history, black women's suffrage in particular, and has published over forty articles in history and women's studies professional journals and anthologies. She is the author or co-editor of several books, including *Afro-American*

Women: Struggles and Images (1978 & 1998); *Women in Africa and the African Diaspora* (1987); *Black Women in America: An Historical Encyclopedia* (1993); *African American Women in the Struggle for the Vote, 1850–1920* (1998); and *Black Women 's History at the Intersection of Knowledge and Power* (2000). She is a founder and first National Director of the Association of Black Women Historians.

HANES WALTON, JR., is a Professor of Political Science at the University of Michigan. His current areas of interest are African American politics, presidential elections, and public policy. He has published numerous articles on black politics. His major books include: *Negro in Third Party Politics* (1969); *Political Philosophy of Martin Luther King, Jr.,* (1971); *Black Political Parties: An Historical and Political Analysis* (1972); *Study and Analysis of Black Politics: A Bibliography* (1973); *Black Republicans: the Politics of the Black and Tan* (1975); *Invisible Politics: Black Political Behavior* (1985); *When the Marching Stopped: the Politics of Civil Rights Regulatory Agencies* (1988); *Native Son Presidential Candidate: The Carter Vote in Georgia* (1992); *Black Politics and Black Political Behavior: A Linkage Analysis* (1994); *African American Power and Politics: the Political Context Variable* (1997); *Reelection: William Jefferson Clinton as a Native-son Presidential Candidate* (2000); and *American Politics and the African American Quest for Universal Freedom* (2000).

ROBERT E. WEEMS, JR., is Professor of History at the University of Missouri at Columbia. Born and raised in Chicago, Illinois, he received his Ph.D. from the University of Wisconsin at Madison. His publications include the following books: *Black Business in the Black Metropolis: The Chicago Metropolitan Assurance Company, 1925–1985; Desegregating the Dollar: African American Consumerism in the Twentieth Century;* and *The African American Experience: An Historiographical and Bibliographical Guide* (co-edited with Arvarh E. Strickland). He is the co-author (with Lewis A. Randolph) of a forthcoming book entitled *Whatever Happened to Black Capitalism: The Rise and Fall of Richard M. Nixon's Plan for Black America.*

OSCAR R. WILLIAMS is an Assistant Professor of History at The State University of New York at Albany. He received his Ph.D. in American History from Ohio State University in 1997. He is the author of "George S. Schuyler: Portrait of a Conservative," in *Africana: An Introduction and Study* (1999); and "From Black Liberal to Black Conservative: George S. Schuyler, 1923–1935," in *Afro-Americans in New York Life and History* (1997). He is currently writing a biography of Schuyler.

RHONDA M. WILLIAMS was an Associate Professor of Economics and Afro-American Studies at the University of Maryland at College Park. She became the Acting Director of the Department of Afro-American Studies in 1999. She graduated cum laude from Harvard-Radcliffe College in 1978 and received her Ph.D in Economics from M.I.T in 1983. She was a political economist noted especially for her work on occupational segregation, wage differentials, social outcomes, wealth, and affirmative action. Her 1996 study, "A Logic Decomposition Analysis of Occupational Segregation: Results for the 1970s and 1980s," was published in the *Review of Radical Political Economics.* She co-edited *Race, Market and Social Outcomes* in 1997. She authored *Beyond Capital: Black Women, Work, and Wages,* as well as two of the nine reports composing the National Urban League's 1999 *State of Black America* report. Beyond her scholarly contributions, she was celebrated for her excellence in teaching by her students; her selflessness by her colleagues; and her inspiration and activism to make the world a better place. She died of lung cancer on November 7, 2000.

FRANK HAROLD WILSON is an Associate Professor of Sociology and Urban Studies at the University of Wisconsin at Milwaukee. He has written several articles on such varied issues as urban inequality, housing, gentrification, poverty, and African American population. His book, *Race, Class, and the Post Industrial City: William Julius Wilson and the Promise of Sociology* is forthcoming.

ACKNOWLEDGMENTS

This volume was the brainchild of Talmadge Anderson, the founding editor of the Western Journal of Black Studies, who believed that the historical, economic, and political dimensions of black conservatism required continuous exploration and analysis. To that end, we gathered together a group of contributing scholars who have made immeasurable contributions, in many ways, to this collective endeavor. We also owe a debt of gratitude to a number of other enthusiastic supporters, including Ernest M. Tate, Jr., Eartha Tate, Charles Tutler, Ruth Ernestine Tutler, Juanita Glasgow, Gloria Burroughs, Lillie Johnson Edwards, Geraldyne Pemberton-Diallo, Shirley Traylor, Elton A. Beckett, Mel Gary, Sheila Jean Walker, William Davis, Jr., Stacia Murphy, William Jordan, Melva D. Burke, Donald Ames, and Gwen Parker Ames, all of whose highly spirited discourse, resources, and archival materials on contemporary black politics contributed to our perspectives. Georgia A. Persons provided invaluable insight, commentary, and analysis on the current political environment facilitating the resurgence of black conservatism. Mary Louise Byrd and Patty Zimmerman provided critical editing of many chapters, improving their overall quality in each instance. Barbara Jo Mitchell contributed her expertise on current computer software which made our job easier.

Karen Wolny, former Senior Editor of St. Martin's Press, provided initial support for the project and Assistant Editor Ella Pearce patiently moved the book from its embryonic stages to completion. To all, we thank you.

INTRODUCTION

GAYLE T. TATE AND LEWIS A. RANDOLPH

With the increasingly visible stratum of black neoconservatives as prominent voices in the body politic, scholars are now revisiting the issue of their significance in black political and social thought as well as the critical implications they pose for African Americans seeking new political alternatives and strategies in this post-civil rights era. Black neoconservatives (the term delineating the rise of black conservatives since the Fairmount Conference in San Francisco, California, in 1980) have distinguished themselves with rhetorical positions that counter racial realities in American society, media visibility, and financial and ideological ties to conservative think tanks, institutions, and foundations, all of which have the combined potential for reshaping the political discourse and future social action in the black community. Just as important, the nature of black neoconservatives' political discourse, particularly their antiliberal stance, may support the political environment for social welfare policies that adversely impact African Americans, women, the poor, and other minorities. Political scientist Mack Jones, commenting on the significance of black conservatives, notes that "[t]he political thought of the new Black conservatives as an important factor could influence the course of the Black struggle for equality in the United States."[1]

Black conservatism has evolved over the centuries, with disparate meanings depending on the time, opportunity, and political condition of African Americans. However, there has been no clear definition of conservatism, and scholars tend to focus on their own ideological perspectives rather than the ambiguities of its meaning. Scholars in this volume are not of one mind either, instead pointing to the complexities in terminology as well as meanings. Jack C. Plano and Milton Greenberg, in *The American Political Dictionary*, note that conservatives are "consistently opposed to governmental regulation of the economy and civil rights legislation, and in favor of state over federal action, fiscal responsibility and decreased governmental spending and lower taxes."[2]

This book seeks to provide both a historical and a contemporary political and ideological framework for the discussion of black conservative thought and praxis. One of the major emphases is on the rise of black neoconservatives since the 1980s. Despite the inherent limitations in attempting to encompass the range of thought and perspectives of black neoconservatives, we have identified four major generalizations about black neoconservatives:

1. They are restructuring the public discourse on black issues by shifting the onus of responsibility on African Americans for their political and economic plight; appealing to whites by denying their culpability in the existing superordinate-subordinate race relations in society; and strengthening their individual and group political and economic alliances with the American conservative movement.
2. They have decisively shifted the terrain of the political discourse from the expansion of civil rights gains to the elimination of those gains by negating racism, sexism, and impoverishment as historical and contemporary determinants in the lives of African Americans.
3. They seek to destabilize the post-civil rights leadership (dubbed the "civil rights establishment") and replace their liberal/progressive critique of systematic discrimination with a discourse on black cultural traditions and values as sources of black inequality.
4. They hope to become the critical voice of new leadership in the black community and ultimately sway a decisive percentage of the black electorate to the Republican Party.

Like most white conservatives, black neoconservatives loosely fall into three main ideological camps, antistatists, organics, and neoconservatives (a subcomponent of the total group of neoconservatives), of the Republican Party. According to Dolbeare and Metcalf, these three ideological perspectives, although dominated by antistatists and organics, most ably represent American conservatism.[3] Historically, the antistatist perspective represents a variation of eighteenth-century Manchester Liberalism, which derived its name from the Manchester (England) School of Thought.[4] As the term implies, those who espoused an antistatist perspective advocate a restrictive role of government, particularly in the areas of social welfare policy and implementation and the economic marketplace, and favor an increased reliance on individual initiatives.[5] Although most antistatists are in opposition to imposing quotas to remedy historic forms of discrimination, some do support the limited implementation of affirmative action programs, such as minority set-asides, and of minority-hiring preferences to promote diversity. This support can be deceptive at times, however, particularly on the local levels, where contractors vying for projects are encouraged to financially support the Republican Party.

David Gergen, former advisor to ex-presidents Nixon, Ford, Reagan, and Clinton, posits that the antistatists represent the "establishment," or the moderate wing, of the Republican Party.[6] Known as the "old right," and producing such prominent Republican leaders as Dwight D. Eisenhower, Richard M. Nixon, and Nelson D. Rockefeller, this wing of the party held sway over national Republican politics until the mid-1960s. In the mid-1960s, the leadership of the antistatist was supplanted by the ultraconservative movement spearheaded by Barry Goldwater and remained in power through the election of Ronald Reagan.[7] The established black conservatives prior to the 1980s, such as Massachusetts Senator Edward Brooks, were identified with this moderate wing of the Republican Party.

The most prominent black antistatists since 1980s include Eileen M. Gardner, Glenn Loury, Thomas Sowell, and Walter Williams. Mostly academicians, this group of black antistatists is much more conservative than the black antistatists of the 1960s and 1970s. Typically, all these conservatives are opposed to government intervention in solving the plight of the poor. Centering their critique on the black urban poor, the most vulnerable members of the society and the ones that can easily generate public condemnation by the tax-burdened middle-class, black antistatists believe that the liberal policies known as the Great Society programs, such as busing, affirmative action, expenditures for public assistance, and quotas, have failed. Left in its wake has been an increased dependency among African Americans and a paucity of moral values, which has weakened the moral fiber of the black community. For Loury, middle-class blacks, not government, can best provide the economic assistance and moral guidance that will empower the black community.[8] Gardner argues that a reversal of educational policies (busing, preferential treatment, and quotas), with a stronger emphasis on rising educational standards, strict behavioral standards among students, and competent teachers, would eliminate the need for government intervention in education.[9] Both Williams and Sowell emphasize the marketplace as the vehicle by which blacks can address their economic plight and gradually gain acceptance by whites.[10] In essence, these antistatists believe that if backs simply work harder, and place more emphasis on achievement rather than the historical and contemporary racial constraints—enslavement, segregation, and racial profiling—and the struggle for social equality, they will ameliorate most of their problems.

Organic conservatives have their roots in the traditional conservatism of Edmund Burke and the fundamental interpretation of Protestantism in early America.[11] Steeped in religious piety as a social, moral, and political barometer, organic conservatives are known as the "religious far right," the ultraconservative wing of the Republican Party. Although their fundamental beliefs have been honed in Christianity and traditional family values, organics offer few redemptive qualities for those left out of the traditional interpretations of societal laws and policies, namely, women, minorities, and the poor. Thus, the organics have gained considerable media visibility in their opposition to liberal or reform policies and programs that are more, rather than less, inclusive. In the 1960s, for example, organic conservatives were strident in their opposition to the Civil Rights Act of 1964 and the Voting Rights Act of 1965, and they have been equally vehement against the extension of these laws. Although they are clearly not the only voice in opposition to liberal reform measures, they are strong supporters of the death penalty but oppose gun control, the Equal Rights Amendment (ERA), abortions, affirmative action, and school desegregation through busing. Their intricate network of foundations, think tanks, institutions, radio and television talk shows, and publishing houses have strengthened and promoted their ideological positions.

Black organics espouse the same positions and beliefs of their white counterparts. This group of conservatives includes Joe Clark, Keith Butler, Elizabeth Wright, Armstrong Williams, Anne Wortham, Alan Keyes, and J. A. Parker. Some scholars criticize black organics, and indeed black conservatives in general for "toadyism" (note chapter 1, "Black Creole Cultures: The Eighteenth-Century Origins of African American Conservatism," by Rhett S. Jones): in addition, the concentration of their critique on the black community obfuscates the culpability of whites for the perpetuation of racism in society. Although all black conservatives emphasize traditional family values, which is the touchstone of the conservative movement, black organics see this as central to their ideological position. They argue that traditional family values, guided by a moral compass, could reverse the hopelessness in inner city communities, inculcate a strong moral fiber and work ethic, and restore the emphasis on black family life.[12] Joseph Perkins, for example, believes that black despair can be reversed by simply "reviving . . . traditional black values . . . and strong moral values shaped by a deep sense of community and religious faith."[13] Negating the material realities that circumscribe the lives of urban blacks, these black organics "blame the victims" for their fate and locate their material problems as deficiencies within the black family and community life. Making blacks responsible for the larger complex issues of poverty, drugs, family cohesiveness, morality, and work ethics, issues that are clearly pervasive in the larger society, fosters a sense of white complacency while simultaneously obfuscating the need for a clear national agenda on social problems.

Neoconservatives, the third type of conservatives, are principally former liberals who were disillusioned with the liberal social agenda of the 1960s and 1970s and are now opposed to liberalism in general, and more specifically, to the government expansion of the welfare state. This group is loosely comprised of former black power advocates, progressive liberals, socialists and communists.[14] Although they strongly emphasize "family values," the traditional party rhetoric that serves to counterpoint the Democratic Party and its present image of loose morality, this group's primary focus is on meritocracy (although they will probably have to revamp their notions of meritocracy considering President George W. Bush's own admission to being a "C" student) and are in opposition to quotas, affirmative action, and minority set-aside programs. Similar to the organics and the antistatists, the neoconservatives also make political and economic alliances with white conservatives.

Black neoconservatives, a group that includes Shelby Steele, Robert Woodson, Roy Innis, Tony Brown, Clarence Thomas, and Stephen Carter, believe that the economic marketplace is the key to upward mobility for African Americans. Undergirding this capitalist thrust is their argument that in order to be successful, blacks must transcend the notion of racial barriers. As all conservatives do, black neoconservatives take a jaundiced view of government support, seeing it as government handouts, and believe that African Americans need a good dose of "do-for-yourselfism."[15] Some of the neoconservatives are recent converts to the conservative movement and have quickly become able to gain media visibility by emphasizing traditional family values, the ineffectiveness of affirmative action, and the viability of capitalism for all Americans. They are also quick to stress merit and individual responsibility, appealing to the stereotypical notions of blacks held by largely white audiences. Their rhetoric places them in direct opposition to the post–civil rights leadership and the existing liberal stance on affirmative action. Stephen Carter, for example, argues that affirmative action perpetuates the "best black syndrome" namely, "[W]e'll tolerate so-and-so at our hospital or in our firm or on our faculty, because she's the best black."[16] Like the organics, however, they see strong family values as the vehicle for economic prosperity and racial equality. And similar to all other black conservatives, black neoconservatives are generally uncritical of the capitalist system and of racial and gender discrimination, and they frequently offer nonracial interpretations of blatant racist incidents.

Overall, black conservatism has been viewed with a great deal of skepticism in the black community. Although black conservatives have always been an integral part of black political and social thought, many blacks have regarded them with a jaundiced eye. In general, black conservatives experience a marked resurgence whenever there is a shift in the economic mode of production, a need for a political and economic alliance between black and white conservatives, a vacuum in black political leadership, or a combination of these factors. Black neoconservatives are not recognized as a part of the long legacy of conservative thought among blacks, but rather as a separate entity that has been "grafted on" to black political and social thought. This perception of being "grafted on" and not being an intrinsic part of the community's dialogue has aroused the ire of the black community.

The critique or upbraiding of the black community by black neoconservatives is also problematic. One of the major cornerstones of their rhetoric is "self-reliance," but in reality, their heavy financial dependence on conservative funding for jobs, media exposure, research monies, publications, and other "self-help initiatives" points to what Hanes Walton, Jr., Robert Smith, and Deborah Toler view as "patron-client" politics, namely, being bought and paid for by the Republican Party.[17] Second, black neoconservaives seek to dismantle affirmative action, which would eventually shrink the black middle class, the very group that is integral to their "self-help initiatives" in the black community. Third, many black neoconservatives have benefited from affirmative action initiatives. Ward Connerly, a member of the University of California Board of Regents, received millions of dollars from the state's Department of Energy's weatherization program as the owner of a minority-owned business.[18] Finally, there is a perception by blacks that this dialogue of black conservatives is separate and apart from the black community. For example, Martin Kilson and Cornel West have argued that black neoconservatives constitute an inauthentic voice with no discernible ties to the black community.[19]

HISTORICAL AND CONTEMPORARY PERSPECTIVES

Conservatism has been infused in black political and social thought for over two hundred years. In locating the origins of black conservatism, Hanes Walton, Jr., states that "the roots of Black conservatism are ambiguous and complex," but purely possessed of American origins. "Thus, for all intents and purposes then Black conservatism emerged on the American continent."[20] Rhett S. Jones, in chapter 1, "Black Creole Cultures: The Eighteenth Century Origins of African American Conservatism," traces the origins of black conservatism. Jones argues that the early Afro-British, who were property owners in the 1600s on Virginia's eastern shore and had conflicting values with the incoming Africans, may have constituted the first black conservatives in the colonial society. Although the Afro-British emulated their white counterparts, incoming African slaves had a different environmental response to the burgeoning slave institution in which they found themselves struggling for their lives. As enslaved Africans created their own transatlantic culture for survival and endurance, the culture became a vehicle for the struggle against slavery and oppression. As the slave institution developed and slaves increasingly began to focus on resistance, the conservatism of the Afro-British declined in importance, although it also began to take root within the slave community. By the eighteenth and nineteenth centuries, blacks had shaped a number of responses to oppression and black conservatism was firmly intertwined in the black struggle for freedom.

Robert E. Weems, Jr., in chapter 2, "The American Moral Reform Society and the Origins of Black Conservative Ideology," traces the conservative ethos of the American Moral Reform Society (AMRS) in the antebellum era. Founded in 1835, the

AMRS was comprised of a group of middle-class black men in Philadelphia, who began to retreat from the racial designation of "African" in favor of the more racially muted "colored" in the hopes of achieving racial integration. These men believed that they could make themselves acceptable to whites with an emphasis on educational uplift and morality as well as espousing universal themes of brotherhood. Samuel Cornish, the editor of *The Colored American* of New York City, used the paper to chided the men on their lack of racial pride and dignity. Cornish was speaking for the black community which perceived these men as having acquiesced to the white power structure. Similar to contemporary conservatives, antebellum conservatives viewed whites as the arbiters of character and morality and sought to appease their racial fears. The men in the AMRS encouraged blacks to work for moral reform, believing that it was linked to decreasing racial prejudice and increasing white acceptance of blacks. The efforts of the AMRS to incorporate white members in their organization failed, and the organization expired in 1841.

Chapter 3, "There is no refuge in conservatism: A Case Study of Black Political Conservatism in Richmond, Virginia" by Gayle T. Tate and Lewis A. Randolph, explores the evolutionary path of black conservatism in Richmond, Virginia, starting with its emergence as individual opportunism by those slaves who believed that an alliance with the master would yield material rewards.[21] By the antebellum era, free blacks and slaves from surrounding plantations were major laborers in Richmond's industrialization process, working in its tobacco factories, iron foundries, flour mills, and domestic service. Although slaves were able to keep only a modicum of their wages, they were able to keep all of their overtime bonuses, thus earning enough to spearhead the development of the city's black community. Prominently featured in the community for sacred and subversive development were five black churches which would become autonomous immediately after the war. The class, color, and ideological cleavages between free blacks and slaves, carryovers from slavery, ebbed and flowed throughout the postemancipation period and resurfaced in the post–civil rights era, when a coalition of black and white conservatives destabilized a progressive black majority council that had established a base of power.

Despite Booker T. Washington's legacy of black political conservatism, which deemphasized the political struggle for racial equality and persisted long after his death in 1915, prominent voices of resistance such as William Monroe Trotter, Ida B. Wells-Barnett, and W. E. B. DuBois continued unabated. As Rosalyn Terborg-Penn notes in chapter 4, "The Politics of the Anti-Woman Suffrage Agenda: African Americans Respond to Conservatism," black women political activists sought out the voters in order to further their cause of social equality for all African Americans. Black suffragettes formed many clubs and initiatives that had numerous functions such as educating black women concerning the vote, supporting candidates in favor of women's suffrage, and forming tentative coalitions with white women to press for the passage of the Nineteenth Amendment. In the midst of this political movement, black women encountered black and white conservatives who were hostile to their efforts, believing that they should be relegated to more traditional gender roles, and be denied the vote, as they were too inferior to vote in their own interests.

The problems of gender, black women, and conservatism persist into the twenty-first century and are symptomatic of not only the sexism inherent in the rhetoric and ideology but the elitism as well. Rhonda M. Williams argues in chapter 5, "If it ain't broke, don't fix it: Thomas Sowell on Black Women, Affirmative Action, and the Death of Discrimination," that Thomas Sowell negated the operation of racism and sexism as factors in the economic marketplace. Rather, he constructed an idealized version of the marketplace, using academe "circa 1969 to 1973" as his case study, in which economic discrimination is short-lived at best because it is irrational in a competitive marketplace that focuses on profit accumulation. Equally, for Sowell, sexism is not a function of the marketplace; rather, "the gender-based division of labor in heterosexual families is the fundamental cause of women's labor-market problems."[22] But as Williams points out, Sowell's analysis of gender-based discrimination in the marketplace applies to white women only; he is totally silent on the labor experiences of black women. Having dismissed the primary forces that inspired affirmative action policies and initiatives, Sowell then dismissed the policy itself as superfluous and unnecessary

In upbraiding the black community for its moral decay and lack of work ethic and individual responsibility, black neoconservatives are implicitly taking aim at black women as well as black men. James B. Stewart, in chapter 6, "The Neo-Conservatives Assault on Black Males: Origins, Objectives, and Outcomes," argues that black neoconservatives have a faulty conceptualization of black males, which contributes to the marginalization of black men in society. For Stewart, the construction of an idealized white nuclear family as the norm poses problems for black families which are then viewed as dysfunctional even though many families, black and white, do not fit into the idealized construction. With black neoconservatives eliminating, transcending, or dismissing slavery, racism, and oppression as past phenomena that are no longer relevant, black males must now bear the burden of being characterized as failures for their inability to surmount the external factors that plague their lives. Unable to fit into the idealized white family construct that has been popularized by the Republican Party and the media, African American males are instead demeaned, caricatured, and viewed as predators in urban society. The "Willie Horton" criminal imagery of black males, concomitant with the disfiguring images of black women as "welfare queens," acts effectively to counter progressive social welfare policies.

Many blacks now view the rhetoric of black neoconservatives with growing consternation. Historically, blacks have viewed black conservatives as an anomaly, but their prominence at a decisive point when there is a vacuum in the national black political leadership has generated a web of suspicion. Chapter 7, Sherri Smith's "The Individual Ethos: A Defining Characteristic of Contemporary Black Conservatism," examines the political rhetoric of black neoconservatives, in terms of, first, their personal transformation and then, second, the utilization of the ideology as a persuasive element in African American politics. The personal transformation ultimately leading to a construction of a new identity is a transcending of racial barriers that effectively renders the black community powerless. Once black neoconservatives have transcended race and experienced a new sense of freedom, they now have the "individual reasoning and honesty" to effectively critique the black community. With the aid of new insights on poverty, self-reliance, individual incentives, and capitalism, all wrapped in the mantle of conservatism as promoted by the Republican Party, the black community can then experience a similar transformation. The obvious tension, Smith argues, is that if black neoconservatives focus on the "individual ethos" in their effort to eliminate "the traditional civil rights advocates and black nationalists as legitimate leaders of the African American community," how can they hope to appeal to a collective community?

According to Hanes Walton, Jr., in chapter 8, "Remaking African American Public Opinion: The Role and Function of the African American Conservatives," the rhetoric of black neoconservatives serves a political function for the Republican Party. The development of this political alliance was intrinsic to the new "Republican Strategy" to lure 10 percent of the black voting electorate to the party to ensure decisive political victories in upcoming elections. The genesis of this partnership, Walton posits, was formalized at the 1980 conference (recognized as the Fairmount Conference), at the Institute of Contemporary Studies, a conservative research organization, whose purpose was to identify approximately 125 black professionals, entrepreneurs, and intellectuals to: (1) create new black Republican leadership in the black community; (2) promote these hand-picked conservatives as spokespersons for the African American community, and (3) utilize their new status to generate black community support for the Republican Party. In addition to molding and shaping public opinion, the black neoconservatives would supplant existing post-civil rights leadership.

Chapter 9, Oscar R. Williams Jr.'s study of George Schuyler entitled "The Lonely Iconoclast: George Schuyler and the Civil Rights Movement," provides us with a lens on the complexities of black conservatism prior to the 1980s. In the 1930s and 1940s, Schuyler advocated liberal and left-wing sympathies particularly as he countered New Deal policies believing that they had been largely ineffectual in ameliorating the plight of African Americans during the depression. By the 1950s, Schuyler was becoming increasingly more controversial in the black community and more conservative writing such pamphlets as *The Communist Conspiracy Against the Negroes* and for conservative magazines including *American Mercury* and the *National Review.* By then Schuyler's conservatism was evident, and his subsequent membership in the John Birch Society reinforced his beliefs. Schuyler's position was in marked contrast to the early civil rights mobilization efforts of the African American community. Many conservatives did not verbally oppose the civil rights movement for fear of being labeled race traitors; Schuyler, however, not only denounced the movement as communist propaganda but his vitriolic attacks on Martin Luther King, Jr., led to his separation from the black newspaper the *Pittsburgh Courier,* after a forty-year association. Although Schuyler subsequently wrote for the ultraconservative *Manchester Union-Leader,* by the mid-1960s he was a lone conservative voice as African Americans pinned their hopes on Democratic Party candidate Lyndon B. Johnson.

Chapter 10, Frank Harold Wilson's "Neoconservatives, Black Conservatives and the Retreat from Social Justice," examines the interlocking components that have been put in place by white conservatives in promoting black neoconservatives to national prominence. Wilson argues that this conservative apparatus of think tanks, foundations, institutions, and publishing houses has contributed to mainstreaming black neoconservatives into positions of high visibility, where they have become household words in the popular culture. Wilson contends that conservative think tanks such as the Hoover Institute on War, Revolution, and Peace; the American Enterprise Institute, and the Heritage Foundation award black neoconservatives fellowships, consultant work, and important staff and administrative positions. Although conservative publications such as the *Wall Street Journal* play a major role in publishing the critiques of black conservatives, the liberal press features their works as well. Coupled with their access to the media and being recognized as radio and television personalities, black neoconservatives are being given legitimacy and validation by the white community far beyond their numbers and meager influence in the black community.

The ideological perspective of black conservatives rests on the elitism and class consciousness inherent in the white male-dominated Republican Party. In chapter 11, Marcus D. Pohlmann, "Black Conservatives and Class Relations," argues that black conservatives' notion that everyone willing to work hard in America can prosper is a flawed one. In fact, Pohlmann posits, the system of "mixed capitalism" not only reinforces existing class relations but relegates African Americans to the bottom of the economic structure. It is not an issue of inherent black dependency on the welfare state, for Pohlmann, but rather that black conservatives are playing to the stereotypes of the black community. Disparate classes, the poor, and black and white working-class and middle-class families, are "conduits" in the process of transferring monies to the welfare state capitalists and elites during the course of their survival and the maintenance of their households. Pohlmann sees little evidence that the "trickle down" supply side of economics has created permanent jobs for disparate classes in the society. Instead, he argues, the capitalist system needs restructuring and a socialist alternative may pose the best alternative.

James Jennings also peers beyond the scope of liberalism and conservatism. In chapter 12, "Beyond Black Neoconservatism and Black Liberalism," he contends that allowing either group to frame the issues that are critical to the black community erodes the philosophical and political bases by which this community shapes its political, economic, and social development. Both groups have failed their African American constituencies by not addressing their needs and by placing them in perennial subordinate positions to the white power structure. For Jennings, blacks must develop a power base, utilizing grassroots initiatives built upon a philosophical basis of black cultural traditions and values that speak to the needs and issues that concern them as a collective community. Thus, for Jennings, blacks, working-class peoples, and Latinos must not give credence to the ideological debates and perspectives of liberals and conservatives, but, instead, must focus on the critical political, economic, and social issues that will allow them to establish communities of power and resources.

Increasingly, as black neoconservatives are infused into the body politic and promoted by the conservative apparatus, they will most assuredly generate discussion and debate in the African American community as to what motivates them and their political and economic alliance with white conservatives. One cannot readily dismiss their individual ethos, nor their political alliance with the white conservative movement. But they occupy a tenuous position at best. In American politics, political relationships change over time as interests and needs change. The fact of the matter is that, despite their rhetoric and media visibility, black neoconservatives, with all of the power of the white conservative apparatus behind them, have not garnered the support of the black electorate for the Republican Party. Indeed, in the recent (2000) presidential election, President George W. Bush "did worse with black voters than any Republican presidential candidate in history except Barry Goldwater."[23] This may prove problematic for black neoconservatives in the future for while they serve a number of other political interests, such as unraveling the "civil rights establishment," they may no longer be as viable to a party that has experienced victory without the black electorate. For the African American community, the challenge may be the larger question of providing a more sustained criticism of the duopoly of American politics and the impact that it has on black thought and praxis.

NOTES

1. Mack Jones, "The Political Thought of the New Black Conservatives: An Analysis, Explanation and Interpretation," in *Readings in American Political Issues*, ed. Franklin D. Jones (Dubuque, IA: Kendall Hunt Publishing Company, 1987), 23.
2. Jack C. Plano and Milton Greenberg, *The American Political Dictionary*, 2nd edition, 4.
3. Kenneth M. Dolbeare and Linda J. Metcalf, *American Ideologies Today*, (New York: McGraw Hill, 1993), 63–72.
4. Ibid.
5. Lewis A. Randolph, "A Historical Analysis and Critique of Contemporary Black Conservatism," *The Western Journal of Black Studies*, 19:3, (Fall 1995): 150.
6. David Gergen, "Republicans before and after Reagan," Columbia Public Broadcasting Company, South Carolina Public Television, October 1988.
7. Ibid.
8. Glenn Loury, "Redirecting Priorities to Help the Black Underclass," *Point of View*, Op. Cit. Summer 1984, p. 4.
9. Eileen M. Gardner, "Back to Basics for Black Education," in *Critical Issues*, ed. Joseph Perkins, (Washington, D.C.: The Heritage Foundation, 1990). pp. 45–46.
10. Walter E. Williams, *The State Against Blacks* (New York: New Press, 1982), pp. 104, 142; and Thomas Sowell, "Politics and Opportunity: The Background," in *The Fairmount Papers: Black Alternatives Conference* (San Francisco: Institute for Contemporary Studies, 1981), pp. 3–12.
11. Dolbeare and Metcalf, *American Ideologies Today*, pp. 63–72.
12. Elizabeth Wright, "Needed: A Moral Revival," in *Critical Issues*, pp. 23–25.
13. Joseph Perkins, in *Critical Issues*, ed. Perkins, p. 1.
14. Dolbeare and Metcalf, *American Ideologies Today*, pp. 63–72.
15. Manning Marable, *How Capitalism Underdeveloped Black America*, (Boston: South End Press, 1983), p. 174.
16. Stephen Carter, *Reflections of an Affirmative Action Baby*, (New York: Basic Books, 1991), p. 48.
17. Robert C. Smith and Hanes Walton Jr., "U-turn: Martin Kilson and Black Conservatives" in *Transition* (1993):62, pp. 209–216; Deborah Toler, "Black Conservatives: Part Two," *The Public Eye Newsletter* (Cambridge, MA: Political Research Associates, 1993), 7:4, p. 46; and note "Remaking African American Public Opinion: The Role and Function of the African American Conservatives" by Hanes Walton, Jr., chapter 8 in this volume.
18. Suzanne Espinosa-Solis, "Affirmative Action Critic Used His Minority Status," *San Francisco Examiner*, A1, May 8, 1995.
19. Cornel West, *Race Matters* (New York: Vintage Press, 1993), pp. 75–85; Martin Kilson, "The Anatomy of Black Conservatism," *Transition* (1992): 59; Peter Eisenstadt, *Black Conservatism: Essays in Intellectual and Political History*, (New York: Garland Publishing, 1999), p. xxvii-xxviii.
20. Hanes Walton, Jr., "Black and Conservative Political Movements," *The Quarterly Review of Higher Education Among Negroes*, 37:4, (October 1969), p. 178.
21. Vernon E. McClean, "Historical Examples of Black Conservatism," *The Western Journal of Black Studies*, 8:3 (Fall 1984): p. 149.
22. See chapter 5, "'If it ain't broke, don't fix it': Thomas Sowell on Black Women, Affirmative Action, and the Death of Discrimination," by Rhonda Williams.
23. Jonathan Tilove, "To Blacks, Bush Means Hard Times," *Star Ledger*, December 1, 2000.

PART I

THE CONTEXT OF BLACK CONSERVATISM

CHAPTER 1

BLACK CREOLE CULTURES: THE EIGHTEENTH-CENTURY ORIGINS OF AFRICAN AMERICAN CONSERVATISM

RHETT S. JONES

Kelly Miller, longtime professor of sociology at Howard University and one of the leading black intellectuals from the turn of the century until his retirement in 1934, begins his 1908 article, "Radicals and Conservatives," as follows:

> When a distinguished Russian was informed that some American Negroes are radical and some conservative, he could not restrain his laughter. The idea of conservative Negroes was more than the Cossack's risibilities could endure. "What on earth," he exclaimed with astonishment, "have they to conserve?" According to a strict use of terms, a "conservative" is one who is satisfied with existing conditions and advocates their continuance; while a "radical" clamors for amelioration of conditions through change. No thoughtful Negro is satisfied with the present status of his race. . . . Radical and conservative Negroes agree as to the end in view, but differ as to the most effective means of attaining it.[1]

Of course, African Americans have a great deal worth conserving. But Miller raises an important issue: Are blacks in agreement as to what they ought to conserve?

Unfortunately, most who seek to answer this question and thereby understand the development of black conservatism begin their analysis in the middle of the story. For the most part, they focus on such African American men as David Walker, Henry Highland Garnett, and Frederick Douglass, who wrote in the nineteenth-century, carefully and, often usefully, sorting them into integrationists or nationalists and placing them along a spectrum that ranges from toadyism through accommodation to armed resistance. But as Jones has pointed out, the roots of black social and political thought are not to be found in the writings of nineteenth-century black intellectuals, but rather in the creation of African American culture over the course of the eighteenth century.[2] Nineteenth-century black writers who led the battle against slavery, for race unity, and against racism were themselves the product of eighteenth century events.

Boles titles a chapter in his book, "The Crucial Eighteenth Century," noting that it was in this century that Euro-American racism and African American culture were born and grew up alongside one another, each having an impact on the other.[3] For most of the seventeenth century, as Jordan clearly demonstrates, North American colonists described themselves as "Christian," but by the early years of the eighteenth century, they had began to refer to themselves as "white." And while they had initially referred to persons of African descent as "heathen" and "savage," by the eighteenth century they increasingly referred to them as "black" or, borrowing the Spanish word, as "Negro."[4] These changes in terminology had great meaning, Jordan argues, as they indicated a shift from a focus on culture, as manifested in religious belief, to a focus on race. After all, a heathen could convert and become a Christian, just as a Christian could reject the faith and become a follower of the anti-Christ. But no matter what terrible things a white person did, he or she could never sink to the level of the Negro because racially, he or she would always remain white. Similarly, no matter what a black person did, he or she could never attain to the level of whiteness. The exact mechanisms of this shift from culture to race, as well as the reasons for it, are much debated by scholars, though Bennett provides a useful, if perhaps oversimplified, explanation.[5]

While whites were laying the foundations of racism, blacks were creating a distinct culture. At the beginning of the eighteenth century, most persons of African ancestry living in North America were African born, but by the century's end, most had been born on this side of the Atlantic. Over the course of the 1700s, Africans became African Americans. The root of black conservatism is to be found in this change. It is not, however, clear what—to return to Miller's question—African Americans sought to conserve. As African American culture underwent a number of changes over the course of the eighteenth century, a number of types of black conservatives were produced, with each one attempting to maintain—in Miller's words—"existing conditions."

After exploring issues important in the understanding of African American culture, this chapter discusses the evolution of black life in North America over the course of the eighteenth century. It concludes by examining the varieties of black conservatisms that resulted from these changes, distinguishing these from their superficial resemblance to white conservatisms.

PROLOGUES: ISSUES IN THE DEVELOPMENT OF AFRICAN AMERICAN CULTURE

A glimpse of what African American culture might have been, and therefore what black American conservatism might have looked like had it not been for the development of racism, is described by Breen and Innes.[6] They describe a group of successful seventeenth-century black families on Virginia's Eastern Shore. These men and women understood that the key to success in the emergent Anglo-American society was property and that the most recognizable and useful form of property was land. The Eastern Shore was divided, not so much between whites and blacks, as between those who owned land and those who did not. Land ownership gave such families as the Paynes, the Drigguses, and the Johnsons standing in the eyes of the law and the right to indenture servants and apprentice children. These families not only held white indentured servants, they served as foster parents for white children, all with the full approval of the colony's government. Breen and Innes's careful review of the court cases in which these blacks were involved shows none of the racial biases of the legal system that black Americans later faced. In disputes with their white neighbors, they were just as likely to win as to lose. The families were in a biracial network of middling landowners like themselves who stood between the property-less lower orders and the large landowners, whom they regarded as patrons. But they had not lost racial consciousness; one of them named his farm, "Angola," and, in the words of Breen and Innes, they "appear[ed] in their most intimate relations to have maintained a conscious black identity."[7] They were in a separate black network of persons like themselves, whom they traveled some distance to visit, supported in various ways, and married. But, conclude Breen and Innes:

> By the 1670s, it would have been nearly impossible for a slave to work himself out of slavery in the manner that Francis Payne had done. The doors to economic opportunity were either shut or fast closing by that time. It was not that Payne's [black] successors were less astute or energetic than he had been. Rather, they lost the possibility to acquire property, the basis of genuine freedom in this society.[8]

The children of these successful blacks were denied the opportunity to emulate their parents. Had it not been for racism, black conservatism might have been just like its white counterpart, as blacks would have fully participated in American political, economic, and legal institutions, and therefore, like white conservatives, been fully committed to maintaining them unchanged.

Scholars differ over why black Americans lost the rights for which these African Virginians worked so hard. Some argue that they never had them and that race bias was always there, simply awaiting economic events to trigger racism. According to Winthrop Jordan, long before Englishmen settled the Americas, they had negative ideas concerning the color black, ideas that were part of their culture.[9] When the New World offered them the opportunity to achieve great wealth if only they could find the necessary labor, they readily turned to the enslavement of Africans. Happily for the colonists, the vulnerability of Africans, the willingness of their fellow Africans to sell them into slavery, their color, and the fact they were not Christians, all combined to make them suitable slaves. Kovel and Welsing, while agreeing that color, not economics, was the root cause of racism, disagree as to its meaning. Welsing argues that whites exploit blacks because they envy blacks their color, whereas Kovel contends that whites hate blacks because the darkness of their skins symbolizes feces. Bennett and Morgan take a position opposite to that of Kovel and Welsing. As they see it, color was of little importance to the settlers; rather, the white elites, fearing that lower order whites and black slaves would join together to challenge their hegemony, succeeded, in Morgan's words, in creating a screen of "racial contempt" between whites and blacks.[10]

Creating this screen took considerable effort, according to Mechal Sobel who argues that Virginia's eighteenth-century slaves and its white lower classes had much in common, sharing ideas about religion, causality, time, and the use of space. Because they agreed on so much, blacks and whites together created a single world in which their shared values united them. Nothing drew them closer, she contends, than their joint commitment to the evangelical Christianity that emerged in Virginia—and else-where in the thirteen colonies—in the 1740s. Whites accepted the idea of heaven as the place where families and friends were reunited, a distinctly West African concep-tion of the afterlife. But this eighteenth-century unity was, as Sobel sees it, shattered, so that by the second decade of the nineteenth century, Virginia was racially divided in ways that would be familiar to twentieth-century Americans.[11]

Although the debate over whether racism came into existence during the eigh-teenth century or had always existed continues, the emergence of African American culture is a little more clear. But because the two are so closely linked, a lack of clar-ity as to the origin and early development of racism means that the related origin and early development of black American culture also remains murky.

Before tracing the evolution of African American culture through the 1700s, it is important to address Native American/African American relations. Much of the scholarly discussion on the stages in the development of eighteenth-century African American culture focuses on the actions of blacks and on relations between whites and blacks. These transformations were driven by slavery, racism, black struggles against both, and the oppositionist tactics of black Americans. But three races, not two, were present in the thirteen colonies. This reality has been neglected in both mainstream histories of colonial America and in histories of black America, as a number of scholars note.[12] Put in another way, in constructing a political agenda, blacks had Indian alternatives to those developed by whites and those they devel-oped themselves. In some cases, individual blacks reflected on Indian actions, cul-ture, and society from the outside, but in others they were admitted as members of Indian nations.[13] In still other cases, persons of African descent managed to take ad-vantage of the eighteenth-century frontier to change, and then change again, their racial identity. Hart explains why this was possible on the New York frontier:

> The frontier made the rejection and reformulation of [racial] categories possible, for by definition the frontier was that space that lay between and beyond the political and cul-tural reaches of the two or more socially and culturally distinct societies in contact that lived on either side of the divide. Because the frontier lay physically remote, interaction among Indians, Euro-Americans, and persons of African ancestry was fluid, creative, and open. Individuals embraced aspects of the "other's" culture and often identified with—and were identified as—the "other." To maneuver easily through the open fron-tier culture, however, required that one be multicultural, which meant, knowing the languages of the cultures in contact, being familiar with their cultures and codes of diplomacy, and claiming kinship in two or more of the cultures.[14]

Hart goes on to describe blacks who were successful and others who were not so successful at shifting racial identities against this backdrop of Native American–Eu-ropean American contact, pointing out that in New York, individual blacks operat-ing along both sides of the frontier sometimes manipulated racial categories to their advantage.

Things were different in the Seminole country of Florida, to which groups of run-away slaves, as well as individuals, escaped. Historians have not agreed on why the Seminole, who were originally part of the Creek nation, were more receptive to, and supportive of black runaways than were other Indians on the eighteenth-century southern frontier. As Unser makes clear, most of the Indians in what is now the southeastern part of the United States were adept at playing the English, French, and Spaniards—each of whom sought to control the area—against one another.[15] When the United States became independent, Native Americans merely added the new nation to the list, taking shrewd advantage of the hostility between Great Britain and its former colonies. But while the Cherokee and other southeastern Indians, for example, rapidly adopted, not only slavery, but the racist justifications for it, the Seminole did not. Most scholars argue that blacks were readily accepted by the Seminole so that the two peoples fused into one nation. But Mulroy finds that as the Seminole, and the blacks who lived among them had different interests, they remained different peoples.[16]

Four groups of persons of African descent lived within the Seminole nation. The first, while often clearly bearing clear physical signs of their African ancestry, were Seminole, having either married into the nation or descended from blacks who were regarded as Seminole. There were two groups of Seminole slaves, one of which lived in Seminole villages under the direct supervision of their Indian masters, while the other group lived in separate villages. This group paid an annual tribute to their Seminole owners but otherwise enjoyed a considerable amount of independence. A fourth group of blacks lived in Seminole territory but were not slaves. For the most part they were either runaway slaves from the English colonies or the descendants of such slaves, and they were regarded both by the Seminole and whites as allies of the Seminole. At a time when both communication and transportation were unreliable and irregular, there is little evidence and less likelihood that slaves in Georgia and the Carolinas were aware of these distinctions among persons of African descent among the Seminole, but they did understand that relations were different between Indians and blacks than between whites and blacks.

No study of the development of the eighteenth-century roots of black conservatism would therefore be complete without recognizing complexity of red-white-black relations or acknowledging that the history of Indians east of the Alleghenies in the 1700s was one of the declining military and political power. Indians, Dowd demonstrates, were aware of this decline, as were blacks.[17] Indian cultural alternatives to the cultures of whites and blacks were therefore less attractive to black Americans at the end of the eighteenth century than they were at the beginning. Further complicating the relationship between Native Americans and the black population was Indian acceptance of antiblack racism. Not all red peoples accepted white ideas on the biological inferiority of Africans, but as Perdue and McLoughlin show, these ideas attracted many.[18] Assimilated southern Indians who purchased slaves found the racist justifications for the cruelties of the peculiar institution as useful as did whites. Moreover, as racist ideology grew in the 1700s, many Indians feared being lumped with blacks. According to Horsman, by the end of the eighteenth century, most white Americans believed there was an unbridgeable gulf between whites and blacks, and that black people could never become the equal of whites.[19] In the early years of independence, while Euro-Americans debated on which side of the racial gulf Indians belonged, the federal government—in conjunction with many Protestant denominations—pursued a vigorous program aimed at incorporating Indians into white society. By the 1830s, however, the majority of European Americans sided with Andrew Jackson, who regarded Indians as a racially inferior folk and therefore forcibly removed them west of the Mississippi along the Trail of Tears.

Space does not permit full and systematic exploration of how the evolution of black ideas in the 1700s was influenced both by direct contact with Native Americans and by changing white ideas about American Indians. It is important, however, to emphasize that both Indians and ideas about Indians had an impact on eighteenth-century African American culture. Beyond the role played by Native Americans in shaping this culture, four points need to be considered before exploring how changes in black American culture produced a variety of black conservatisms.

First, although it seems paradoxical, in some respects black Americans were freer than whites. No African state exercised power in the Americas which means that, unlike the colonists, who had to cope with orders from London, Madrid, Paris, or even private, European-based companies, the slaves only had to deal with their owners and the colonial governments behind them. Moreover, as Olwell's study makes clear, the slaves understood that their masters and these governments were themselves subordinate to the European powers.[20] The settlers were constrained both by the governments of Europe and by European culture. The powers of state and culture did not always manifest themselves in the same ways in differing parts of North America. In an innovative argument, Fisher demonstrates that various parts of British North America were settled by immigrants who came from parts of Britain with diverse cultural expectations and social structures.[21] Beyond these more general cultural differences, the colonists sometimes had particular religious or other goals. The Pilgrims who settled Plymouth and the Puritans who settled Boston each had their differences with the Church of England, but they also differed from each other. Maryland was established as a refuge for persecuted English Catholics. Georgia, the original charter of which forbade slavery, was founded to enable Germans and Scots to escape persecution. Roger Williams established Rhode Island as a place where there would be no state-supported church, and all could enjoy liberty of conscience. But these settlements, though different in important ways, were all ruled by European nations.

Although there was no place in the Americas where Africans confronted power exercised by an African state, in some parts of the New World (Brazil, Cuba, Jamaica, and Haiti are obvious examples), African nations exercised considerable cultural influence. Murphy explains what happened in Cuba:

> The Yoruba were quick to establish a strong community in Havana. They came to be called "Lucumi" after their way greeting each other, *oluku mi*, "my friend." They formed guild and dance halls, taverns and fraternities, where they would dance the old dances. More than ever they needed the *orishas* [gods of the Yoruba] and their ways of power, and they found ingenious ways of keeping them alive. This story of survival involved an unlikely partnership between the *orishas* and the Roman Catholic Church.[22]

Murphy goes on to explain that the Church, in conjunction with the Spanish government, encouraged the Yoruba and other African nations to continue their traditional ways, both as a means of keeping slaves divided from one another and as a means of linking them, through Catholic sponsored religious organizations, to the Church. The purpose of both goals was social control. Encouraging African national rivalries and customs prevented the slaves from acting in union against their common oppressor, while church organizations encouraged their assimilation into, and submission to, Catholic institutions. Similar policies were adopted in many of the other Spanish settlements as well as in Portuguese Brazil and French Haiti. But even in the absence of deliberate policies in such Protestant settlements as Barbados and Antigua, the sheer number of slaves from certain regions of Africa made it possible for the Fanti, Ashanti, and others to continue many of their customs.[23]

Typically, slaves in North America were drawn from so wide a variety of African cultures that it was impossible for them to emulate Havana's Yoruba. There may, however, have been exceptions to this general rule. Thornton accounts for the 1739 Stono Rebellion by attributing it to slaves who were, for the most part, from Angola and therefore able to act in military, cultural, and religious unity.[24] But this was apparently the exception to the rule. Most American slaves were therefore doubly emancipated, from the authority of an African state and, similarly, from a particular African culture.

A second consideration in tracing the development of American culture has to do with the absence of pomp, circumstance, wealth, and conspicuous consumption in the way of life created by American slaves. Eighteenth-century West Europe and West Africa shared a love of materialism and a respect for wealth. The businessman was admired in both regions, and in both, the ruling classes dressed in costly garments, wore expensive jewelry, and insisted on elaborate rituals. To be sure there were, in both areas, entire regions where people were either too poor for, or little interested in, the public display of wealth. But the ruling classes in both regions shared a love of high-sounding titles, elaborate ceremonies, and displays of wealth intended to demonstrate to their subjects, enemies, and friends that they were persons of importance. This public display of wealth as manifested in dress and ritual was used in West Africa and West Europe as a means of commanding respect. American slaves needed respect, but as they could not own property, claim titles, nor participate in costly ceremonies, they had to develop other ways manifesting respect for one another.

In the eighteenth century in both Europe and Africa it was easy to determine a person's status. Those who owned property, lived in a certain area, had servants (or slaves), and possessed a title or a degree were awarded deference as people of high position. If they lacked these things, they lacked status and were not entitled to deference. North America's slaves developed a different means of delivering respect to one another. Slaves gained the respect of their fellows when they loved children, honored the elderly, publicly acknowledged God, and served the community. These various activities have in common that there are no ready social markers of them. In West African and West Europe it was possible to tell at a glance whether people deserved respect by learning where they lived or seeing how they dressed. But in the world of African American slaves, people had to be watched for some time before they earned respect. There were no clothes that would signal that one respected the elderly, nor a residential area reserved for those who cared for children. Free from the restraints of Africa and Europe by their enslavement, the slaves imposed a watchfulness on themselves. There were no shortcuts to deference in the slave communities of North America, each person had to earn respect.

Third, in tracing the evolution of black American culture, it is important to understand that a good part of it was oppositionist. Blacks resented what was happening to them in British North America and while many of them sought to overcome racism by modeling themselves on whites, others sought to distance themselves from whites and their Anglo-American culture. Nash writes of Philadelphia's blacks at the end of the eighteenth century:

[In addition to Philadelphia's black elite] was a mass of city dwellers, many of them recent arrivals. Some of them spoke in Southern dialect, drank and gambled, dressed
flamboyantly, sometimes ran afoul of the law, and affected a body language—the saun-
tering gait, unrestrained singing and laughing, and exuberant dancing—that set them
apart from "respectable" black society. Theirs was a precarious world, but they made the
best of it in ways that whites and some blacks found offensive. . . . For these dispossessed
urban refugees, "reputation" in the streets and privately created self-image figured more
importantly than "respectability" in the community.[25]

These black men and women developed a set of strategies for dealing with Anglo-
American slavery and racism that separated them both from whites and from assim-
ilating blacks. Piersen suggests that black organizations in Boston and other cities in
New England that began as groups to facilitate the integration of blacks into American society gradually despaired and transformed themselves instead into institutions
that advocated black separatism.[26]

African American culture differed from its European American counterpart because of slavery and racism. Because most blacks were enslaved, they adopted
strategies different from those of whites, and as racism grew in strength, black
Americans developed tactics to deal with it as well. But, as the passage from Nash
demonstrates, some African Americans were deliberately oppositionist and developed ways of walking, talking, dressing, speaking, and dancing intended to challenge
and confront European Americans. African American culture was therefore shaped
by the African heritage, slavery, racism, and by the deliberate adversarial position
some blacks took.

Fourth, African Americans were reflective. All the immigrants to British North
America, as well as the Indians who coped with both white colonists and black slaves,
were reflective. The term *New World* is a particularly apt one, for in an age when most
persons lived and died no more than twenty miles—if that—from where they had
been born, this meeting of races and cultures was unprecedented. All those involved
reflected on the meaning of their encounters, as they not only speculated on reasons
for color and cultural differences, but developed strategies for coping with them. Indians and whites differed from blacks, however, in that their reflectivity was exercised
within the framework of existent cultures. These cultures and the political institutions that supported them placed some constraints on the thoughts and actions of
Native Americans, Europeans, and European Americans. For example, in deciding
how they would cope with the oppressive Protestant majority in British North America, English Catholics were constrained by the British state and by their own religion
and culture. The very fact that they were in a new environment encouraged reflectivity and the creation of a culture that was different from the one left behind in England, but Anglo-Catholics' continued links to, and control by, this culture placed
restraints on them.

The reflections of Africans and African Americans were less restrained than those
of others in the thirteen colonies because they were emancipated from the cultural
and political control of the African states. Neither the African nor the European
model was useful for slaves who had to establish a means of delivering respect to one
another in the absence of the common culture and shared political system that most
human beings took for granted. Reflectivity was the essence of the African American
experience, as, lacking power, black Americans had to be ever watchful, always sort-

ing out the meaning of one another's actions and those of whites and Indians, in a society in which race became ever more important.

EVENTS: THE EVOLUTION OF AFRICAN AMERICAN CULTURE

The reflective watchfulness characteristic of blacks in North America shaped each stage in the development of their culture. As a powerless people, African Americans had no choice but to be a watchful one, ever calculating how to behave. In turn, this collective decision as to how they ought to act shaped black American culture to a greater extent than their African heritage or the examples set before them by white Americans. The beliefs of Europeans were irrelevant to African Americans, the beliefs of European Americans only a little less so, and those of Africans, while they helped to shape their ideas in a general way, were also irrelevant. The ancient, well-organized societies of Europe and Africa, with their clear cultural guidelines and self-conscious perspectives on their long pasts, were of little use to a people who were slaves. African American culture was, therefore, built from the ground up, painfully put together by slaves who created a culture that suited their way of life, not one that continued the cultural patterns of Africa or Europe. At the same time, the West African orientation of the first slaves made them flexible, open-minded, and willing to learn from others. This predisposition to openness stood in dialectical opposition to the reality that, as slaves, black women and men had little choice in their every-day lives.

While they had to develop a way of life that served themselves, slaves also had to create a way of life that enabled them to survive and even get ahead in the social orders controlled by whites. In writing of race relations in the Spanish settlements, Klein observes that the slaves operated in two cultures.[27] They were fully committed to, and comfortable in, their own culture, yet fully committed to and able to function well in the larger white culture. Klein's observation holds for the entire hemisphere as blacks moved back and forth between two societies, that of the slave quarters and that of their white masters. In tracing the evolution of African American culture, it is important to keep in mind that blacks shuttled back and forth between the lives they were creating for themselves and the lives their masters wished them to live.

The first step in the evolution of African American culture was taken in the 1600s, during a time when the number of slaves was small and racism was not yet a powerful force. Blacks in British North America created an African British culture. Although these were involuntary immigrants, like most immigrants they quickly and readily adapted to the English ways of their new land. It seems reasonable to argue that they did so with more readiness than did, say, Germans or Scots, who retained ties to their homelands. Mention has already been made of the aggressive, fast-rising blacks of Virginia's Eastern Shore as described by Breen and Innes.[28] According to Higginbotham, in seventeenth-century Dutch- controlled New Netherlands:

> Negroes were able to own real property and to serve in the militia; slaves had certain
> tangible rights in the society. . . . In the courts, the status of a slave was nearly the same
> as that of a free man and woman. A slave could testify against other blacks and even in
> cases in which one or both of the litigating parties was white. Black slaves were able to
> seek judicial relief when they were unlawfully held in bondage.[29]

In Rhode Island, "for most of the seventeenth century, [blacks] were treated as servants and released after ten years."[30] Under these circumstances, it is not surprising that many blacks rapidly adopted the ways of the English, creating their own variety of Anglo-American culture. They adopted Christianity, learned English, mastered a trade, purchased property, and in general took advantage of a social order that was fluid and open when compared to those of Africa and Europe.

Three forces swamped this African British culture: the growth of slavery as an economic institution, a sizable increase in the number of slaves, and racism, all of which were characteristic of the 1700s. Kulikoff writes of the Chesapeake:

> From roughly 1650 to 1690, blacks assimilated the norms of white society, but the growth of the number of blacks also triggered white repression. The period from 1690 to 1740 was an era of heavy slave imports, small plantation sizes, and social conflicts among blacks. The infusion of Africans often disrupted newly formed slave communities.[31]

With this increase in their numbers, "Africans were able better to retain aspects of their own culture and began to develop creative adaptations of it."[32] This culture placed the new arrivals in conflict with whites, who increasingly regarded them as "outlandish" as compared to their more familiar, more English-like, "country-born" slaves. And it placed them in conflict with these American-born slaves, who sought to retain their African British culture and who, in that sense, may fairly be regarded as North America's first Black conservatives.

It should be emphasized that African British culture was not completely washed away by the influx of Africans; it simply became less important. It was succeeded, in the 1700s, by what is here termed African Creole culture, but it was never completely eliminated. African Creole culture, emerging around the end of the seventeenth century, embodied the understanding of African Americans that they were not like the other Americans, that the majority of whites intended to keep them and their descendants in slavery, and that European Americans were working out justifications for their brutal treatment of blacks. This culture reflected the confidence produced by the increased numbers of blacks and their discovery of commonalties among themselves, produced. Piersen explains:

> [T]he wide varieties of ethnically specific African traditions carried across the ocean were being reshaped into a new generalized African American culture. The intragroup compromises worked out between Africans of differing nationalities combined with external ones forced on them by alien white masters created something brand-new—the first truly American culture.[33]

The exact shape of this culture, it must be stressed, varied according to the African ethnic origin of the slaves, their percentage of the total population, the work to which they were assigned, the nationality and religion of their masters, and the larger social, political, and economic structures within which they lived.

Black communities in the large rice plantations of South Carolina differed from the mixed farming communities of Pennsylvania, and these in turn differed from communities in urban Boston. The "first real slave community in Monmouth [County, New Jersey] was industrial rather than agricultural, being established at Lewis Morris' iron mine and forge."[34] Cottrol found three different patterns of slave-holding in tiny Rhode Island: one in Newport, where most slaves were house servants; one in Providence, where slaves worked at a variety of tasks; and one in rural Narraganset Country, where slaves produced wood, dairy products, corn, and tobacco.[35] Regardless of where the eighteenth century slaves lived, they worked together to create a number of African Creole societies, which, because they were shaped by the same forces, strongly resembled one another.

Sobel finds the African influence strong, noting that it profoundly and deeply affected white attitudes in eighteenth-century Virginia, and Berlin notes that while African cultures manifested themselves in different ways in the varied parts of seventeenth- and eighteenth-century British North America, they had a deep impact on blacks in all the thirteen colonies.[36] Fitts shows how blacks in Rhode Island worked together to maintain African names.[37] Gomez concludes a chapter by noting that social divisions within the black community "were to a degree informed by conditions growing out of the African antecedent,"[38] thereby suggesting that the slaves themselves were so strongly influenced by their separate African cultures that they often divided along African cultural lines. Despite these divisions and regional variations, the slaves created, by the early years of the eighteenth century, an African Creole culture.

The conservatives this culture produced were strikingly different from their African British predecessors in that their culture was shaped by the tightening up of the racial system, the growth of racism, and increasing restrictions placed on blacks, whether slave or free. Unlike their seventeenth century ancestors, these black Americans realized they were not going to have the opportunities enjoyed by whites. Yet, as Olwell clearly demonstrates, they also understood that their masters were themselves the subjects of others and so were not all-powerful.[39] The improvisational ability of slaves to subvert white restrictions, legal and otherwise, their growing awareness of the concept of race; and the common strategies they adopted served to cement the loyalty of many of them to their new culture.

But this culture in turn was swamped in the 1740s when hundreds of thousands of blacks committed themselves to a new African American culture based on Christianity. The First Great Awakening, which was characterized by evangelic preaching, mass conversions, bible-readings, prayer meetings, as well as shoutings, speaking in tongues, and enthusiastic singing, appealed to masses of whites and blacks in a way the more staid forms of existent American Christianity had not. Prior to the Great Awakening, most blacks practiced some kind of religion, but the only thing that can be certain is that it was not Christianity. The observations of the whites of the time suggest it was probably an amalgamation of the various West African religions the slaves had brought with them, and as a part of the African Creole culture it was almost certainly African centered. Explanations for the mass conversion of blacks in the 1740s, some four generations after their arrival in North America, vary. Some scholars suggest that this energetic Christianity reminded blacks of the similar religions of West Africa, affording the slaves the opportunity to participate in services in an African manner in a way that the rituals of Anglicans, Congregationalists, Moravians, and Quakers did not. Others argue that the ideologies of the new religions— both the Baptists and the Methodists initially condemned slavery—appealed to slaves, whereas still others believe the slaves appreciated the opportunity for religious leadership that the new religions offered. Finally, there are scholars who suggest that some opportunistic blacks only pretended to join in the religious fervor and that, as the Great Awakening placed emphasis on individual reading and interpretation of the Bible, blacks pretended conversion in order to learn how to read. Lambert argues that white evangelicals, while welcoming black converts, nevertheless feared that these men and women would find in their independent interpretations of the Bible a mandate for ending slavery. In this they were right. Lambert concludes, "Listening to the message of evangelicalism, slaves heard the strains of emancipation from slavery as well as spiritual deliverance."[40]

African American culture was forever transformed by this eighteenth-century black commitment to Christendom. To be sure, conversion of African Americans to Christianity had little impact on either slavery or its racist underpinnings. While some blacks remained within white churches, others separated from them, establishing their own, separate, black churches. Whether they chose to remain in white Christendom, separate themselves into black Christendom, or reject Christianity, black Americans forever after grappled with the Christian faith. But as the vast majority of them became Christians, and African Christian culture replaced the African Creole, non-Christian culture among most blacks.

The Christianity of the era was patriarchal. Men controlled the religious institutions of British North America. Women had no public voice in either church or state. But while European American women occupied a subordinate position, controlled by their fathers, husbands, brothers, and even sons, things were different on the other side of the race line. Historians do not agree on whether the position of black women as compared to black men was different from the position of white women as compared to white men in eighteenth-century British North America. Gundersen argued that as black and white women performed much the same tasks, they occupied much the same position and, indeed, were part of the same culture.[41] Shammas, on the other hand, found that slavery and the kind of work it forced on black women meant that white women and their families often profited at the expense of black women and their families.[42]

Slavery and a number of other forces produced black gender relations that were more egalitarian than their white counterparts. Some scholars argue that in the West African societies from which most of the slaves were drawn, women had more of a voice in economic, political, and religious affairs than was the case in West Europe at the time and that emergent African American societies, however much subject to white control and influence, therefore accorded women a more equal role. Moreover, black men and women frequently worked together in the fields in a (white) enforced gender equality that carried over into their everyday lives. Black families were often separated by sale, and though it was relatively uncommon to sell young children away from their mothers, fathers were typically separated from their families. Black women were therefore central in the survival of black families. Newman's study of black women in Philadelphia demonstrated that they were equal partners with black men in the construction of self-help societies, schools, and other black organizations established to uplift the race.[43] But African American culture was influenced by its European American counterpart, with some blacks seeking respectability by building a way of life that was modeled on the patriarchal structures of white society in general and white Christianity in particular. For example, black women who sought to preach in black churches frequently encountered the same barriers that white women met in white churches. But African American males, the majority of whom were slaves, lacked the power to replicate the kind of dominance European American males exercised over women, even had they been mindful to do so. Around the same time that the majority of black Americans became Christians, they also created a culture in which the sexes stood on a more equal footing than was the case among white Americans.

By the middle of the eighteenth century then, an African American, Creole, Christian culture, tilted toward gender equality, existed. As communication and transportation within the thirteen colonies improved, blacks gradually developed an awareness that slavery and racism were not limited to their particular locale, but were instead characteristic of all the colonies. Free blacks responded to this awareness by creating institutions that were intended to facilitate their integration into white America, or provide blacks support in the separate black world whites were forcing on them. Slaves, of course, lacked the privilege of creating formal public institutions and instead developed a range of ways of both resisting, and accommodating themselves to, the rising tide of racism that was characteristic of British North America. At the same time that blacks were developing these options and solidifying their culture, numbers of whites in the thirteen colonies were convincing themselves that Great Britain had trampled on their rights, had abused them, and were compelling them to formally separate themselves from England. Drawing on a mixture of Enlightenment ideology and their own experiences, some of the colonists argued that their needs were neither understood nor appreciated in England and that all men were created equal, endowed by their creator with certain rights. Americans should not, they argued, be regarded as second class Britons.

In making such a declaration, Higginbotham argues, most European Americans did not mean to include their slaves.[44] Though many of the rebels recognized the inconsistency of championing the rights of liberty for themselves while denying it to enslaved blacks they nevertheless refused to abandon the impressive rhetoric of universal equality. African Americans were quick to seize on these beliefs. According to Jones:

> Black Americans were successful in using Enlightenment beliefs against whites. If the country, Blacks argued, rested on the ideological basis that all men were equal and therefore entitled to freedom, liberty and justice, then America was false to herself in denying Blacks rights routinely given whites. Lacking an ideology of their own, Blacks used the ideology of Euro-Americans against whites.[45]

Black Americans may not have been able to create a distinct ideology of their own, but they demonstrated that they were extraordinarily adept at using the ideology that had been developed by white Americans against racism and slavery. They also succeeded in incorporating European American ideology into their culture, convincing one another that, as blacks were just like whites, they deserved the same opportunities. In taking this position, African Americans denied much of their own history. Blacks were nothing like whites. White had not been enslaved, nor had they been subjected to the vicious doctrine of racism, which insisted that their enslavement was morally, biologically, and legally legitimate.

At the end of the eighteenth century, then, African American culture was rooted in the experience of black Creoles, Christian, slanted toward gender equality, and strongly committed to the ideals of the American Revolution. This commitment to Revolutionary ideals returned black Americans to the African British culture characteristic of the seventeenth century, before racism became so powerful. The genesis of the American Revolution was the argument that the British Crown was depriving its American subjects of rights they ought to have enjoyed as freeborn Englishmen. That they lived an ocean apart from their fellows in England did not mean the Americans had surrendered these rights, and as the English government oppressed them, the colonists argued, they had no alternative but to go their own way. Just as white Americans were divided over whether they should rebel, so, too, were black Americans. Some black conservatives of the time remained committed to British rule in North America, and thousands of them fought on the side of the British. When the English lost the war, many of these blacks departed with British loyalists to Canada, the West Indies, and other parts of the British Empire.

LEGACIES: BLACK CONSERVATISMS

Each step in the evolution of African American culture over the course of the eighteenth century produced its own set of black conservatives, women and men who were committed to the ways of their time. For example, the radicals of one era, who broke with the African Creole culture to adopt Christianity, became the conservatives of the next, as some black Christians, in turn, resisted giving black women a role in church and society equal to that of black men. By the beginning of the nineteenth century, a variety of black conservatives existed, sometimes battling, sometimes cooperating with one another. Little of this black conservatism matches what many in the twentieth century regard as white conservatism. For, as Kelly Miller wrote in 1908: "No thoughtful Negro is satisfied with the present status of his race. . . . Radical and conservative Negroes agree as to the end in view, but differ as the most effective means of attaining it."[46] White conservatism has about it a certain smugness, much of which—though certainly not all—is rooted in the belief that whites are biologically superior to blacks. On the surface, this is a political ideology, one of many competing systems of thought among which men and women may choose in a nation that prides itself on the right of political choice. But the link between varieties of white conservatism and racism is no accident, for it rests on the eighteenth-century decisions made by whites such as Thomas Jefferson and other planters of the era, who, while publicly presenting an argument for personal liberty, selfishly served their own ends by retaining slavery. That a nation supposedly committed to freedom continues to honor slaveholders such as Thomas Jefferson and George Washington may surprise, but the commitment of contemporary European American conservatives to the founding fathers' rationalizations for racism should not. Most, though not all, white conservatives celebrate and root their ideology in a period near the end of eighteenth century, when the nation as a whole decided that Native Americans, blacks, and certain persons of European descent who were then not regarded as white were not Americans. Racism, therefore, remains their lodestar. It excuses, not only the hypocrisy of the nation's founders, but slavery, the moral failure of white Christianity, and continuing discrimination against African Americans.

Black conservatives share no agreed-upon and agreeable period of the past around which they can rally. Identifying with white America and having little understanding of the role of Africa in the shaping of African American culture, black conservatives ignore, in their ideological constructions, the formation of African Creole culture. Nor do they include, in any meaningful sense, the early and important role of black

women in the development of ideas about gender equality. And although it is curi-
ous, given their Eurocentrism, they also give little attention to the African British
culture formed by free blacks in the seventeenth century. The achievements of these
men and women ought to be celebrated by black conservatives, and should serve as
the foundation of the black conservatism which so many of them view as simply a
darker version of its white counterpart. Free blacks in the seventeenth century
worked hard, educated themselves, worshipped the Christian God, supported their
family members, participated in community affairs, served in the militia, asked no
special favors based on race, and so, by every possible measure important to the black
conservatives who imitate whites, achieved. But to focus on these people would force
black conservatives to acknowledge that this seventeenth century black commitment
to white conservative values ill served black people. The rising tide of racism and
slavery swept African Britons away, rendering all their hard work and commitment
to the emergent American culture worthless and now largely forgotten.

As black conservatives encourage blacks to behave as whites do, they ignore these
early African Britons, just as they ignore the remarkable achievement of enslaved
Africans in creating an African Creole culture and the accomplishments of black
women, despite the double discrimination based on gender and color. Left for black
conservatives in their search for tradition is the choice between focusing on the early
eighteenth-century conversion of masses of black Americans to Christianity and the
later eighteenth-century black commitment to the ideology of the Revolution. They
must chose, then, either between religion or politics, and so the choices they make
superficially resemble those made by white conservatives, who adopt either the programs of Christian fundamentalists or those of right-wing capitalists. As current differences in the Republican Party clearly demonstrate, while it is sometimes possible
to bring these groups together, they differ in significant ways.

But for all the differences among white conservatives, it is legitimate to say that
their ideologies reflect and embody a not unreasonable assessment of white life and
history in the United States and the thirteen British colonies that preceded its formation. For this reason, they have been able to root their ideas in the eighteenth century in general and in the statements of the founding fathers in particular. Because
black conservatism, in its emulation of white conservatism, ignores so much of eigh-
teenth- century African American life and history, its ideas are inevitably distorted
and for this reason have little appeal to the masses of black people. Black conservatism will attract black Americans only when it clearly understands and publicly ad-
dresses the evolution of African American political and social culture in the century
in which the United States was formed.

NOTES

1. Kelly Miller, *Radicals and Conservatives and Other Essays on the Negro in America* (New
   York: Schocken Books, 1968), pp. 25–26.
2. Rhett S. Jones, "Structural Isolation and the Genesis of Black Nationalism in North
   America," *Colby Library Quarterly,* 15 (December, 1979): 252–66.
3. John B. Boles, *Black Southerners, 1619–1869* (Cambridge: Harvard University Press,
   1984).
4. Winthrop D. Jordan, *White over Black: American Attitudes toward the Negro, 1550–1812*
   (Chapel Hill: University of North Carolina Press, 1968).
5. Lerone Bennett, Jr., "The Road Not Taken," *Ebony,* 25 (10) (August, 1970): 71–76.

6. T. H. Breen and Stephen Innes, *"Myne Own Ground:" Race and Freedom on Virginia's Eastern Shore* (New York: Oxford University Press, 1982).

7. Ibid., p. 18.

8. Ibid., p. 114.

9. Frances Cress Welsing, *The Cress Theory of Color Confrontation and Racism* (Washington: n.p., 1971).

10. Joel Kovel, *White Racism: A Psychohistory* (New York: Vintage Books, 1971); Bennett, "The Road Not Taken"; Edmund S. Morgan, *American Slavery, American Freedom: The Ordeal of Colonial Virginia* (New York: Norton, 1975).

11. Morgan, *American Slavery, American Freedom*, p. 316.

12. See, for example, Gary B. Nash, *Red, White and Black: The Peoples of Early America* (Englewood Cliffs, NJ): Prentice-Hall, 1974); Rhett S. Jones, "Black over Red: The Image of Native Americans in Black History," *Umoja* (Summer, 1977), 13–29; Theda Perdue, *Slavery and the Evolution of Cherokee Society* (Knoxville: University of Tennessee Press, 1979); and Daniel K. Richter, "Whose Indian History?" *William and Mary Quarterly* 50:2 (April, 1993): pp. 379–393.

13. Two discussions of this among the Creek are J. Leitch Wright, *Creeks and Seminoles* (Lincoln: University of Nebraska Press, 1986) and Kathryn E. H. Braund, "The Creek Indians, Blacks, and Slavery," *Journal of Southern History* 57 (November, 1991): pp. 601–36.

14. William Hart, "Black 'Go-Betweens' and the Mutability of 'Race,' Status, and Identity on New York's Frontier, 1750–1775," (unpublished paper), p. 1.

15. Daniel H. Unser, Jr., "Frontier Exchange in the Lower Mississippi Valley" (unpublished Ph.D. dissertation, Department of History, Duke University, 1981).

16. Kevin Mulroy, *Freedom on the Border: The Seminole Maroons* (Lubbock: Texas Tech University Press, 1993).

17. Gregory Evans Dowd, *A Spirited Resistance: The North American Indian Struggle for Unity* (Baltimore: Johns Hopkins University Press, 1992); Rhett S. Jones, "Mirroring the Double Failure: African and Native American Roots of Oppugnancy," *New England Journal of Black Studies* 9 (1990): pp. 1–17.

18. Perdue, *Slavery*; William G. McLoughlin, *Cherokee Renascence in the New Republic* (Princeton, NJ: Princeton University Press, 1986).

19. Reginald Horsman, *Race and Manifest Destiny* (Cambridge: Harvard University Press, 1981).

20. Robert Olwell, *Masters, Slaves, and Subjects: The Culture of Power in the South Carolina Low Country* (Ithaca, NY): Cornell University Press, 1998).

21. David Hackett Fisher, *Albion's Seed: Four British Folkways in America* (New York: Oxford University Press, 1989).

22. Joseph M. Murphy, *Santeria: African Spirits in America* (Boston: Beacon Press, 1993), p. 27.

23. For a discussion of this in Barbados see Gary A. Puckrein, *Little England: Plantation Society and Anglo-Barbadian Politics* (New York: New York University Press, 1984). For Antigua see David Barry Gaspar, *Bondsmen and Rebels: A Study of Master-Slave Relations in Antiqua* (Baltimore: Johns Hopkins University Press, 1985).

24. John K. Thornton, "African Dimensions of the Stono Rebellion," *American Historical Review* 96 (October, 1991): 1101–13.

25. Gary B. Nash, *Forging Freedom: The Formation of Philadelphia's Black Community* (Cambridge: Harvard University Press, 1988), p. 219.

26. William D. Piersen, *Black Yankees: The Development of an Afro-American Sub-Culture in Eighteenth Century New England* (Amherst: University of Massachusetts Press, 1988).

27. Herbert S. Klein, *African Slavery in Latin America and the Caribbean* (New York: Oxford University Press, 1986).

28. Breen and Innes, *"Myne Owne Ground."*

29. A. Leon Higginbotham, Jr. *In the Matter of Color: Race and the American Legal Process* (New York: Oxford University Press, 1980), p.104.

30. Robert J. Cottrol, *The Afro-Yankees: Providence's Black Community in the Antebellum* Era (Westport, CT: Greenwood Press, 1982), p. 14.

31. Allan Kulikoff, *Tobacco and Slaves: The Development of Southern Culture in the Chesapeake* (Chapel Hill: University of North Carolina Press, 1986), p. 319.

32. Boles, *Black Southerners*, pp. 19–20.

33. William D. Piersen, *From Africa to America: African American History from the Colonial Era to the Early Republic* (New York: Twayne Publishers, 1996), pp. 86–87.

34. Graham Russell Hodges, *Slavery and Freedom in the Rural North* (Madison, WI: Madison House, 1997), p. 16.

35. Cottrol, *The Afro-Yankees*, p. 16.

36. Mechal Sobel, *The World They Made Together: Black and White Values in Eighteenth Century Virginia* (Princeton, NJ: Princeton University Press, 1987); Ira Berlin, *Many Thousands Gone: The First Two Centuries of Slavery in North Carolina* (Cambridge: Harvard University Press, 1998).

37, Robert K. Fitts, *Inventing New England's Slave Paradise* (New York: Garland, 1998).

38. Michael A. Gomez, *Exchanging Our Country's Marks: The Transformation of African Identities in the Colonial and Antebellum South* (Chapel Hill: University of North Carolina Press, 1998), p. 87.

39. Olwell, *Masters, Slaves, and Subjects.*

40. Frank Lambert, "I Saw the Book Talk: Slave Readings of the First Great Awakening," *Journal of Negro History* 77 (Fall 1992): 195.

41. Joan Gundersen, "The Double Bonds of Race and Sex: Black and White Women in a Colonel Virginia Parish," *Journal of Southern History* 52 (August 1986): 351–72.

42. Carole Shammas, "Black Women's Work and the Evolution of Plantation Society in Virginia," *Labor History* 26 (Winter 1985): 5–27.

43. Debra L. Newman, "Black Women in the Era of the American Revolution in Pennsylvania," *Journal of Negro History* 61 (July 1976): 276–89.

44. Higginbotham, *In the Matter of Color.*

45. R. S. Jones, "In the Absence of Ideology: Blacks in Colonial America and the Modern Black Experience," *Western Journal of Black Studies* (Spring, 1988), p. 35.

46. Kelly Miller, *Radicals and Conservatives and Other Essays on the Negro in America*, p. 25.

CHAPTER 2

THE AMERICAN MORAL REFORM SOCIETY AND THE ORIGINS OF BLACK CONSERVATIVE IDEOLOGY

ROBERT E. WEEMS, JR.

Webster's Dictionary defines a conservative as someone "disposed to preserve existing conditions, institutions, etc. and to resist change."[1] From the standpoint of both the historic and contemporary black experience, it seems contradictory, if not unimaginable, for an African American to be conservative. Yet, during the past twenty- five years, an increasing number of blacks have publicly embraced and espoused the conservative designation. Although black conservative ideology may be unpalatable to most African Americans, this does not negate conservatism's long standing presence, if not popularity, in the African American community. The American Moral Reform Society (AMRS), of the mid- to late 1830s, represents one important aspect of the African American conservative tradition.

The American Moral Reform Society, first and foremost, epitomized what today's political scientists refer to as "organic" conservatism. Although there exists a tendency within the general public to lump conservatives (both black and white) into a homogenous ideological category, philosophical variance does, indeed, exist among those who consider themselves "conservative." Lewis Randolph's 1995 essay, "A Historical Analysis and Critique of Contemporary Black Conservatism," provided a helpful clarification of the differences between "antistatist" conservatives, "organic" conservatives, and "neoconservatives."[2]

Organic black conservatives, from the members of the American Moral Reform Society to such contemporary figures as Alan Keyes and Armstrong Williams, tend to believe that African Americans' problems stem from internal, rather than external, factors. Specifically, organic black conservatives view "immorality" within the African American community, rather than white racism, as the primary impediment to racial progress. Moreover, when one observes how today's organic black conservatives want to be referred to as simply an "American," rather than as a "black American" or an "African American," this sentiment, too, can be traced back to the American Moral Reform Society. In fact, a closer examination of the AMRS further validates the maxim, "There is nothing new under the sun."

The American Moral Reform Society grew out of the African American convention movement that commenced in 1830. Early on, "the American Society of Free People of Colour" considered a number of options to aid northern free blacks in an increasingly hostile environment. Chief among the proposals debated between 1830 and 1833 was the feasibility of promoting large-scale black emigration to Canada.[3]

Although the 1830 meeting produced a organizational constitution that described one of the group's aims as "purchasing lands . . . for the establishment of a settlement in the Province of Upper Canada,"[4] by 1833 emigration to Canada appeared to be a dead issue. In a clear reversal of sentiment expressed three years earlier, the 1833 meeting resolved:

> that there is not now, and probably never will be actual necessity for a large emigration of the present race of free people . . . this Convention most respectfully recommend(s) to their constituents, to devote their thoughts and energies to the improvement of their condition, *and to the elevation of their character*, in this their native land.[5] (emphasis added)

The 1833 Free People of Colour Convention's dramatic turnabout regarding emigration reflected the growing power of the organization's Philadelphia contingent.

Although free blacks throughout the northern states experienced similar discrimination, blacks, especially in Philadelphia and New York City, disagreed as to how they should respond to this mistreatment. New York City black leaders, such as publisher Samuel Cornish, actively promoted the establishment of separate African American schools and churches, being convinced that mainstream institutions would never allow blacks equal access.[6] Conversely, Philadelphia's black leadership, personified by businessman William Whipper, asserted that blacks should not focus on their insular needs and problems. Rather than establish separate institutions, Whipper argued that African Americans should focus upon achieving total integration in American society. Moreover, Whipper believed that blacks could make themselves more acceptable to whites by concentrating on educational uplift and morality.[7]

Besides the 1833 Free People of Colour Convention's dramatic disavowal of emigration, another report presented to the meeting, related to temperance, provided even greater evidence of the Philadelphia contingent's burgeoning influence. After calling for the establishment of an entity to be called "The Colored American Conventional Temperance Society," the Committee on Temperance's report declared to delegates:

> The utility of such an organization is obvious . . . not that intemperance abounds more among us, than among others . . . but notwithstanding, it, more than any thing under our control, tends to perpetuate that *relentless prejudice*, which arrays itself against our dearest interests; frowns us away from the avenues of useful knowledge and of wealth; and which with a cruel hand wrenches from us our political rights.[8] (emphasis in original)

This linkage of alcohol consumption with the degraded socioeconomic status of free blacks during the early nineteenth century provides a valuable revelation about the nuances of both historic and contemporary organic black conservatism. Specifically, organic black conservatives tend to (consciously or unconsciously) view whites as indisputable arbiters of morality. Thus, if whites discriminate against African Americans, they must do so for a good reason. In the early nineteenth century, they believed (as the 1833 report on temperance absurdly asserted), that *all* blacks were denied basic human and civil rights because *some* blacks consumed alcohol. Likewise, today's organic black conservatives would have us believe that drug abuse, rather than ongoing white racism and the transferral of industrial jobs overseas, should be Black America's chief concern.

Organic black conservatives' simultaneous inclination to both absolve whites and blame blacks for problems facing the African American community indicates, among other things, their profound naiveté, if not self-hatred. Again, the history of the American Moral Reform Society provides documentation for this assertion.

After their successful coup at the 1833 People of Colour Convention, the organization's Philadelphia membership sought to extend its influence over the group's agenda. At the 1834 meeting, William Whipper delivered the keynote address. His speech did acknowledge white wrongdoing associated with the institution of slavery. Still, Whipper contended that until black moral elevation evaporated the ill effects of white racism, African Americans should accept whatever indignities came their way:

> We have observed, that in no country under Heaven have descendants of an ancestry once enrolled in the history of fame; whose glittering monuments stood forth as beacons, disseminating light and knowledge to the utter-most parts of the earth, (been) reduced to such degrading servitude as that under which we labor from the effect of *American slavery* and *American prejudice*. . . . Let us not lament, that under the present constituted powers of this government, we are disfranchised; better far than to be partakers of its guilt. . . . We therefore declare to the world, that our object is to extend the principles of universal peace and good will to all mankind, by promoting sound morality, by the influence of education, temperance and economy, and all those virtues that alone can render man acceptable in the eyes of God or the civilized world.[9] (emphasis in original)

Whipper's comments, among other things, prompted some delegates, especially those from New York, to abandon the Free People Of Colour national organization. Thus, Philadelphia moral reformers gained even more control over the 1835 convention. With muted opposition, two controversial resolutions were passed at this pivotal meeting. First, the organization approved the following Whipper motion: That we recommend as far as possible, to our people to abandon the use of the word colored, when either speaking or writing concerning themselves; and especially to remove the title of African from their institutions, the marbles of churches etc."[10] Also, in keeping with the spirit of denigrating racial identification, the meeting agreed to change the organization's name to the racially neutral American Moral Reform Society.[11]

Although the 1835 convention, in a report entitled, "To The American People," criticized white racism, it stated that, in the name of moral reform, free blacks would be urged to: "bear with Christian fortitude the scoffs and indignation that may be cast upon them on account of their complexion, and pity the source from whence it emanates, knowing it is the offspring of wickedness and ignorance."[12]

By 1836, the free black convention movement had been totally transformed. Perhaps the most striking aspect of this new reality was the fact that whites were invited to participate as delegates to the American Moral Reform Society's inaugural meeting. As one historian described this phenomenon: "Conceding that this [inviting white delegates] was a radical departure from previous practice, Whipper and his fellow directors explained that their organization spurned 'complexional distinctions in the prosecution of moral action.'"[13]

The victory achieved by William Whipper and his fellow moral reformers in taking over the national black convention movement proved to be short-lived. Between 1836 and 1841, the official years of the American Moral Reform Society's existence, the group fought an ultimately unsuccessful battle to convert the majority of free blacks to their cause. There were three major reasons for the AMRS's failure.

First, in the context of the times, the American Moral Reform Society's belief that moral reform could eradicate racial animosity seemed totally unrealistic. In fact, an examination of AMRS literature suggests that Whipper and other members may have been delusional. For example, the Preamble of the American Moral Reform Society's constitution, approved at the watershed 1835 meeting of free blacks, included the following:

> We, the subscribers, citizens of the United States of America, in Convention assembled, believing that the successful resuscitation of our country from moral degeneracy depends upon a vigilant prosecution of the holy cause of Moral Reform, as in its promotion is involved the interest, happiness, and prosperity of this great Republic, and also that the moral elevation of this nation will accelerate the extension of righteousness, justice, truth, and evangelical principles throughout the world . . . do agree to form ourselves into a National Society.[14]

If most free blacks were skeptical of the American Moral Reform Society's self-appointed role as the vanguard of global moral regeneration, they were even more uneasy about specific aspects of the AMRS strategy for achieving utopia. For instance, at the group's 1837 annual meeting, one of the approved resolutions stated "that the practice of non-resistance to physical aggression, is not only consistent with reason, but the surest method of obtaining a speedy triumph of the principles of universal peace."[15] Afterward, in a lengthy speech endorsing the resolution, William Whipper contended:

> There is scarcely a single fact more worthy of indelible record than the utter inefficiency of human punishments to cure human ills. The history of wars exhibits a hopeless, as well as fatal, lesson to all such enterprises. . . . If mankind ever expects to enjoy a state of peace and quietude, they must at all times be ready to sacrifice on the altar of principle, the rude passions that animate them. . . . I am aware that there are those who consider non-resistance wholly impractical. But I trust that but few can be found that have adopted the injunction of our Messiah for their guide and future hope, for he commands us to "love our enemies, bless them that curse you, pray for them that despitefully use you, and persecute you" . . . I rest my argument on the ground that whatever is *scriptural* is *right* and whatever is right, is reasonable, and from this invulnerable position I mean not to stray, for the sake of any expediency whatever. . . . We must be prepared at all times to meet the scoffs and scorns of the vulgar and indecent—the

contemptible frowns of haughty tyrants and the blighting mildew of a popular and sinful prejudice. If amidst these difficulties we can but possess our souls in patience, we shall finally triumph over our enemies.[16] (emphasis in original)

Although William Whipper and his organization based their beliefs on Christian principles, other black Christians of this period frowned on this platform of non-resistance to racial oppression. For example, David Walker's famous 1829 *Appeal*, which espoused slave revolts in the South, included the following religious reference:

The man who would not fight under our Lord and Master Jesus Christ, in the glorious and heavenly cause of freedom and of God—to be delivered from the most wretched, abject, and servile slavery, that ever a people was afflicted with since the foundation of the world, to the present day—ought to be kept with all his children or family, in slavery, or in chains, to be butchered by his *cruel enemies*.[17] (emphasis in original)

Likewise, Nat Turner, who was, among other things, an itinerant Baptist preacher, believed he had divine approval to pursue his aborted 1831 attack against slavery.[18] Consequently, the American Moral Reform Society's overall inability to attract new members[19] suggests that most free blacks, similar to David Walker and Nat Turner, were guided by the belief that "God helps those who help themselves."

Perhaps, the aspect of the American Moral Reform Society's agenda most anathema to the larger free black community was the AMRS's denigration of both racial identification and racially based institutions. This issue, in fact, generated well-publicized, heated discussion at the AMRS's 1837 meeting in Philadelphia.

An Agenda Committee resolution recommending that "free people of colour" form societies to provide educational opportunities for their youth sparked intense debate for several days. William Whipper and the majority of AMRS members present condemned the proposal's wording. They contended that the term "people of colour" represented degradation and discrimination. Moreover, Whipper and his allies believed the American Moral Reform Society should also consider the needs of white youth.[20]

When word spread throughout northern black communities regarding the AMRS debate over the term "free people of colour" and the term's subsequent deletion from the youth education resolution, there was an immediate outcry. Still, despite mounting criticism of the American Moral Reform Society, William Whipper remained steadfast in his disavowal of such terms as "colored" and "people of color."

Thomas M. Lessl, who has analyzed William Whipper's public oratory, provides important insights as to why Whipper prioritized African American moral reform over race-based protest and institution-building. Specifically, Lessl has asserted:

[Whipper] reads . . . as one imbued with a substantial measure of Enlightenment faith in the emancipatory powers of reason. . . . Whipper believed that the emancipation of African Americans, both slave and free, could be accomplished through moral and intellectual development alone. . . . Whipper believed that the ability of his race to show forth its moral and rational integrity would demonstrate the futility and error of all prejudice. . . . The influence of the Enlightenment ideals in Whipper's oratory . . . is most evident in his argument that the oppression of African-Americans was a product of their condition rather than their complexion.[21]

Although Whipper may have both denigrated African American racial self-iden-
tification and believed that the repression of blacks resulted from their lack of moral
and intellectual development (rather than racism), other members of the AMRS apparently did not agree. Feeling the sting of public criticism, they compromised by
using such terms as "Oppressed Americans" to refer to people of African descent.[22]

Samuel Cornish, cofounder of the New York-based *Freedom's Journal* (the first
African American newspaper) in 1827 and a staunch critic of the American Moral
Reform Society, blasted the group's "identity" problem in a March 15, 1838, editor-
ial in the *Colored American* (a successor to *Freedom's Journal*). This essay, entitled
"Our Brethren in Philadelphia," included the following:

> The good sense of some of our brethren in Philadelphia, seems to have forsaken them.
> They are quarreling over trifles, while our enemies are robbing them of diamonds and
> gold. Nothing can be more ridiculous nor ludicrous, than their contentions about
> NAMES—if they quarrel it should be about THINGS. . . . But what caps the climax is, that
> while these sages are frightened half to death, at the idea of being called COLORED, their
> FRIENDS and their FOES, in the convention, in the Assembly and in the Senate; through-
> out the pulpit and the press, call them nothing else but NEGROES, NEGROES, THE NEGROES
> of Pennsylvania. . . . Oppressed Americans! who are they? nonsense brethren!! You are
> COLORED AMERICANS. The Indians are RED AMERICANS, and the white people are WHITE
> AMERICANS and *you are as good as they, and they are no better than you*—God has made all
> of the same blood.[23] (emphasis in original)

By 1839, because of the growing and varied attacks on the American Moral Reform Society, the organization stood at the brink of extinction. To forestall the
AMRS's seemingly imminent collapse, the 1839 annual meeting amended the group's
constitution to admit female members. Still, the 1840 meeting in Philadelphia, despite an invitation to all supporters of moral reform (regardless of their race or gender), attracted only five delegates.[24]

In an apparent last-ditch attempt to resurrect the fortunes of the American Moral
Reform Society, William Whipper used three letters published in the *Colored American* to plead his organization's case to the African American community. In response
to a recent convention of New York African Americans in Albany, Whipper wrote
the following in a January 3, 1841, letter (which appeared in the January 30, 1841,
issue of the *Colored American*):

> Through the kindness of a friend, I have just received for perusal, a copy of the "Min-
> utes of the Albany Convention of Colored Citizens." . . . As I am opposed to the man-
> ner of organization, I cannot therefore subscribe to the proceedings, as a whole, but I
> find in many of the reports and resolutions, principles and sentiments that are eternal
> and immutable. . . . The first resolution will be admired by the friends of liberty and
> equality in all future generations, viz: Resolved, That ALL LAWS established for human
> government, and ALL SYSTEMS, of whatever KIND, founded in the SPIRIT OF COMPLEX-
> IONAL CAST, are in *violation of the fundamental principles of* DIVINE LAW, *evil in their ten-
> dencies,* and should, therefore, be EFFECTUALLY DESTROYED. . . . The convention in
> passing this resolution, not only aided in bringing odium on the title of your paper [*The
> Colored American*], . . . but ushered forth a withering condemnation on the form of their
> own organization.[25] (emphasis in original)

In response, Charles B. Ray, then editor of *The Colored American*, asserted that African Americans formed separate institutions (churches, fraternal societies, etc.), not based upon "the spirit of complexional cast," but because of "*desperate necessity.*"[26]

Undaunted, the irrepressible Whipper wrote a January 12, 1841, letter to Charles B. Ray that elaborated upon his first communique:

> As a people we are deeply afflicted with "colorphobia." . . . It is an evil that must be met, *and we must meet it now.* . . . We must throw off the distinctive features in the charters of our churches and other institutions. We have refused to hear ministers preach from the pulpit, because they would not preach against slavery. We must pursue the same course respecting prejudice against complexion.[27]

For his part, Charles Ray, with undisguised sarcasm and derision, dismissed Whipper's latest assertions with the following:

> Friend Whipper appears again this week, on our first page, like some distant planet, whose reflected light is hardly discoverable, on account of some opaque spots, nearly covering its disk, and the few rays which do escape, are too feeble to produce either light, heat, or effect. . . . It is indeed a pity to have such a noble mind and sweet temper thus in the dark.[28]

Whipper's final letter to Charles Ray, dated January 17, 1841 (which appeared in the February 20, 1841, issue of the *Colored American*), sought to clarify the similarities and differences between the American Moral Reform Society and other black organizations:

> The A.M.R. Society, which sprang from the "Convention of free people of color" adopted principles, the exact antipode of those of the call of the convention in Albany, and yet it would have been in strict accordance with the Society's principles, to have adopted every resolution passed by that body [Albany convention]. Now sir, we see plainly that there is no difference of opinion with the principles that ought to be maintained, it is only as to the *method of organization.*[29] (emphasis in original)

The recorded responses to Whipper's three letters to *The Colored American* included a front page article in the March 3, 1841, issue of the paper authored by an unknown writer with the pen name "Sidney." While "Sidney's" identity remains a mystery, he (or she), as the following excerpt indicates, clearly questioned Whipper's aversion to racial identification:

> That we are colored, is a fact, an undeniable fact. That we are descendants of Africans—colored people—negroes if you will, is true. We affirm there is nothing in it that we need to be ashamed of, yea, rather much that we may be proud of. There is, then, on our part, as identified with the negro race, no reason why the term [colored] should be repudiated. . . . Discontinue the use of the term—does prejudice die? Oh no, Leviathan is not so tamed.[30]

Among other things, "Sidney's" repudiation of William Whipper, along with that of Charles B. Ray (and most northern free blacks), contributed to the American Moral Reform Society's official demise in August, 1841.[31]

One important postscript to the American Moral Reform Society's story was the subsequent ideological transformation of its leading figure, William Whipper. In the final issue of the *National Reformer*, the AMRS's official, but short-lived publication, Whipper made the following shocking declaration:

> We have been advocates of the doctrine that we must be "elevated" before we could expect to enjoy the privileges of America citizenship. . . . We now utterly discard it, and ask for pardon for our former errors . . . not lack of elevation, but complexion . . . deprived the man of color of equal treatment.[32]

It is worth noting that if a committed organic conservative like William Whipper could, ultimately, see the error of his ways, perhaps, there is hope, after all, for such individuals as Armstrong Williams and Alan Keyes.

The failure of the American Moral Reform Society to develop into a truly viable organization, as well as the failure of contemporary black conservatives to attract a significant constituency within the African American community, does not reflect a historic (or ongoing) lack of interest among blacks in issues related to morality. What it does reflect is an African American suspicion of organizations and individuals that link moral reform with a repudiation of group consciousness.

Philadelphia's Free African Society, which was founded in 1787 and regarded as the first African American mutual aid society, clearly revealed that moral reform and racial consciousness are not necessarily mutually exclusive characteristics. For instance, the organization's financial rules included the following stipulation: "And it is further agreed that no drunkard or disorderly person be admitted as a member, and if they should prove disorderly after having been received, the said disorderly person shall be disjoined from us."[33]

Similarly, the United Order of True Reformers, arguably the most significant African American fraternal organization of the late nineteenth century, was a consciously black organization that stressed both morality and collective African American economic development. The True Reformers, under the leadership of William Washington Browne, urged African Americans to eschew the consumption of alcohol and to use monies saved for collective economic development. The True Reformers' subsequent multifaceted economic program included ownership of a bank, an impressive meeting hall, a retirement home, and a newspaper. Besides these auxiliary enterprises, the organization provided its members with insurance options ranging from simple burial insurance to survivors' benefits of up to $1,000.[34]

At the March 4, 1894, dedication of a True Reformers meeting hall in Lynchburg, Virginia, William Washington Browne clearly articulated his philosophy. After telling the crowd that "with a mind full of industry, there is no room for the barroom and other vices,"[35] he turned the crowd's attention to the True Reformers' latest achievement, focusing on how the group could help the black church resuscitate black America:

> This building cost twenty-four thousand dollars. I can find you ten thousand men who have drunk the cost of this building, seven times this year, at five cents a drink. Ten thousand men at five cents a day will drink up in one year one hundred eighty-two thousand, five hundred dollars. Which is best for the Church to have; an army of ten thousand and spending one hundred eighty-two thousand, five hundred dollars a year

impoverishing their families and the Church . . . or to have an industrious organization going forth in every community, putting her sermons, songs, and prayers into practice, taking care of the sick, burying the dead . . . teaching the people to save their money, buy homes, [and to] circulate their money one with the other.[36]

Browne, who viewed African American alcohol consumption as another form of enslavement,[37] exulted in the fact that, unlike many late nineteenth century black leaders (who were of mixed racial ancestry), he was of pure African ancestry. Moreover, as David M. Fahey noted, Browne often boasted that he "never mingled" with whites and asserted, "You do not see me among them [whites] except on business."[38]

The Nation of Islam represents a more recent indication that an African American organization can be both pro-black and pro–moral reform. An examination of its famous convict rehabilitation program among black convicts and parolees (especially males), graphically verifies this assertion.

Malcolm Little's transformation from a two-bit hoodlum named "Detroit Red" into the articulate and ascetic Malcolm X represents the most spectacular historic example of the Nation of Islam's positive work in this area. As one commentator described this "moral reform" program:

Their [Nation of Islam's] rehabilitation program is nothing short of miraculous. They start out by convincing the ex-convict that he fell into crime because he was ashamed of being black, that the white man had so psychologically conditioned him that he was unable to respect himself. Then they convince the one-time prisoner that being black is a blessing, not a curse, and that in keeping with that blessing he, the ex-convict, must clean himself up and live a life of decency and respect. As a result:

You never see a Muslim without a clean shirt and tie and coat.

You never see a Muslim drink.

You never see a Muslim smoke.

You never see a Muslim dance.

You never see a Muslim use dope.

You never see a Muslim woman with a non-Muslim man.

You never see a Muslim man with a woman other than his wife.

You never see a Muslim without some means of income.

You never see a Muslim who will not stop and come to the aid of any black woman he sees in trouble.

You seldom see a Muslim lapse back into crime. (A close friend of mine is a lawyer with Muslim clients and he tells me that he has known of only four Muslims who have returned to crime in the past five years. This is remarkable when one remembers that some six hundred convicts in prison join the Black Muslims each year. The Muslim leaders arrange parole for their converts and take them in hand. Parole and police officers have told me that the Black Muslims are the best rehabilitation agency at work among Negro criminals today).[39]

Considering the historic and contemporary examples represented by the Free African Society, the True Reformers, and the Nation of Islam, it is clear that an African American organization can be both pro-black and pro–moral reform. Moreover, both historical and contemporary evidence suggests that the majority of African Americans concur.

If it is indeed true that most African Americans have valued, and continue to value, their racial heritage, what does the future hold for today's organic black conservatives who, like the American Moral Reform Society, tend to denigrate notions of African American racial pride and identity? To propose a possible answer, it is not far-fetched to suggest that today's (white-financed) organic black conservatives, similar to the American Moral Reform Society, appear headed for historical obscurity. Despite their media exposure and vehemence, today's organic black conservatives, similar to the earlier American Moral Reform Society, have no real constituency in the African American community. In fact, many contemporary African Americans find it ludicrous, if not insulting, for the black agents of the people who enslaved millions of Africans and stole the land of Native Americans to offer African Americans instruction in the area of morality.

NOTES

1. *Webster's Desk Dictionary of the English Language* (New York: Portland House, 1990), 194.
2. Lewis A. Randolph, "A Historical Analysis and Critique of Contemporary Black Conservatism," *The Western Journal of Black Studies*, 19 (Fall 1995): 150–51.
3. Phillip S. Foner, *History of Black Americans: From the Emergence of the Cotton Kingdom to the Eve of the Compromise of 1850* (Westport, CT: Greenwood Press, 1983), pp. 311–12; Howard H. Bell, "The American Moral Reform Society, 1836–1841," *Journal of Negro Education*, 27 (Winter 1958): 34.
4. Howard H. Bell, ed., *Minutes of the Proceedings of the National Negro Conventions, 1830–1864* (New York: Arno Press, 1969), p. 5.
5. Ibid., pp. 22–23.
6. For an overview of the experiences of northern free blacks in early- to mid-nineteenth-century America, see Leon Litwack, *North of Slavery: The Negro in the Free States, 1790–1860* (Chicago: University of Chicago Press, 1961), and Leonard Curry, *The Free Black in Urban America, 1800–1850* (Chicago: University of Chicago Press, 1981).
7. Foner, *History of Black Americans*, p. 313.
8. Bell, *Minutes of the National Negro Conventions*, 1833 meeting, pp. 17–18.
9. Ibid., 1834 meeting, pp. 27–29, 31.
10. Ibid., 1835 meeting, pp. 14–15.
11. Ibid., 1835 meeting, pp. 25–32.
12. Ibid., 1835 meeting, p. 29.
13. Julie Winch, *Philadelphia's Black Elite: Activism, Accommodation, and the Struggle for Autonomy, 1787–1848* (Philadelphia: Temple University Press, 1988), p. 109.
14. Bell, *Minutes of the National Negro Conventions*, 1835 meeting, p. 31.
15. C. Peter Ripley, ed., *The Black Abolitionist Papers, Volume III: The United States, 1830–1846* (Chapel Hill: University of North Carolina Press, 1991), p. 238.
16. Ibid., pp. 242, 243, 245
17. David Walker, *David Walker's Appeal, in Four Articles, Together with A Preamble, to the Colored Citizens of the World, But in Particular, and Very Expressly, to Those of the United States of America*, with an introduction by James Turner (Baltimore: Black Classics Press, 1993; originally published in 1829), p. 32.
18. Stephen B. Oates, *The Fires of Jubilee: Nat Turner's Fierce Rebellion* (New York: Harper and Row, 1975). Perhaps the most famous story involving Nat Turner's religiosity was his response, "was not Christ crucified?" when asked about his impending execution for leading a slave revolt. (pp.121–22)
19. Foner, *History of Black Americans*, p. 314.

20. Ibid.

21. Thomas M. Lessl, "William Whipper," in Richard W. Leeman, ed., *African American Orators: A Bio-Critical Sourcebook* (Westport, CT: Greenwood Press, 1996), p. 377.

22. Bell, "The American Moral Reform Society," p. 38.

23. Ripley, *The Black Abolitionist Papers*, pp. 263–64.

24. Foner, *History of Black Americans*, p. 314.

25. "Letter from William Whipper to Charles B. Ray," *The Colored American*, January 30, 1841, pp. 1–2.

26. Editorial comment, *The Colored American*, January 30, 1841, p. 2.

27. "Letter from William Whipper to Charles B. Ray," *The Colored American*, February 6, 1841, p. 1.

28. Editorial comment, *The Colored American*, February 6, 1841, p. 2.

29. "Letter from William Whipper to Charles B. Ray," *The Colored American*, February 20, 1841, p. 1.

30. Sidney, "Response to the William Whipper Letters," *The Colored American*, March 13, 1841, p. 1.

31. Foner, *History of Black Americans*, p. 314.

32. Ibid., p. 315; Ripley, *The Black Abolitionist Papers*, p. 129. Whipper's movement from nonracialist moral reform peaked during the 1850s, when he publicly accepted the need for separate black schools and endorsed Henry Highland Garnet's African Civilization Society (which promoted emigration to Africa). See Ripley, *The Black Abolitionist Papers*, pp. 129–30.

33. Herbert Aptheker, ed., *A Documentary History of the Negro People in the United States* (New York: The Citadel Press, 1969), p. 18.

34. For a complete examination of the True Reformers and William Washington Browne, see David M. Fahey's *The Black Lodge in White America: "True Reformer" Browne and His Economic Strategy* (Dayton, OH: Wright State University Press, 1994).

35. Ibid., p. 210.

36. Ibid.

37. Ibid., p. 111.

38. Ibid., p. 3.

39. Louis E. Lomax, *The Negro Revolt* (New York: Signet Books, 1963), pp. 190–91.

CHAPTER 3

"THERE IS NO REFUGE IN CONSERVATISM": A CASE STUDY OF BLACK POLITICAL CONSERVATISM IN RICHMOND, VIRGINIA

GAYLE T. TATE AND LEWIS A. RANDOLPH

RESISTANCE, CONSERVATISM, AND PLANTATION SLAVERY

Much of the discussion on the origins of black conservatism in Virginia must be traced to the myriad of responses that Africans had to their enslavement in the Chesapeake and Piedmont regions of the state. Over time, these responses were shaped by the confluences of plantation slavery, industrial slavery, the importation of African slaves, and the development of the planter aristocracy. Undoubtedly, such factors as the "slave fever" that swept the South and the constant migration of middle class slaveholders for fertile land as they sought to reconcile their dreams of wealth on the backs of black labor fed the larger currents of slave resistance.[1] Black resistance was a far more dominant expression by Virginia slaves, and it ebbed and flowed over several centuries of oppression. In contrast, the incipient forms of black conservatism were far lesser expressions, and they, too, changed over the enslavement period in the larger exigencies of black struggle and cash crop-commodity production. Ironically, black resistance, until the last few decades, had been somewhat muted in historical treatments of the period, while the complacency of slaves, a conservative feature, was widely accepted as the slaves' prevailing response to oppression.

Black resistance and black conservatism were both rooted in the dynamics of change that was integral to the construction of a slave society in Virginia. By the eighteenth century, the Virginia colony had imported a substantial slave population. "[F]rom 1700 to 1740, roughly 43,000 blacks entered Virginia, about 39,000 of whom were Africans."[2] Coming chiefly from Biafra and Angola, these African slaves "shared a similar ethnic identity" which, in turn, facilitated the retention of an African world-view as well as African traditions and values. Sterling Stuckey notes, "Since the overwhelming majority of the slaves brought into Virginia until the end of the trade were African born, they provided the foundation of values from which slave culture was erected, New World experience being interpreted largely from the African point of view."[3]

As Africans developed a cohesive slave community, they also forged a common solidarity in other forms of resistance. Historian Allan Kulikoff comments on the resistance taking shape in early Virginia among the slaves:

> In the mid-1700s, late 1710s, mid-1720s, and mid-1730s, when unusually large numbers of blacks entered Virginia, these Africans, united by their common experiences and able to communicate through the heavily African pidgin they probably created, ran off to the woods together, formed temporary settlements in wilderness, and several times conspired to overthrow their white masters.[4]

Although some scholars view the development of the transatlantic slave community and African retentiveness as ways in which the slaves were conservatizing their traditions, particularly the patriarchal family structure, that is only partly accurate.[5] Although slave women were locked into a patriarchal family structure in which they performed gender-specific tasks associated with their roles in Africa and reinforced by plantation slavery, there were underlying elements of resistance. Jacqueline Jones points out that slave women's voluntary labor on behalf of their families and their dignity was an act of defiance against a system that relegated them to chattel property.[6] The slaves' determination to pass on their ancestral legacy in a hostile environment, to transform their "living space" to embrace the historical memories of Africa as well as the new European American cultural remnants, constituted the very essence of resistance to domination. The slave community's cohesiveness, which was largely fueled by their resistance to slavery was also stabilized by elements of conservatism.

But the negative components of black conservatism, which Vernon McClean states were slaves "who identified their fortunes with those of their masters," were deleterious to slave community cohesiveness.[7] While some slaves simply tried to exist in the slave system, McClean argues that "a few Blacks knowingly and willfully, for monetary and ideological reasons, embraced a philosophical orientation which can be termed conservative."[8] Planters selected, fostered, and reinforced this aspect of conservatism by promoting slave divisiveness "through a complex system of rewards, incentives, and punishment, including bonuses, such as cast-off dresses, better food, better housing quarters, etc."[9]

Many slaves who sought willingly to maximize their advantage in the plantation system by aligning themselves with their masters had shifted their allegiance and loyalties to the planter class. In this process, "favored slaves," who psychologically distanced themselves from the rest of the slave community in their attempts to identify with a more powerful group, were merely supplanting one form of oppression for another, more comprehensive form of racial subordination. The new status of "favorite slave," which was recognized by both the slave community and the planter, meant that the role of these slaves expanded exponentially. In return for his supposed largesse, the master had the expectation of complete obedience, a liaison to the slave quarters, and, sometimes, community betrayal. In the slave community, the individual was frequently regarded with suspicion, distrust, and outright contempt. Depending on the nature and substance of the favored slave status, these slaves had to navigate a difficult terrain on the plantation.

Masters determined the special status of favorite slaves based on their profit motives in cash crop–commodity production and their skills at plantation management. Although such factors as color, gender, division of labor, and the productive and reproductive capacity of slaves proved to be major determinants in according slaves' status, masters knew that their prosperity depended on how much divisiveness they could create in the slave community. Once slaves engaged willingly in this more subtle form of exploitation, masters could exercise better control of the labor force. Despite the boasting of Robert Ellett, a Virginia ex-slave, "We was favored slaves. . . . I am a mixture of Negro-Indian-French and white blood. My father's grandfather was Governor of the State of Virginia, Governor Ellett, yessir! [No Ellett was ever governor of Virginia],"[10] these relationships were always determined by the planter and could prove hazardous for the slave at any moment. Allen Crawford, another Virginia ex-slave, recalls that the relationship between Austin Sykes, a favorite slave, and his master, John Biggs, was mired in contempt and betrayal.

> Lemme tell you dis. Dar was a slave named Austin Sykes belonging to ole man John Biggs. John Biggs promised to protect him when he was out from boteration of paterrollers. So dis particular time I was setting dar by marse, saw ole paterrollers take Sykes down woods—See, his master went back on 'im. Didn't 'tect him dis time.—Arter while, I jes heard 'em beating Sykes and I up and tole marse like dis: "Dam ef dey ain't giving Austin hell down dar!" Marse's mother, who was setting dar too, up and spoke: "He ought to kill dat nigger!"[11]

Black resistance and black conservatism were intertwining factors in plantation communities, which stabilized the community as blacks forged a transatlantic culture to preserve African traditions, withstand the onslaught of their enslavement, and fortify a resistance against oppression. Simultaneously, slaves' resistance to their enslavement necessitated masters creating divisiveness among the slaves as an essential component of plantation management—through the rape of black women, corporal punishment, intensive labor, and the sale of slaves among other tactics—to assert domination and control, instill compliance, and stabilize the work force. Opportunistic slaves, who willingly complied with the masters' attempts at forging disunity in the slave quarters, reinforced the negative trappings of early black conservatism by separating themselves from the group, seeking individual gain, and creating an alliance with the white power structure that held blacks in bondage. These negative elements of black conservatism, which reinforced the patriarchal, authoritative power of the white planter elite, were transformed into class and ideological cleavages as slaves and free blacks migrated to Richmond, Virginia to become part of the city's industrial labor force.

RICHMOND, INDUSTRIAL SLAVERY, AND THE BLACK ELITE

Countless African slaves had already shaped the confluences of Virginia's slave society for well over a century before Richmond became the state capital in 1779.

African slaves dominated the state's labor force and, as agricultural producers, played pivotal roles in tobacco and cereal grain production, which not only defined class, gender, and race relations but fueled the state's market economy and early industrialization. From the outset, then, Richmond's indigenous history was shaped just as much by the social and economic forces of slavery, the city's lucrative slave markets, and the concomitant development of the white planter aristocracy as it was by being located in a temperate climate that was conducive to tobacco cultivation. The city's growth industries soon included the processing and packaging of tobacco, iron foundries, flour mills, and canal and railroad construction, enabling the distribution of the richly desired Virginia sweet tobacco, cereal products, and heavy equipment to domestic and international markets.[12] But as was typical of many southern cities, the die had already been cast: by the time Richmond had emerged as an urban center depending heavily on industrial slavery, the construction of Virginia's slave society had been in progress for more than a century and was integral to the city's future.

Before the antebellum period, the Richmond mercantilists had shaped the city's growth and prosperity through their political leadership on Richmond's city council and control of the dominant economic initiatives. These early leaders had possessed visions of making the city a center of trade and commerce connecting Europe, the North, and the South, but Richmond's commercialism was gradually being replaced by a growing industrial economy. This industrial development conducted by the established mercantile elite was gradually being infiltrated by new industrialists with more progressive ideas regarding the city's internal improvements, new technology, and, ultimately, political and economic leadership. Although the alliance between the established elite and new entrepreneurs would be an uneasy one at times, both classes were cut from the same cloth in their aristocractic pretensions and support of southern slavery. As both groups were seeking to dominate the region's economy and politics, their alliance proved critical in creating the Richmond oligarchy.

The Richmond oligarchy (dubbed the Richmond Junta), which emerged in the early 1800s, typified two centuries of white supremacy in Virginia. Political scientist V. O. Key, Jr., described Virginia's oligarchical structure, which dominated the state's political apparatus: "Political power has been closely held by a small group of leaders who, themselves and their predecessors, have subverted democratic institutions and deprived most Virginians of a voice in their government."[13] The political environment in Richmond, which was created by the Richmond Junta and buttressed by Virginia's ideology of white supremacy, laid the foundation for the superordinate-subordinate relations between blacks and whites in the city. By the antebellum era, 1830–1860, this planter-industrialist class of judges, editors, and bank presidents (most of whom were members of the planter elite) dominated the city's conservative agenda, espousing antipathies toward immigrants and a pseudo-aristocratic superiority toward their urban slaves and toward free blacks as well.[14]

By the 1840s, Richmond was considered the major industrial city in the South. Such factors as the agricultural production of tobacco, the pig iron from the trans-Allegheny region and northern cities, a pool of German and Irish immigrant laborers, and an even cheaper pool of urban slave and free black laborers spearheaded the city's factory development. The city's strategic location on the fault line of the James River and the Kanawha Canal, as well as the fact that five railroads terminated in the city, allowed entrepreneurs and manufacturers to easily export finished products to international and domestic markets. Federal government contracts, particularly in the iron industry, led to frequent plant expansion and the increased purchasing and hiring of more slaves to stabilize the labor force.

This rapidly expanding industrialization created an acute need for an aggregate labor force, which was solved partly by the large influx of white Irish and Germany immigrants who came to Richmond seeking jobs and solidified their positions as wage laborers in industrial production. "Northern and European ironworkers were reluctant to settle in slave states and could only be lured south by premium wages."[15] The other part of the industrial need for labor was remedied by the slave and free black labor force. The slave laborers, artisans, and agricultural producers, were drawn from the surplus of slave labor that occurred on some plantations where there was a shift away from staple crop production to a more diversified economy. Slaves, both skilled and unskilled, who were purchased by factory owners or "hired out" by their masters on an annual contract basis and came into the city from a slave culture steeped in African traditions and now removed from the regimentation of plantation labor, were eager to experience this new quasi-independence. These slaves went to work in artisan shops, tobacco factories, flour and iron mills, building and construction, and stone quarries, as well as on the railroads. Other slaves were hired as domestic servants to perform household labor for upper-class white Richmonders. Although the hiring of slaves was always integral to interplantation life, industrial slavery placed blacks into an urban milieu, which distanced the planter from the control of his property and thereby weakened the bonds between master and slave.[16]

Richmond's urban environment transformed the lives of free black and slave laborers who came from the surrounding rural areas to work in the city's industrial factories. Richmond's fifty-two tobacco factories, of which forty-nine produced two popular chewing tobaccos, "plug" and "twist," placed almost a total reliance on slave labor.[17] Just as slaves worked in the cash-crop production of tobacco, black men, women, and children worked at the manufacturing and processing end as well. "By the mid-1850s, 3,400 slaves worked in the city's tobacco factories."[18] Slaves were also employed in significant numbers in the seventy-seven iron foundries, machine shops, forges, and rolling mills in the skilled positions of puddlers, heaters, and rollers, and in semiskilled jobs as well. Manufacturers, such as Joseph T. Anderson, the head of Tredegar Iron Works, sought to reduce his labor cost and enhance his advantage when competing with northern and European manufacturers for government and business contracts by employing mostly slave labor.[19]

Despite the intense labor of factory production, slaves and free blacks experienced a tenuous, quasi-free status by living and working in the cities. Slaves who worked in factories could receive wages for overtime work as well as a stipend for room and board in the city. Factory owners found that slaves were zealous in their productivity when performing overtime work, which allowed them to earn monies for themselves. Although slaves were initially forced to live in the master's "compound," which was "the urban equivalent of the plantation," this system soon broke down, and some of the physical and social control of the slaves was lost.[20] "Living out" meant that slaves sought rented rooms, basements, back alleys, sheds or anywhere where there was a modicum of privacy and freedom.[21] Despite the diligent effort on the part of Richmond to curb the slaves' behavior with restrictive codes, as well as the watchful eyes of white citizens, the inability to control blacks in the urban environment, as well as blacks' attempts to expand their freedom at every turn, weakened the urban slave system.

Just as Richmond's emerging industrialization created the impetus for quasi-independence for some slaves, it also changed the context and strategies of black resistance by enabling more free blacks to be incorporated into rebellion efforts. Urban resistance also included the participation of slaves and free blacks from several towns and cities, an extension network of communication, and heavy reliance on black seamen and other blacks who were mobile and harbored a clear resentment against the planter-industrialist aristocracy. In 1793, the "Secret Keeper," a conspiracy rumored to include several thousand insurrectionists in Richmond, Norfolk, and Charleston, planned a revolution to overthrow slavery.[22] Although the conspiracy was discovered and aborted, it engendered fear in white southerners, leading to increased societal proscriptions for blacks.

By 1800, Gabriel Prosser (a blacksmith on the Prosser plantation in Brookfield, a few miles from Richmond), who was inspired by the Haitian rebellion, planned a revolt. Encouraged by the schism between the Democrat-Republicans and Federalists in Richmond, Prosser crafted a plan that included slaves from nearby plantations as well as slaves and free blacks in the port cities of Richmond, Petersburg, Charlottesville, Suffolk, and Norfolk, hoping to "inspir[e] a general uprising among thousands of Africans."[23] Although a terrible storm spoiled the attack strategies on August 30, 1800, and the plot was betrayed before Prosser could reassemble his troops, the seeds of urban resistance had been planted. By August 1831, Nat Turner's rebellion in Southhampton County, three decades after the aborted Prosser rebellion, signaled the continuity of black resistance into the antebellum era. Although it was a southern slave rebellion, it promoted fear in whites, who then imposed greater restrictions on blacks as far away as Philadelphia, Pennsylvania.[24] The systematic slaughtering of whites by Turner and his slave rebels as they moved from house to house was curtailed by a county-wide alarm, which permitted a now alerted militia and vigilante groups to give chase and, ultimately, capture the slaves.[25] These rebellions, as well as individual acts of resistance and courage via the Underground Railroad, which was very active in Richmond, inspired the heroism of other blacks, just as their oppressors chose to interpret black resistance as demonic anomalies rather than a struggle for justice and freedom.

Just as black resistance provided the major context for plantation and urban struggle, black conservative traditions and values were instilling influences that were moderating, but still defiant, in the free black community in the city. As many of these semiautonomous urban slaves made their transition from slavery to freedom, they contributed to the free black community's expansion and development. With the "bonus" or "overtime" monies received by these factory workers, they were able to purchase themselves and family members, rent lodging, purchase provisions, and become members of the black church and one or more of the community's "secret societies" in the free black community. Subsequent to gaining their freedom, some ex-slaves sought to accumulate real estate, often with the legal title resting in some white person's name.[26] "By 1860 seventy-one free Negroes in Richmond held property of a minimum value of $1000. . . . Fifteen of these, by frequent purchases of real estate, accumulated property worth $4000 or $5000."[27] This small group of free property owners would form the core of Richmond's black elite after emancipation.

EMANCIPATION, MOBILIZATION AND DISENFRANCHISEMENT

After nearly 250 years of enslavement, black men and women could experience freedom for the first time when the city fell to the Union troops on April 3, 1865. Despite the occupied forces, there were already signs that black progress would be thwarted and compromised. For one thing, the antebellum planter-industrialist oligarchy was not destabilized after the Civil War but continued to dominate and control the city. Once former white officials of the Confederacy had sworn loyalty oaths to the U.S. Constitution, Governor Francis N. Pierpont, leader of the Restored government of Virginia, reinstated all antebellum officials to their former offices and repealed all wartime provisos that disenfranchised former Confederate officials. The collusion between the federal troops and the white oligarchy allowed the continuation of the customary treatment of blacks. Moreover, the doctrine of white supremacy in Richmond was merely transformed so that white southerners could still maintain domination and control over blacks while they exploited their labor in order to resuscitate the southern economy. Charles Wynes, in his book, *Race Relations in Virginia, 1870–1902*, aptly characterized black-white relations in Richmond, Virginia, after emancipation, stating that "white Virginians believe that the only way to address the Negro problem was through segregation, subordination or if necessary, extermination."[28]

Despite the chaos of war and its aftermath, black Richmonders immediately mobilized for social change. Pooling their collective resources, they established four hundred secret societies and quasi-trade union organizations and quickly expanded the hegemony of the five black churches that had been founded in the antebellum era. "They seized control of their churches by June 1865, named new pastors, and used church buildings for schools, employment offices, and staging areas for organizing public protests and celebrations."[29] Embedded in the institutionalization of the black church in the postbellum era was the construction of a black male hierarchy of leadership. Black women's base of leadership was frequently tied to the family, church organizations, work, and community activism. Most, if not all, black women worked as household domestics or factory workers and performed the double duty of caring for the home and, frequently, boarders as well.

Nevertheless, black women were active grassroots organizers, participating in constitutional convention deliberations of the Republican Party in 1867, the elections of delegates to the constitutional conventions, public protests, streetcar demonstrations, and, increasingly, militant emancipation celebrations. Although black women were denied suffrage, it did not exclude them from political participation, and they made their mark on the political spectrum in campaigning for candidates, educating the community around the issues, organizing political fundraisers and voter mobilization, and bridging the gap between political, benevolent, and church societies. Despite their activism and organizational expertise, by the 1880s middle-class black men were encouraging them to take a more traditional role in the black community. However, black women sagaciously focused on an independent course of black female entrepreneurship, faith, economic nationalism, protest, and race consciousness and argued that "race men" were defenders of black womanhood. "Their arguments redefined not only the roles of women but also the roles and notions of manhood. . . . In her 'Address for Men' [Maggie Lena] Walker argued that one could not defend the race unless one defended black women."[30] Ironically, the attempts to silence black women's political voices occurred as the final planks of social segregation and disenfranchisement were being put in place for African Americans.

Class and political alignments in the African American community in Richmond became more prevalent in the decade following emancipation and embodied different ideological and pragmatic perspectives. Black conservatism was expressed among the black elite, who quickly distanced themselves from the newly freed slaves pouring into Richmond, instead taking solace in their real estate, access to education, and economic opportunities, all gained before the Civil War. Boasting of their miscegenated family tree (although comprised frequently of the group that Roi Ottley termed the "mulatto nobodies" and pseudoalliances with whites), they were seen by the black masses as disloyal to the race.[31] This black elite solidified its economic interests under the rubric of racial solidarity, although its bourgeois respectability pivoted on economic prosperity, light skin color, notions of "southern gentility," and conservatism. In marked contrast, recently freed persons were of darker hues, totally penniless, displaced during the war, lacking social graces, and strident in seeking political inclusion and wider distributions of economic resources. Black conservatives, many of whom were totally dependent on white patronage, were either conservative in their politics or shunned politics altogether for fear of offending their white benefactors, and they encouraged the black community toward moderate political and social change.

The newly freed urban slaves were far more strident in their press for social and political change and quickly assumed the mantle of black community leadership in protest activities until the 1880s.[32] As former slaves picked up the fragment of their lives and got the same factory jobs that most had held during slavery, they quickly realized that Reconstruction for black Richmonders held meager benefits and that freedom and struggle were intertwined. Two months after emancipation in Richmond, black Richmonders galvanized the community to protest against the "pass system," which had formerly been a slave law to limit their mobility and was now reinstated for free blacks and perceived as an eggregious affront to the entire black community. A letter of protest to the *New York Tribune*, a meeting with President Andrew Johnson, and protest forums at First African Baptist Church led to the abolishment of the system.[33] Even though the black masses' allegiance was to the radical wing of the Republican Party, they continued to demonstrate their independence and militancy. Emancipation Day celebrations proved to be another vehicle for blacks to demonstrate their growing independence and to create a political forum for community issues. Although black men, women, and children actively participated in Republican Party convention deliberations, simultaneously they organized a successful mass political action to desegregate the city's streetcars.[34]

The class cleavages and ideological perspectives in the black community quickly became evident in the political arena and served as political opportunities for both the Republican Party and the newly constituted Conservative Party to exacerbate the schisms and betray all black Richmonders. During Reconstruction (1865–1870), the oligarchy prevailing under the guise of the Conservative Party, the military rule of the Union troops, and the Republican Party made pseudoalliances with an emerging black political elite as they sought to maintain white supremacy in Richmond. But the black elite did not possess the reins of power in the black community. The working-class group of artisans that emerged as leaders was not receptive to any proposal suggested by the Conservative Party. Although many of its members emulated the social mores and culture of white southern society, most of the black elite identified its political interests with the rest of the black community but were approachable by the Conservatives. By 1871, the Conservative Party had carefully constructed a plan to limit black political effectiveness. Toward this end, they created Jackson Ward, in which the "new ward boundaries were skillfully gerrymandered to include much of the black population and very few whites,"[35] to limit black political effectiveness. Then the Conservative Party carefully "created" and handpicked black moderate leaders to serve on the city council and control black political gains. "The black councilmen occupied the middle ground politically and economically, although socially they ranked higher in the black community that did many postwar white councilmen in white society."[36]

Except for a brief period during the Readjuster campaign (1879–1883), when the Republican-black axis rallied after a Conservative Party-Democratic Party split, dominated the state legislature, and passed progressive reforms, the disenfranchisement of blacks by the Conservative Party that had begun its constitutional process in 1869 proceeded apace. James T. Moore commented on this period:

This relentless machine hammered the blacks with poll taxes, gerrymanders, and election frauds, reducing the number of Negroes in the state legislature from thirty in 1870 to only five in 1878. County officials excluded blacks from jury duty; local school boards employed white teachers for black schools, rejecting the applications of qualified Negroes. . . . Political impotence paved the way for public humiliation.[37]

By the 1880s, as the Democrats were establishing one-party rule and relegating the Republican Party to oblivion, they were simultaneously finalizing plans for the complete political and social subordination of blacks. The Democrats reinstituted the former Conservative Party's use of threats, physical violence, and economic reprisals against blacks and strengthened the legal apparatus of oppression. Adding outright intimidation throughout the state, gerrymandering in all congressional districts to assure complete political control, and embracing the Anderson-McCormick election law, enabled the Democrats to accomplish the almost total disenfranchisemment of black Virginians. The Anderson-McCormick law, once amended, provided that in 1884 and thereafter, three persons would be elected for each city and county, who could then appoint local election officials.[38] "The Anderson-McCormack bill was passed in the interest of the white people of Virginia. . . . It is a white man's law. It operates to perpetuate the role of the white man in Virginia."[39] Although the law enabled the Democrats to gain political control of state and local officials, it also paved the way for fraud, widespread corruption, and the manipulation of every election with the expressed intent of black political exclusion.

Richmond's black industrial workers grew increasingly alarmed after the Democratic sweep to victory in 1883. As the Democrats began to dismantle the Readjuster's policies, black Richmonders' gains began to diminish in the city. "When Democrats returned to power in 1883, many of Richmond's black teachers and all three of the city's black school principals were fired."[40] This rapid erosion of black political gains made black workers anxious to build an independent political and economic base that grew out of their cultural nationalism, namely, existing black cultural institutions, and attracted them to the Knights of Labor. The Knights of Labor (founded in 1884 in Richmond, it was a a nationally based interracial trade union that included male and female workers), experienced unprecedented growth in the city, and in one year it had grown to 12 black assemblies and two female local chapters.[41] The Knights' success at initiating mass consumer boycotts eventually found them in opposition to the city's industrial-planter alliance. Despite forming the Workingmen's Reform Party and winning the city elections in 1886 with an all-white slate, their inability to hold the reins of government and their unresponsiveness to the needs of black citizens and workers' interests caused their disappearance from the political landscape by 1888.

Black Richmonders continued their fight for political inclusion with broad-based nationalist strategies that emphasized their racial pride, which had been honed by their cultural institutions. Gradually, the black working-class leadership in Richmond was being supplanted by a new middle-class black professional leadership, whose members were born directly before or after emancipation. This latter group was termed "new issue Negroes" by Michael B. Chesson and proved somewhat more moderate than the former, more strident, working-class leaders.[42] Whereas the masses wedded their nationalism to a working-class ideology that included race, gender, and class, the rising middle class supported economic nationalism, encouraging black institutional development and "buy black campaigns" as a bulwark against the rising racism. John T. Mitchell, Jr., editor of the *Richmond Planet,* the largest black weekly in Virginia, was supporting Booker T. Washington's economic nationalism when he stated: "Colored men, continue to save money and property. . . . Any colored man who opposes race enterprises among the colored people is his own worst enemy."[43]

Black Richmonders' focus on "race enterprises" evince strong progress in the 1880s and 1890s. They founded the Savings Bank of the Grand Fountain United Order of True Reformers, the first black bank, in 1888. This was followed in 1893 by the founding of Southern Aid and Life Insurance Company, one of the first black insurance companies in the United States, as well as the founding of the Saint Luke Penny Savings Bank in the same year by Maggie Lena Walker, the first woman bank president in the United States. Walker bought a renewed emphasis on black women's economic development and social reform activities. Class distinctions were often blurred when black women engaged in collective endeavors to "uplift the race" and improve the quality of people's lives. Rosa Dixon Bowser, for example, was widely known for being a teacher at Navy Hill School in the 1880s and established a plethora of clubs and associations to benefit young men and women.[44] Similarly, Ora Brown Stokes, another social activist in Richmond, had a lifelong commitment to "gender and race work." Despite the trepidations of middle-class black men about black women's clubs, black women continued to use these vehicles to promote a consciousness of race and gender concerns.

The 1890s brought renewed vigor on black disenfranchisement and social segregation, and already blacks had begun to migrate to northern cities to escape the oppression. Social segregation was rigidly enforced throughout the city; black schools were declining rapidly; low wages for black males and females persisted; and there was a step-up of police brutality to reinforce the oppressive laws and quell black protest. In 1894, the Walton Act, which was designed to keep preliterate blacks away from the polls in local elections, coupled with the stalling tactics of Democrats of closing polls down while hundreds of blacks waited to vote, crippled black political participation, especially on Richmond's Common Council. The United States Supreme Court's decision in *Plessy v. Ferguson* in 1896 legalized the social segregation that was already a fact of life throughout the South. For black Richmonders, the realities of segregation and the Plessy decision were compounded by the Virginia Constitution (established at the 1901–1902 constitutional convention), which eliminated blacks from the political process.

Black Richmonders were outraged over the introduction into their lives of de jure segregation by 1902. In 1904, they collectively protested the segregation of Virginia's streetcars. Prodded by John Mitchell, the editor of the *Richmond Planet*, African Americans boycotted the Virginia Passenger and Power Company, which operated the streetcars.[45] Richmond's streetcar boycott was one of the first mass-based, organized protest movements by African Americans in the twentieth century. It was organized primarily by John T. Michell, Maggie Lena Walker, and other Richmond African American newspaper editors, Mitchell argued that "[a] people who willingly accept discrimination. . . . are not sufficiently advanced to be entitled to the liberties of a free people."[46] By advocating nonviolence, Mitchell employed a strategy that would prove successful some fifty years later. The boycott was initially 90 percent succsssful, organizing working-class and middleclass blacks around de jure segregation but eventually failed because the community was being attacked on two political fronts. During this protracted strike, which lasted until 1906, the Virginia Assembly introduced legislation to eliminate appropriations for black schools.[47] Blacks were forced to shift their limited resources from asserting their civil rights to safeguarding black education for their children. But the oral account of the boycot has been passed down generationally in Richmond's African American community and provided much of the historical context for contemporary political struggle.

Despite black Richmonders' best efforts at fighting social segregation, the realities of the system were becoming increasingly a fact of life in both the North and South, leaving black Richmonders few political options. By 1906, Virginia's General Assembly mandated segregation on all streetcars in Virginia. Although black Richmonders still opposed all vestiges of Virginia's "Jim Crow" society, by the 1930s even Gordon Blaine Hancock, "who was probably the most articulate and popular champion of his race in Virginia for over a quarter century preceding the Brown decision of 1954,"[48] acknowledged the political realities of black life. "Racially speaking . . . we oppose segregation, but economically speaking it forms the basis of our professional and business life. There is nothing at present to indicate . . . the slightest change in this bi-racial attitude."[49]

As black Richmonders engaged in the complex struggle for social and political equality, they faced the reality that it would be long-term and that just beneath the surface of Virginia's gentility was the force of the Ku Klux Klan and other white terrorists who could quickly mobilize to stymy their progress. Even Marcus Garvey's arousing speech to the largest gathering ever of black Richmonders in 1922 failed to persuade those in attendance to join his movement.[50] Apparently, the position of John T. Mitchell, a progressive black leader who supported Garvey's self-help programs while expressing opposition to his back-to-Africa philosophy, resonated with this strong, working-class community. While other southern communities actively formed Garvey chapters, what most black Richmonders wanted, according to Hancock, "was freedom in Richmond."[51] Despite the street and legal assaults testing the constitutionality of 1902 Constitution by black Richmonders, social segregation and the denial of suffrage defined "southern culture" for most of the twentieth century.

HARRY F. BYRD AND THE RICHMOND AFRICAN-AMERICAN COMMUNITY, 1925–1966

The rise, decline, and reemergence of contemporary southern black conservatism in Richmond was evinced from the "Byrd era" (1925–1966) to the election and demise of the African American political majority on city council (1977–1982). The "Byrd machine" benefited from the de jure segregation in Virginia that was firmly entrenched by 1902. The four decades that witnessed the development and consolidation of the Byrd machine over the Virginia electorate reestablished the fragile relationships of whites, who had been politically divided between Democrats and Republicans, perpetuated the legacy of white supremacy, and suppressed the black electorate until the rise of the civil rights movement. According to Derrick A. Bell, Jr., blacks are "involuntarily sacrificed" whenever whites seek to reestablish their racial solidarity and, ultimately, domination.[52] This political environment, which circumscribed all political and social relations between blacks and whites, was deemed necessary to transcend class cleavages among whites, stabilize racial polarization, and ensure white supremacy. Harry F. Byrd was elected governor of Virginia from 1925 to 1929 and U.S. senator from 1933 to 1966, elections that were facilitated by his establishment and control of the Byrd machine. "Although many Virginians are too genteel to use the term, Senator Byrd is the boss of the machine and of the state. . . . Power in the hands of the Senator's field marshal, as one informed observer puts it, keeps local government officials in an understanding and sympathetic frame of mind."[53]

The Byrd machine rested on the appearance of progressive politics while it employed legal and extralegal measures to suppress the black electorate. On the progressive side, Byrd eliminated the state's financial deficit, "abolished the state tax on land, and promoted rural electrification, conservation and the tourist trade."[54] Byrd "sponsored strict legislation which made lynching a state offense and all members of a lynch mob subject to murder charges,"[55] and advocated strict enforcement of the poll tax to restrict black suffrage. As V. O. Key Jr., noted, Byrd vigorously supported the poll tax because between 1925 and 1945, "[t]he machine owed its existence to a competent management and a restricted electorate."[56] Key hypothesized that "[u]nder the conditions in Virginia, the small number of voters definitely contributes to the manageability of elections."[57] Although Byrd did not publicly engage in "race-baiting" campaign tactics, which was standard fare in Virginia politics whether blacks could vote or not, his support of the poll tax effectively stifled black political participation.

The Byrd machine led to a splintering of racial solidarity among black Richmonders and an increased visibility of black conservatism. Undoubtedly, the shift in black political leadership also played a pivotal role. As the mantle of leadership shifted from organizations that had initially been dominated by the black working class to those dominated by the black professional and middle classes, there was also a change in the way in which the new leadership related to white politicians. Thus, the shift in leadership from the working class to the professional and middle classes occurred when the latter allied themselves with powerful local white political figures in order to wrestle leadership away from the black working class. Once this biracial alliance was made, black Richmonders, now bereft of the city's strident political leadership, could only make a scattered response to the encroaching disenfranchisement and social segregation.

There was a decided conservative shift by black Richmonders, which lasted until the 1950s as they fashioned a political response to the Byrd Machine. Of those black Richmonders who could vote, some lodged subtle forms of protests by opposing the Byrd Democrats at the state and local levels while simultaneously supporting the Democratic Party at the national level. Some black Richmonders who sought to retain their suffrage rights frequently voted with the local arms of the Byrd Machine viewing the oligarchy as the lesser of southern evils. Other middle-class blacks, who were feted by the machine as "leaders," maintained discreet associations with these politicians, which reflected the existing class cleavages and political schisms in Jackson Ward dating back to the antebellum era. The most conservative group of black Richmonders consisted of realtors and ministers, who formed a covetous relationship with the Byrd machine and were used as mouthpieces in the black community. According to A. J. Dickinson, a reporter revealed to him that "he saw a list of Negro ministers and real estate men who could be bought, a list which was kept [by the Byrd people] until at least up to the late 1950s."[58] Whether black Richmonders were attempting to prevent the further erosion of their rights seeking to lessen the impact of institutional racism upon their lives, or attempting to engage in duplicitous political participation, black politics was severely fractionalized, thus undermining racial unity.

While the Byrd machine suppressed the black electorate and thwarted black political development, it simultaneously engendered black political mobilization for social and political change. As Charles Tilly argues, segregated groups who are bound by a common identity perceive themselves as a collective "we" against the dominant oligarchy, which is identified as "the enemy." This perception among group members of a common identity against an outside world facilitates a "defensive mobilization" strategy toward collective goals.[59] In this "collective activation" process, Doug McAdam noted, the group mobilizes the community for the successful redistribution of power resources.[60] Minion K. C. Morrison argued that African Americans were "especially susceptible to [this] type of mobilization" because their "political exclusion was coupled with a virulent hatred and social isolation."[61] As black Richmonders began to mobilize the community for social change, they became more vocal in regard to those whom they suspected of collaboration with the white power structure.

Moderate and conservative black leaders adopted several strategies to deal with social segregation and disenfranchisement. From 1942 to 1954, moderate leaders such as Dr. Gordon Blaine Hancock from Virginia Union University; Dr. Benjamin Mays, former president of Morehouse College in Atlanta; and Lieutenant George Washington Lee, a black Republican and a major black member of the Edward C. Crump political machine in Memphis, Tennessee, sought, through formal interracial dialogues, to influence southern white moderates in making concessions in race relations. Black leaders refused to allow the participation of northern black leaders, believing that their presence would doom the meetings and curtail any efforts to gradually reform the "Jim Crow" system. Southern black leaders

> urged the white South to demonstrate greater fairness to blacks and to provide evidence of greater opportunities for southern blacks, although they stopped short of calling for an end to segregation. They made it clear that without some tangible evidence that white leaders were willingly to make some concessions, the black masses would begin to turn increasingly to black "extremists" outside the South who would demand nothing less than complete abolition of all segregation and discrimination.[62]

The long-range implication of southern moderate black leaders excluding their black northern brethren from their meetings to placate the interests of white southern moderates is that their strategy would eventually backfire on them. Although the meetings lasted until 1954, southern moderate white leaders were not persuaded to address major racial issues. Despite this failed alliance, the meetings still drew fire from both whites and blacks. Southern white conservatives such as Eugene Talmadge, former governor of Georgia, labeled the meetings as communist inspired. But these moderate leaders had also lost credibility within the black community. Blacks saw them as "accommodationists" (accommodating the interests of white segregationists) for their inability to broker a political arrangement with moderate southern white leaders to reform the Jim Crow system after more than a decade of negotiations. J. Saunders Redding, in his article, "A Negro Speaks For His People" in the *Atlantic Monthly* offered a trenchant analysis of established moderate black leadership that had been in place in the south in varying degrees for over 50 years:

> In the first place, the old Negro leadership in the South was outstripped by its (theoretical) following. The old leadership had been chosen and maintained by the white South because it was too weak to make encroachments upon the basic assumption of Negro inferiority or upon the racial status quo. The old leadership was maintained because it threatened no change and no essential modification of the mores of the South. . . . It was a leadership meant to be effective for progress in a world in which black would remain forever unequal to white. . . . There is no refuge in conservatism.[63]

Ironically, as black Richmonders became more critical of southern moderate black leadership in general, they were also critically analyzing organizations such as The Richmond Civic Council that was designed to mobilize black voter registration. The Richmond Civic Council, a decentralized triumvirate of black moderate middle class civic associations, fraternal societies, and religious groups, was founded during the 1940s to mobilize voter registration for black representation on the city council. Even under a ward/district system, Richmond's old district system had been gerrymandered by the white power structure to effectively restrict black representation on the city council since 1895. Coupled with subjection to the poll tax, blacks were effectively disenfranchised from city politics. The mobilization efforts of the black community and some liberal whites led to the election of Attorney Oliver Hill in 1948. But the RCC's political alliance with white conservatives led to a betrayal in the endorsement of black candidates, a split in the organization when it attempted to foster unity by endorsing two black candidates, and a loss of political capital and credibility in the black community. Consequently, some in the African American community began, privately and publicly, to accuse the ministers who controlled the RCC of aligning themselves with white conservatives and supplementing their incomes by taking money from the white conservatives and selling out the black community for personal gain.[64]

The Massive Resistance campaign, which was promoted by white segregationists to thwart the integration of Virginia's public schools and, ultimately, the dismantling of the Jim Crow system, was officially born on May 31, 1955. Immediately, segregationists moved to destroy the influence of the "radical" National Association for the Advancement of Colored People (NAACP) by the adoption of anti-NAACP laws in Virginia and most of the southern states. Richard K. Scher notes: "The southern circling of wagons took place quickly and forcefully. Its effect was to eliminate moderate voices and pragmatic political discussion from most areas of the South."[65]

Ironically, the Massive Resistance campaign also destabilized moderate and conservative black leadership throughout the South and especially in Virginia. After their political debacles and the rise of Massive Resistance, these black leaders who were already perceived by black Richmonders as "accommodationists," felt their credibility rapidly eroding. These moderate and conservative leaders quickly ran afoul of the white power structure as well. Now they were of no use to the white power structure because they had lost their political credibility with the black masses and thereby destroyed white southern complacency, domination, and control. Although the moderate and conservative black leadership was losing political capital, it did pave the way for some of the "quiet integration" or token integration (1947–1956) that was achieved in southern cities before the civil rights movement.[66] However, it would be the gathering storm of marching feet of more militant blacks that spurred most token integration efforts, even though the interracial dialogues between blacks and whites did pointed to blacks' dissatisfaction with the Jim Crow system. As the influence of RCC began to wane, young black activists, dubbed the "new turks," pushed for a new organization, the Richmond Crusade for Voters (RCV), which would challenge Massive Resistance to the mandates of the *Brown v. Board of Education* (I and II) independent of the city's white leadership.[67] It was not lost on those in power that RCV was also challenging the authority of Harry F. Byrd.

The long-term consequence of the Massive Resistance campaign in Virginia triggered a black insurgency and mobilization among black Richmonders. The white power structure thwarted the integration of Richmond's public schools by placing a referendum on the ballot that allowed local communities to close their schools. The referendum passed, whereupon the RCV was born as a countermovement in the black community around 1956.[68] Under the RCV, the African American community's approach to politics shifted from voter registration to electoral politics. The RCV leadership was closely aligned with the NAACP's local leadership of mostly male, highly educated, upper-and middle class professionals in Richmond's black community. Ministers were members of the RCV, and although they did not dominate, as they had in RCC, they still maintained their behind-the-scenes access to the white power structure. However, after the Brown decision (*Brown v. Board of Education* I and II, 1954–1955) desegregated the public schools, a federal district court ruling that Virginia's anti-NAACP laws violated the Fourteenth amendment, as did the rulings in *Harrison v. Day* and *James v. Almond*, which had officially ended the Massive Resistance campaigns and the RCV began to make tentative inroads into state and local politics.

But it was the mobilization activities by black women, who proved essential to the civil rights movement in Richmond, that transformed the political environment and, later, the electoral arena. Janet Ballard, Ethel L. Overby, Ruby Clayton Walker, and Ora Lomax were some of the early civil rights activists who were instrumental in defining areas of individual and collective protest, and all of these women emerged as "bridge leaders," leaders who occupied the informal "free space" connecting the goals of the community with those articulated by the black leadership.[69] Ballard's leadership in desegregating the Thalhimer's Department Store beauty salon and Overby's undermining of the white educational administration's efforts to get black parents to sign Pupil Placement Sheets in support of segregation alerted the community to the vulnerability of the segregation system and paved the way for the civil rights movement in Richmond.[70] Lomax integrated the sales counters of some of the most fashionable white clothing stores, and Walker's organizational leadership proved fortuitous for the movement. During the boycott, these women were civil rights activists who solidified the infrastructure of the protest.

As the civil rights movement gained momentum in Richmond, it dismantled de jure segregation and, at the same time, exacerbated the existing gender and class cleavages in the community. On February 20, 1960, the sit-ins by students from Virginia Union University in Woolworth's Department Store on Broad Street, as well as six other downtown lunch counters initiated the boycott. It was the arrest of these students, however, on February 22, 1960, at Thalhimer's in front of five hundred supporters, that launched the two-year boycott campaign. Black women and college students walked the picket lines with women walking during their lunch hours and students walking between classes. Although the black press placed greater emphasis on this boycott, primarily owing to its middle-class origins, Harmon Buskey simultaneously led a similar boycott by working-class participants, called the East End Neighborhood Association, against Springer Drug Company, a major local drugstore chain, which was successfully desegregated seven months before the agreement was reached in the Thalhimer's boycott on August 30, 1961.

THE RISE AND DECLINE OF THE BLACK MAJORITY COUNCIL

In the community's transformation from political protest to electoral politics, organizations such as the Richmond Crusade for Voters were facilitated by new federal laws. The Twenty-Fourth Amendment to the U.S. Constitution (passed in 1964), which outlawed the use of poll taxes in federal elections, the passage of the Civil Rights Act of 1964, and the Voting Rights Act of 1965, and the federal courts' banning of the use of poll taxes in state and local elections in 1966 legitimized the black struggle for political enfranchisement.[71] As the RCV shifted from a crisis-oriented to a franchise-oriented organization, becoming an intermediary between the white political elite and Richmond's black community, other more conservative groups, such as the Voters' Voice and the People's Political and Civic League, emerged, creating political schisms in the black community. Now that the critical battle had been fought in the courts and in the streets to dismantle de jure segregation, competing conservative ideologies surfaced, jockeying for a political power base in the electoral arena. Simultaneously, as political realignments and tenuous biracial coalitions were forged, they threatened the fragile racial solidarity in the black community.

Black conservatives garnered political capital by providing a buffer between the white power structure and the black community, which seeks political and social equality. Their credibility rested on quelling the black masses into accommodating their political aspirations within the segregationist system. Conservatives prospered, both economically and politically, from their positions within the body politic, which were derived from their handpicked status by white conservatives as well as their viable economic positions in black Richmond society. These black conservatives were not dormant during the Byrd era but instead affiliated with black moderates in their quest for reforms of the Jim Crow system. Because the Byrd era typified blatant racial hostility, black conservatives had few incentives in publicly supporting the Byrd machine and arch segregationists. By the 1950s, Byrd's "massive resistance" strategy was supported by both Republicans and Democrats, forcing black conservatives to support the national Republican Party while opposing the state and local machine.

By the 1960s, white conservatives were speaking out in opposition to the Civil Rights Act of 1964 and the Voting Rights Act of 1965, arguing that this legislation was an intrusion on individual rights and a violation of state's rights. Black conservatives were hesitant to openly challenge the civil rights movement because of its overwhelming support among African Americans nationwide as well as its conscious appeal to liberal whites. Some black conservatives found themselves forced to support the national Democratic presidential candidate, Lyndon B. Johnson (LBJ), because of the hostility to civil rights for blacks within the Republican Party. Clarence Towns, a native Richmonder, supported LBJ in the 1964 presidential elections because he could not consciously support Barry Goldwater, his party's nominee. Andrew Buni noted:

> For Virginia Negroes, the Republican National Convention in San Francisco held little hope. Senator Barry Goldwater, who had voted against the 1964 Civil Rights Bill, was nominated on the first ballot. Though his past civil rights record was creditable and he promised to uphold the law, Negroes looked upon him as against civil rights. Clarence Towns, Jr., a Richmond Negro representing the Virginia G.O.P. [Republican Party] as an alternate delegate (a history-making precedent, as it is believed he was the first of his race to do so in either party since the turn of the century), openly stated that he could not follow his fellow delegates as they voted for Goldwater, 20 to 1.[72]

Class, gender, and racial cleavages began to define Richmond's political landscape after the civil rights movement and paved the way for a resurgence of black conservatism to dominate and control black politics in Richmond. By 1968, the mobilization of the black community by the Richmond Crusade for Voters had resulted in one black, Henry Marsh, and two white liberals, Howard H. Carwine and Reverend James G. Carpenter, being elected to the city council. Two years later, the city's white elite, fearing the black majority population would create a black majority council, annexed nearby Chesterfield County, a suburb of 47,000 white, middle-class residents, in order to dilute the voting strength of the black electorate.[73] Curtis Holt, a grassroots organizer and already a potent voice in the working-class community, became a major force in the annexation controversy by filing a lawsuit against the city of Richmond and thus changing the face of the city's politics. In *Richmond v. United States* (1974), the U.S. Supreme Court ruled that the intention of the city's annexation of Chesterfield County was to dilute the voting strength of black Richmonders.[74] In *Richmond v. United States* (1977), the Court accepted a proposed compromise to change the city's representation from an at-large system to a single-member ward, or district, system in order to ensure African American representation on the city council.[75] The adoption of a nine-seat, single-member district system in 1977 led to a special councilman election on March 8, 1977, resulting in an African American majority on the city council and the election of the city's first black mayor, Henry Marsh.

Historical divisions that included the class and gender schisms in the black community as well as white intransigence to black political leadership foreshadowed the demise of the black majority council. The catalyst that eclipsed the black majority council's brief (five-year) history (1977–1982) was the racial confrontation in 1978 over the selection of a hotel for the proposed Project One convention center and office complex strongly favored by the white business community.[76] The white business community favored the Hilton Hotel chain, whereas the Council supported the Mariott Hotel Corporation. The conflict escalated when the city council passed an ordinance requiring that all private development be assessed a development fee based on potential impact on Project One. With the ordinance, the council sought to protect the city's investment in the Mariott Hotel chain by keeping the area from being oversaturated with other hotels.[77] The Hilton Hotel chain sued the city and was awarded $5 million for racial bias. The city's loss of credibility over the development issue rekindled myths of incompetent black leadership, triggered a vote of "no confidence" in the press, and exacerbated existing class and gender tensions in the black community.

The Project One fiasco was the harbinger of the shift in black politics from a progressive black majority city council to the conservative biracial coalition that would ultimately dominate city politics. Councilperson Willie Dell's upcoming 1982 reelection as councilperson was perceived by the coalition as their most vulnerable target. The 1982 defeat of Willie Dell, a liberal African American female member of the city council, paved the way for the election of Roy West, a black conservative, as councilperson and, ultimately, mayor of Richmond. Black conservatives quickly took advantage of the emerging tensions in the city council, forming biracial alliances with white conservatives that would ultimately shift political power back to the white established elite. Although many believed that Dell was the sacrificial lamb of the Project One controversy (and the council's detractors were really aiming at Henry Marsh), Dell's reputation as a "radical" on the city council and the growing speculation that she would succeed Mayor Henry Marsh as the first black female mayor, caused considerable dismay among black and white conservatives. Widely known for her outspoken leadership for the disenfranchised and her initiatives to remedy the lives of the "poor, blacks, elders, and women," Dell's initiatives drew both praise and criticism.[78] One white conservative frankly informed Dell that she was considered too black by white conservatives and that they were searching for the "whitest" black person that they could find to capture her council seat.[79]

There were several significant factors contributing to Dell's defeat. Dell was running against black conservative Roy West, heavily favored by then-Governor L. Douglas Wilder and the white power structure. For many, Wilder's public criticism of Dell contoured the political environment and her defeat.[80] Another major factor was the redrawing of Dell's district, formerly comprised of largely working-class blacks, which now became 69 percent black and 31 percent white. This redrawn district, presumably to protect a more vulnerable councilperson, reflected a decided ideological shift with more middle-class and upper-class blacks who considered Dell an "outsider," and conservative whites who feared her growing popularity and progressive initiatives for the city. During the campaign, the barrage of criticism against Dell, such as remarks that "she was looking for a man" and was "wearing the pants" in her house, revealed the gender bias of the campaign as well as the desperation of her opponents. Given the charged political atmosphere and the anti-Marsh sentiment, the resurgence of conservatism, and the media's endorsement of West, it may indeed have been impossible for Dell to mobilize her constituency and launch a strong counteroffensive. And Dell suffered from the fact that her new poor black voters did not have the same allegiance and close working relationship with her as those who were in the boundaries of her old district. Such salient factors as low voter turnout and West's support among new members of the district also contributed to her defeat, and she lost her council seat by 497 votes.[81]

Willie Dell's loss of her council seat in 1982 and the election of Roy West, first to the city council and then as mayor in the same year, signaled the encroaching destabilization of the political power of Richmond's Crusade for Voters and its black majority council along with a new wave of black conservatism in Richmond's city government. Peter A. Bailey notes: "The Crusade at one time was probably the best example of the use of African American bloc voting in the United States, says Said El-Amin. Dell, whose defeat by West is considered by some to have signaled the beginning of the Crusade's decline. . . ."[82]

Some African American leaders suggested to John V. Moeser that West was succeeded in being elected mayor in the same year by politically aligning himself with the white council members and casting the tie-breaking vote for his own election, thereby precipitating the downfall of the black majority on the city council.[83] But West had astutely aligned himself with white conservatives throughout his campaign and was participating in a brokered political deal between himself and the white conservatives who wished to regain control of the city council. Quickly restoring the council's credibility, the new conservative majority publicly declared that it would work more closely with the private sector, especially on development matters.[84] At the same time, as the more progressive minority programs were being dismantled, the city saw a collusion of black and white conservatives in control of the city council. Dell made another unsuccessful bid for her council seat in 1984, running again against black conservative Roy West. West's conservative leadership signaled a profound change in the city; and, just as important, perhaps, was the fact that many of West's contributors were white conservatives, including J. Smith Ferebee, a white conservative businessman who was a staunch supporter of the Byrd machine. Oliver Hill, a civil rights attorney and former council member, noted:

> This is one of the things that makes West's acceptance of the power play by his white carry-me-back-to-the-pre-ward-days supporters so tragic. It serves to strengthen their resolve to keep blacks in their place. Before July 1, Richmond stood as a splendid example of how blacks, through unity, could use the political process to improve the atmosphere of the city. In a single day, Roy West destroyed what took many years to build.[85]

CONCLUSIONS

Black political and social activism in Richmond, Virginia, was informed by the prevailing forces of cash-crop commodity production, industrial slavery, social segregation, and disenfranchisement over approximately four hundred years. Integral to this activism has been the intertwining dynamics of black resistance and black conservatism, manifested initially in incipient forms in Virginia's slave communities, which has been critical to the evolution of black political development. In local political arenas such as Richmond, where politics were characterized by competing interest groups, predominantly along racial lines, black conservatism fosters racial, gender, and ideological schisms and thwarts the reallocation of power resources for the black community.

The erosion of racial solidarity and the perennial class and ideological schisms (which may prove less significant in regional and national politics), destabilized black collective gains in the city. Black conservatives in Richmond effectively used black community schisms for personal and political gains in forming organic relationships with the prevailing white power structure. Often approached by white politicians, black conservatives were required to either manipulate black suffrage, thwart black political participation, quell black protest, or promote themselves (with able white assistance) as leaders. The junior/senior partner relationship that black conservatives formed with white segregationists not only proved divisive in dismantling political gains won through decades of black struggle but, ultimately, marginalized a significant portion of the black community from the electoral arena.

NOTES

1. James Oakes, *The Ruling Race: A History of American Slaveholders* (New York: Vintage Books, 1982), pp. 72–76, 86–87.
2. Allan Kulikoff, "The Origins of Afro-American Society in Tidewater Maryland and Virginia, 1700 to 1790," *William and Mary Quarterly*, 35:2 (April 1978): 230.
3. Sterling Stuckey, *Slave Culture: Nationalist Theory and the Foundations of Black America* (New York: Oxford University Press, 1987), p. 31.
4. Kulikoff, "Afro-American Society," p. 237.
5. Claire Robertson, "Africa into the Americas? Slavery and Women, the Family, and the Gender Division of Labor," in *More Than Chattel: Black Women and Slavery in the Americas*, ed. David Barry Gaspar and Darlene Clark Hine (Bloomington: Indiana University Press, 1996), pp. 15–17; Jacqueline Jones, "'My Mother Was Much of a Woman': Black Women, Work and the Family under Slavery," *Feminist Studies* 8:2 (1982): 261.
6. Jacqueline Jones, *Labor of Love, Labor of Sorrow: Black Women, Work and the Family, from Slavery to the Present* (New York: Vintage, 1985), pp. 29–32; and Mitchelle D. Wright, "African American Sisterhood: The Impact of the Female Slave Population on American Political Movements," *The Western Journal of Black Studies*, 15:1 (Spring 1991): 34–35.
7. Vernon E. McClean, "Historical Examples of Black Conservatism," *The Western Journal of Black Studies*, 8:3 (Fall 1984): 149.
8. Ibid.
9. Ibid.
10. Charles L. Perdue, Jr., Thomas E. Barden, and Robert K. Philips, eds., *Weevils in the Wheat: Interviews with Virginia Ex-Slaves* (Charlottesville: University Press of Virginia, 1976), p. 84.
11. Ibid., p. 75.
12. Peter J. Rachleff, *Black Labor in the South: Richmond, Virginia, 1865–1890* (Philadelphia: Temple University Press, 1984), pp. 5–6; and Jeffrey R. Kerr-Ritchie, *Freedpeople in the Tobacco South: Virginia, 1860–1900* (Chapel Hill: The University of North Carolina Press, 1999), pp. 13–30.
13. V. O. Key, Jr., *Southern Politics in State and Nation* (New York: Vintage Books, 1949), p. 19.
14. Michael B. Chesson, *Richmond after the War, 1865–1890* (Richmond: Virginia State Library), p. 20.
15. Charles B. Dew, *Ironmaker to the Confederacy: Joseph R. Anderson and the Tredegar Iron Works* (New Haven: Yale University Press, 1966), p. 22.
16. Clement Eaton, "Slave-Hiring in the Upper South: A Step towards Freedom" *Mississippi Valley Historical Review*, 46:4 (March 1960): 664; Richard C. Wade, *Slavery in the Cities: The South 1820–1860* (New York: Oxford University Press, 1964), pp. 42–43.
17. Peter J. Rachleff, *Black Labor in the South: Richmond, Virginia, 1865–1890* (Philadelphia: Temple University Press, 1984), p. 6.

18. Ibid.

19. Dey, *Ironmaker*, pp. 28–32.

20. Wade, *Slavery*, p. 61.

21. Ibid., pp. 66–67.

22. James Sidbury, "Saint Domingue in Virginia: Ideology, Local Meanings, and Resistance to Slavery, 1790–1800," *The Journal of Southern History* 63:3 (August 1997): 540; and Alfred N. Hunt, *Haiti's Influence on Antebellum America: Slumbering Volcano in the Caribbean* (Baton Rouge: Louisiana State University Press, 1988), pp. 115–116.

23. Vincent Harding, *There Is a River: The Black Struggle for Freedom in America* (New York: Harcourt Brace Jovanovich, 1981), p. 55: and Douglas R. Egerton, "Gabriel's Conspiracy and the Election of 1800," *The Journal of Southern History* 56:2 (May 1990): 194–95.

24. Julie Winch, *Philadelphia's Black Elite: Activism, Accommodation, and the Struggle for Autonomy, 1787–1848* (Philadelphia: Temple University Press, 1988), pp. 130–31.

25. Vincent Harding, *There Is a River*, pp. 77–81, 95–97.

26. Luther P. Jackson, *Free Negro Labor and Property Holding in Virginia 1830–1860* (New York: D. Appleton-Century, 1942), pp. 174, 181.

27. Ibid., p. 151.

28. Charles E. Wynes, *Race Relations in Virginia, 1870–1902* (Charlottesville: University of Virginia Press, 1961), p. 108.

29. John T. O'Brien, "Factory, Church, and Community: Blacks in Antebellum Richmond," *The Journal of Southern History* 44:4 (November 1978), p. 535.

30. Elsa Barkley Brown, "Womanist Consciousness: Maggie Lena Walker and the Independent Order of Saint Luke," in *Black Women in America: Social Science Perspectives*, ed. Micheline R. Malson, Elisabeth Mudimbe-Boyi, Jean F. O'Barr, and Mary Wyer, (Chicago: The University of Chicago Press, 1988), p. 192.

31. Roi Ottley, *'New World A-Coming': Inside Black America* (Boston: Houghton Mifflin, 1943), p. 177; and Willard B. Gatewood, *Aristocrats of Color: The Black Elite, 1880–1920* (Bloomington: Indiana University Press, 1990), pp. 7–29.

32. Gregg D. Kimball, "Race and Class in a Southern City: Richmond, 1865–1920" (unpublished paper presented at the Organization of American Historians [OAH] annual conference, Spring 1992), p. 2.

33. *New York Tribune*, June 17, 1865.

34. *Richmond Dispatch*, April 12, 1867; April 24, 1867.

35. Michael B. Chesson, "Richmond's Black Councilmen, 1871–96" in *Southern Black Leaders of the Reconstruction Era*, ed. Howard N. Rabinowitz (Urbana: University of Illinois Press, 1982), p. 192.

36. Ibid., p. 196.

37. James T. Moore, "Black Militancy in Readjuster Virginia," *The Journal of Southern History* x1i:2 (May 1975): 168–169.

38. Andrew Buni, *The Negro in Virginia Politics, 1902–1965* (Charlottesville: University Press of Virginia, 1967), p. 7: Charles E. Wynes, *Race Relations in Virginia, 1870–1902* (Charlottesville: University Press of Virginia, 1961), p.108.

39. Robert E. Martin, *Negro Disfranchisement in Virginia: Volume 1 in* The Howard University Studies in the Social Sciences (Washington, D.C.: 1938), p. 100.

40. Dwight Carter Holton, "Power to the People: The Struggle for Black Political Power in Richmond, Virginia," (unpublished honors B.A. degree thesis, Brown University, 1987), p. 8.

41. Peter J. Rachleff, *Black Labor in the South: Richmond, Virginia, 1865–1890* (Philadelphia: Temple University Press, 1984), pp.117–38, 143–46.

42. Michael B. Chesson, *Richmond after the War, 1865–1890* (Richmond: Virginia State Library, 1981), p. 190.

43. *Richmond* Planet, March 14, 1903.

44. Lauranett Lee, "More Than an Image: Black Women Reformers in Richmond, Virginia, 1910–1928," (master's thesis, Virginia State University, 1993), p. 25.

45. Ann Field Alexander, "Black Protest in the New South: John Mitchell, Jr. (1863–1929) and the Richmond Planet," (Ph.D diss., Duke University, 1972), pp. 327–29.

46. Ibid., p. 328.

47. Ibid., pp. 329, 286.

48. Raymond Gavins, *The Perils and Prospects of Southern Black Leadership: Gordon Blaine Hancock, 1884–1970* (Durham, NC: Duke University Press, 1977), p. viii.

49. Ibid., p. 69.

50. Ibid., p. 43.

51. Ibid.

52. Derrick A. Bell, Jr., *Race, Racism and American Law* (Boston: Little, Brown and Company, 1980), p. 29.

53. V. O. Key, Jr., *Southern Politics in State and Nation* (New York: Vintage Books, 1949), p. 21.

54. J. H. Wilkinson, *Harry Byrd and the Changing Face of Virginia Politics, 1945–1966* (Charlottesville: University of Virginia Press, 1968), p. 6.

55. Ibid.

56. Key, *Southern Politics*, p. 20.

57. Ibid.

58. A. J. Dickinson, "Myth and Manipulation: The Story of the Crusade for Voters in Richmond, Virginia," (B.A. degree thesis, unpublished Scholar of the House paper, Yale University, 1967), p. 14.

59. Charles Tilly, *From Mobilization to Revolution* (Reading, MA: Addison Wesley, 1978), p. 73.

60. Doug McAdam, *Political Process and the Development of Black Insurgency* (Chicago: University of Chicago Press, 1985), pp. 41–44.

61. Minion K.C. Morrison, *Black Political Mobilization: Leadership, Power and Mass Behavior* (New York: State University of New York Press, 1987), p. 11.

62. John V. Moeser and Chris Silver, *The Separate City: Black Communities in the Urban South, 1940–1968* (Lexington: University Press of Kentucky, 1995), p. 65.

63. J. Saunders Redding, "A Negro Speaks for His People," *Atlantic Monthly,* 151, January–June 1943. pp. 25–31.

64. John V. Moeser, interview by author, August 23, 1991.

65. Richard K. Scher, *Politics in the New South: Republicanism, Race and Leadership in the Twentieth Century,* 2nd ed. (New York: M. E. Sharpe, 1997), p. 200.

66. The term was taken from an article written by Virginius Dabney which he praised the capital of the confederacy for its voluntary efforts at integration. See "Richmond's Quiet Revolution," *Saturday Review,* 1964, p. 26.

67. John V. Moeser and Rutledge M. Dennis, *The Politics of Annexation: Oligarchic Power in a Southern City* (Cambridge: Schenkman Publishing Company,1982), p. 34.

68. Dickinson, "Myth and Manipulation," 1967, pp. 24–27.

69. Belinda Robnett, *How Long? How Long?: African-American Women in the Struggle for Civil Rights* (New York: Oxford University Press, 1997), p. 19.

70. Janet Ballard, interview by author, August 3, 1993; Ethel Thompson Overby, *It's Better to Light a Candle Than to Curse the Darkness: The Autobiographical Notes of Ethel Thompson Overby* (Richmond, VA: Ethel Thompson Overby, 1975), p. 32.

71. J. Rupert Picott and Edward H. Peeples, "Prince Edward County, Virginia," *Phi Delta Kappan,* 45:8 (1964), pp. 4–7; Robert A. Pratt, *The Color of Their Skin: Education and Race in Richmond, Virginia, 1954–1989* (Charlottesville, VA: University Press of Virginia, 1992), p. 11.

72. Andrew Buni, *The Negro in Virginia Politics, 1902–1965* (Charlottesville: University of Virginia Press, 1967), p. 219.
73. Moeser and Dennis, *The Politics of Annexation*, pp. 143–44.
74. John V. Moeser, telephone interview by author, July 7, 1991.
75. Moeser and Dennis, *The Politics of Annexation*, pp. 159–88.
76. Lewis A. Randolph and Gayle T. Tate, "The Rise and Decline of African American Political Power in Richmond: Race, Class, and Gender," in *Urban Affairs Annual Review* 42, ed. Judith A. Garber and Robyn S. Turner, pp. 143–44.
77. John V. Moeser, interview with author, September 11, 1989.
78. Henry Marsh, interview with author, December 5, 1991.
79. Willie Dell, interview with author, July 28, 1993.
80. Dell interview.
81. Margaret Edds, *Free at Last: What Really Happened When Civil Rights Came to Southern Politics* (Bethesda, MD: Alder and Alder, 1987), p.143.
82. Peter A. Bailey, "Challenging Richmond's Crusade for Voters," *Richmond Surroundings*, 3:6 (November/December 1988).
83. John V. Moeser, interviews with author, September 11, 1989, August 23, 1991; Said El-Amin, interview with author, December 5,1991; Michael Williams, interview with author, August 24, 1991; and Martin Jewell, interview with author August 21, 1991.
84. Michael Williams, interview with author, August 24, 1991.
85. Oliver W. Hill, "Did He Sell Out to Whites?" in "Close to Home," *Washington Post*, July 25, 1982, p. B8.

PART II

GENDER, FAMILY, AND SOCIAL POLICY

CHAPTER 4

THE POLITICS OF THE ANTI–WOMAN SUFFRAGE AGENDA: AFRICAN AMERICANS RESPOND TO CONSERVATISM

ROSALYN TERBORG-PENN

Throughout the woman suffrage movement, African American spokeswomen and their male supporters refuted the conservative anti–woman suffrage arguments. They discredited these views made mainly by individual white males and females in their antisuffrage organizations. They also responded to the argument of those African Americans who questioned the motives of early twentieth-century white suffragists or who doubted how effective woman suffrage goals could be to blacks. Woman suffrage, like all controversial issues, had its skeptics and its opponents. The antisuffrage argument was based on the belief that women did not need, did not want, or could not handle the responsibility of voting.

Although the overwhelming majority of African Americans who commented on woman suffrage supported it, as the accounts of the woman suffrage movement developed over the years, there was a popular view in the nineteenth century that blacks were against women voting, or at best, indifferent to the cause of the enfranchisement of females. Moreover, the popular view evolving among feminist writers who generalized about blacks who critiqued the movement made little distinction between those who chose universal suffrage over woman suffrage versus the minority of blacks who chose to oppose women voting entirely.[1]

By the 1890s, the "antis"—those who opposed granting women the right to vote—had founded organizations throughout the nation and their influence remained apparent for the duration of the struggle for woman's rights to the vote. Their views reflected the long tradition of political conservatism in the United States—a tradition that the nation would experience again in the 1970s as conservative politicians mobilized to stop the Equal Rights Amendment.

As the antisuffrage forces mobilized nationally in the 1890s, "educated suffrage" became an important argument used to exclude black women from the movement. At the same time, southern white women were taking greater interest in the woman suffrage movement. Simultaneously, anti–black woman suffrage arguments developed, not only among those who basically opposed the movement, but among some white suffragists who had spoken on behalf of African American women in the past. Although anti–black suffrage sentiments did not come only from southern white women who believed in white supremacy, some northern suffragists said that it was expedient to ignore black women while wooing support for the movement in the South.

Exclusionary sentiments came from woman suffrage leaders outside the South, revealing how for some, their expressed fear of alienating white southern suffragists was merely a scheme for covering up the racism among women suffragists generally. Historian Marjorie Spruill Wheeler confirms that many white suffragists believed that votes for white women could be used as a way for countering African American voters in the South.[2] Even the editors of a national journal, *The Suffragists*, published several news items aimed to show white southern suffragists how even with a federal woman suffrage amendment, black votes would be countered by white female votes in the South.[3]

Nevertheless, African American women persisted in their efforts, not only to gain membership in the national woman suffrage organizations, but to assist all black women in gaining the right to vote. It soon became evident to white politicians that African American women would resist any attempt to disenfranchise blacks. As a result, white Democratic Party southerners in particular feared the political clout that Republican Party African American females could develop, not only for themselves and for their race as a whole, but against the southern Democrats.

It is not surprising that many feared the impact of African American female voters on the politics of the nation. Demographic data from the late nineteenth century to the decade of the woman suffrage blitz (1910–1920) revealed the steady growth of the black female population. In 1890 there were approximately 1.6 million black females aged twenty-one or over in the nation. By 1910, in fifteen southern states that were surveyed, there were 4.4 million black women of voting age, compared to 10.6 million white women of voting age. Although the National Woman's Party (NWP) reported that a federal suffrage amendment would not "complicate the race problem" in the South as whites outnumbered blacks, white supremacists maintained their misgivings despite NWP attempts to calm their fears. On local levels, white suffragists responded similarly, as Suzanne Lebsock found among members of the Equal Suffrage League of Virginia.[4]

As black women responded to the two antisuffrage arguments, for the most part, black men joined their women by reporting in the black press about woman suffrage policies and activities that discriminated against African American women. Together they were determined to make it difficult for the forces of racism to keep black women from the polls. The handful of black men who publicly opposed women's right to the franchise were in the minority among their race. However, their conservatism can be contextualized within the broader tradition of U. S. gender conventions usually associated with white males.

Gender conventions tradition was only the tip of the iceberg when we survey the anti-woman suffrage agenda over time. On the other hand, most of the antiblack tactics among whites reflected the perceived threats of the so-called lower classes and lower races of women living in the United States, fears among conservatives that can be traced back to the nineteenth century, especially in response to African American attempts to unite peoples, who were disfranchised because of race and/or gender.

Beginning in the nineteenth century, throughout much of the first generation of the woman suffrage movement, blacks attempted to demonstrate that disenfranchised African Americans and disenfranchised white women shared the common plight of oppression. In doing so, they aimed to unite the two groups for a greater drive toward universal suffrage. As black suffrage advocates adopted this strategy, many woman suffrage advocates among whites moved further away from the universal suffrage cause and more toward the goal of enfranchising only white women. During the post–Civil War years, the cry from white women to enfranchise black women lasted about ten years. For some this cry appeared to have been merely a ploy to gain sympathy from Republicans who supported the "Negro suffrage" cause. Once the argument seemed no longer expedient, some white women of the first generation ended their call for men to enfranchise black women. Although African American women such as Sojourner Truth, Frances Harper, and Mary Ann Shadd Cary called for the ballot as a means of protecting themselves and the women of the race, the strongest outcry among black men and black women on behalf of the latter became evident during the last two decades of the nineteenth century, after white feminists ceased to call for the enfranchisement of black women.[5]

Overt discrimination against African Americans in the suffrage movement became most apparent in the 1890s. While stirring northern black women to join the suffrage movement, on one hand, suffragist Henry Blackwell publicly advocated "educated suffrage" as a means of eliminating the southern black female voter, on the other. In 1903 the National American Woman Suffrage Association (NAWSA), the largest suffrage organization in the nation, passed a resolution stating that there were more white native-born women who could read and write than all black and foreign-born voters combined, so that "the enfranchisement of such women would settle the vexed question of rule by literacy, whether of home grown or foreign-born production."[6]

In spite of their personal opinions, suffrage leaders of the NAWSA such as Susan B. Anthony accepted the resolution. For political reasons, they were willing to sacrifice principle for the sake of expediency. Anthony had even taken similar stands based on political expediency before 1903. In a 1894 meeting with Chicago black suffragists Ida B. Wells-Barnett, Anthony explained why she had compromised her ideals against racial discrimination. Anthony had asked her longtime political ally Frederick Douglass not to attend the forth-coming NAWSA convention scheduled for Atlanta, Georgia, which was to be the first southern-held convention. Anthony did this, so she said, to avoid embarrassment for Douglass as well as to avoid jeopardizing support of woman suffrage from southern white women. [7] "Expediency" appeared to mean sacrificing the chance to mobilize black women to join the national woman suffrage association in order to placate potential southern supporters. In response, Wells-Barnett criticized Anthony for sustaining the prejudice of white southern suffragists. Wells-Barnett felt that although Anthony may have made gains for woman suffrage by her behavior, "she had also confirmed white women in their attitude of segregation."[8] Susan B. Anthony's normally radical feminist politics appeared to be compromised as she succumbed to the southern conservative political agenda aimed at maintaining white supremacy.

The same year, Elizabeth Cady Stanton attacked the concept of universal suffrage in the South and once again denounced the enfranchisement of illiterate people everywhere. During the NAWSA Convention held in Atlanta in 1895, she expressed her concerns about the danger in enfranchising illiterate women, whose votes, Stanton presumed, would be manipulated by politicians. Her sentiments appealed to the southern audience because of its racist connotations; however, Harriet Stanton Blatch, Susan B. Anthony, and William Lloyd Garrison, Jr., opposed the idea. Needless to say, Stanton's view prevailed.[9]

Although Susan Anthony was not a proponent of "educated suffrage," she wanted to remove the race question from the woman suffrage campaign. However, conservative forces in the movement continually entertained questions. For example, Carrie Chapman Catt of New York, who later became an NAWSA president, and Alabama suffragist Frances A. Griffin were invited to speak to a group of white men and women in New Orleans about how to use woman suffrage as a means to secure white supremacy. Historian Adele Logan Alexander found that by 1904, Catt had written in the *Woman's Journal*, "It is little wonder that the North is beginning to question the wisdom of the indiscriminate enfranchisement of the Negro."[10] These sentiments do not make it clear whether Catt was merely rationalizing the expedient strategy of scapegoating African Americans in order to win southern support or whether Catt truly believed blacks to be unworthy of voting. Unlike Anthony, Catt used the race question frequently. As for Frances A. Griffin, at the NAWSA meeting at Grand Rapids, Michigan, in 1899, she addressed the national woman suffrage platform for the first time and set the tone for antiblack sentiments when she spoke bitterly about her "Negro boy" gardener who, at twenty-three, was illiterate but enfranchised.[11]

As the woman suffrage movement gained more popularity on a national level, leaders did not require members to agree on any women's rights issues other than woman suffrage. In an attempt to woo male support as well as southern white female support, suffragists demonstrated that white women's views about race were the same as white male views. Consequently, some suffragists were willing to argue that nonwhite women held no claim to suffrage.[12]

Opposition to the racism of individual suffragists or other reformers did not negate black support for the ideals of the woman suffrage cause. As a result, African American women championed the suffrage movement in much the same way that blacks generally supported the Populists and the Progressive movement—bypassing elements of the movements that deterred them, but defending basic and inclusive, democratic concepts. Similarly, blacks accepted some, but rejected other sides of woman suffrage leaders such as Susan B. Anthony, who had been an ardent abolitionist and onetime friend of universal suffrage. Like Ida B. Wells-Barnett, other African American suffragists admonished Anthony for what they perceived as racist behavior, but some also forgave her expedient course of action because of her past loyalty.[13]

"Educated suffrage" was just one of the issues argued by those who opposed the enfranchisement of black women. There was also the general anti-woman suffrage rationale, which rested firmly on a conservative position for gender conventions among all men and women. African American women responded, primarily in the black press, to the general anti-woman suffrage rationale. In 1895 Josephine St. Pierre Ruffin challenged the woman suffrage opposition in Boston when "antis" attempted to sabotage municipal suffrage. In an editorial prepared for her black women's newspaper, *Woman's Era* (co-authored with her daughter, Florida Ridley), Ruffin wrote sarcastically:

> The friends of equal rights owe a deep debt of gratitude to the Man Suffrage Association for the impetus their organized opposition to woman suffrage has given to the cause. Not for many years has so much interest and enthusiasm been shown in the annual meeting of the Massachusetts Woman Suffrage Association as in these held in Association Hall the week ending January [1896].[14]

By the early twentieth century, the opposition of black females to the antisuffrage argument became even more pronounced. In 1900 Mary Church Terrell, then president of the National Association of Colored Women (NACW), addressed the NAWSA and opposed the anti–woman suffrage argument that it was "unnatural for women to vote." Proceedings chroniclers said that she called the discrimination against women as voters unjust and predicted that "the political disenfranchisement of woman shall be removed." In 1905, Ella Wheeler Wilcox, a prominent white feminist and poet from South Carolina, responded to an anti–woman suffrage editorial in the *Beaufort County News* by asserting: "Women's suffrage must and will come before another decade." Black journalist Grace Lucas-Thompson, who wrote for the *(Indianapolis) Freeman*, concurred with this view and published Wilcox's statement in her women's column of the *Freeman*.[15] In the case of both Ruffin and Lucas-Thompson, we hear the voices of Black women journalists specifically targeting African American women readers in their discussion about the politics of the "antis" debates.

The same year, Adella Hunt Logan wrote the most comprehensive attack on the anti-woman suffrage argument from an African American woman of the time. In referring to the Fourteenth Amendment, she quoted the section on citizenship and argued that women should be included. She denounced those men who claimed to love the principles of the American Revolution, but failed to apply these ideals to women. In rejecting the argument that women were too modest to be seen in public at the polling booth, Logan declared that "every man who thinks knows that every woman who thinks just a little sees through this screen to her modesty."[16] In addition, she cited the success of woman suffrage in western states, where the evils predicted by antisuffragists had not occurred. Like other blacks before her, such as Philadelphia journalist Gertrude Mossell, Logan used the printed media to discredit the myth that woman did not want to vote. Some did not, she claimed, but many more did. If that was a valid reason for disfranchising a group, then, she reasoned, the ballot should be taken from the men who did not choose to cast their votes. Logan resented being treated as a minor and challenged all the other excuses for denying women the ballot, such as that husbands represent their wives; women could never understand politics; and women were not interested in politics. In this remarkable argument, we have an attack upon the "antis" expressed, in *The Colored American Magazine*, by an African American woman.[17]

A decade later, as the debate over suffrage intensified, black women continued to refute the critics. Many responded in 1915 when W. E. B. Du Bois called for essays to be published in *The Crisis* magazine's special woman suffrage issue. For example, Minnesota club woman Lillian A. Turner wrote facetiously: "I have ceased to tremble when I hear dire predictions of the ruin that is expected to follow the rapid approach of woman's franchise." In the same issue, Rhode Island club woman Mary E.

Jackson wrote: "Looked at from a sane point of view, all objections to the ballot for women are but protests against progress, civilization and good sense."[18]

In their own words, these early twentieth century African American spokeswomen expressed views quite similar to those that white women suffragists voiced against the "antis." Although all these women were leaders in the NACW, they also affiliated with predominantly white suffrage groups such as the NAWSA and the National Woman's Party. For the most part, these suffragists had to contend with conservative elements, who were fearful of removing middle-class women from their "proper place"—at home.

As Congress debated the amendment in summer 1919, Black women whose men voted Republican in Ohio took action against the male elected officials who refused to support the Beatty Equal Rights Bill in the lower house of the state legislature. The bill failed by a vote of thirty-five to sixteen. As a result, the Colored Women's Republican Club in Columbus severed its party affiliation. This bold action was indicative of woman suffragists throughout the nation, who organized politically, yet without having the right to vote.[19]

Despite the evidence that most blacks had opposed anti–woman suffrage arguments since the nineteenth century, national suffrage leaders needed to be reminded of that fact again and again. Du Bois, editorializing in The Crisis, made it his business to continually do the reminding. In 1911, for example, he refuted a statement made by NAWSA president Anna Shaw indicting blacks for opposing woman suffrage. Du Bois accused Shaw of a "barefaced falsehood." In addition, he chastised her for not attempting to enlighten those who she felt did not support woman suffrage. At the same time, Du Bois noted the hypocrisy among suffrage leaders who criticized blacks for opposing woman suffrage on one hand, but not whites who opposed enfranchising blacks, on the other.[20]

Many African American men and women supported Du Bois's position on the matter. In 1915, when he invited black leaders and intellectuals to write articles supporting woman suffrage for The Crisis, many responded. Among those who specifically addressed the anti-woman suffrage rationale was the highly respected Washington, D.C., minister, the Reverend Francis Grimke, husband of feminist Charlotte Forten Grimke. Her family had been universal suffragists since the antebellum years. Francis Grimke attacked the antisuffrage advocates and argued that women were as able, if not more able, than men to make sound political decisions. He also opposed the view that men were superior in any way to women.[21]

Similar criticism of the antisuffrage argument also came from historian Benjamin Brawley, who encouraged the men of the nation to stop hiding behind the excuse that they were protecting their women from the evils of politics when they opposed enfranchising them. In referring to Henrik Ibsen's play, The Doll's House, Brawley agreed with the heroine when she refuted her husband's contention that her most important role in life was that of wife and mother. Brawley felt it was time to bring the American woman out of the "doll's house."[22] Sentiments of this kind were expressed in the same Crisis issue by leaders such as NACW activist Alice Dunbar Nelson from Delaware, NAACP secretary James Weldon Johnson, and the Crisis editor W. E. B. Du Bois.[23]

Thirty-two African Americans had responded to Du Bois's call for essays in support of woman suffrage. As the voice of the NAACP, Du Bois used The Crisis to spread his equalitarian views about gender conventions and woman suffrage. He also felt that both sides of the woman suffrage question should be heard, so he invited African American conservatives to express their opposing views. Only one dared to respond to Du Bois's call for essays—Howard University professor Kelly Miller, who represented the black conservatism of the era.

In essence, Miller felt that the best place for women was in the home. Of the family, he wrote, "[W]oman suffrage could not possibly enhance the harmoniousness of this relationship, but might seriously jeopardize it."[24] He also contended that women were weaker than men and were unable to compete in the strenuous activities demanded of political life. In his view of woman's role in society, Miller's argument was similar to those of the "antis." With respect to the argument that women voters would reform society, Miller noted that by 1915, in the twelve states where woman suffrage had been in effect, there was no noticeable improvement in the status of women. He also refuted the thesis, enunciated by such black leaders as Du Bois, Mary Church Terrell, her husband Judge Robert Terrell, and socialist journalists A. Philip Randolph and Chandler Owen, that the plight of black women was similar to the plight of all women. Miller saw the gender issue separately from the race issue. Combining the old abolitionist-Republican argument of the 1860s with the "anti" argument of the 1890s, Miller asserted that "the negro" (man) could not get justice without the right to suffrage, but (white) women were privileged, and therefore held no such claim to protection.[25] Here we see the conservative view of race and gender conventions held by some among the black elite, who viewed blacks in terms of men and whites in terms of women. In this paradigm, there is no room for black women unless they have affluent husbands who, despite their risky position in society as black men, can protect their wives as do white men.

In an editorial published in the same *Crisis* issue, Du Bois took issue with Miller. Du Bois found Miller's argument about the weak woman who belonged in the home under the protection of male suffrage to be an irrational contention, especially for black families and for the many families with single mothers who did not have a male protector. He considered Miller's position to be "ancient."[26]

Similarly, James Dudley, president of Greensboro A & T College in North Carolina, was another African American conservative on the woman suffrage issue. During the 1920 elections, Dudley discouraged black women in Greensboro from going to the polls. Like other "antis," he argued that woman's place was in the home, not the polling place. However, he added a more practical dimension to his argument, one that Miller did not express. Dudley felt that it was unwise for blacks in general to "meddle in politics," voicing the many fears of violent reprisals of southern African American men who had witnessed white intimidation against them when in the past they had attempted to vote. In commenting on Dudley's advice, Du Bois felt that black women in Greensboro as well as in the South as a whole, disregard such advice; and indeed they did. NAACP statistics indicated that black women had voted in large numbers throughout the nation and even in the South, where many were purposely discouraged by white registrars.[27]

The NAACP, like many institutions serving the African American community, understood the politics of the woman suffrage movement, part of which was, not only to intimidate, but to defame African Americans so that they would be excluded from the franchise entirely. As a result, the efforts African Americans had made since the post–Civil War period to discredit the anti-woman suffrage arguments appeared to make little difference to those conservatives who refused to accept them.

Black women's responses to the gendered and racialized politics of the times varied over time. Many individual African Americans in both the nineteenth and the twentieth centuries endorsed woman suffrage because it seemed to be a vehicle for helping the race. At the same time, others were discouraged from joining the national suffrage movement because they were suspicious of the leadership's position about enfranchising black women. Nonetheless, African American women discussed the woman suffrage issues and usually resolved that they could accomplish more for the race by supporting the movement. As a result, they were obliged to counter the anti–black woman suffrage strategies.

In 1899, Adella Hunt Logan wrote of her concerns about the southern states' determination to disfranchise black men and keep women from gaining the right to the ballot. In a letter to a white northern friend, Logan wrote that she held little hope for white southern women's enfranchisement "and none for the black woman."[28] She clearly foresaw the bitter fight during the next two decades to include black women in the woman suffrage amendment.

In 1904, Mary Church Terrell attended the NAWSA convention held in the District of Columbia. During the proceedings, the white delegates spoke of the problems of child and animal abuse. In response to a call for federal legislation to protect children and animals, Terrell spoke out, noting the irony of suffragists who, while pleading for the just treatment of animals, could not concede to "give fair play to the colored race."[29]

Other African American women expressed similar sentiments when given the opportunity to speak at NAWSA conventions. At the convention held in Louisville, Kentucky, in 1911, a Black female delegate attempted to formulate a resolution condemning disenfranchisement on the grounds of either sex or race. Du Bois and Martha Gruening, a white NAACP leader and a suffragist, alleged that Anna Shaw aborted the resolution attempt. According to Gruening, Shaw gave two reasons for her actions. First, the suffragists did not want to offend their southern hostesses with a resolution that opposed the doctrine of white supremacy. Second, Shaw accused black men of being the number one enemy of the woman suffrage amendment. Consequently, she refused to introduce the resolution.[30]

Assessing the validity of the Shaw accusation is difficult because statistics are not available. Nonetheless, the black male electorate could never have made the impact that she claimed that it could because the majority of black males lived in the South and their votes had been substantially reduced by the turn of the century. It appears that African American men were being used as scapegoats—but then, so were their women. In reply to accusations that black women's clubs opposed woman suffrage, a black suffragist from Vineland, New Jersey, stated: "It was the Labor Union, and the white women's clubs of New Jersey which defeated the Amendment." She claimed further that in her borough there were 722 votes for woman suffrage and that she had personally secured 300 of them.[31]

Although white suffragists exaggerated the anti–woman suffrage activity among African Americans, there were a few black men, such as Kelly Miller, who voiced reservations, if not opposition, to the movement. Oftentimes, what appeared to be anti–woman suffrage sentiments was actually opposition to white women suffragists, whose racism black men feared. In North Carolina, for example, some middle-class black men, such as James Dudley, were fearful that if their women attempted to vote, they would face the same intimidation and indignities black men had faced at the polls. For this reason, others expressed antisuffrage views.[32]

Perhaps the most vocal black woman to write on this subject was Mary Church Terrell. In 1912 she wrote: "If I were a colored man, and were unfortunate enough not to grasp the absurdity of opposing suffrage because of the sex of a human being, I should at least be consistent enough never to raise my voice against those who have disenfranchised my brothers and myself on account of race." However, Terrell observed in her travels that "the intelligent colored man who opposed woman suffrage is very rare indeed." In discussing woman suffrage, Terrell said that the majority of men, whom she described as the "leading citizens" in their communities, advocated it.[33]

Writing for *The Crisis* in 1915, Terrell compared the plight of blacks and women. Her aim was to obtain support from blacks who, because they distrusted white suffragists, failed to support the woman suffrage cause. She felt that the same antisuffrage argument that was used to withhold the ballot from women was also being used to prove that black men should remain disenfranchised. For this reason alone, she argued, African Americans should support woman suffrage. Likewise, writing in *The Crisis* the same year, Washington, D.C. educator and club woman Coralie Cook reminded skeptical black men that "disenfranchisement because of sex is curiously like disenfranchisement because of color. It cripples the individual; it handicaps progress; it sets a limitation upon mental and spiritual development." [34]

Nonetheless, African American fears went beyond misgivings about white women, particularly in the South. There black women resisted the idea that woman suffrage truly represented enfranchising all women, because they trusted the white power structure's promise to keep blacks, both men and women, disenfranchised. As the debates about enfranchising African American women intensified, southern suffragists such as Margaret Murray Washington became even more disillusioned by the movement. In 1912 she wrote a friend that most men and women of the race had other priorities. As for woman suffrage, she felt that black women would "try hard to take our stand," but only when the nation reached the point of giving African American women equal rights with all other citizens.[35] Other black women, however, refused to be disillusioned and sought to gain the vote particularly, as whites had feared, to establish universal suffrage for all black adults.

Clearly there was a nationwide, not just a southern, prejudice against allowing African American women to vote. As for the woman suffrage leadership, it appears that white women outside the South used southern white women's overt prejudice as an excuse for the NAWSA's discriminatory policies, while hiding their own similar feelings about black women, even though they shared many of the black women's goals for reform and women's political equity. African American woman suffragists were quite aware of their position, and they were determined to move beyond the attempts to keep them disenfranchised.

Black suffragists knew that although those national suffrage leaders who courted black support endorsed equal suffrage among the races while in African American circles, their public actions and statements to the mainstream society often contradicted their professed equalitarianism. One example involves one of the most famous incidents of direct confrontation among the so-called radical woman suffragists of the early twentieth century—the famous suffrage parade in front of the White House. It was co-sponsored in 1913 by the NAWSA and the Congressional Union for Woman Suffrage (National Woman's Party) at Washington, D.C. Alice Paul, founder of the NWP, was the parade organizer.

When Adella Hunt Logan read in the NAWSA newspaper, the *Woman's Journal*, that white women said they could not march in the parade if any African American women participated, she immediately went into action to subvert the exclusionary plan. Logan wrote Mary Church Terrell and other black woman suffragists in the District of Columbia, encouraging them to march. News of the forthcoming black participation must have forced the NAWSA to compromise its racial exclusionary strategy, and it was decided to segregate the black suffragists at the back of the parade instead.[36]

The Crisis reported that despite efforts to exclude black women, "they made such an admirable showing in the first great national parade."[37] Du Bois was pleased about the way in which African American women persisted in their attempts to participate, because NAWSA officials had asked Ida B. Wells-Barnett, who was representing the Alpha Suffrage Club, not to march with the white Chicago delegation. The reason advanced was fear of offending "certain unnamed southern women," who had pledged not to march in a racially integrated parade. This request was made publicly of all the black marchers. Nonetheless, Wells-Barnett integrated the Illinois delegation, despite the rebuff.[38]

In the meantime, white suffragists Virginia Brooks and Belle Squire agreed with Wells-Barnett; however, other whites in the Illinois delegation admonished her for not being willing to march with the other women of her race. This disclosure about Illinois suffragists reveals that, not only southern white suffragists, but some northern ones too felt that black women should be segregated in the march. Shortly after the admonishment, Wells-Barnett disappeared from the parade, but as the delegates began marching down Pennsylvania Avenue, she stepped out of the crowd and joined Brooks and Squires in the parade. Historian Wanda Hendericks believes that Wells-Barnett's refusal to be segregated in the march impeded the white "prerogative of discriminating against African American Women." Yet she argues that white women's endorsement of segregation blinded them to the way in which they had forced African American women to separate their blackness from their femaleness.[39]

In the meantime, the rest of the Chicago delegation and the other black women delegates were relegated to the end of the line. For example, Mary Church Terrell, who had marched in the parade with African American Delta Sigma Theta Sorority women from Howard University, assembled in the area reserved for black women— at the end of the line. Several years later, Terrell confided her feelings about the NAWSA and about Alice Paul to Walter White of the NAACP. Both questioned, in particular, Paul's loyalty to black women and concluded that if she and other white suffragist leaders could get the Anthony suffrage amendment through without enfranchising African American women, they would.[40]

In contextualizing this discussion, it does not matter if contemporary historians debate whether white suffragists were racist. Although northern suffragist leaders accepted the southern strategy in varying degrees, even those who did not personally endorse the idea could not announce from a NAWSA platform that black women should be enfranchised equally with white women. The South was against a national policy of woman suffrage because it would include black women. Northern suffragists realized that a national amendment needed some southern support in order to be successful. On the other hand, many northern white suffragists hid behind the South in justifying racial prejudice. For example, although militant suffragist Alice Paul rejected both male and female Democrats who were known for their antiblack views, she did not publicly support black female suffrage and, consequently, has been charged with being prejudiced against black women. On the other hand, New York suffrage leaders Alva Belmont, Mrs. John Dewey, and Harriet Blatch encouraged African American participation. However, the New York suffrage leaders appear to be in the minority.[41]

There was a congressional debate over granting white women (not all women) the suffrage. In testifying before the Senate Committee on Woman Suffrage against the proposed amendment, the National Association Opposed to Woman Suffrage asserted: "The first fruits of the Amendment would be to admit Negro women to the polls, when eleven states have successfully defied the Federal Government in any effort to admit Negro men to the polls."[42]

Not surprising, steps to disenfranchise African American females who already had the vote revealed another antiblack strategy observable in many localities throughout the country. As early as 1902 Kentucky had taken away the school vote from the women of the state in order to eliminate the black female vote.[43] In 1914 the Illinois legislature was considering the woman suffrage question, and according to the recollections of Ida B. Wells-Barnett, there was talk of limiting the legislation to include white women only. This threat led black women, who in the past had been reluctant to join the Illinois Woman Suffrage Association, to join the Alpha Suffrage Club. The significance of this club's influence on Chicago elections could be seen as far South as Alabama, where periodicals published pictures of black Chicago women campaigning for African American candidates. Antisuffrage fliers read: "Five Million of These Ladies Will Vote!" "How Many of These Will Your County and State Produce under Federal Suffrage?" Black woman suffragists of Chicago's second ward were said to have helped to defeat the candidate chosen by white suffragists. "Antis" predicted the advent of "Negro rule" throughout the South should a federal amendment enfranchise all women.[44]

Although in Virginia, legislative debates between 1912 and 1920 infrequently raised the issue of race, outside of legislative halls the news media fanned the fears of "negro rule." "Antis" referred to the 1910 census showing more blacks than whites in twenty-nine Virginia counties. Virginia "antis" predicted that a woman suffrage amendment would bring an end to the Democratic Party in Virginia because the black electorate would vote for the Republican Party. Historian Suzanne Lebsock notes how in 1915 the Equal Suffrage League of Virginia responded to the "antis" by contending that white supremacy was in no danger. The suffragists argued that through poll taxes and literacy tests, the black women would be prevented from registering to vote just like their men.[45]

Nonetheless, African Americans stood ready for these impediments to their enfranchisement. With such fears among white southern politicians, their reaction in 1918, the year Texas women won the right to vote, is not surprising. The black editor of the *Houston Observer* responded to fears on the part of black people about disfranchisement when he called upon the men and women of the race to register to vote in spite of the poll tax, which, he felt, was designed especially to exclude black voters. In urging African Americans to vote, the editor implored them to pay the poll tax so that they could "perform that sacred duty."[46]

As a result of these developments, Mrs. A. W. Blackwell, a Georgia woman missionary of the African Methodist Episcopal Church (AME), predicted that white suffragists would institute a "grandmother's" clause once they obtain the vote in order

to keep the more than three million black women from voting. Blackwell was the corresponding secretary of the AME Church Women's Home and Foreign Mission Society in Atlanta, and she expressed views similar to those of Mary Church Terrell.
Blackwell wrote that justice would not prevail, even with the ballot, until white
women learned to teach their children respect for black people and all other citizens.
In addition to the AME, the leaders of the National Baptist Women's Convention
called, not only for white women to cooperate with black women, but for whites to
teach their youth respect for all women. Moreover, they declared that "the longer
and farther apart the women of the races remain, the greater will be the encroach-
ment by white men."[47] By November 1918, African American men and women in
the North, in particular, watched the press carefully for the congressional debates
about the Anthony amendment, to which they responded critically. An anonymous
African American correspondent, whose letter was signed "J.K.L.," wrote to a
Philadelphia newspaper and charged white Americans with political hypocrisy, as
while they called for U.S. leadership in making the world safe for democracy, southern U.S. senators proposed a woman suffrage amendment to exclude black women.[48]

The closer the woman suffrage legislation came to passage, the more white supremacists in the South resorted to tactics designed to sabotage it. In 1918 James
Callaway wrote an article in the *Macon Telegraph* (reprinted in NWP literature), in
which he attempted to discredit Susan B. Anthony. He recounted "some strange history" about the late suffrage hero and printed photographs of people he called "the
three immediate women friends of the Anthony family." Two women were prominent, white suffragists who were in the nation's eye—Carrie Catt and Anna Howard
Shaw. The third woman was Mrs. R. Jerome Jeffrey (the black woman's club leader
from Rochester), who was pictured with the caption "negro" below her name. Callaway indicted Anthony and other suffragists close to her because of their friendship
with Jeffrey and other blacks such as Frederick Douglass, Robert Purvis, and Booker
T. Washington (all of whom were deceased). Callaway supported his claim that Anthony had betrayed the white women of the South by quoting excerpts from her biography that revealed her relationship with black suffragists. Callaway ended his
article with a plea to the Senate not to endorse woman suffrage, for to do so would
be to affirm the beliefs of people such as Anthony, whom he believed to be immoral.
He wrote: "All who have the interest of the white woman of the rural districts at
heart pray that the Senate will have the wisdom to stand firm for the liberties of the
women on the farm. It is a critical hour for the South—a crisis that involves her future civilization, her tranquility and her prosperity."[49]

The year 1919 marked the adoption of the Anthony bill by Congress, as
anti–black woman suffrage sentiments continued to plague the suffrage movement.
The substantial opposition to the ratification of the Nineteenth Amendment
throughout the South was due to the perception of many whites that black women
were eager to win the right to vote in the entire region. The overwhelming majority
of negative votes in Congress against the amendment in 1919 came from Mississippi,
South Carolina, Alabama, Georgia, Louisiana, and North Carolina. Although there
were several other reasons for southern opposition, it was widely believed that Black
women wanted the ballot more than white women. Black women were expected to
register and vote in larger numbers than white women; thus, the ballot would soon
be returned to black men. Opponents of black female suffrage believed that the result would be the return of the two-party system in the South and that if African

Americans gained the vote, they would consistently vote Republican. These fears were realized in Florida when, following the passage of the Nineteenth Amendment, black women in Jacksonville registered in greater numbers than white women. As a result, the Woman Suffrage League in Jacksonville was reorganized into the Duval County League of Democratic Women Voters whose members were dedicated to maintain white supremacy and to register white women voters.[50]

Five months before ratification, white supremacists had circulated pro–black woman suffrage articles from black periodicals such as *The New York Age* and *The Crisis* in order to show whites how effective the woman suffrage amendment would be in strengthening the black electorate. One report pictured Annie Simms Banks, a black woman from Winchester, Kentucky, who became the "first Negro Woman delegate to a political convention." Another report, copied from *The Crisis*, enumerated the black women who were eligible to vote in the thirty-one states that had ratified the proposed woman suffrage amendment by March 1920. The report estimated that 750,000 black women were eligible to vote in those states alone. Antiblack propaganda accompanied these reprinted articles to fuel the fire of the "antis" with predictions about black women voters taking over the South.[51]

Even had African American women united and flooded the polls as predicted, the enemy would have remained overwhelming. In hindsight, we know that the ballot could not have protected black women for very long in most of the South. Yet in 1920, African American women continued to resist and were determined to get the vote. Nonetheless, they were virtually abandoned by most white female suffragists. Calls for interracial cooperation to assist black women win the vote coming from black women such as Josephine St. Pierre Ruffin, Mrs. A. W. Blackwell, Mary Church Terrell, and S. Willie Layton went unheeded. Hence, the words of Frederick Douglass and of Frances Harper in 1869 were shown to still be valid fifty years later. Douglass had said that in America, a black woman is victimized, "not because she is a woman, but because she is black." Harper had felt that for white women, the priorities in the struggle for human rights were "for sex, letting race occupy a minor position."[52]

Despite the racism in the movement, among the African Americans who responded to the woman suffrage arguments and activities, the vast majority supported the cause and rejected conservatism. Throughout the period of the woman suffrage movement, only three out of eighty-three black men were found to have publicly opposed woman suffrage. Not one of the black women who spoke out about woman suffrage opposed it.[53] Although African American leaders expressed concern about the motives of white suffragists, they encouraged others to support the ideas of the woman suffrage argument. In recognizing that their people needed a political voice in order to bring about changes, some leaders encouraged blacks to put aside their fears about the racism apparent among many white woman suffragists and to support the movement for the good of the black race.

As a consequence of the growing racism among whites, on one hand, and the increasing mobilization of black women for the suffrage cause, on the other, African American women turned more to themselves to find solutions for their own problems. The support black women received from the men of their race seemed inversely proportionate to the amount of backlash black women received from white women. Male efforts to assist African American suffragists were especially notable in calling attention to white discrimination against black women in the suffrage movement.

Whatever their reasons, most African American men publicly championed their women's struggle for the vote.

In reflecting on the political characteristics of anti-woman suffragists, issues surface about the interaction between traditional nineteenth-century racial and gender conventions in the United States as a whole and not only in the South. As conservatives attempted to maintain these conventions during the early twentieth century, African American women nationwide experienced social and political proscriptions based on two birth-determined characteristics. As a result, they were subordinated by both their race and their gender. As African American women resisted proscribed roles, they contested conservative beliefs and practices, inspiring more fear among those who could not yield to progress.

NOTES

1. See Miriam Gurko, *The Ladies of Seneca Falls: The Birth of the Woman's Rights Movement* (New York: MacMillan Publishing Co., 1974), p. 215; Carrie Chapmen Catt and Nettie Rogers Shuler, *Woman Suffrage and Politics: The Inner Story of the Suffrage Movement* (New York: Charles Scribner's Sons, 1926), pp. 54–60; Robert L. Allen and Pamela P. Allen, *Reluctant Reformers: Movements in the United States* (Washington, D.C.: Howard University Press, 1974), pp. 142, 145. For details on the black male response to those who accused them of opposing woman suffrage, and for an analysis of the myth of anti–woman suffrage sentiments among black men, Rosalyn Terborg-Penn, "Afro-Americans in the Struggle for Woman Suffrage" (Ph. D. diss., Howard University, 1977), chaps. 3, 6.

2. Marjorie Spruill Wheeler, *New Women of the New South: The Leaders of the Woman Suffrage Movement in the Southern States* (New York: Oxford University Press, 1993), pp. 101–2.

3. "The Southern States Woman Suffrage Conference," *The Suffragists*, 14 (November 1914), p. 2; "Chief Justice Clark on Woman Suffrage and the Race Problem," *The Suffragists*, 16 (October 1915), p. 2; "Southern Chiva'ry," *The Suffragists*, 1 (January 1916), p. 2.

4. U.S. Department of the Interior, *Eleventh Census, 1890*, 1:3, (Washington, D.C.: U.S. GPO, 1890), p. 166; "Will the Federal Suffrage Amendment Complicate the Race Problem?" (1890 flier, National Woman's Party, National Literature, Anti–Woman Suffrage Folder, Political History Division, Smithsonian Institution). For a good analysis of anti–black woman suffrage activities in the South, see Bettina Aptheker, *Woman's Legacy: Essays on Race, Sex, and Class in American History* (Amherst: University of Massachusetts Press, 1982), chap.3; Suzanne Lebsock, "Woman Suffrage and White Supremacy: A Virginia Case Study," in *Visible Women*, edited by Nancy A. Hewitt and Suzanne Lebsock (Urbana: University of Illinois Press, 1993), pp. 75–76.

5. Elizabeth Cady Stanton et al. eds., *The History of Woman Suffrage* (hereafter HWS) (New York: Fowler and Wells, 1881–1882), 2:94–95, 216, 396, 443–44; *New York Tribune*, January 13, 1869; *New National Era*, October 24, 1872.

6. *Woman's Era*, 2 (August 1985): 19; HWS 4:216, 246; James M. McPherson, *Abolitionist Legacy: From Reconstruction to the NAACP* (Princeton: Princeton University Press, 1975), pp. 320–21.

7. Ida B. Wells-Barnett, *Crusade for Justice: The Autobiography of Ida B. Wells*, ed. by Alfreda Duster (Chicago: University of Chicago Press, 1970), p. 230.

8. Ibid.

9. McPherson, *Abolitionist Legacy*, p. 319–320. "Educated suffrage" continued to be popular among white suffragists in the twentieth century. See, for example, Margaret De-

land, "The Third Way in Woman Suffrage," *Ladies' Home Journal*, 30 (January 1913): pp. 11–12.

10. Adele Logan Alexander, "Adella Hunt Logan, the Tuskegee Woman's Club and African American Women in the Woman Suffrage Movement," in *Votes for Women: the Woman Suffrage Movement in Tennessee, the South and the Nation*, ed. Marjorie Spruill Wheeler (Knoxville: University of Tennessee Press, 1995), p. 102, n 34.

11. McPherson, *Abolitionist Legacy*, p. 321; HWS, 4:341, 678, 680–81.

12. Allen and Allen, *Reluctant Reformers*, pp. 155–56.

13. See: *Negro Year Book, 1918* (Tuskegee: Tuskegee Institute, 1918–1921); and *Woman's Era*, 1894–1897; Aileen Kraditor, *The Ideas of the Woman Suffrage Movement, 1890–1920* (Garden City, NY: Anchor Books, 1971), p. 213.

14. *Woman's Era*, 2 (January 1896):12.

15. HWS, 4:359; *(Indianapolis) Freeman*, July 1905; National Baptist Convention, *Thirteenth Annual Report, Women's Convention, 1913* (Nashville: National Baptist Convention, 1913), p. 33.

16. Adella Hunt Logan, "Woman Suffrage," *Colored American Magazine*, 9 (September 1905): p. 487.

17. Ibid., pp. 487–88.

18. Lillian A. Turner, "Votes for Housewives," *The Crisis*, 10 (August 1915): 192; Mary E. Jackson, "The Self-Supporting Woman and the Ballot," *The Crisis*, 10 (August 1915): 187.

19. *The Crisis*, 18 (July 1919); 17.

20. Editorial, *The Crisis*, 3 (October 1911): 243–44.

21. Francis Grimke, "The Logic of Woman Suffrage," *The Crisis*, 10 (August 1915): 178–79.

22. Benjamin Brawley, "Politics and Womanliness," *The Crisis*, 10 (August 1915): 179.

23. *The Crisis*, 10 (August 1915): 180, 187, 192.

24. Kelly Miller, "The Risk of Woman Suffrage," *The Crisis*, 11 (November 1915): 37. Ironically, Miller's daughter, Harlem Renaissance playwright Mae Miller, was the antithesis of her father's perception about the place for women. She was the most widely published black woman playwright of the times. A Howard University graduate, she became a professional woman and moved away from her home in the District of Columbia to live as a single woman and teach drama at Frederick Douglass High School in Baltimore. There she wrote most of her plays focusing on social and political issues. An Alpha Kappa Alpha Sorority woman, Miller helped found the Morgan College chapter shortly after she moved to Baltimore. A single woman for most of her adult life, Miller waited until she was forty-one years of age before marrying and soon after changed her creative genre, becoming a poet as her father had been before her. Kathy A. Perkins, "Mae Miller," in *Black Women in America: An Historical Encyclopedia*, ed. Darlene Clark Hine, Elsa Barkley Brown, and Rosalyn Terborg-Penn (Bloomington: Indiana University Press, 1994), 2: 797–98.

25. Kelly Miller, "The Risk of Woman Suffrage," 38.

26. Editorial, *The Crisis*, 11 (November 1915): 29–30.

27. Editorial, *The Crisis*, 21 (March 1921): 200.

28. Alexander, "Adella Hunt Logan," p. 73.

29. HWS, 5:105–6.

30. *The Crisis*, 4 (June 1912): 76–77.

31. *Negro Year Book, 1916*, 37–38.

32. Quoted in Alexander, "Adella Hunt Logan," 103 n. 47.

33. Mary Church Terrell, "The Justice of Women Suffrage," *The Crisis*, 4 (September 1912): 191.

34. Ibid.; Coralee Franklin Cook, "Votes for Mothers," *The Crisis*, 10 (August 1915):185.

35. Quoted in Alexander, "Adella Hunt Logan," pp. 101–02, n. 29.

36. Ibid., p. 78.
37. *The Crisis*, 5 (April 1913): 298.
38. Kraditor, *Ideas of the Woman Suffrage Movement*, pp. 167–68.
39. Ibid., 270.
40. Walter White to Mary Church Terrell, March 14, 1919, (Mary Church Terrell Papers, The Library of Congress, Manuscript Division, Washington, D.C.).
41. David Morgan, *Suffragists and Democrats: The Politics of Woman Suffrage in America* (East Lansing: Michigan State University Press, 1972), p. 92; author's conversation with Edith Mayo, Curator, Woman's Collection, Division of Political History, Smithsonian Institution, June 30, 1976, Washington, D.C.
42. Morgan, *Suffragists and Democrats*, pp. 93–94; quoted in *Negro Year Book 1914*, p. 43.
43. Wheeler, New Women, pp. 100–105, 143.
44. *HWS* 4:27; Wells-Barnett, *Crusade*, 345; "Five Million of These Ladies Will Vote," (1890 flier, Anti–Woman Suffrage folder, Political History Division, Smithsonian Institution).
45. Lebsock, "Woman Suffrage," pp. 70–71.
46. Quoted in the *Negro Year Book 1918* (Tuskegee Institute, 1918–1921), 60.
47. Blackwell was identified only by her picture and organizational title. Her undated pamphlet is located in the Trevor Arnett Library at Clark-Atlanta University and was originally contained in the Slaughter Collection; Mrs. A. W. Blackwell, *The Responsibility and Opportunity of the Twentieth Century Woman* (n.p., n.d.), pp. 3–4; National Baptist Convention, *Woman's Convention 1916* (Nashville: National Baptist Convention, 1916), pp. 31–33.
48. *The Crisis* 17 (November 1918): 25.
49. James Callaway, "Some Strange History," *Macon Telegraph*, May 26, 1918, (reprinted in National Woman's Party literature, Anti-Woman Suffrage folder, Political History Division, Smithsonian Institution).
50. Kenneth R. Johnson, "White Racial Attitudes as a Factor in the Arguments Against the Nineteenth Amendment," *Phylon* 31 (Spring 1970): 31–32, 35–37.
51. *The New York Age*, March 31, 1920, *The Crisis* 18 (March 1920) (reprinted in National Woman's Party literature, Anti-Woman Suffrage folder, Political History Division, Smithsonian Institution).
52. *HWS*, 2:383, 385.
53. See Rosalyn Terborg-Penn, "Afro-Americans in the Struggle for Woman Suffrage," appendices.

CHAPTER 5

"IF IT AIN'T BROKE, DON'T FIX IT": THOMAS SOWELL ON BLACK WOMEN, AFFIRMATIVE ACTION, AND THE DEATH OF DISCRIMINATION

RHONDA M. WILLIAMS

Economists have been, and continue to be, prominent critics of affirmative action. Professional economists are very visible among those crafting narratives that question the very existence of discrimination, and thus challenge the need for any antidiscrimination policy whatsoever.[1] Politicians, court officials, journalists, talk-show hosts, and ordinary people look to the profession for "expertise" on the mysterious workings of labor markets. In debates on affirmative action, economists' accounts of race, gender, and labor-market outcomes have become important referents that inform the construction of a shared "common sense."

This chapter posits that there is more to economists' prominence than meets the eye. In other words, the profession's importance in articulating the case against affirmative action in part derives from the ideological content of the labor-market stories provided by the dominant paradigm. In the neoclassical tradition, merit and choice are the primary determinants of occupational and earnings outcomes. The mainstream narrative theoretically validates the popular notion that the Unites States is fundamentally a meritocratic social order.

In the dramas of the neoclassical mainstream, African Americans, Latinos, and white women are characters who affirm the market's capacities to mirror moral substance and reflect "preexisting" social norms.[2] Viewed from this perspective, today's distribution of economic rewards, particularly the racial, ethnic, and gender dimensions thereof, simply reflects the distributions of abilities, character, and cultural norms largely determined prior to labor-market engagements. In such a world, affirmative action is, at best, unnecessary. In a worst-case scenario, it is an exercise in folly, an unjust and stigmatizing practice.

This chapter critically reads one of Thomas Sowell's early challenges to the need for, and effectiveness of, affirmative action. I suggest that Thomas Sowell's exposé on affirmative action functions as an allegory for the workings of race and gender in U.S. labor markets. In both style and substance, "'Affirmative Action' Reconsidered" (1976) foreshadows twenty years of neoconservative parables of market life.[3]

First and foremost, Sowell's narrative affirms racism as a phenomenon of the past; his dismissal of discrimination as a contemporary phenomenon renders absurd the actions of those who seek or support race-based affirmative action policies. Gender-based discrimination all but disappears in Sowell's story; rather, the gender-based divisions of labor in heterosexual families is the fundamental cause of women's labor-market problems.

Sowell concludes that ability and preference guide labor markets. A limited domain of acceptable evidence supports his reasoning: he makes his case with a subset of information that effectively "disappears" the possibility that labor markets might have ever functioned to further white male authority, power, and privilege. Moreover, his choice of the academy as the site from which to conduct his evaluation makes invisible the pervasive race and gender-based occupational segregation that first inspired affirmative action policies.

Of particular interest is black women's status as nonsubjects in Sowell's essay. Like much of his later writing, this essay conjures a world in which "blacks" seem distinctively male and "women" are universally white.[4] Viewed from the perspectives of a generation of black feminist writers, Sowell's essay is more than just another piece of labor-market analysis that excludes women of color. His critique suggests an absence of commonly shared economic narratives, either that examine black women's work or that imagine or that examine the particularities of the discriminations that black women encounter.[5]

This absence is particularly significant when viewed in hindsight—that is, when viewed from the perspective of twenty years of U.S. policy discussions that *indeed* foreground very specific constructs of African American women as economic agents. I have in mind popular racialized representations of the prototypical Aid to Families with Dependent Children (AFDC) client and the professional black woman. The former is a degenerate black woman, an unbridled breeder whose imagined hypersexuality and aversion to work made necessary the "ending of welfare as we know it" in 1996. The "welfare mother" who haunts public spaces is the antithesis of the productive citizen-worker. She is a black woman who neither raises proper national subjects, the obligation of the citizen-mother, nor earns a wage. Her ritualistically circulated image thus fosters the notion that black women are anathema to social reproduction, both marginal and unproductive subjects. These constructs make less plausible the notion that the state should be accountable to black women.

The "welfare mother" has a troublesome twin, the "two-fer." The "two-fer" is the employed African American woman who has undeservedly benefited from affirmative action, here understood as widespread, government-supported compulsory hiring of "minorities" and "women" ("two-fer" meaning "two for one"). This construct again insists that black women in the United States lack a proper engagement with capitalist labor markets; it suggests that their labor-market successes are intrinsically suspect and their problems deserved.

This chapter argues that Sowell's essay foreshadows twenty years of neoconservative narratives of affirmative action and assaults on it. Two contextual discussions provide a prelude to a critical assessment of Sowell's essay. The first briefly explains my choice of Sowell's essay as an entry point. I then present a short compendium of labor-force data that reveal the incompleteness of labor-market studies and serve to "de-racialize" women and "de-gender" African Americans. The remaining sections examine Sowell's narrative on policy and the workings of race and gender in academic labor markets.

WHY THIS GUY?

Although he would probably score low on most name-recognition surveys, Thomas Sowell is well known to those who regularly engage the conservative political economy and to those who read the footnotes of anti–affirmative-action treatises. Although *The New York Times Book Review* has occasionally reviewed his work, he is both more prolific and less publicly visible than kindred spirit and fellow black neo-conservative economist Glenn Loury.[6] As a former student of Nobel laureate and conservative economist Milton Friedman, Sowell has his mentor's propensity to theorize race and gender within an idealized free market economy.

In this ideal-type construction, all market agents are maximizing subjects relentlessly pursuing economic gain. In this world, race and sex discrimination are irrational and short lived: would-be discriminators ultimately fall prey to nondiscriminating competitive adversaries. Because the latter hire "qualified," yet underpaid, women and minorities at the prevailing wage (a wage lowered by discrimination), they operate with lower costs and earn higher profits than do their erstwhile discriminating counterparts. Thus, competitive rivalry erodes discriminatory wage gaps and drives the discriminators from the marketplace.

Like many in the profession, Sowell is theoretically predisposed to believe that economic discrimination cannot be a long-standing and ongoing phenomenon. And, like his peers, he has looked elsewhere for explanations of long-standing race and gender differentials in employment and earnings.

WHITHER THE SISTERS?

There is little real question that if one goes back a number of years one finds a pervasive pattern of discrimination against minorities in academic employment. . . . The situation with respect to women is somewhat more complicated and will be deferred for the moment.[7]

Among antiracist and multiracial feminist scholars, it is by now conventional wisdom that race and class divisions (to name but two) among women significantly differentiate life conditions and the distribution of power and well-being.[8] In keeping with this spirit, many feminist economists in the United States continue to argue that gendered identity and social relations are a necessary component of race and class analysis.[9]

Sowell's comparison of "minorities" and "women" typifies the kind of scholarship that called forth multiracial feminisms. He models a discursive practice that has become normative in twenty years of affirmative action dialogues: discrimination is something that happens to two distinct populations, "minorities" and "women." Implicitly, the men under consideration are of color; the women are white.

The price of labor-market studies that neither genderize racial economies nor racialize gender is the obliteration of the working lives of women of color. If their work lives were comparable to those of black men or white women, then the price would be low. However, even a cursory compilation of labor-force artifacts demonstrates the difference that difference makes. These data suggest that a systematic erasure of black women's labor-market experiences can function as a silent narrative; one that suggests that black women are either disengaged from wage work or are only insignificantly present.

Labor-force participation rates offer a window into a world of working women in which race makes a difference.[10] Sowell's study uses data from 1968 to 1973. In 1970, adult black women were much more likely than their white peers to be either working (employed) or seeking work (unemployed) and therefore counted among the nation's labor-force participants. Among those aged twenty-five to thirty-four years, the black/white labor-force participation gap was 57.6 percent versus 43.2 percent, in the age thirty-five to forty-four cohort, the gap was slightly smaller but still ten points, 59.9 percent versus 49.9 percent.[11]

Black and white women also have different work histories during their childbearing and child-rearing years. Although white wives with live-in husbands had already begun to increase their rates of labor-force participation at the time of Sowell's writing, they still spent less time in paid employment than did their black counterparts.[12] Black women were also more likely than white women to be household heads and, whether working full or part time, faced much higher unemployment rates. Among those who worked full time, black women averaged weekly earnings much lower than those of their white female and black male counterparts. In 1970, whereas black men and white women averaged weekly earnings of $113 and $95, respectively, black women earned only $81.[13] Older black women workers dominated the ranks of private-household workers, comprising 53 percent of retirees in 1970. Among new workers, only 8 percent worked as domestics. At the other end of the wage hierarchy, only 6 percent of retiring women worked in professional and technical occupations, in contrast to 15 percent of new entrants.

Although black women considerably upgraded their occupational status during the 1960s, the legacy and practice of race and gender job segregation were still very much alive in the early 1970s. Black women were still 50 percent more likely than white women to work in service occupations, remained very concentrated in the lowest tiers of clerical work, and were more likely to be supervised than to supervise.[14]

Black men and women also worked in very different occupations in the late 1960s and early 1970s. Women were concentrated in clerical and service occupations and noticeably absent from transportation and material-moving occupations. Among professional and technical workers, black women, but not black men, were disproportionately employed as teachers and nurses. In every major industry group, fewer black women than black men were high earners, and, compared to black men, black women were more likely to be ranked among the working poor. Because working-class black men were heavily concentrated in manufacturing employment, they were especially hard hit by the decline in blue-collar jobs during the 1980s.[15]

Black women's labor-market experience also differs from those of Puerto Rican women, recent Vietnamese immigrants, and Chinese Americans of both sexes. The historical evidence continues to accumulate; race, ethnicity, gender, and nationality are important factors in shaping the labor-market experiences of working peoples. This brief descriptive foray can only hint at the incompleteness of labor-market statistics, whicht fail to disaggregate women by race and blacks by gender. Accounts of women's work that subsume race will most likely overstate black women's economic well-being, as will descriptions of African Americans that focus only on men's work. I now turn to the particulars of Sowell's treatise. His discussion of minorities, women, and affirmative action both dismisses discrimination and masks black women's subordinate status in the U.S. labor markets. His narrative makes implausible the notion that discrimination is a significant factor in the operations of labor markets, circa 1970.

SOWELL ON "THE PAST" AND "POLICY"

Before he corrects popular misconceptions about the workings of academic labor markets, Sowell engages his reader with a brief hypothetical on how discrimination might work in the world-as-it-is. *If* a firm has been practicing racial discrimination for years, then a simple government "cease and desist" order will not change the status quo. Such a statute would neither undo prior harms nor prevent further harm, "as long as the firm continues to hire by word-of-mouth referrals to its current employees' friends and relatives. (Many firms hire in just this way, regardless of their racial policies.)."[16] In this passage, Sowell simultaneously defines for readers a commonplace employment practice (whom you know matters) and tells us how discrimination might persist under these conditions. It is worth noting that he chooses not to offer supporting evidence for this assertion. I read this choice as indicative of Sowell's belief that his readers held this view—it is "common knowledge" that needs no further elaboration. Although I hold both beliefs—that social networks matter and that many people believe that they matter—neither appears in the worldview that states, "merit + hard work = job." To the extent that Sowell asks his readers to embrace both stories of success, one that suggests something more than merit adjudicates employment decisions, and the other suggesting that merit is necessary and sufficient, he asks them to partake of contradiction.[17] Ironically, critics of the meritocratic model, including many supporters of affirmative actions, have produced a vast literature that affirms the importance of social networks in the securing of employment.[18]

In a world where "word of mouth" referrals are the norm and employers and workers have actively engaged in discrimination, Sowell concedes that some kind of positive affirmative steps against discrimination might be reasonable; "which is not to say that the particular policies actually followed make sense." Having constructed a scenario in which all-white work forces can be self-perpetuating *in the absence of intentional discrimination*, Sowell then moves on to address the effects of past discrimination on the current racial distribution of abilities. What is remarkable here is his choice to omit any discussion of *intentional discrimination*. Sowell's decision to eschew that discussion constitutes yet another silent story, this time one that sets aside or trivializes U.S. histories that accord significance to historic white racism, racist cultures, and black resistance theoreto.[19]

It is important to recall that Sowell wrote his chapter only a decade after the passage of major national civil rights legislation, a political development preceded by open, and sometimes violent, white resistance. It is implausible that the generations-old white practices of excluding blacks from preferred jobs, schools, and neighborhoods could have vanished in less than a generation. Given the absence of an antiracist cultural revolution that challenged and discredited recurring popular and "scientific" narratives of black laziness, criminality, and stupidity, the notion that intentional discrimination could have vanished in the mid-1970s requires, at the very least, a vigorous defense; it is by no means a self-evident proposition. Yet Sowell's narrative suggests precisely that.

His historical silences notwithstanding, Sowell's omissions serve larger strategic and ideological ends. Strategically, they shift attention away from meaningful consideration of overt racial discrimination as a present-day reality. Discrimination is, at worst, a benign phenomenon, manifested by race-based social networks that are no longer intentionally racist. Ideologically, Sowell's story opens the door to the possibility that, even absent a collective naming and rejection of the cultural practices of white supremacy, we are nonetheless free to imagine ourselves living and working in a nonracist world.

And what exactly are we to do about the tragedy of past racism? Sowell ponders, " . . . what to do when the effects of past discrimination are incorporated in the current capabilities of individuals? Is equal opportunity itself discriminatory under such circumstances?"[20] Here again, Sowell raises an issue that continues to resonate deeply in political and policy debates about equal employment opportunity. Many supporters of antidiscrimination policy do indeed argue that we cannot make sense of skewed black wealth, income, educational, and occupational distributions apart from the historical practices of white racial domination.[21]

Sowell's passing reference demonstrates an awareness of his opposition's concerns. In so doing, he calls to mind literature that questions the justice of procedural equality when individuals and groups are differentially endowed with the attributes necessary for effective competition. However, his analysis remains individualized. Sowell avoids explicit references, both to race, which would tell us whose capabilities are of interest, and to class, which would connect the black class distinction to the economic and social histories of White racism. His only additional comments verify that the legislative advocates for the 1964 Civil Rights Act targeted only intentional discrimination and were content to let racism's "historic disadvantages" persist. The absence of further interrogation leaves the reader hanging, fostering the notion that, however important these questions might be, they, like the possibility of ongoing discrimination, are not worth pursuing.

Sowell closes this discussion with a warning to those grappling with unintentional discrimination and intergenerational inequalities: "As important as the question of whether a legal basis exists for any compensatory or preferential treatment is the question of who should bear the inevitable costs of giving some citizens more than equal treatment."[22] Here he makes a major analytic leap. Discrimination may be problematic, but its remedy, labeled "preferential treatment," is also anathema because of the attendant costs. Thus, Sowell partly answers the question that he posed earlier: we can address the past effects of discrimination, but only with "inevitable costs." Both the possibility of present-day discrimination and its costs vanish; the possible social, economic, or cultural benefits of ending discrimination remain unimagined. The remedy is just as bad, perhaps worse, than the disease itself.

"MINORITIES," "WOMEN," AND DISCRIMINATION IN AMERICA

Sowell's case study is "academic" circa 1969 to 1973. It is here that he plunges fully into a discussion of the wages and employment conditions facing "minorities" (blacks, Asians, and Jews) and "women." He acknowledges "pervasive discrimination" against blacks and other minorities in academia in the dark past, "back a number of years," but he questions the necessity and effect of affirmative action during the years in question. For women, Sowell offers a story familiar to feminist critics of neoclassical labor-markets analysis: "for women, the situation is somewhat more complicated . . . the crucial variable for women's academic careers is marriage."[23]

As noted at the outset, black women's absence from Sowell's analysis functions as silent narrative on black women's work; black women are nonplayers in the work force, their remarkable work histories notwithstanding. In 1970, very few black women (or men) had Ph.D.'s and worked as college or university professors.[24] By choosing Ph.D.- holding academies as his case study, Sowell seemingly steps into the belly of the beast. If affirmative action is not needed in this field, one of the most white-male dominated jobs in the United States, then what is the point?

For "minorities," Sowell's argument is twofold. First, lawmakers imposed their requirements on universities and colleges without a knowledge base; according to Sowell, "virtually nothing" was known about black academic employment conditions prior to 1971, when the federal government required universities and colleges to provide specific employment goals and timetables. Second, he presents data intended to show black/white and male/female wage and employment parity, comprising a knowledge base intended to demonstrate the folly of affirmative-action policies in higher education.

Sowell's assertion that we knew nothing about black academic employment conditions prior to 1971 is remarkable. At the very least, it suggests that the historical realities of state-supported educational segregation are a piece of noninformation. At worst, his blanket statement casts African American scholarship on the matter into the historical waste bin.[25]

Sowell offers Kent Mommsen's 1974 article as the beginning of significant knowledge.[26] He uses Mommsen's survey results to affirm the power of "choice," that is, that black professors were not pining away for jobs in the white schools and were, in effect, "choosing" segregation in labor markets unmarred by overt racism. The notion that many African American professors who worked in historically black colleges and universities would have done so absent racist exclusion is quite plausible. Yet U.S. education history being as it is, many professors did not have a choice. This is precisely the political reality that Sowell's narrative "disappears": his interpretation completely denies the employment barriers enforced by racist segregation and denies historical relevance to the segregationist roots of the historically Black colleges and universities. By proclamation, he erases the experiences of professors who were rebuffed when seeking employment in white institutions and those who never sought such jobs on the basis of a knowledge of whites-only employment policies. Such a conclusion belies forty years of black-led struggles against segregation.[27]

Sowell's construction of a radically truncated knowledge rests on a singular definition of knowledge: absent *statistical* studies, the knowledge set is empty. Historical and legal scholarship matter naught to Sowell and should not matter to his readers. Thus, he constructs affirmative-action programs in higher education as ill-conceived policy "going to full blast for years before anyone knew the dimensions of the problem to be solved."[28] In the world according to Sowell, there was only one legitimate source of information on the employment conditions of black academics circa 1975 to 1976: the previously mentioned Mommsen study.

Sowell's use of Mommsen's employment data is alarming. Citing Mommsen's finding that blacks held less than 1 percent of Ph.D.s but comprised more than 2 percent of academics, he argues that the figures "suggest that the *cause* of underrepresentation is not necessarily employer discrimination."[29] I believe that Sowell is right: This data alone does not convincingly demonstrate employer discrimination. Further evidence would be needed.

Yet Mommsen's data are easily consistent with a world in which the vast majority of African Americans both worked in the black colleges and universities and were excluded from white institutions. Sowell's citing of the combined data on black and white universities makes it impossible to document racial discrimination in hiring at the white schools; the story makes little sense without some consideration of segregation.

My examination of Mommsen's essay revealed that his data do shed light on a world of segregated academics. Mommsen's Table 1 identifies the educational origins, and the first and current positions of a subset of his sample of 785 Ph.D.s. He lists the "top 10" institutions according to their frequency in the sample. Given the historical era, it is not surprising that the top ten undergraduate institutions for his Ph.D.s were all (historically black colleges and universities (HBCUs). Although the top ten Ph.D.- granting institutions for his sample were all traditionally white institutions, four private institutions and six public universities, all in the North, all top ten *employing* institutions, in both the "first position" list and the "present position" list were black schools! His data indicate that very few black Ph.D.s worked in traditionally white institutions. Mommsen described the black Ph.D.'s "returning" to predominately black colleges. Like Sowell, he eschews a consideration of any possible relation between historically documented patterns of employment discrimination in traditionally white colleges and universities and this systematic pattern of "returns."

Sowell also cites Mommsen's salary data as further evidence that affirmative-action policies in the academy are highly suspect. En route to analyzing black/white gaps, he poses the following question: "But in the real world, where prejudice obviously exists, how much concrete difference remains when career characteristics are the same?"[30] Sowell presents a table that shows virtual parity between the average salaries of black academics and those of white academics in 1969 to 1970 when sorted by field (natural science, social sciences, and humanities). What is remarkable here is the absence of information on the careers of the sampled subjects. We have no idea of their rank, seniority, service, or publication records, which are indicators of productivity usually cited by mainstream economists. In the absence of this information, we do not know the extent to which blacks and whites are similarly rewarded for their professional accomplishments.[31]

Because the "black" data include both genders, we cannot use it to independently identify black women's relative standing. We cannot ascertain their wage or employment position vis-à-vis black men, white women, or white men. Furthermore, both the Mommsen data and Sowell's discussion fail to address gender-based discrimination in the determination of access to specific Ph.D. programs. In other words, the salary data obscure male professors' historically documented practice of rejecting black (and nonblack) women candidates in specific fields and disciplines.

Sowell's discussion of "women" in the academy is equally problematic. He informs his readers that *before* the onset of affirmative action, it was the case that "Single academic women with a Ph.D. achieve the rank of full professor *more often* than do other academics with similar years of experience—through married female Ph.D.'s achieve that rank far less frequently."[32] Furthermore, never-married women earn more than their never-married male peers; it is married women who pull down the women's averages. Sowell's explanation of this phenomenon is vintage mainstream economics: married women earn less because compared to married men, they put more time into home and family, more often interrupt their careers for family needs, and subordinate their professional goals to those of their husbands. These factors diminish their on-the-job productivity and thus "explain" (that is, render acceptable and fair) the male/female wage gap.

Sowell's hypotheses have been subjected to much econometric testing through the years. Critics of human-capital explanations of male/female wage and employment inequalities continue to amass case-study, theoretical, and statistical evidence that consistently yields variations on the same theme: that employer and employee-based gender discrimination matters, and, that it impairs women's labor-market outcomes.[33] Here, again, Sowell makes assertions without supplying evidence. He does not tell us what percentage of the total male/female wage gap is statistically explained by marriage or time out of the labor force. We are also given no information about the time required for single women to earn full professor status relative to their male peers. Nor does he engage the oft-cited feminist response to this line of reasoning: if discrimination exists and women are rewarded less than men for the attributes that they bring to the market, it would make sense for some women to eschew careers and invest more of their productive energies in family care. Thus, the results themselves could easily be an indication of women's responses to discrimination.

In the male/female data, Sowell does not sort the sample by discipline. The aggregate data could therefore easily mask substantive pay and employment gaps between single men and women in the same field of scholarship.[34] As was the case in his discussion of blacks and whites, Sowell's effort to demonstrate gender-based employment parity is, at best, highly questionable.

His case rests on the observation that women hold about 10 percent of all Ph.D.s but make up 20 percent of all academics. Yet these numbers are completely consistent with widespread occupational and employment discrimination. Suppose that ten women earned Ph.D.s in education and all secured employment in the same fifty-member faculty, where they were the only women in the faculty. Although the ten education professors constitute 20 percent of the faculty, their presence does not prove the absence of discrimination against women seeking graduate training or employment as for example, historians, literature professors, economists, and physicists.

This basic gender-based narrative also disallows for women's racial ethnic diversity and the presence of racial discrimination in spheres of academic training employment more heavily controlled by women—for example, teacher training and nursing. The aggregate data do not allow us to see how black women fared, compared to white women, in either male or female-dominated specializations. Sowell asserts that marriage is the determining factor for women's wages; race and class differences among married women disappear.

Those wondering how marriage affected the career paths of black women academics in the 1960s are left high and dry. In contrast with their white peers, married black women circa 1970 had higher percentages in labor-force participation than those of their single counterparts. Between 1948 and 1968, this difference was particularly true of both married black women with young children and married black women with sixteen or more years of education.[35] What implications, if any, did this disparity have for the career experiences of married black women professors? Once again, Sowell is long on compelling narratives and theoretical constructs but very short on the evidence needed either to strongly affirm his worldview or to challenge other perspectives.

In this case, the fact that black women are not identified in the data not only obscures their very different labor- market histories but also undermines a cornerstone of Sowell's thesis and his dismissal of women's need for affirmative-action remedies. If college-educated, married black women were less likely to interrupt their careers than were their white counterparts, then they should have fared better than that group. The interiors of black women's work lives suggest a greater, not lesser, need for affirmative action.

"Gone but Not Forgotten": Black Women and Public-Policy Narratives

Sowell's exclusion of black women from his affirmative-action analysis anticipates a generation of conservative debate. The economic realities facing wage and salary-earning black women suggest communities in dire straits. After occupational gains in the late 1960s and early 1970s, black women's economic progress slowed considerably in the 1980s. They still experience unemployment rates twice those of white men and women, experience greater difficulty finding full-time employment, and are much more likely to be concentrated in the economy's lowest-paying jobs. Compared to white women, African American women are also much more likely to be the sole supporters of their families. Because they often share lives and resources with black men, black women were also hurt by the increasing economic marginalization of working-class black men in the 1980s.[36]

Although conservative narratives and texts rarely represent black women as legitimate beneficiaries of affirmative action, they are by no means unrepresented in public dialogue on work and policy: academics and journalists have saturated the public space with narratives of African American women as deficient mothers, welfare dependents, and suspect overachievers. As many scholars have noted, the corporate media and policy scholars continue to recycle representations of black women that signify an impaired humanity.[37]

Today African American AFDC clients must negotiate the paradoxes of a world that questions their 'work ethic" yet frowns on the employed single mother whose work takes her away from her children for many hours of the day.[38] Meanwhile, unmarried black women who achieve some modicum of professional success run the risk of being cast as particularly unworthy beneficiaries of affirmative action, the notorious "two-fer," hired to work in an imaginary world governed by strictly enforced race and gender quotas.

In their 1992 essays on the Clarence Thomas/Anita Hill hearings, Kimberly Crenshaw and Nell Painter addressed the absence of widely shared public narratives that speak to the prevalence of racist and sexist discrimination in black women's lives. In the same book, Lubiano argued that Anita Hill's opponents damaged her credibility by implication: hers was ill-gotten gain. Hill's position as an attorney on the Equal

Employment Opportunity Commission (EEOC) reeked of undeserved affirmative-action politics. She was, in other words, the suspiciously overachieving "black lady," a potential two-fer hired because she satisfied the needs of an unspecified employer (perhaps Clarence Thomas) seeking to fill race and gender employment quotas. [39]

Two-fer stories are at root stories of black incompetence: a two-fer is not deserving of a job and has it only because her employer can check both the "minority" and "women" boxes in the firm's affirmative-action report. Two-fer stories, engendered as a women-specific version of the more generic story of stigmatization, are now widespread among both black and white critics of affirmative action. Here, too, Sowell's writing anticipates a recurring narrative: "But it [affirmative action] has side effects which are negative in the short run and perhaps poisonous in the long run. While doing little or nothing to advance the position of minorities and females, it creates the impression that the hard-won *achievements* of these groups are *conferred* benefits."[40]

Sowell goes on to note that, in regard to blacks, affirmative action is especially problematic: its stigmatizing effects perpetuate racism, averting what would otherwise be its natural death. This, then, is why discrimination's imagined cure is deadly: bad medicine will make a healthy patient sick. Racism is a problem, but, he prophesizes, it is one that will die in the wake of black advances through equal employment opportunity laws and the telos of humanity's progress toward antiracist thinking.

The stigmatization thesis remains very much with us today and is much sustained by a small, but prominent, cadre of black academics.[41] And here we come full circle. Those who hold fast to the notion that affirmative action creates the impression that African American employment gains are "conferred" but not "earned" harbor a vision of post-1965 labor markets as filters of merit and virtue, rewarding the deserving and sanctioning the unwashed. If we look deeper, this vision also presupposes that the passage of antidiscrimination laws vanquished the ideologies and practices of white supremacy.

Yet Sowell himself argued that "cease and desist" orders are not enough! How can Thomas Sowell oppose both discrimination and enforced remedies? The answer is clear: discrimination is not a substantive real-world problem: it is a historical phenomenon, but not one sustainable in competitive labor markets. So what is all the fuss about? If it ain't broke, don't fix it.

NOTES

1. See C. Juhn, K. Murphy, and B. Pierce, "Accounting for the Slowdown in Black-White Wage Convergence" in *Workers and Their Wages*, ed. M. Kosters (Washington, D.C.: The AEI Press, 1991), pp. 107–143; J. O'Neill, "The Role of Human Capital and Earnings Differences between Black and White Men," *Journal of Economic Perspectives*, vol. 44 (1990): 25–45; T. Sowell, *Affirmative Action Reconsidered: Was it Necessary in Academia?* (Washington, D.C.: American Enterprise Institute for Public Policy Research, 1975); T. Sowell, *Markets and Minorities* (Basic Books, 1981); T. Sowell, *Civil Rights: Rhetoric or Reality?* (New York: William Morrow, 1984); and G. Loury, *One by One from the Inside Out: Essays and Reviews on Race and Responsibility in America* (New York: Free Press,1995). The economists who write in support of affirmative action are many in number but they are not the focus of this chapter.
2. In other words, from a neoclassical perspective successful participation in the labor market is an example of how properly functioning competitive markets reward hard

work and deferred gratification, and unsuccessful participation is explained by lack of hard work (thus the market mirrors moral substance). At the same time, labor market outcomes such as women's segregation into certain occupations reflect women's choices to specialize in the care of husband, hearth, and children (thus reflecting pre-existing social norms).

3. T. Sowell, "'Affirmative Action' Reconsidered," *The Public Interest*, 42 (Winter 1976): 47–65

4. Gloria Hull, Patricia Bell Scott, and Barbara Smith, *All the Women Are White, All the Blacks Are Men, But But Some of Us Are Brave: Black Women's Studies* (Feminist Press, 1986).

5. A substantive literature makes the case that black women encounter race- and gender-specific forms of labor market discrimination. Because black women in the United States are a heterogeneous lot, their experiences of discrimination display intragroup variation. See Phyllis Wallace (with Linda Datcher and Julianne Malveaux), *Black Women in the Labor Force* (Cambridge: The MIT Press, 1980); Randy Albelda, "Nice Work If You Can Get It: Segmentation of Black and White Women Workers in the Post World War II Period," *Review of Radical Political Economics*, 17:3 (1985): 72–85; E. Glenn, "Racial Ethnic Women's Labor: The Intersection of Race, Gender and Class Oppression," *Review of Radical Political Economics*, 17:3 (1985): 86–108; R. Terborg-Penn, *Women in Africa and the African Diaspora* (Washington, D.C.: Howard University Press, 1988); R. Williams, "Capital, Competition, and Discrimination: A Reconsideration of Racial Earnings Inequality," *Review of Radical Political Economics*, 19:2 (1987): 1–15; R. Williams, "Beyond 'Bad Luck': The Racial Dimensions of Deindustrialization," Technical Paper (Washington, D.C.: Joint Center for Political Studies, 1990); R. Williams, "Race, Deconstruction, and the Emergent Agenda of Feminist Economic Theory," in *Beyond Economic Man: Feminist Theory and Economics*, ed. Marianne A. Ferber and Julie A. Nelson (Chicago: University of Chicago Press, 1993), pp. 144–153; E. McCrate and L. Leete, "Black-White Wage Differences Among Young Women, 1977–1986, *Industrial Relations*, 33:2 (April 1994): 168–83.

6. Loury published widely in the popular press in the 1980s. His work appeared in *The Public Interest, The New Republic, Commentary,* and *Playboy,* as well as traditionally academic publications. After a short absence, he has returned to the public scene as an editorialist, television commentator, active academic, and author of *One of One from the Inside Out* (New York: Free Press, 1995). Sowell, in contrast, is much more the recluse, all but shunning public appearances and dialogue with his colleagues. He has amassed a vast publication record. Like Loury, he publishes in the popular press (*Forbes, Newsweek, The Wall Street Journal*) and academic journals. Sowell also has written more than a dozen books in the last twenty-one years, most of which address matters of race, discrimination, human capital, culture, and ethnicity.

7. Sowell, "'Affirmative Action' Reconsidered," p. 52.

8. See Bonnie Thornton Dill and Maxine Baca Zinn, "Theorizing Difference from Multiracial Feminism," *Feminist Studies* 22:2 (Summer 1996): 321–31. Zinn and Dill provide an insightful analysis of the historical emergence and distinguishing features of multiracial feminism in the United States. The authors argue that, its complexities and controversies notwithstanding, the multiracial feminisms developed by women of color in the United State "cohere in their treatment of race as a basic social division, a structure of power, a focus of political struggle, and hence a fundamental force in shaping women's and men's lives." (p. 324).

9. See J. Matthaei, *An Economic History of Women in America: Women's Work, the Sexual Division of Labor and the Development of Capitalism* (New York: Schocken Books, Incorporated, 1987); J. Matthaei, "Why Marxist, Feminist and Anti-Racist Econo-

mists Should be Marxist-Feminist-Anti-Racist Economists," *Feminist Economics* 2 (Spring 1996): 1–21; T. Amott, *Caught in the Crisis: Women and the U.S. Economy Today* (New York: Monthly Review Press, 1993); R. Albelda and C. Tilly, "Toward a Broader Vision: Race, Gender and Labor Market Segmentation in the Social Structure of Accumulation Framework," in *Social Structures of Accumulation: The Political Economy of Growth and Crisis*, ed. T. McDonough, M. Reich and D. Kotz (Cambridge: Cambridge University Press, 1994); pp. 212–30; T. Amott and J. Matthaei, *Race, Gender, and Work: A Multicultural Economic History of Women in the United States* (Boston: South End Press, 1996); R. Williams, "Race, Deconstruction, and the Emergent Agenda of Feminist Economic Theory" in *Beyond Economic Man: Feminist Theory and Economics*, ed. M. A. Ferber and J. A. Nelson (Chicago: University of Chicago Press, 1993), pp. 144–53; R. Williams, "Racial Inequality and Racial Conflict: Recent Developments in Radical Theory," in *Labor Economics: Problems in Analyzing Labor Markets*, ed. William Danty, Jr. (Norwell, MA: Kluwer Academic Publishers, 1993), pp. 209–35. R. Williams, "Culturally Bereft, Naturally Unfit: African Americans and the Current Social Policy," *Journal of Intergroup Relations* 23:4 (1996): 3–8.

10. See Amott and Matthaei, *Race, Gender and Work* for a thorough history of women's work in the United States that accords centrality to women's heterogeneity by race, ethnicity, and class. B. T. Dill and M. B. Zinn, "Difference and Domination," in *Women of Color in U.S. Society*, ed. M. B. Zinn and B. T. Dill (Philadephia: Temple University Press, 1994), provides an overview for women of color. Also see B. Dill, "Fictive Kin, Paper Sons, and Compadrazgo: Women of Color and the Struggle for Family Survival," in the same volume (Zinn and Dill, 1994).

11. Wallace, Datcher, and Malveaux, *Black Women in the Labor Force* (1980), Table R4, p. 111. This raw data does not sort women by age, education level, marital status, or occupation.

12. Ibid., pp. 34–36.

13. B. Bergmann, *The Economic Emergence of Women* (New York: Basic Books, 1985), p. 69.

14. Wallace, Datcher, and Malveaux, *Black Women in the Labor Force*, pp. 24–25.

15. See R. Williams, "Beyond 'Bad Luck.'"

16. Sowell, "Affirmative Action' Reconsidered," p. 48.

17. The work of neoclassical theorists to date suggests that evidence of the importance of networks appears as evidence of imperfect competition. That is, employers lack perfect information about possible hires and use networks as a means to reduce risk and secure information economies. See W. Darity, Jr., "Underclass and Overclass: Race, Class and Economic Inequality in the Managerial Age" in *Essays on the Economics of Discrimination*, ed. Emily P. Hoffman (Kalamazoo, MI: W. E. Upjohn Institute, 1991), pp. 67–84, for a discussion of the modeling of information problems in mainstream theory and its problematic application to discrimination.

18. P. Mason, "The Divide-and-Conquer and Employer/Employee Models of Discrimination: Neoclassical Competition as a Familial Defect," *Review of Black Political Economy* 20 (Spring 1992): 73–89; P. Mason, "Race, Competition and Differential Wages," *Cambridge Journal of Economics*, 19:4 (August 1995): 545–568; Williams, "Capital, Competition, and Discrimination; Williams, "Competition, Discrimination and Differential Wage Rates: On the Continued Relevance of Marxian Theory to the Analysis of Earnings and Employment Inequality," in *New Approaches to the Economic and Social Analysis of Discrimination*, ed. R. Cornwall and P. Wunnava 65–92 (New York: Praeger, 1991); pp. 65–92; R. Williams, "Culturally Bereft, Naturally Unfit," pp. 3–8; and W. Darity, Jr., "What's Left of the Economic Theory of Discrimination?," in *The Question of Discrimination: Racial Inequality in the U.S. Labor Market*, ed. W. Darity and Steve Shulman (Wesleyan, CT: Wesleyan University Press,

1989) argue that race-identified white workers acting to exclude blacks from their jobs are part of the past and present discrimination. B. Bergmann, *In Defense of Affirmative Action* (New York: Basic Books, 1996), pp. 78–81.

19. Examples of these histories and cultural analyses abound. See for example, M. F. Berry and J. Blassingame, *Long Memory: The Black Experience in America* (Oxford: Oxford University Press, 1982); J.H. Franklin and A. Moss, Jr., *From Slavery to Freedom: A History of African Americans*, 6th ed. (New York: Knopf, 1988).

20. Sowell, "'Affirmative Action' Reconsidered," p. 52.

21. The literature here is vast and interdisciplinary. See for example, O. Cox, *Caste, Class and Race* (New York: Monthly Review Press, 1990); H. Baron, "The Demand for Black Labor: Historical Notes on the Political Economy of Racism," *Radical America* (March–April 1971),. 1–46; B.T. Dill, "The Dialectics of Black Womanhood," *Signs*, 4(3)(1979); 545–55; M. Reich, *Racial Inequality: A Political-Economic Analysis* (Princeton: Princeton University Press, 1981); M. Marable, *How Capitalism Underdeveloped Black America: Problems in Race, Political Economy and Society* (Boston: South End Press, 1983); E. Glenn, "Racial Ethnic Women's Labor" *Review of Black Political Economics* 19(2) (1985): 86–108; M. Simms and J. Malveaux, *Slipping Through the Cracks: The Status of Black Women* (New Brunswick, NJ: Transactions Books, 1986); W. Darity, Jr., "What's Left of the Economic Theory of Discrimination?" (1989); *Black Wealth, White Wealth: A New Perspective on Racial Inequality*, ed. M. Oliver and T. Shapiro (New York: Routledge, 1995); and R. Brewer, "Theorizing Race, Gender and Class," in *Theorizing Black Feminisms*, ed. S. M. James and A. P. A. Busia (New York: Routledge, 1993).

22. Sowell, "'Affirmative Action' Reconsidered," p. 49.

23. Ibid., pp. 52, 55.

24. In 1970, the U.S. Census classified 11.3 percent of working black women as employed in "professional, technical and kindred occupations. Of these 373,713 women, approximately 173,502 were teachers in elementary and secondary schools. Only 7,735 (0.2 percent of all employed black women) were college and university teachers.

25. Histories of segregated education and the education of African Americans abound. Both J.H. Franklin and A. Moss, Jr., *From Slavery to Freedom: A History of Negro Americans*, 6th edition (New York: Knopf, 1988), Chapters 14 and 20, and the annotated bibliographies, pp. 517–518 and pp. 523–524; and M.F. Berry and J. Blassingame, *Long Memory*, Chapter 8 and pp. 445–47 provide standard overviews and bibliographies.

26. K. G. Mommsen, "Black Ph.D.'s in the Academic Marketplace," *Journal of Higher Education*, 45(4) (April 1974): 253–67.

27. My reference point here is the beginning of the NAACP's legal struggle against educational racial inequality in 1934. See M.F. Berry and J. Blassingame, *Long Memory*, Chapter 8.

28. Sowell, "'Affirmative Action' Reconsidered," p. 42.

29. Ibid., p. 55.

30. Ibid., p. 54.

31. Sowell does assert that, on average, black academics had fewer publications than their white peers. He does not, however, document this assertion.

32. Sowell, "'Affirmative Action' Reconsidered," p. 55.

33. The literature here is vast. For example, P. England, "The Failure of Human Capital Theory to Explain Occupational Sex Segregation," *Journal of Human Resources* (Summer 1982): 358–70; and B. Bergman, *The Economic Emergence of Women* (New York: Basic Books,1986); offer solid feminist critiques of the mainstream perspective.

34. In his closing discussion of the ineffectiveness of affirmative action, Sowell does compare women and men in similar fields, but only to note that the gender-based pay gaps in the social and natural sciences did not change between 1970 and 1973.

35. Wallace, Datcher, and Malveaux, *Black Women in the Labor Force,* Chapter 2 and p. 108.

36. R. Williams, "Beyond Human Capital: Black Women, Work and Wages," Working Paper 183 (Wellesley, MA: Wellesley Center for Research on Women, 1988); and R. Williams, "Race, Deconstruction, and the Emergent Agenda . . ." (1993).

37. See R. Brewer, "Theorizing Race, Gender and Class," in *Theorizing Black Feminisms,* ed. S. M. James and A. P. A Busia (New York: Routledge, 1993) among others.

38. See the *Time* article on the disappearing Black family.

39. See their essays in *Race-ing Justice, En-gendering Power: Essays on Anita Hill, Clarence Thomas, and the Construction of Social Reality,* ed. T. Morrison (New York: Pantheon Books, 1992).

40. Sowell, "'Affirmative Action' Reconsidered,'" 63.

41. See S. Steele, *The Content of Our Character: A New Vision of Race in America* (New York: St. Martin's Press, 1990); S. Carter, *Reflections of an Affirmative Action Baby* (New York: Basic Books, 1991); G. Loury, *One By One from the Inside Out* (New York: Free Press, 1995).

CHAPTER 6

THE NEOCONSERVATIVE
ASSAULT ON BLACK MALES:
ORIGINS, OBJECTIVES, AND OUTCOMES

JAMES B. STEWART

This chapter offers a critique of the treatment of African American males in the analyses and public policy prescriptions advanced by neoconservative writers. As noted by Robert Nisbet, neoconservative conservative thought, as a distinct modality, is a product of the 1960s.[1] Although it includes many of the elements of traditional conservative thought, there are also some key differences. In both traditional and neoconservative thought, males are ascribed the dominant role in all social relationships. Special importance is attached to the family as a primary social unit, and males are seen as the principal mediators between the family and external institutions, particularly political-economic structures. As a consequence, neoconservative portrayals of black males attack the perceived retrogression from this traditional role.

In addition to the primacy role attached to the family, neoconservatives have the traditional conservative aversion to redistributive governmental policies designed to promote equality. Efforts through law and government to counteract differences in outcomes resulting from variations in innate talents and abilities are seen to cripple the liberties of all, "especially the liberties of the strongest and the most brilliant."[2]

Conservatives and neoconservatives believe that intermediate groups, rather than government, have the responsibility to provide direct aid to those in need. The rationale is that, compared to government, these groups are closer to the individual person. By extension, the primary purpose of government is seen as nurturing the strength of intermediate groups. To bypass these groups and provide aid directly is argued to be an invitation to discrimination and inefficiency, as well as a source of group erosion.[3]

Neoconservatives differ from traditional conservatives in their willingness to invoke governmental action to propagate conservative values and regulate the activities of families. To illustrate, Nisbet argues that "tireless crusades to ban abortion categorically, to bring the Department of Justice in on every Baby Doe, to mandate by Constitution the imposition of 'voluntary' prayers in the public schools, and so on" are inconsistent with the views of conservatives that "the surest way of weakening the family. . . . is for the government to assume, and then monopolize, the family's historic functions."[4]

Some of the most aggressive neoconservative interventionist tendencies have targeted African American males and, by extension, African American families. The logic of the attack is that African Americans have proved unable to maintain a pattern of family functioning that warrants the type of family nonintervention policy typically advocated by conservatives. Black males are portrayed as the equivalent of Frankenstein's monsters, created by permissive social policies. These social policies have allegedly produced a rejection of the fundamental values and beliefs required for acceptance as functioning members of society. As a consequence, neoconservatives advocate, not only a reversal of permissive social policies, but, in fact, punitive social policies targeted at black males.

The image of black males projected in neoconservative thought has historical roots in the ideology of racial oppression that has undergirded race relations in the United States. Its historical intellectual roots have been a mirror image of that ideology. These intellectual roots gained new life in the early 1980s in the writings of George Gilder and Charles Murray, and they have regained their former luster in the recent work of Dinesh D'Souza.[5] However, neoconservatives have been able to build their case, in part, on selected analyses by black sociologist E. Franklin Frazier. Although Frazier could hardly be described as a conservative, he laid the groundwork for the contemporary wedding of quasiconservative ideology and a distorted image of black males through his decidedly negative portrayal of black family life and black males.

Given the significance of Frazier's work, it is examined in more detail in the next section, in which a critique of Frazier's model based on an alternative perspective advanced by W. E. B. Du Bois, is offered. A critique of neoconservative analyses of black family life and black males is presented in the third section. Despite critical flaws in the assessments by neoconservatives, their prescriptions have been increasingly integrated into public policy. A discussion of the reasons for the attractiveness of these policies is followed by an examination of the effects of these policies on Black males. The analysis concludes with a projection of the likely prospects for Black males in the next millennium if current policies are continued.

E. Franklin Frazier's Contribution to Neoconservative Perspectives on Black Life

Although Frazier maintained that investigations of African American families must both take a historical approach and apply the method of cultural analysis, which was designed to take "into account all the factors, psychological, social, and economic, which determine the character of any group,"[6] his analyses of black families can be easily incorporated into a contemporary neoconservative tract. Black families, in his view, suffer from a "lack of traditions, knowledge, and ideals which all people acquire by living in the social and physical environment to which they have become adopted."[7]

Assessing how this proposed methodology would relate to the study of black families, Frazier claimed that the black family "would not present the unique characteristics which a family group like the Chinese, where the family is based upon blood, land, law, and religion, and is the 'practical unit of social control in the village,' would present if placed in the American social environment."[8] In accord with his line of reasoning, there is no need for a separate analysis of African American culture because European American culture is the only appropriate frame of reference. "Generally," he suggested, "when two different cultures come into contact, each modifies the other. But in the case of the Negro in America it meant the total destruction of the African social heritage."[9] Frazier argued that African Americans had failed, not only to introduce innovative familial adaptations, but also to conform to European American norms. For Frazier, then, pathology was endemic in African American families rather than an institutionalized feature of the social structures that constrained the opportunities of blacks.

Frazier went so far as to suggest that only within the context of the American milieu does black life have meaning:

> When one views in retrospect the waste of human life, the immorality, delinquency, desertions, and broken homes which have been involved in the development of Negro family life in the United States. . . . The Negro has found within the patterns of the white man's culture a purpose in life and a significance for his strivings which have involved sacrifices for his children, and the curbing of individual desires and impulses indicates he has become assimilated to a new mode of life.[10]

In Frazier's view, the institution of slavery was the source of the deculturation of African Americans. As a consequence, it is no surprise that, when Frazier looked for positive examples of family life during the era of enslavement, he could locate them only among free blacks. He insisted that it was within this group "that family traditions became firmly established before the Civil War."[11] This desirable pattern of family development was contrasted with a matriarchal pattern that Frazier saw as the norm. He argued that "only the bond between the mother and her child continually resisted the disruptive effect of economic interests that were often inimical to family life among slaves. Consequently, under all conditions of slavery, the Negro mother remained the most dependable and important figure in the family."[12]

The modal pattern of development described by Frazier was clearly inconsistent with the ideal of family centrality and stability projected through traditional conservative thought. Only the experiences of the free black family remotely resembled the conservative image of the family. Frazier maintained that the two distinct lines of family development continued to diverge after the Civil War. One line of development extended the tradition of free blacks such that "the authority of the father was firmly established . . . the woman in the role of mother and wife fitted into the pattern of the patriarchal household . . . [and] the father became the chief, if not the sole breadwinner."[13] The other line of family development entailed "women becoming responsible for the maintenance of the family group [after severance of] the loose ties that had held men and women together in a nominal marriage relation during slavery."[14]

Frazier applauded the urbanization of blacks in the early twentieth century, although he recognized the potential for the exacerbation of problems of family organization and functioning. His positive assessment stemmed from his belief that urbanization, combined with a transformation of the linkage of black males to the new economic order, would strengthen patriarchal family structures. Thus, he argued that "the most significant element in the new social structure of Negro life is the Black industrial proletariat. As the Negro has become an industrial worker and received adequate compensation, the father has become the chief breadwinner and assumed a responsible place in his family."[15] Unfortunately, the industrial sector did not generate the magnitude of employment opportunities for black males that Frazier had envisioned, and a new chapter in the continuing history of economic subordination was written.

Frazier's model of underdeveloped patriarchal family life among African Americans was adopted by Daniel Moynihan to describe subsequent developments.[16] Neoconservatives have resurrected Moynihan but have been less forthcoming about the legacy of Frazier. Given the significance of Frazier's work as a foundation for neoconservative projections of black families and black males, it is important to understand the limitations of his analysis. These limitations can be identified by contrasting Frazier's analytical framework with that of a contemporary—W. E. B. Du Bois. Like Frazier, Du Bois understood that black family life had undergone extraordinary stress in the American environs. Du Bois acknowledged that "we have striking evidence of the needs of the Negro American home. The broken families indicated by the abnormal number of widowed and separated, and the late age of marriage, show sexual irregularity and economic pressure."[17] However, Du Bois argued that "these things all go to prove not the disintegration of Negro family life but the distance which integration has gone and has yet to go."[18]

Although Du Bois was very much an integrationist and held many of Frazier's views about the "civilizing" effect of slavery, he did not advocate a total assimilation of values and behaviors. As an example, in discussing sexual mores he argued that

> the Negro attitude in these matters is in many respects healthier and more reasonable. Their sexual passions are strong and frank, but they are, despite example and temptation, only to a limited degree perverted or merely commercial. The Negro mother-love and family instinct is strong, and it regards the family as a means, not an end, and although the end in the present Negro mind is usually personal happiness rather than social order, yet even here radical reformers of divorce courts have something to learn.[19]

The major difference between the views of Du Bois and Frazier is in the assessment of the implications of integration into the industrial order. Du Bois warned that "low wages and a rising economic standard are postponing marriage to an age dangerously late for a folk in the Negro's present moral development" and that "present economic demand draws the [N]egro women to the city and keeps the men in the country, causing a dangerous disproportion of the sexes."[20] Thus, even in the early period of industrialization, in some cities males had less access to employment opportunities created by industrialization and urbanization than black women.

Unlike conservatives and neoconservatives, Du Bois saw the movement of black women into the labor market as a harbinger of future developments rather than an indicator of incomplete assimilation of the norms of white family life: "The Negro woman more than the women of any other group in America is the protagonist in the fight for an economically independent womanhood in modern countries. Her fight has not been willing or for the most part conscious but it has, nevertheless, been curiously effective in its influence on the working world."[21]

Du Bois thus offered a direct challenge to the model of family organization advocated by Frazier and conservatives. Du Bois's model, which rejects traditional patriarchal organization and recognizes the complex manner in which economic forces influence family life, serves as the basis for the critique of contemporary neoconservative analyses of African American families and African American males undertaken in the next section.[22]

NEOCONSERVATIVISM, BLACK FAMILIES, AND BLACK MALES

Denial of Persisting Structural Barriers

The foundation of neoconservative examinations of black life and culture is the frontal assault on the public policies associated with the Great Society and the War on Poverty programs initiated in the 1960s. In the early 1980s, the vanguard in this attack consisted of neoconservatives such as George Gilder and Charles Murray. These neoconservatives argued that previously existing overt discriminatory behavior and social disadvantages had been eradicated by Civil Rights laws. This argument was extended to claim that progress was then threatened by the perpetuation of existing policies because they engender dysfunctional behavior and handicap the potential for further improvement that could be accomplished through the deregulation of market mechanisms. This theme was endorsed by such black conservatives as Walter Williams, who insisted that "when choices are made in the market arena, people, including poor people, have a higher probability of getting some of what they want, even if they are a minority. When choices are made through the political arena, they very well may get *none* of what they want."[23]

Public Assistance, Sex Roles, and Family Functioning

Neoconservatives' unbridled faith in the market mechanism is complemented by an equally intense disdain for public assistance. George Gilder criticized the expansion of public assistance on the grounds that "the benefit levels destroy the father's key role and authority."[24] As described by Gilder, these circumstances violate basic societal organizational norms in which the male is the provider, "the definitive male activity from the primal days of the hunt through the industrial revolution and on into modern life."[25] He argued that "unlike the mother's role, which is largely shaped by biology, the father's breadwinner duties must be defined and affirmed by the culture."[26]

The male's response to the weakening of his role is described by Gilder as a "combination of resignation and rage, escapism and violence, short horizons and promiscuous sexuality." But in this instance, Gilder maintained, "the pattern is often not so much a necessary reflection of economic conditions as an arbitrary imposition of policy—a policy that by depriving poor families of strong fathers both dooms them to poverty and damages the economic prospects of the children."[27]

In the end, however, Gilder's principal concern was not with the micro-level behaviors themselves, but with the idea that

welfare, by far the largest economic influence in the ghetto, exerts a constant, seductive, erosive pressure on the marriages and work habits of the poor, and over the years, in poor communities, it fosters a durable "welfare culture" [that] continuously mutes and misrepresents the necessities of life that prompted previous generations of poor people to escape poverty through the invariable routes of work, family, and faith.[28]

The critical question, however, is, if the primal-urge and sex-roles dictates that Gilder ascribed to African Americans are so ingrained in the long history of humankind, how can twenty-five years of public policy so easily distort and misdirect them? The failure to address this question is highly problematic, because Gilder relied heavily on argumentation implying that changes in sex roles explain trends in earnings and labor-force participation. But he references only contemporary phenomena and abstracts from what is supposed to be primal conditioning.

The solution proposed by Gilder is fascinating because it would entail the reinforcement of existing stereotypes of black males as hyperaggressive. Gilder actually advocated that African American men reduce "the emphasis on credentials and qualifications in the American economy and . . . [increase the] stress on aggressiveness, competitiveness, and the drive to get ahead." His rationale was that "[i]t is the greater aggressiveness of men, biologically determined but statistically incalculable, that accounts for much of their earnings superiority."[29]

Gilder's resort to biological determinism is problematic for several reasons. Historically, such arguments have been associated with claims about the genetic inferiority of blacks. To suggest that black males should diminish efforts to obtain higher levels of schooling in an era in which the black male presence in higher education is declining borders on the ludicrous. Even in the early 1980s, the acquisition of higher education credentials constituted a strategic competitive advantage in the labor market. The consensus of scholars who examine patterns of marriage formation is that comparability in educational attainment and social status increases marriage probabilities.[30] Finally, a declining emphasis on academic achievement serves simply to reinforce the arguments of proponents of the genetic intellectual inferiority of blacks who use differences in educational achievement to buttress their position.

Gilder, in fact, introduced a variant of the genetic inferiority thesis to develop his position. He observed, for example, that

> the biological factor is particularly important in giving black men their small edge over black women. Unlike the larger advantage of white men over white women, the black male superiority, according to statistical analysis, is almost entirely attributable to sexism. Because of the difficulty female-headed families face in disciplining boys, black women are several times more likely to have high IQs than black men and are substantially superior in academic performance. On credentials alone, black men would not be able to compete with either black or white women in employment or to function as preferable providers.[31]

Thus, in Gilder's view, black males are inferior intellectually to all females and to all other racial groups and must compensate by increased aggressiveness if the traditional male role is to be reestablished. For Gilder, the critical question is why "the black males' edge over their women . . . is so inadequate to sustain the male role as provider and the father's place in the home."[32] The policy implications of his views follow directly:

> Even if disguised by regular litigation in favor of black men, the antidiscrimination drive can only reap a harvest of demoralization, work-force withdrawal, and family breakdown, and a decay in the spirit of work, family, and faith on which enduring upward mo-

bility depends. The crucial goal of an antipoverty policy must be to lift the incomes of males providing for families and to release the current poor from the honeyed snares of government jobs and subsidies.[33]

Segregation and Labor-Market Behavior

Other neoconservatives commentators, especially black neoconservatives, have shied away from such overtly biological models that confidently pronounce the inferiority of blacks. As an illustration, Glenn Loury withdrew his membership in the American Enterprise Institute in protest of the publication of Dinesh D'Souza's monograph.[34] Instead, some black conservatives mask their adherence to the neoconservative orthodoxy through an emphasis on voluntary segregation, arguing that racial segregation is not a critical source of persisting inequality. According to this view, public policy initiatives to reduce segregation violate the rights of individuals to associate voluntarily. As an illustration, Williams insisted that "it is efficient for people with similar tastes and the means to pay for public goods to reside together. If communities exhibit a high degree of homogeneity, it is less likely that local budget and expenditure decisions will be highly offensive to any one individual's set of tastes."[35] But Williams ignored the extent to which limited choices for blacks produce involuntary location relative to access to public goods.

The issue of segregation and its effects is closely linked to the question of the labor-market behavior of black males and the general economic condition of peoples of African descent. As noted by Thomas Boston: "To conservatives numerous factors explain this [disadvantage] better than racial discrimination. These include ethnic differences in age, education, geographical location, job experience, occupational distribution, family size, and culture." Unconvinced by neoconservative arguments, Boston asserted that "not only are qualified blacks relegated disproportionately to lower status jobs, but their concentration in such positions is reinforced by occupational mobility barriers."[36] More generally, a variety of studies convincingly documented continuing barriers to employment for black males during the 1980s resulting from their disproportionate residence in central cities.[37]

ILLICIT ECONOMIC ACTIVITY (CRIME)

Conservatives and neoconservatives regard the high level of criminal activity in black communities as an indicator of the breakdown of traditional civic values rather than an outcome of limited labor force opportunities. However, this view is at odds with the findings that have emerged from economists' analyses of criminal activity. As noted by W. Kip Vicusi,

> although minor changes in the economic environment may not dramatically alter the overall youth crime problem, the criminality among those who are not in school or employed is very sensitive to economic incentives. Since members of this group are responsible for most of the youth crime, they comprise a major, economically responsive component of the criminal population.[38]

The larger issue at stake is the model of criminality that underlies both neoconservative and economic theories. Daniel Georges-Abeyie claimed that "the current array of popular criminological and criminal justice theories fail, for the most part, to offer insight into the dynamic of Black criminality, and criminal justice processing."[39] Georges-Abeyie advocated a socialecological model that attributes above-average rates of Black criminality in large part to "the fact that blacks reside in 'natural areas' of crime" that possess the following characteristics:

> (1) deteriorated or deteriorating housing, (2) limited or nonexistent legitimate employment and recreational opportunities, (3) anomic behavior patterns, (4) a local criminal tradition (which started prior to the duration of the current Black ethnic group in residence), (5) abnormally high incidence of transient or psychopathological individuals, (6) a disproportionate number of opportunities (due to mixed land use) to engage in criminal deviance or to develop subcultures that are extra-legal (criminal or quasi criminal), and (7) . . . poverty and limited wealth [are] the norm rather than the exception.[40]

Summary

The preceding discussion of the tenets of neoconservative examinations of the experiences of African Americans reveals a significant disconnection between the ideological stance of conservative pundits and the consensus of findings from detailed social scientific investigations. Nevertheless, the policies directed at African Americans since the early 1980s have been influenced significantly by neoconservative perspectives. This disjunction raises the important question of why neoconservative formulations have been so attractive to policymakers.

THE SOCIAL FUNCTION OF NEOCONSERVATIVE ANALYSES OF BLACK LIFE

Throughout the sojourn of peoples of African descent in the West, intellectual justifications have been an integral dimension of the implementation of policies designed to control potentially disruptive segments of the population. The types of policies common in previous eras are well known and include (1) restriction of political rights, (2) regulation of access to markets and public goods, and (3) regulation of conditions of entry into, and remuneration from, labor markets. Intellectual justifications have been advanced for all these policies in a manner similar to the function of neoconservative thought in the current era. These intellectual arguments disguise the actual direction and results of public policy.

To illustrate, significant improvement in access to higher paying jobs for blacks has generally occurred only when other labor supplies are limited as, for example, during World Wars I and II. In general,

> the overall impact of economic policy on the black experience has been, and continues to be, the exploitation of black labor coupled with parallel exploitation of black consumer purchasing power. The aggregate policy thrust can be seen by examining policies affecting the structure and functioning of labor markets, policies shaping the configuration of the economy and the location of economic activity, and policies affecting the acquisition of skills and general training.[41]

During periods in which labor shortages do not exist, African Americans are perceived as social liabilities rather than social assets and the proverbial question asked by Sidney Willhelm, "Who Needs the Negro?"[42] is again posed. The concept of "institutional decimation" characterizes the processes that reduce the survival rate of African American males. Institutional decimation "leads to the temporary and permanent removal of black males from the civilian population through the operation of labor market mechanisms, the educational system, the health care delivery system, the public assistance complex, the subliminal institutions of crime and vice, the penal correction system, and the military."[43] The suggestion is that the process operates organically rather than as a result of some complex conspiracy. Even in the absence of a formal means of coordinating the mechanisms of exploitation, however, the interests of the dominant group are clearly served in part by "contain[ing] pressures in Black communities in which the potential for violent uprising exists [and] maintain[ing] a balance between the number of Black and white males."[44]

A similar perspective was advanced by Barbara Solomon, who used the "endangered species" metaphor, to indict public policy as the source of "difficulties for black males in social functioning generated by circular and dysfunctional transactions vis-à-vis family, school, and work."[45] In a complementary manner, Jewel Taylor Gibbs argued that black males have been "miseducated by the educational system, mishandled by the criminal justice system, mislabeled by the mental health system, and mistreated by the social welfare system."[46]

Frances Fox Piven and Richard Cloward argued that welfare is used as one component of labor regulation and social control. During periods of labor shortage or limited activism among disadvantaged groups, public assistance is reduced. In contrast, during periods of social upheaval or high unemployment that might lead to unrest, or both, welfare policies are liberalized.[47] William Darity and Samuel Myers declared:

> We agree with Piven and Cloward that the changing demographics of the poverty population had an important influence on the politics of poverty policy. Thus, the coincidental rise in single-parent families with the expansion of welfare was really the reflection of policy responding to demographics rather than demographics instantaneously responding to policy.[48]

These perspectives directly challenge the policy interpretations advanced by neoconservatives to the effect that traditional patterns of discrimination have been eliminated. In fact, the counterinterpretation suggests that, not only has discrimination not been eliminated, there has been no intention of altering patterns of black oppression in any significant manner. The inherent limitations of the policies implemented during the 1960s were cogently described by Charles Killingsworth, who argued:

> Certain broad implications for policy are rather obvious from the conclusion of this analysis. The first is that some of the remedies most often prescribed for Negro unemployment are to yield disappointingly small results. Anti-discrimination laws, higher rates of attendance at today's schools, faster economic growth, the normal push-pull forces in the labor market. . . . none of these seem to hold the promise of substantial impact on the basic source of Negro disadvantage. A second implication is that the mere passage of time without the application of powerful remedial measures will probably increase Negro disadvantage.[49]

Given such an assessment, an actual function of neoconservative attacks on African Americans is to facilitate reductions in public expenditures for social support that are disproportionately received by blacks but actually serve greater numbers of whites. By creating imagery that equates welfare recipiency and criminality with blacks and by demonizing policies such as Affirmative Action, such attacks encourage the public not only to be less likely to resist major cuts in social programs, but also to endorse the increasing introduction of coercive policies.

To illustrate, reductions in welfare outlays implemented in President Ronald Reagan's 1981 budget led to an increase of more than 135,000 in the number of persons living in poverty.[50] Another example is provided by federal funding for elementary, secondary, and vocational programs, which, in fiscal year 1986, was approximately 30 percent lower than in 1981.[51] These reductions dramatically worsened the existing funding inequities between urban and suburban school districts. Black students, in particular, were disproportionately affected because in twenty-six of the fifty states, more than 40 percent of black students were attending segregated schools.[52]

Major changes in the economy in the 1980s created unprecedented uncertainty for many Americans, and blacks served as convenient scapegoats to disguise the true sources of worsening economic prospects. As an example, in 1982 alone, 2.7 million full-time workers were displaced, primarily from manufacturing jobs. The annual number of displaced workers remained above 1.5 million until 1988.[53] The vast majority of these workers were white; and 20 percent of dislocated or displaced workers were 45 years old or older, 60 percent were males, and the percentage with schooling beyond high school grew from about 30 to 40 percent.[54] Blue- and white-collar nonwhite men and women had lower probabilities of reemployment and lower postdisplacement earnings than whites, as well as longer unemployment durations.[55]

It is important to recognize that, even though the service sector now far outstrips manufacturing as an employment base in the American economy, this service sector, too, is vulnerable to international competition. Black and Hispanic men employed in the service sector have in common the experience of being much more likely to be employed in those industries with the largest employment losses.[56] Despite the significant growth in service-sector employment, Blacks and Latinos continue to be underrepresented in white-collar occupations and overrepresented in blue-collar occupations. Blacks tend to be overrepresented among union members and, although black union members earn less than white union members do, the gap is less than is the case for nonunion workers.

Incarceration became an increasingly important public policy as expenditures for education, training, and job creation declined. In fiscal year 1992, federal, state, and local governments spent $94 billion for civil and criminal justice, a 59 percent increase over expenditures in 1987, at a time when public outlays for social support were either stagnant or growing at a slow pace. Federal spending for justice increased 132 percent, twice as fast as the growth rate for state and local spending.[57]

It is important to note that there is a direct connection between increasing incarceration rates and the available supply of workers. Of all inmates in state prisons in 1991, two-thirds of state prison inmates were employed during the month before they were arrested and more than half were employed full time.[58] Moreover, 65 percent of state prison inmates belonged to racial or ethnic minority groups in 1991, compared with 60 percent in 1986.[59] Thus, as traditional employment opportunities eroded, there was a disproportionate increase in the incarceration of racial and ethnic minority group members in the context of strong competition for the remaining employment opportunities. This overrepresentation of black and Latino males in correctional institutions and under other types of criminal justice system control is related directly to the ongoing global transformation whereby manufacturing facilities and other "old economy" activities are relocated to countries with lower-cost production costs. This process also affects white workers, particularly those living in more rural areas. The effect on a significant number of rural white communities is, however, ameliorated to some degree by constructing correctional institutions in these communities, thereby providing alternative employment to that lost by the decline in manufacturing, mining, and agriculture. The high degree of urbanization of Blacks and Latinos precludes the accrual of any direct employment benefits from the large federal and state expenditures on new prison construction.

THE EFFECTS OF NEOCONSERVATIVES POLICIES ON BLACK LIFE

Table 6.1 lists selected indicators of the effects of neoconservative policies on black life in the early 1990s. In particular, significant gaps in employment, unemployment rates, earnings by educational level, poverty rates, and wealth holdings remain.

The patterns in Table 6.1 are confirmed by more recent economic statistics. In February 1999, the civilian unemployment rate had fallen to 4.4 percent. The rates for whites, blacks, and Hispanics were, respectively, 3.8 percent, 8.3 percent, and 6.7 percent. The rate for all teenagers (aged 16–19) was 14.1 percent, whereas that for black teens was 29.2 percent.[60] Although the official unemployment count was 6.1 million, hidden unemployment accounted for an additional 8.2 million workers. In addition, millions more were working full-time year-round, yet earned less than the official poverty level for a family of four. In the latest year for which data are available, 1997, that number was 16.8 million, comprising 18 percent of full-time workers.[61] Roughly one in four women and one in seven men who had full-time jobs the year round earned less than the poverty level for a family of four.

The effects of these patterns on the growth of the number of prisoners follows the patterns discussed previously. At the end of 1996, 5.5 million people were on probation, in jail or prison, or on parole. Lifetime chances of a person going to prison were 16.2 percent for blacks, 9.2 percent for Hispanics, and 2.5 percent for whites. On the basis of current rates of first incarceration, an estimated 28 percent of black males will enter state or federal prison during their lifetime, compared to 16 percent of Hispanic males and 4.4 percent of white males.[62]

Currently, more black males are under the control of the criminal justice system than are enrolled in institutions of higher education. Although the proportion of degrees awarded to males has been declining for all groups, for blacks, the decline (from 42.9 percent in 1977 to 36.0 percent in 1996) is far lower than for any other group, a pattern directly attributable to the high incarceration rate of black males.[63]

BLACK MALES: AN UNCERTAIN FUTURE

The preceding examination of the effects of neoconservative policies on black life and black males suggests that a continuation of these policies will further erode the educational attainment of black males and increase their incarceration rates. The policy interpretation presented earlier as an alternative to the neoconservative pronouncements

Table 6.1 Comparison of Selected Economic Indicators: Blacks and Whites, Selected Years

Economic Indicator	Black (B)	White (W)	Ratio B/W
Employment-to-population ratio (1995)			
Total	.56	.64	.88
Male	.60	.71	.85
Female	.53	.57	.93
Unemployment rates			
1960s average	9.0	4.3	2.09
1970s average	11.1	5.5	2.02
1980s average	14.9	6.3	2.37
1990	11.3	4.7	2.40
1991	12.4	6.0	2.07
1992	14.1	6.5	2.17
1993	12.9	6.0	2.15
1994	11.5	5.3	2.17
1995	10.3	4.7	2.19
Median earnings (1994)			
Not a H.S. graduate	$16,523	$19,808	.834
Males	$19,941	$22,466	.887
Females	$13,949	$14,928	.934
H.S. graduate	$20,023	$24,806	.807
Males	$22,028	$29,321	.751
Females	$17,754	$20,039	.886
B.A. degree or more	$33,899	$41,475	.817
Males	$36,072	$48,591	.742
Females	$31,890	$33,720	.946
Poverty rates (1994)			
All persons	30.6	9.4	3.26
Metropolitan areas	29.8	8.4	3.55
Central cities	34.2	11.0	3.11
Outside	22.3	7.3	3.06
Nonmetro areas	35.4	12.8	2.77
Wealth (1994)			
Pct. with 0 or negative net worth	30	8	3.75
Median net worth	$10,329	$76,519	.135

Source: Employment, unemployment, earnings, poverty rates—J. Jeffries and R. Schaffer, "Changes in Labor Economy and Labor Market State of Black Americans," in The State of Black America 1996, ed. A. Rowe and J. Jeffries (New York: National Urban League, 1996), pp. 12–77; Wealth—E. Hurst, M. Luoh, and F. Stafford, "Wealth Dynamics of American Families, 1984–1994" available on-line at: http://www.umich.edu/~psid.

suggests that there is no momentum for changing current directions. If there were, the policy outlines for accomplishing this change would certainly bear no resemblance to that advocated by neoconservatives. Rather, as Bennett Harrison noted, there is a need "for a change in emphasis away from concentration on the alleged defects of the ghetto poor themselves toward the investigation of defects in the market system which constrain the poor from realizing their potential."[64] Movements toward such an approach, according to Harrison, are likely to be incremental, but short-term changes should be "consistent with the long-range vision of more radical reform involving guaranteed employment, . . . vocational training, . . . and family allowances."[65] More recent proposals to enhance labor market outcomes for African Americans can be found in *African Americans and Post-Industrial Labor Markets*, edited by J. B. Stewart.[66]

Given the limited likelihood that an alternative focus will emerge from public policy circles, it will likely be left to forces within black communities to develop self-help approaches.

Afrocentric perspectives have demonstrated some usefulness in altering the current socialization patterns that lead black males down the path of eventual capture by the criminal justice system. One of the approaches enjoying some success is an adaptation of the tradition of socializing cohorts of males in African societies through structured rites of passage. This approach is now being explored in many communities.

Ultimately, all peoples within the orbit of the American economy have a stake in the empowerment and elevation of African American males. Collectively, perhaps people of conscience can help promote a policy agenda incorporating the vision offered by Gibbs: "[If] black youth are given real opportunities for education, if they are provided with meaningful jobs, if they have adequate income to care for their families, if they have hope for future mobility, then they will act responsibly and will contribute their fair share to the larger community."[67]

Whether the policy mix proposed by Gibbs is sufficient to achieve the desired results is, of course, an open question. The option of maintaining current directions, however, can only have the effect of adding momentum to the current downward spiral, which, if unchecked, will eventually produce a national and global disaster of unprecedented proportions.

NOTES

1. R. Nisbet, *Conservatism: Dream and Reality* (Minneapolis: University of Minnesota Press, 1986).
2. Ibid., p. 47.
3. Ibid., p. 62.
4. Ibid., p. 104.
5. D. D'Souza, *The End of Racism: Principles for a Multiracial Society* (New York: Free Press, 1995).
6. E. F. Frazier, "Is the Negro Family a Unique Sociological Unit?" *Opportunity*, 5 (June 1927): 165–166.
7. E. F. Frazier, "Three Scourges of the Negro Family," *Opportunity*, 4 (1926): 210.
8. Frazier, "Unique Sociological Unit," p. 166.
9. Ibid.
10. E. F. Frazier, *The Negro Family in the United States* (1939; revised and abridged edition, Chicago: University of Chicago Press, 1966), p. 367.
11. Ibid., p. 362.
12. Ibid., p. 32.
13. Ibid., p. 88.
14. Ibid.
15. Ibid., p. 366.
16. D. Moynihan, *The Negro Family: The Case for National Action* (Washington, D.C.: United States Department of Labor, Office of Policy Planning and Research, 1965).

17. W. E. B. Du Bois, *The Negro American Family* (Atlanta: Atlanta University Press, 1908), p. 31. This is the report of a social study made principally by the college class of 1909 and 1910 of Atlanta University, under the patronage of the trustees of the John F. Slater Fund, printed together with *the Proceedings of the Thirteenth Annual Conference for the Study of the Negro Problems*.

18. Ibid., p. 31.

19. Ibid., p. 42.

20. Ibid., p. 36.

21. W. E. B. Du Bois, *The Gift of Black Folk: The Negro in the Making of America* (1924; reprint, New York: Washington Square Press, 1970), p. 142.

22. For a more detailed discussion of Du Bois's and Frazier's analyses of black families, see J. Stewart, "Back to Basics: The Significance of Du Bois' and Frazier's Contributions for Contemporary Research on Black Families," in *Black Families: Interdisciplinary Perspectives*, ed. H. Cheatham and J. Stewart (New Brunswick, NJ: Transaction Consortium, 1990).

23. W. Williams, *The State Against Blacks* (New York: New Press, 1982), p. 2.

24. Ibid., p. 142.

25. G. Gilder, *Wealth and Poverty* (New York: Basic Books, 1981), p. 114.

26. Ibid., p. 115.

27. Ibid.

28. Ibid., p. 122.

29. Ibid., p. 137.

30. For a discussion of this research, see D. Macpherson and J. Stewart, "Racial Differences in Married Female Labor Force Participation Behavior: An Analysis Using Inter-Racial Marriages," *The Review of Black Political Economy*, 21 (1) (1991): 59–68.

31. Gilder, *Wealth and Poverty*, p. 136.

32. Ibid., p. 137.

33. Ibid., p. 152.

34. D'Souza, *The End of Racism*.

35. Williams, *The State against Blacks*, p. 10.

36. T. Boston, *Race, Class and Conservatism* (Winchester, MA: Unwin Hyman, 1988), p. 159.

37. See G. Cain and R. Finnie, "The Black-White Difference in Youth Employment: Evidence for Demand-Side Factors," *Journal of Labor Economics* 8 (1, part 2) (1990): S364-S395; J. Farley, "Disproportionate Black and Hispanic Unemployment in U.S. Metropolitan Areas: The Roles of Racial Inequality, Segregation and Discrimination in Male Joblessness," *American Journal of Economics and Sociology*, 46 (2) (1987): 129–50; M. Hughes and J. Madden, "Residential Segregation and the Economic Status of Black Workers: New Evidence for an Old Debate," *Journal of Urban Economics* 29 (1991): 110–30; K. Ihanfeldt and D. Sjoquist, "The Impact of Job Decentralization on the Economic Welfare of Central City Blacks," *Journal of Urban Economics* 26 (1989): 110–30; and J. Leonard, "The Interaction of Residential Segregation and Employment Discrimination," *Journal of Urban Economics*, 21 (1987): 323–46.

38. W. K. Vicusi, "Market Incentives for Criminal Behavior," in *The Black Youth Employment Crisis*, ed. R. Freeman and H. Holzer (Chicago: University of Chicago Press, 1986), p. 344.

39. D. Georges-Abeyie, "Race, Ethnicity and the Spatial Dynamic: Toward a Realistic Study of Black Crime, Crime Victimization, and Criminal Processing of Blacks," *Social Justice* 16 (4) (1989): 37.

40. D. Georges-Abeyie, "Studying Black Crime: A Realistic Approach," in *Environmental Criminology*, ed. by P. J. Brantingham and P. L. Brantingham (Beverly Hills, CA: Sage, 1981), p. 99.

41. J. B. Stewart, "Economic Policy and Black America," in *Contemporary Public Policy Perspectives and Black Americans: Issues in an Era of Retrenchment Politics*, ed. M. F. Rice and W. Jones (Westport, CT: Greenwood Press, 1984), p. 142.

42. S. Willhelm, *Who Needs the Negro?* (Cambridge, MA: Schenkman, 1970).

43. J. Stewart and J. Scott, "The Institutional Decimation of Black American Males," *Western Journal of Black Studies*, 2 (1978): 90.

44. Ibid., p. 83.

45. B. Solomon, "The Impact of Public Policy on the Status of Young Black Males," in *Young, Black and Male in America: An Endangered Species*, ed. by J. T. Gibbs (Dover, MA: Auburn House, 1988), p. 304.

46. J. T. Gibbs, ed., *Young, Black and Male in America: An Endangered Species* (Dover, MA: Auburn House, 1988), pp. 1–2.

47. F. F. Piven and R. Cloward, *Regulating the Poor: The Function of Public Welfare* (New York: Pantheon, 1971).

48. W. Darity and S. Myers, "Review of Losing Ground: American Social Policy, 1950–1980," in *Slipping Through the Cracks: The Status of Black Women*, ed. by M. Simms and J. Malveaux (New Brunswick, NJ: Transaction Books, 1986), pp. 173–174. See also C. Murray, *Losing Ground: American Social Policy, 1950–1980* (New York: Basic Books, 1984).

49. C. Killingsworth, "Negroes in a Changing Labor Market," in *Employment, Race and Poverty*, ed. by A. Ross and H. I. Hill (New York: Harcourt Brace and World, 1967), pp. 71–72.

50. J. Storey, "Income Security," in *The Reagan Experiment: An Examination of Economic and Social Policies under the Reagan Administration*, ed. by J. Palmer and I. Sawhill (Washington, D.C.: The Urban Institute Press, 1982), pp. 361–92.

51. J. O'Neill and M. Simms, "Education," in *The Reagan Experiment: An Examination of Economic and Social Policies under the Reagan Administration*, ed. by J. Palmer and I. Sawhill (Washington, D.C.: The Urban Institute Press, 1982),pp. 329–59.

52. A. Hacker, *Two Nations: Black and White, Separate, Hostile, Unequal* (New York: Scribner's, 1992).

53. Congressional Budget Office, *Displaced Workers: Trends in the 1980s and Implications for the Future* (Washington, D.C.: Congressional Budget Office, February 1993), p. 5.

54. Ibid., p. 40.

55. L. Kletzer, "Earnings after Job Displacement: Job Tenure, Industry, and Occupation"; and P. Swaim and M. Podgursky, "Displacement and Unemployment," in *Job Displacement: Consequences and Implications for Policy*, ed. by J. Addison (Detroit: Wayne State University Press, 1991), pp. 136–61; pp. 107–35.

56. B. Armah, "The Demographics of Trade-Affected Services and Manufacturing Workers (1987–1990): A Comparative Analysis," *The Review of Black Political Economy* 23 (4)(Spring 1995): 243–68.

57. U.S. Department of Justice, Bureau of Justice Statistics, *Justice Expenditure and Employment Extracts, 1992*, Washington, D.C.: U.S. Government Printing Office, January 1992.

58. U.S. Department of Justice, Bureau of Justice Statistics, *Survey of State Prison Inmates*, 1991, Washington, D.C.: U.S. Government Printing Office, May 1993.

59. Ibid.

60. U.S. Department of Labor, Bureau of Labor Statistics, Bureau of the Census, Economics and Statistics, Washington, D.C.: U.S. Government Printing Office, February 1999.

61. Estimated from U.S. Bureau of the Census, *Money Income in the United States* (Washington, D.C., U.S. Government Printing Office, September 1998), Table 10.

62. U.S. Department of Justice, Bureau of Justice Statistics, *Lifetime Likelihood of Going to State or Federal Prison* Washington, D.C.: (U.S. Government Printing Office, March 1997).

63. T. Mortensen, "Men Behaving Badly: Where Are the Guys?" *Postsecondary Education, Opportunity* 76 (October 1998): 1–8.

64. B. Harrison, "Education and Underemployment in the Urban Ghetto," in *Problems in Political Economy: An Urban Perspective,* ed. by A. Ross and H. Hill (Lexington, MA: D. C. Heath, 1977), pp. 262–63.

65. Ibid., p. 314.

66. J. B. Stewart, ed., *African-Americans and Post-Industrial Labor Markets* (New Brunswick, NJ: Transaction Consortium, 1997).

67. Gibbs, *Young, Black and Male in America,* p. 360.

PART III

RHETORIC, MEDIA,
AND PUBLIC OPINION

CHAPTER 7

THE INDIVIDUAL ETHOS: A DEFINING CHARACTERISTIC OF CONTEMPORARY BLACK CONSERVATISM

SHERRI SMITH

The 1991 nomination and confirmation of Clarence Thomas as associate justice of the U.S. Supreme Court brought national attention to contemporary black conservatives. Both black and white journalists tried to situate Thomas in a tradition of black conservatism. Leaders from Frederick Douglass[1] to Malcolm X[2] to Martin Luther King[3] were labeled as black conservatives by both black and white journalists. These media reports and the confirmation hearings culminated in scholarly articles, essays, books, and book chapters by African Americans attempting to "demystify" black conservatives and their philosophies.[4] As Claudia Butts, White House liaison to blacks for former President George Bush said of the hearings, "Now is the safest time ever [for black conservatives] to come out of the closet."[5]

One of the reasons for the interests in black conservatism is the current "crisis of black leadership."[6] There has been a void of African American leadership in the post-civil rights era. The ousting of Benjamin Chavis as executive director of the National Association for the Advancement of Colored People (NAACP), the perceived co-opting of Jesse Jackson, and the middle-class bias of civil rights organizations have resulted in disillusionment with the traditional establishment.[7] The negative publicity that Khallid Muhummad brought the Nation of Islam has called into question black nationalist leadership. The Republican landslide in the 1994 mid-term elections has dissipated the political potency of the nearly all-Democratic Congressional Black Caucus.[8] It is at this juncture in American history that contemporary black conservatives make their bid for political and intellectual hegemony in the African American community.[9] Black conservatives are making a concerted attack on the civil rights establishment[10] and challenging the legitimacy of the black nationalist movement.[11]

The elimination of the traditional civil rights advocates and black nationalists as legitimate leaders of the African American community clears the way for conservative hegemony in African American leadership. It is necessary for black conservatives to discredit and neutralize these two groups because of the African American community's unwillingness to recognize black conservatives as potential leaders. Although the community recognizes there is a crisis in black leadership, as Henry Louis Gates argues, "The underlying question is who counts as a black leader."[12] Although twenty-five of the Republican nominees for the mid-term elections in Congress were black, only one was elected. Therefore, it would appear as though the problem is not a lack of people who want to lead the African American community. The problem for black conservatives is that the rest of the community does not want to recognize them as leaders. Black conservatives must construct an identity that declares who they are and why they are capable of being leaders.

This chapter explores contemporary black conservative rhetoric in light of black conservatives bid for the hearts and minds of African Americans. The chapter attempts to answer the following set of questions: How does black conservative rhetoric function to call into being a group that can be labeled black conservatives? How do black conservatives define themselves? How do black conservatives define others?

This set of questions examines black conservative rhetoric as it applies to the construction of group identity. Views of rhetoric as constitutive provide the framework for this set of questions. Constitutive rhetoric relates to how individuals or groups identify themselves, and sometimes how they identify others as well. In his discussion of Burke's use of the term "identification" as an alternative to "persuasion," Charland points out that social identifications "are rhetorical, for they are discursive effects that induce human cooperation."[13] He points out why we must understand "how those in Athens come to experience themselves as Athenians"[14] before we can understand why it is easier to praise Athens before a group of Athenians than before another group. It follows that an account of how black conservatives come to experience themselves as such must be given before one can theorize about the persuasive potential of black conservative rhetoric on other African Americans. Stated another way, the identification process (self or internal persuasion) precedes the external persuasion process. Studies have indicated that individuals and groups can identify themselves in relation to others "to locate themselves positively in the symbolic and social hierarchy."[15] An examination of how black conservatives define themselves in relation to other leaders (e.g., civil rights leaders and black nationalists) is necessary for understanding their persuasive potential among members of the African American community.

Many argue that the concept of self-help is what separates black conservatives from other black leaders and organizations, as reflected in such comments as, "The bedrock of black conservatives is self-help."[16] However, self-help has been an essential element of the African American community for centuries. Leaders such as W.E.B. DuBois, Marcus Garvey, and Ida B. Wells spoke frequently about the internal problems confronting the black community and the need for community members to find solutions to these problems. Contemporary intellectual and political leaders such as law professor Derrick Bell, former Black Panther Angela Davis, Nation of Islam leader Louis Farrakhan, feminist author bell hooks, Rainbow Coalition president Jesse Jackson, economist and columnist Julianne Malveaux, and Harvard professor Cornel West speak to the importance of self-help. Certainly one would hesitate to refer to these people as black conservatives. Stated simply, advocating changes in

African American behavior or calling for African Americans to do more for themselves may be a necessary, but certainly not a sufficient condition for labeling one a black conservative. It is my contention that black conservative individualism is the theme that separates black conservatives from other black leaders who also emphasize that African Americans need to help themselves. The meaning and value of individualism is articulated in several interrelated components of black conservative rhetoric. These components serve to declare publicly who black conservatives are and how they come to experience themselves as black conservatives.

BLACK CONSERVATIVES AND INDIVIDUALISM

Dolbeare and Medcalf (1993) point out in their discussion of the basic values that provide the foundation for American ideologies that "[t]he individual serves as the self-evident starting point for thinking about the nature and purposes of social life."[17] The authors are careful to point out that this perspective is uniquely American stating that "[n]ot even the European countries from which the United States was initially settled hold these values [i. e., individualism, property rights, contracts and law, freedom and equality] in the way that Americans do. Europeans start from quite different social histories and political principles."[18] By extension, Africans and those of African descent start with even greater differences in social histories and political principles. These differences can become problematic for those of African descent in America. African American scholar W. E. B. Du Bois (1903) articulated this problem in his discussion of the "double consciousness," or psychic duality, of African Americans:

> It is a peculiar sensation, this double-consciousness, this source of always looking at one's self through the eyes of others, of measuring one's soul by the tape of a world that looks on in amused contempt and pity. One ever feels his twoness—as an American, a Negro; two warring ideals in one dark body, whose dogged strength alone keeps him from being torn asunder.[19]

African Americans embody both the spirit and tradition of African worldviews and the special experience of being born in America. Being an American of African descent can put us in a double bind because often the principles of Americanism and the Western world view are in conflict with the principles of our African heritage. One such conflict is the "two warring ideals" of "individualism" and "collective unity." In his discussion of West African kinship, Nobles describes the African emphasis upon the collective:

> Unlike Western philosophical systems, the African philosophical tradition does not place heavy emphasis on the "individual." Indeed one might say that in a sense it does not allow for individuals. . . . Only through others does one learn his duties and responsibilities toward himself and others. Most initiation rites were designed to instill a sense of corporate responsibility and collective destiny. Thus, when one member of the tribe suffered, the entire tribe suffered; when one member of the tribe rejoiced, all of his kinsmen living, dead, and still unborn rejoiced with him.[20]

This West African philosophical tradition has been firmly rooted in many African Americans. We are oriented to think in terms of the collective good of the many rather than the individual. The long-standing tradition of the African American community is clear in Molefi K. Asante's notion of collective consciousness: "[T]he particular nature of this consciousness expresses our shared commitments, fraternal reactions to assaults on our humanity, collective awareness of our destiny, and respect for our ancestors."[21] This collective consciousness manifests itself in many ways. From the notion of the extended family as opposed to the nuclear family, to the choice of a service career rather than one that will generate great individual wealth, many private decisions of African Americans are based on the individual's desire to help the collective community.

For black conservatives, the notion of the collective is problematic because it supposedly undermines the heterogeneity of the African American community. "Shared commitments" indicate having the same life experiences. "Fraternal reactions to assaults on our humanity" imply a victim status. A "collective awareness of our destiny" suggests that racial unity, interpreted as racial homogeneity, is the key to our survival. In place of what they consider to be a homogeneous racial collective that emphasizes a victim status and collective oppression, black conservatives offer the individual. This call for individualism is a recurring theme of black conservative rhetoric. Although individualism is a difficult concept to define, we can look to the writings of several black conservatives for components of black conservative individualism. In her preface to her study of *The Other Side of Racism*, Anne Wortham argues:

> I am not against Negroes and neither am I for Negroes; and this holds for any other group of people. I am for the individual, and what I have to say is always in defense of a particular kind of individual: the self-created person of authentic self-esteem, integrity, and honesty, whose individuality is endowed with a free spirit and an active commitment to reason as his only tool of knowledge.[22]

From her description of "a particular kind of individual," we can glean several components of individualism that are in contrast to the collective consciousness notion of Asante. First, black conservatives are individuals who transcend race. Second, they are individuals who are honest with themselves and with others. Third, they are individuals who recognize that knowledge comes from individual reasoning rather than from a collective awareness.

These components of black conservative individualism are interdependent. Black conservatives' ability to transcend race and experience themselves as individuals gives them the courage and the honesty to base their knowledge on facts and their own experiences rather than succumbing to a collective awareness. This theme of individualism and its components also accounts for black conservatives dissent from other leaders in the African American community (civil rights leaders and black nationalists) and their advocacy of certain social policies (e.g., deregulation and the dismantling of affirmative action programs).

REAL TRANSCENDENCE

In their admonition of racial transcendence, black conservatives stress that the individual is self-created rather than created by his or her race category. In other words, the individual is deracialized. Wortham defines this deracialization:

Deracialization . . . does not mean the deculturalization that many claim has robbed Negroes of their self-esteem. It means the de-emphasis of race as the measure of a person's self-identity, his ideas, and his behavior. A man of authentic pride has no need of this measure—not because he is ashamed of it, as black-identity advocates would claim, but because it is irrelevant, inappropriate, and insignificant to the maintenance of a free-functioning life. The truly proud man requires maximum freedom of spirit and would find the racial approach (or, indeed any form of collectivism) too confining and its cost in self-denial too great.[23]

Wortham's discussion points to one area of contention that many African Americans have with black conservatives—black conservatives deny, forget, or are ashamed of the fact that they are black. Wortham confronts this accusation head on and argues that she acknowledges her racial identity but recognizes that it is of secondary importance, if not "irrelevant." Many black conservatives echo this theme. In the introduction of his text, *The Content of our Character: A New Vision of Race in America*, Shelby Steele remarks, "In the writing, I have had both to remember and forget that I am black."[24] Near the end of the book, he is able to conclude that "being 'black' in no way spared me the necessity of being myself."[25] According to black conservatives, it is not that they deny that they are indeed black or that they are ashamed of their blackness. It is that they do not define themselves by their blackness. They are able to transcend race. Black conservatives point out that they are individuals or humans who happen to be black. As economist Glenn Loury argues:

The empathetic exchange of survivors tales among brothers, even the collective struggle against the clear wrong of racism, does not provide a tableau sufficiently rich to give meaning and definition to the totality of my life. I am so much more than the one who has been wronged, misunderstood, underestimated, derided, or ignored by whites. I am more than the one who has struggled against this oppression and indifference; more than a descendant of slaves, now claiming freedom. . . .

Who am I then? Foremost, I am a child of God, created in his image, imbued with His spirit, endowed with His gifts, set free by His grace. The most important challenges and opportunities which confront me derive not from my racial condition, but rather from my human condition. I am a husband, a father, a son, a teacher, an intellectual, a Christian, a citizen. In none of these roles is my race irrelevant, but neither can racial identity alone provide much guidance for me in discharging these responsibilities adequately.[26]

In his characterization of himself, Loury indicates that many of the expressions of a racial "collective consciousness" are not sufficient for daily living. If we are to have a collective consciousness, he argues it should revolve around our humanity or Christianity rather than our racial experiences. It is interesting to note that white Americans are not the ones who are blamed for diminishing his humanity. Loury makes the culprit clear. It is "the empathetic exchange of survivors' tales among 'brothers,'" or what Asante describes as our collective consciousness. In other words, it is not racism that is at fault, it is our collective response to racism.

This notion of a punishing black community that resents individuality is a prominent feature of black conservative rhetoric. As Steele remarks, they become the targets of "one of the most damning things one black can say about another black—'so-and-so is not really black, so-and-so is an 'Oreo.'"[27] According to Steele, black conservatives are "marginalized," "humiliated," and "too often disregarded rather than debated."[28] They have become prisoners of a war being waged by other blacks. "When we [successful blacks] first meet, we experience a trapped feeling, as if we had walked into a cage of racial expectations that would rob us of our individuality by reducing us to an exclusively racial dimension."[29]

This "trap" is an interesting rhetorical construction. The implication is that this trap is set by other blacks. Black conservatives are outsiders because they emphasize individuality over collectivism. According to black conservatives, they are outsiders because other blacks force them out, not because of their own choosing or because of a preference to be with whites. They are "trapped" because they have walked into a cage of racial expectations. They are not running away from blackness to whiteness. They have innocently fallen into a trap laid for them. Traps, however, must be set by someone. Usually, when we think of African Americans being "trapped," we think of white Americans as responsible for setting the trap. In this case, however, the trap is laid by members of Steele's own race. The implication is that this trap is laid because "so-and-so is more successful than other blacks and more comfortable as an individual in the mainstream."[30]

Although the "cage" and the "trapped feeling" are not literal, they nevertheless conjure up all the sympathy associated with helpless creatures that are robbed of their lives by evil, stronger creatures (e.g., humans). In this case, black conservatives are robbed of their individuality by fellow African Americans. The cage may not exist physically, but it is a powerful rhetorical image.

HONESTY WITH SELF AND OTHERS

A second component of individualism espoused by Wortham is the preeminence of honesty with oneself and with others. As Wortham says of her work: "This study aims to lift the shroud of social sanctity from racial victimization to reveal the other side of the coin of American racism-the side which few are courageous enough to admit is there and has always been there."[31] Black conservatives pride themselves on their courage and often brutal honesty about (1) the problems confronting the African American community and (2) the opportunities that America presents to the African American community. The assumption is that black conservatives are able to be this honest and courageous because their individualism has allowed them to transcend race. For this reason, the "rules of racial standing" as articulated by Derrick Bell do not apply to them. With regard to objectivity, Bell asserts that society has the following two premises about blacks: (1) No matter their experience or expertise, blacks statements involving race are deemed "special pleading" and thus not entitled to serious consideration and (2) there is a widespread assumption that blacks, unlike whites, cannot be objective on racial issues and will favor their own no matter what.[32]

Because black conservatives have supposedly transcended race, they are able to be brutally honest and not "favor their own no matter what."[33] The following jacket cover quotes found on the back of their respective books allude to this honesty:

- *The New York Times* says of Shelby Steele in reference to his *The Content of Our Character: A New Vision of Race in America*: "Steele has given eloquent voice to painful truths that are almost always left unspoken in the nation's circumscribed public discourse on race."[34]

- *The Los Angeles Times* in its review of *The Content of Our Character* describes Steele as "the perfect voice of reason in a sea of hate."[35]
- Mary Ann Glendon, author of *Rights Talk*, says of Glenn Loury's *One by One from the Inside Out*, "At a time when many doubt the possibility of rational discussion concerning issues involving race, Glenn Loury's forthright and intelligent essays arrive on the wings of cautious hope."[36]
- Former Education Secretary William J. Bennett writes of *One by One from the Inside Out*, "Race is one of the most contentious issues in modern American politics. Which is why we are fortunate to have Glenn Loury's clear and compelling voice as part of that debate."[37]
- In reference to Thomas Sowell's *The Economics and Politics of Race*, the back cover reads: "Emotional controversies concerning the Third World, racism, and population growth are examined in factual terms, with many myths being exploded along the way."[38]
- Sociologist William Julius Wilson says in the *New York Times* that Sowell's *Civil Rights: Rhetoric or Reality?* "is a brutally frank, perceptive and important contribution to the national debate over the means to achieve equality and social justice for minorities and women."[39]
- The U. S. Commission on Civil Rights says of *Civil Rights: Rhetoric or Reality?*, "Sowell has forced civil rights advocates to take a hard look at what has, and has not, been accomplished in the three decades since the struggle for racial equality began."
- Also, the *Reporter-News* of Abilene, Texas says of Sowell's *Compassion Versus Guilt and Other Essays* is "incisive and straightforward, written to show the fallacies of such phenomena as media hype, liberal guilt, affirmative action, judicial activism, and comparable worth."[40]
- Rondo Cameron of Emory University says of Sowell's *Race and Culture: A World View*, "Thomas Sowell's views on race and culture must command the respect of any informed, unbiased person. In *Race and Culture: A World View*, they are stated with the clarity and objectivity that mark all of his writing."[41]

Book jacket covers use the testimony of others to argue that a book is worth reading. These particular jacket cover quotes work together to legitimize black conservatives' discussions of problems in the African American community. Usually, the word *brutal* describes cruel savagery or one with a predatory nature. However, when coupled with the term *frank*, as in being *brutally frank*, distances the term from cruelty. At the most, simply those who are brutally frank do not employ politically correct speech. When associated with frankness and truth, words like *brutal* and *painful*, which are usually characteristics that one is criticized for having, become positive characteristics. Instead of avoiding people with these characteristics, we should seek them out and emulate them. The same legitimizing function is in operation with the activities black conservatives are described as engaging in. Destructive action such as exploding (e.g., "with many myths being exploded along the way") and dominating actions such as forcing (e.g., "Sowell has forced civil rights advocates") become constructive activities that the "informed, unbiased person" should respect. This legitimizing function is important because black conservatives, along with their white counterparts, are generally perceived and portrayed as bullies who pick on the poor, and the black poor especially.[42] Many feel that a ruthless attack on black poor mothers is at the heart of (black and white) conservative discourse.[43] The quotes from these jacket covers, however, serve to recast the works of black conservatives as well-intentioned attempts to help the black poor. According to black conservatives and their supporters, they can help the black poor by first exposing painful truths about the problems that African Americans create for themselves.

Black conservatives argue that we must stop blaming racism for the poverty and social problems of our community. They suggest that other leaders in the African American community do not have the courage to tell their constituents that it is their own lifestyles, their own street culture,[44] and their own lack of "human capital"[45] that perpetuate poverty. In fact, black conservatives argue that other leaders encourage us in these destructive behaviors by denying their hazardous nature. As Harvard sociologist Orlando Patterson says of liberal black intellectuals:

> Black American ethnicity has encouraged the intellectual reinforcement of some of the worst sociological problems of the group and an incapacity to distinguish the things that are worthwhile in black life from those that are just plain rotten. The street culture of petty crime, drug addiction, paternal irresponsibility, whoring, pimping and super-fly inanity, all of which damage and destroy only fellow blacks, instead of being condemned by black ethnic leaders has, until recently, been hailed as the embodiment of black soul.[46]

The implication here is that the inability to transcend race causes black leaders to glorify immoral and destructive behaviors simply because they are performed by black people. Other black leaders are not honest or courageous enough to condemn these lifestyles. Steele takes this lack of courage a bit further and suggests that other leaders are purposely deceitful. They tell the community one thing and their own families another:

> Our leaders must take a risk. They must tell us the truth, tell us of the freedom and opportunity they have discovered in their own lives. They must tell us what they tell their own children when they go home at night: to study hard, pursue their dreams with discipline and effort, to be responsible for themselves, to have concern for others, to cherish their race and at the same time make their own lives as Americans. When our leaders put a spotlight on our victimization and seize upon our suffering to gain us ineffectual concessions, they inadvertently turn themselves into enemies of the truth, not to mention enemies of their own people.[47]

While Steele describes these leaders as "inadvertently" becoming enemies of the truth and of their own people, the inconsistency between what they tell their own children and what they tell the general public seems deliberate and hypocritical. The implication is they want the best for their own children, but not for the rest of us. Black conservatives, on the other hand, are not afraid to reveal the true causes of our problems.

To be consistent with the notion of racial transcendence, black conservatives must support the belief that America is the land of equal opportunity, regardless of race. A very important component of black conservatives individualism is success, specifically material success. This success can only be garnered through individual initiative. Black conservatives are quick to point to their own lives as examples of the opportunity that America affords African Americans.[48] As admirers Conti and Stetson assert, "They [black conservatives] know, from their own experience, that there is no impermeable wall separating the individual who grows up in a ghetto from full participation in larger society."[49] Black conservatives stress that individual initiative can help African Americans overcome insurmountable odds. However, they point out that this individual initiative is often at odds with collective consciousness. As Steele argues,

> I think this identity [a victim-focused, collective racial identity] is a weight on blacks because it is built around our collective insecurity rather than our faith in our human capacity to seize opportunity as individuals. It amounts to a self-protective collectivism that obsesses us with black unity instead of individual initiative. . . . Not only is personal initiative unnecessary for being black, but the successful exercise of initiative working ones way into the middle class, becoming well-off, gaining an important position may in fact jeopardize one's blackness, make one somehow less black. The poor black is the true black; the successful black is more marginally black unless he (or she) frequently announces his solidarity with the race in the way politicians declare their patriotism. This sort of identity never works, never translates into the actual uplift of black people. It confuses racial unity with initiative by relying on unity to do what only individual initiative can do. Uplift can only come when many millions of blacks seize the possibilities inside the sphere of their personal lives and use them to take themselves forward. Collectively, we can resist oppression, but racial development will always be, as Ralph Ellison once put it, the gift of its individuals.[50]

From this passage we can draw out several contrasts between the individualist and the collectivist. Individualism is linked with success. Collectivism is linked with being poor. Those who are individualists seize opportunities and seize the possibilities; those who are collectivists obsesses us with black unity. Individualists anticipate and prepare for opportunity and success. Collectivists fear opportunity and resent success on the part of others. In essence, those who advocate a collective consciousness fear their freedom.

This fear of freedom on the part of other black leaders is mentioned frequently by black conservatives. In an interesting play on words, Wortham describes both civil rights leaders and black nationalists as "nonviolent freedom fighters—fighters *against* freedom."[51] She describes the 1964 Civil Rights Bill as civil rights leaders' leveled "legislative" assault on freedom. She accuses Afrocentrists of waging intellectual and psychocultural assaults on freedom through their emphasis on black culture in education, social sciences, and the arts. The Congressional Black Caucus is accused of waging a political assault on freedom.[52] According to Wortham, it is an irrational fear of freedom that precedes these legislative, intellectual, psycho-cultural, and political assaults on freedom. She speaks of this fear of freedom with the following analogy to slavery:

> In a sense their dilemma is like that of the slaves who chose to remain on the plantation upon being told they were free to go: while they had been granted physical freedom, they did not have the political freedom needed to take advantage of it. While

many contemporary Negroes have been granted political freedom, many do not have the psycho-intellectual freedom necessary to take advantage of it. . . . Much of the cultural, political, and economic activity among Negroes is not an expression of increased freedom, but an expression of the conflict between their lack of internal freedom and the increased external socio-political freedom. Theirs is not an embrace of freedom, but a desperate flight from freedom.[53]

This slave-remaining-on-the-plantation metaphor is prominent in black conservative writings and speeches. Armstrong Williams warns, "We need to break away from the crippling political orthodoxy that has kept us begging for crumbs at the back stoop of the Democratic plantation."[54] After the Republican takeover of Congress, he admonished African Americans to come home to the Grand Old Party of Lincoln: "They [black Americans] can come out of the kitchen of the Democratic party and stop taking crumbs off the table because if they want to come home they can."[55] In a brochure of the black conservative Lincoln Institute for Research and Education, Jay Parker remarks: "As president of The Lincoln Institute, I invite you to help us continue our work of building support for conservative principles in the black community and thereby free more black Americans from the liberal plantation."[56] Black conservatives argue that it is a slave-like mentality that causes us to be blind to our new freedoms.

According to black conservatives, they are the only ones who realize that whites are not an omnipotent power. In an interview with Bill Moyers, Anne Wortham declared,

> My view of whites was not that they were so all-powerful as individual people. They never became a stereotype in my mind. I never gave them the power that it seemed the civil rights message had to impute to them to make its redress. And I felt that I was being asked to somehow diminish myself by attributing to just another human being who was doing terrible things that he was somehow much more powerful and a different kind of human being than me. And I was not going to make whites that important. They aren't that important. They never were that important.[57]

When Moyers stated that whites were important enough to exercise state power over her, she responded: "They were important to have power. But they were not important to define who I am and I thought I was hearing this and of course, later I saw that I was."[58]

According to Steele, it is not only civil rights leaders and conventional integrationists who ask us to "diminish" ourselves while granting white Americans all power.[59] In a response to activist Amiri Baraka's criticism of black neoconservatism, Steele writes:

> The problem with Baraka and his fellow travelers is that they are stuck in a mode of thinking peculiar to the slave. They believe, as the slaves had to believe on pain of death, that the white man is omnipotent, that white racism is intractable and impenetrable. More than a belief, this is the cornerstone of their identity. Thus Baraka's affection for the ideologies of oppression. . . . Baraka suffers from a common and insidious confusion: He equates black success with Uncle Tomism. In his revolutionary vision it is preferable that we all be losers, lining up at the welfare office as we wait for the revolution. Only Uncle Toms succeed by making it off the collective back of their people

and becoming rookie functionaries for the man. But this formula only makes Baraka a
functionary in a black cult of failure. . . . Baraka is black now and only waiting to be
human. While he waits, he consoles himself with the gibberish of various isms, black nationalism one day and Marxism the next. He can't be fully human now. He is waiting
for the negotiations with the white man to work out so that the conditions for his humanity will be conducive.[60]

I quote from Steele at length because this passage contains many explicit and implicit themes about individualism versus collectivism. Those who insist on a racially
collective identity make white people omnipotent. They prefer that we all be losers.
Instead of being revolutionaries, they become functionaries "in a black cult of failure." They console themselves with "gibberish." They must negotiate their humanity
with whites. The implied contrast is that black conservatives view whites as humans,
not as omnipotent or divine. They prefer that we all be winners through individual
initiative. They do not define themselves by "isms," not even conservatism, but
through their humanity. Finally, they refuse to negotiate their humanity with white
people. While it was excusable for the slave, because "the slave had to believe on
pain of death," contemporary "slave" thinking has no justification.

This association of other black leaders with a slave mentality works well rhetori-
cally for black conservatives because traditionally they are the ones who are viewed
as "identifying their fortunes with those of their masters."[61] Contemporary black conservatives are often viewed in the same light as those in the African American community who had participated in the European slave trade, helped squash slave
revolts, and served as allies to the Confederate Army. To recast other black leaders
(e.g., the civil rights message) in this light and simultaneously portray themselves as
the only free thinkers of our community is indeed a rhetorical feat. The implication
is that black conservatives are able to be free thinkers because they have the ability
to transcend race and to be honest with themselves and others about the problems
in our community and the opportunities America offers. All of this would not be possible, they suggest, if they were to succumb to a collective mentality rather than rely
on their individual experiences and reasoning for their base of knowledge.

INDIVIDUAL REASONING RATHER
THAN COLLECTIVE SENTIMENT

A third component of black conservative individualism, as articulated by Wortham,
is that knowledge comes from individual reasoning rather than from a collective
awareness, which she argues involves the suspension of purposeful awareness.[62] Black
conservatives argue that their individualism allows them to depart from flawed collective thinking. They suggest that other potential leaders in the African American
community hold on to outdated beliefs simply because they are commonly accepted
although unsubstantiated. Black conservatives, on the other hand, base their beliefs
on evidence. That evidence can be empirical, historical, anecdotal, or personal.

With regard to empirical evidence, black conservatives articulate the contrast as
competing visions—one based on facts, the other based on propaganda. Economist
Thomas Sowell is perhaps the most outspoken with this theme. His body of work is
considered by many to be a debunking project.[63] For example, in *Civil Rights:
Rhetoric or Reality?*, Sowell attempts to discredit the beliefs that affirmative action

has increased the number of minority professionals, that women are paid less for doing the same work as men, and that education is the key to the advancement of African Americans. He argues that these beliefs are "established through repetition and vehemence, rather than evidence."[64]

In contrast, Sowell presents his work as a challenge to the "received wisdom" of the civil rights vision. Instead of "social science," he employs empirical evidence in the form of historical and statistical analyses to support his claims. He challenges the "illusion of a dominant majority and peculiar minorities" with statistics from the U.S. Census Bureau. He discredits the belief that color prejudice and lack of social acceptance prevent non-white groups from rising out of poverty with histories of the "overseas Chinese" and the wandering Jews.[65] He undermines the view that employment and income disparities are results of racism and sexism by detailing the equalizing effect of the marketplace.[66] He argues that his empirical evidence "corresponds to reality" whereas the civil rights "vision" does not.

Empirical evidence is not the only evidence marshaled in support of black conservative claims. Personal experience is also called on. Armstrong Williams calls on personal experience to justify his relationship with Senator Strom Thurmond and combat the commonly held belief that Thurmond is a racist. In response to a question asked about his association with Strom Thurmond, he makes this reply to his nearly entirely African American audience at Howard University Law School:

> During the time of the voting rights act, when Senator Thurmond held nine votes that would determine the future of that Voting Rights Act and he was going to vote against it, I said to him, look, I'm a young man. I am not as knowledgeable on this subject as a lot of people in this country. Let me bring in Art Fletcher, Sam Cornelius, Clarence Pendleton and tell you why you should vote for that Voting Rights Act. They convinced the Senator. He brought nine votes to the table and he supported the bill. That's how you make a difference, not standing out in the street. You've got to go inside with these people who have the power and who can determine the future of this country and talk to them and tell them why they should change. That's how I choose to do it.[67]

Through his own personal experience with the Senator, Williams is able to portray Thurmond as a reasonable man who listens to and respects the opinion of African Americans. Not only does this personal experience challenge the collective sentiment against Thurmond, it demonstrates how an individual can get things done. Williams's individual initiative resulted in nine votes in favor of the voting rights act. According to Williams it was individual initiative on his part that brought about his association with Thurmond. He describes their first encounter as follows: "I first met him when I was 16 years old and I asked him whether he was a racist. And he said to me, you seem like a bright young man. Why don't you send your resume and come to Washington to intern for me when you graduate from high school and find out for yourself." [68] Although he has taken an unpopular position (supporting Strom Thurmond), Williams argues that the position comes from his personal experience and should be respected. Personal experience, in other words, should take precedence over collective thinking.

Personal experience is not the only thing that black conservatives believe should take precedence over collective thinking. Individual expertise in interpreting historical American documents also takes precedent. This understanding allows Anne

Wortham to take an unpopular position that goes against the collective sentiment of the African American community, and in this case, the larger American community. In her discussion of the rights of the discrimination, she details the case of Lester G. Maddox, a restaurant owner who in 1964 refused to serve black customers despite the public accommodations clause of the Civil Rights Act. Armed with pistol and pick handle, Maddox refused to serve the black customers and ordered them off his property. Wortham writes this of the encounter:

> Most twentieth-century Americans have no sympathy for Maddox's position and every Supreme Court since 1964 would surely rule against his assertion of his right to property. But at that moment Lester Maddox, the dissenter, was championing a fundamental principle of human survival and human liberty and in so doing joined the ranks of the men who signed the Declaration of Independence and the Constitution of the United States. The drama of the moment Maddox, wielding gun and pick handle as the blacks approached him, was unpleasant and ugly, to be sure, and its star, a contemptible fellow to many; but none of these elements have any bearing on the fact that Maddox was justified in his disobedience.[69]

Maddox becomes a champion who is equated with the signers of the Declaration of Independence and the U.S. Constitution. Wortham's individual reasoning, which, she would argue, is grounded in those sacred documents, allows her to support a man whom many found contemptible and a three-judge federal panel in Atlanta and the Supreme Court found to be in violation of the Civil Rights Act of 1964. Going against both public sentiment and legal rulings, Wortham asserted her own individual thinking.

The *Hudson v. McMillian* case brought before the Supreme Court in February 1992 gave Associate Justice Clarence Thomas the same opportunity to assert his own individual thinking over the collective sentiment of the general population and the constitutional interpretation of seven other Justices. Keith Hudson, a black inmate in a Louisiana prison had sued for eight hundred dollars for being beaten by prison guards while he was shackled. In a dissenting opinion Thomas claimed that Hudson had not been subjected to cruel and unusual punishment because he had not suffered a significant injury. Responding to the majority opinion, he wrote:

> Today's expansion of the Cruel and Unusual Punishment Clause beyond all bounds of history and precedent is, I suspect, yet another manifestation of the pervasive view that the federal Constitution must address all ills in our society. Abusive behavior by prison guards is deplorable conduct that properly evokes outrage and contempt. But that does not mean that it is invariably unconstitutional. The Eighth Amendment is not, and should not be turned into, a National Code of Prison Regulation.[70]

The quote outraged civil rights leaders[71] and caused Republicans who had supported Thomas in 1991 to reconsider their position.[72]

I cite the two examples of Wortham and Thomas because they are both cases in which the collective sentiment of African Americans and, for that matter, Americans in general was that African Americans' rights were violated by white persons. If there were any occasion where an individual might go along with the collective sentiment of his or her race, either of these cases would seem to be such an occasion. However, both Wortham and Thomas privilege individual reasoning—in this case, individual interpretation of the Constitution, over collective sentiment. They suggest that the collective sentiment is flawed in some way or another and only they are courageous enough to depart from it. This is important for black conservatives. Not only do they espouse an individualism (racial transcendence, honesty, individual reasoning), but they also enact it. Black conservatives stress their individualism both in their discourse, their attitudes, and their behavior. It is this individualism, they argue that differentiates them from the traditional black leadership. The next section discusses these differences.

POINTS OF CONTRAST

From their own discussions of the importance of individualism we can gather several points of contrast black conservatives use to distinguish themselves from other potential leaders of the African American community, namely, civil rights leaders and black nationalists. These contrasts cluster around the issue of intellectual, cultural, and political freedom. We (black conservatives) seize opportunities whereas they (civil rights advocates and black nationalists) fear opportunities. We prepare for success but they resent it. We prefer for African Americans to be winners; they encourage us to be losers. We value individual experience and knowledge; they gauge their beliefs by collective popular sentiment. We are true to ourselves; they are true to no one. We reject a victim status; those leaders encourage a victim status. We are independent thinkers who recognize the humanity of whites; they are slaves who believe whites and white racism to be omnipotent. Finally, we fight for intellectual, cultural, and political freedom; they fear this freedom and fight against it. These identifications allow black conservatives to align themselves with freedom. Black conservatives perceive themselves as champions of freedom, and civil rights leaders and black nationalists as opponents of freedom.

TENSIONS WITHIN BLACK CONSERVATIVE INDIVIDUALISM

From the previous discussion, we can see that individualism is a major theme of contemporary black conservative rhetoric. This theme is consistent with contemporary neoconservative public discourse. On the other hand, this theme of individualism is somewhat inconsistent with the African American ideal of collective unity. Black conservatives must somehow negotiate the tensions of individualism and collective unity as they vie to direct the future of American blacks. However, black conservatives must also confront and negotiate the tensions that arise with the theme of individualism.

There are several inconsistencies in black conservatives' claims to transcend race and the consequent claims of being penalized for it. Comments from syndicated talk-show host Armstrong Williams highlight some of these inconsistencies:

> The fact is that I cannot ignore the fact that even though I am a syndicated talk show host and ninety percent of my audience right now just happens to be white Americans, I cannot ignore the fact when I look in the mirror every morning that I am still a black man. I would like to say that we can get away from seeing issues such as black issues and white issues. I would say that there's no such thing as black issues and white issues. It's

the issue that affects you the most that becomes your issue. We play too much on race in this country. But I do realize that there are those who are consumed by race and they define everything in black and white.[73]

Williams made these comments during a press conference, entitled "Minorities and the Mid-term Elections" held with the National Press Club. Although black conservatives argue that we should transcend race, they have gained much of their notoriety because of the particular ways in which they talk about race. They are called on mainly to speak as black experts on black issues such as minorities in politics, the effectiveness (or lack thereof) of the Congressional Black Caucus and the civil rights establishment, economics in the African American community, and the dangers of black racial pride and black criminal behavior. Even issues that are not officially labeled black issues are privately understood as black. For example, "public" is often reinterpreted as "black,"and so black conservatives are requested to speak about the evils of public housing and public support (welfare). Issues such as affirmative action and multiculturalism are recast as issues of black versus white. In an interesting turn, black conservatives become the defenders of endangered white males and white male culture. As economist Thomas Sowell says of multiculturalism:

> There is, for example, the whole Alice-in-Wonderland world of multiculturalism, where the very photographs and drawings in textbooks must propagandize the multi-cultural message. There are math textbooks where the pictures of famous mathematicians and scientists would suggest that virtually no white male had ever had anything to do with either of these fields.[74]

Black conservatives, in their efforts to transcend race, do not account for the many instances in which the majority of their audiences "just happen to be white Americans." If their message has transcended race, why are their readers and listeners mainly white? Can it only be attributed to the rest of African Americans' inability to transcend race?

Black conservatives also face problems with the perception that it is not individual reasoning that makes them arrive at conservatism as the key to black advancement, but their association with white conservatives. Black conservatives are often funded by right-wing institutions such as the Heritage Foundation, the Free Congress Foundation, and the National Center for Public Policy Research.[75] These foundations extensively fund black conservatives to challenge the NAACP and other civil rights organizations. On the state and local level, conservative foundations fund black community programs that support a new right agenda.[76] Conservative foundations and conservative leaders often provide both monetary support and political power for black conservatives.

These associations with prominent, well-financed conservative foundations, conservative leaders, and conservative publications (e.g., *Commentary, Forbes, Policy Review,* and *The New Republic*) make the labels "dissenters,"[77] "dissidents,"[78] "radicals"[79] suspect. Dissenters, dissidents, and radicals usually confront a power structure they are outside of. They are challengers of, rather than members of, the status quo. Black conservatives, on the other hand, are seen as part of the status quo. While claiming individualism and the transcendence of race, black conservatives must somehow explain their relationship with powerful white conservative collectives.

Like most African Americans, black conservatives must negotiate the tensions of being Americans of African descent. The National Black Election Study of 1984 revealed that 73 percent of African Americans said that both their American and their black identities were important to them.[80] A related problem that comes with black conservatives' attempts to transcend race is that this racial transcendence is often interpreted as thinking that being black or African American is somehow being second-rate or second-class. Much of black conservative discourse is critical of Afrocentric and nationalist movements that emphasize an "African-centered" identity. Along with Thomas Sowell, Anne Wortham dismisses Black Studies courses and programs as being "soft" and as "arresting [students'] thinking at the level of concrete particulars."[81] Black conservatives do not seem to be as capable of critiquing the problems of America as they are with critiquing the problems of the African American community. As Cornel West asserts, black conservatives rightly argue that a blind race loyalty is unacceptable.[82] However, they replace a blind race loyalty with a blind American loyalty. When experiencing the psychic duality that W. E. B. Du Bois speaks of, the American side tends to win out with black conservatives. If black conservatives hope to gain inroads into the African American community, they must be careful that their discourse does not imply that their black identity is in some way inferior to their American identity.

Implied in black conservatives' claim that African Americans should transcend race and be more honest about the opportunities that America presents us is the rejection of a victim status. Much of black conservative rhetoric castigates civil rights leaders and others in the African American community for clinging to a victim status. Black conservatives argue that we should reject such a status. This rejection of a racial group victim status is one of the central reasons why many black conservatives oppose group affirmative action strategies. Phyllis Berry-Myers of Black America's Political Action Committee argued: "When there are group preferences, I disagree vehemently with that. That just because you're black, you're disadvantaged. You're a woman, you're disadvantaged. You're Hispanic, you're disadvantaged."[83]

While black conservatives argue that the rest of the community should not cling to a group identity of victimage based on one's racial category, a group identity of victimage based on one's political affiliation is prevalent in the written and oral discourse of black conservatives. In what would appear to be an uncharacteristic move, Thomas Sowell devotes the epilogue of his *Civil Rights: Rhetoric or Reality?* to proclaiming the ways in which he and others have been the victim of straw men attacks. He laments:

> The poisonous atmosphere surrounding any attempt to debate issues involving race and ethnicity is demonstrated in many ways. In addition to the usual ad hominem attacks and overheated rhetoric, there has also developed a fundamental disregard for the truth, which has become widespread not only among some journalists, but is even beginning to creep into scholarly publications. Not since the days of Senator Joe McCarthy has the drive to discredit so overridden every other consideration.[84]

He goes on to point out how he has been misquoted, taken out of context, and lied about. He suggests that this is all because he "dares to question publicly the prevailing vision."[85] He and others like him become the victims of what he labels "the new McCarthyism." Like the original McCarthyism, this new strand depends on the cooperation of several groups. In black conservatives' view, the media, white liberals, and African American elites are working together to destroy them. Steele speaks of the "quasi-secrecy"[86] of the courts, universities, corporations, foundations, and the Equal Employment Opportunity Commission. Loury speaks of the "conspiracy of silence"[87] among black American intellectuals and politicians. Clarence Thomas described the second round of his Supreme Court nomination hearings as "a high-tech lynching for uppity blacks who in any way deign to think for themselves, to do for themselves, to have different ideas."[88] While encouraging other African Americans to reject a victim status, black conservatives imply that they are the victims of a vicious conspiracy to discredit and silence them.

SUMMARY

This chapter has examined the constitutive nature of contemporary black conservative rhetoric. It was argued that individualism and its components of racial transcendence, honesty, and individual reasoning best explain how black conservatives come to experience themselves as black conservatives. These components illuminate several points of contrast black conservatives use to distinguish themselves from civil rights leaders and black nationalists.

It seems ironic that members of a group would call themselves into being by saying that what makes them a distinct group is their emphasis on being individuals. With this emphasis on individualism, one could question whether these black conservatives truly think of themselves as a group. From their own writings however, it appears that they do. The black conservatives analyzed in this chapter borrow from, and expand on one another's ideas. Loury's discussion of "social capital" borrows from Sowell's discussion of "human capital." Many of the claims about race consciousness in Steele's *The Content of Our Character* were discussed nearly a decade earlier in Wortham's *The Other Side of Racism*. Both Steele and Loury discuss the tensions of being black and middle class. Steele terms this tension "black middle-class isolation" whereas Loury refers to it as "the guilt of the survivor."

These black conservatives frequently refer to one another, usually as fellow warriors in a battle against liberalism and the media. This is ironic considering that black conservatives chastise other African Americans for focusing on being victimized as a racial group. This tendency to declare themselves as victims also points out some inherent contradictions in their emphasis on individualism. Black conservatives warn against clinging to a victim identity. Yet, they suggest that they are penalized as a group of conservatives. Sowell mentions himself and Wortham as a victims of the new McCarthyism.[89] Loury cites Sowell as a victim of the "intolerance for critical discourse by black American intellectuals at variance with the racial party line."[90] Sowell spoke out in support of Clarence Thomas's nomination to the Supreme Court and criticized those who were opposed to the nomination.[91]

At times, it seems that black conservatives are making a collectivist argument and that what separates them from other black leaders is that theirs is a collective based on something other than race. Their frequent references to one another and to each other's ideas suggest that they think of themselves as a group. In their discussion of differential black identity patterns, Cross and Fhagen-Smith argue that in order to be mentally healthy, a black person must have some sense of connection with some type of reference group.[92] They note that this is true of all people. In the case of many

African Americans, this reference group is fellow African Americans, making race or ethnicity a central feature of their identity. However, as this chapter demonstrates, this is not the case with black conservatives. They argue that their identity transcends race. It is not absolutely clear who their reference group is. Some speculate that it is white America in general and white conservatives in particular. I would argue that my findings indicate that their primary reference group is one another. I believe their shared theme of individualism and its related components provides personal clarification and internal consistency for them. It serves to create individual identities for them. Their public discourse (written and oral) surrounding this theme creates and sustains a group identity for them, indicating how they come to experience themselves as black conservatives. By articulating certain themes to define who they are as a collective and how they are different from civil rights leaders and black nationalists, black conservatives announce that they are vying to direct the future of American blacks—and possibly the country as a whole.

NOTES

1. S. Macedo, "Douglas to Thomas," *The New Republic* September 30, 1991, pp. 23–25; M. Rees, "Black and Right," *The New Republic* September 30, 1991, p. 21.
2. Juan Williams, "Was Malcolm X a Republican?" *Gentlemen's Quarterly*, December, 1992, pp. 190–95.
3. Clint Bolick, "Blacks and Whites on Common Ground," *Wall Street Journal* August 5th, 1992, p. A14.
4. R. Chrisman & Robert L. Allen, *Court of Appeal: The Black Community Speaks Out on the Racial and Sexual Politics of Thomas vs. Hill* (New York: Ballantine, 1992); R. E. Childs, "Afrocentrism vs. Black Conservatism: Searching for Some Common Ground," *Ebony Man*, January. 1993, pp. 58–62; Martin Kilson, "Anatomy of Black Conservatism," *Transition*, 3 (1993): pp. 4–19; Toni Morrison, *Race-ing Justice, En-gendering Power: Essays on Anita Hill, Clarence Thomas, and the Construction of Social Reality.* (NewYork: Pantheon Books, 1992); Cornel West, *Race Matters.* (New York: Vintage Books 1994), pp. 36–43.
5. Fred Barnes, "The Minority Minority," *The New Republic*, September, 30th, 1991, p. 20.
6. West, Race Matters, pp. 36–43.
7. Coleman, "Assault from the Right," *Emerge* February, 1994, pp. 49–52.
8. E. Clift, "The Black Power Outrage," *Newsweek* November 28, 1994, p. 32.
9. J. G. Conti and B. Stetson, *Challenging the Civil Rights Establishment: Profiles of a New Black Vanguard* (Westport, CT: Praeger, 1993), pp. 1–19; Armstrong Williams, "Black Conservatives: We are the Future," *USA Today* November 22nd, 1994, p. 10A.
10. Coleman, "Assault from the Right," pp. 49–52; Conti and Stetson, *Challenging the Civil Rights Establishment*, pp. 1–19.
11. Shelby Steele, *The Content of Our Character: A New Vision of Race in America* (New York: St. Martin's Press, 1990), pp. 21–35; Steel, "A Race Divided," *Emerge* February 1991, 30–31; Anne Wortham, "Afrocentrism Isn't the Answer for Black Students in American Society," *Education Digest* November,1992, pp. 63–66.
12. Henry L. Gates, "The Black Leadership Myth," *The New Yorker* October 24, 1994, p. 8.
13. M. Charland, "Constitutive Rhetoric: The Case of the Pueple Quebecois," *Quarterly Journal of Speech*,73 (1987): 133.
14. Ibid.,134.
15. C. J. Stewart, "The Ego Function of Protest Songs: An Application of Gregg's Theory of Protest Rhetoric," *Communication Studies* 42 (1991): 241.

16. Barnes, "The Minority Minority," p. 22.
17. Kenneth M. Dolbeare and Linda J. Medcalf, *American Ideologies Today: Shaping the New Politics of the 1990s* (New York: McGraw-Hill, 1993), p. 13.
18. Ibid.
19. W.E.B. DuBois, *The Souls of Black Folks* (Chicago: A.C. McClury and Co., 1903), p. 214.
20. Wade A. Nobles, "African Philosophy: Foundations for Black Psychology," *Black Psychology* ed. R. L. Jones, 3rd ed. (Berkeley, CA: Cobb and Henry, 1991), p. 55.
21. Molefi K. Asante, *Afrocentricity,* 5th ed. (Trenton, NJ: Africa World Press, 1992), 26.
22. Anne Wortham, *The Other Side of Racism: A Philosophical Study of Black Race Consciousness* (Columbus, Ohio State University Press, 1981), Preface, xii.
23. Ibid., p. 218.
24. Steele, *The Content of Our Character,* (Preface, p. xi).
25. Ibid., p. 168.
26. Glenn Loury, "Free at Last?" *Commentary,* Oct. 1, 1992, p. 32.
27. Steele, *The Content of Our Character,* p. 171.
28. Ibid., p. 74.
29. Ibid., p. 22.
30. Ibid., p. 171.
31. Wortham, *The Other Side of Racism,* p. 5.
32. Derrick Bell, *Faces at the Bottom of the Well: The Permanence of Racism* (New York: Basic Books, 1992), pp.111–18.
33. Ibid.
34. Ibid.
35. Ibid.
36. Glenn C. Loury, *One by One from the Inside Out: Essays and Reviews on Race and Responsibility in America* (New York: The Free Press, 1995), book jacket cover.
37. Ibid.
38. Thomas Sowell, *The Economics and Politics of Race: An International Perspective* (New York: Quill, 1983), book jacket cover.
39. Thomas Sowell, *Civil Rights: Rhetoric or Reality* (New York: Quill, 1984), book jacket cover.
40. Thomas Sowell, *Civil Rights,* book jacket cover; Thomas Sowell, *Compassion Versus Guilt and Other Essays.* (New York: Basic Books, 1987), book jacket cover.
41. Thomas Sowell, *Race and Culture: A World View.* (New York: Basic Books, 1994), book jacket cover.
42. W. Henderson, "Contract with America," *Emerge* No. 6 (March 1995): 48–51; R. Lacayo, "Down on the Downtrodden," *Time* 144 (December 19, 1994), pp. 30–34.
43. Conti and Stetson, *Challenging the Civil Rights Establishment,* 41; Mark Shields, "So, Senator, Tell Us What You Really Think," *Washington Post* May 6th,1995, p. A15.
44. Orlando Patterson, *Ethnic Chauvinism* (New York: Stein and Day, 1977), pp.155–56.
45. Sowell, *The Economics and Politics of Race,* pp. 234–37.
46. Patterson, *Ethnic Chauvinism,* pp. 155–56.
47. Steele, *The Content of Our Character,* pp. 170–71.
48. Black Entertainment Television, "Assault on Affirmative Action," March 16, 1995; Sowell, *Civil Rights,* pp.112–14; Steel, *The Content of Our Character,* pp. 168–69; Clarence Thomas, "No Room at the Inn," *Policy Review* 58 (1991): 72–78.
49. Conti and Stetson, *Challenging the Civil Rights Establishment,* 41.
50. Steele, *The Content of Our Character,* pp. 170–71.
51. Wortham, *The Other Side of Racism,* 134.
52. Ibid.
53. Ibid., p. 127.

54. Armstrong Williams, "Black Conservatives: We are the Future," *USA Today* November 11, 1994, p. 10A.

55. Ibid.

56. J. A. Parker, *Freeing Black Americans from the Liberal Plantation* (Pamphlet, Washington, D.C.:The Lincoln Institute for Research and Education, 1994).

57. Bill Moyers, "Interview with Anne Wortham," *A World of Ideas* produced by Bill Moyers, Public Affairs Television, Chicago and New York, 1988.

58. Moyers, Wortham interview.

59. Shelby Steele, "A Race Divided," p. 31.

60. Ibid.

61. V. E. McClean, "Historical Examples of Black Conservatism," *Western Journal of Black Studies* 8 (1984): 150.

62. Wortham, *The Other Side of Racism*, p. 12.

63. P. Brimelow, "A Man Alone," *Forbes* August 24, 1987, pp. 40–46; Conti and Stetson Challenging the Civil Rights Establishment, pp. 85–122.; W. A. Henry, "Sowell on the Firing Line," *Time* August 24, 1981, p. 25; J. Merwin, "The Rights Attitude," *Forbes* September 14, 1981, pp. 98–104.

64. Sowell, *Civil Rights*, p. 50.

65. Sowell, *Race and Culture*, (New York: Basic Books, 1994), p. 36.

66. Sowell, *Civil Rights*, p. 50.

67. Black Entertainment Television, *"Assault on Affirmative Action:" William's response* March 16, 1995

68. B. J. Woerner, "Thomas Emerges as Strong Voice," *Washington Times* June 19, 1995; p. A6.

69. Wortham, *The Other Side,* pp. 304–5.

70. F. J. Murray, "Thomas Emerges as Strong Voice," *Washington Times* June 19, 1995, p. A6.

71. P. Jordan, "Clarence T and Camp J.," *Commonwealth* (March 27, 1992): 5–6, 119; "Thomas Disagrees with Court Ruling Curbing the Beating of Prisoners," *Jet* 81 (March 16, 1992): 5.

72. F. J. Murray, "Hatch Applauds Justice Thomas' Court Record," *Washington Times* June 19, 1995, p. A6.

73. Armstrong Williams, "Minorities and the Midterm Elections," *National Press Club Conference Club,* C-Span, November 26, 1994.

74. Sowell, "Indoctrinating the Children," *Forbes* February 1, 1993, p. 65.

75. Coleman, "Assault from the Right," pp. 49–52; Kilson, "Anatomy of Black Conservative," pp. 4–19.

76. S. G. Greene and J. Moore, "Conservative Foundation on the Move," *The Chronicle of Philanthropy* February 2, 1995, pp. 1, 10, 13, 16.

77. Steven L. Carter, *Reflections of an Affirmative Action Baby* (New York: Basic Books, 1991), prefaces, pp. x-xiii.

78. Conti and Stetson, *Challenging the Civil Rights Establishment,* pp.1–21; Clarence Thomas, "No Room at the Inn," *Policy Review* 58 (1991): 72–78.

79. Walter Williams, "Speech for Meeting of Young Americans For Freedom," at Pennsylvania State University, University Park, Pennsylvania, March 24, 1994.

80. Katherine Tate, "Black Politics as a Collective Struggle: The Impact of Race and Class in 1984," *DAI* 50 (1989); AAC 8920624 (University of Michigan).

81. Wortham, "Afrocentrism Isn't the Answer for Black Students in American Society," p. 65.

82. West, *Race Matters*, pp. 49–59.

83. Black Entertainment Television *"Assault On Affirmative Action," Williams' Response* March 16, 1995.

84. Sowell, *Civil Rights* p. 123.
85. Ibid., p.127.
86. Shelby Steele, "Malcolm Little," *The New Republic*, December 21, 1992, pp. 27–31.
87. Loury, *One by One from the Inside Out*, p.190.
88. Chrisman and Allen, *Court of Appeal*, p. 22.
89. Sowell, *Civil Rights*, p. 127.
90. Loury, *One by One from the Inside Out*, p. 191.
91. Sowell, "Quotas or No, Thomas Is Best Choice," *Detroit News*, July 8, 1991, p. A6; Sowell, "Thomas Threatens the Black Elite's Self-Help Program," *Wall Street Journal* 27 August 27, 1991, p. A18.
92. W. E. Cross and P. Fhagen-Smith, "Nigrescence and Ego-identity Development: Accounting for Differential Black Identity Patterns," *Counseling Across America*, eds. P. Pedersen, J. Drugun, W. Lonner, and J. Trimble (Thousand Oaks, CA: Sage, 1996), pp. 108–23.

CHAPTER 8

REMAKING AFRICAN AMERICAN PUBLIC OPINION: THE ROLE AND FUNCTION OF THE AFRICAN AMERICAN CONSERVATIVES

HANES WALTON, JR.

Pollster Louis Harris wrote a book, amid the two massive Eisenhower election victories, entitled *Is there a Republican Majority?*[1] Harris's answer was that this was not the case. Political Scientist V. O. Key, Jr., in his now-classic work *The Responsible Electorate,* raised the same question and revealed that the Eisenhower victories were no more than an aberration. He gave chapter 5 the title "The Republican Interlude." In fact, he wrote, "Eisenhower's victory seems to have been at bottom a victory that rested on a transient majority which could exist no longer than the issues around which it was built."[2] Thus, in the very next chapter, "Democratic Return to Power," he described how the Republican interlude coalition fell apart.

Subsequent to this political forecast was the work of analyst and journalist Samuel Lubell. He described the Eisenhower victories as the "revolt of the moderates," led in part by General Eisenhower's popularity and charisma. It was, as Lubell saw it, a personal, instead of a partisan, victory.[3] The Republican presidential hold on the White House had come to an end. It would be nearly a decade before they recaptured the White House. And even that was short-lived. Democrat James Earl Carter won the presidency in 1976. Thus, the Republican losses caused the party elites and officeholders to engage in a major strategic effort to build a substantial electoral majority. They would begin with the Reagan presidential victory in 1980. And to ensure the building of this majority, the party would deliberately enlist the support of African American conservatives. Of this group's role, John Saloma writes that "the Conservatives and the Republican Party, as part of their effort to form a new political majority, have solicited the support of racial and ethnic minority groups. Their largest and to date most successful achievement has been the backing of a distinctly conservative black political movement."[4]

Therefore, the purpose of this chapter is to describe and explain how the African American conservatives were deployed as a political pressure group to aid or assist the emerging Republican party majority.

DATA AND METHODOLOGY

To explore the role and functions of a partisan created, motivated, and substantially pressured groups such as the African American conservatives requires the creation and construction of a different data set and, to say the least, a host of methodologies so that the data set will reveal systematic patterns and trends. Out of these systematic patterns and trends, a set of testable propositions can be developed.

First, the data set must include systematic information on how the reconstituted Republican Party sought to attract and attach the African American community to its effort to create and sustain a new electoral majority. Then, information needs to be gathered on elements of the Republican coalition that worked to make the party's new strategy for the African American community effective and successful. Hence data on the Republican Party strategy and machinery is crucial.

Once data on the making and mapping of a plan to create this African American pressure group is assembled, data must be gathered on the political recruitment and political utilization of this group. African Americans had to be attracted to this new partisan banner and thrust, and they had to have both material and ideological incentives to carry out these partisan concerns. Mere data on who was recruited are not nearly as important as how they were recruited and when they were introduced to the governing process.

Finally, with the African American pressure group activated, data must then be gathered on their techniques and tactics for shaping African American public opinion. How did the African American conservatives try to reorient and remold African American political theory and ideology? What tactics did this surrogate pressure group and its network of partisan supporters attempt to roll back or bring in, congruent with the Republican thrust?

However, techniques and tactics are not enough in this phase of the data gathering; one must also try to attain data on the very nature of the group's success. Was there a conversion and shift in public opinion in the African American community? Were African Americans moved on the public-opinion spectrum?

As conceptualized, to analyze and interpret how the Republican Party's African American conservative pressure group sought to remake and shift public opinion in the African American community overall, it is essential to collect data in a threefold fashion. The complete data set will consist of (1) data on the Republican Party's African American strategy, (2) the party's mobilization and creation of this pressure group, and (3) the African American conservatives' tactics and success in influencing the public opinion in their community.

There is one other factor: the political context variable. Data gathered only on the Republican Party's strategy through their African American conservatives to shift public opinion in the African American community takes such information out of the political and social context in which it operates and functions. Hence, it is necessary to set the political and electoral context so that one can understand the political motives and purposes behind the Republican Party's most recent strategy. Hardball politics against African Americans in this political system and process rides not on theory but on practice. Political failures in the past lead inevitably to new ones. The African American conservative pressure groups grew out of the failed strategy of the Barry Goldwater presidential campaign of 1964.

With this diverse data set, the methodology will be multilevel. First, there will be a content analysis of the materials on the Republican Party's strategy. Second, there will be a content analysis on the Republican Party's mobilization and recruitment materials, particular the Fairmont Conference papers. Third, observational studies of mass media outlets and publications will be sources of insight into the techniques and tactics employed by African American conservatives to influence public opinion in the African American community. This observational procedure will be used with content analysis of various secondary courses on the thrust and input of the African American conservatives.

Then, scholarly materials on conservatism in the African American community will provide an opportunity for a secondary analysis of this primary information to shape it into some type of pattern and trend about the nature and scope of the pressure group success and failures.

Finally, an unvariate statistical analysis will be made of African American electoral data in presidential and congressional elections to provide a view over time of the electoral and political variables in the African American community. Such an analysis will be a source of insight into the patterned nature of electoral support for the Republican Party in the community.

Collectively, these different methodological techniques will provide an empirical rendering of the data analysis and interpretation and permit a set of testable propositions to be empirically derived. It will be a first-of-a-kind analysis of the procedures seeking to influence African American public opinion in a counterrevolution.

THE EVOLUTION OF THE REPUBLICAN PARTY'S AFRICAN AMERICAN STRATEGY

In the 1928 and 1932 presidential elections, Republican candidate Herbert Hoover began mapping out a southern strategy. And embedded in this southern strategy was an African American strategy.[5] The one required the other, which was essential because, ever since the Civil War and Reconstruction, the Republican Party had tried to win the South. At first, it appealed essentially to the newly enfranchised African American voters, but after the Compromise of 1877 and the era of disenfranchisement, the African American voter became a minor force in the region. There the resurrection and rebirth of the party had to have another political base—the white electorate. Therein resided the problem: how to appeal to the white electorate and the African American electorate simultaneously. Hoover's strategy sought to solve the dilemma by appealing to the southern white electorate and disregarding the African American one with promises for the latter group made in private and behind closed doors. Given the Democratic candidate Al Smith's Catholic religion, the strategy partially succeeded.

In 1948, Republican candidate Thomas Dewey broke with this southern and African American strategy. He reached out in public for the African American vote and endorsed the older Republican stance on equality for all races. His efforts met with no success because of the Democratic Party's stronger efforts. Enter General Dwight Eisenhower in 1952 and 1956. His two campaigns redeployed the Hoover strategy and quietly added components of the Dewey strategy. It was a mixed approach and, like the Hoover strategy, it met with partial success in both the South and the African American community of the North and South. But in the 1960 reelection campaign, as they had done in 1948, the Democrats outdid the Republicans in their outreach to the African American community. During that campaign, on October 19, 1960, Martin Luther King, Jr.,"was arrested at a lunch counter sit-in" in Atlanta. The students were released, but a local white judge held King on the grounds that he had "violated the probation terms of an earlier minor traffic violation." The judge eventually sentenced King "to four months of hard labor for driving with an expired license," and King was "abruptly transferred from the DeKalb County jail to a rural state prison in Reidsville."[6] The jailing became a major campaign problem. Senator John F. Kennedy called Dr. King's wife, Coretta, and Robert F. Kennedy called the sentencing judge. These calls were made at the request of African American Democratic operative, Louis Martin.[7]

As for the Republicans, "Eisenhower drafted a statement announcing that his attorney general would take proper steps to join with Dr. King in an appropriate application for his release. But the statement was never released, and the president took no action." As for presidential candidate Richard M. Nixon, he "complained that Kennedy's civil rights gestures were just grandstanding and that if he himself had called the judge, he might have won."[8] Thus, in this election, vice president Nixon had drifted back toward Hoover's southern strategy and its implicit African American one. The shift had started.

The next innovation in the southern and African American strategies came in the very next presidential election. The Republican candidate, observing what Alabama Governor George Wallace had accomplished in the Democratic primaries of that year, fully and completely embraced Hoover's lily-white southern strategy. His opposition to, and vote against, the 1964 Civil Rights Bill won him the electoral votes of five states in the Deep South. In this campaign, Goldwater had separated the southern and African American strategies from each other.

After having separated the two strategies and blatantly refusing to appeal to the African American community, Goldwater moved forthrightly to neutralize the African American vote. His operative in the 1964 campaign ran Martin Luther King, Jr., for president. Of that incident, the Democratic operative Louis Martin wrote: "The most troubling event of the campaign concerned a black Republican ploy to use Martin Luther King's name to syphon off votes that would otherwise go to Johnson."[9] On the same matter, an African American political scientist (the present author) says:

> In the 1964 national election, the Republican party strategists and some of its black Republican leaders designed a "King for President" strategy. The plan was developed in the belief that the Republicans would not get any of the black vote that year because of Republican presidential hopeful Barry Goldwater's stand on civil rights. Therefore, it was decided that if the black bloc vote for the Democrats could be split, a Goldwater victory was possible.[10]

Thus, with Goldwater's candidacy had come the forthright appeal to southern Whites and a tactic to neutralize or "fake out" the African American electorate. Al-

though Goldwater lost, the Nixon elections of 1968 and 1972 enabled Nixon to re-
fashion the Republican Party's southern strategy on the basis of what he had seen in
the George Wallace–for president campaigns in 1964 and 1968.[11] According to
Nixon, Goldwater had deliberately appealed to what he called the foaming-at-the-
mouth racists in the South. Here is how Wallace's biographer describes Nixon's reflections on the matter:

> By 1964, however, the civil rights movement had galvanized angry whites within the re-
> gion, nowhere more intensely than in the Deep South. Goldwater had been drawn to
> that constituency like a moth to a flame [and]. Goldwater's decision to identify with . . .
> the "foam-at-the-mouth segregationists" weakened Republicans' appeal to moderates.[12]

Such an appeal, as Nixon saw it, was both too limited and too restrictive. Hence,
Nixon's southern strategy was designed to win the entire southern and the African
American community. The South, Nixon offered policy reversals of civil rights reforms, and to African Americans, he offered economic policies known as "Black Capitalism."[13] It was a new mixture with something for both groups. African Americans
were offered a substitute. For the loss of their civil rights, they would be economically
compensated (at least a few of them). Nixon's strategy succeeded with the South. It
failed with the African American community, as expected, if not planned.

President Gerald Ford's 1976 campaign reverted back to the Goldwater strategy.
The effort to neutralize the African American vote began "on the day before the November 3 election, [when] someone in the organization sent telegrams to 400 black
ministers around the nation, trying to capitalize on an incident in Plains, Georgia, at
the Baptist Church to which Governor Carter belonged."[14] At the Plains Baptist
Church, the "deacons canceled services when several blacks . . . tried to integrate the
church. The telegram suggested that Governor Carter 'could not manage the affairs
of his own church' and that this incident showed up some of the inconsistencies in
Governor Carter's beliefs on civil rights and religion."[15] Like Goldwater's neutraliza-
tion plan, this one failed.

Between 1977 and 1980, the Republican Party, under its new chairman William
Brock, decided to build a "new majority" and hired an African American public relations firm to develop an overall outreach strategy for the African American community.[16] However, the Republican National Committee's in-house "public relations"
plan was scrapped when the conservative Ronald Reagan captured the party's nomination and won the election over incumbent president Carter. In fact, long before
his capture of the Republican Party's presidential nomination, Reagan had been developing a southern strategy of his own.[17] And he had personally nominated Goldwater at the 1964 Convention as well as campaigned for him throughout the South
in that election. Hence, in 1980, presidential candidate Reagan's southern strategy
was a forthright appeal to the South, and it was launched in Philadelphia, Mississippi,
the home of the slain civil rights students, with discussions of states' rights and governmental intrusion. However, instead of an appeal to the African American community, Reagan went after a specific and selected cache of African American
philosophical conservatives; that is, he pursued the black conservatives. And this
group would "go after" the African community but in a unique and different manner.
They would attack the African American civil rights leaders and simultaneously tell
the African American masses that they held the wrong public opinions, that their

public opinion was too liberal. And then they would tell that community that their salvation rested on individual instead of governmental initiatives. Such a pressure would function to support the Republican Party's southern strategy. Southern Whites could hear from those whom they opposed that they were loved.

This was old stuff. Booker T. Washington did it at the turn of the century, so did Joseph Holly in the 1940s. The modern African American spokespersons justified white denial and oppression, North and South, of African American civil rights and liberties. African Americans became responsible for their own lack of civil rights. Additionally, with these spokespersons, not only did the Republican Party not have to offer African Americans any policies or programs, but they could rescind those granted by the Democratic Party. And, finally, this approach would further weaken the African American community by setting off an intense set of factional rivalries. African Americans could not present a united or common front. Here was the perfect pressure group. Here was a bold, an innovative Republican Party African American strategy. It was launched with the Fairmont Conference, less than one month after Ronald Reagan's 1980 election, at the Fairmont Hotel in San Francisco.

THE POLITICAL CONTEXT OF THE REPUBLICAN PARTY'S AFRICAN AMERICAN STRATEGY

It is accepted common knowledge and a significant part of academic conventional wisdom that the African American electorate's coalition with the Republican Party collapsed sometime during the New Deal era. On this matter, it was noted in *The American Voter,* by Campbell, Converse, Miller and Stokes, that "prior to the 1930's . . . the prevailing political preference among Negroes was Republican. . . . During the 1930's . . . the conversion of Negroes to the Democratic party was very substantial."[18]

A study of this coalition in Boston found that "it was not mobilization, but a large scale conversion of former Republicans, that fueled the development of a Democratic majority in the black community in Boston."[19] Beyond the scholarly studies, a leading journalistic study reports that by 1936 "in major cities, two out of every three Negro voters were for Roosevelt."[20]

Whatever the scholars and the journalists found, the Republican National Committee became so concerned that, in 1939, it asked African American political scientist Ralph Bunche to undertake a study of why African Americans were no longer voting for the Republican Party.[21] They wanted to know what caused the rupture. In that report, Bunche wrote:

> To attract the Negro Vote the Republican party will need to offer more than the Democratic Party and will be asked to give concrete evidence in its program of a determination to fully integrate the Negro in American life . . . and . . . the Republican Party will need to decide whether it prefers to court the dissident white vote of the Democratic South, through continuance of its lily-white program and an obscure Negro policy, or really design the Negro vote. It cannot seduce both.[22]

Although these different studies do not agree on the date of the collapse of the coalition, each marks the New Deal era as the time when this electoral union became unraveled. However, when all of the studies of this era are taken collectively, most,

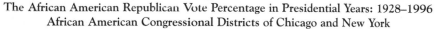

Figure 8.1
The African American Republican Vote Percentage in Presidential Years: 1928–1996
African American Congressional Districts of Chicago and New York

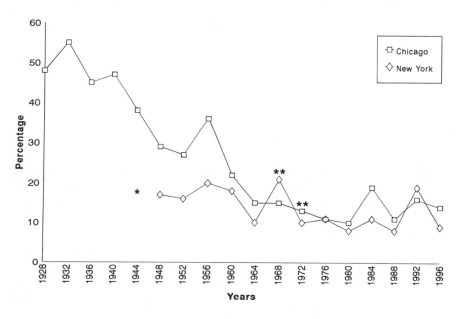

Source: Hanes Walton, Jr. *Invisible Politics* (Albany: State University of New York Press, 1985) for the
1928–1984 data. Congressional Quarterly *Guide to U.S. Elections 3rd Edition* (Washington, D.C.: Congressional Quarterly, 1993), for the 1988–1992 data. And the Congressional Quarterly Weekly Report,
1997 for the 1996 data.
*In this year, Congressman Adam Clayton Powell got all of the Democratic and Republican votes
combined.
**In these and subsequent years, the vote percentage is the mean percentage of all the African American Congressional candidates.

but not all, analysts of this critical election credit the 1936 election as the moment
of rupture and collapse.

Figure 8.1 attempts an empirical rendering of this political context. By examining the African American Republican vote from the ghetto congressional districts
of Chicago and New York, one can get a rudimentary sense of African American
voter support for Republican presidential candidates. Figure 8.1 refers to only the
presidential election, and not the congressional elections, so that some comparative judgment can be made on these different Republican presidential candidates.
The African American voters in Chicago elected the first African American Republican to Congress in the twentieth century, Oscar Depriest. And, in 1932, the
majority of African Americans voted for the Republican candidate. However, two
years later, in 1934, that district elected an African American Democrat to Congress, Arthur Mitchell, and one or more ever since. Notable about Figure 8.1 is the
decline in the vote for Republican congresspersons, even in presidential years,
when turnout is the greatest. The story from Chicago is a near-linear decline in
support for the party. After 1960, the vote percentage dropped to the teens and has

not been above that since then. Reagan's reelection saw a sharp increase, but it was short-lived.

In New York, the vote rose to 20 percent in 1956, the year that the Democratic Congressman Adam Clayton Powell urged his constituents to vote for President Eisenhower. It rose again to that level in 1968, brought on by the fact that popular civil rights leader James Farmer of the Congress of Racial Equality (CORE), a Nixon supporter, ran in a new congressional district against newcomer Shirley Chisholm. Although Chisholm won, Farmer made a significant showing, with a quarter of the total vote cast. During the Reagan-Bush years, the vote for the Republican candidate dropped into the single digits.

Collectively, it can be derived from this aggregate election data that the support for African American Republican congressional candidates is minimal and declining. All of the Republican presidential candidates since the advent of the civil rights years have failed to enhance and improve the prospects of their congressional candidates with their presidential coattails. Nor have the conservative ideologies of the Reagan-Bush years energized or mobilized the African American voters in this ideological and partisan direction.

If these electoral data are used as surrogate indicators of the mind and mood of the African American community, the current crop of African American conservatives has done less well in remaking and changing African American public opinion than did the old party activists and canvass workers. Instead of a turnaround, which would have been seen in a larger vote percentage, what is seen is a decline and drop off.

THE FORMATION AND PLACEMENT OF THE AFRICAN AMERICAN CONSERVATIVE PRESSURE GROUP

African American conservatives have long been in the community's life and its politics. Some in this group appeared long before the Civil War but their conservative positions and posturing addressed issues other than civil rights and the reform techniques designed to acquire them. In the pre–Civil war era, African American conservatives spoke to other issues and realities and did not readily link up with the present-day groups. Nevertheless they were there.[23]

However, the founding fathers of this current and contemporary group can be traced to the counterrevolutionary movement that was created to justify the era of disenfranchisement and the rise of white supremacy. Chief among this group was Booker T. Washington, along with a host of lesser lights. And most of this group of early African American conservatives were sponsored by white clients. Historian David Levering Lewis writes of these white philanthropists that:

> It is even possible that Booker T. Washington was their idea. For Booker Washington, the man . . . was railroad magnate William H. Baldwin, Jr. . . . nervous, impatient, intolerant of contrary opinions, and decisively convinced of African-American inferiority, Baldwin saw the solution to the South's race problem in salvation through work and rights after obedience.[24]

Several of this group of African American conservatives had no sponsoring clients, and they made their anti–civil rights pronouncements in the hope that such statements and speeches would eventually attract a client. But those who found themselves in the self-sponsorship mode struggled; a few such as Joseph Holly, president of Albany State College in Georgia, worked their way into institutionalized positions and, with conservative tracts supporting southern white supremacy, attained momentary sponsorship.[25] Others, such as northern-based George Schuyler, did not meet with the same success and ended up being their own sponsors.[26] Thus, in the post-Washington era, self-sponsors became the main pattern until the rise of the Reagan era.

Therefore, it should come as no surprise that a personal friend and advisor to the newly elected President Reagan would, on December 12 and 13, 1980, set up and finance the Fairmont Conference. The conservative Institute for Contemporary Studies "played official host," and attorney Edwin Meese, then legal counsel to the president, and Tony Brown edited the Conference proceedings.[27]

Scholar Georgia Persons wrote that "the objectives of the conference were clear: to establish a cadre of blacks of some prominence who could speak to a new thrust in domestic policies in regard to black Americans, with the hope and anticipation that they would emerge as alternative leaders to the civil rights leadership group."[28] What this conference did was to pull together, for the first time since the Booker T. Washington era, all of those African Americans struggling as self-sponsors and operating on the fringes of African American and white society and legitimate them, giving them national exposure.

The conference announced to this group, and more broadly to the activist cadre in the African American community, that conservative ideology would be quickly fused with political patronage and governmental appointments. Beyond appointments, there would be federal funds and grants, instant national success, and promises of more federal funds. Fringe spokespersons would now become mainstream players with official governmental support. But there was more.

The federal government was just one part of the new conservative labyrinth. Conservative think tanks and foundations now fell into line behind the Republican Party's new African American strategy. Foundations such as the American Enterprises Institute, the Cato Institute, the Hoover Institute, the Manhattan Institute, and others would open their doors and positions to this new group of conservatives. And following the foundations, there would be the conservative media establishment. They would provide national exposure.

Finally, this was, as President Reagan's Attorney General Ed Meese promised, a ground floor entrance. Older African American Republican partisans would be set aside for these newly ideologically committed supporters.[29] There would be no waiting in line behind the older party regulars. Newcomers could start immediately at the top. Thus, the African American conservative pressure group was formed and set into motion at the Fairmont Conference and placed within moments into the new Reagan administration.[30]

Immediately after the Fairmont Conference, "[the] Reagan administration appointed several of these blacks to top governmental positions. Samuel Pierce went to Housing and Urban Development (HUD), Clarence Pendleton was named Chairman of the Civil Rights Commission, and Clarence Thomas was named to head the Equal Employment Opportunity Commission (EEOC)."[31] Numerous African American conservatives went to sub-cabinet posts. Others went into the federal judiciary. In fact, not only were African American conservative appointees placed in the executive and judiciary branches of the federal government, but, eventually, an African

American, Gary Franks from Connecticut's fifth district, was elected to the 1990 House of Representatives. Another came in 1994: J. C. Watts from Oklahoma.

Beyond these official governmental spokespersons were those such as Thomas Sowell, Glenn Loury, Walter Williams, and Robert Woodson, to name a few, who obtained positions at conservative think tanks and foundations. A smaller group found places inside the academy.

In a very short time, this conservative pressure group had been formed and well placed. All that was now needed was for them to spring into action. And, at the sound of the Reagan presidential bell, they did so.

THE TECHNIQUES OF REMAKING AFRICAN AMERICAN PUBLIC OPINION

African American public opinion, "while individually held, is not individually derived. It emerges from systemic and individual factors." Moreover, "various groups have . . . engineered public opinion since the beginning of political democracy in government and are likely to continue in this role long into the future." Hence, "the manipulations of [African American public] opinion include the government itself, public relations firms, and majority and minority groups and their leaders."[32] In the 1980s, it was the Republican Party and its collaborators in the conservative establishment. Basically, they worked with and through their pressure group, the African American conservatives. Professor Georgia Persons indicates: "As reported by Washington journalist Fred Barnes, the Reagan White House developed a strategy which they committed to written memorandum, for identifying and bestowing publicity upon blacks who could in turn be anointed as credible, alternative black leaders."[33]

The Fairmont Conference identified, organized, and motivated through political patronage and political appointment, such a group of leaders. And out of this group "a small cadre of very articulate black intellectuals emerged to lend their voices to a cacophony of conservative voices seeking to lend intellectual support for what was to become known as the Reagan revolution in regard to domestic policy generally, including the traditional black agenda."[34] Concerning this last matter, the intent was to change African American public opinion about their traditional policy agenda, civil rights.

In regards to the traditional policy agenda, a survey of African American attitudes just prior to the Reagan-Bush era found that "a near majority of blacks, voters and non-voters, classified themselves ideologically as liberals. However, on racial matters with all other concerns excluded . . . blacks in both categories are overwhelmingly liberal, with only a very small segment labeling themselves as conservatives."[35]

Moreover, when one explores these ideological preferences by sex, as in table 8.1, the liberal policy preferences remained the same. In Table 8.1, the "data reveal blacks not only to have ideological positions on political issues . . . but . . . that nearly three-fourths of black men and women see themselves as liberals and moderates. Slightly less than one-fourth see themselves as conservatives."[36]

The point here is that African American public opinion on their policy agenda was skewed toward the liberal ideological spectrum.[37] And this usually meant that, in national elections and in many state elections, African Americans were the most consistent liberal voters.[38] Therefore, the task of this cadre of African American conservatives was to reverse or shift African Americans toward the conservative end of the ideological spectrum.

Table 8.1 Self-Identified Ideological Positions in the Black Community by Sex,
          1972–1982

Ideological Position	Black Men %	Black Women %
Liberals*	44% (179)	39% (225)
Moderates	32% (132)	39% (221)
Conservatives*	24% (97)	22% (125)
Totals	100% (408)	100% (571)

Source: Hanes Walton, Jr., *Invisible Politics* (Albany, New York: State University of New York Press, 1985), p. 33.
Note: In order to get fairly representatvie cell entries, the numbers for each year were pooled and treated in a cumulative fashion
*The NORC Survey questionnaire used a seven-point scale, including three liberal and three conservative positions. Each of these three positions has been merged to present a more simplified table.

Being appointees in the national administration ensured this partisan group developed and deployed pressure group's access to the national media. When the media showed up for interviews, discussion, remarks, reflections, and public discourse, this pressure group, which operated "within the mainstream a political institution . . . argued for a reduced and restricted role of the federal government in the black community, particularly in the area of social programs."[39]

This group told the morning news programs, the midday news programs, the evening news shows, the news magazines, and the twenty-four-hour news stations, "that governmental intervention in the lives of blacks has been more detrimental than helpful to the interests and well being of blacks, especially the black poor."[40] In regard to the solution for the one-third of the African American community that emerged out of the civil rights revolution and found itself still "mired in the misery and degradation of the so-called underclass,"[41] this group of conservatives favored instead "a laissez-faire capitalism with a presumed rectifying hand of the free market," and a restoration of a moral foundation and commitment.[42]

These were the governmental appointees. The think tank and foundation appointees populated the talk show circuit and local media, where the intellectual centers existed. These individuals became debaters, providing the "other" side. Supposedly, they offered a balance to the old-line and civil rights leaders and exponents. Despite the facts that the "other" side was a fiction and that the reach for balance and objectivity was "jive," the burlesques continued. On talk show after talk show, the promoted intellectuals from the right wing think tank who were obvious advocates were accepted because of credentials as uninterested nonpartisans. Both groups, the governmental and foundation appointees, covered the electronic media.

As for the print media, this same pressure group turned to op-ed journalism. It had long been a tradition in newspaper journalism to permit readers to write letters to the editor that would be published on the editorial pages of the newspaper.[43] By the 1980s, this institution had been expanded. It had become fashionable for individuals both in and out of government to specifically write opinion pieces for the editorial pages. The African American pressure group made great use of these op-ed pieces. In all of the major newspapers and in minor-market ones as well, the African

American conservatives promoted their argument that all governmental intervention was bad. They did not differentiate. Governmental protection of African American civil rights was not singled out as necessary or essential, even though the news media continually reported that African American civil rights were violated with impunity. The die had been cast. The op-ed technique went on unabated.

In addition to the talk show circuit and news programs, as well as the op-ed technique, the pressure groups used book publishing. Nearly all of the think tank appointees wrote books expressing their ideas. Thomas Sowell, the most prolific of the group, was followed by Walter Williams, Glenn Loury, Alan Keyes, Shelby Steele, and later Armstrong Williams. The books came out in political science, literature, economics, and philosophy, and also as personal memoirs. The last genre was flooded with books. In fact, the personal memoirs became a substitute for academic research and careful scholarship. In these works, barely literate individuals became philosopher kings. But there was more.

These advocacy tracts, which were written by academics and offered partisan posturing as objective scholarship, were given numerous awards and honors. Shelby Steele's book, written, not in his own academic specialization, but as a personal memoir presented as a Gunnar Myrdal treatise on race relations, won the National Book Award; Carole Swain's books on African American congressmen as obsolete entities received the two top awards in political science. Moreover, Justice Clarence Thomas's work in his Supreme Court decisions was praised. And the discussion of these advocacy tracts gave these pressure group members another reason to be on television. Here was another opportunity to demand an end to all governmental intervention on behalf of the African American community. Such a technique enhanced and increased their chances of being seen and heard.

The fourth technique employed by the African American conservatives to remake African American public opinion was the use of radio talk shows. Talk radio had in the wake of the television revolution given radio a rebirth and second chance. In the major media markets, African American conservative talk-show hosts replaced or competed with the "DJ" rhythm and blues shows. Such hosts attracted large numbers of conservatives listeners, and they accentuated the virtues of not having the government intervene to protect civil rights for the community. One of these shows, the "personal memoir," became the road map for ghetto salutation. It was shamelessly promoted and touted.

Next, came the cable news channel C-Span 1 and 2. Because this government-sponsored media outlet covers conferences, seminars, panels, and special educational events, conservative think tanks and academic organizations and groups constantly put on these African American conservatives as speakers, participating in admiring love feasts at which white audiences told the African American presenters how wise, enlightened and profound they were as thinkers. In the coverage of these events, the C-Span camera would, more often than not, reveal the presence of a few African Americans in the audience. But such a technique did have a significant purpose. It showed to the African American community the fiction that African American spokespersons had something to say to the white community and that the white community would listen and act appreciatively. There was never anyone there to say that the African American spokesperson was saying exactly what the white community wanted to hear, and none of the programs offered any pretense at balance or objectively. Yet the C-Span outlet gave this pressure group one more mass media avenue.

Besides these techniques to manipulate African American public opinion were the outlets of this pressure group itself. Chief among these outlets was, and is, *The Lincoln Review.*[44] This African American conservative quarterly is published by J. Y. Parker and offers an outlet for all of the pressure group's ranting and raving that did not reach the mainstream media or a speciality outlet. Article after article pours forth from this journal, which itself received only modest attention in the conservative counterrevolution. And despite its minimal position in the remaking of African American public opinion, it did attract some attention in the community.

Next, there were the conservative publications themselves. Here the conservative journals, newspapers, television shows, and monograph publishers afforded the pressure group reliable outlets.[45] When the mainstream and specialty outlets did present the pressure group with avenues for influencing the community's attitude, the conservative outlets pushed up the stock. The existence of conservative outlets meant that the pressure group was always ensured a public outlet. For example, the Manhattan Institute collected all of Thomas Sowell's books, packaged them in one offering, and sent out a mass mailing offering what they called the Thomas Sowell Library to interested readers. The conservative outlets found unique ways and means to keep this pressure group before the public. It is to this innovation that we can now turn.

One of the most unique techniques in the long list of public opinion weapons was the deliberate promotion and selling of this pressure group when the Reagan revolution began to wane with the defeat of President George H. Bush in his reelection effort. There appeared a small batch of books extolling the virtues of this pressure group.[46] These books push away criticism from the African American community and defend these conservative spokespersons as being in the American tradition of Thomas Paine—individuals who are willing to endure criticism, scorn, and snipes for the greater good of their community and society.[47] Despite the fact that such reasoning—if it can be called that—was sheer nonsense, these works continued to trickle out. African American conservatives, these promoters maintained, were brave and courageous activists. They were the new heroes and heroines for the community—greater than Martin Luther King, Jr., and Frederick Douglass. Here were the role models for the present and future. With this technique, white conservatives and Republican partisans gave the community a new list of heroes and heroines. They said to members of that community, "change your thinking and ideology and you, too, can become a new community icon." This technique turned liars and false prophets into patron saints and idols.

The last major technique for shifting public opinion was the use of a demonstration project. "Throughout third world and first world nations, Western powers use 'demonstration elections' to say to the world that these once totalitarian nations and dictatorships were now evolving democracies."[48] One event demonstrated how things had turned around. During the Reagan-Bush era, this international political technique to fashion and structure world public opinion was deployed domestically.

Robert Woodson, "who ran the National Center for Neighborhood and Enterprise" and had an appointment at the American Enterprise Institute in Washington, D.C. would use the conservative model-cities programs as a tool to show the ghetto how to rebuild and turn the inner city communities around. Woodson soon followed the theorist on the media circuit with statements about how to do it.[49] Here was the model conservative project for the inner cities. Here was something that could be done for those trapped in the inner city without governmental help and intervention.

But what was most troubling about this "demonstration" project was that it had been set into motion by federal grants to Woodson and had been supplemented by grants from private conservative foundations. Thus, the fundamental flaw with Woodson's "demonstration" project, was that he neither denied, nor revealed, the source of his funding to his listeners.

Overall, these sundry techniques to influence and reshape African American public opinion were designed to reach both the elite and the mass segments of the community in an effort to shift their opinions toward the conservative end of the continuum. Thus, the essential question at this moment is whether this new pressure group actually remade opinion in the African American community. Was there a shift? At the elite segment, two disciples of Dr. Martin Luther King, Jr.—Reverend Ralph David Abernathy and Hosea Williams—became Reagan supporters.[50] Other leaders were less publicly visible and vocal.

In regard to what happened at the mass level in the African American community, it is necessary to turn to polling and survey evidence for our empirical insights. However, it should be noted once again at this point that there were no major national polls and surveys monitoring the change in African American mass attitudes between 1981 and 1996. Hence, our analysis will have to rely on a secondary analysis of the few data base findings that did emerge (See Tables 8.2 and 8.3).

THE EMPIRICAL ASSESSMENT OF CONSERVATISM IN THE AFRICAN AMERICAN PUBLIC OPINION

Did events occur as the Republican partisans and their fellow travelers and companions had hoped? Was their underlying assumption that African American public opinion is malleable correct? And did this new African American strategy work?

Elsewhere it has been noted that there is an "extremely limited literature on African American conservatives" but, since the Reagan-Bush era, that literature has expanded significantly.[51] Along with this massive expansion of literature have been several scholarly and academic efforts to gain empirical insights into conservative attitudes and opinion in the African American community. Although scattered and limited, a composite of this literature should help us assess the efforts of the remaking techniques.

First to appear was Charles Hamilton's article, "Measuring Black Conservatism," in 1982.[52] Its publication was followed by Richard Seltzer and Robert Smith's article titled Race and Ideology: A Research Note Measuring Liberalism and Conservatism in Black America[53] and their book titled Race, Class, and Culture: A Study in Afro-American Mass Opinion. Then came the article by Susan Welch and Lorn Foster, "Class and Conservatism in the Black Community" in 1987.[54] There were a few limited studies in the 1990s.

Overall, these assessments cover both past and recent years. These data are therefore supplemented from the survey of African Americans in the 1984 and 1988 National Black Election studies and the 1991 National Black Political Study. This time dimension permits the reader to look at the past and the Reagan-Bush years.

Table 8.2 is a composite of the research of numerous others who have analyzed different aspects of the topic. In the past, another summary and composite piece, Charles V. Hamilton's essay, began the probe of the attitudinal dimension of the African American conservatives. However, that initial work was not only poorly con-

Table 8.2 The Empirical Assessment of African American Conservatism: A Composite Portrait, 1964–1988

Authors	Years of the Study	Attitudinal Evidence		Behavior Evidence	
		Self-Identified Conservatives	Issue Conservatives	Presidential Conservatives	Electoral Conservatives
Walton	1964				0.6%
Walton	1972–1974	16%			
Walton	1972–1982		10%		
Hamilton	1961–1981				
	1961–1973		5%		
	1964–1978		9%		
	1973–1980		42%		
	1972–1980		67%		
	1980–1981	23%	11%		0.1%
Seltzer and Smith	1982	**	**		
NBES	1984–1988				
	1984	35.3%			
	1988				

Sources: See Table 8.3.
*This datum refers to votes in congressional districts and single elections.
**Data in these works do not lend themselves to recalculation for Tables 8.2 and 8.3.

ceptualized but quite limited in its perspective. It left a very jumbled portrait of this pressure group and set into motion a circumscribed legacy of analysis. Hamilton's initial essay set up only two categories of African American conservatives: (1) those who had been self-identified in the polls and surveys, and (2) the issue conservatives, African Americans who had given their opinions on numerous governmental programs and spending. Thus, Hamilton's conceptualization failed to establish categories for (1) African American approval ratings for Republican presidential candidates and (2) voting for African American conservative candidates the Republican presidential candidates, or both. In regard to the latter category, Hamilton's essay does include a sentence on the vote for such a candidate but does not develop it into a full-blown category. Thus, the sentence is jumbled in with issue matters, despite the fact that it does not logically fit into the paper's discourse. Hence, it was a throw-in. Thus, with a limited set of categories, one got a limited set of insights.

However, the limited set of categories that Hamilton developed have been put to use by other academics who followed in his wake—notably Susan Welch and Leon Foster—and have not been enlarged upon or expanded. Hence, Table 8.3 includes the new categories for a broader perspective and comprehensive view.

From the information in Table 8.3, it becomes quite clear that roughly less than one-fifth of the African American community describes itself as conservative. And in the late 1980s, when this proportion seemingly goes up, the increase is due to the manner in which the question was asked. In fact, the question wording and extended categories set up in the National Black Election Studies (NBES) programs are responsible for the one-third of the community calling itself conservative.

Table 8.3 The Empirical Assessment of African American Conservatism: A Composite
Portrait (1986–1992)

Authors	Years of the Study	Attitudinal Evidence		Behavior Evidence	
		Self-Identified Conservatives	Issue Conservatives	Presidential Conservatives	Electoral Conservatives
Welch & Foster	1986		24%		
Dawson	1961–1988			**	4%
Edwards & Gallup	1953–1988			33%	
Walton	1964–1992				
NBPS	1991				
Bositis	1984–1992				
	1984				13%
	1988				15%
	1992				12%

Source: To develop this summary for Tables 8.2 and 8.3 from the literature so that it will reflect an
overtime perspective, 1964–1992, the fragmentary data had to be compiled from numerous sources. They
are: Hanes Walton, Jr., *Invisible Politics* (Albany: State University of New York Press, 1985), pp. 31–39, for
1964–1982 Florida registration data, Hanes Walton, Jr., *African American Power and Politics: The Political
Context Variable* (New York: Columbia University Press, 1997), pp. 217–219. Charles V. Hamilton,
"Measuring Black Conservatism," *The State of Black America* (New York: Urban League, 1982), for the
data from 1961–1981, pp. 113–40. Richard Seltzer and Robert Smith, "Race and Ideology: A Research
Note Measuring Liberalism and Conservatism in Black America," *Phylon* Vol. 46 (June 1985), pp. 98–105.
The National Black Election Studies (NBES) were carried out by James Jackson, Katherine Tate, Ronald
Brown, and Michael Dawson at the Institute of Social Research, the Program for Black Americans at the
University of Michigan. Susan Welch and Lorn Foster, "Class and Conservatism, in the Black Commu-
nity," *American Politics Quarterly* Vol. 15 (October 1987), pp. 445–70. Michael Dawson, "African
American Political Opinion: Volatility in the Reagan-Bush Era," in Walton, *African American Power and
Politics*, pp. 135–53. George C. Edwards III and Alex Gallup, *Presidential Approval: A Source Book*
(Baltimore: Johns Hopkins University Press, 1990), for the 1953–1988 data, pp. 2–113. David Bositis,
"Meyerson Confused," *Policy Review* (Summer 1994), for the 1984–1992 data, pp. 87–89. The National
Black Political Study (NBPS) was carried out by James Jackson, Ronald Brown, and Michael Dawson at
the Institute of Social Research, the Program for Black Americans at the University of Michigan.
*This datum refers to votes in congressional districts and single elections.
**Data in these works do not lend themselves to recalculation for Tables 8.2 and 8.3.

"Issue conservatives" prevail in the community, and the percentage rises and falls
depending on the issues. On spending issues, African Americans tended to be most
liberal, whereas on most social issues, they are quite conservative. As to matters of
political and civil rights, they are quite liberal.

Shifting to the approval of Republican presidents we find that African Americans
have tended on the whole to rate Republican presidents much lower than Democratic ones. And recent presidents such as Reagan have received very low ratings. Although George H. Bush fared better than did Reagan, he, too, remained inside the
low range given to Republicans.

Finally, the last indicator in Table 8.3 is that of electoral conservatives. The composite data tell us that, in the past and at the present, Republican candidates do not

fare well with the African American electorate. And this information is quite congruent with the data presented in Figure 8.1

Therefore, the suggestive interpretation is that, at the mass level, African American public opinion was not significantly remade or reshaped by the African American conservatives.

CONCLUSION: REMAKING AFRICAN AMERICAN PUBLIC OPINION: SOME TESTABLE PROPOSITIONS

At this point in the study, the logical, historical, observational, contextual, and statistical evidence lends support to an evidential base interpretation. After every African American social and political revolution for their civil and political rights, a white conservative elites, drawn from the political, economic, legal, academic, media, and social sectors of society, coalesces into an anti- civil rights coalition. This loose coalition forms into a broader confederation and sets into motion a counterrevolution that includes the transformation of public opinion in the African American community.

Why is this transformation of central importance? During the African American social revolution, a near consensus of opinion within that community supported its drive for civil and political rights. Such a seemingly coherent and united voice made for a determined opponent. That public opinion consensus had to be weakened. A weakened public opinion consensus would mean a weakened opponent, particularly in a context in which the major political leaders had been killed off.[55]

The public opinion consensus that civil rights leaders had taken decades to build could be weakened by voices speaking at variance with that consensus.[56] Older civil rights leaders knew the score on this matter. However, some of the mobilized African American conservatives truly believed that they needed to remake the public opinion consensus in their community. However, their white clients knew that history was against them. They were less interested in the remaking of opinion. They wanted division, dissension, disunity, conflict, controversy, and intra-group conflict. Such well-publicized contentious and combative public discourse would create an aura of serious divisions and different beliefs in that community. And, on the bases of these "public fights," the white community could roll back and reverse civil and political gains. The African American conservatives were merely used in a major power gambit.

To provide future empirical support for this interpretation Table 8.4 sets forth the testable propositions that were derived from this last round of African American conservatives. Table 8.4 contains measurable observations about the African American conservative pressure group and its client and benefactors. Moreover, it contains measurable observations about the techniques of this mobilized interest group. Finally, it contains measurable observations about the influence and effects of this group in relation to of African American and white public opinion.

As for the matter of public-policy reversals and rollback, there are measurable observations showing that there is little linkage between remade opinion and policy change.

In closing, it should be noted that the techniques to remake African American public opinion do induce intra group in-fighting and that these "public fights" result in less societal support for recent governmental expansion of rights for the African

Table 8.4 The Testable Propositions Empirically Deduced from the African American Conservatives' Efforts to Remake African American Public Opinion

Number	Hypotheses
1.	Governmental expansion of African American civil and political rights will lead to the countermobilization of white political, economic and media elites.
2.	White elites will emerge from the minority political coalition that failed to stop and/or limit the governmental expansion.
3.	White elites who launch this counter-mobilization will find a political base in the South.
4.	This mobilized elite will have a conservative and/or racist ideology, or both.
5.	This mobilized elite will develop an organizational base in a cadre of right wing pressure groups.
6.	This mobilized elite will develop an organizational base in one of the major and in minor political parties.
7.	This mobilized elite, once empowered, will enlist the support of African Americans in this public opinion reversal.
8.	This mobilized African American pressure group will affect only a minor change in African American public opinion.
9.	The mobilized African American pressure group will employ a technique to affect a change in public opinions.
10.	The techniques for change will create a perception of division and disunity in the African American public opinion.
11.	The mobilized white elite exaggerate such intragroup divisions in order to generate support in the white community for policy reversals.
12.	The African American conservative pressure group's failure to effect a remaking of African American public opinion will not affect the rollback and reversals of civil and political rights.
13.	The role and function of the African American conservative pressure groups is to create the perceptions of divisions and disunity in the African American community.

American community. This method is, indeed, a new way to re-empower the white community.

NOTES

1. Louis Harris, Is There a Republican Majority? (New York: Harper and Row, 1954).
2. V. O. Key, Jr., *The Responsible Electorate* (Cambridge: Harvard University Press, 1966), p. 71.
3. Samuel Lubell, *The Revolt of the Moderates* (New York: Harper and Row, 1956).
4. John Saloma, *Ominous Politics: the New Conservative Labyrinth* (New York: Hill and Wang, 1984), pp. 130–137.
5. Hanes Walton, Jr., *Black Republicans: The Politics of the Black and Tans* (Metuchen, NJ: Scarecrow Press, 1975), pp. 45–141. And Donald Lisio, *Hoover, Blacks and Lily: Whites: A study of Southern Strategies* (Chapel Hill: University of North Carolina Press, 1985), pp. 41, 61, 66, 135, 158, and 163.
6. Alex Poinsett, *Walking with Presidents: Louis Martin and the Rise of Black Political Power* (Lanham, MD: Madison Books, 1997), p. 80.

7. Ibid.
8. Ibid., p. 86.
9. Ibid., p. 146.
10. Hanes Walton, Jr., *Invisible Politics: Black Political Behavior* (Albany: State University of New York Press, 1985), p. 137.
11. Dan T. Carter, *The Politics of Rage: George Wallace, the Origins of the New Conservatives, and the Transformation of American Politics* (Baton Rouge: Louisiana State University Press, 1995), pp. 325–27.
12. Dan T. Carter, *From George Wallace to Newt Gingrich: Race in the Conservative Counterrevolution, 1963–1994*, (Baton Rouge: Louisiana State University Press, 1996), p. 27.
13. Theodore Cross, *Black Capitalism* (New York: Atheneum, 1969).
14. Walton, *Invisible Politics*, p. 138.
15. Ibid.
16. Pearl Robinson, "Whither the Future of Blacks in the Republican Party?" *Political Science Quarterly* (Summer, 1982): 207–31.
17. Wayne Greenshaw, *Elephants in the Cotton fields: Ronald Reagan and the New Republican South* (New York: Macmillan, 1982).
18. A Campbell, P. Converse, W. Miller, and D. Stokes, *The American Voter* (New York: John Wiley, 1960), p. 160.
19. Gerald Gamm, *The Making of New Deal Democrats: Voting Behavior and Realignment in Boston, 1920–1940* (Chicago: University of Chicago Press, 1986), p. 94.
20. Samuel Lubell, *The Future of American Politics* (New York: Harper and Brothers, 1951), p. 48.
21. See Charles Henry, ed., *Ralph Bunche: Selected Speeches and Writings* (Ann Arbor: University of Michigan Press, 1995), pp. 85–92.
22. "Introduction to Confidential Report to Republican Party, in *Ralph Bunche*, ed. Henry, p. 91.
23. Hanes Walton, Jr., "Blacks and Conservative Political Movements," in Lenneal Henderson, Jr., ed., *Black Political Life in the United States* (San Francisco: Chandler Publishing Company, 1972), pp. 216–18.
24. David Levering Lewis, *W. E. B. DuBois: Biography of a Race* (New York: Henry Holt and Company, 1993), pp. 240–41.
25. Institute for Contemporary Studies, *The Fairmont Papers: Black Alternatives Conference* (San Francisco: Institute for Contemporary Studies, 1981); Georgia Persons, *Dilemmas of Black Politics* (New York: HarperCollins, 1993), p. 199.
26. George Schuyler, *Black and Conservative* (New York: Arlington House, 1966).
27. Persons, *Dilemmas*, p. 199.
28. Ibid.
29. Quoted in Hanes Walton, Jr., *When the Marching Stopped: The Politics of Civil Rights Regulatory Agencies* (Albany: State University of New York Press, 1988), p. 171.
30. Ibid.
31. Ibid., p. 172.
32. Walton, *Invisible Politics*, pp. 55–56.
33. Georgia Persons, "The Election of Gary Franks and the ascendancy of the New Black Conservatives"; in her *Dilemmas of Black Politics* (New York: Harper Collins, 1993)
34. Ibid.
35. Walton, *Invisible Politics*, p. 32.
36. Ibid., p. 33.
37. Ibid., pp. 33–34. See table 2.4 for "African American Evaluation of Governmental expenditures."
38. See Figure 8.1 and Table 8.1 in this chapter.

39. Walton, *Invisible Politics*, pp. 30–31.

40. Persons, *Dilemmas*, p. 199.

41. Ibid.

42. Ibid.

43. Leila Sussman, "Mass Political Letter Writing in America: The Growth of an Institution," in *Public Opinion Quarterly*, Vol. 23 (1959): pp. 203–13.

44. Walton, *When the Marching Stopped*, p. 173.

45. Ibid.

46. Hanes Walton, Jr., "Defending the Indefensible: The African American Conservative Client, Spokesperson of the Reagan-Bush Era," in *The Black Scholar* (Fall 1994): pp. 46–50.

47. Ibid.

48. Persons, *Dilemmas*, p. 199.

49. Robert Woodson, *On the Road to Economic Freedom: An agenda for Black Progress* (Washington, D.C.: Regency Galway, 1987).

50. Walton, *When the Marching Stopped*, p. 172.

51. Ibid.

52. Charles V. Hamilton, "Measuring Black Conservatism" in *The State of Black America* (New York: National Urban League, 1982), pp. 113–140.

53. Richard Seltzer and Robert C. Smith, "Race and Ideology: A Research Note Measuring Liberalism and Conservatism and Black America," *Phylon* (June 1985), pp. 98–115.

54. Susan Welch and Lorn Foster, "Class and Conservatism in the Black Community," *American Politics Quarterly*, Vol. 15 (October 1987): 445–70.

55. Robert Smith, *We Have No Leaders: African Americans in the Post–Civil Rights Era* (Albany: State University of New York Press, 1996).

56. Walton, *Invisible Politics*, p. 247.

PART IV

STRUGGLE, CLASS, AND IDEOLOGY

CHAPTER 9

THE LONELY ICONOCLAST: GEORGE SCHUYLER AND THE CIVIL RIGHTS MOVEMENT

OSCAR R. WILLIAMS JR.

In 1954, the U.S. Supreme Court declared segregation unconstitutional in the famous *Brown vs. Board of Education* decision, thus ushering in the modern civil rights movement. George Samuel Schuyler, associate editor of the *Pittsburgh Courier*, praised the decision in an editorial: "Has any other country with a comparable racial, religious or nationalist problem met it more forthrightly and in keeping with the principles of republicanism?"[1] In another *Courier* editorial, Schuyler prophesied that Thurgood Marshall would be the next appointee to the Supreme Court.[2] In a 1960 interview, Schuyler had a more somber view of the *Brown* decision. He replied that the success of desegregation would be dependent on whites, adding that "sometimes all you do is frighten and alarm people, and that makes them get up their defenses sooner than they ordinarily would have."[3]

Schuyler's analysis of the *Brown vs. Board of Education* decision reflected his increasingly conservative views on race. Throughout his career, Schuyler earned a reputation as a controversial journalist who blindly criticized African American culture. In the 1960s Schuyler became the most prominent African American critic of the civil rights movement and a weapon for the growing conservative movement. A review of his life and career is needed in order to understand how an African American who grew up in the Jim Crow era could become one of the bitterest opponents of the civil rights movement.

Schuyler was born February 25, 1895, in Providence, Rhode Island, and reared in Syracuse, New York. Schuyler's parents were domestics, but within the fragile African American class system in Syracuse, they were considered middle class. His family reflected conservative views of assimilation that had a profound effect on him. Most influential was his mother, who proved to be a model for his discriminating attitude toward African American southerners, referring them to as "illiterate, ignorant, ill-bred and amoral."[4] She preferred the company of white northerners who were, according to Schuyler, "her kind of people."[5] His mother's dislike of southern African Americans may have stemmed from factors real and imagined: An influx of African Americans would result in increased job competition between African Americans, possibly resulting in Fisher losing out on domestic jobs she coveted. Another reason was a possible white backlash in Syracuse, which could result in a loss of jobs for African Americans or racial violence.[6] Therefore, she favored preservation of the racial status quo in Syracuse.

Despite Fisher's lessons of conservatism, a teenage Schuyler realized that his prospects for a meaningful life in Syracuse were greatly limited. As an African American in early twentieth century Syracuse, he could hope for no more than the domestic jobs that his parents held. In 1912, at the age of seventeen, Schuyler dropped out of high school and enlisted in the U.S. Army, serving in the famous, all-black, 1st Battalion, 25th U.S. Infantry.[7]

During his service, Schuyler was exposed for the first time to a large number of African Americans, many of them southerners. Although Schuyler eventually made friends and associates among his army comrades, he felt separate from his fellow soldiers: "They came from areas where the mores were different from those of my area, and the fact that we were all colored was somewhat beside the point," explained Schuyler. "When you're among people who haven't read anything and have nothing particular to talk about, it makes you a little lonesome."[8]

During World War I, Schuyler was chosen to be among the few African Americans to attend the Army's officer training camp for African American candidates at Fort Des Moines, Iowa. In October 1917, Schuyler was commissioned as a first lieutenant.[9] Despite the achievement, the young lieutenant's military career ended on a sour note. In 1918, Schuyler deserted the Army after a Greek shoeshine boy in a Philadelphia railroad station refused to serve him. He eventually wound up on a California ranch working as a dishwasher before he gave himself up after three months as a deserter. He was sentenced to five years in prison at Castle William, New York. Fortunately, the commandant was a former officer in Schuyler's regiment, and as a result his sentence was reduced to nine months, which he served while working in the commandant's office.[10]

From 1919 to 1923, Schuyler was adrift between New York City and Syracuse, working a number of odd jobs, from a temporary clerical position as a civil service worker to a dishwasher in a restaurant. While in Syracuse, he became a member of the Socialist Party of America and was elected its educational director. For his first meeting, Schuyler presented a lecture titled, "An Intelligent Program for Intelligent Negro Workers," to an audience of ten people.[11] Initially, Schuyler joined the party to seek out intellectual stimulation and interracial acceptance in white working-class Syracuse. Subsequently, Schuyler began to question socialism, arguing that it still had not improved the situation of the poor and was out of touch with reality.[12] In addition, Schuyler may have become disenchanted with his limited role as an African American in the Socialist Party. He eventually quit the party and left Syracuse for good. Finding himself in New York City once again, Schuyler was adrift as a common laborer living in a basement with the unemployed and homeless in 1922 when he met Asa Philip Randolph and Chandler Owen.[13]

Schuyler met Randolph and Owen at a meeting of the Friends of Negro Freedom, a socialist-based organization. In addition, they were editors of The Messenger, a socialist, African American magazine. Establishing a good relationship with Randolph, Schuyler soon found himself secretary for the Friends of Negro Freedom and began submitting articles for *The Messenger* in 1923. Shortly after his arrival, Schuyler was regularly featured in his own column, titled "Shafts and Darts: A Page of Calumny and Satire." Teamed with fellow writer Theophilus Lewis, Schuyler proceeded to mercilessly lampoon mainstream American and African American society. Nothing was above ridicule and "Shafts and Darts" attacked issues of race, religion, politics, and culture.[14]

As a columnist, Schuyler exercised his power to humiliate and denigrate individuals and organizations that clashed with his ideologies. One of his targets was Pan-Africanist Marcus Garvey, head of the Universal Negro Improvement Association (UNIA). Garvey ran into troubles in 1922 when he was arrested on charges of mail fraud. He had sold tickets for one of his ships, the *S.S. Phyliss Wheatley*, but the ship had not been purchased yet and angry stockholders demanded an answer.[15] These developments pleased Owen and Randolph, who detested Garvey.[16] Subsequently, Schuyler was given the green light to humiliate Garvey as much as possible in the *Messenger*.

In a July 1924 *Messenger* article, Schuyler portrayed Garvey as a fraud and satirized him for being skillful enough to convince UNIA members to support a failing shipping line that had "the finest rat-trap [the *S.S. Shadyside*] in the Harlem River."[17] Schuyler concluded by stating that he would not expect any special favors for his "tribute" to the UNIA leader: "I have never refused any material rewards, because, like Brother Marcus, my motto is: One God, One Aim, One Destiny—The Almighty Dollar."[18]

In 1926, Schuyler critiqued the Harlem Renaissance in his famous article, "The Negro-Art Hokum." He declared that the idea of "Negro art" existing in America was foolishness and that:

> the Aframerican is merely a lampblacked Anglo-Saxon. If the European immigrant after two or three generations of exposure to our schools, politics, advertising, moral crusades, and restaurants becomes indistinguishable from the mass of Americans of the older stock, . . . how much truer must it be of the sons of Ham who have been subjected to what the uplifters call Americanism for the last three hundred years. Aside from his color, . . . your American Negro is just plain American.[19]

In 1924, Schuyler began to write for the *Pittsburgh Courier*, the leading African American newspaper of the period, and quickly established himself as one of the major critics and satirists of African American culture. Schuyler also managed to publish two critically acclaimed novels: *Black No More*, a biting satire of the Harlem Renaissance and American race relations; and *Slaves Today*, a fictional account of slavery in Liberia.

After World War II, Schuyler became more conservative as he began to associate with right-wing conservatives, becoming actively involved with the growing anti-communist movement. Shrewdly, the enterprising journalist saw his chance to be part of the American mainstream and to possibly be accepted and known among the white conservative of the world, such as James Burnham, John Dos Passos, and William Buckley. Consequently, Schuyler reinvented himself as an African American patriot and became the most prominent African American anticommunist during the

Cold War period.[20] In 1950, he joined the American Committee for Cultural Freedom (ACCF) and attended the first meeting in Berlin.[21] During the early 1950s, Schuyler used his "Shafts and Darts" as a sounding board for Senator Joseph McCarthy and his campaign of anticommunism. In the mid-1950s, he turned his attention to the growing civil rights movement.

Tensions flared in the South when white opponents organized against the *Brown vs. Board of Education* decision and enacted a campaign of terror against innocent African American victims. Schuyler deplored the violence, but he criticized civil rights leaders and organizations for a lack of strategy: "Due to our misleadership which has mistaken legal shadow for economic substance and orations for organization, we have not used the weapons and resources we possess for the warfare which was implicit in the prematurely accelerated drive for integration."[22] As an alternative, he argued for a more economically secure African American society to combat segregation:

> Were we possessed of as many cooperative societies, credit unions, business enterprises, factories and banks in Hog and Hominy Land and North, East and West as we have social clubs, fraternities, churches and NAACP branches, we could laugh at the crackers' threats. As it is, we can't and there's no point in pretending that we can. You can't bring about equality . . . not even from the Supreme Court.[23]

Schuyler criticized other significant movements such as the 1956 Montgomery, Alabama, Bus Boycott. A longstanding critic of boycotts, he chastised those who did not enfranchise African American businesses and practice self-help capitalism: "Why do they discriminate against their own professional and business folk who live in the community, are identified with the community, rear families in the community and whose success aids the community?" [24] Although the boycott resulted in desegregation of the city busses, he remained critical: "The Montgomery bus boycott might have been a noble experiment but now that it has been 'won' . . . so what? Montgomery Negroes could have owned the bus company without doing all that walking if they had used their heads instead of their feet and their tonsils."[25]

Predictably, Schuyler was critical of Martin Luther King, Jr., and his organization, the Southern Christian Leadership Conference (SCLC). Carrying a longtime grudge against the African American clergy, Schuyler found himself ideologically opposed to events such as the SCLC Prayer Pilgrimage March in May 1957: "A much more fruitful pilgrimage led by the reverend clergy would be one to the registration booth, making possible the greatest use of the Negro's potential political power."[26]

In 1959, when King suggested a march in Mississippi to protest a lynching,[27] Schuyler criticized the plan, calling it irrational and that an attempted march in Mississippi would only "enrich the undertakers in the volatile region."[28] In 1960, the journalist denounced King's statement that unjust laws should not be obeyed:

> Obviously if citizens are to choose the laws they want to obey, the result will be anarchy and chaos, with Negroes the worst sufferers. . . . They have reached their present state of development because the majority of white people were tolerant and helpful, and willing to obey most of the laws enacted in the Negro's behalf and supported by the courts.[29]

Schuyler additionally opposed black militant organizations of the period. Although he shared their disdain of nonviolent resistance, Schuyler did not approve of black nationalism. One particular example was his criticism of the Nation Of Islam (NOI) and its prominent leaders Elijah Muhammad and Malcolm X. Interestingly, Schuyler praised the NOI's self-improvement programs in a 1959 *Courier* editorial:

> Mr. Muhammad may be a rogue and a charlatan, but when anybody can get tens of thousands of Negroes to practice economic solidarity, respect their women, alter their atrocious diet, give up liquor, stop crime, juvenile delinquency and adultery, he is doing more for the Negro's welfare than any current Negro leader I know.[30]

In 1961, Schuyler took part in a radio broadcast debate with Malcolm X, James Baldwin, and C. Eric Lincoln, author of *The Black Muslims in America*. Hosted by Eric Goldman of Princeton University, the program centered on the NOI and its impact on African Americans. Goldman asked panelists their opinion of the NOI. Predictably, Schuyler came out against the organization's nationalistic approach to solving African Americans' social problems. When Malcolm X discussed the NOI's goal of separatism from white America, Schuyler was moved to comment, thereby leading to a discourse between the two:

> Schuyler: Just wait a minute, now. At the risk of going into politics, I would like to know how any group in the United States is going to separate part of the United States for them to live in without having something to do with politics. Do you plan to do this through warfare?
>
> Malcolm X: Sir, I don't think that it's necessary to bring about any warfare. If the ex-slave in America has to go to war with his former slavemaster to get what is his by right, then that in itself is a condemnation of the former slavemaster. If Lincoln issued the Emancipation Proclamation a hundred years ago . . . and yet at the same time today the so-called Negro is knocking at the White House door, still begging his master to pass legislation that will give him recognition or protection by the constitution that is supposed to represent him, I think sir that the man who is depriving him of these rights cannot open up his mouth and say that it would be war.[31]

During the debate Schuyler did praise the NOI for its self-improvement programs and its emphasis on economic uplift. Nonetheless, Schuyler's overall position was that the NOI was a dictatorial black nationalist organization that thrived on a hatred of whites. When Malcolm X replied to Schuyler's criticism by quoting an editorial in which he praised the NOI, Schuyler lightheartedly commented, "Well you see there, that's what you get for being nice."[32] Interestingly, Roy Wilkins commented that the only man who could keep up with Malcolm X's sharp wit was Schuyler. "I always thought that Malcolm and George made a splendid set of antipodes," commented Wilkins.[33]

Although Schuyler and Malcolm X may have been similar in their intellectual gymnastics, the journalist did not share any affection or admiration for the slain leader years after his assassination in 1965. In an 1973 *American Opinion* article, Schuyler called Malcolm X "a bold, outspoken, ignorant man of no occupation after he gave up pimping, gambling, and dope-selling to follow Mr. [Elijah] Muhammad."[34] Dismissing the NOI as an insignificant group of no more than ten thousand, he categorized other African American organizations as "insignificant groups of hustlers and braggarts organized to bulldoze white people into handing out charity or to snatch a little transient graft."[35] Schuyler concluded by saying efforts to honor Malcolm X were akin to celebrating the birthday of Benedict Arnold or memorializing Alger Hiss.[36]

Eventually, Schuyler's hard-line editorials against the civil rights movement aroused the ire of readers and *Courier* management. In 1962, Schuyler received a memo from editor William G. Nunn, instructing him and other reporters to "lay off" of criticizing King.[37] Schuyler was unmoved by Nunn's request.

> If, as you say, there is a tendency on the part of *Courier* reporters "to continue sniping at Martin Luther King Jr." . . . it is undoubtedly due to the fact that they have detected the essential fraudulence of that demagogue and recognize that he and his ilk will do the Negro's cause a great deal of harm in the long run.[38]

Commenting on Nunn's statement of King being the most articulate voice for Negroes, Schuyler replied:

> Being articulate also means nothing in itself. Some of the worst enemies of the Negro have been articulate. And you are quite wrong if you think that Rev. King and his crackpot ilk are accomplishing more for Negroes than the NAACP and the Urban League, which have a more definite policy based on experience and intelligence. As for my personal opinion, I shall continue to express it in my signed column regardless of whether others agree or not. I do not regard the purpose of a column to be a rubber stamp for management, a sort of affirmation of the paper's policy. . . . I cannot accept the belief that anybody who leads thousands of Negroes to be [fined] whatever white courts think they should be [fined] is doing the impoverished Negro community any good, whether in Albany, Ga. or Pittsburgh, Pa. If the column is distasteful, it can be left out; but I personally deplore running a newspaper like a plantation—and that's what the *Courier* risks.[39]

Schuyler's conflict with *Courier* management finally came to an end in 1964, when his sentiment with the far right became more prevalent. During the spring, Schuyler announced his candidacy for U.S. congressman in the Eighteenth District (Harlem) of Manhattan, the congressional district of then incumbent congressman Adam Clayton Powell, Jr. Running on the Conservative Party ticket, Schuyler attacked Powell by calling him as "playboy," declaring him irresponsible, and labeling him to be "New York's Number One demagogue."[40] Schuyler's hostility toward Powell was deeply rooted in a longtime resentment of the charismatic politician. Inquiring about Powell to journalists, Schuyler often said, "I wonder what that yellow nigger is up to now."[41] Running more on principle and visibility rather than a realistic chance to win, Schuyler came in last, with 6% of the popular vote (637 votes) compared to Powell's overwhelming reelection with 84.6% of the popular vote (94,222).[42]

Another infuriating issue was Schuyler's membership on the grand jury that failed to indict New York City Police Lieutenant Thomas Gilligan for shooting James Powell, a fifteen year old African American teenager whose death caused six days of rioting in Harlem and Bedford-Stuyvestant in Brooklyn.[43] As one of two African Americans on the grand jury, Schuyler supported the majority opinion and defended his decision: "I did the right thing and so did the rest of the jury. We heard everything and we're more expert on the subject because we were there."[44]

The breaking point was Schuyler's open support for presidential Republican candidate and right wing conservative Barry Goldwater. The *Courier* overwhelmingly supported President Lyndon B. Johnson and disapproved of Goldwater's anti–civil rights position. Schuyler openly supported and praised the Arizona Senator. "Goldwater is an honest straightforward man who does not gull the mob and shift ground to cadge votes."[45] In August 1964, the journalist appeared on radio station KMOX in St. Louis, Missouri and campaigned for Goldwater.[46]

The radio program made *Courier* editor P. L. Prattis furious when he received word of readers canceling subscriptions and of one man in Washington D.C. bought all the copies of the *Courier* from a newsstand, tore them up, and threw them into a trash can.[47] Prattis scolded Schuyler for his position: "Your KMOX interview has done us incalculable harm. We can't believe that you had any idea what the reaction would be or that your opinions and position would be taken to be those of *The Courier*."[48] Schuyler was typically indifferent to Prattis: "I think the damage you mention is [somewhat] exaggerated vis a vis [sic] circulation. Losing subscribers is an occupational hazard which occurs only when something worthwhile is being said."[49] In turn, Schuyler urged Prattis to feature more debates on civil rights, President Lyndon Johnson's War On Poverty, urban riots, and other controversial topics: "An Article by George Wallace would not be amiss!"[50]

Between Schuyler's unbending support for the right and the *Courier*'s support for civil rights, it was a matter of time before the two factions would clash. In September 1964, the *Courier* announced that it would demote Schuyler from the title of associate editor. Arguing that Schuyler's title was more honorary than real, Prattis told Schuyler that he would be allowed to continue his editorials in the *Courier*.[51] Schuyler was naturally disappointed, calling Prattis' letter "needlessly dishonest and libelous."[52] Two months later, when Schuyler submitted an editorial criticizing the awarding of the Nobel Peace Prize to King, the *Courier* rejected it and told the aged newspaperman not to submit editorials any longer to the newspaper.[53] Nonetheless, his editorials appeared in the *Courier* until November 1966 when the newspaper came under new management.[54] Despite the gesture, the feud between Prattis and Schuyler meant the end of a productive yet tempestuous forty-two year career with one of the leading African American newspapers of the pre–civil rights era.

In truth, Schuyler's relationship with the *Courier* had ended long before the Goldwater incident. Since the late 1940s, Schuyler had flirted with conservatism and the far right, hoping to become part of that clique. The ambitious journalist had worked for mainstream acceptance throughout his career by seeking approval from established white intellectuals. In the 1920s, he gained the attention and mentorship of *American Mercury* editor and social critic H. L. Mencken, who considered Schuyler "the most competent Negro journalist ever heard of."[55] After Mencken's death in 1956, Schuyler continued to search for a mentor and mainstream acceptance. His dual quest was fulfilled when newspaper editor and right-wing conservative William Loeb approached him after Schuyler's demotion from the *Courier*.

Loeb, editor of the *Manchester (New Hampshire) Union Leader*, was an admirer of Schuyler and felt that he would be an ideal weapon of choice against the civil rights movement. Loeb shrewdly exploited the situation in a letter to Schuyler: "Frankly I am surprised that they haven't come sooner. As you know, there is a really filthy campaign against you. You have a great amount of guts. Very few people would stick out their necks the way you are doing. My hat is off to you, sir."[56]

Loeb pushed for immediate syndication of Schuyler's editorials in several newspapers. In a letter to Brady Black of the *Cincinnati Enquirer,* he asked for ten newspapers to syndicate Schuyler's editorials. He also confirmed Schuyler's political stance: "George is very much of a conservative and writes intelligently and vividly on the Negro question. While he is naturally proud of his race, he takes the attitude that acceptance must be earned and what Negroes should do is become competent and acceptance would then take care of himself."[57]

On November 10, 1964, an editorial by Schuyler criticizing the awarding of the Nobel Peace Prize to Dr. Martin Luther King, Jr., appeared in the *Union Leader.* Initially rejected by the *Courier,* Schuyler submitted it to Loeb, who eagerly printed the diatribe against King. In the editorial, Schuyler argued that King was not worthy of the award nor had he made a contribution to domestic and world peace. "Methinks the Lenin Prize would have been more appropriate," quipped Schuyler.[58] Similar to his ideological criticism of Marcus Garvey forty years before, Schuyler proceeded to debunk and belittle King's strategy of civil disobedience and nonviolent resistance:

> Dr. King's principal contribution to world peace has been to roam the country like some sable Typhoid Mary, infecting the mentally disturbed with perversion of Christian doctrine, and grabbing fat lecture fees from the shallow pated . . . His incitement packed jails with Negroes and some whites, getting them beaten, bitten and firehosed, thereby bankrupting communities raising bail and fines, to the vast enrichment of Southern "law 'n' order'" . . . Alfred Bernard Nobel will probably whirl in his tomb on Dec. 10 when Dr. King receives the bauble and the bankroll.[59]

Schuyler received praise for his editorial from several conservatives, namely Loeb. "You are a wonderful writer," exclaimed the editor. "I don't know when I have enjoyed anything as much as your piece on the ridiculousness of Martin Luther King being given the Nobel Peace Prize."[60] He also gained the attention of Theodore Lit, Senior Editor of Arlington House Publishers. In late November, he contacted Schuyler and proposed an autobiography tailored to Schuyler's circumstance of being African American and conservative. "What are the experiences of being at once a Negro and Conservative?" asked Lit. "How do people react and how do you react to *their* reactions?"[61] Schuyler answered his inquiry: "I do not look upon these matters as a Negro but simply as an American individual. I think that there is much to conserve in American society, including what Negroes have (which happens to be more than anywhere else I know)."[62] Two years later, Arlington House published Schuyler's autobiography *Black and Conservative.*

In 1965, Sidney Goldberg, president of the North American Newspaper Alliance (NANA), hired Schuyler to have his editorials syndicated in over 150 newspapers.[63] Reaching his largest audience to date, Schuyler proceeded to continue his one-man campaign against the civil rights movement. In August 1965, Watts predominantly African American section of Los Angeles, California, exploded in a riot, resulting in 34 deaths, 1,032 injured, 3,952 arrested, and approximately $40 million in property destruction.[64] The journalist wasted little time in condemning the violence and laying blame in his first NANA-syndicated editorial.

Titled "Anatomy of Black Insurrection," Schuyler harped on a familiar theme: irresponsible civil rights leaders and organizations were to blame for Watts: "The net result of this long encouragement of civil disobedience, disdain for authority and general disrespect for public morals was to set the stage for the successive disgraceful orgies of burning, looting, vandalism and death, with the criminal elements of the slum proletariat taking over."[65] Predictably, Schuyler blamed Martin Luther King, Jr. for: "infecting the mentally retarded with the germs of civil disobedience, camouflaged as non-violence and love of white people . . . Phony prayers for the salvation of white 'oppressors' and chanting slave songs fooled nobody except possibly the utopians of the National Council Of Churches and the socialist Roman Catholics."[66] Schuyler ended the diatribe with the following message:

> What this country badly needs is public officials who will not temporize with illegality and disorder garbed in the mantle of civil rights and equality; who will not suppress crime and violence regardless of color; judges who will act with speed and vigor to jail disturbers of the peace; and a more responsible communications media that will refrain from persistently exciting the idle, envious and lawless.[67]

Shortly after the release of the editorial, the NAACP magazine *The Crisis* dismissed Schuyler's analysis of the Watts riot: "Under the Schuyler formula, all the multiple evils which beset the Negro community might possibly begin to be ameliorated after 2065, if only, in the meanwhile, Negroes sit quiet and stop rocking the boat."[68] Emphasizing that Schuyler did not speak for African Americans, the editorial concluded: "Mr. Schuyler does not even comprehend the depth and fury of the Negro's resentment against the restrictions imposed upon him solely because of his race. All in his years, Mr. Schuyler has been too busy breaking idols to learn this lesson."[69]

Despite the criticism, Schuyler continued to lend his talents to the conservative movement. In October 1965, Robert Welch, president of the John Birch Society, encouraged Schuyler to become a member of his ultraconservative organization.[70] He eagerly accepted the offer, stating in his reply "I could have been (a member) a long time ago because I feel that's where I belong, so here it is without any ado."[71] Shortly afterward, Welch invited Schuyler to speak at the organization's National Council Meeting the following December in New York. Once again, the eager journalist accepted the offer. Interestingly, Schuyler was featured with fellow speaker Jim Clark, the Selma, Alabama Sheriff who gained notoriety for his strong-arm tactics against civil rights demonstrators.[72]

Schuyler's career was revitalized when he claimed a new professional home with *American Opinion* and *Review of the News*, two John Birch publications. Schuyler also wrote for *Human Events*, another conservative publication. In addition, he leased his speaking talents to *American Opinion*'s speakers bureau, lecturing at several college campuses, universities, and organizations throughout the U.S. against the civil rights and emerging black power movements. Coupled with his NANA articles, Schuyler amassed a massive amount of anti–civil rights literature that was mostly read by his audience of predominantly white, upper-middle class, conservative Americans who desired to hear an African American criticize the movement.

The journalist did not disappoint his audience as he attacked several issues such as urban riots, welfare, public housing, and other related issues. In April 1968, Schuyler received his greatest acclaim as an ultra conservative journalist when he wrote an essay addressing the life and career of Martin Luther King, Jr. Felled by an assassin's bullet, King's death set off a period of rioting in more than one hundred cities, and mass mourning by black and white Americans.[73] Schuyler, a longtime critic of King, was not swayed by the emotions of the moment, and wrote a critical essay that was published by NANA shortly after the leader's death.

Coldly titled, "He Reaped The Whirlwind: A Cool And Critical Appraisal of Martin Luther King's Works," the essay began by asserting that nonviolent resistance causes violence: "Countless mass demonstrations which started to advance a good cause have ended in clashes with police, looting, vandalism and killing rather than the goodwill and understanding originally intended."[74] Schuyler argued for moderation and compromise as an alternative to protest:

> Wherever the Negro lives in the United States, he prospers only to the extent that he has the goodwill, tolerance and acceptance of his white neighbors and fellow workers. This is a necessarily slow process, when trying to maintain the most delicate balance. It cannot be speeded by razzle-dazzle tactics which arouse suspicion and lend support to the propaganda of Negrophobes.[75]

Schuyler also criticized King's protest of the Vietnam War and felt that his tactics resulted in attracting "retarded, half-witted, criminally-inclined people" in the movement.[76] He concluded the literary rampage with the declaration that continued demonstrations would result in further racial violence. "Dr King, tragically, never learned this. His followers had better."[77]

Shortly after its release, Schuyler received several letters from critics and admirers. Most of his critics were African Americans who were incensed over his remarks. One Chicago reader addressed Schuyler as a "black traitor" and vehemently disagreed with his analysis of King:

> I say because [King] didn't compromise, we sit on the front of Montgomery busses, eat in the best Southern restaurants and vote in every county of America. I ask you Old Man, what had your approaches done for America before King? Perpetuated a system of bowing, humble, "Nigras," happy to be second-class citizens. You ought to write speeches to George Wallace.[78]

Admirers of Schuyler were mostly white conservatives who showered the journalist with accolades and gratitude for his indictment of King. "I cannot help but tell you the words therein had more meaning than anything I have observed, editorially, for years and years," exclaimed one reader from Chicago.[79] One letter from Nashville, Tennessee, declared, "I know there are many Negroes who feel the same as you do, and I truly hope your life will be long and fruitful."[80] Another Chicago reader asked Schuyler the proverbial yet racially patronizing question: "Why can't all Negro people be like you? Then, they would have a man to be proud of and proud to be called an American."[81]

Many letters from admirers were revealing yet paradoxical in their analysis of King and the Civil Rights movement. One minister from Tennessee stated, "If he had the truth of God to preach, he should have rendered unto God as a Minister, the things of God, and not been in the things of Caesar."[82] Another reader acknowledged that all races should have equality but "should not expect things on a silver platter."[83] Lastly, a Nebraska couple shared their views of civil rights: "I think most of the so-called Civil Rights legislation does more harm than good. Most of them build up the hope of Utopia in many Negroes . . . Most of our problems are moral and must be corrected by a change of heart, not by laws."[84]

Schuyler had reached the summit of his ultra-conservative career. Syndicated in several American newspapers and right wing publications, the journalist received the recognition, fame, and attention he desired. In 1968 and 1969, Schuyler received respectively the American Legion Award and the Catholic War Veterans Award.[85] Ironically, Schuyler's professional apex coincided with the most tragic period of his personal life.

His daughter and only child, Philippa, a child prodigy and product of an interracial marriage, was a pianist who became a journalist for the *Union Leader*. Initially, the talented, young, and beautiful journalist shared many of her father's political views throughout her life. However, her views changed when she went to Vietnam in 1966 as a foreign correspondent. Philippa Schuyler reconsidered her views on the Vietnam War and race relations because of three factors: (1) The rough treatment of South Vietnamese civilians by American soldiers; (2) the treatment of African American soldiers by fellow white soldiers and officers; and (3) her own treatment by the American embassy and white American military personnel.[86]

She also began to sympathize with the civil rights movement and condemned her father in her last letter to her mother:

> Now if George, instead of letting himself be segregated all his life, had the guts to go forth into integration and try to thrust his way into white companies and white neighborhoods, he would have found out why the Stokley Carmichaels are necessary now as a pressure valve. I am not going to cravenly accept segregation. Nor will I bring any child up into segregation.[87]

Tragically, the talented journalist did not have the chance to explore her newfound identity. On May 9, 1967, Philippa Duke Schuyler was instantly killed in a helicopter crash that claimed three lives. On a mission rescuing Vietnamese children, Schuyler was on her way back to Da Nang when the helicopter descended rapidly, crashing into Da Nang Bay.[88] Philippa's stunned and grief-stricken parents made the somber preparations for their daughter's funeral. On May 17, she was given an elaborate funeral procession that began in Harlem and ended at St. Patrick's Cathedral, where she was laid to rest.[89]

Philippa's death took a toll on both parents, particularly Schuyler's wife Josephine. Suffering from depression, her health rapidly declined. On May 2, 1969, a few days before the second anniversary of Philippa's death, Schuyler walked into Josephine's bedroom to find his wife hanging in the doorway and a suicide note.[90]

Over a period of approximately two years, George Schuyler had lost his entire family. For the usually stoic journalist, the loss proved to be unbearable. Although he kept busy with his career, he confessed his personal anguish to his new mentor and confidant William Loeb:

> Yes, I truly expected that both Josephine and Philippa would outlive me, and now it is the reverse. But I doubt that I shall be here very long. I have tried to fight the good fight for what I have considered right, but now the long battle has worn me down. It is hard to hold one's head high and to carry on under crushing burdens of responsibility.[91]

It was eight years later, on August 31, 1977, that George Samuel Schuyler joined his family when he passed away at New York Hospital at the age of 82.[92]

Since Schuyler's death, the rise in American conservatism has been complimented with a revival of black conservatism. Schuyler's relevance to contemporary black conservatism is that many of them are echoing the same sentiments he shared years ago. In the 1960s, Schuyler argued that civil rights bills and laws would not end racism but rather only increase it. Today, many black conservatives have echoed Schuyler's declarations, arguing that civil rights and affirmative action have worked to create a racial backlash in whites while creating inferiority in blacks.[93] Similar to Schuyler's association with the right in the 1950s and 1960s, they have been given a pulpit in the media to voice their objections to civil rights and African American protest, greatly increasing their notoriety.

At the same time, Schuyler differs from most black conservatives of today in that his conservative views were formed during the age of Jim Crow, making his conversion more remarkable. Most black conservatives today came of age during the end of the civil rights or post civil rights period. Also, he was closely associated with the civil rights vanguard of the 1920s through the 1940s, whereas most black conservatives of today did not share the same association with comparable civil rights spokespersons.

In the final analysis of George S. Schuyler, one can interpret him in two ways. On a positive note, the political odyssey of Schuyler represents the desire of one voice striving to be different from others, and a declaration that African Americans are not a monolithic intellectual body. The dilemma of Schuyler also forces civil rights activists to vigorously defend and strengthen their own beliefs of militant activism for African Americans.

At the same time, Schuyler's philosophies denote a disturbing characteristic of black conservatism. Motivated by a desire for mainstream, Schuyler analyzed African American issues in a narrow, prejudicial manner: He created a superficial, false picture that often ignored the significance of race in American society. As a result, Schuyler blamed African Americans for their own dilemma rather than indict white supremacy. Despite his own bitter experiences with racism during the Jim Crow era, Schuyler chose to ignore and repress them in the inner depths of his soul. Yet they haunted him throughout his life.

At best, Schuyler's dilemma can be explained by the classic thesis introduced by W. E. B. Du Bois in 1903: "One ever feels his twoness—an American, a Negro; two souls, two thoughts, two unreconciled strivings; two warring ideals in one dark body, whose dogged strength alone keeps it from being torn asunder."[94] Schuyler constantly warred with his twoness, struggling to be part of the American mainstream while trying to resist the call of his African American contemporaries to join the struggle. In the end, Schuyler chose to be American, sacrificing his identity and, eventually, his family.

In summation, Schuyler's life should be viewed as a challenge. Although his philosophies can be easily dismissed as the writings of a bitter, self-hating, caustic individual, they challenge African American society to look at itself and examine its own beliefs. In order to understand the complexity and diversity of African American intellectual history, a study of black conservatism must be taken into consideration. It is hoped that the life of George Samuel Schuyler will be included in future discussions.

NOTES

1. George S. Schuyler, "Views and Reviews: High Court Decision Was No Surprise To Him," *Pittsburgh Courier*, May 29, 1954.
2. George S. Schuyler, "The World Today," *Pittsburgh Courier*, May 29, 1954, p. 4.
3. William Ingersoll, interview with George S. Schuyler, November 6, 1960; cited in "The Reminscences Of George S. Schuyler," Oral History Research Office, Columbia University, 1962, p. 621.
4. George S. Schuyler, *Black and Conservative: The Autobiography of George S. Schuyler* (New Rochelle, NY: Arlington House Publishers, 1966), p. 4.
5. Ibid., pp. 11–12.
6. Although there is no indication that race riots occurred in Syracuse during Schuyler's childhood, there was still racial hostility against African Americans during the early 1900s. An unidentified article from August 10, 1917, states: "The influx of Southern Negroes is becoming serious in Syracuse. While many of them have gone to the larger cities, at least 150 and probably many more located in that city within the last two months. They are looking for work and although laborers are needed, many people will not employ the Negroes because their white laborers quit rather than work with them." (Onondaga Historical Society, Syracuse, New York.)
7. Schuyler, *Black and Conservative*, p.31.
8. "Reminiscences of George S. Schuyler," p. 31.
9. Schuyler, *Black and Conservative*, pp. 89–91.
10. Kathryn Talalay, *Composition in Black And White: The Life Of Philippa Schuyler* (New York: Oxford University Press, 1995), pp. 67–68.
11. Ibid., pp. 113–14.
12. Schuyler, *Black And Conservative*, p. 114
13. Ibid., p. 133.
14. Ibid., pp. 137–39.
15. Edmund David Cronon, *Black Moses: The Story of Marcus Garvey and the Universal Negro Improvement Association* (Madison: the University of Wisconsin Press, 1955, pp. 92–99, 114–15.
16. Theodore Kornweibel, Jr., *No Crystal Stair: Black Life and the Messenger, 1917–1928* (Westport, CT: Greenwood Press, 1975), pp. 140–141.
17. George S. Schuyler, "A Tribute to Caesar," *The Messenger*, July 1925, pp. 225–31.
18. Ibid.
19. George S. Schuyler, "The Negro-Art Hokum," *The Nation*, June 16, 1926, p. 662.
20. Rudolph Von Herald, "The Reaction of The African American Press To Fears of Un-American Activities, 1947–1952" (M.A. thesis, The Ohio State University, 1992), pp. 18–19.
21. Schuyler, *Black and Conservative*, p. 317.
22. George S. Schuyler, "Views and Reviews," *Pittsburgh Courier*, December 10, 1955, p. 11.
23. Ibid.
24. George S. Schuyler, "Views and Reviews," *Pittsburgh Courier*, February 18, 1956, p. 11.
25. George S. Schuyler, "Views and Reviews," *Pittsburgh Courier*, December 14, 1957.
26. George S. Schuyler, "Views and Reviews," *Pittsburgh Courier*, May 25, 1957, p. 9.
27. This was probably a reference to the lynching of Mack Charles Parker, a black man suspected of raping a white woman who was taken out of a Mississippi jail cell and murdered by a mob of white men. The Federal Bureau of Investigation (FBI) sent a team of agents to investigate the murder, but because of the refusal of the Mississippi courts to comply with the investigation, the case was dismissed. See Taylor Branch, *Parting the Waters: America in the King Years, 1954–63* (New York: Simon and Schuster, 1988),

258–59. For a detailed analysis of the Parker lynching, see Howard Smead, *Blood Justice: The Lynching of Mack Charles Parker* (New York: Oxford University Press, 1986).

28. George S. Schuyler, "Views and Reviews," *Pittsburgh Courier*, June 6, 1959; cited in Williams, "When Black Is Right," p. 350.

29. George S. Schuyler, "Views and Reviews," *Pittsburgh Courier*, December 31, 1960.

30. George S. Schuyler, "Views and Reviews," May 30, 1959; cited in C. Eric Lincoln, *The Black Muslims in America* (Boston: Beacon Press, 1961), p. 142.

31. Malcolm X and George Schuyler, excerpts from roundtable discussion "The Black Muslims In America," April 23, 1961; Malcolm X: The Great Debate With James Baldwin and Others, Cassette 161, Paul Winley Records.

32. *Malcolm X.*

33. Roy Wilkins, *Standing Fast: The Autobiography Of Roy Wilkins* (New York: Viking Press, 1982) p. 317

34. George S. Schuyler, "Malcolm X: Better To Memorialize Benedict Arnold," *American Opinion*, February 1973, p.35.

35. Ibid.

36. Ibid., p.36.

37. Letter from William G. Nunn to George S. Schuyler, July 25, 1962, Schuyler Papers-Syracuse University.

38. Letter from George S. Schuyler to William G. Nunn, 27 July, 1962, Schuyler Papers, Syracuse University.

39. Ibid.

40. J. Daniel Mahoney, *Actions Speak Louder* (New Rochelle, New York: Arlington House, 1968), 214; Harry McKinley Williams, Jr., "When Black Is Right: The Life and Writings Of George S. Schuyler," (Ph.D. diss., Brown University), 1988, p.356.

41. Another source of Schuyler's hostility toward Powell may have been the experience he and Roy Wilkins had in Powell Sr.'s Abyssinian Baptist Church in January 1933. Arriving from Mississippi to discuss their investigation of levee workers, hecklers from the Communist Party in Harlem disrupted their presentation and called them fakes and frauds. Even more disheartening, Powell failed to defend Schuyler and Wilkins, sowing the seeds of resentment in the bitter journalist. Will Haygood, *King of The Cats: The Life and Times of Adam Clayton Powell, Jr.* (New York: Houghton Mifflin Company, 1993), pp. 55–56; Wilkins, *Standing Fast*, p.125.

42. Lenneal J. Henderson, Jr., ed., *Black Political Life in the United States* (San Francisco: Chandler Publishing Company, 1972), p. 220.

43. The grand jury concluded that because Powell was armed with a knife and confronted Gilligan, the officer was acting in an official manner and therefore was not liable for the teenager's death. The toll from the riot was 1 person dead, 118 injured, and 465 arrested. See Fred C. Shapiro and James W. Sullivan, *Race Riots: New York, 1964* (New York: Thomas Y. Crowell Company, 1964), pp. 1–2. The District Attorney's report of the grand jury's findings can be found in the Appendix, pp. 209–22.

44. Ibid., p. 16.

45. It is interesting to note that a disclaimer, which had appeared above Schuyler's column years ago reappeared, stating that Schuyler's views were completely separate from the *Courier*. See George S. Schuyler, "Views and Reviews," *Pittsburgh Courier*, August 1, 1964.

46. "Courier Relieves George Schuyler of Title over 'Goldwater Incident,'" *Philadelphia Tribune*, September 22, 1964, p. 6; Claude A. Barnett Papers, Library Of Congress, Washington, D.C.

47. Letter from P. L. Prattis to George S. Schuyler, August 7, 1964, Schuyler Papers Syracuse University.

48. Ibid.

49. Letter from George S. Schuyler to Eleanor A. Lofton,August 13, 1964, Schuyler Papers, Syracuse University.

50. Alabama Governor George Wallace, whose symbolic refusal to allow two African American students to desegregate the University of Alabama in 1963 established him as one of the major opponents of desegregation.

51. "*Courier* Relieves George Schuyler," Schuyler Papers, Syracuse University.

52. Letter from George S. Schuyler to P. L. Prattis, September 11, 1964, Schuyler Papers, Syracuse University.

53. Letter from P. L. Prattis, to George S. Schuyler, November 10, 1964, Schuyler Papers, Syracuse University.

54. Williams, "When Black Is Right," p. 365.

55. H. L. Mencken, typed diary entry, September 24, 1945, H. L. Mencken Papers: quoted in Williams, "When Black Is Right," p. 241.

56. Letter from William Loeb to George S. Schuyler, September 17, 1964, Schuyler Papers, Syracuse University. For a detailed analysis of Loeb's conservatism, see Kevin Richard Cash, *Who in the Hell is William Loeb?* (Hooksett, NH: Amoskeag Press), 1983.

57. Letter from William Loeb to Brady Black, September 17, 1964, Schuyler Papers, Syracuse University.

58. George S. Schuyler, "King No Help to Peace," *Manchester Union Leader,* November 10, 1964, p. 25.

59. Ibid.

60. Letter from William Loeb to George S. Schuyler, November 5, 1964, Schuyler Papers, Syracuse University.

61. Letter from Theodore Lit to George S. Schuyler, November 23, 1964, Schuyler Papers, Syracuse University.

62. Letter from George S. Schuyler to Theodore Lit, December 16, 1964, Schuyler Papers, Syracuse University.

63. Williams, "When Black Is Right," p. 364.

64. John Hope Franklin and Alfred A. Moss, *From Slavery to Freedom: A History of African Americans* (New York: McGraw Hill, 1994), p. 514.

65. George S. Schuyler, Transcript, NANA Article, "Anatomy Of A Black Insurrection," August 18, 1965, Schuyler Papers—Syracuse, p.3.

66. Ibid., pp. 2–3.

67. Ibid., p.6.

68. George S. Schuyler, "Iconoclast," *The Crisis,* October 1965, p. 485.

69. Ibid.

70. Letter from Robert Welch to George S. Schuyler, October 29, 1965, Schuyler Papers, Syracuse University. For more information on Robert Welch and the John Birch Society, see Donald Janson and Bernard Eismann, *The Far Right* (New York: McGraw-Hill, 1963), pp. 25–54.

71. Letter from George S. Schuyler to Robert Welch, November 1, 1965, Schuyler Papers, Syracuse University.

72. Letter from Robert Welch to George S. Schuyler, November 23, 1965; Letter from George S. Schuyler to Robert Welch, November 24, 1965, Schuyler Papers, Syracuse University.

73. Franklin and Moss, *From Slavery To Freedom,* p. 518.

74. George S. Schuyler, transcript of NANA article, "He Reaped the Whirlwind: A Cool and Critical Appraisal of Martin Luther King's Works," April 6, 1968, p. 1, Schuyler Papers, Syracuse University.

75. Ibid., p. 2.

76. Ibid., p. 3.

77. Ibid., p. 4.

78. Letter from Judson C. Mitchell to George S. Schuyler, April 8, 1968, Schuyler Papers, Syracuse University.

79. Letter from Mrs. Edward M. Ray to George S. Schuyler, April 12, 1968, Schuyler Papers, Syracuse University.

80. Letter from U.B. Overton to George S. Schuyler, April 15, 1968, Schuyler Papers, Syracuse University.

81. Letter from Clara Whisenant to George S. Schuyler, April 10, 1968, Schuyler Papers, Syracuse University.

82. Letter From H.V. Massey to George S. Schuyler, April 10, 1968, Schuyler Papers, Syracuse University.

83. Letter from Bernan Loracc to George S. Schuyler, April 12, 1968, Schuyler Papers, Syracuse University.

84. Letter from Mr. and Mrs. Larry Davis to George S. Schuyler, April 8, 1968, Schuyler Papers, Syracuse University.

85. Michael W. Peplow, *George S. Schuyler* (Boston: Twayne Publishers, 1980), pp. 14–15.

86. Talalay, *Composition in Black and White,* p. 273.

87. Letter from Philippa Schuyler to Josephine Schuyler, May 6, 1967; cited in Ibid., p. 274.

88. Ibid., pp. 3–4.

89. Ibid., p 7.

90. Ibid., p. 278; the suicide note is among the George Schuyler Papers, Syracuse University.

91. Letter from George Schuyler to William Loeb, May 5, 1969; cited in Talalay, *Composition in Black and White,* p. 278.

92. Hollie I. West, "George S. Schuyler, Writer, Satirist On Race Problems," *Washington Post,* September 9, 1977.

93. See Shelby Steele, *The Content of Our Character: A New Vision Of Race in America,* (New York: St. Martin's Press, 1990).

94. W. E. B. Du Bois, *The Souls of Black Folk;* cited in *Three Negro Classics,* p. 215.

CHAPTER 10

NEOCONSERVATIVES, BLACK CONSERVATIVES, AND THE RETREAT FROM SOCIAL JUSTICE

FRANK HAROLD WILSON

In *The Crisis of the Negro Intellectual* (1967), Harold Cruse described the dualism in challenges confronting black intellectuals. Cruse noted that black intellectuals were expected to be acutely attuned to the white power structure, its cultural institutions, and larger dynamics of economics, politics, and social class in order to control or affect them. At the same time, these black intellectuals were challenged to define and negotiate a role that would combine cultural and political criticism and include programs and demands.[1] Cruse recognized that the institutional resources supportive of black intellectuals existed outside the black community and that these resources constrained black intellectuals to play a narrower role. Cruse's critique of black intellectuals focused on their uncritical embracing of liberalism and integration.

In the past few decades, the emergence of black conservative intellectuals and celebrities has grown out of institutional changes in the economy, the government, technology, and mass communications which have been accompanied by the growth and mobilization of conservative institutions, politics, and social movements. Although conservative-right social movements and politics have always been a part of the American experience alongside liberal-left social movements and politics, these recent developments are historically specific and unprecedented. Conservative institutions, foundations, organizations, networks of organizations, political actors, celebrities, and constituencies have developed and mobilized in response to changing institutional contradictions and social-class conflicts that are frequently articulated in the politics of race, privilege, resentment, and the new inequality.

Black conservative intellectuals provide an illustration of these continuing structural, social-class, and cultural contradictions. Although they have partly heeded Cruse's challenge and provided critiques of liberalism and integration, the intellectual roles that they have negotiated are largely constrained, dependent, and narrow with respect to cultural and political criticism, and their analyses are characterized by a retreat from social justice.

The title of this chapter, "NeoConservatives, Black Conservatives, and the Retreat from Social Justice" describes an attempt to contextualize and critically appraise black conservative intellectuals. Progressive and independent intellectuals have underestimated the role of conservative theorists, and particularly neoconservative intellectuals, who have been the most important links in connecting conservative analyses, opinions, and public-policy perspectives with journals and the academy. Simultaneously, the contributions of black conservative celebrities, who are important symbols in popular culture, have been seriously underestimated.

In this chapter, the emergence and growth of the contemporary black conservative intellectuals are viewed as having derived from the larger neoconservative and conservative movements. Whereas black conservatives depend on larger conservative institutions and structures, black conservative intellectuals have struggled for independence and freedom. In this effort, I will be addressing several concerns. First, who are these neoconservatives, and what is their vision of American society? What are the principles, beliefs, and assumptions that underlie this vision? How has the growth of conservative institutions and structures contributed to this phenomenon? Second, what is the role of black conservatives in recent intellectual controversies. In particular, what are their perspectives of individualism, self-reliance, and social structure? Third, what are the possibilities and limitations of these black conservative social analyses with respect to social justice questions and African Americans? My interests in black conservatives is only part of a continuing interest in the history of sociology in general and black intellectual history specifically.

NEOCONSERVATIVES AND CONSERVATIVES

Neoconservatives were early defined by Michael Harrington as "those who came to their position from a liberal or socialist background, after being disillusioned of their Great Society dreams."[2] Jurgen Habermas defined neoconservatism as "a movement dedicated to supporting capitalism and the democratic rule of elites."[3] Gary Dorrien expanded on these definitions to define neoconservatism as "an intellectual movement originated by former leftists that promotes militant anticommunism, capitalist economics, a minimal welfare-state, the rule of traditional elites, and a return to traditional cultural values."[4] Neoconservatism has its roots in the anti-Stalinist Marxism (Trotskyists) of New York intellectuals during the late 1930s.[5]

Neoconservatives may be partly defined by their publications, which address culture, politics, economics, history, and other concerns. These publications reflect intersecting foundations, think tanks, organizations, and social networks. The most important include *Commentary, The Public Interest, The New Leader, The American Spectator, The American Scholar, The American Enterprise, Public Opinion,* and *Society.* Neoconservatives control or significantly influence corporate-funded policy centers such as the Manhattan Institute, the Institute for the Study of Economic Culture, the Institute for Contemporary Studies, the Institute on Religion and Public Life, the American Enterprise Institute, the Ethics and Public-policy Center, the Center for Strategic and International Studies, the National Forum Foundation, and the Center for Security Policy.[6] Among them, the most important is the American Enterprise Institute, which was established to promote free-market economics in opposition to the New Deal.

The intellectual actors and celebrities of neoconservatism partly define this move-ment. Included in most discussions are Irving Kristol, Norman Podhoretz, and Michael Novack. Kristol, a former professor at New York University who is some-times referred to as the "godfather" of neoconservatism, founded the *Public Interest* and frequently contributes to the *Wall Street Journal*. Included in this movement were Edward Banfield, James Q. Wilson, Seymour Martin Lipset, and Lewis Feuer. During the 1970s, at least three leading sociologists were included in most discussions of neo-conservatives: Daniel Patrick Moynihan, Daniel Bell, and Nathan Glazer. Moynihan has since moved toward the center and liberal-left, Bell has continually repudiated any association with the neoconservatives, and Glazer has held firm. More recently, sociologist Peter Berger is discussed at length in the book by Dorrien.

The neoconservative movement may also be defined by its institutions and foun-dations. The leading foundations, which are called the "four sisters," include the John M. Olin Foundation (Olin chemical and munitions), the Smith Richardson Foundation (Vicks Vaporub and Smith Brothers Cough Drops), the Sarah Mellon Scaife Foundation (Mellon Industrial Oil and Banking), and the Lynde and Harry Bradley Foundation (Bradley automation equipment).[7] Other important foundations include the Adolph Coors Foundation, the Noble Foundation, the David Koch and Charles Koch Foundation, the Bechtel Foundation, the Lilly Endowment, the Howard Pew Freedom Trust, and the Annie Casey Foundation.[8] The major think tanks funded through these foundations include the Heritage Foundation, the Amer-ican Enterprise Institute for Public-policy Research, the Free Congress Research and Education Foundation, the Madison Center for Educational Affairs, the Philan-thropy Roundtable, the National Association of Scholars, the Hudson Institute, the Heartland Institute, the Manhattan Institute for Policy Research, and the Wisconsin Policy Research Institute.[9]

One of the leading conservative foundations, the Bradley Foundation, is based in Milwaukee.[10] The Bradley Foundation is sponsored by the Allen Bradley Company, a manufacturer of electronic and radio components and was incorporated in 1942 as a nonprofit devoted to strengthening American democratic capitalism and its insti-tutions. Since Allen Bradley was bought by Rockwell International in 1985, a large part of the proceeds have gone to the Bradley Foundation, with assets growing from less than $14 million (1985) to $461 million in 1995. The Bradley Foundation has been a principal funder of think tanks such as the Heritage Foundation, the Ameri-can Enterprise Institute, the Hudson Institute, the Manhattan Institute, and the Na-tional Association of Scholars. It is instructive that the Bradley Foundation helped underwrite Charles Murray's *Losing Ground* and *The Bell Curve*. The Bradley Foun-dation has also underwritten important research and demonstration programs related to the anti affirmative action policy in California, the welfare reform initiatives in Wisconsin, school choice voucher alternatives to public schools, and the like.[11]

Neoconservatives are usually distinguished from conservatives on the basis of their minimal support for welfare-state policies. In contrast, conservatives tend to be unequivocal in their call for dismantling the welfare state. Conservative theorists, po-litical actors, and celebrities were more visible than neoconservatives during the Ronald Reagan revolution. Leading actors of the conservative New Right during the 1980s included Richard Viguerie, Paul Weyrich, Howard Phillips (Conservative Cau-cus), John T. Dolan (National Conservative Political Action Committee), Reverend Jerry Falwell (Moral Majority), Jesse Helms (founder of the Congressional Club), and

Phyllis Schlafly (Eagle Forum). Among the conservative intellectuals, William F. Buckley, George Will, George Gilder, Charles Murray, Lawrence Meade, and Dinesh D'Souza were particularly visible during the 1980s. In the 1990s, Newt Gingrich, Oliver North, Rush Limbaugh, and G. Gordon Liddy were important celebrities.

Neoconservatives are made up disproportionately of academics, and most appear to be social scientists. By contrast, most conservatives are generally hostile to the social sciences, and particularly sociology. Neoconservatives as intellectuals are often generalists, whereas many of the conservative activists are focused on single-issue moral crusades and critical of secular humanism. Both neoconservatives and conservatives converge on issues of free-market capitalism, the elimination of the welfare policies, and the introduction of workfare.

More recently, neoconservatives have moved closer to the right in politics. Earlier recognitions of a limited welfare-state in the 1970s and 1980s have been recently characterized by increased acquiescence in social injustice. Recent publications such as Richard Herrnstein and Charles Murray's *The Bell Curve* and Dinesh D'Souza's *The End of Racism* signal a theater of the absurd in discussions of racial injustice.

THE SOCIOLOGY OF NEOCONSERVATIVES

Built into neoconservatism is an implicit sociology of modern American society. According to Steinfels, neoconservatives advance an analysis of American society that is based on several important principles, beliefs, and assumptions and committed to political change. A major part of the neoconservative analysis and prescription focuses on a critique of post–World War II policies addressing inequality. Although neoconservatives are not necessarily hostile to the welfare state (in fact, many are comfortable with New Deal reforms), they are most critical of the Great Society reforms of the 1960s. The Great Society was repudiated for creating a new class of bureaucrats and social workers. These neoconservatives, who claimed to be "true liberals," were particularly critical of the transformation of civil rights into black power and the growth of black nationalism.[12] Three main domain assumptions or beliefs underscore this sociology.

First, neoconservatives hold that a crisis of authority has overtaken America and the West generally. To the extent that governing institutions have lost their legitimacy, the confidence of leading elites has been undermined. Social stability and the legacy of liberal civilization are threatened. A continuing concern with the question of stability is expressed in "crisis" discourses both written and spoken.[13]

Second, neoconservatives view the current crisis as primarily a cultural crisis of values, morals, and manners. Although neoconservatives concede that this crisis has causes and consequences that are institutional and socioeconomic, what is particularly problematic is that "our convictions have gone slack, our morals gone loose, and our morals have become corrupt."[14] Behind this crisis of authority is an adversary and nihilistic culture that is the ruling spirit of a "new class" of professionals, technicians, and bureaucrats.[15]

Third, neoconservatives view the government as excessively democratic and use the metaphor of "overload" to describe the breakdown of traditional means of control, the delegitimation of political and other forms of authority, and the unrestrained pressures and demands of citizens. Because the government has attempted to do too much, it has failed and undermined its own authority.[16] This "overload" is derived from liberal attitudes of the "New Society" (which are optimistic, socially sensitive, confident, and naive), the emergence of an urban underclass that has been so deeply deprived, unemployable, and alien to middle class norms that it threatens the entire society,[17] and the Western demand for ever-increasing equality of social and economic condition. This new demand for equality is to be distinguished from simple legal and political equality or traditional equality of opportunity.[18]

Neoconservatives advance several political prescriptions of how society should be reorganized to meet their visions. They prescribe that authority must be reasserted and government protected at the levels of the government, the public, and ruling elites.[19] At the level of government, governmental reforms are advocated that will foresee, forestall, or relieve destabilizing social tensions. Because increased demands on the New Deal welfare state might increase aspirations of egalitarianism and lead to a crisis, the previous authority and responsibility of the federal government should be dispersed to state and local governments.

The marketplace is increasingly seen as a most likely source of progressive social change.[20] At the level of the public, neoconservatives expect a lowering of the public's expectations. Despite its rhetoric and pronouncements to the contrary, neoconservativism, like conservatism, is an elite rather than a popular movement. It offers intellectual rationalizations for "hard decisions" and "tough-minded" measures and offers an analysis of the burdens of lowered expectations and how they are distributed. An important target of these political changes is the "New Class" of decision-making elites, which must be tamed.[21]

The neoconservative critique has become part of the conventional wisdom because of its resonance with the dominant American cultural belief system, public opinion, and conservative political administrations. The historical and social science evidence indicates that this analysis is partial, ideological, and problematic. As Michael Harrington has correctly noted, the failures of the welfare state are due more to its conservatism than to excessive liberalism or radicalism. He indicates further that the American welfare state, among advanced industrial nations, is the most conservative and antistatist, with smaller percentages of the gross national product spent on social programs.[22]

One of the more important sociological analyses by a neoconservative sociologist is that of Peter Berger, a former professor at Rutgers University. In the early 1970s, Berger was best known for *The Social Construction of Reality* which he co-authored with Thomas Luckmann.[23] This classic in the sociology of knowledge was followed by numerous other books on religion, modernization, and democracy. By the late 1970s, Berger had appropriated the concept of empowerment from the left and found within the role of mediating structures one of the most seminal projects for neoconservatives.[24]

Berger would articulate these mediating structures as private, voluntary organizations such as families, churches, schools, and unions, and charitable organizations which provide meaning, sustenance, and support to individuals outside of government.[25] Although these groups start locally, they nurture the qualities that are necessary for participation in larger communities, ultimately ending in the state and civil society.[26]

Currently a university professor of sociology at Boston University, Berger provides an analysis of conservative humanism which grows out a dialectic of humanity and society. In this undertaking, he recognizes the role of society in making humans and that of humans in the making of society. This social construction follows a three-step process: (1) externalization—an outpouring of human and physical energies into the world; (2) objectification—when the products of human physical and mental efforts attained a reality that confronted its creators as facility outside themselves); and (3) internalization—when objective reality was subjectively reappropriated by human agents, transforming it once again from structures of the objective world into structures of the subjective consciousness.

As a conservative humanist, Berger is both irreverent toward existing institutions and skeptical toward most efforts to change society. According to Berger, sociologists must be aware of what Max Weber called the "law of unintended consequences of social action"; that is, social crusades of any kind, no matter how well meaning, nearly always produced a greater mess than the one that they addressed.[27]

It is instructive that Berger criticized the new left of the anti–Vietnam War movement as being essentially anti-intellectual, antiliberal, and a variation of fascism. He opposed the Vietnam War on the basis of humanistic reasons such as compassion for the victims as distinct from the anti-imperialistic objectives of the left. Berger's conservative humanism would urge conservatives to accept and preserve the basic status quo of American society as a "practical political goal" while refusing to glorify these structures or embrace liberal ideology.[28]

THE RISE OF THE NEW BLACK CONSERVATIVE INTELLECTUALS, COMMENTATORS, AND CELEBRITIES

Black conservatism has been a tradition within business, education, political and literary circles. More than fifty years ago in an essay titled "Patterns of Negro Leadership," sociologist Oliver Cox noted that "the conservative leader never makes a direct protest, and he always avoids the common cause of Negroes."[29] Cox emphasized that these leaders were expected to counter the criticisms and attacks of black and white protest leaders. The rhetorical strategies of conservatives were instructive. While expecting material benefits for themselves and their people, conservatives never demand these benefits as rights. Black conservatives, according to Cox, were careful not to offend the ruling class and, when complaints are necessary, these complaints are made philosophically to the self-interests of the ruling class.

With respect to the political aspirations of blacks, Cox indicated that "conservative political leaders make an artificial disassociation of politics from economics and then conclude that the latter outweighs the former in importance." Politically, the conservative views the friendship of those in power as the dominant wish and aim of black people, and to insist on political, economic, and social issues that might offend these persons is to be avoided.[30] With respect to discrimination, the conservative must minimize it or explain it away. To the extent that Blacks experience oppression, the burden of blame is made their own responsibility. Cox identified this intellectual strategy particularly with black business leaders and school administrators such as Booker T. Washington, W. H. Council, and Joseph W. Holley. However, Cox's characterizations did not anticipate the conservative black intellectual movements following the civil rights movement.

The emergence, growth, and visibility of the new black conservatives have accompanied the conservative movements of the post civil rights years and, in particular, the Reagan revolution of the 1980s. Although there are fundamental similarities to the black conservatives described by Cox, there are also considerable differentiation. Manning Marable identified at least four categories of black conservatives during the Reagan era: conservative black politicians (who were subordinates of the Rockefeller liberal wing of the party such as Arthur Fletcher, Samuel Pierce, and William Coleman and more recent appointees such as Melvin Bradley and Thadeus Garrett); black corporate executives, business managers, and Reagan administration appointees; former black power activists and nationalists who became closely aligned but did not fully embrace Reaganism (Tony Brown); and the philosophical conservatives (Thomas Sowell, Walter Williams, Glenn Loury).[31]

Although describing the philosophical conservatives as problematic, Marable predicted that the black corporate executives and bureaucrats were potentially more dangerous because they had no ideological commitment to civil rights or affirmative action. These black conservatives were seen as more opportunistic in that their support for conservative policies was rooted in increased power and profits.[32] The black conservatives who are the focus of this essay are primarily represented by the conservative intellectuals (philosophical conservatives) and secondarily by corporate executives, business managers, and administrative appointees.

The distinguishing characteristics of the new black conservative intellectuals derive in part from their alliances with conservative and neoconservative institutions, foundations, and publications. In some instances, they have developed separate institutions and agencies such as the Center for New Black Leadership, the Center of the American Experiment, the National Center for Neighborhood Enterprise, the David Institute, the Lincoln Institute, and the Black Alternatives Association, Incorporated. Although most of these persons grew up in the era of the civil rights movement and the Great Society programs, most have acquired perspectives that are independent and critical of these programs. The social backgrounds and social mobility of these intellectuals did not differ from those of their generation who have become part of the post–World War II black middle class. Strong principles of self-reliance, individualism, and independence enter their interpretations of social reality. However, pessimism, cynicism, and opportunism are frequently their means of observation and actualization. At the same time, these intellectuals are both alienated and isolated from the mainstream black society and public opinion that they have attempted to influence.

Most of these black conservative intellectuals are academics. Black conservatives have carried the criticisms of conservatives and neoconservatives into discussions of economics, the state, culture, and civil rights. They are particularly visible in debates concerning unemployment, poverty, welfare, and the underclass. Furthermore, black conservatives offer radically different conceptualizations of American institutions and race. Among the most visible are three economists, Thomas Sowell, Walter Williams, and Glenn Loury, as well as a neighborhood activist (Robert Woodson) and an English professor (Shelby Steele).[33] The most visible administrative appointees include Clarence Pendleton, former director of the U.S. Civil Rights Commission and Ward Connerly of the University of California Board of Regents. Radio and television talk show "infotainment" have been the medium for personalities such as Armstrong Williams and Larry Elder. Roy Innis, former national director of the Congress of Racial Equality (CORE) during the late 1960s, has been occasionally visible on talk shows. The most enduring symbol of black conservatism is probably Clarence Thomas, the Supreme Court justice. There has been an important convergence between black conservatives and more centrist and liberal voices.

Compared with mainstream black leaders and intellectuals, black conservative intellectuals offer radically different assessments of the social and economic conditions of African Americans and the question of race in America. Publicly, they share the civil rights movement's goals of eradicating racial discrimination and improving the quality of life for blacks. Black conservatives emphasize that their differences are not with goals of freedom, justice, and equality, but they are opposed to the reliance of mainstream civil rights leaders on government programs.

Closer inspection reveals that the Black conservatives embracing of the civil rights movement's goals is more symbolic and rhetorical. They are much more accommodationist and conciliatory than are traditional conservative and liberal leaders. Alongside their philosophical similarities and organizational relations with conservatives and neoconservatives, they are united in perspectives and world views that signify a retreat from racial justice. For purposes of illustrating these perspectives, this examination focuses on Thomas Sowell, Glenn Loury, Robert Woodson, and Shelby Steele as exemplars of black conservative intellectuals.

BLACK ECONOMISTS AS SOCIAL COMMENTATORS

Among the black conservative intellectuals, economists would play a central role in formulating their perspectives. These economists offered critiques of liberal pragmatism and Keynesian economics that extended to the social reforms attempted by the civil rights movement. Their affirmations of American society grew out of conservative economic theories of the marketplace and social ethics.

THOMAS SOWELL AND THE BLACK CONSERVATIVE ALTERNATIVES

Thomas Sowell is an economist and social commentator at Stanford University and a senior fellow at the Hoover Institute on War, Revolution, and Peace. Sowell briefly attended Howard University, graduated magna cum laude from Harvard University (where he wrote his senior honors thesis on Karl Marx),[34] and earned his doctorate in economics at the University of Chicago, where he was intellectually influenced by Milton Friedman and George Stigler.[35] Sowell's early teaching experiences at Cornell University during the late 1960s were problematic and alienating. He viewed both the black militant students and the white liberal faculty and administrators as problematic and excessive. Consequently, Sowell became critical of black studies and the post–civil rights attempts to bring ghetto blacks to universities.[36]

In the 1970s, Sowell was a frequent critic of busing and affirmative action. By 1980, he organized the Black Alternatives Conference and served on President Ronald Reagan's Economic Policy Advisory Board.[37] Behind Sowell's social analysis is a person who began with humble beginnings in North Carolina and grew up in Harlem, New York. This biography includes family economic difficulties that required him to drop out of high school in tenth grade, enter military service, and begin college as a night school student. Partly from this background, Sowell derived a social vision based on self-reliance (or individualism) and supraindividual mediating structures such as the family, church, schools, social clubs, and neighborhoods.

In much of his writings, Sowell advances a human-capital theory of social structure and social change.[38] The family is the key mediating structure in the development of self (and self reliance) and is communally nested.[39] As such, this self reliance is not individually or "bootstrap generated" but rather derived from social forces. Other social forces, such as a centralized government, the government and academic elites, and centralized public policies are problematic. The central place of human capital and self-reliance explains Sowell's resistance to governmentally implemented policies of civil rights.[40]

Sowell's scholarship combines both normative and empirical analyses. It is instructive that his recent writings are almost exclusively focused on race and sociology rather than the complex mathematical models that characterize mainstream economics. In Sowell's alternative analysis, he emphasizes that the human and cultural capital between ethnic groups, not discrimination, historically affect income differences. It critiques the "victimization hypothesis" (which transfers the burden of responsibility from the "oppressing class" to individual members of the "victimized class"), the black civil rights leadership devaluation of self help, and the excessive reliance on black political empowerment.

GLENN LOURY AND THE NEW BLACK LEADERSHIP

Another proponent of the black conservative alternative is the economist Glenn C. Loury. Loury was a mathematics major as an undergraduate and completed his doctorate in economics at Northwestern University. Loury has taught at the University of Michigan and at Harvard University and is currently at Boston University. Loury's biography is one of mobility from the Chicago ghetto to the ivory tower. An important part of this rapid mobility has been his relations with the American Enterprise Institute and the Heritage Foundation.

Loury is appreciative of the role of free enterprise and limited government intervention and is preoccupied with preserving the American tradition of self-help. For Loury, self-help has been uniquely tied to conservative political philosophy and the history of African American achievement more than to pragmatism.[41] The possibilities of democratic capitalism and socioeconomic mobility are best manifested in the growth of the black middle class. Of particular concern in many of his earlier writings is a moral concern for the black poor. Yet Loury has also been critical of liberal and neoconservative analyses that make use of the historic victimization of blacks in the service of their own cultural critique of "bourgeois America." He notes that these liberal scholars are not so much concerned with the challenges facing American blacks, especially poor ones, as with establishing the necessity of their political agenda.[42]

Loury sees limits in the law and social justice in addressing racial discrimination. He does not appeal to social justice in his analyses, because he believes that justice no longer demands that government introduce any reforms to benefit blacks.[43] Although such justice once existed (the civil rights legislation of the past), it no longer does and we consequently live in a "post civil rights era."[44] Even though past justice inflicted serious injuries on blacks and present-day blacks still suffer from the evil effects of these injuries, compensatory justice can do little to bring blacks to the condition that they would have enjoyed had they not been injured.

In Loury's analysis, because the liberal political heritage provides legal protection of various freedoms, any further governmental reforms to benefit blacks is likely to

violate these freedoms. Built into his analysis is a zero-sum analysis of the relation between equality and liberty, with the latter weighing more strongly. For Loury, not only
does compensatory justice have limits, but these limits no longer require governmental reforms for the benefit of blacks. While acknowledging that the history of
racial discrimination accounts for an important part of the current socioeconomic
differences between blacks and whites and the black underclass, Loury advances the
notion that fault and responsibility are separable.[45] The responsibility for overcoming
these injuries falls on blacks not whites. In this analysis, corporate liberalism is anathema, and individual liberalism is sacred. By implication, people have only those oblig-
ations that they have created for themselves by voluntary actions.

The dilemmas facing Loury as a black conservative surfaced clearly after the publication of Dinesh D'Souza's *The End of Racism* when Loury resigned from the board
of the American Enterprise Institute. In an article in *Common Quest*, Loury began to
come to grips with the dilemmas growing out of the ideas held by neoconservative intellectuals and expressed in journals such as *Commentary*, *The Public Interest*, and *The
New Republic*, in which he developed his independent critical analysis free from pressures to conform to the civil rights orthodoxy.[46]

The new black leadership, according to Loury, seeks to encourage individual initiative, personal responsibility, and traditional solutions to social and economic problems in the black community.

ROBERT WOODSON AND THE NATIONAL
CENTER FOR NEIGHBORHOOD ENTERPRISE

Robert Woodson is founder and president of the National Center for Neighborhood
Enterprise and the former director of the National Urban League's Administration of
Justice Division. Woodson's biography is one of a high-school dropout who earned his
high-school equivalency degree in the air force. Working at night in a juvenile deten-
tion center to help pay his way through college, he eventually received a full scholarship to earn a masters degree in social work at the University of Pennsylvania.[47]

The National Center for Neighborhood Enterprise has been described as "the
most successful pro-free enterprise grass roots organization dedicated to solving Black
and urban problems."[48] The National Center "is a non-profit research and demonstration organization dedicated to assisting low-income Americans in developing and
implementing solutions to the problems of their communities." [49]

Woodson is also chairman of the National Leadership Task Force on Grass Roots
Alternatives for Public policy.[50] This task force produced a report titled, "Grass Roots
Alternatives for Public Policy (GAPP) Report—Bridging the Gap—Strategies to
Prompt Self-Sufficiency among Low-Income Americans." [51] The larger economic and
geographic goal behind the report is the enterprise zone, which, in principle, brings
in businesses free of excessive government regulations. At the same time, it encourages the recruitment of subsidized or free workers who are part of the welfare-reform
programs, and it establishes community-based service providers (who are deregulated
and need not be trained, educated, certified, or inspected). The report recommended
that federal money intended to help the poor should bypass both state and local government and go directly to community-based organizations. Deregulation is recommended with respect to federally assisted housing programs and the right of
construction companies to hire at less than union wages.

Woodson has several problems with the civil rights leadership, which he sees as out of touch with black people. With respect to racism, these black leaders are seen as using race as an excuse for not forthrightly addressing the needs of poor blacks. Civil rights leaders and black politicians are cited by Woodson for "using affirmative action to pad their pockets and then pull out their civil-rights credit card and plead race when they get caught."[52] For Woodson, racism cannot be a controlling factor in the lives of black Americans, and some of the evidence of white racism is not valid. He views criticisms of black leadership as affirming a common humanity rather than racial betrayal. Black unity and racial pride are behind his belief that "black people can think for themselves and manage their own affairs."[53] To him, a social policy that insists that "black people need to be 'rescued by outsiders' borders on bigotry and is historically naive."[54] To Woodson, the extent to which neighborhoods deal with their problems is related to ethnic, racial, and class identity. Policymakers need to build on the strengths of these social and cultural dynamics of neighborhood.

Woodson's neighborhood programs are theoretically informed by the intermediating structural theories of the sociologist Peter Berger. Woodson notes that Berger believed that intermediary institutions such as neighborhood groups, families, ethnic subgroups play a critical role that has been overlooked in our public policy and I provided empirical support for his theories.[55] The most important units of care and responsibility are family, friends, neighbors, associations connect inner city residents into communities which are viewed as more effective in administering distributive programs than big government.[56] Unlike Berger, Woodson's intermediary institutions do not appear to include unions or public schools.

SHELBY STEELE AND "THE CONTENT OF OUR CHARACTER"

Shelby Steele is a professor of English at San Jose State University. Steele's conservative analyses of race are based on highly personal and intuitive observations. These analyses are presented in his critically acclaimed *The Content of Our Character*. What is problematic for Steele? Steele argues that many blacks, particularly in the black middle class, exaggerate the current role of racism as a cause of black failure. In Steele's analysis, these exaggerations are not traceable to macrosociological economic or cultural sources but rather are reduced and decontextualized to psychological traits. Although these psychological problems are the legacy of past discrimination, they cannot be explained by current discrimination because discrimination has declined.

A vicious cycle of internalized victimization has, both morally and psychologically, constrained blacks' human potential. In particular, Steele sees three main problems among blacks: (1) racial anxiety makes blacks afraid to try, because trying involves the possibility of failure and failure is a confirmation of racial inferiority; (2) racial vulnerability makes blacks doubt their abilities and achievements and makes them apprehensive that they are inferior; and (3) many blacks see themselves as the victims of racial injustice. Furthermore, Steele believes that "memories and imagined memories of racial oppression [are the factor] that sustains and feeds the psychological problems that hamstring middle class blacks and explain their faltering advance."[57] These marks of oppression persist because they are functional and reinforcing for those who feel oppressed. For Steele, "when blacks choose to believe in their inferiority," they gain "the comforts and rationalizations

[that] their racial inferiority" affords them. Thus, when blacks insist on seeing themselves as victims, they are spared guilt and responsibility for their condition and acquire a sense of authority and power.[58]

In Steele's analysis, "one of the greatest problems blacks currently face—one of the greatest barriers to our development in society—is that our memory of oppression has such power, magnitude, depth, and nuance that it constantly drains our best resources into more defense than is strictly necessary."[59] While acknowledging that the real enemy has not disappeared, he cautions that the irresistible lure of the past for Blacks can render opportunities in the present all but invisible.[60]

For Steele, other problems exist among African Americans, in their excessive focus on collective action at the expense of individual development and responsibility."[61] There is a theory of the heroic and rebellious individual who is both isolated and integrated in his or her idealized role of the intellectual.

A CRITICAL APPRAISAL OF BLACK CONSERVATIVES

The emergence and increased visibility of the Black conservative intellectuals have accompanied macrosociological changes in the economy, the government, technology, and mass communications. In this larger context there has been a growth and mobilization of conservative institutions, politics, and social movements. Within the conservative social movements, a neoconservative intellectual movement made up largely of former liberals has been the primary source of criticism of post–World War II civil rights and of rationalizations for the retreat from social justice.

The black conservative intellectuals have reflected and reproduced these neoconservative analyses, adding to them a "black spin." The new black conservatives provide both possibilities and limitations in their social analysis, programs, and policy prescriptions. However, the limitations appear to heavily outweigh the possibilities.

The possibilities for black conservatives are found in their provision of a new and more accurate understanding of what constitutes conservatism in the black experience; at the same time, they have raised important questions and criticisms of liberalism. First, they advance, both theoretically and programmatically, a commitment to capitalism as an economic system and the possibilities of black participation. The commitment to capitalism as an economic system is increasingly seen as being stronger in black communities than is a commitment to those who seek its overthrow and destruction. Although political conservatism is usually rejected in the black community, moral conservatism has a resonance that transcends several features of black institutional and organized life.

Second, black conservatives advance a coalition with conservative white business leaders, political leaders, and, on occasion, black community leaders. This coalition includes, not the largest and most established multinational corporations, but rather smaller, more domestically and regionally based corporations. Their perspectives on economics and politics are more regional and local (and the national and international framing of issues including race are avoided). Black conservatives view as inadequate the liberal coalitions among blacks, other minorities, labor, white women, and the "rainbow coalition." Liberal coalitions are not seen as empowering blacks and strengthening local intermediary institutions such as the church and family.

Third, to the extent that black conservatives have raised questions of culture and human agency (responsibility), they challenge sociological analyses to make use of more reflexive analyses of social issues, which move beyond oversocialized, structurally deterministic, and victimization conceptions. Sociologists who have been susceptible to structuralist assumptions are challenged to increasingly bring culture "back in" to discourses and analyses. This does not suggest that conservative emphases on values and choice are the appropriate starting point. In fact, conservative perspectives of culture are usually decontextualized from historic and sociological contexts.

Fourth, in advancing critiques of civil rights and affirmative action, black conservative intellectuals have challenged progressive and independent scholars to reexamine the civil rights era and its policy reforms and to develop a more adequate analysis, synthesis, and resolution. They will need to focus, not only on the constraints of conservative resistance, but also on other constraints, such as those involving liberal support and allies.

The increased visibility of black conservatives in the mainstream media, including black newspapers, has meant that these perspectives have gained in familiarity and legitimacy. Black conservatives' opinions and analyses appear frequently in magazines such as *Forbes, Harper's, The New Republic,* and *Reader's Digest.* The appropriation of several of their analyses and arguments by black intellectuals, who are more liberal and progressive, suggests that these black conservatives have at least captured the symbolic and moral higher ground. There is a convergence in some of their ideas with a longer conservative tradition stemming from Booker T. Washington, which is exemplified in more respected bourgeois- and cultural-nationalism positions such as those of John Johnson, Tony Brown, Sybil Mobley, and the Nation of Islam.

Conservative celebrities and pundits—most notably the late Clarence Pendleton, former chair of the U.S. Civil Rights Commission—have introduced "down home" barbershop debate and logic into public-policy discourses. "Barbershop debate," which usually places a premium on long-windedness, rhythm, cleverness, and the use of a single focus, moves beyond parliamentary and legal forms of discourse. These debate forms have been picked up in television and radio talk-show programs.

The limitations of these black conservative intellectual productions may be analyzed normatively, empirically, and programmatically. These limitations grow out of how they have accounted for institutional contradictions of post industrial capitalism, their explanations of changing social class and interracial struggles, and how they have connected and resolved their biographical and interpersonal troubles in public controversies.

In normative terms, in their analyses these black conservatives retreat significantly from the long tradition of the black struggle for social justice. Although most black conservative intellectuals recognize the historic effects of racial oppression and discrimination on blacks and some recognize the persisting effects of race, these issues are not to be raised forthrightly. A historicist discourse of these issues recognizes the prominence of race in the past (or near past) but suggests that race currently has less bearing or none at all. The persistence of race may be taken as a given, to the extent that they have conceded the impracticality of addressing race-specific issues or the principle that race has no place in a color-blind society in which the prescription is confused with the objective social fact. To the extent that these black conservatives have addressed normative questions of race, the attempt is to put the problem behind us.

In *Blacks and Social Justice* Bernard Boxill argued that these black conservative intellectuals essentially surrender to injustice. Through their arguments of the divisive effects of racial equality through affirmative action and busing, as well as their critiques of minimum-wage legislation, these black conservatives rationalize the deregulation of civil rights and progressive labor policy.[62]

Cornell West, in "Unmasking the Black Conservatives," indicated that black conservative intellectuals are correct in identifying the moral breakdown of the society but incorrect blaming the victims instead of the perpetrators. In supporting the dismantling of affirmative action and social programs for the poor, West saw black conservatives as offering unacceptable and less adequate remedies.[63]

In empirical terms, the evidence used by black economic conservatives is only partly based on social science. Black conservatives usually have advanced their points through anecdotes, illustrations, correlational arguments, and the selective use of history. When providing empirical evidence, these are usually delimited to micro economics. Human capital, more so than institutional economics, becomes the main prism for analysis.

Thomas Boston, in *Race, Class, and Conservatism* (1988), critiques the theory, historical evidence, and empirical research behind the work of the black neoconservative economists.[64] At great length, he debunks the conservative conventional wisdom that "everything but discrimination" explains the wage, employment, and occupational differentials between blacks and whites. These conservative propositions are particularly evident in the work of Thomas Sowell and Walter Williams. These propositions are as follows: First, racial differences are not a function of discrimination but rather are due to the inability of researchers to adequately control other human capital and demographic variables, such as age, geography, education, and job experience. Second, in competitive markets, it is theoretically impossible to have racial wage differences without their being due to individual job-related characteristics, and systematic errors (including racial hiring preferences) cannot continue over the long run. Third, ethnic groups having the same color as blacks have succeeded in ways that blacks have not, suggesting that culture rather than race is the important factor (for conservatives, further evidence is found in the fact that some ethnic groups have experienced more oppression than blacks yet have advanced farther). Fourth, without discrimination, racial groups would still be different in their wealth, income, and jobs (meaning that numerical inequality does not provide evidence of discrimination). Fifth, several factors, such as government regulations, affirmative action, and minimum wages, that regulate and retard the market are detrimental rather than beneficial to blacks. Sixth, the denial of civil rights cannot be viewed as the universal explanation of racial problems because the battle for civil rights was fought and won decades ago. Seventh, class differences are misinterpreted as racial discrimination. Much, if not most, inequality can be explained by the greater distribution of blacks in the lower class.[65]

Harold Cruse, in *Plural but Equal* (1987), critiques the economic history and sociological analysis of the black conservatives. Although Cruse considers their ethnic group comparisons to be enlightening as generalizations, the black conservatives ignore specific events that relate to their generalizations.[66] With respect to Sowell, who attempts to explain the differences in entrepreneurial success between African Americans and West Indians with respect to cultural differences, not only does he not mention the selective populations of West Indians in these comparisons, but he presents essentially a cultural deficits analysis that is out of context (for example, involving rotating credit associations). Before the establishment of West Indian entrepreneurs there were important entries of African American businesspeople, including those in real estate. Cruse further notes correctly that Sowell's analysis of West Indians in the United States (which is restricted to New York) is not opened up cross-culturally. In other historical situations, such as in Canada and England, the history of West Indian entrepreneurs did not match their history in New York. Cruse does note that civil rights movements among West Indians in both Canada and England did exist during the 1960s and 1970s.[67]

Other fallacies in some of these social analyses and policy statements confuse what is sociologically in fact a "class struggle" (in which race is a major public issue) with an "ass struggle" (which is focused on interpersonal and personal troubles). The assessments of these individual's coping adaptations, such as interracial cooperation, accommodation, miscegenation, and submission, are overstated, confused, and projected socially. Such projection is exemplified in part in Ward Connerly's statement concerning the effects of continuous blending in the melting pot as putting behind the question of race. Connerly, in a *New York Times* interview, noted that "in 10 to 15 years, intermarriage will make this entire debate [race] a moot one anyhow, and we'll wonder why we didn't see it coming."[68] In accounting for the authenticity of his analyses of black victimization, Shelby Steele credits his wife's specialized knowledge as a clinical psychologist as helping immensely in his search for the "human universals that explain the racial specifics."[69]

The programmatic objectives of black conservative intellectuals reveal further limitations. Most of these black neoconservative intellectuals and celebrities have relatively small constituents in the national black community. The strongest exception is Robert Woodson, who comes closest to the conservative activist tradition. It is as public intellectuals that these scholars have carved a niche. Within the constraints of conservative politics, conservative foundations, and neoconservative academic networks, these intellectuals have provided, to some degree, an independent black perspective. In the larger context, however, these black conservatives do not appear to have their own voices. In fact, they exemplify what I call "intellectual ventriloquism." In this contemporary puppetry, there are no visible strings, but postmodern dummies are needed.

In regard to conservative and neoconservative leaders, they are expected to comment only on the domestic and microsociological questions. Cultural concerns bearing on race and ethnicity, including critiques of affirmative action and multiculturalism, are their niches. However, there are situations in which underlying tensions between white conservative intellectuals and black conservatives are evident. Clarence Thomas has mentioned that early on, black conservatives were not generally received by white conservatives in public-policy discussions aside from caricatures and sideshows. With white conservative resistance and indifference, black conservatives were expected to constantly and adamantly oppose affirmative action and welfare.[70] The origins of Thomas's oppositional views to affirmative action are partly found in his adaptations to early experiences of racism, his hatred of civil rights leaders, whom he saw as a light-skinned elite excluding him, his attempts to hide his own affirmative action admissions at Holy Cross and Yale, and aspirations of professional mobility through political networking.[71] Ironically, it is not clear to what extent other black conservative intellectuals see their intellectual contributions as genuine or rather as caricatures and sideshows for their audiences. If they are taking part in intellectual theater, there are indications that earlier requirements of comedy and tragedy in their performances are being challenged by new requirements to participate in a theater of the absurd. Both Glenn Loury and Robert Woodson resigned as fellows at the American Enterprise Institute in protest of its publication of Dinesh D'Souza's *The End of Racism.* During the controversy over Herrnstein and Murray's *The Bell Curve,* both Sowell and Lowery critiqued the genetic implications from cultural assimilationist and individualistic perspectives.

Black conservative intellectuals usually embrace the role of the intellectual as heroic individual. To the extent that intellectuals make important contributions, these black conservatives argue that these contributions are based on exceptionalism, competition, and compatibility with mainstream intellectuals. Because black communities do not significantly support intellectual activities, accountability to this constituency is not necessary except in symbolic and rhetorical terms. These patterns run through most of the analyses of conservative intellectuals and to a large extent are embraced by a majority of the celebrities. Their marginality as conservatives functions to rationalize their isolation and alienation while cushioning them from any intellectual and social accountability.

Where do these black conservative intellectuals stand with respect to the challenges outlined in Cruse's *The Crisis of the Negro Intellectual?* Although they have provided critiques of liberalism and civil rights, there is little or nothing to suggest that these critiques extend to social and racial justice. Nor have they developed an intellectual role that has combined a cultural and political criticism that is inclusive of programs and demands.

There is an old saying that, whatever it is, conservatives do not believe it necessary, and, even if it were, they would oppose it. People are conservative when they are least vigorous or when conditions are most luxurious. They are conservatives after dinner or before taking their rest; when they are sick or aged. These black conservative intellectuals alert us again to the continuing challenges and work ahead.

NOTES

This chapter was originally presented at the Conference on "The Crisis of the Negro Intellectual: Past, Present, and Future," University of Michigan, Ann Arbor, Michigan, March 13–14, 1998.

1. H. Cruse, *The Crisis of the Negro Intellectual: From Its Origins to the Present* (New York: William Morrow, 1967).
2. M. Harrington, "The New Class and the Left," in *The New Class?* ed. B. B. Biggs. (New Brunswick, NJ: Transaction Books, 1979), p. 137.
3. J. Habermas, *The New Conservatism: Cultural Criticism and the Historians' Debate* (Cambridge: MIT Press, 1989), p. 24.
4. G. Dorrien, *The NeoConservative Mind: Politics, Culture, and the War of Ideology* (Philadelphia: Temple University Press, 1993), p. 8.
5. P. Steinfels, *The NeoConservatives* (New York: Simon and Schuster. 1979).
6. Dorrien, *The NeoConservative Mind,* pp. 9–10.
7. P. Wilayto, *The Feeding Trough: The Bradley Foundation, "The Bell Curve," and the Real Story behind W-2, Wisconsin's National Model for Welfare Reform* (Milwaukee: A Job Is a Right Campaign, 1997), pp. 13–14. See also P. Wilayto, "Report Reveals Bradley Foundation Behind W-2," *Milwaukee Courier* April 26, 1997, pp. 1, 5, 12.

8. Ibid., pp. 14–15.

9. Ibid., pp. 23–27.

10. B. Miner, "The Power and the Money: Bradley Foundation Bankrolls Conservative Agenda," *Rethinking Schools* 8, (3) (Spring 1994): p. 16.

11. Wilayto, *The Feeding Trough.*

12. Steinfels, *The NeoConservatives.*

13. Ibid., p. 53.

14. Ibid., p. 55.

15. Ibid., pp. 56–57.

16. Ibid., pp. 58–59.

17. Ibid., pp. 61–62.

18. Ibid., p. 62.

19. Ibid., p. 63.

20. Ibid., p. 64.

21. Ibid., 65.

22. M. Harrington, "The Welfare State and Its NeoConservative Critics" in *The New Conservatives: A Critique from the Left,* eds. L. Coser and I. Howe (New York: Quadrangle/New York Times Book Company, 1974), pp. 29–63.

23. P. Berger and T. Luckmann, *The Social Construction of Reality: A Treatise in the Sociology of Knowledge* (Garden City, NJ: Anchor Books, 1971).

24. P. Berger and J. Neuhaus, *To Empower People: The Role of Mediating Structures in Public Policy* (Washington, D.C.: American Enterprise Institute for Public Policy Research, 1977).

25. Ibid.

26. P. Berger and J. Neuhaus, *To Empower People: From State to Civil Society* (Washington, D.C.: American Enterprise Institute, 1996).

27. Dorrien, *The NeoConservative Mind,* p. 284.

28. Ibid., p. 286.

29. O. Cox, "Leadership among Negroes in the United States," in *Studies of Leadership: Leadership and Democratic Action,* ed. by Alvin Gouldner (New York: Harper, 1950), pp. 228–271.

30. Ibid., pp. 251–252.

31. M. Marable, *How Capitalism Underdeveloped Black America* (Boston: South End Press. 1983).

32. Ibid., p. 175.

33. See A. Williams, "Black and Conservative?" *Reader's Digest,* November 1995: pp. 157–59; R. Woodson, *On the Road to Economic Freedom* (Washington, D.C.: Regnery-Gateway, 1987); and S. Steele, "A Conversation with Shelby Steele" in *Black and Right: The Bold New Voice of Black Conservatives in America,* eds. by S. Faryna, B. Stetson, and J. G. Conti (Westport, CT: Praeger, 1997), pp.143–51.

34. J. Singer, "With a Friend in the White House, Black Conservatives Are Speaking Out," *National Journal,* March 14, 1981, pp. 435–39.

35. J. G. Conti and B. Stetson. *Challenging the Civil Rights Establishment: Profiles of a New Black Vanguard* (Westport, CT: Praeger, 1993), p. 87.

36. T. Sowell, *Black Education: Myths and Tragedies.* (New York: MacKay, 1972).

37. Singer, "With a Friend in the White House"; Conti and Stetson. *Challenging the Civil Rights Establishment.*

38. T. Sowell, *Race and Economics* (New York: Longman. 1975).

39. Conti and Stetson, *Challenging the Civil Rights Establishment,* p. 90.

40. T. Sowell, *Civil Rights: Rhetoric or Reality?* (New York: William Morrow, 1983).

41. G. Loury, "The Moral Quandary of the Black Community." *The Public Interest,* 79 (Spring 1985): 9–22.

42. G. Loury, "Responsibility and Race," *Vital Speeches*. April 15, 1983, pp. 398–400; "Who Speaks for American Blacks?" *Commentary,* January, 1987, pp. 34–38; "Individualism before Multiculturalism," *The Public Interest* Fall, 1995, pp. 92–106.

43. G. Loury, "Responsibility and Race"; Loury, "The Moral Quandary of the Black Community."

44. G. Loury, "Responsibility and Race"; Loury, "The Moral Quandary of the Black Community," p. 13.

45. Loury, "The Moral Quandary of the Black Community," p. 11.

46. G. Loury, "Going Home." *Common Quest: The Magazine of Black Jewish Relations* 1, (2) (Fall 1996): 11–14.

47. Singer, "With a Friend in the White House, Black Conservatives Are Speaking Out," p. 439.

48. Conti and Stetson. *Challenging the Civil Rights Establishment: Profiles of a New Black Vanguard* (Westport, Connecticut: Praeger. 1993), 165.

49. P. Wilayto *The Feeding Trough*, p. 57.

50. Ibid., 59.

51. Ibid., p. 60.

52. Conti and Stetson. *Challenging the Civil Rights Establishment,* p. 82.

53. Ibid., pp. 166–67.

54. Ibid., p. 167.

55. Singer, "With a Friend in the White House," p. 429.

56. Conti and Stetson. *Challenging the Civil Rights Establishment,* pp. 170–71.

57. S. Steele, *The Content of Our Character: A New Vision of Race in America,* (New York: Harper Perennial, 1990.

58. Ibid., p. 67.

59. Ibid., p. 151.

60. Ibid., p. 152.

61. Ibid., pp. 161–62.

62. B. Boxill, *Blacks and Social Justice* (Boston: Rowman and Littlefield, 1992).

63. C. West, "Unmasking the Black Conservatives," *The Christian Century,* July, 16–23, 1986, pp. 644–48.

64. T. D. Boston, *Race, Class, and Conservatism* (Boston: Unwin Hyman, 1988).

65. Ibid., pp. 55–57.

66. H. Cruse. *Plural but Equal: Blacks and Minorities in America's Plural Society* (New York: William Morrow, 1987).

67. Ibid., p. 320.

68. B. Bearack, "Questions of Race Run Deep for Foe of Preferences," *New York Times* July 27, 1997, pp. 1, 20–21.

69. R. S. Roberts, *Clarence Thomas and the Tough Love Crowd: Counterfeit Heroes and Unhappy Truths* (New York: New York University Press, 1993), pp.31–32.

70. C. Thomas, "No Room at the Inn: The Loneliness of the Black Conservative," in *Black and Right: The Bold New Voice of Black Conservatives in America,* eds. by S. Faryna, B. Stetson, and J. G. Conti (Westport, CT: Praeger, 1997), p. 9.

71. J. Mayer, *Strange Justice: The Selling of Clarence Thomas* (Boston: Houghton Mifflin, 1994).

CHAPTER 11

BLACK CONSERVATIVES AND CLASS RELATIONS

Marcus D. Pohlmann

Through numerous successful attacks, private property and individual liberty are mere skeletons of their past. Thomas Jefferson anticipated this, saying, "the actual progress of things is for government to gain ground and for liberty to yield." An easy measure of how government is gaining ground is to look at the time spent earning money for which we have no claim. The average taxpayer works from January 1 to May 6 to pay federal, state, and local taxes. . . . We should not forget that a working definition of slavery is that one works all year and has no claim to the fruits of his toil. . . . The ultimate end of this process is totalitarianism, which is no more than a reduced form of servitude.[1]

Black conservatives such as Walter E. Williams, quoted here, tend to oppose governmental intervention in the capitalist marketplace. They also espouse the traditional view that the American system is open to anyone willing to work hard enough. The obvious corollary is that those who fail do so because of their own weaknesses, while governmental social programs only create and perpetuate dependence on the part of those too unmotivated to compete.[2]

What they fail to acknowledge, however, is just who benefits most from the current system of "mixed capitalism" practiced in the United States. As the following analysis will demonstrate, the current system does a very effective job of reinforcing class relations that leave most African Americans trapped toward the bottom of the economic pyramid. The wealth of this nation is essentially owned by a relatively small number of white men, who will continue to dominate as long as we retain a primarily capitalist economy. In point of fact, reducing the role of government is likely only to enhance that domination.

THE CONCEPT OF CLASS

The term *economic classes* refers to the subgroupings within a society that delineate that society's most basic power relationships as it decides how to produce and distribute its goods and services. Under a capitalistic economic arrangement like the one championed by Walter Williams, most goods and services are produced by privately owned companies and distributed according to people's ability to pay. The owners of these companies, referred to as capitalists, directly or indirectly hire others to work for them and pay those workers a wage. That wage, however, is not set at the full market value of what the workers produce. Instead, the capitalist sells the fruits of the workers' labors for more than the workers are paid and thus extracts a "profit" in the bargain.

The end result in terms of power is that the workers are dependent on the capitalist owners for their very livelihoods. And out of that dependence comes subordination. It is, after all, the owner's company, and the owner's interest in maximization of profits will ultimately be the interest that controls the workers. Workers' needs, to the contrary, must be subordinated or the workers risk losing their livelihoods.

Such subordination also has implications for self-expression and security. By having control over decisions as to what is to be produced and how one's work provides an opportunity for self-expression. By contrast, when one must work exclusively to maximize the owner's profits, those opportunities are reduced and there is a tendency to become alienated from the work, and ultimately, from oneself.[3] In addition, there is little personal security without the cushion of accumulated wealth, as one can become destitute virtually overnight due to a layoff, extended illness, or large medical bills.[4]

These economic class relationships become an *economic class structure* when the boundary lines between the classes begin to solidfy. In the capitalist context, this would be true when there becomes almost no likelihood that one can move from the nonowning class, to the owning class or vice versa. The evidence, then, is in the intergenerational reproduction of existing class positions. In a class structure, one is born, lives, and dies a member of a certain class, for example, as do one's children, grandchildren, and so on. That results in large part because class positions are inherited. For example, one inherits one's parents, values, connections, wealth, and other attributes. Thus, it becomes highly unlikely that a member of the owning class will slip to the nonowning class, regardless of abilities, efforts, and the value of his or her skills to the society. Nonowners are similarly likely to remain nonowners no matter how talented and productive they are.[5]

BLACKS' SHARE OF CAPITALIST AMERICA

"America belongs to the white man." That statement is nearly correct. But to be even more accurate, "America belongs to a very small number of white men." They are the tiny fraction of the population that owns the bulk of the nation's property, corporate stock, and financial accounts.

To begin with, the nation's corporate assets are highly concentrated. The one hundred largest manufacturers, for example, control more than two thirds of the nation's manufacturing capital. Meanwhile, fifty banks hold two thirds of the banking assets and fifty insurers hold eighty percent of all insurance assets.[6] Combining manufacturers and nonmanufacturers, fewer than one percent of the nation's corporations produce over eighty percent of the nation's corporate output.[7]

Beyond that, the ownership of corporate assets is also quite concentrated. Compiled from a variety of sources, some of the best available data suggests that fewer than 20 percent of Americans have ever directly owned any stock. Of even more importance is the fact that a far smaller number of them have held nearly all the available shares. By relatively conservative estimates, the top 1 percent of the American adult population has held nearly 40 percent of all corporate stock since at least 1922. The top 5 percent of Americans has continued to hold the majority of all the stock, with the top 10 percent possessing more than 80 percent of it.[8]

Meanwhile, African Americans own very few of the nation's corporate assets, meaning almost total subordination to the interests of the white owning class. Only 1 percent of all black households possess more than $250,000 worth of wealth, while more than 30 percent either own nothing or owe more than they own. Where wealth has been accumulated, it has most often reflected a small amount of equity in a house or automobile. Only six percent of black households hold any corporate stock or mutual funds, and the median holding is only $4,013—most likely small individual retirement accounts (IRAs). The mean holding is only $7,841, which indicates some variation in size of holdings but very few large accumulations.[9]

From a different perspective, blacks hold only about 2 percent of the nation's capital stock.[10] And although they own 3 percent of the businesses,[11] those businesses received only 1 percent of all gross receipts. Only 17 percent had even one paid employee, whereas less than 0.4 percent (189 firms) employed more than one hundred people. As telling as anything is the fact that 94 percent were sole proprietorships, most of which operated on capital drawn from the owner's personal savings or borrowed from friends.[12] Although there has been some recent expansion in areas such as heavy construction, professional and business services, finance, insurance, and real estate,[13] black-owned businesses generally continue to be restaurants, car dealerships, laundries, funeral parlors, gas stations, barber shops, hair salons, shoe repair shops, neighborhood grocery stores, and other service-producing enterprises, most of which are small and operate on the economic margin; more than three-fourths of these go bankrupt within three years of opening.[14]

WELFARE STATE CAPITALISM

In fall of 1972, Charles V. Hamilton published an article entitled, "Conduit Colonialism and Public Policy" in which he set out a model that had four basic components: taxpayers, government, welfare recipients, and "welfare beneficiaries"—wealthy individuals who make sizable profits selling goods and services to the welfare-receiving poor. A primary point was to show how governmental welfare programs caused their recipients to function as channels for transferring money from the paychecks of the average taxpayer to the pockets of a group of wealthy elites. This pass-through occurred when the recipients paid inflated amounts of taxpayer-provided money to the welfare beneficiaries: the landlords, pharmacists, doctors, and other vendors who served them. Consequently, the recipient was a "conduit" and was being "colonized" in the process—left dependent on others for subsistence and, at the same time, absorbing much of the wrath of the average taxpayer.[15]

By using an extended version of Hamilton's "conduit colonialism" model, I will attempt to estimate the degree to which America's capitalist political economy functions to enrich an "owning class" at the expense of the rest of American society. But whereas Hamilton focused on the systemic functions of the poor as welfare recipients, this analysis will extend his model to focus on the systemic functions of the black and white middle and working classes.

Where Walter Williams and other conservatives focus on the taxes government extracts from the paychecks of working people, I will attempt to estimate the amount of money that gets transferred annually from the black and white middle and working classes to the bank accounts of the small white owning class. This transfer takes a variety of forms, among them private-sector profits from sales to governmental and private consumers and direct transfers from government in the form of grants and credit subsidies.

Average Americans, black and white, do pay a sizable share of their paychecks to government each year, just as Walter Williams noted. Somewhat less obvious, however, is the fact that a significant portion of those paychecks also goes to the owners of corporate capital, as a sort of "tribute" for the privilege of living in the country they own. Government, welfare recipients, and the owning class interrelate to create that reality.

Where is the opposition to such an arrangement? The last sections will present evidence that much middle- and working-class anger is diverted toward the poor. In addition, many in the exploited population are co-opted by their faith in a mythology that holds out the hope of interclass mobility as a reward for talent, hard work, and frugality.

Before beginning, let me make two methodological qualifications. First, it is clear that the operation of the economic system is a dynamic process. Corporate profits, for example, generally are not hoarded away in the vaults of the owning class. Instead, they are often spun back into the economy in the form of purchases and investments. What this analysis attempts to provide is a reasonable indication of which class groupings have been gaining and which have been losing in the course of this dynamic process.

Second, along those same lines, it is important to note that governmental policy is also a moving target in its own right. We are living through a period of considerable political instability, reflected in the varying partisan control of Congress and the White House, and consequently in taxing and spending priorities. Whether the issue is welfare reform, corporate subsidies, or tax rates, it is difficult to precisely describe a process that changes almost daily.

THE CONCEPTUAL MODEL

The primary components of my adaptation of Charles V. Hamilton's model are described next.

Government

In domestic policymaking, it can be argued that government (meaning federal, state, and local levels combined) has come to play accumulation and legitimation functions. Government assists the process of capital accumulation by attempting to guarantee an adequate supply of venture capital and productive labor so that the owners of capital can, and will, invest in ways that will lead to stable economic growth—for example, by providing tax breaks and subsidies to corporations ("social investment") or to help minimize corporate transportation costs ("social consumption"). In legitimation, government compensates people who become economically dislocated, so that the necessary level of social harmony can be maintained, as by providing maintenance services and social-welfare programs ("social expenditures").

As the ownership of capital becomes more concentrated, the capitalist class can coerce the government into socializing even more of the costs of capital accumulation and production, while the benefits remain largely private. This, however, requires that the government also spend more and more on social expenditures in order to retain legitimacy with the non-owners. Thus, the role of government continues to expand, whereupon it serves essentially stabilizes a system that smiles most favorably on the owning class.[16]

The Owning Class (Hamilton's "Welfare Beneficiaries")

As defined here, the *owning class* represents the top 1 percent of American households in terms of wealth, with average assets of nearly $7 million in value.[17] As a group, it has consistently owned a clear majority of the nation's business assets[18] and, wealth holdings guarantee that virtually all of its members enough unearned income to keep them in the nation's top 5 percent of income earners even if they do not work.[19] They make 16.4 percent of all national income,[20] averaging nearly $700,000 per household.[21] By contrast, fewer than 1 percent of all black households have ever fallen into this category. Thus, for empirical convenience, these black households have been included in the middle and working-class grouping.

Besides wages, interest, gifts, and inheritance, the owning class derives its income from at least three other sources: the work of their employees, direct government aid, and indirect government aid. To begin with, they make profits from investments of their capital by charging more for products and services than employees are paid to produce and distribute them. Direct government aid includes government subsidies such as low-interest loans and tax abatements and profits derived from contracts with government for building things like highways, bombers, housing, and other durable goods. Indirect government aid, for the purposes of this chapter, is the profit realized when selling goods and services to the publicly subsidized indigent (called "welfare recipients" from here on).

Welfare Recipients (The Lower Class)

The lower class has been defined as the bottom 20 percent of American families in terms of wealth, with the average household owing more than it owns.[22] As a group, its members made 3.1 percent of the nation's income, averaging $6,000 per household; and, rarely making more than 125 percent of the federal poverty level, they have generally been eligible to receive one or more forms of public assistance from the welfare state.[23] Approximately 40 percent of all black households and a majority of black children fall into this category.[24]

Middle- and Working-Class (MC/WC) Work Force and Tax Base

The 79 percent of American households between the owning and lower classes, including 60 percent of America's black households, constitute the "middle and working class." This group has an average net worth of $157,000; but most of this is owned by those at the very top of the group. For example, that amount is nearly cut in half if you omit the top 10 percent of these households, and it falls by nearly two thirds if the top quarter is excluded. It also should be noted that for most members, virtually all of this wealth is tied up in their houses and cars, with very little invested in financial assets like stocks and bonds.[25] Meanwhile, the group makes just over 80 percent of the nation's income, averaging $43,000 per year;[26] however, increasingly it requires the paychecks of at least two wage earners in the household in order to remain in this category, especially for African Americans.[27]

Working in either the private or public sector to produce the nation's goods and services, the members of this group also find themselves caught in two additional economic predicaments. Most are employees of the owning class, working for a wage that is less than the market value of what they produce. Second, taxation deprives them of a significant portion of their incomes, while billions of those dollars end up in the pockets of the owning class.[28]

WELFARE STATE CAPITALISM IN ACTION

Much of this should become clearer by examination the "welfare state capitalism" model as applied to the United States.

Private-Sector Corporate Profits

When the owning class invests its money in corporations, it expects something in return. What it gets in return are profits. These derive from paying workers less than the market value of what they have produced. In other words, this is a return to capital, not to labor.

These corporate profits have accounted for approximately 10 percent or more of all national income throughout most of this century.[29] Corporate profits from domestic industries alone reached $256.2 billion in 1994, even after subtracting the owners' taxes, adjustments for inventory valuation and capital consumption, and profits from transactions with both government and welfare recipients (considered later in this model).[30]

Focusing on African Americans, such private profit taking has allowed the white owning class to acquire billions of dollars of income each year as profits from its sales of goods and services to the black middle and working class. In 1994, the white owning class extracted more than $7 billion in profits as a result of these transactions— nearly $128 billion when combined with sales to the white middle and working class.[31]

Personal Taxes

When tax burdens imposed by federal, state, and local governments are combined, it is quite clear that the United States does not begin to have a *progressive* tax system. Americans who make most of the money still have most of the money after government is paid. In 1985, for instance, the poorest one-tenth of American families made 1.3 percent of all adjusted family income before taxes, and 1.3 percent afterward. At the other end of the income spectrum, the wealthiest one-tenth made 33.1 percent of all adjusted family income before taxes but had 33.9 percent after all taxes had been paid.[32] Ten years later, Thomas Dye continued to find that "before-tax and after-tax income distributions are nearly identical."[33]

Now add the fact that the United States has no wealth tax as such. In other words, besides local real estate taxes, individuals are taxed only on the yearly income derived from their stocks, trust funds, bank accounts, and so on, instead of being taxed annually on the overall value of such wealth. Inheritance and estate taxes are applied once the individual dies, but even those are fraught with loopholes. Prior to death, for instance, a wealthy person may (1) gradually liquidate the estate by giving it away in untaxed annual gifts to each heir, (2) sell property to the inheritor(s) for a nominal fee, or (3) create trust funds that will be taxed only when the inheritors collect their yearly allotment. The entire estate is also granted a $1 million dollar federal estate tax deduction ($1.3 million if farms or businesses are involved), and the estate is subject to inheritance taxation only when first put into trusts. (Unspent trust money can be passed along to the next heirs without incurring any inheritance taxation.) In addition, *lead trusts* can be established, which allow wealth to be inherited tax free as long as interest income goes to charitable causes for a fixed period of time.[34] Beyond that, a number of highly wealthy Americans have managed to avoid capital gains and estate taxes altogether by renouncing their citizenship and moving abroad. Tax consultant William Zabel refers to such expatriation as "the ultimate estate plan."[35]

In the end, then, estate and gift taxes have been providing less than 1 percent of all governmental revenues, despite the billions of dollars' worth of wealth that exists and is passed on every year. Thus, huge family fortunes often can be amassed and handed down from generation to generation with little government interference.[36] It also should come as no surprise that thousands of the nation's wealthiest individuals pay few if any personal income taxes either, once all tax breaks have been utilized.[37] Meanwhile, average Americans working for a wage or salary wind up paying the lion's share of the ever-increasing (nonprogressive) government tax burden.

By 1994, Americans were paying more than $1.2 trillion in taxes every year. In that year, the black middle and working class paid nearly $54 billion in taxes, while black and white workers combined paid more than $978 billion.[38]

Corporate Subsidies

Direct Subsidies.   Each year the *Survey of Current Business* compiles the amount of governmental subsidies paid to enterprises primarily in the agricultural, construction, and transportation industries. In 1994, the owning class's share of those subsidies amounted to more than $21.5 billion. This meant that the black middle and working class transferred more than $955 million to the white owners by means of these governmental subsidies, with black and white workers combined contributing more than $17 billion.[39]

Contract Profits.   The owning class also reaps profits from business transactions with government, as its corporations sell various goods and services to the federal, state, and local governments. These profits were estimated to be more than $7.5 billion in 1994. This cost the black middle and working class nearly $336 million, with the total middle and working class contributing more than $6 billion.[40]

Interest Profits.   Government indebtedness has mounted into the trillions of dollars, and thus government continues to pay considerable interest to its lenders. In 1994, these interest payments meant more than $6.5 billion in income for the white owning class. As a result of this vehicle, that year the owning class extracted nearly

$300 million dollars from the paychecks of the black middle and working class, and more than $5 billion from the middle and working class as a whole.[41]

Public Assistance

Public assistance refers to those governmental programs historically designed to ease the burden of being indigent in the United States, including family assistance, Medicaid, food stamps, rent subsidies, and the Supplemental Security Income program. They have provided low-income Americans with money and vouchers with which to purchase necessities such as food, shelter, clothing, and medical assistance. Beginning primarily with Franklin Roosevelt's New Deal and accelerating dramatically during and after Lyndon Johnson's Great Society era, such relief payments grew to sizable proportions. In 1984, for example, some 74 need-based programs provided millions of indigents with over $134 billion worth of "relief."[42] By 1994, the total spent on all "cash and non-cash benefits for persons with limited incomes" exceeded $306 billion.[43] But the story does not end there, for the recipients do not eat, wear, and live under these checks and coupons. They spend them, and in the process, they provide additional profit for the owning class.

Conduit Capitalism

Charles V. Hamilton was one of the first to note the "conduit" function played by nearly all relief recipients.[44] This occurs when various proportions of relief recipients' governmentally funded purchases flow on to the owning class—wealthy landlords, nursing home operators, the stockholders of pharmaceutical companies—as profits from these transactions. Although it is difficult to determine how much money each of these vendors makes by serving the poor, it is possible to estimate what the owning-class vendors as a group have made. For example, by applying the average corporate profit rates to the billions spent on need-based public assistance programs, it can be seen that the owning class garnered nearly $180 million from the pockets of the black middle and working class and more than $3 billion from the entire middle and working class.[45]

Now, none of this is meant to suggest that a considerable amount of good has not come from governmental relief programs. Public assistance has provided badly needed items, such as food, shelter, clothing and medical assistance, to many who would have been significantly worse off otherwise. As long practiced, however, such assistance also has allowed for a considerable amount of profit-taking on the part of the owning class.

Summary

America's political-economic system does seem to reinforce existing class relationships. This becomes even more obvious when all of the previous figures are combined. In 1994, nearly $9 billion was transferred from the paychecks of the black middle and working class to the investment portfolios of the white owning class. That figure climbed to nearly $160 billion when considering the black and white middle and working classes combined. This amounts to a "tribute" of sorts for the privilege of living and working in the country owned by the white elites.[46]

Government was directly involved in one-fifth of this transfer. It was also indirectly involved in the amount transferred through private-sector profits, given its nonprogressive tax system, economic regulations or lack thereof, many of its maintenance services, and so on.

Most recently, welfare reform efforts have been designed to coerce many of the poor into low-wage employment as a condition of receiving relief. This, too, will enhance the position of the owning class by providing them with an easily exploitable group of workers in what essentially will amount to a condition of indentured servitude. If successful, then, private-sector corporate profits will increase as conduit profits are reduced, leaving the overall tribute levels pretty much unchanged.

The Trickle-down Fallacy

Conservatives, both black and white, have espoused varying versions of supply-side economics as at least partial justification for such a tribute system. This is an economic theory based on the premise that if the wealthy are allowed to get wealthier, a reasonable amount will trickle down to everyone else, making the entire society better off.[47]

Reality, however, poses some serious problems for that theory. First of all, there is no guarantee that such increased wealth will necessarily be invested in job-producing endeavors in the United States. Instead, much of it may well be invested abroad or spent here on such things as collectibles or quick-profit speculations. Second, even if the wealth is invested in a manner that produces American jobs, there is little guarantee that such new jobs will necessarily pay the kinds of wages and benefits needed to provide middle class lifestyles for the employees.

As a test, it should be noted that the rich have indeed been getting considerably richer, by both absolute and relative measures. Looking at families ranked by income, for example, the poorest family among the nation's top 5 percent of families made $92,158 (1993 dollars) in 1980 and $113,182 by 1993, an increase of nearly 23 percent. In relative terms, the top 5 percent of American families increased their proportion of all family income from 15.3 percent in 1980 to 19.1 percent by 1993.[48] In addition, at the very top of that group, the number of centimillionaires more than tripled over this time frame, while the period also produced the first U.S. billionaires.[49]

Meanwhile, the income of the median white family grew some 2 percent, seeming at least minimally, to support the trickle down concept. By contrast, however, the median income for black families actually declined 3 percent; and, as will be demonstrated next, the gain for white families tended to fall disproportionately to a fortunate few.[50] Also, in relative terms, as the top 5 percent of American families were increasing their portion of national income, the bottom 80 percent saw their income share decline rather uniformly across the board.[51] Susan Mayer and Christopher Jencks concluded that the distribution of income has become "more unequal than at any time since the Census Bureau began collecting such data in 1947."[52]

Now, there is some inter-group movement occurring over time, for example, households moving from the middle to higher group when a wage earner is added or down from the middle to the lower group following a divorce or layoff. Nevertheless, society as a whole continues to end up with pretty much the same class configuration trends after those movements occur.[53] And, as Duncan, Smeeding, and Rogers concluded, "A middle income adult's chances of falling from the middle to the bottom of the distribution increasingly [have] exceeded [the] chances of moving from the middle to the top."[54]

Beyond all that, these figures actually understate the declining position of much of the middle and working class for a variety of reasons:

1. The large baby boom generation has begun to reach its peak earning years.
2. The number of multiple-income families has been growing markedly.[55]
3. Individuals are working longer hours, at the expense of leisure time.[56]
4. Baby boomers have married later and had smaller families than their predecessors, allowing for more discretionary per capita income, even when hourly wages were declining.[57]
5. Savings have declined and short-term borrowing has increased in an attempt to maintain existing living standards.[58]
6. Welfare reform has cast the working class into competition with former welfare recipients for a variety of low-wage jobs in an economy where the Federal Reserve Board is inclined to increase interest rates in order to slow growth if unemployment shrinks much below 6 percent.[59]

Thus, the present situation is even worse than it appears, and the future looks even less promising for many in the next generation of middle- and working-class families. But even for the present, this situation only appears to be intensified by the next development.

Real-dollar governmental spending has continued to increase. Therefore, given a nonprogressive tax structure, the corresponding growth in taxes has consumed much of what little the middle and working class gained as a result of any expanded economic pie. The average owning-class family, by contrast, received enough from their disproportionate share of increased income so that they could pay their taxes and still emerge with a sizable increase in after-tax income.[60]

In conclusion, there simply is not much recent evidence to support the supply-side economic theory; in fact, the opposite has seemed to be true of late. As tribute has grown since 1980, the income level of most people has remained where it was or dropped, while income gaps increased. According to Felix Rohatyn, "What is occurring is a huge transfer of wealth from lower-skilled middle-class American workers to the owners of capital assets and to the new technological aristocracy."[61] As Duncan, Smeeding, and Rogers summarized, "the rising tide of economic growth . . . appears to have lifted the yachts, but neither the tugboats nor the rowboats."[62]

Meanwhile, there is reason to believe that tribute will continue to rise. The advent of the postindustrial economy has further strengthened the bargaining position of the owners of capital. With expanding opportunities to invest virtually anyplace on the face of the earth, venture capitalists are likely to be increasingly successful at extracting concessions from government. Consequently, given the capitalist economic system favored by Walter Williams and his black conservative cohorts, wealth and income gaps appear destined to continue to widen. The rich will get richer and more powerful while most of the remainder of society becomes relatively poorer and more subordinate.

Directed Wrath

Watching its overall standard of living decline since the mid-1970s, much of the middle and working class has become frustrated. It is instructive, however, to note how and why the poor, and particularly welfare recipients, end up as a primary target of this wrath.

A *New York Times* survey found that nearly two-thirds of its nationwide respondents believed that welfare "encourages people to have larger families than they would have had otherwise," and a clear majority were convinced that welfare discourages "pregnant women from getting married."[63] Consequently, it should not be surprising that a near majority favored "requiring welfare mothers to accept contraceptive implants,"[64] despite the lack of credible empirical evidence that poor women have additional children in order to receive more welfare.[65]

At the time it was eliminated, AFDC remained the lightening rod of the relief package. Yet the average monthly benefit was only $373.[66] The entire program comprised less than one tenth of total welfare spending. At least two thirds of the recipients were children.[67] Most heads of those households were single mothers, and more than one third of them had been employed during the previous year.[68] The number of able-bodied adult males receiving such relief had been estimated at 1 to 2 percent of the caseload[69]—not a particularly high figure in a period when more than 5 percent of those actively seeking work could not find it. In addition, contrary to popular belief, intergenerational welfare dependence was highly unusual;[70] and despite public fears to the contrary, there was very little evidence of actual welfare fraud. Of New York City's 1.1 million recipients, for example, there were only 184 arrests for welfare fraud in 1993—less than .02 percent.[71] If there was waste, it may well have been in the amount of resources expended in overseeing such programs. Cook County, Illinois, for instance, spent some two thirds of its poverty funds on administration.[72]

There is also the persistent belief that most able-bodied recipients of any type of welfare are simply too lazy to work their way out of poverty. In other words, most end up on welfare due to their own character flaws.[73] Characterizing this attitude, when California Governor Pete Wilson signed a welfare payment cut, he asserted that this would mean "one less six-pack per week."[74]

There is no denying that personal irresponsibility contributes to some of the underemployment and poverty that leads to welfare reliance; yet, despite the monetary disincentives discussed below, a majority of these households have at least one wage earner and two thirds of those who leave the relief roles do not return.[75] Lou Harris found what the poor most wanted was (1) better job opportunities, (2) more schooling, and (3) more job training, while their single biggest regret was not being adequately trained to support themselves.[76] And as for welfare, the poor hold virtually the same views as everyone else. For example, 88 percent of them believe the able-bodied should be required to attend school or training in order to receive welfare and that poor people who have more children should not automatically receive more public aid.[77]

Another myth is that these recipients have lived quite comfortably on public assistance. To begin with, the median Aid to Families with Dependent Children (AFDC) and food stamp allotments combined still left household income at less than three quarters of the federal government's poverty level.[78] In Illinois, for example, a single mother with one child was eligible to receive a monthly maximum of $313 in AFDC payments, $187 in food stamps, and a Medicaid card. That was less than $400 per month, or $5,000 per year.[79]

Nevertheless, in apparent response to such misguided frustration, the amount of real-dollar expenditures on public assistance stopped growing in the 1980s. For example, a combination of governmental assistance and tax policies lifted 30 percent of individuals in single-parent families out of poverty in 1979, but only 20 percent by 1990. The proportion of the poor receiving AFDC shrunk from 55 percent in 1973 to 49 percent by 1992 (81 percent to 63 percent for poor children). The typical state's maximum AFDC benefit was cut nearly in half between 1970 and 1994; eligibility for unemployment compensation was narrowed; and Medicaid cuts meant the poor would have an increasingly difficult time finding medical treatment.[80] Then, in summer 1996, Congress passed, and the president signed, sweeping welfare reform legislation that further reduced the government's commitment of funds while ending the AFDC program entirely. Not surprisingly, the posttransfer income of the bottom one-fifth of American families has been declining in real dollars.[81]

In absolute terms, the rich are getting richer and the poor are getting poorer, a reality that is both reinforced and enhanced by the functioning of welfare state capitalism. So, just what keeps people in the middle and working class and in the lower class going in the face of the political-economic realities just described? At least part of it can be explained by a faith in another long-standing bit of mythology.

THE HORATIO ALGER MYTH

Americans seem willing to tolerate wide gaps between rich and poor so long as they view the door of opportunity as open.[82]

Horatio Alger (1834–1899) was a successful author who inspired generations of American youth with tales about Ragged Dick, Tattered Tom, and Luck and Pluck, penniless heroes gained wealth and fame through a combination of goodness and courage. Thus the Horatio Alger myth comes to read something like this:

It is possible to go from rags to riches in the United States if one displays the right combination of abilities, hard work, thrift, and wise investment. Conversely, the existence of considerable economic inequality must be taken as a given, the necessary result of healthy competition between free, variably talented individuals.

A century later, the myth seems alive and well, for rich and poor, black and white. In a Gallup Poll, for instance, nearly two-thirds of all adults under thirty years of age considered themselves at least somewhat likely to be rich someday.[83] Now consider the realities of a capitalist system that black conservatives wish was even less regulated.

Acquiring Riches

To begin with, the ranks of the owning class are not impenetrable. However, how one usually enters these ranks today might well cause poor Horatio Alger to turn uncomfortably in his grave.

Lester Thurow, studying families with incomes of more than $100,000 and wealth holdings averaging $1.5 million, found a sizable majority of these families to have inherited substantial amounts of these estates.[84]

In an in-depth study of Connecticut probate records, Paul Menchik found much the same thing. Comparing children's estates to those of their parents, he estimated that some 30 percent of a child's estate will be directly left over from the parents' estate. However, if one assumes that the child invests the inheritance, the figure jumps to 50 percent at bond rates and well over 50 percent if stock market indexes are employed. He also noted that the larger the inheritance, the more of it is likely to survive; for example, if one person's lifetime resources are 10 percent higher than another person's, the first person's estate will be some 25 percent higher because a higher proportion of those resources can be saved and invested. The end result of all this is that the median child dies possessing 85 percent as much wealth (in real dollars) as his or her parents had accumulated by the time they died. The correlation coefficient is .635, meaning that a full 40 percent of a child's wealth is statistically determined solely by the level of parental wealth. Menchik concludes that if one is born to parents who are ten times wealthier than someone else's, one is likely to die at least eight times wealthier than the other person.[85]

It is also true, however, that more than 40 percent of the "great" and "less great" fortunes have been compiled without the benefit of substantial inheritance; but Thurow found that this economic success is rarely the result of a lifetime of scrimping and saving. Rather, it comes as virtually "instant wealth." The person gambles or invests and happens to win, which is obvious when one looks at how quickly most of these fortunes were accumulated, often in a matter of a few years and seldom in two or more leaps. Therefore, this success comes to be seen much more as a matter of luck and seldom as the result of lifelong hard work and frugality.

Thurow concluded that only about 10 percent of economic success is explicable by how hard one works or how frugal one has been. The rest is determined by a society's population trends, unemployment level, tastes, and so on, leaving some 70 to 80 percent of economic success unexplained by the standard variables such as education, experience, and personality traits. Hard work may be necessary but it is certainly not sufficient and there is little indication that it is even necessary. A person may well work hard and even save, but that is not likely to place that person on the path to a great fortune. Rather, the latter tends to be a "random walk": One happened to be fortunate enough to have chosen to invest in Xerox or IBM in the 1950s rather than the broad array of other possible choices—and, of course, one was among the small minority that had much of anything to invest in the first place.[86]

More recently, inheritance appears to be increasingly critical to capital accumulation. Looking at 35 to 39 year olds in 1973, for example, some 56 percent of their wealth had been inherited. By the mid-1980s, however, that figure had jumped to 86 percent.[87] And as for its distribution, the richest 1 percent of baby boomers stand to inherit more than $2 trillion by the year 2011—some $3.6 million apiece. Each Boomer in the next highest 9 percent should garner roughly $396,000; while the bottom 90 percent will average only $40,000—and most of that will fall to those at the top of the group.[88]

In sum, it is possible to become wealthy other than by inheritance, but that leap requires luck more than anything else. Alger's goodness and courage seem to play very little part in the process. Consequently, short of inheriting a healthy sum of money from a long-lost relative or hitting a number in the lottery, the odds are that the hardworking, penny- pinching janitor from the ghetto simply has no realistic hope of acquiring a fortune in his or her lifetime. His or her children and grandchildren will not see one either. As a matter of fact, they will almost certainly find themselves punching a time clock as well.

If a child's wage-earning parent is in the bottom 5 percent of wage earners, for example, that child has only a one in twenty chance of earning his or her way into the top quintile—let alone the owning class. Except for the normal income fluctuations associated with age, most Americans simply do not move very far up or down over the course of their lifetimes. As for trends, it is actually becoming more and more difficult to fall from the top or rise from the bottom, despite the modicum of mobility apparent in the upper strata of the middle and working class.[89] And, this is particularly true for African Americans.[90]

Focusing on males, both black and white, an earlier Department of Commerce study revealed that nearly two out of three sons will end up working at a job of the same general status as their fathers. And when the white-collar category is limited to professionals and managers, almost three in four sons will remain outside of this group, just as their fathers did.[91]

So, if hard work and frugality do not really help much in scaling the class wall, must the overwhelming majority of Americans be content to "bet on the horses" as their only realistic hope of gaining a share of the means of production? Even though Thurow has indicated that all the abilities in the world are nowhere near the surest ticket to a ride on the wealth train, it seems reasonable to believe that if nurtured, such abilities might help increase income as a step toward attaining wealth. Indeed, as discussed when analyzing postindustrial trends above, there is empirical evidence that schooling helps determine one's job, which in turn should help determine income and wealth.[92]

Education and Mobility

To begin with, financial position is indeed related to educational attainment, regardless of a person's age. A college graduate makes an average of 59 percent more than a high school graduate and more than three times that of a grade school graduate. The same is even truer for wealth accumulation, where the college graduate has more than seven times the financial assets of a high school graduate and some thirty two times that of a grade school graduate.[93]

But who gets the higher levels of education? To begin with, the more income parents have, the more likely it is that their children will be afforded the opportunity to further their educations.[94] As a matter of fact, even more recent trend data suggest that the gap in educational attainment between the children of the haves and have nots has increased significantly since the late 1970s, especially with rising tuition costs and a decline in government tuition assistance.[95] Then, when the impediments of race and poverty come together, we find scarcely more than 1 percent of African-American students from the poorest category of households attending college full time.[96] Not surprisingly, weak students from well off families stand a better chance of attending college than better students coming from poorer backgrounds.[97] And there are some indications that the ante has been going up.

The technological prerequisites of postindustrial success have prompted ever more of the population to both finish high school and find a way to attend college. But as an increasing proportion of the middle and working class has managed to work its way into college classrooms, a veritable elite bastion until relatively recently, a mere college degree is no longer enough to open the most desirable of the postindustrial doors of employment.[98]

In 1960, for example, 29 percent of America's full-time workers had high school educations and another 13 percent had managed to attain college degrees. Those figures jumped to 38 percent and 30 percent respectively, by 1990.[99] Meanwhile, the number of high- skill jobs has not kept pace with this proliferation of educated workers, which led to at least two important developments. First, in a process called *downward substitution*, better educated workers have displaced those who are less well educated in jobs requiring few skills.[100] Related to that, it now requires an advanced degree from a prestigious college in order to compete successfully for many of the more desirable positions that used to require only a college diploma. And, not too surprisingly, it is the wealthier who are more likely to attend the more expensive, elite institutions.[101]

Educational attainment does seem to be intergenerationally linked, at least in part by the socioeconomic position of the student's parents. But looking beneath the opportunity to study a greater number of years, it is just as revealing to note that the quality of the person's elementary and secondary educational experiences may well be affected by the socioeconomic status of that person's parents.

Because nearly one-half of all school funding comes from local property taxes, there are substantial discrepancies in the amount of money available to spend on the public schools. In the state of Texas, prior to judicial intervention, one district spent $2,337 per pupil, while another was able to spend more than $56,791 and still enjoy a much lower tax rate.[102] As a result, the wealthy schools have the latest textbooks, full libraries, science laboratories, and state-of-the-art computer equipment and can attract the better teachers. Meanwhile, at the other end of town, children often must make do with out-of-date textbooks and other hand-me-down resources, while many teachers eschew teaching there.[103] Then, comparing teacher salaries to student achievement, Harvard's Ronald Ferguson found a considerable correlation. Students at better funded schools simply score higher on such tests.[104]

A Class System

Americans do not like to talk about economic classes and class differences, in large part because they hold staunchly to the belief that there are no fundamental class barriers to advancement in the United States.[105] As the black conservatives continually remind us, anyone can rise from rags to riches in a capitalist system. However, it seems safe to say that in today's real world of capitalism, a person who is not born in the owning class will almost certainly never end up there, regardless of abilities, hard work, thrift, and a knack for making wise investments. When there is nothing left at the end of the month to invest in either the stock market or further education for one's children, the family simply lacks the ante even to get into the game—a reality that appears even more hard and fast for African Americans.[106]

Each generation is likely to have its superrich entrepreneurs, such as J. Paul Getty, H. L. Hunt, and Daniel Ludwig (oil); Howard Hughes (aerospace); Edward Land (photography); John Kluge (mass media); Sam Walton (retail); William Gates, Paul Allen, and H. Ross Perot (computers). And, in extremely rare cases, a Samuel Newhouse, Henry Kaiser, W. Clement Stone, or Tom Monoghan will actually rise from rags to riches largely by virtue of his own efforts.[107] Such examples help keep the Horatio Alger myth alive and spur support for the existing system. Stated another way, capitalism's limited permeability serves as an important reinforcing device. Meanwhile, virtually every American will work very hard to make profits for someone else and will remain essentially locked into the class position into which he or she was born. Indeed, there is a light at the end of the tunnel, but for the overwhelming majority of Americans it simply amounts to a false hope, a cruel hoax, as they continue to bite the bullet of their own economic exploitation.

CONCLUSIONS

Black people cannot afford the social injustices of capitalism. They cannot afford a system which creates privileged classes within an already superexploited and underprivileged community. They cannot afford a system which organizes community resources and then distributes the resulting wealth in a hierarchical fashion, with those who need least getting most.[108]

Overall, the welfare state capitalism model found a system that exploits the middle and working class, struggles to maintain the lower class at subsistence, further enhances the dominant position of the capital-owning class, and leads to an at least temporary diversion of middle and working class wrath toward the lower class while maintaining essentially groundless hopes of interclass mobility.

But what is the alternative? The black conservatives argue for reducing the role of government and letting capitalism function even more freely. However, reducing the role of government in an already exploitative economic system is not the answer. Not only would there be more hardships, but the white owning class would become even more dominant. Instead, I will argue for altering the underlying economic system itself. The real challenge to our liberty is not coming primarily from government, as the conservatives would have us believe, but from the class system inherent in capitalism itself.

"Why are there 40 million poor people in America?" And when you begin to ask that question you are raising questions about the economic system, about a broader distribution of wealth. When you ask that question, you begin to question the capitalistic economy. . . . But one day we must come to see that an edifice which produces beggars needs restructuring.[109]

At about the very same time that Martin Luther King, Jr., made that pronouncement, a young delegate to the 1967 Newark Black Power Conference took it a step further when he stated: "The capitalist system hasn't worked for us in the four hundred years we've been under it. . . . Capitalism is the most successful system of enforced exploitation in the world, I agree. It's the latest model of slavery."[110]

The alternative is socialism. Socialists reject the economic system of capitalism. As Manning Marable put it, "The road to black liberation must also be a road to socialist revolution."[111]

In general, socialists argue that capitalism generates a small capital-owning class that possesses the controlling shares of the nation's wealth and power. As a consequence, the political and economic systems come to function primarily in the owners' interests. Robert Allen warns that "simple transference of business ownership into black hands . . . is in itself no guarantee that this will benefit the total community. Blacks are capable of exploiting one another just as easily as whites."[112]

According to the socialists, a new economic system must be fashioned that will democratize the ownership of capital and thus allow all citizens to have more control over the political and economic decisions that affect their lives. Stated more concretely, a socialist society would be distinguishable, first and foremost, by worker control of the means of production. That, however, has come to mean at least two significantly different things, depending on the analyst. Some put their emphasis on democratizing the decisions of existing corporations, while others maintain that the means of production must also be owned, either directly or indirectly, by the workers themselves.

Economic Democracy

Members of the Congressional Black Caucus and prominent black spokespersons such as Coretta Scott King have called for more centralized government planning of the existing American economy, in particular to create full employment.[113] Ralph Nader, on the other hand, has proposed what he terms his Corporate Democracy Act, which would require all corporations to be chartered by the federal government, subject to regular independent audits, have a majority of the board of directors be chosen independently of the stockholders, and have a "community impact analysis" undertaken and approved should an industrial enterprise intend to expand or relocate. Countries like West Germany, for example, already have *codetermination* laws, which mandate worker representation on the boards of large corporations.[114]

In point of fact, however, these are only left liberal approaches, as much of the means of production would remain in the hands of the small owning class. The owners of capital could still exert ultimate influence by the threat to withhold essential investments. The workers, nonetheless, would have more control than they do at present.

Socialism

The more traditional socialist approach is to move towards collective ownership of at least the major means of production. As Manning Marable describes one such scenario:

> Socialism . . . would involve radical changes. . . . The state would assume the ownership of major corporations, and their direction would be left in the hands of those best qualified to make decisions at the point of production, the working class. Socialism would mean the expropriation of wealth from the capitalist class, and the guarantee of employment, decent housing, education, and health care to all citizens.[115]

Full conversion to a socialist economic system would involve most, if not all, of the following:

1. *Wage labor*, as presently defined, would come to an end, for there would no longer be a separate, capital-owning class. Workers would, directly or at least indirectly, own the companies where they worked, and thus by definition work for themselves.
2. With no separate owning class, the extraction of *surplus value* would also come to an end, as the people actually working in the businesses would collectively receive the full market value of what they were producing.
3. The *workplace would be democratized* in that the worker-owners would have far greater control over such decisions as what products they were to produce, where, at what pace, under what conditions, for what wages, and under what kind of management system.
4. Some centralized *economic planning* would be necessary, such as for allocating scarce basic natural resources, coordinating the nation's large primary industries, and determining which worker-entrepreneurs get start-up loans to form other businesses. Nevertheless, the planners would at least be democratically elected, which is certainly not the case for those who currently control most of the nation's capital.
5. Government also would see to it that *distribution of products* would be based more on people's needs, with guaranteed rights to food, shelter, clothing, and both medical and social services.
6. Finally, the *educational system* would have to help prepare people for creative work as well as for a more active political life, to help purge them of a variety of social prejudices, and to teach them to structure their personal needs within the requirements of society.

Implementation could include having the federal government employ the power of eminent domain in order to nationalize the most basic major industries, such as steel, autos, and oil. The tax system could be used to dismantle monopolies, as well as to raise money in order to spur and sustain cooperative businesses. As a vehicle for the latter, a National Cooperative Bank already exists and could be significantly expanded with renewed assistance from the federal government.[116] In addition, federal, state, and local governments already have the experience of owning and operating significant components of the nation's education, utilities, and mass transportation industries, as well as providing most of our police, fire, sanitation, and military services.[117]

To opt for a less hierarchical political-economic system, however, does entail a trade-off. It would mean trading a system that allows a few to succeed in exploitive positions and for a less exploitive system with fewer extremes of wealth and power. That flies in the face of many fundamental beliefs long held in America. But when the American dream for a few amounts to a nightmare for far more and insomnia for many of the rest, there can be no justice. It is time for a fundamental change in the political economic structures, so that blacks—and all other citizens currently excluded from the American dream—can find justice and dignity in a system based not on exploitation but on a fair distribution of wealth and power.

Nevertheless, it is also clear that such structural alterations are necessary, but not sufficient, to achieve racial justice in America. Racism will continue to stall progressive change even if major structural alterations can be implemented immediately. Racist individuals in positions of power will continue to find ways to discriminate. Yet these structural changes will still accomplish two very important ends. First, they will help clear the way for far more equal economic and political opportunity if, and when, racism diminishes. Second, they will take some of the sting out of existing racism by forcibly providing more equity for most African Americans.

NOTES

1. Walter E. Williams, *Do the Right Thing: the People's Economist Speaks* (Stanford, CA.: Hoover Institute, 1995), pp. viii–ix.

2. See, for example, Mack Jones, "The Political Thought of the New Black Conservatives," in *Readings in American Political Issues,* ed. Franklin Jones (Dubuque, IA.: Kendall/Hunt, 1987); Cornell West, "Assessing Black Neoconservatism," in *The Turbulent Voyage: Readings in African-American Studies,* ed. Floyd Hayes (San Diego, CA: Collegiate Press, 1992); Martin Kilson, "The Gang That Couldn't Shoot Straight," *Transition* 62 (1993); Lewis Randolph, "The New African-American Conservatives or the Same Old Song with A Few New Twists?" (unpublished paper presented at the First National Conference on Civil and Human Rights of African Americans, Memphis, Tennessee, August 1995).

   For original works by these black conservatives, see Joseph Perkins, ed., *A Conservative Agenda for Black Americans* (Washington, D.C.: Heritage Foundation, 1990); *The Fairmont Papers* (San Francisco: Institute for Contemporary Studies, 1981); Walter Williams, *The State Against Blacks* (New York: New Press, 1982); Thomas Sowell, *Markets and Minorities* (New York: Basic Books, 1981); Shelby Steele, *The Content of Our Character: A New Vision of Race in America* (New York: St. Martin's, 1990); Stephen Carter, *Reflections of an Affirmative Action Baby* (New York: Basic Books, 1991).

3. See David McLellan, *The Thought of Karl Marx* (New York: Harper & Row, 1971), pp.105–21.

4. For a more complete discussion of the value of holding "wealth" (bank accounts, stock, bonds, real estate, etc.), see David Swinton, "The Economic Status of African Americans: Limited Ownership and Persistent Inequality," *The State of Black America 1992,*ed. National Urban League (New York: National Urban League, 1992), pp. 62–63.

5. Self-employed workers are conceptually troublesome. Yet the proportion of the American population that is self-employed, and has no nonfamily members working for them has shrunk steadily since the nation began and is now less than 9 percent. Yet this is still a sizable number of people, and as a group they remain difficult to categorize. They are clearly not capitalists, as they do not extract profits from the labor of others. By the same token, they are not really workers either, as their labor is not exploited by a capitalist. Thus, they end up as a group in-between. On the other hand, they also can be seen as a small-scale glimpse of a socialist-type economic arrangement in which all would control the businesses within which they labored. See U.S. Department of Commerce, Bureau of the Census, *1995 Statistical Abstracts of the United States* (Washington, D.C.: GPO, 1995), pp. 407–10.

6. Thomas Dye, *Who's Running America?* (Englewood Cliffs, NJ: Prentice-Hall, 1995), pp. 20–21.

7. Michael Parenti, *Democracy for the Few* (New York: St. Martin's, 1995), p. 10.

8. U.S. Department of Commerce, *1995 Statistical Abstracts,* pp. 515–17; U.S. Department of Commerce, Bureau of the Census, Current Population Reports, Series P-60, No. 179, *Income, Poverty and Wealth in the United States* (Washington, D.C.: GPO, 1992); U.S. Federal Reserve Board and Internal Revenue Service, *Survey of Consumer Finances* (Washington, D.C.: GPO, 1992); New York Stock Exchange Survey (November 1983).

Figures for the top 1 percent of Americans come from James D. Smith and Stephen D. Franklin, "The Concentration of Wealth, 1922–1969," *American Economic Review,* May 1974; figures for the top 5 percent were estimated by taking Smith and Franklin's calculation for the top 1 percent in 1962 and dividing it by a calculation for the top 5 percent from the *Survey of Financial Characteristics of Consumers* (1962). The resulting ratio was then applied to Smith and Franklin's other figures to attain the corresponding estimates for the top 5 percent, extrapolated for the years skipped over in the Smith and Franklin article.

Reference is to direct ownership, although a large number of people indirectly hold shares through banks, insurance companies, and pension funds. Most of the latter group, however, have not controlled these shares in a way that has threatened the dominant power of those who directly hold large individual holdings.

Stock is defined as common and preferred issues in domestic and foreign firms, certificates or shares of building and loan and savings and loan associations, federal land bank stocks, accrued dividends, and other investments reporting equity in an enterprise, as well as stock held in trust (though understated).

9. U.S. Department of Commerce, Bureau of the Census, *Household Wealth and Asset Ownership: 1991* (Washington, D.C.: GPO, 1994); U.S. Department of Commerce, *Income, Poverty and Wealth.* Also see, for example, Abram Harris, *The Negro as Capitalist* (New York: Haskell, 1936); Timothy Bates, *Black Capitalism* (New York: Praeger, 1973); Roger Ransom and Richard Sutch, *One Kind of Freedom* (Cambridge: Cambridge University Press, 1977); Melvin Oliver and Thomas Shapiro, *Black Wealth/White Wealth: A New Perspective on Racial Equality* (New York: Routledge, 1995), pp. 62–65.

10. Jeremiah Cotton, "Towards a Theory and Strategy for Black Economic Development," in James Jennings, ed., *Race, Politics, and Economic Development,* ed. James Jennings, (New York: Verso, 1992), p. 13.

11. *Wall Street Journal,* April 3, 1992, p. R6.

12. U.S. Department of Commerce, Bureau of the Census, *1990 Survey of Minority Owned Business Enterprises: Black* (Washington, D.C.: GPO, 1990).

13. Timothy Bates, *Banking on Black Enterprise: The Potential of Emerging Firms for Revitalizing Urban Economies* (Washington, D.C.: Joint Center for Political and Economic Studies, 1993).

14. *U.S. Department of Commerce 1990 Survey of Minority Owned Business Enterprises.*

15. Charles V. Hamilton, "Conduit Colonialism and Public Policy," *Black World,* October 1972, pp. 40–45.

16. James O' Connor, *The Fiscal Crisis of the State* (New York: St. Martin's Press, 1973), pp. 6–7.

17. The top 1% of households owned $5.7 trillion in net wealth—which averages out to more than $6.8 million per household. See U.S. Department of Commerces *1989 Survey of Consumer Finances.*

18. See *1992 Survey of Consumer Finances;* Edward N. Wolff, "Trends in Household Wealth in the United States, 1962–83 and 1983–89," *Review of Income and Wealth,* June 1994.

19. See John Harrigan, *Empty Dreams, Empty Pockets: Class and Bias in American Politics* (New York: Macmillan, 1993), p. 10.

20. Wolff, "Trends in Household Wealth."

21. Estimated from 1989 Congressional Budget Office figures reported in the *New York Times,* March 5, 1992.

22. Wolff, "Trends in Household Wealth," *New York Times,* June 22, 1996.

23. Wolff, "Trends in Household Wealth," *1995 Statistical Abstracts,* p. 373.

24. Mack Jones, "The Black Underclass as Systemic Phenomenon," in Jennings, *Race, Politics, and Economic Development,* pp. 53–65.

25. Wolff, "Trends in Household Wealth."
26. Wolff, "Trends in Household Wealth." Although not as skewed as wealth holdings, the income average of $47,000 is inflated by the higher incomes at the top of the group. The average drops to $34,000 when the top 10 percent is excluded, and to $29,000 when the top 25 percent is excluded.
27. See *New York Times,* November 26, 1990; *New York Times,* August 16, 1994.
28. Note that a sizable minority of the "lower class" also works for a wage. See U.S. Department of Commerce, Bureau of the Census, *Workers and Low Earnings: 1964–1990* (Washington, D.C.: GPO, March 1992). Thus, in a sense, these people also end up in the middle/working-class category. They, too, are paid less than the market value of what they produce, thus contributing to owner profits. And they, too. pay taxes, some of which find their way to the bank accounts of the owning class. Nonetheless, this total transfer is relatively small, as even including public assistance, this group earns less than 4 percent of all national income. And as they own virtually no property, members of the lower class pay very little in property taxes.
29. For an example, see Paul Samuelson and William Nordhaus, *Economics* (New York: McGraw-Hill, 1995), pp. 202–3.
30. The May 1996 Survey of Current *Business* (Washington, D.C.: GPO, 1996), p. 21, listed domestic corporate profits at $465.3 billion for 1994. Using a corporate income tax rate of .386 (derived from figures in the *1995 Statistical Abstracts,* p. 564), $179 billion was subtracted at corporate income taxes, along with $10.5 billion for profits from lending to government, $12.2 billion for profits from government contracts, and $6.5 billion for profits from serving the poor.
31. Adjusted domestic corporate profit figures from the *Survey of Current Business* (March 1996). Interest profit, contract profit, and conduit profit amounts, as calculated in this note, were then subtracted to avoid double-counting. Profits derived from foreign investments and sales were also excluded, as they generally involved extracting money from transactions with foreign workers and consumers. Lastly, corporate taxes were subtracted as well, using a 38.6 percent tax rate derived from figures in the *1995 Statistical Abstracts,* p. 564.

Estimates of the percentage of business assets held by the top 1 percent of American households were used to calculate the share of these profits garnered by the owning class. These figures exclude profits made by partnerships and proprietorships, which tend to be small firms with relatively few employees and account for only approximately 10 percent of all sales. Inasmuch as a number of their white owners would fall into the owning-class category, ignoring profits from these firms makes the private-sector profit figure slightly more conservative.

Population statistics were used to calculate African Americans as a percentage of the total middle and working classes from which owning-class profits were extracted. Because blacks have regularly made less income than their white counterparts, their proportionate contribution to the corporate profit figure was deflated by multiplying it by a ratio of average black middle/working class (MC/WC) income divided by average middle/working class income as a whole:

$$BD = TD \times \frac{BF}{TF} \times \frac{BI}{AI}$$

where   BD = total black MC/WC dollars involved at this juncture
                       TD = total dollars involved at this juncture
                       BF = black MC/WC families (60 percent of all black families)
                       TF = total MC/WC families (79 percent of all U.S. families)
                       BI = average black MC/WC family income
                       AI = average MC/WC family income

In 1994, domestic corporate profits were $465.3 billion, before subtracting corporate income taxes ($179.9 billion), profits from loans to government ($10.5 billion), profits from sales and services to government ($12.2 billion), and profits made from transactions with welfare recipients ($6.5 billion). That left $256.2 billion in adjusted, after-tax, owning class corporate profits. The owning class's share was estimated to be $158.844 billion—and calculating the owning class's share via its share of business assets that year resulted in 62 percent. The proportion of that share contributed by the total middle/working class was estimated by taking the middle/working class share of all taxes paid, which was 80.5 percent; and the black middle/working class was derived by using the formula in this note.

32. Joseph Pechman, *Who Paid the Taxes, 1966–1985?* (Washington, D.C.: Brookings Institution, 1985), p. 52.

33. Dye, *Who's Running America?* p. 55.

34. See Teresa Odendahl, "A Thousand Pointless Lights?" *New York Times*, July 21, 1990.

35. Karen De Witt, "One Way to Save a Bundle," *New York Times*, April 12, 1995.

36. *1995 Statistical Abstracts*, p. 300.

37. In 1993, for example, of those individuals or couples making $200,000 or more, 2,400 paid no federal income taxes at all, and 18,000 paid less than 5 percent of their incomes in federal income taxes. See David Cay Johnston, "More U.S. Wealthy Sidestepping I.R.S.," *New York Times*, April 18, 1994.

38. Figures from *1995 Statistical Abstracts* for all taxes paid were multiplied by middle/working class percentage of national income for all taxpayers, with black middle/working class taxes derived as in note 31. Given the nation's nonprogressive tax structure, it was assumed that these middle/working classes were paying taxes in proportion to their national income share.

These figures are conservative estimates, not only for the reason cited in the text but also because federal social security payments are not included as taxes even though they are not optional payments. For example, see Kevin Phillips, *Boiling Point: Democrats, Republicans, and the Decline of Middle Class Prosperity* (New York: Harper, 1993), pp. 42–9.

39. The *Survey of Current Business* "subsidy" figure was used despite the fact that it includes subsidies paid to governmental enterprises. Nonetheless, when considering that the figure excludes items such as benefits-in-kind, tax expenditures, loan guarantees, and sales below market value made to private businesses, this best available indicator appears to be a conservative estimate of the amount of tax dollars flowing to private-sector enterprises.

The precise calculation for 1994 took the $34.7 billion "subsidy" figure, arriving at the owning class's share via their share of business assets, with the proportion of that share contributed by the total middle/working class and the black middle/working class derived by the same methods used in note 31.

40. *Survey of Current Business* figures on federal, state, and local government purchases of services and durable and nondurable goods and structures, less all money going directly to employee compensation—conservatively assuming that the owning class was not receiving any of this compensation. In 1994, this amounted to $1,175.3–$602.8 = $572.5 billion (*1995 Statistical Abstracts*, pp. 451, 457).

An indicator for a national profits-to-sales ratio was calculated using *Survey of Current Business* figures for the combined manufacturing and trade industries—profits from the January/February 1996 survey, p. 79, and sales from the October 1995 survey, p. C-41. As the latest available data was from the 1993 calendar year, those numbers were multiplied by a cost-of-living factor to create a 1994 estimate. The resulting calculation was $174.4 billion (in profits) divided by $8,156.9 billion (in sales) = 2.13 percent profit-to-sales rate. This is a conservative estimate, as a sizable majority of these purchases were made without competitive bidding; and thus profit rates are no doubt higher than usual in this governmental arena (see *New York Times*, March 8,1985; *New York Times*, April 9,1985; *New York Times*, May 30,1988).

Corporate profits were then calculated as a proportion of government purchases each year, and the shares captured by the owning class and paid by the black middle/working class were calculated as done in note 31.

41. According to the *1995 Statistical Abstracts*, p. 519, federally insured banks earned a net profit margin of 4.36 percent on their loans and investments. This profit margin was then applied to the $241.3 billion in net interest government paid to domestic persons and businesses in 1994 (*Survey of Current Business*, March 1996, p. 12). The resulting profits from lending to government were then reduced to the share gained by the owning class and paid by the black middle/working class, as calculated above in note 31.

Overall, these, too, are seen as reasonably conservative estimates in that semi-private corporations like the Farm Credit System do additional borrowing and transferring, while members of the owning class likely make more than 4.36 percent net interest when they personally loan money directly to government via purchases of government securities, as opposed to reaping profits via the bank shares they own when banks do the lending.

42. See Vee Burke, *Cash and Non-cash Benefits for Persons with Limited Income*, Congressional Research Service Report No. 85–194 (Washington, D.C.: GPO, 1984).

43. *1995 Statistical Abstracts*, p. 377. Nearly half of this amount is spent on Medicaid. The federal government did pass significant welfare reform in August of 1996, for example, converting Aid to Families with Dependent Children (AFDC) into block grants to allow more state control of this spending. Nevertheless, as this analysis combines the amounts spent at all levels of government, it is anticipated that these numbers will not change much. In the end, the federal reforms ultimately will do little more than shift the cost burden to the states. See, for example, Jason DeParle, "U.S. Welfare System Dies as State Programs Emerge," *New York Times*, June 30, 1997.

44. Hamilton, "Conduit Colonialism and Public Policy."

45. The focus is on cash paid to welfare recipients and items and services purchased for them, such as school lunches and medical care. It is presumed that the cash is spent and not saved or invested. The 1994 public assistance total ($306,113.28 million) is actually an estimate derived from using the latest available figures (from 1992) and multiplying those by a cost-of-living factor. The estimated 1994 figures were then multiplied by the average corporate profit of 2.13 percent, and the shares going to the owning class and paid for by the black middle/working class and the total middle/working class were calculated as in note 31.

It is also assumed that the administrative portion of these government expenditures is offset by the higher-than-average profits gained in many of these transactions. In addition, there are some indications that the administrative costs of these programs are actually relatively low; See for example, *Social Security Bulletin Annual Statistical Supplement*, 1972, p. 57.

There is some overlap between the "conduit profits" and the "contract profits" discussed earlier. Nonetheless, the earlier figures are conservative enough to more than compensate.

46. These numbers are slightly inflated by the fact that some welfare recipients also work for a wage and thus supply a portion of this tribute. Nonetheless, these numbers are conservative estimates for the variety of reasons discussed in the notes and text. Thus, they provide a reasonable estimate of the total transferred to the owning class from the paychecks of the middle and working class.

47. See Jude Wanninski, *The Way the World Works* (New York: Basic Books, 1978).

48. *1995 Statistical Abstracts*, pp. 474–75. The 1980–1993 time frame was chosen because 1993 family data was the most recent and most complete available, whereas 1980 was the first year in which the census bureau employed a new definition of *family*. Actually, I would have preferred to have used household data subdivided by the wealth categories employed previously; however, this was simply the closest that the existing data would allow me to come if I wanted to make meaningful comparisons over time.

49. Kevin Phillips, *The Politics of Rich and Poor* (New York: Harper, 1990), pp. 157–72. The number of billionaires had grown to 135 by 1996. See *Forbes*, October 14, 1996.

50. See, for example, *New York Times*, April 15, 1992.

51. *1995 Statistical Abstracts*, pp. 474–75; Harrigan, *Empty Dreams*, p. 19.

52. Susan Mayer and Christopher Jencks, "Recent Trends in Economic Inequality in the United States: Income versus Expenditures versus Material Well-being," in *Poverty and Prosperity in the USA in the Late Twentieth Century*, eds. Dimitri Papadimitriou and Edward Wolff, (New York: St. Martin's, 1993), p. 121.

53. Greg Duncan, Timothy Smeeding, and Willard Rodgers, "W(h)ither the Middle Class? A Dynamic View," in *Poverty and Prosperity*, eds. Papadimitriou and Wolff, chap. 7; Sylvia Nasar, "One Study's Rags to Riches Is Another's Rut of Poverty," *New York Times*, May 18, 1992.

54. Duncan, "W(h)ither the Middle Class?, p. 263; *New York Times*, December 16, 1990; *New York Times*, January 12, 1992.

55. See for example, Louis Uchitelle, "Moonlighting Plus: 3-Job Families on the Rise," *New York Times*, August 16, 1994. As for the special position of African Americans, see for example, *New York Times*, November 26, 1990, p. A11; Wade Nobles, "Public Policy and the African-American Family," in *Race: Twentieth Century Dilemmas—Twenty-First Century Prognoses*, Winston Van Horne (ed.), (Madison: University of Wisconsin, 1989), p 105.

56. See for example, Juliet Schor, *The Overworked American: The Unexpected Decline of Leisure* (New York: Basic, 1991); Phillips, *Boiling Point*, pp. 161–62.

57. Duncan, "Whither the Middle Class?"; Frank Levy, "The Vanishing Middle Class and Related Issues," *PS* Summer 1987, pp. 650–55.

58. Pension savings have declined as well, e.g., see for example *New York Times*, April 13, 1992.

59. See for example, Bob Herbert, "Bogeyman Economics," *New York Times*, April 4, 1997.

60. For example, see Phillips, *Boiling Point*, pp. 175–77.

61. Quoted in A. M. Rosenthal,"American Class Struggle," *New York Times*, March 22, 1995.

62. Duncan, "Whither the Middle Class?," p. 248.

63. Cited in Richard Morin, "Sociologist Takes on the 'welfare myth'," *Memphis Commercial Appeal*, April 29, 1994.

64. Yankelovich Clancy Shulman poll (1992), reported in *Memphis Commercial Appeal*, April 29, 1994.

65. *Report of the U.S. Department of Health and Human Services*, October 1995.

66. Average benefit for 1993. See *New York Times*, March 23, 1995. This ranged from $923 in Alaska to $120 in Mississippi. See *National Journal* June 10, 1995, pp. 1385–86; *New York Times*, July 5, 1992.

67. *New York Times*, March 23, 1995; Holly Sklar, *Chaos or Community?: Seeking Solutions, Not Scapegoats For Bad Economics* (Boston: South End, 1995), p. 94.

68. Sklar, *Chaos or Community?*, p. 99. See also Harrell Rodgers, *Poor Women, Poor Families: The Economic Plight of America's Female-Headed Households* (New York: Sharpe, 1990).

69. Parenti, *Democracy for the Few*, pp. 101–2; U.S. News and World Report, April 3, 1972, p. 57.

70. See Fred Block, Richard Cloward, Barbara Ehrenreich, and Francis Fox Piven, *The Mean Season* (New York: Pantheon, 1987), chap. 2; Sklar, *Chaos or Community?*, p. 96.
71. See *New York Times*, March 3, 1994.
72. *National Journal*, December 1, 1990, p. 2931.
73. See, for example, Herbert Gans, *The War Against the Poor: The Underclass and Anti-Poverty Policy* (New York: Basic Books, 1995).
74. Quoted in Sklar, *Chaos or Community?* p. 96.
75. Mary Jo Bane and David Ellwood, *Welfare Realities: From Rhetoric to Reform* (Cambridge, Mass.: Harvard University Press, 1994), chap. 2.
76. Lou Harris poll, published May 19, 1989.
77. NORC poll, reported in the *New York Times*, January 4, 1993. For more on the character and values of the poor, see Charles Henry, "Understanding The Underclass: The Role of Culture and Economic Progress," in, *Race, Politics and Economic Development*, ed. Jennings, chap. 4.
78. Sklar, *Chaos or Community?*, p. 95.
79. Christopher Jencks, *Rethinking Social Policy* (Cambridge.: Harvard University Press, 1992), p. 205. Jenck's 1988 figures have been converted to 1994 dollars.
80. Sklar, *Chaos or Community?*, pp. 94–95; *New York Times* December 2, 1990; *New York Times* April 2, 1991; *New York Times* November 19, 1996.
81. The high-income cutoff point for the bottom 20 percent of American families was $17,535 in 1980 but had declined to $16,952 by 1993 (in 1993 dollars). See 1995 Statistical Abstracts.
82. Paul Starobin, "Unequal Shares," *National Journal*, September 11, 1993, p. 2179.
83. Gallup poll (July 1990), cited in Harrigan, *Empty Dreams*, p. 22.
84. Lester Thurow, *Generating Inequality*, (New York: Basic Books, 1975), ch. 6.
85. Paul Menchik, *Conference on Research in Income and Wealth* (New York: National Bureau of Economic Research, 1979).
86. Thurow, *Generating Inequality*, esp. chaps. 5, 6.
87. Phillips, *Boiling Point*, pp. 191–92.
88. Nick Ravo, "A Windfall Nears In Inheritances from The Richest Generation," *New York Times*, July 22, 1990; Keith Bradsher, "For Most U.S. Households, Inheritances Hardly Count," *New York Times*, July 25, 1995.
89. Sylvia Nasar, "Those Born Wealthy or Poor Usually Stay So, Studies Say," *New York Times*, May 18, 1992. See also Greg Duncan and James Morgan, "An Overview of Family Economic Mobility," in *Years of Poverty*, eds. Greg Duncan and James Morgan, (Ann Arbor, Mich.: University of Michigan Press, 1984).
90. See, for example, Gary Orfield and Carole Ashkinaze, *The Closing Door: Conservative Policy and Black Opportunity* (Chicago: University of Chicago Press, 1991); Martin Kilson, "Black Social Classes and Intergenerational Poverty," *Public Interest* 64 (Summer 1981), pp. 58–78.
91. See for example, U.S. Department of Commerce, Bureau of the Census, *Current Population Surveys; Occupational Changes in a Generation Survey* (1973).
92. See *National Journal*, September 28, 1991, pp. 2321–2; Richard Coleman and Lee Rainwater, *Social Standing in America*, (New York: Basic Books, 1978).
93. Oliver and Shapiro, *Black Wealth/White Wealth*, p. 196; Also see *New York Times*, December 13, 1993.
94. See for example, *New York Times*, June 17, 1996; Oliver and Shapiro, *Black Wealth/White Wealth*, pp. 152–153; U.S. Department of Commerce, Bureau of the Census, "School Enrollment—Social and Economic Characteristics: October 1993," in *Current Population Reports* p. 20–479 (Washington, D.C.: GPO, 1994), p. 69.
95. See for example, Karen Arenson, "Cuts in Tuition Assistance Put College Beyond Reach of Poorest Students," *New York Times*, January 27, 1997.

96. See *U.S. Department of Commerce,* "School Enrollment."

97. See for example, Benjamin DeMott, *The Imperial Middle: Why Americans Can't Think Straight about Class* (New York: William Morrow, 1990), pp. 139–40.

98. See for example, Phillips, *Boiling Point,* p. 12.

99. See Martin Carnoy, *Faded Dreams: The Politics and Economics of Race in America* (New York: Cambridge University Press, 1994), p. 107.

100. See for example, Schor, *The Overworked American,* pp. 39–40.

101. See for example, Jones, "The Black Underclass," pp. 60–61. Lucius Barker and Mack Jones *African Americans and the American Political System,* (Englewood Cliffs, N.J.: Prentice-Hall, 1994), pp. 337–338; Alexander Astin, *The Myth of Equal Access to Higher Education* (Atlanta: Southern Education Foundation, 1975).

102. Sklar, *Chaos or Community?,* p. 107; *New York Times,* March 11, 1990; June 6, 1990; June 10, 1990.

103. Sklar, *Chaos or Community?,* pp. 106–9. Specifically for racial implications, see, for example, Andrew Hacker, *Two Nations* (New York: Scribner's, 1992), p. 173; E.D. Hirsch, Jr., "Good Genes, Bad Schools," *New York Times,* October 29, 1994.

104. See Ronald Ferguson, "Paying for Public Education: Evidence on How and Why Money Matters," *Harvard Journal of Legislation* (Summer 1991).

105. See for example, DeMott, *The Imperial Middle;* Harrigan, *Empty Dreams,* pp. 6–24; Susan Ostrander, "Upper Class Women," in *Power Structure Research* in William Domhoff ed., (Beverly Hills: Sage, 1980), p. 79.

106. See Oliver and Shapiro, *Black Wealth/White Wealth,* pp. 152–70; William J. Wilson, *The Truly Disadvantaged* (Chicago: University of Chicago Press, 1987); Douglas Glasgow, *The Black Underclass* (San Francisco: Jossey-Bass, 1980); Douglas Glasgow, "The Black Underclass in Perspective," in *The State of Black America, 1987,* ed. National Urban League, (New York: National Urban League, 1987), pp. 129–44.

107. Monoghan, for instance, grew up in an orphanage, yet went on to found Domino Pizza and own the Detroit Tigers major league baseball team. See Harrigan, *Empty Dreams,* p. 9.

108. Robert Allen, *Black Awakening in Capitalist America: An Analytical History* (Garden City, N.Y.: Anchor Doubleday, 1969), p. 274.

109. Martin Luther King, Jr., "The President's Address to the 10th Anniversary Convention of the Southern Christian Leadership Conference (August 16, 1967)," in *The Rhetoric of Black Power,* eds. Robert Scott and Wayne Brockreide (New York: Harper and Row, 1969), pp. 161–62. For further discussion of King's socialist leanings, see James Cone, *For My People: Black Theology and the Black Church* (Maryknoll, N.Y.: Orbis, 1984), p. 96.

110. Quoted in Allen, *Black Awakening,* p. 159.

111. Manning Marable, *How Capitalism Underdeveloped Black America* (Boston: South End Press, 1983), p. 256. See also W. E. B. Du Bois, "Is Man Free?" *Scientific Monthly* May 1948; W. E. B. Du Bois, "There Must Come a Vast Social Change in the United States," *National Guardian,* July 11, 1951; Wilson Record, *Race and Radicalism* (Ithaca, NY: Cornell University Press, 1964); Phillip Foner (ed.), *The Black Panthers Speak* (Philadelphia: Lippincott, 1970); Earl Ofari, "Marxist-Leninism: The Key to Black Liberation," *Black Scholar* 4 (1972); pp. 35–46; I. A. Baraka, "Why I Changed My Ideology: Black Nationalism and Socialist Revolution," *Black World,* 24 (1975): pp. 30–42; Cedric Robinson, *Black Marxism: The Making of the Black Radical Tradition* (London: Zed Books,1983); Lloyd Hogan, "the Role of Land and African-Centered Values in Black Economic Development," in *Race, Politics, and Economic Development,* ed. James Jennings, (New York: Verso, 1992).

112. Allen, *Black Awakening,* p. 153.

113. Coretta King and others have advocated this position in organizations such as the Full Employment Action Council.

114. *Village Voice,* September 29, 1975.

115. Marable, *How Capitalism Underdeveloped Black America,* p. 16.

116. On August 20, 1978, Congress created the National Consumer Cooperative Bank (Public Law 95–351). See the National Cooperative Bank's web page at www.ncb.com/day/a9a.htm.

117. For a detailed fictional account of how such a revolution and transformation might take place, see Kenneth Dolbeare and Janette Hubbell, *USA 2012: After the Middle-Class Revolution* (Chatham, NJ: Chatham House, 1996).

CHAPTER 12

BEYOND BLACK NEOCONSERVATISM AND BLACK LIBERALISM

JAMES JENNINGS

Since the time of the New Deal period, the U.S. government has experimented with economic development and social welfare strategies and programs molded by liberals and conservatives and embodied in the policies and politics of both major parties. Presumably these policies provide spillover, or trickle-down, benefits that can improve the living conditions for people of color and their neighborhoods. Given continuing social and economic crisis facing relatively large sectors of blacks and Latinos in urban locations, apparently the approaches of both liberals and conservatives have been inadequate for many people and families in these groups.[1]

The ideological framework utilized by black neoconservatives as a response to continuing inequality contains conceptual and historical flaws that become evident in efforts to implement an ideologically conservative political and economic agenda in black communities.[2] But have liberal thinkers in the black community accomplished better and more in terms of answers for improving black life? I believe that the answer is negative for both schools of thought. Due to the apparent failure of certain policy and political strategies in terms of improving living conditions, and narrowing social and economic gaps between blacks, Latinos, and whites, civic and activists' debate in the black community should move from disagreements between liberals and conservatives, or Democrats and Republicans, toward the question of what kinds of new philosophical principles and mobilization should guide political, educational, and economic activism.

The National Congress of Black Conservatives was founded in September 1997 in order "to fill the leadership vacuum in the Black community as we move into the 21st century. Seeds of Black conservatism, rooted hundreds of years ago during slavery, and blossoming at a time when America is undergoing a fundamental power shift."[3] While this statement is correct in pointing out that a "fundamental power shift" is occurring in U.S. society, and that there does exist a certain kind of leadership vacuum in the black community, it may not be on the mark in claiming that black conservatism as a response to this situation is blossoming, at least based on numerous black opinion polls and surveys.[4] Yet this claim is made continually in a number of Black conservative venues. For example, note the preface to a recent book, *Black and Right: The Bold New Voice of Black Conservatives in America*, edited by Stan Faryna, Brad Stetson, and Joseph G. Conti:

> The newness of the black conservative voice lies not in some nouveau quality to their ideas but rather in their burgeoning numbers and social influence. This will perhaps be one of he most politically significant trends in American public life as the century in which this country began to live out the true meaning of its creed—"All men are created equal"—comes to a close.[5]

Interestingly, the claim of burgeoning numbers and social influence is not discussed further in the anthology. Certainly the 1998 national elections make this claim a bit hyperbolic. Black voters, for example, overwhelmingly tended to support liberal Democratic party candidates for a range of local and state offices. New York City offers another example that serves to question the claims of some black neoconservatives that black public opinion is swaying in their direction. Current reports in the media indicate that Mayor Rudolph Giuliani is concentrating his U.S. senatorial efforts in upstate New York, perhaps conceding the black (and Latino) vote in his own home base of New York City to the Democratic Party rival, Hillary Clinton. Why would he do this if there were really a swing of support among blacks towards conservative and Republican Party issue positions? Related to this are the efforts of various Democratic Party contenders for major office to woo the support of the Reverend Al Sharpton in this same city. Again, this indicates that Sharpton, who is certainly not known for any conservative or Republican party issue positions, carries much weight in the black community, which would not be the case if the contention of black neoconservatives is accurate. This also raises the issue of Alan Keyes's candidacy for the Republican Party presidential nomination. Here is a black conservative who did not generate significant support among black or white voters during his campaign. But if the claims of some black neoconservatives are accurate, then surely Keyes should have done much better than the five or so percentage points he received in the primaries in 2000.

Aside from these and other pragmatic examples indicating that Blacks are not moving toward conservative or Republican Party issue positions en mass, there are opinion polls that could be cited. For example, in reviewing the attitudes of blacks regarding redistributive policies as well as racial policies, this group is consistently and significantly more liberal than whites, as reported by Michael C. Dawson in his book, *Behind the Mule: Race and Class in African-American Politics*.[6] But some have contended that it is black leadership that is liberal leaning rather than the majority of black people. This issue was investigated by political scientists Ronald W. Walters and Robert C. Smith. They discovered that while there are class and ideological differences among African-American leadership as many scholars have observed, there is also a degree of consensus on issues such as the role of government in addressing racial and social inequalities, affirmative action, and other redistributive social welfare and economic policies.[7]

Now, how do black liberals respond to the fact that the black community continues to face serious community-wide social and economic problems? Blacks, compared to whites, are characterized by persistently greater levels of poverty, unemployment, inferior housing, inadequate education, and poor health, including high levels of infant mortality. Even in places where blacks have made important political gains, major social and economic problems remain steadfast and, in fact, may be intensifying in some ways. Moreover, a significant racial divide, manifested in terms of education, housing, health, and wealth indicators, continues to characterize almost all aspects of life in the United States. One need but visit many black neighborhoods in cities such as New York, Philadelphia, Detroit, Los Angeles, and Chicago.[8] It is apparent that black liberal leaders, like the black neoconservatives, have failed to develop strategies or generate political mobilization to change these kinds of conditions.

The substance of a racially based social and economic hierarchy has been documented and analyzed in several national studies, including the volume published by the National Academy of Sciences, *A Common Destiny*, and the Trotter Institute's five volume study, *Assessment of the Status of African Americans*.[9] These studies and others show that, although some individuals and sectors in the black community have been able to realize a limited degree of racial progress, other, larger sectors of this community continue to be characterized by poverty and related problems such as high unemployment, poor housing, high incarceration rates, and poor health. For example, a recent report issued by the Council of Economic Advisors reiterated the findings reported in the earlier studies. The median family income of blacks remains much lower than that of white families; the poverty rates of black children remains much higher than that of white children (in 1995 registering 40 percent versus 17 percent); black women and men continue to be unemployed at twice the rate of white men, even factoring in similar levels of education; home ownership rates for blacks have remained essentially at the same level as that noted in 1983 but have increased for whites; and the infant mortality rate of blacks also continues to register at a rate twice that of whites. This and other studies provide a wealth of data illustrating the extent and persistence of these kinds of problems.[10]

A range of reasons have been offered by black neoconservations and black liberals for the contemporary state of racial affairs in the United States. Some in the black liberal camp, such as Hugh Price, president of the Urban League, and Roy Wilkins, Jr., professor of history at George Mason University, believe that these problems reflect a moral and political problem on the part of society that maintains social and economic inequality. Individuals in this camp propose that the civil rights movement during the mid-1960s was too short-lived, but that nevertheless, it was an effective period of social and government activism in which policies and practices associated with racism and discrimination were reduced to a limited extent. Black neoconservatives, such as the economist Thomas Sowell and Reverend Earl Jackson of the Christian Coalition, believe the essential causes of these kinds of problems are the fault of individual blacks whose cultural or group attitudes prevent them from pushing hard enough to succeed. Along this neoconservative line, a few commentators such as the economist Walter Williams and the literary critic Shelby Steele have raised doubts about the effectiveness or strategies of the civil rights movement during the 1960s in resolving current social and economic problems facing massive numbers of impoverished black citizens today. In fact, they suggest that the civil rights movement actually contributed to the negative and deteriorated living conditions in the 1980s and 1990s.

Persisting negative living conditions and inequalities between blacks and whites historically have generated intense ideological debates about the current and future status of blacks in the United States. In earlier periods such debates usually took place within a racial and social order that made it possible to identify common problems facing blacks, as well as the source of such problems. For instance, during slavery, the focus of debates among blacks had to do with the abolition of slavery or challenging this system by utilizing a range of tactics. While some leaders advocated self-defense, others sought the path of assimilation and accommodation and yet others, emigration.[11] But during slavery, the black agenda was clearly the abolition of this institution. Abolition was the glue for black protest and mass mobilization directed against the system of slavery. Certainly a range of tactical responses to this agenda were offered, but the bottom line was that slavery had to be abolished and challenged in all possible ways by the African American community.

This prevailing issue is what defined political friends and enemies for the black community. It was this "permanent" interest during the pre–Civil War era that served as a philosophical reference point. An aspect of the crisis of black leadership today is that many individuals begin their analysis with identifying whom they perceive to be a political friend or enemy rather than what may serve the current interests of the black community, to borrow a quip from a Chicago congressman of the 1950s and 1960s, William Dawson.

For seventy or eighty years after emancipation, the major item on the black agenda was physical and cultural survival within a legally sanctioned oppressive and segregated society. During this period antilynching campaigns were prominent, as was the building of cultural and economic, albeit forced "separatist" institutions, including businesses, hospitals, and schools. For many in the black community in the decades of the 1940s, 1950s, and 1960s, the major item on the racial and political agenda was desegregation. Thus, many black leaders and activists could develop strategies directed against a common enemy: official and de facto segregation. Such a strategic umbrella, if not a source of tactical unity, nonetheless made it easier to mobilize greater numbers of blacks for specific actions. Today, and perhaps unlike earlier periods, black America no longer has a clearly defined social enemy that helps to frame or clarify a philosophical map for political mobilization and action. Such a reference would facilitate a degree of concerted political, economic, and cultural strategies aimed at mobilizing significant numbers of black people. Moreover, the absence of such a common realization of the problems facing blacks has produced debates about the in current and future status that are confined philosophically to what is known today as liberalism and conservatism. Alas, as Harold Cruse pointed out, this confinement represents a major problem for the effective political mobilization of the black community.[12] Although liberal and conservative policies have not significantly furthered the racial and class interests of the black community, black leadership today remains ensconced in debates focusing on the relative merits of both schools. This is one reason for the crisis of black leadership that has been bemoaned by many in the black community. Actually, the crisis is rather that neither black liberal or conservative apologists have been able to enhance the political and economic power of the black community vis-à-vis white power in the United States.

At the same time that black neoconservatives' calls for self-help and family values have hit a respondent cultural chord in the black community, although less effectively than many who might be described as liberal or even left, they have not been able to expand their political base. This is due partially to the fact that connections to the political right and accompanying but periodic fiscal resources has its institutional ebb and flow, and it tends to benefits individuals rather than masses of black citizens. But, more fundamentally, black neoconservatives do not have a concrete grassroots program to operationalize politically or economically the values they espouse. Errol Smith, described as a "black conservative" radio talk host in Los Angeles, observed: "Significant political and social influence has eluded Black conservatives. The black right has demonstrated precious little ability to profoundly influence politics within the black community, or to mobilize black Americans behind a generally conservative agenda."[13]

Additionally, black conservatives implicitly accept a second-class status for blacks vis-à-vis the building of multiracial coalitions. Such coalitions, according to many black conservatives and their apologists, must be based on blacks not antagonizing whites. This is pointed out in the critique of Stephen L. Carter's *Reflections of an Affirmative Action Baby* by political scientist Martin Kilson. He writes that

> Carter's discussion of the need for blacks to appease white voters' anxiety toward affirmative action never mentions a reciprocal obligation on the part of whites, nor does he probe the possible political methodologies that might ensure this. Presumably, the injury done by affirmative action policy to whites' mobility interests and normative sensibilities—relating to presumptively pristine values of achievement and merit—negates the right of blacks to expect a reciprocal obligation.[14]

Thus, and again, blacks must be careful not to disrupt the social and dominant racial order of "white as right."

On the other side of the isle, black liberal leaders have become nothing more than cheerleaders for the so-called moderate wing of the Democratic Party. They, too, accept a second-class citizenship—of sorts. The ideological framework of the latter sector is captured partially by Hanes Walton, Jr., in a recent article for the journal *Black Scholar*, "Social Policy: The Politics of Disappearances." Walton states that the essence of black liberal thinking about social policy and politics is reflected in the black public intellectuals that have recently emerged:

> Coming into the public sphere where the debate and discourse are raging, are a cacophony African American voices. Liberals, such as Mary Francis Berry, Marian Wright Edelman, and William J. Wilson, for example, give vigorous voice to the position that some of the New Deal social policies were beneficial to the African-American community. As they see it, some of the policies should be copied, extended and made to enhance racial and minority communities. Jesse Jackson, the NAACP, the National Urban League, the congressional Black Caucus, and a host of civil rights leaders have suggested various ways to fund and finance such policies.[15]

One astonishing example of this is reference to former President Bill Clinton as a sort of first black president of the United States.[16] This silly and defeatist notion is exactly the kind of sentiment that widens the gap between black public intellectuals and grassroots sectors involved with local activism aimed at institutionally and culturally strengthening the black community. According to some observers, another example of this response on the part of the black elite is the kind of "opposition" directed at the former president and the Democratic Party by the Reverend Jesse Jackson during the second Clinton administration, as well as the unflappable loyalty of blacks to this party. Jackson has been criticized for essentially abandoning an independent and progressive, rainbow strategy for mobilizing "left-out" sectors. Although he is driven by moral outrage at important issues involving race and class, community mobilization seems to be always pursued in ways that are not harmful to the electoral interests of the Democratic Party. One cannot but help to conclude from these actions that blacks really do have a permanent friend: the Democratic Party.

Reverend Jackson has a widely respected and legitimate base in the black community. Unlike Jackson and like many black neoconservatives, however, other black liberals and public intellectuals do not have substantial political or economic linkages with poor and working-class sectors and organizations in black urban communities. Their major function and role is merely to provide a black voice for whites in power who reflect the liberal school of politics. This is exactly the function that black neoconservatives perform for conservative whites. Usually these voices, whether conservative or liberal, are expressed forthrightly and loudly in the nation's elite media such as *The New Yorker, The Atlantic,* and the *New York Times,* but hardly ever heard in other power arenas such as corporate institutions. The "voices" of both black liberals and neoconservatives are merely used to talk (and rap?) innocuously to white audiences, rather than as a vehicle to mobilize poor or working-class people in the black community.

Black conservatives and liberals have failed to provide a political or social policy framework that could serve to change racial and class hierarchies in this society, as currently reflected in social and economic inequality. These leaders have failed to mobilize the black community—or, generally, poor and working-class sectors in society. They have refused to use existing social and economic inequalities as a moral and political leverage for pursuing the expansion of social democracy for all people. Essentially, many of the struggles of black leadership has been reduced to the politics of getting "a piece of the pie."

Black conservatives, as is the case with liberals, have overlook or sacrificed certain lessons from U.S. history that could serve to build a more effective intellectual and ideological framework aimed at the expansion of social and economic democracy, not just for blacks but other groups as well. Perhaps what makes black liberalism more appealing to black people, however, is the failure of black conservatives to challenge a social and economic system of white privilege. Whereas black liberals believe that such a system could be reformed to include black interests, conservatives seem to merely wink at structures of power and wealth built on the idea of white supremacy. As one example, note the lack of outcry about how white students have benefited from policies of privilege in higher education, compared to the outcry against affirmative action.

Some black conservatives have criticized admissions policies with goals of increasing the racial and ethnic diversity of elite universities on the basis that we live in a color-blind society. In this way, they conveniently overlook the continuing benefits for the children whose grandparents, if not parents, lived, worked, and realized benefits during segregation in this society. In 1997, for instance, 267 students were admitted to Harvard University as "legacy" admissions, that is, on the basis of where their parents attended college. In that same year, a total of 132 black students were admitted to Harvard University. The *Journal of Blacks in Higher Education* reported:

The conservative position is that [racial preferences] should be abolished because we live in, and must be faithful to, a meritocratic society. Accordingly, it is said that students should be admitted to educational institutions solely on the basis of individual merit or personal qualifications. But this statement is pure hypocrisy. In fact, the number of academically underqualified white students admitted each year to college for political, family legacy, or financial influence far exceeds the number of black students admitted under racial preference.[17]

Although black conservatives are anxious, as are some whites, to criticize policies that support some preferences for blacks and other people of color, they are quite silent about policies and practices that support white privileges in U.S. society. The lawyer and writer Stephanie M. Wildman offered a personal account as a white woman confirming how a social system based on white skin privileges operates in higher education, and especially at law schools. She described a range of informal practices, coupled with stereotypical attitudes held by those in power, against people of color, and also women, that uphold a sometimes invisible system of white privileges in this sector. In her book, *Privilege Revealed: How Invisible Preference Undermines America*, she gives several examples of how this system operates in terms of outreach, recruitment, and evaluation of people of color in such ways as to give advantages to whites.[18]

Writers and speakers reflecting both schools of thought, conservatism and liberalism, have generally dismissed the importance of institution-building in black or Latino communities. Many spokespersons of both schools, furthermore, do not have direct hands-on knowledge or experiences about what works, or does not work, in terms of policy and politics or economic and community development at the local level. An example of this weakness can be illustrated by noting how both black conservatives and black liberals approach the question of "self-help." Certainly the idea of self-help in the black community represents an important value and a popular tradition. The historian V. P. Franklin described this tradition in his work, *Black Self-Determination*.[19] Prominent historian John Hope Franklin and civic activist Eleanor Holmes Norton made a similar observation years later: "[T]he 'self-help' tradition is so embedded in the Black heritage as to be virtually synonymous with it."[20]

The idea for self-help among blacks is a powerful one, which black conservatives have assiduously and effectively used as a way to enhance their legitimacy. But this camp has not pursued the political and economic resources that U.S. history suggests are necessary to achieve it, nor have they offered an analysis of how black self-help has been resisted and feared as a political and economic development throughout national history. Black liberals, on the other hand, tend to continue calling for racially benevolent and trickle-down programs to be obtained from friendly government administrations, forgetting that power rests on concrete, community-based resources built on strategies of self-help and independence, rather than proximity to friendly or racially liberal democrats. As a matter of fact, some have derided the call for black self-help as conservative or unworthy. These positions on self-help can be explained by the fact that in the current racial order, both black neoconservatives and black liberals simply serve as racial point persons, and at times racial gatekeepers, for one or the other school of power, which is sometimes correlated with the Democratic and Republican Parties. Thus, both types have little need for self-help strategies built on political independence because this would be inimical to the interests of white wealth and power, whether liberal or conservative in orientation.

TOWARD A RENAISSANCE BLACK AGENDA

There are other important ideas emerging from a review of the historical struggles of blacks that can be noted here. But the theme of this short chapter is that the black community, through its leadership and activism, must again build a *philosophical map* for the community. Such a map, reflecting the lessons learned from earlier historical struggles, could help produce a conceptualization of strategies and tactical initiatives for improving living conditions in ways that would enhance the quality of mass mobilization. The call for a philosophical framework is not new, as indicated by the work of Philip S. Foner and George E. Walker in their collection, *Proceedings of the Black State Conventions, 1840–1865.*[21] As previously noted, in earlier periods, obvious problems facing the black community facilitated a framework for mobilizing against adverse political and economic situation or conditions.

The absence of such an agenda represents a critical political and cultural disadvantage for the black community today. It is associated with a fundamental crisis in lack of direction regarding the regarding principles and values that could be the basis of political, economic, and cultural strategies for community empowerment. As a matter of fact, it is such a social change agenda that has represented the cultural glue for black mobilization in earlier periods. Today, the development of a black agenda incorporating democratic principles and values can lead to more effective strategies for mobilizing people at a grassroots level.

A historically and culturally relevant black agenda can provide the symbolism and substance that serves to unite and mobilize large numbers of blacks to focus on tactics directed at social change today in the United States. Such an agenda, also utilized as a political reference for holding leadership accountable, can serve as a counterpoint to the staid strategy confined to debates about whether to support—loyally and blindly—the Democrats or the Republicans. It is precisely due to the political fact that both Republican and Democrats, whether conservatives or liberals, are unreliable in terms of racial and social justice that the black community must again develop and advocate for a vision of society that does not sacrifice equality and justice for political expediency or access to the powerful.

There are certain key principles and values reflected in earlier historical struggles to challenge the nation's racial hierarchy that are still relevant today. Two important principles are the development of political and economic power, rather than mere access to such; and the cultural strengthening and preservation of the black community as fundamental to the economic wellbeing of black people. A general theme emerging from a review of historical documents is that many of the problems facing the black community have required the community's political strengthening or "empowerment." The political muscle and respect of the black community (and not merely its electoral influence) must be enhanced in the contemporary period for any kind of social advancement that benefits poor and working-class people. Understanding these principles enhances the collective political consciousness of the black community, especially among young people. It expands the consciousness of activists to address the role of power in society, especially regarding how it is used to depress the wellbeing of the black community. This kind of political and historical consciousness is far more important than electoral influence or access to the powerful.

Another lesson emerging from a review of earlier historical struggles is that the pursuit of both political and economic development cannot be separated. The effective pursuit of one goal cannot be accomplished without the other. But as Cruse so eloquently showed, these two principles have been separated and thereby have weakened the possibility of effective black-led strategies in the pursuit of either political or economic power. Generally, whereas liberals would argue that an expanding economy and a responsible government (usually run by Democrats), would take care of the needs of blacks, poor people, and working-class people, conservatives believe that it is an expanding economy via the free market and a noninterfering government (usually run by Republicans), that would actually accomplish these objectives. Both these perspectives presuppose a politically passive black community. Blacks, however, must be politicized, regardless of whether liberal or conservative administrations are in control of government and regardless of the number of black faces or appointees. A corollary to both principles is that black political strategies and tactical decisions should be aimed at the development of power, rather than merely access to the powerful. This observation provides a guide by which to critique or endorse specific actions of individuals and groups. An acknowledgment of this need shifts discussion and debate from simply personal or "party-based" disagreements about the decisions made by individuals to a more focused discussion on whether the action taken reflects movement toward power for the black community. This also "forces" a discussion of the nature of power and its manifestations. Actions by individuals representing the black community therefore should be evaluated in terms of greater movement toward group power, not simply greater access to the powerful.

Another idea inherent in earlier historical struggles that continues to have relevancy today is the preservation of the culture and historical knowledge of the black community. Cultural efforts in the black community must be expanded and strengthened for this community to realize significant economic progress. Many have pointed to the economic progress of groups such as Koreans, Cubans, and others in poor and working-class communities and have queried why blacks have not progressed similarly. There are many systematic reasons for this uneven progress. But perhaps one explanatory factor is the cultural basis on which some of the successful efforts of other groups are built. It seems that groups that reflect the acknowledgment or appreciation of their cultural context and utilize it as a base for mobility have advantages over blacks who pursue economic initiatives as culturally disconnected individuals.[22] This does not mean that blacks are culturally or genetically deficient, as suggested in the writings of Edward C. Banfield, Thomas Sowell, Charles Murray, and others.[23] It does mean that in the pursuit of integrating into mainstream America, some blacks rely on meritocratic and individualistic approaches rather than utilizing their group and related cultural manifestations as part of the base for advancement.

In response to the political appeals of representatives of both neoconservatives and liberal electoral camps, whether Democratic or Republican, national and local organizations in the black community should begin sponsoring public forums, town meetings, and summits to discuss the state and future status of race relations. Activists must involve young people, religious institutions, educators, and health workers in a myriad of meetings to begin enunciating and debating the needs of the black community and appropriate political and economic responses. If anything, such civic forums can begin to counter the message of mainstream media, including television, radio, and newspapers, that assert that black political opinion and even activism are insignificant because they are managed and controlled. Black leadership interested in strengthening black communities politically and economically can make a major contribution in struggles toward the democratization of U.S. society by reviewing the principles that undergirded strategies for social change in earlier periods, which too many black neoconservatives and liberals have forgotten or abandoned.

NOTES

1. For examples and critiques of both liberal and conservative responses to social and urban issues, see the two volumes edited by James Jennings, *Race, Politics, and Economic Development: Community Perspectives* (London: Verso Press, 1992), and, *Race and Politics* (London: Verso Press, 1997).
2. See Walter Stafford's essay, "Whither the Great Neo-Conservative Experiment in New York City?" in Jennings, *Race, Politics, and Economic Development,* which describes the failures of attempts to operationalize an urban agenda on the basis on neoconservative ideology in New York City. I provide a summary of these neoconservative views in "The New Black Neo-Conservatism: A Critique," *Trotter Review,* 1 (2) (Fall 1987).
3. Editorial, "Moving Black Conservatives from the Margins to the Mainstream," *The Tuskegee Rail,* 1 (1) (June/July 1998).
4. See, for example, the following essays describing black public opinion on a range of issues: Robert Smith and Richard Seltzer, *Race, Class, and Culture* (New York: State University of New York Press, 1992), Michael C. Dawson, Riaz Khan, and John Baughman, *"Black Discontent": The Final Report on the 1993–1994 National Black Politics Study,* Working Paper no. 1 (Chicago: University of Chicago, Center for the Study of Race, Politics, and Culture, 1996), and Martin Carnoy, *Faded Dreams* (London: Cambridge University Press, 1994).
5. Stan Faryna, Brad Stetson, and Joseph G. Conti, eds., *Black and Right: The Bold New Voice of Black Conservatives in America* (Westport, CT: Praeger Publishers, 1997)
6. Michael C. Dawson, *Behind the Mule: Race and Class in African-American Politics* (Princeton, NJ: Princeton University Press, 1994), especially the chapter, "Group Interests, Class Divisions, and African-American Policy Preferences." See also Smith and Seltzer, *Race, Class, and Culture,* Dawson, Khan, and Baughman, *Black Discontent;* and Carnoy, *Faded Dreams.*
7. Ronald W. Walters and Robert C. Smith, *African American Leadership* (Albany: State University of New York Press, 1999)
8. See, for example, Douglas S. Massey and Nancy A. Denton, *American Apartheid: Segregation and the Making of the Underclass* (Cambridge: Harvard University Press, 1993), for an overview and history of social and economic problems that continue to characterize many predominantly black urban locations.
9. See Gerald D. Jaynes and Robin M. Williams, Jr., eds., *A Common Destiny: Blacks and American Society* (Washington, D.C.: National Academy Press, 1989); and Wornie L. Reed, *Assessment of the Status of African Americans,* Vols. 1–5 (Boston: W. M. Trotter Institute, 1992).
10. Council of Economic Advisors, *Changing America: Indicators of Social and Economic Well-Being by Race and Hispanic Origin* (Washington, D.C.: U.S. Government Printing Office, 1998).
11. For an overview of these various ideologies and strategic perspectives, see Howard Brotz, ed., *Negro Social and Political Thought, 1850–1920* (New York: Basic Books, 1966); another important work is Charles V. Hamilton, *Black Political Thought* (New York: Capricorn Books, 1973).
12. Harold Cruse, *Plural, but Equal: Blacks and Minorities in America's Plural Society* (New York: Morrow and Co., 1987).

13. Cited in Elwood Watson, "Guess What Came to American Politics: Contemporary Black Conservatism," *Journal of Black Studies*, 29(1) (September 1998: 88).
14. Martin Kilson, "Thoughts on Black Conservatism: A Review Essay," *The Trotter Review*, 6(1) (Winter/Spring 1992).
15. Hanes Walton, Jr., "Social Policy: The Politics of Disappearances," *Black Scholar*, 27(3/4) (1997): p.73.
16. See Toni Morrison, "Talk of the Town," *New Yorker*, October 5, 1998.
17. "Naked Hypocrisy: The Nationwide System of Affirmative Action for Whites," *Journal of Black Higher Education*, no. 18 (Winter 1997/1998): 40.
18. Stephanie M. Wildman, *Privilege Revealed: How Invisible Preference Undermines America* (New York: New York University Press, 1996).
19. Vincent P. Franklin, *Black Self-Determination* (Brooklyn: Lawrence Hill Books, 1992).
20. John Hope Franklin and Eleanor Holmes Norton, *Black Initiative and Governmental Responsibility* (Washington, DC: Joint Center for Political and Economic Studies, 1987), p. 40.
21. Philip S. Foner and George E. Walker, eds., *Proceedings of the Black State Conventions, 1840–1865*, Vols. 1 and 2 (Philadelphia: Temple University Press, 1979–1980), and Philip S. Foner and George E. Walker, eds., *Proceedings of the Black National and State Conventions, 1865–1900* (Philadelphia: Temple University Press, 1986).
22. See my discussion of this point in "Understanding Relations between Blacks and Korean-Americans," *Urban Affairs Quarterly* (March 2000).
23. See the classic example and application of this argument as reflected in many later works by neoconservative writers in Edward C. Banfield, *The Unheavenly City* (Boston: Little, Brown, and Co., 1973).

INDEX

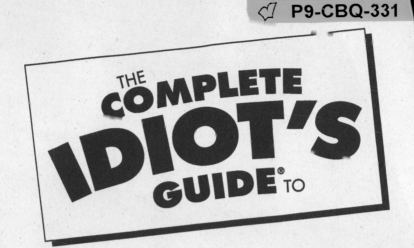

Spices and Herbs

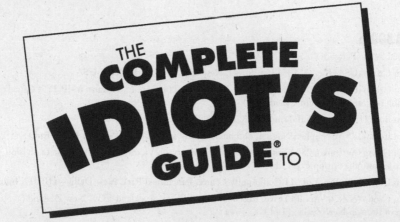

THE COMPLETE IDIOT'S GUIDE® TO

Spices and Herbs

by Leslie Bilderback, CMB

ALPHA

A member of Penguin Group (USA) Inc.

ALPHA BOOKS

Published by the Penguin Group

Penguin Group (USA) Inc., 375 Hudson Street, New York, New York 10014, USA

Penguin Group (Canada), 90 Eglinton Avenue East, Suite 700, Toronto, Ontario M4P 2Y3, Canada (a division of Pearson Penguin Canada Inc.)

Penguin Books Ltd., 80 Strand, London WC2R 0RL, England

Penguin Ireland, 25 St. Stephen's Green, Dublin 2, Ireland (a division of Penguin Books Ltd.)

Penguin Group (Australia), 250 Camberwell Road, Camberwell, Victoria 3124, Australia (a division of Pearson Australia Group Pty. Ltd.)

Penguin Books India Pvt. Ltd., 11 Community Centre, Panchsheel Park, New Delhi—110 017, India

Penguin Group (NZ), 67 Apollo Drive, Rosedale, North Shore, Auckland 1311, New Zealand (a division of Pearson New Zealand Ltd.)

Penguin Books (South Africa) (Pty.) Ltd., 24 Sturdee Avenue, Rosebank, Johannesburg 2196, South Africa

Penguin Books Ltd., Registered Offices: 80 Strand, London WC2R 0RL, England

Copyright © 2007 by Leslie Bilderback, CMB

International Standard Book Number: 978-1-59257-674-6
Library of Congress Catalog Card Number: 2007930853

13   12   8   7   6   5

Interpretation of the printing code: The rightmost number of the first series of numbers is the year of the book's printing; the rightmost number of the second series of numbers is the number of the book's printing. For example, a printing code of 07-1 shows that the first printing occurred in 2007.

Printed in the United States of America

Publisher: *Marie Butler-Knight*
Editorial Director: *Mike Sanders*
Managing Editor: *Billy Fields*
Senior Acquisitions Editor: *Paul Dinas*
Senior Development Editor: *Christy Wagner*
Production Editor: *Megan Douglass*

Copy Editor: *Jan Zoya*
Cartoonist: *Shannon Wheeler*
Cover Designer: *Kurt Owens*
Book Designer: *Becky Harmon*
Layout: *Ayanna Lacey*
Proofreader: *Mary Hunt*

Contents at a Glance

Contents

Appendixes

Introduction

Do you every wander down the herb and spice aisle at your grocery store and wonder what people do with all those powders and seeds? When you dine out, do you ever wonder what makes a particular dish taste the way it does? If so, you're in luck! This book unlocks those mysteries and emboldens you to experiment with spices, herbs, tastes, and flavors like you never have before.

Spices and herbs have an ancient and honorable history. The search for, and marketing of, spices has been creating wealth for centuries. Spices were so valuable that in ancient Egypt, Greece, and Rome, they were used as currency. Herbs were also coveted for their medicinal and magical properties. Many of these ancient remedies are still in use today. But more than an interesting past, spices and herbs have changed eating from simply providing sustenance into an art form. Seasoning is no longer for preservation or palatability. It is done for fun.

Modern cookery has not only advanced technologically, but culinarily as well. And thanks to television and the Internet, even if you live in the middle of nowhere, your neighborhood is global. Within a 5-mile radius of my house (not counting fast food), I have several Mexican restaurants, 2 barbecue restaurants, 2 Thai restaurants, an Indian restaurant, 3 Chinese restaurants, 2 Japanese restaurants, 2 Italian restaurants, a Jamaican restaurant, and a classic French restaurant. Each of these establishments serves chicken, but thanks to spices and herbs, not one is the same. They are defined by the seasonings, the cuisine, the culture, and the chef.

The cuisine of a particular country is first defined by the regional availability of foods and the way people utilized what they had on hand to fulfill their basic nutritional needs. For instance, corn, beans, and chiles are native to Central and South America, and so these foods are utilized in many of their regional specialties. Coastal civilizations utilize the bounty of the sea. Inland people learned to hunt. Agriculture took hold, and people learned to grow what they needed. As civilizations progressed, and basic needs were met, taste gained importance. Spices and herbs, fruits, and vegetables were gathered or cultivated and used to add interest to food.

As people began to wander, they shared ingredients and insights, introducing new foods and flavors to each other. Chiles from the New World ended up in Europe and became a vital element in the cuisines of Hungary and Spain. Citrus moved from Asia to Europe, to the New World, where it thrived. Melons, yams, and sesame came from Africa to the New World with the slaves and became an integral part of the American culture.

Consequently, we have developed a global palate. Demand has increased for foods from far-off lands. We want to learn how to cook like the peasants of Germany and Argentina and Morocco. We want to eat like the kings of Russia and Persia and Siam. Thankfully, we can. Extravagant ingredients aren't all that extravagant anymore, and they are relatively easy to come by. Through the Internet, and a global market that brings the weird and wonderful foods of the world to our local markets, we can experience the wonders of international cuisine in the comfort of our own homes.

How to Use This Book

This book is divided into two parts. In **Part 1, "The Spice of Life,"** you learn how to buy spices and herbs at their freshest, how to store them, and how to use them to their best advantage. And if you're interested in the freshest possible ingredients, you'll learn how to grow spices and herbs yourself, in the backyard or on the windowsill. There are recipes, too, for flavoring vinegars, oils, butters, and even potpourri, all designed to preserve the flavor and aroma of spices and herbs.

This first section also delves into the how and why of taste and flavor. It discusses the basic elements of taste and how they combine to give each food its unique qualities.

In **Part 2, "Flavor at Your Fingertips,"** you'll find an exhaustive list of all the common, and many not-so-common, spices and herbs. It explains what they look like, taste like, and how they are used. It also provides sources for the more unusual, hard-to-get entries. Scattered throughout the list are a few ingredients that do not fall into the category of spice or herb, such as baking soda. But because it's found on the same shelf in your market (and your pantry), I've included it.

Recipes are sprinkled throughout the list as well—beverages, soups, meat dishes, snacks, and desserts, all designed to whet your appetite for the new and different. The recipes illustrate how the spice or herb is classically used, or give some ideas for more unusual ways to use the flavor.

The appendixes contain recipes for spice and herb blends. Some are interpretations of commonly available mixes, like Italian Herbs or Cajun Spice. Others are exotic blends from far-off lands. You'll also find information on the form and function of fresh and dried chiles, including their heat levels.

Extras

Throughout the book you'll see sidebars sprinkled here and there. They provide just a little more information you might find useful.

Tidbit

These sidebars include tips and general notes about a spice or an herb.

Chefspeak

These boxes explain culinary-specific terminology you might not be familiar with.

Hot Stuff

"Hot stuff!" is a classic warning in professional kitchens. What better name for these warning boxes that alert you to potential problems or hazards.

Acknowledgments

Thanks to Paul Dinas for thinking of me for this project. You have reawakened my desire to travel afar and taste the world. Thanks, as always, to my supportive family, Bill, Emma, and Claire, who take extra good care of me when I've had too much curry. (Is there ever too much, really?) Thanks to Mom, for teaching me that one should never be without cardamom.

Trademarks

All terms mentioned in this book that are known to be or are suspected of being trademarks or service marks have been appropriately capitalized. Alpha Books and Penguin Group (USA) Inc. cannot attest to the accuracy of this information. Use of a term in this book should not be regarded as affecting the validity of any trademark or service mark.

Part 1

The Spice of Life

Spices make the world go 'round. At least they did 500 years ago. It was for want of spice that the great Portuguese mariners set out on quests for riches. They spread their spice lust throughout Europe, and a New World was discovered.

Why did flavor carry so much influence, and how does it influence us today? Why do we crave something sweet at one time and something salty another? Why does one person love a flavor, while another avoids it like the plague? And what makes one flavor complement another? These mysteries of taste will unravel before you in the following chapters.

In Part 1, you learn how to choose and use herbs and spices to their best advantage, in traditional ways as well as recipes and food pairings you might not have considered. You'll also learn how to grow them for yourself, and what to do with your first bumper crop.

Using Spices and Herbs

In This Chapter

- ◆ Understanding the influence spices and herbs have had on civilization
- ◆ How to best buy, use, and store spices and herbs
- ◆ The mystique of spices and herbs
- ◆ Spice and herb flavor compatibility

Some might see them as simply the contents of little jars in our kitchen cabinets we pull out from time to time when we're feeling culinarily creative. But throughout human history, spices and herbs have meant much more. For centuries, spices and herbs have defined cultures and ethnic diversity. They displayed wealth and civic pride. They were the impetus of modern trade, the rationale behind decisions of settlement, and reasons for the discovery of new worlds.

A Brief History

Today, as throughout history, herbs are used for their fragrance, flavor, color, and medicinal properties. Five thousand years ago, the Sumerians documented medicinal uses of a few herbs. Four thousand years ago, the Chinese used more than 300 herbs for their healing properties. Three thousand years ago, the Egyptians expanded use from the merely pharmaceutical (including mummification) to culinary and cosmetic use. The Greeks used herbs to adorn the heads of their heroes, and the ancient Romans used herbs for magic and sorcery. The Old Testament includes much about herbs, and the Middle Ages saw herb cultivation, with studies revolving around the monasteries. Superstitions surrounded herbs well into the eighteenth and nineteenth centuries, until modern chemistry and the study of the physical sciences began to advance.

In the ancient world, herbs were largely medicinal and spiritual and were grown or gathered easily. Spices were a luxury item and, consequently, one of the world's most valuable trade goods. They were light and didn't require special preservation like other foods. That, combined with their multiple uses, made spices a hot commodity. And while we still use spices for dyes, medicines, and cosmetics, their most beloved characteristic is their flavor.

> ### Tidbit
>
> It's long been thought that the use of spices and herbs in cookery began out of necessity. If large animals were not consumed soon after a kill, the meat had to be preserved. With no refrigeration, poorly preserved meat began to rot. It was once thought that spices were used to mask foul flavors and increase palatability. However, most scholars today agree that spices were luxury items, and those who could afford them could certainly also afford fresh meat.

While black pepper appears profusely in the fifth century C.E. Roman cookbook *De re Coquinaria* (*On the Subject of Cooking*, commonly known as *Apicius*), the spice trade didn't really begin in earnest until the third century, when trade from Malaysia to China began. Alexander the Great began exchanging rice and cotton for spices to please the Greeks.

The Muslims controlled the overland spice route from approximately 700 to 1000 C.E. Crusaders passing through brought the desire for spices home to Europe.

During the Middle Ages, cinnamon, clove, nutmeg, and pepper were most prized by medieval traders. In the late fourteenth and early fifteenth centuries, the Spanish and Portuguese began searching for ways to get in on the spice-trade action. Thus began the age of exploration. While looking for a trade route, Marco Polo found China, Christopher Columbus found the New World, and Ferdinand Magellan circumnavigated the globe. All this, spurred on by the love of spice and the promise of wealth.

Spices

Spices are the bark, seed, resin, root, stem, fruit, or bud of a plant, tree, or shrub. They count amongst their rank the familiar, such as *cinnamon, mustard, ginger, licorice, juniper*, and *cloves*. Also included are the strange and exotic, including *asafetida, nigella, silphium*, and *grains of paradise*. Many can be found at your neighborhood market, and some can only be obtained on the other side of the globe.

In the ancient world, spice merchants held all the cards. Middlemen of Phoenicia (modern Syria and Lebanon), Cairo, Alexandria, Venice, and Genoa befriended pharaoh's and kings in an attempt to monopolize the lucrative spice market. In a time when a human being could be traded for a handful of pepper, you can bet it was a competitive business. Before the age of exploration, spice sources were closely held secrets.

Spices spread more than flavor and wealth. The prophet Mohammed used spice trade as a platform from which to spread his message, capturing attention with his spices and then captivating with his words. And three kings are said to have traveled to Bethlehem bearing at least two spices, *frankincense* and *myrrh*.

> **Tidbit**
>
> Early records give us a glimpse into the practice, ethical or not, of cutting spices with sawdust, dirt, and rocks. They also show penalties for such behavior, which often included a toasty death.

Cooking With Spices

Spices are available whole and ground. They begin to lose their flavor and aroma as soon as they are ground, and the longer they sit on the shelf, the weaker they get. The most economical and flavorful way to purchase spice is in whole form. Spices kept whole will last for years with little loss of flavor and can be ground as needed.

Hot Stuff

If you're going to use a coffee grinder, consider keeping a separate grinder for your spices. Otherwise, your coffee will start tasting weird.

In centuries past, a *mortar* was used to grind whole spices. A classic chef's method called *mignonette* uses a sauté pan to rub and crush whole spices against a cutting board. There are special spice graters and grinders at every gourmet gadget shop. But perhaps the easiest way to grind spices today is with a coffee grinder.

Some spices, especially seeds, benefit from light toasting prior to grinding to help release their aromatic oils. You can do this in a dry sauté pan on top of the stove. Keep the spices moving as they heat up, and remove them from the heat, and the hot pan, as soon as you smell the spice. Let the toasted spices cool down for a few minutes before you grind them.

Chefspeak

A **mortar** is a bowl, usually made of ceramic or stone, into which spices, herbs, vegetables, or pharmaceuticals are put to be crushed by a *pestle*, a hard instrument shaped like a small baseball bat. **Macerate** means to soak food, usually fruit, in liquid to infuse flavor.

Other spices such as *annatto* or *saffron* should be heated in oil or other liquid to release and trap their essence. Others, like mustard, don't have much flavor at all until they're moistened and allowed to *macerate*.

Larger spices, like *nutmeg* and *cinnamon*, can be broken into smaller pieces before being ground. A meat mallet is a perfect tool for this. If you're into gadgets, you can buy special graters designed especially for large spices.

More Bang for Your Spice Buck

Smaller ethnic markets usually have the best spice prices. Buy them in tiny cellophane packages and empty them into clean, airtight jars when you get home. Store spices in a cool, dark, dry place to prolong their flavor. You can also find many online sources for whole and ground spices and spice blends. In Part 2, I suggest online sources for many of the spices and herbs listed.

To get their maximum effect in your recipes, add spices early in the cooking process. Because fat is a natural flavor carrier, adding your spices to oil or butter brings out the flavors and permeates a recipe.

Herbs

Herbs are green, leafy plants. With a few exceptions (such as *bay* and *rosemary*), they have delicate, nonwoody stems. If allowed to grow to maturity, herbs develop into flowers and seeds. Many of these seeds are then reclassified as spices when dried.

You can purchase herbs in fresh or dried forms, and although they can be substituted for one another, the two forms have very different characteristics that are worth noting.

Dried Herbs

When herbs are dried, the water in the leaves evaporates and the oils intensify, which is why dried herbs tend to have stronger flavor than their fresh counterparts. However, dried herbs lose their flavor very quickly. Ground and powdered herbs have an increased surface area that allows the oils to dissipate faster.

Buy dried herbs in small quantities, rather than in large life-time supply–size containers. Store them in a cool, dry, dark space to maximize their lifespan. To release more of the dried herb oil, rub it in your hands before adding it to a recipe. Dried herbs that are powdered tend to be stronger than those that are granulated, crushed, or crumbled.

Hot Stuff

If you can't smell your dried herbs after rubbing them in your hand, replace them.

Cooking dried herbs for prolonged periods diminishes their flavor. Add dried herbs in the last 30 minutes of a recipe for maximum effect. In cold recipes, like salads and marinades, the longer the herb is in contact with the food, the more intense the flavor will be. In baking, incorporate herbs with the fat in the recipe for more even distribution throughout the batter or dough.

Fresh Herbs

When gathering fresh herbs (in the grocery store or the garden), look for bright green leaves that stay on the stem. You shouldn't see any bruised or dried leaves, and the stems should be straight and firm. Limp, dry, bruised, or sad-looking herbs are rarely worth the price you pay.

 Tidbit

Fresh herbs can be costly in supermarkets, so look for better deals at farmers' markets and neighborhood ethnic grocers. Most large markets sell a couple stems of herbs carefully sealed and beautifully packaged. But purveyors who cater to a specific culture buy the most sought-after herbs in much larger quantities and sell them cheaper. Within 4 miles of my house, one store sells cilantro for $2.49 a bunch, while another sells 3 bunches for 99 cents. Guess where I shop.

It's easy to waste fresh herbs unless you know how to store them and how to utilize the leftovers. When the fresh herbs come home, wash them right away—thoroughly, but gently. I like to submerge them in water for a minute to be sure all the sand, soil, and bugs are removed. Shake them dry and let them drain in a colander for a few minutes before refrigerating.

There are several excellent ways to store fresh herbs in the fridge. A good rule is to think of your herbs as fresh flowers. You can stand them upright in a glass of water and loosely cover the top with a plastic bag to keep the moisture in. You can also wrap the washed herbs loosely in paper towels and store them in the produce drawer. As a professional chef, I used to hang my herbs from a clothesline rigged up in the back of the walk-in refrigerator, loosely wrapped in plastic bags. Use any method that will keep them from getting smashed.

When adding fresh herbs into recipes, keep in mind that you need more fresh herbs than dried. A general conversion rule is 3 parts fresh herb to 1 part dry. Chopping them very fine—such as in a *chiffonade* or *julienne*—exposes as much surface area as possible, which in turn allows the most flavor to be released. When garnishing with sprigs of herbs, remember that they contain a lot of water and will wilt if they get hot and dry. And like any green vegetable, herbs discolor if overcooked. Add them into recipes at the very end of cooking to maximize flavor and appearance.

Leftover herbs are easily stored for later use. Freeze chopped herbs in plastic bags, or mix them with water and freeze them in an ice cube tray. You can dry them yourself in the microwave between paper towels, or preserve their flavor in oils, vinegars, and compound butters.

> **Chefspeak**
>
> Cutting large-leafed herbs into strips is called a **chiffonade.** You do it by stacking the leaves, rolling them into a log, and slicing off coin shapes, which uncoil into **julienne** strips.

> **Tidbit**
>
> Herbs are easily cultivated from seeds or plants in a garden, indoors or out. See Chapter 2 for instructions on growing and preserving spices and herbs.

Ancient Remedies and Power

Herb gardening and cultivation is an ancient tradition. Egyptians, Greeks, and Romans, kept herbs close at hand, growing them in ornamental courtyards, pots, and public areas. In the ninth century, Emperor Charlemagne regulated agriculture, detailing 73 herbs to be planted in gardens at each of his estates throughout the Empire. In the 1500s, gardens filled with medicinal herbs were planted throughout Europe. Called *physic gardens*, they were planted specifically by and for apothecaries.

There's no question that spices and herbs played a major role in the history of medicine. Due, perhaps, to their seemingly magical powers of altering the physical state, they took on mystical significance as well. The following list gives a glimpse into the flavorful folklore of the more common spices and herbs.

Allspice   Caribbean folk medicine included the use of allspice to cure colds, cramps, and upset stomach, and the Mayans included it in their embalming ritual. Once introduced to Europe, allspice was believed to bring about good luck and financial prosperity.

Basil   Native to Africa and India, basil was probably brought from India to Greece by early trade of Alexander the Great. It's a sacred plant in India, associated with the Hindu goddess Tulasi, and remains a symbol of love, faithfulness, and eternal life. Basil is a symbol of love in Italy and Eastern Europe, thought to be an aphrodisiac and a love potion. The name Basil comes from the Greek *basileus*, which means "king." In France, the herb is still known as *herbe royale*.

Basil is also associated with the scorpion, thought to protect against them in some cultures, and attract them in others. In England, it was used to ward off evil spirits and insects. Christians believe basil grew at the sight of the cross, which is why it's found on the altar and in the Holy Water at the Greek Orthodox Church.

Coriander   One of the first herbs grown by the colonists in the New World, coriander is said to relieve abdominal pain. The Chinese associated it with immortality, and the in the Middle Ages, it was commonly used as an aphrodisiac.

Cumin   Cumin was used as a bit of marital insurance, carried in ceremonies to ensure happiness and used to keep lovers from straying. It was also used as a remedy for the common cold.

Dill   The Greeks saw dill as a sign of wealth. It was used to aid digestion and calm the nerves. Europeans hung it about the home and made it into potions as protection against witchcraft. Bathing in water infused with dill was said to make you irresistible to your lover.

Fennel   The ancient Greek named this herb Marathon, after the battle that took place in a field of fennel. The Romans chewed fennel as an appetite suppressant, and puritans chewed it during fasting to keep hunger at bay. Fennel was hung throughout medieval homes for luck and to keep away ghosts.

Marjoram   Ancient Greeks set their sheep and goats to graze on hillsides of marjoram, believing it made the meat tender and delicious. A favorite herb of Aphrodite, marjoram was once believed to induce dreams of one's future mate. As a symbol of love and happiness, marjoram wreaths crowned the wedding couple and adorned gravesites. Hippocrates used it as an antiseptic, and the Egyptians used it as a disinfectant. In the Middle Ages, it was chewed to relieve toothaches and indigestion.

Mint   Minthe is the name of Hades' lover. In retaliation, she was turned into a low-growing herb by his wife Persephone, destined to be stepped upon for all eternity. Despite this mythology, mint has been considered a symbol of hospitality since Roman times. The Greeks believed that mint stirred up bodily lust, and soldiers were warned to stay away from it, lest they lose courage and strength from increased lovemaking.

Parsley   This herb has been used to anoint champions, celebrate spring, and curse enemies. The natural ability of chlorophyll to absorb foul odor was put to good use in the Middle Ages, when parsley was strewn about tables and people. Its absorption potential was also employed as an antidote to poison and as hangover prevention.

Rosemary   The Greeks believed rosemary improved their memory. Students carried it to examinations, and lovers used it to ensure fidelity. The smoke of burning rosemary was used to ward off sickness and evil demons, and the herb was hung around the home for protection and luck. Unmarried women believed the name of their future husband would come to them during sleep if they placed rosemary under their pillow.

It's said that Mary placed her blue cloak atop a rosemary bush, changing its white flowers to blue. Still more Christian association says the rosemary shrub will never grow taller than Christ's height and never live longer than 33 years.

Sage   The ancient Greeks, Romans, and Arabs all believed sage to induce immortality and wisdom. Thus, it was used to treat memory loss and a host of illnesses, including fever and stomach disorders. It symbolized domestic virtue and skill, and as such, a house with a garden overflowing with sage was said to contain a strong-willed woman.

Tarragon   The name, derived from the French *esdragon*, meaning "little dragon," is a reference to its serpentine root system, which led medieval healers to use it as a remedy for snake bites. The ancient Greeks used tarragon as a cure for toothaches, and it was considered a calming herb. Also referred to as a *banishing herb*, tarragon was used as incense while the name of one's nemesis was written on a piece of paper and then burned.

Thyme   Native to Southern Europe and the Mediterranean, thyme has long been associated with courage. Ancient Egyptians used it in embalming, and the ancient Greeks believed it would make them brave. They burnt it as incense, bathed in it, and used it as treatment for shyness and depression. In the Middle Ages, thyme was given to knights to encourage bravery and hidden under pillows to ward off nightmares. Shakespeare wrote of the fairy queen, Tatiana, who slept in a bed of wild thyme, and English folklore includes recipes using thyme designed to lure fairies out into the open.

Cooking Creatively with Spices and Herbs

After reading about spices and herbs, you're probably itching to taste some. (Throughout the writing of this book, I have experienced several severe cravings for Indian food.) Before you go pair the first spice or herb you find with the first dish of food placed in front of you, a little more reading first. The following list includes the most common spices and herbs and, in general, the types of foods they're compatible with:

Allspice   Apples, beets, cabbage, caramel, cardamom, cinnamon, foie gras, game meats, ginger, juniper, nuts, nutmeg, onions, pears, poultry, pumpkin, root vegetables, seafood

Anise   Apples, beets, beef, caramel, carrots, chocolate, citrus, cinnamon, coconut, cranberry, figs, foie gras, game meats, root vegetables, seafood, stone fruits, tea

Basil   Artichokes, beef, blue cheese, coconut, eggplant, figs, garlic, leafy vegetables, mint, mushrooms, olives, oregano, parsley, peaches, poultry, raspberries, rosemary, seafood, thyme, tomato, vinegar

Bay   Artichokes, apples, bananas, beans, beef, blue cheese, citrus, dates, figs, game meats, grains, mushrooms, nuts, potatoes, poultry, seafood, stone fruits, tamarind, thyme, tomatoes

Caraway   Beets, cabbage, cheese, cured meats, dill, fennel, garlic, nuts, mushrooms, onions, oregano, potatoes, root vegetables, sausage, seafood, yeast breads

Cardamom   Apples, bananas, beans, caramel, cinnamon, citrus, coconut, coffee, coriander, curry, dates, ginger, grains, grains of paradise, nuts, pepper, pumpkin, sugar, squash, yeast breads

Chervil   Artichokes, asparagus, carrots, cheese, chives, citrus, eggs, grains, green beans, leafy vegetables, mushrooms, nuts, onions, parsley, pasta, potatoes, seafood, tarragon, thyme, vinegar

Chiles   Bananas, beans, cheese, cilantro, cinnamon, citrus, chocolate, coconut, corn, cumin, basil, beef, garlic, ginger, grains, oregano, potatoes, poultry, seafood, tropical fruits

Chives   Asparagus, beets, blue cheese, chervil, dill, eggs, horseradish, leafy greens, mushrooms, olives, pasta, parsley, potatoes, seafood, tarragon

Cilantro   Avocados, beef, chiles, citrus, coconut, coriander, corn, cumin, curry, dates, fennel, figs, garlic, mint, oregano, pepper, sausage, seafood, tomatoes, yogurt

Cinnamon   Allspice, apples, bananas, beans, caramel, cardamom, chiles, chocolate, clove, coffee, cranberry, curry, dates, game meats, figs, foie gras, ginger, grains, nutmeg, pumpkin, stone fruit, sugar, squash, tea, vanilla

Clove   Apples, beets, cinnamon, citrus, foie gras, game meats, ginger, grains of paradise, nuts, nutmeg, peaches, pineapple, pumpkin, root vegetables, sausages, stone fruit, tomatoes, vanilla

Coriander   Bananas, beans, cilantro, cumin, cured meats, curry, game meats, mint, parsley, poultry, root vegetables, seafood, tomatoes

Cumin   Avocados, beans, beef, cilantro, citrus, coconut, cucumber, garlic, grains, mango, mint, onion, parsley, poultry, sausages, seafood, tomatoes

Dill   Anise, beets, blue cheese, cabbage, caraway, carrots, chives, cucumbers, eggs, fennel, mint, oregano, parsley, potatoes, seafood, tarragon, tomatoes, veal, yeast bread

Fennel   Artichokes, anise, apples, artichokes, basil, beans, blue cheese, cabbage, cilantro, dill, eggplant, figs, garlic, olives, onions, oregano, parsley, potatoes, thyme, tomato, sausage, seafood, veal

Fenugreek   Allspice, beans, cumin, cardamom, chiles, cinnamon, curry, game meats, ginger, potatoes, poultry

Ginger   Allspice, anise, asparagus, bananas, carrots, chiles, chives, chocolate, cinnamon, citrus, cloves, coconut, coriander, cranberry, cumin, curry, dates, fennel, figs, garlic, jasmine, nutmeg, onions, pears, pepper, poultry, pumpkin, raisins, root vegetables, rose, seafood, stone fruits, sugar, tea, tropical fruits

Horseradish   Apples, beef, beets, blue cheese, capers, chives, citrus, cured meats, dill, nuts, mustard, onions, potatoes, sausage, seafood, root vegetables, vinegar

Juniper   Allspice, beef, blue cheese, cabbage, cilantro, cured meats, game meats, garlic, lavender, olives, oregano, pepper, poultry, rosemary, veal, vinegar

Lavender   Anise, apples, berries, cranberry, fennel, figs, foie gras, game meats, garlic, juniper, rose, rosemary, thyme, olives, oregano, potato, sage, stone fruit, sugar, tarragon, tea

Lemongrass   Berries, carrots, chiles, cilantro, coriander, coconut, curry, garlic, onions, pepper, poultry, parsley, seafood, tea, thyme, tomato

Mint   Basil, beans, beef, carrots, chocolate, cilantro, citrus, coconut, coriander, cranberry, eggplant, fennel, figs, game meats, garlic, grains, parsley, poultry, seafood, tea, yogurt

Mustard   Anchovy, anise, asparagus, beef, beets, blue cheese, cabbage, capers, chiles, cured meats, fennel, honey, poultry, root vegetables, sausage, seafood, vinegar, yeast bread

Nutmeg   Allspice, asparagus, blue cheese, cabbage, carrots, cinnamon, cheese, clove, coffee, cranberries, cumin, eggs, foie gras, ginger, green beans, pasta, peaches, pumpkin, potato, sausage, sugar, vanilla, veal

Oregano   Artichokes, basil, beans, beef, blue cheese, cinnamon, cumin, eggplant, fennel, garlic, mushrooms, nuts, parsley, pasta, poultry, seafood, squash, thyme, tomatoes, veal

Parsley   Artichokes, asparagus, basil, bay, beans, beef, chervil, chives, dill, game meats, garlic, mushrooms, grains, onions, oregano, pasta, potatoes, poultry, seafood, thyme, tomatoes

Pepper   Allspice, artichokes, asparagus, beef, blue cheese, cheese, cinnamon, citrus, eggs, figs, foie gras, game meats, ginger, mushrooms, pineapple, poultry, seafood, sugar, tomatoes

Rosemary   Apples, asparagus, basil, beans, beef, blue cheese, caramel, citrus, cranberry, game meats, garlic, grains, fennel, figs, mushrooms, nuts, onion, oregano, parsley, potatoes, poultry, raisins, sage, seafood, sugar, thyme, tomatoes

Saffron   Basil, bay, berries, chives, cinnamon, cloves, coriander, cumin, curry, fennel, garlic, ginger, grains, mint, parsley, poultry, sausage, seafood, tomatoes

Sage   Anchovy, capers, citrus, cranberry, beef, blue cheese, game meats, garlic, green beans, lavender, mushrooms, nuts, parsley, plums, poultry, rosemary, seafood, thyme, veal

Sesame   Bananas, beans, cinnamon, citrus, coconut, eggplant, game meats, garlic, ginger, leafy greens, nuts, mustard, onions, pasta, pepper, poultry, root vegetables, rosemary, seafood, stone fruits, thyme, vinegar, yeast bread

Sorrel   Chives, beans, beef, blue cheese, eggs, leafy greens, oregano, parsley, poultry, thyme, seafood, squash

Tarragon   Artichokes, carrots, chervil, citrus, eggs, foie gras, garlic, leafy greens, mushrooms, onion, oregano, parsley, potatoes, poultry, seafood, thyme, tomatoes, veal

Thyme   Artichokes, bananas, basil, bay, beans, blue cheese, carrots, chervil, citrus, cranberry, dates, dill, figs, mint, mushrooms, nuts, onion, oregano, parsley, potatoes, poultry, raisins, sage, seafood, stone fruit, tomatoes

Vanilla   Apples, bananas, caramel, chocolate, chiles, cinnamon, citrus, coconut, coffee, dates, figs, lavender, nuts, shell fish, stone fruit, tropical fruit

The list is a compilation of common and unique flavor combinations gathered from regional and international cuisine, as well as a 20-year career of cooking with creative, innovative chefs. Some will seem obvious, such as basil and garlic. Others you might find a little more out-there. I urge you to give those more unusual combinations some thought, and perhaps a try. They are listed because they work together, each flavor bringing out interesting qualities of the other.

The list is not nearly as complete as the encyclopedic bulk of this book (Part 2) because many of the herbs and spices carry similar flavor characteristics. For instance, marjoram is very similar to oregano and could be paired with the same foods that appear on the *oregano* list. Similarly, lemon verbena, lemon balm, lemon myrtle, and lemons could all pair with the foods on the *lemongrass* list. Use the list as a guideline for experimentation with all the entries in this book.

Tidbit

Some of these parings work better than others. The more you cook, the more you will develop your own preferences for food pairings.

The foods on the list are generalized. For instance, poultry could be chicken, duck, turkey, quail, or ostrich. Citrus includes lemons, limes, oranges, and the like. Grains could be rice, oatmeal, or quinoa. Of course, those foods do not all taste the same, but they all combine favorably with the title flavor.

There are also foods that do not appear on the list. For instance, pork is not here, because it will usually work with the flavors that complement poultry. Rhubarb isn't here, but foods with a similar effect—like citrus, cranberries, tamarind, and tropical fruits—are. Experiment accordingly.

Finally, the list is not meant to be recipes. The foods that appear on a given list won't necessarily all work together. The title herb or spice enhances each food, individually. In some cases you can make combinations, but that is up to you, the cook, to experiment with. If you doubt the compatibility of foods on the list, test them before you commit to a full-blown recipe. Gather a small quantity of the foods, and taste them together. Try them in different proportions, and add some of the basic taste elements, like salt, sugar, or acid. Rinse your mouth well with water and chew a piece of bland bread or cracker to cleanse your palette between each taste. This exercise can help you understand how flavors work together, and may spark your culinary creativity.

The Least You Need to Know

- ◆ Herbs and spices played an important role in the evolution of mankind, influencing trade, settlement, and medicine.

- ◆ Spices are best bought whole and ground as needed.

- ◆ Choose the freshest herbs you can find, and buy dried herbs often, in small quantities you can use before they go stale.

- ◆ Dozens of interesting flavor combinations utilize spices and herbs.

Spices and Herbs at Home

In This Chapter

◆ Herb gardening, indoors and out

◆ Drying and freezing herbs and spices

◆ Infusing vinegar, oil, butter, and tea

◆ Using herbs throughout your home

Once you begin investigating spices and herbs, you quickly realize that they're not always easy to come by. Grocery stores stock
fresh herbs—but the herbs are frequently overpriced and often of
poor quality. Even dried herbs and spices can be weak and pale,
often having been left on the shelf for weeks or longer. As for the
more exotic spice varieties, unless you live near a major metropolitan center, finding them is next to impossible. Sure, there are
Internet sources. But if you intend to use an herb or spice more
than once, the cost can be prohibitive.

You may have already decided that it would be well worth
your time and energy to grow your own. And luckily, most herbs

are easy crops. Grow them inside or out, from seeds or small plants, in small quantities or in huge fields. They can be preserved or used fresh. In this chapter, I show you how.

Choosing Your Crop

The hardest part about growing herbs is deciding what to plant, so why not let your recipe book dictate the herbs you choose? Several standard herbs like *thyme*, *mint*, and *cilantro* can be used in a multitude of cuisines. Others, like *angelica* or *costmary*, have much more limited use, but can add interest to a garden.

Consider choosing a small variety of herbs with different characteristics. Balance the stronger herbs, like *rosemary* and *basil*, with a few more delicate ones, such as *chives* and *chervil*. It's also nice to combine some hearty perennials with a few tender annuals.

Annuals are plants that bloom for one season and then die. It might seem like a waste of a good plant, but most annuals produce prolific seeds and are easily started again next season. *Biennials* live a little longer, generally two seasons, blooming in the second and then dying. *Perennials* are the long-lasting plants that, once established, bloom year after year. The tricky part of categorizing plants in this manner is that their status might change depending on your *climate zone*. While certain plants are annuals in a cooler climate, they can become biennials or even perennials where the weather is hot. Within the plant's botanical family may be several species of annuals, biennials, and perennials. In most cases, the seed or plant packaging will indicate its life span. When in doubt, ask a professional gardener.

 Tidbit

Space is an important determining factor when selecting herbs to grow at home. Check the seed packet or ask the nursery staff how large your herb is likely to grow or how wide it can spread.

Knowing your climate zone is an important step in understanding what type of plants your garden can support. For the most part, your zone also indicates what plants and seeds are available to you at your local garden center. (Nurseries don't typically sell plants that won't grow.) But with today's global Internet shopping, knowing your zone can be helpful. The United States Department of Agriculture (USDA) has designated the following zones, based on the average annual minimum temperature.

Climate Zone	Temperature Range
1	below −50°F (−45.6°C)
2a	−50 to −45°F (−42.8 to −45.5°C)
2b	−45 to −40°F (−40 to −42.7°C)
3a	−40 to −35°F (−37.3 to −39.9°C)
3b	−35 to −30°F (−34.5 to −37.2°C)
4a	−30 to −25°F (−31.7 to −34.4°C)
4b	−25 to −20°F (−28.9 to −31.6°C)
5a	−20 to −15°F (−26.2 to −28.8°C)
5b	−15 to −10°F (−23.4 to −26.1°C)
6a	−10 to −5°F (−20.6 to −23.3°C)
6b	−5 to 0°F (−17.8 to −20°C)
7a	0 to 5°F (−15.0 to −17.7°C)
7b	5 to 10°F (−12.3 to −14.9°C)
8a	10 to 15°F (−9.5 to −12.2°C)
8b	15 to 20°F (−6.7 to −9.4°C)
9a	20 to 25°F (−3.9 to −6.6°C)
9b	25 to 30°F (−1.2 to −3.8°C)
10a	30 to 35°F (1.6 to −1.1°C)
10b	35 to 40°F (4.4 to 1.7°C)
11	40°F and above (4.5°C and above)

Once you identify your zone, consider your surroundings. Urban centers tend to be warmer than their surrounding areas. High elevations, where temperatures may be mild, do not promote the same growing conditions as lower elevations. High wind, high or low humidity, and the supply of sunlight should all be factored in. For more specific details about your local zone, visit a local garden center, or check out *Sunset National Garden Book* (Sunset Publishing, 1997).

Outdoor Gardens

When planning the size and shape of your garden, consider the available space, available light, and your intended crops. Choose the sunniest location you've got. For most common garden herbs, the plot should receive at least 6 hours of direct sunlight each day. More exotic species may require varying amounts of sun. Check with your local nursery staff.

Soil is the next crucial element. There's little you can do to change the amount of sun your garden receives, but poor soil can be easily amended. Your garden plot should be fertile and well drained; few herbs grow well in wet soil. Dig a hole and fill it with water. If it drains within a few minutes, your drainage is good. If it takes a few hours, you should consider planting in a raised bed.

A raised bed is essentially a giant flower pot. All you need is a frame at least 10 inches high, in any shape and made out of any material. Wood planks, logs, railroad ties, bricks, barrels, and even old tires work as sides to hold in the soil. Place your frame on the ground in your garden plot and fill it with a healthy soil mixture: $\frac{1}{3}$ should be composted material, whether homemade or purchased at the garden center; another $\frac{1}{3}$ should be sand, which lightens the mix; the remaining $\frac{1}{3}$ should be filled with top soil.

Tidbit

There's nothing better for your garden than compost. If you have space and patience, it's easy to make: accumulate a good mixture of green and brown yard waste, like grass clippings and dried leaves, in an unused corner of your yard or a compost bin. Add kitchen scraps like coffee grounds, egg shells, and vegetable trimmings—no meat, bones, or fat. Layer these ingredients for 3 or 4 months, watering it occasionally, and stirring it around with a pitchfork or shovel. After 4 months, the bottom and inner layers will be a nicely decomposed compost, ready to feed your garden. Remove the big chunks, and stir it into your garden soil.

If your soil drains well, it will still take a little preparation to ensure it's fertile enough to sustain your planting. Dig out your garden plot to about 1½ feet. Fill the cavity with 2 or 3 inches of crushed stone or pebbles for drainage. Create the same mixture as a raised bed, with ⅓ compost, ⅓ sand, and ⅓ topsoil, which can be the original soil from the plot or purchased. Refill the plot with your new soil mix. It will mound higher than before, which is fine and allows for settling.

Planters are a good option when space is limited. Pots, window boxes, hanging baskets, barrels, and even old buckets and wheel barrels work well. Whatever you choose, be sure it has good drainage. If your container of choice has no holes, punch some in. (For planting in containers, use the instructions that follow for indoor gardening.)

> **Hot Stuff**
>
> Don't use plastic planters in sunny locations because plastic is an insulator. It holds the heat inside the soil and can cook the plants on hot summer days.

Indoor Gardens

Planting inside is essentially the same as outside, but on a much smaller scale. The same elements are important: sunlight, drainage, and soil.

For maximum sunshine, look for a sunny window facing south or west. If light is a problem where you live, fluorescent or *grow lights* work well as a supplemental light source.

You can use any type of container as a planter, as long as it has adequate drainage holes. A layer of pebbles at the bottom of your pots keeps the soil and water from draining too quickly. Potting soil is generally rich in nutrients, so an indoor mix should consist of 1 part sand to 2 parts potting soil.

> **Chefspeak**
>
> A **grow light** produces light specifically to encourage photosynthesis. Spectrums of light can be adjusted to benefit the plant throughout its lifecycle.

Special Plantings

Why not plant a garden with a theme? You see them in arboretums all the time. Shakespeare gardens contain plants mentioned by the Bard, like Ophelia's *rosemary* from Hamlet, and *thyme* from *A Midsummer Night's Dream*. Medieval gardens are another favorite, filled with ancient medicinal herbs. Here are some practical suggestions for the culinary gardener.

Garden Theme	What to Plant
French Herb Garden	
For the bouquet garni	parsley, thyme, marjoram, leek
For fines herbes	parsley, chive, tarragon, chervil
For herbes de Provençe	chervil, marjoram, tarragon, basil, lavender, thyme
Italian Kitchen Garden	oregano, sage, rosemary, fennel, basil, garlic
Middle Eastern Garden	mint, coriander, cumin, parsley, dill, anise, oregano, thyme, sumac
Asian Garden	anise, basil, cumin, coriander, fennel, grains of paradise, ginger, cardamom, mustard, nigella (love-in-the-mist)
Barbecue Garden	celery, cumin, coriander, garlic, mustard, New Mexico chiles, oregano, onions, thyme
South-of-the-Border Garden	agave, cumin, cilantro, epazote, garlic, Mexican oregano, sage, serrano chiles

Planting

You can start herbs from seeds, or purchase small plants at a garden center or online. Small plants are the easiest way to get started, because the plant is already established and it won't take long for it to feel at home in its new pot.

For small plants, dig a hole slightly larger than the plastic pot the plant came in. Carefully remove the herb by squeezing the sides of the pot gently, turning the plant upside down, and pulling from the base of the stems. If the herb's been in the pot for a long time, it may have a lot of roots, possibly growing in and out of the pot's drainage holes. Do your best to dislodge the plant, and if necessary, cut the sides of the pot and peel it off. Loosen the roots a little by gently tearing the bottom of the pot-shaped roots open with your hands. This allows the new soil and nutrients to reach all the roots.

> **Tidbit**
>
> You can purchase a wide variety of common and not-so-common plants from these Internet suppliers: Mulberrycreek.com, Crimson-sage.com, or Mountainvalleygrowers.com.

Place the plant in the hole, pack new soil in around the top, and give it a little water. Don't drench the plant, but keep it moist and humid. Too much water makes the roots soggy and can drown the poor thing. If a good compost is used, fertilizer should not be necessary. In fact, too much fertilizer makes the foliage bushier, but reduces the herb's flavor.

Sowing Seeds

Sowing seeds is the most economical way to garden. It's easy, but it requires patience. Some seeds can be sown directly into the garden, while others benefit from indoor germination first. Check the seed packet for recommendations.

Seeds can be sown inside or out. Either way, the smaller the seed, the less soil it needs on top. Really fine seeds can be mixed with sand for more even sowing. Plan out your planting rows, and remember to leave space for you to move in. You'll need a path of some kind to access the plants once they're grown.

> **Hot Stuff**
>
> Creeping herbs, like mint, can easily take over a garden. To keep them in check, bury a large can or bucket at surface level, pierced with lots of drainage holes. Sow the seeds inside, and the can will prevent the roots from spreading willy-nilly throughout your garden.

To help germination, you can cover the seeds with burlap or newspaper to keep them moist until they sprout. If your seeds are planted outdoors, watch out after they sprout for hungry critters who like to eat tiny shoots. Fences or netting may be in order.

For indoor sowing, use a shallow planter in a sunny location. Seeds sown indoors in winter can be transplanted into the garden come spring or transferred into larger pots for indoor or outdoor gardens.

Collecting Seeds

One of the fun things about planting from seed is the endless possibilities. You are by no means limited to the plethora of packets available at your garden center. Anything with seeds in it is fair game. A weekend walk on a local trail or a visit to the farmers' market may inspire you.

Wild herbs and flowers generally produce seeds after their blooms have begun to fade. This is an indication that pollination is complete and the seeds are ripening, often inside a seed pod. Shake the withered blooms into a paper bag to loosen their seeds, or snip off the seed pod. Spread them out on trays to dry completely.

Tidbit

Tomato seeds need special treatment. They must be soaked in water for 3 or 4 days to ferment. After that time, the good ones will have sunk to the bottom of the dish. Dry them out completely before storing or planting.

You can also find seeds inside fleshy fruits and vegetables. Remove, rinse, and spread the seeds on trays a single layer to dry.

Once dried, plant your seeds or store them, well labeled, in paper envelopes. Exotic, wild, and heirloom seeds such as these make for an interesting garden, as well as a fun gift for your gardening friends.

Extended Care

As your herbs grow, you'll want to utilize them for your culinary creations. For the best flavor, harvest the leaves just before the flower buds open. If the plant is outdoors, harvest in the morning, before the dew has evaporated. These conditions produce the most aromatic oils within the plants leaves.

If you have no use for the herbs right now, prune them as if you did (and then freeze or dry the herb; more on this coming up in later sections). A regular trim keeps your plants producing healthy, flavorful foliage.

Annuals die off after the first season, but perennials and biennials last longer, which means you must consider winter care. Unless the temperature in your area dips below 0 for prolonged periods, most herbs survive well with mulching. Cover the ground around the plant with straw, leaves, or pine needles. (Branches from your Christmas tree work great.) Mulching isn't necessary for plants that die back, like *chives*, *mint*, and *tarragon*. They prefer a month or two of freezing temperature to regenerate next year's growth.

In colder climates, you can dig up and pot your herbs for a winter indoors. Prune branches and trim the inner foliage to let light and air circulate. Rinse off any bugs, and plant the herbs in roomy pots, using 1 part sand to 2 parts potting soil. Keep the herbs in a sunny location and prune regularly. Replant them in the garden when spring warms up your dirt.

Potted perennials and biennials, whether indoor or outdoor, grow as time goes by. Make them comfy by moving them into larger containers from time to time.

Tidbit

It is entirely possible that you have neither ample garden space outside, nor optimal conditions inside. Never fear! There are more than 15,000 community gardens throughout the United States and Canada. To find one in your area, check your local city administration or visit the American Community Garden Association at communitygarden.org.

Preserving Flavor

Using herbs in your kitchen is great, but when supply exceeds demand, it seems a shame to let all that flavor go to waste. That's where herb preservation comes in.

In the olden days, people were forced to eat bland foods in the winter if they failed to preserve summer's bounty. But today, just because the basil is at its peak doesn't necessarily mean you have time to use it *right now*. If you have a little spare time, you can set the flavor aside for later.

Drying Herbs

Moisture removal is essential for preservation of herbs. For best results, harvest your herbs right before they flower, when they're at the peak of flavor. Cut them in the morning before the dew has dried, when their oils are at their highest concentration. Trim the stems of perennials about halfway down the stem, and cut annuals at ground level. Wash the stems and leaves thoroughly in cool running water to remove dirt and bugs. Shake them off and spread them out in a single layer on paper towels to dry completely for a couple hours. When the rinse water has evaporated, the real drying can begin.

You can dry herbs naturally or with the help of a microwave, dehydrator, or oven. If time and space allow, natural drying is preferred, as the herbs retain more of the natural oils.

Natural Drying

Hanging herbs is a great drying method if you have the space. Gravity helps the oils flow from the stem into the leaves, giving your dried herbs maximum flavor.

Tie small bunches of herbs together tightly at the stems with a rubber band or wire twist-tie, and hang them in a clean, well-ventilated spot. The herbs will be ready to store in about 2 weeks, when the leaves are brittle.

To preserve more of the herb's natural color, place them in a paper bag, with the stems exposed, before tying and hanging. To collect the herbs when they're dried, simply shake the bag and remove the stems.

Hot Stuff

Be sure the room where you hang your herbs to dry is no warmer than 80 degrees or you'll find yourself with moldy herbs.

Tray drying works, too, although it is a little more labor-intensive. Remove the leaves from the stems and spread them out in a single layer on trays or screens. Store them in a dark, ventilated room, and turn the leaves over every few days to dry evenly.

Salt curing is another method of naturally preserving herbs. Layer clean and dried leaves with regular table salt or kosher salt in a shallow pan or dish. Be sure the leaves are completely covered. In 2 or 3 weeks, remove the leaves, shake off the salt, and test the leaves for a brittle texture.

Ovens and Dehydrators

Speed is the only advantage to using ovens to dry herbs. And it's tricky because the herbs are actually being cooked. But if monitored carefully, the results are pretty good.

To dry in the microwave, layer rinsed and dried herbs between two paper towels. Cook on a medium setting for about 3 minutes, checking frequently until the herbs are dry and brittle. Stir them a bit if they seem to be drying unevenly.

Herbs can also be dried in a regular oven at very low temperatures. Layer them on baking sheets and bake at 150°F for 2 or 3 hours, stirring periodically for even drying. To test for doneness, remove a leaf from the oven. It will be crisper when it cools.

Hot Stuff

It's easy to overcook and brown the herbs when drying them in the oven, so watch them carefully.

Dehydrators are another option. They don't heat up as much as an oven, they don't actually cook the herbs like a microwave does, and they don't require constant monitoring. To use, spread the leaves out in the trays in a single layer and follow the manufacturer's instructions. Generally, herbs will completely dry in a dehydrator after a few hours.

Storing Dried Herbs

The purpose of drying herbs is to remove the moisture so they can be stored for long periods of time without deteriorating. After putting in all the effort to grow and dry your herbs, be sure to store them properly in airtight containers. I prefer canning jars with lids that seal tightly. Don't use paper or cardboard, as they will absorb the herbs' oil. Seeds and leaves should be left whole to retain as much flavor as possible. They will last for months stored this way and kept in a cool, dark cupboard.

Hot Stuff

Even if the herbs appear dry, it's always possible that they could have retained a little moisture. Check the jars every day for the first week or so for any sign of moisture. If you see condensation or signs of any mold, remove the herbs and repeat the drying process.

Freezing Herbs

One way to preserve the fresh-picked flavor of your herbs is to freeze them. Once frozen, herbs are not pretty enough for garnish, but they work well in most recipes.

To freeze herbs, first wash and dry them and strip the leaves off the stems. Chop the leaves fine, as you would for a recipe. Divide the herbs into small quantities, as you would likely use in one recipe, such as 1 or 2 tablespoons. Put them into small plastic zipper bags, and force out the air before you seal it to minimize the formation of ice crystals. Label each bag so you can identify the herb later.

You could also place 1 or 2 tablespoons of the chopped herb into each section of an ice cube tray, cover with water, and freeze. After the cubes are frozen, remove them from the tray and store in labeled zipper bags.

Tidbit

Freezing herbs in ice cube trays only works for recipes that can stand a little extra water, like soups or stews. It won't work for preparations like chicken salad that would get soggy with the extra moisture.

Herbs can also be frozen in a purée form, as with pesto. Using a blender, purée herbs with just enough oil to get the mixture moving. Freeze in small plastic tubs or ice cube trays.

Blending Tea

Tea is an excellent use of dried spices and herbs. Besides the everyday chamomile or mint, why not try an original concoction? I like to use ¼ cup spices and herbs for every 3 cups not quite boiling water. The following table lists some of my favorite blends. (Measurements are given in parts so they can be made easily in any quantity. All ingredients are dried, unless otherwise specified.)

Tea Blend	Ingredients
Floral Tea	1 part each rose petals, violets, lavender buds, orange blossoms, red bergamot
Tummy-Soothing After-Dinner Teaseed	2 parts peppermint; 1 part each fennel seed, anise seed, lemon balm
Exotic Spiced Tea	2 parts rose petals; 1 part each fennel, cardamom, peppermint; 1 cinnamon stick; 1 slice fresh ginger
Refreshing Spa Tea	1 part each rosemary, sage, mint, lemon myrtle (Serve over ice and sliced cucumber.)
Citrus Tea	3 parts kaffir lime leaves; 2 parts lemon grass or lemon verbena; 1 part each orange blossom, allspice; 1 cinnamon stick (Serve with a wedge of orange.)

   To brew the tea, crush and chop the spices and herbs just before the hot water is added, and let it steep for 5 minutes. Strain into your cup, use a tea ball, or make your own tea bags from cheesecloth. Don't forget—the tea can be served hot or cold!

A Garden in Your Pantry

An easy way to preserve the flavor of herbs is to infuse them into oil or vinegar. Oils and fats carry flavor in recipes, so any flavor infused into oil spreads throughout the dish, often more than the herb would on its own. And because vinegars are acidic, they accentuate the flavors they're infused with.

Flavored vinegars and oils make terrific salad dressings. But don't just limit their use to salad greens. Roasted root vegetables, slow cooked beans, and even fruits benefit from these bright flavors. By themselves they make delicious marinades or great dips for veggies and breads, and they add something extra to your everyday cooking.

Safety First

Infused oils and vinegars make wonderful gifts. But you don't want to give your friends *E. coli* or *botulism*. As with any type of food canning, sanitation is critical. Everything the oils and vinegars come in contact with needs to be impeccably clean. This begins with the herbs themselves. Fresh herbs, especially those you didn't grow yourself, should be thoroughly cleaned. To be sure no bacteria are present, a quick dip in a sanitizing solution is recommended. The FDA recommends 1 teaspoon household bleach dissolved in 6 cups water. (Diluting and rinsing make this perfectly safe.) Dip the herbs in and then rinse them in cold running water. Dry them completely before adding to oils.

While there are many attractive decorative bottles available, it's easier to make your infusions in wide-mouth canning jars first and then strain them into the pretty bottles. Jars, bottles, lids, and corks must all be sanitized before you begin. The easiest way to do this is to run them through a dishwasher. Another easy method is to set the jars and lids in boiling water and cook them for 10 minutes. Carefully remove them from the boil with tongs and allow them to drain and cool on clean towels before filling.

Flavored oils and vinegars are often seen gracing the counters of well-groomed kitchens and gourmet shops. But it takes more than a decorative sprig to get the flavorful infusions that make a difference in your recipes. For both oils and vinegar, herbs should be chopped, bruised, and packed tightly into glass jars, filling them at least ¾ full. The more leaves you use, and the more they are bruised, the more aromatic oil escapes into the infusion.

Flavored Vinegars

Infused vinegars show off the herbs and spices best if the vinegar chosen is light in flavor. Distilled white vinegar is too harsh, but white wine vinegar is a good choice, as is rice vinegar. Cider vinegar can work, too, if the spices and herbs are strong in flavor. Red wine and balsamic vinegar are much too strong, and their flavor will compete with your infusions.

Thoroughly cleaning and sanitizing the herbs and jars is an important step in preventing E. coli contamination. To ensure no harmful bacteria are present, bring your vinegar to a simmer before pouring it into a sanitized jar packed with herbs and spices. Cover it loosely with cheesecloth or a clean towel. When completely cool, seal it with a sterilized lid and set it in a cool dark spot for 2 to 4 weeks to infuse.

When you think its ready, strain out the herbs and give the vinegar a taste. If it's not strong enough, repeat the process with a new batch of chopped herbs. If it tastes ready, strain out any small particles and cloudiness through a coffee filter or several layers of cheesecloth. Place a few decorative sprigs of clean herbs inside a sanitized decorative bottle and fill with the vinegar. Seal with a sanitized cork or cap.

Hot Stuff

Be sure the bottle seal is not made of metal or rubber, which are both easily corroded by acid.

You can use a single herb or spice to create a terrific flavored vinegar, but don't overlook the combinations in the following table. They can stand alone as a dressing, glaze, or dip. (Measurements are given in parts so they can be made easily in any quantity. All herbs are used fresh, unless otherwise specified.)

Flavored Vinegar	Ingredients
Garden Herb Vinegar	4 parts parsley; 3 parts chives; 2 parts each thyme, tarragon; 1 part each sage, celery seed; white wine vinegar

continues

continued

Flavored Vinegar	Ingredients
Chile Spice Vinegar	3 parts dried guajillo chiles; 2 parts each coriander, cumin; 1 part each garlic, thyme, oregano, cumin; cider vinegar
Minted Vinegar	2 parts each peppermint, spearmint, wintergreen; 1 part each lemon verbena, anise seed; 1 part sugar; rice vinegar
Winter Spice Vinegar	2 parts each rosemary, thyme; 1 part each mint, allspice berries, chopped ginger, cardamom; 1 cinnamon stick; 3 cloves; 1 tonka bean or $\frac{1}{4}$ vanilla bean; white wine vinegar
Eastern Vinegar	3 parts each kaffir lime leaves, cilantro, scallion; 2 parts toasted sesame seed; 1 part each chopped garlic, chopped ginger, star anise, Szechwan peppercorns; rice vinegar
Fruit Vinegar	3 parts raspberries; 1 part each opal basil, lemon verbena, lemon thyme; 1 cinnamon stick; white wine vinegar

Flavored Oils

The preparation for infusing spices and herbs into oil is similar to that of vinegar, but the dangers are a little different. Acidic vinegar is an inhospitable environment for botulism, but a little moisture trapped in an oxygen-free bottle of oil is a perfect host. Sanitizing the bottles and herbs is an important step, but further precaution should be taken, too. Take care to completely dry foods you plan to infuse into the oil. Oil with infusions of foods like garlic or chiles, with a lot of internal moisture, are especially susceptible to botulism. Make these oils in small batches and store them in the refrigerator. If they haven't been used in 2 weeks, freeze or discard them.

To accentuate the flavors of the spices and herbs in your oil, choose a neutral oil as your base, one that has a very light, nondescript flavor, such as canola, safflower, or vegetable oil. Unlike infused vinegars, oil should not be heated before it's infused. Pour it cool into a sanitized jar of clean spices and chopped herbs. Seal it tightly with a sanitized lid and let it sit in a cool dark spot for 2 weeks. Shake the jar daily to blend the aromatic oils with the base oil. After 2 weeks, taste the oil. If the flavor is lacking, strain the oil into another sterilized jar full of spices and herbs and repeat the process.

> **Tidbit**
>
> Olive oil and nut oils are generally too strong for flavored oils ... unless you want the flavor of the olives and the nuts to be a part of your flavor blend.

The following table lists some ideas for uniquely flavored oils. Drizzle them over grilled meat and seafood, roasted vegetables, or cook with them instead of your plain old olive oil. They are guaranteed to spice up your meal. (Measurements are given in parts so they can be made easily in any quantity. All herbs are used fresh, unless otherwise specified.)

Flavored Oil	Ingredients
Herbaceous Olive Oil	2 parts each rosemary, basil, sage; 1 part each chopped garlic, fennel seed, basil; 1 pequin chile; olive oil
Spicy Barbecue Oil	2 parts each oregano, thyme, cilantro; 1 part each cumin, coriander, chile arbol, kaffir lime leaves, brown sugar, garlic, mustard seed; 1 cinnamon stick; peanut oil
Savory Oil for Seafood	2 parts each bay leaves, celery seeds; 1 part each cardamom, allspice, chopped ginger; 1 vanilla bean; 1 cinnamon stick; corn oil
Lemon Pepper Oil	3 parts lemongrass; 1 part each pink peppercorn, Szechwan peppercorn, chopped ginger; corn oil

continues

continued

Flavored Oil	Ingredients
Annatto Oil	1 part each annatto seed, garlic, sautéed in an equal amount of safflower oil until warmed and then cooled completely; 1 part each bay leaves, cinnamon sticks, black pepper; safflower oil
Caribbean Oil	2 parts each juniper berries, cilantro, thyme; 1 part each chopped garlic, chopped ginger; 1 scotch bonnet chile; 1 cinnamon stick; peanut oil

Compound Butter

Adding spices and herbs to butter is an unexpected way to incorporate their aromatic essence into a recipe. Flavored butters can be used as a sauce melted over broiled fish, grilled meats, steamed vegetables, potatoes, or noodles. They can also become part of another recipe. Add them into a sauce, use them in baking, or simply set them on the table as an accompaniment to your dinner rolls.

For best results, start with room temperature unsalted butter. For every pound of butter, you can add up to 1½ cups of flavorings. Mince the herbs very fine, and grind the spices. Stir the flavorings into the softened butter thoroughly. Be sure anything that has been heated, such as sautéed shallots, is completely cooled before it's added to the butter. Roll the butter into a 1- or 2-inch thick log on a piece of parchment paper or waxed paper. Wrap the paper around the butter log and twist the ends tightly, like a sausage. Chill your compound butter completely or freeze for up to a week.

> **Hot Stuff**
>
> Don't add more than the recommended quantity of spices and herbs, or the butter will lose its structural integrity and fall apart too easily when it's cut or spread.

To use your butter, unwrap and slice off ¹/₂-inch coins. For an alternate presentation, pipe the butter through a pastry bag fitted with a decorative tip into rosettes. As an accompaniment to baked goods, pack it into small ramekins and chill, or roll it into butter balls and serve it in a small dish over a few ice cubes.

The classic compound butter is Beurre Maître d'Hôtel (see recipe in Chapter 4 under *Parsley*), but you need not be limited to that old standard. Try some of the ideas in the following table or create your own. (Measurements are given in parts so they can be made easily in any quantity. All herbs are used fresh, unless otherwise specified. Use unsalted butter, but add a pinch of salt for every pound of butter to bring out the natural flavors.)

Compound Butter	Ingredients
Flower Butter	1 part each rose petals, lavender buds, violets
Gingerbread Butter	2 parts each ground cinnamon, ground nutmeg; 1 part each ground cardamom, ground nutmeg, ground allspice; grated zest of 1 orange and 1 lemon
Pesto Butter	3 parts basil; 1 part each parsley, chervil, chopped garlic, toasted walnuts
Roasted Pepper Butter	3 parts cilantro; 2 parts each epazote, cumin, ground white peppercorns, chopped garlic; 1 Anaheim chile, roasted, peeled and chopped fine
Lemon Mint Butter	1 part each peppermint, lemon balm, lemon thyme, ground pink peppercorns; zest of 1 lemon

Fragrance Throughout Your Home

Spices and herbs were used to heal and cleanse long before we began adding them to our food. The recent boom in aromatherapy is nothing new at all. Here are some easy, nonedible ways to utilize your bountiful harvest.

Potpourri

Placed about a room in decorative bowls, or sewn tight into sachet pillows, the colorful dried petals of *potpourri* are a wonderfully aromatic use for your spices and herbs.

Chefspeak

The word *potpourri* means "rotten pot," and that's what it was. Ceramic and porcelain lidded containers were filled with herbs, spices, and some distilled spirits. The vegetation would emit fragrance as it decomposed. The containers were set near the fire, and the lid was lifted when someone entered the room. Small potpourri buckets were even hung about one's person, tucked under petticoats for fragrance to go.

Dry the herbs as described earlier in this chapter. Flowers and flower petals can be dried in a similar manner. Thick flower heads, like roses, are best broken apart and dried as individual petals. Whole roses and rose buds can be used, but take care that they have dried completely. It's essential to thoroughly dry all your potpourri ingredients. The tiniest amount of moisture left in a leaf, if buried in the mix, can easily turn to mold and spread very quickly.

Tidbit

Many recipes for potpourri include a small amount of imitation fragrance. As with imitation flavorings, the effect is good, but not necessarily natural. A well-chosen mixture of freshly dried natural ingredients can lend just as much fragrance as any imitation oil. Be sure to stir the mixture occasionally to break up the ingredients and release the natural oils.

Sachets, Simmers, and Soaks

A small amount is all that's needed to add fragrance to a room. Fill a bowl with a cup or two, and keep the unused potpourri stored in an airtight container. An even smaller amount can be sewn into small fabric pillows to make fragrant sachets. Tuck them into dresser drawers, linen cupboards, and suitcases. Hang them in closets, bathrooms, laundry rooms, and from your rearview mirror. Or simmer potpourri on the stove. This method is a good idea in dry climates, where the aromatic oils tend to dissipate quickly into the air.

Herbal mixtures can be used to fragrance yourself, too. Combine soothing blends in a muslin bag and toss it in the tub for a soothing bath, or add to your hand-washing rinse water. Mix them with Epsom salts for a skin-softening foot soak, or combine them with vinegar for a refreshing skin toner.

Freshen each room in your home with the essence of your garden. Seasonal availability can also dictate your ingredients. Use the recipes in the following table as a guide and then come up with your own blends. (Measurements are given in parts so they can be made easily in any quantity. All herbs are used dried.)

Potpourri Blend	Ingredients
Floral Potpourri	4 parts rose petals; 2 parts lavender buds; 1 part each rosemary, lemon verbena, tarragon, allspice
Citrus Spice Potpourri	3 parts each dried orange peel, myrtle blossoms; 2 parts each bay leaf, rosemary, peppermint; 1 part each cinnamon stick, fennel seed, cloves; 1 tonka bean or 1/4 vanilla bean
Autumn Potpourri	2 parts each pine needles, rosemary, bay leaves; 1 part each cinnamon stick, clove, allspice, orange peel, rose petals (Use this as a steaming potpourri as well.)
Headache Sachet	3 parts lavender; 2 parts rosemary; 1 part each lemon thyme, lemon verbena, sage, woodruff
Refreshing Face Wash	1 part each chamomile, rose petals, lavender, lemon balm, thyme, white vinegar (Steep in 6 parts warm water for 15 minutes before use.)
Soothing Herbal Bath	2 parts Epsom salt; 1 part each rosemary, lavender, peppermint, lemon verbena (Mix and store in an airtight container for 1 week before use.)

Your recipes take on a whole new dimension when you consider the meanings of your ingredients:

Basil = good wishes	Marjoram = happiness
Bay = victory	Mugwort = happy travels
Borage = courage	Myrtle = true love
Caraway = remembrance	Oregano = joy
Chamomile = comfort	Parsley = festive
Cloves = dignity	Peppermint = affection
Coriander = hidden worth	Rose = love
Cumin = engagement	Rosemary = remembrance
Hyssop = cleanliness	Rue = protection
Dill = power against witchcraft	Sage = wisdom
Fennel = strength	Thyme = courage
Juniper = protection	Violet = faithfulness
Lavender = luck	Wormwood = absence
Lemon verbena = unity	Yarrow = everlasting love

Once you discover all the pleasure spices and herbs can add to your everyday life, be sure to share them with friends. Gifts made from herbs and spices are especially cherished when they're made with love. You can even choose herbs with special meanings to personalize your gifts.

The Least You Need to Know

◆ For the best and freshest selection of spices and herbs, grow them yourself.

◆ Herbs are easy to cultivate outdoors or in.

◆ Preserve the essence of home-grown spices and herbs with careful drying, freezing, infusion into vinegar and oils, and blending into butter and tea.

◆ Dried spices and herbs can be used throughout your home to add freshness and fragrance in unexpected places.

Chapter 3

The Science of Flavor

In This Chapter

- ◆ Mapping the tongue
- ◆ The basic elements of taste
- ◆ Combining senses to determine flavor

Someone with a sense of style is said to "have good taste." Calling something "tasteful" is a compliment. As modern humans, we have evolved away from the survival values of basic taste to a notion that taste is primarily a sense of pleasure. Eating is no longer simply about the need to sustain life. It is a cultural, social, and familial event, built around flavor.

Let's explore taste and flavor. They are different, but intertwined.

Stick Out Your Tongue

At the turn of the twentieth century, German research scientist D. P. Hänig published a map of the tongue. It illustrated the tongue perimeter and the intensity of sensitivity to four basic sensations: sweet, salty, bitter, and sour. The original drawings show clearly that the entire perimeter of the tongue was sensitive to all flavors but that certain areas had greater sensitivity to one of the four specific sensations.

The Tongue Map

From that first map evolved the simple tongue map seen in textbooks across the country. No longer were the tastes perceived around the entire tongue. Instead, the sensation of bitter was focused in the back of the tongue, sweet on the tip, salt on the front sides, and sour on the back sides.

If you've ever tried to experiment with taste based on this map, you'll know right away that it's false. You taste things throughout your *entire* mouth. The modern tongue map is now widely refuted.

 Tidbit

Debunk the tongue map yourself. Gather a few elements representing each basic taste, like salt, lemon juice, cold coffee, and sugar. Taste them, one at a time. Swirl the taste throughout your entire mouth, and concentrate on where you feel the taste. Rinse your mouth well with water and chew a piece of bland bread or cracker to cleanse your palette between each taste. Carefully record your findings.

How Your Taste Buds Work

Your tongue, soft palate, and epiglottis are covered with about 10,000 taste buds. They are found on those visible bumps, called *papillae*. Each taste bud has about 100 taste cells, on which are taste receptors. The things we taste include a number of molecular structures, such as ions, organic molecules, carbohydrates, amino acids, and proteins. The molecules are carried by saliva into the receptors, which respond to a few basic taste sensations and transmit the taste information to the brain.

Each taste bud recognizes all the taste sensations. Each one has a preference and responds to one of the tastes more strongly than the others. But the increased sensitivity is minor and not nearly as defined as the modern tongue map would have us believe.

Humans inherit different levels of sensory responsiveness, which influences what we eat. Some taste less, some more. Babies and the elderly have less tolerance for strong tastes. Hormones affect how we taste and what we crave. (Consider the eating habits of pregnant women and teenagers.) Drugs, both legal and illegal, affect our sense of taste and alter our perception of flavor.

> **Tidbit**
> Some people called super-tasters perceive taste with intense reaction. For them, capsaicin, bitterness, and artificial sweeteners are not easily tolerated.

An Explanation of Taste

We eat the foods we like, and avoid the ones we don't. But why? And why do some people love foods that others despise? Our preferences stem from physiological traits that have evolved with our species. It started as a means for survival. Taste drives our appetite. We crave certain foods because our body needs them. Sweets are rich in energy-giving carbohydrates. Salt balances our body fluids and carries nutrition throughout the body. Bitterness and acidity are warnings of toxins and spoiled foods. Nature is an amazing thing.

Of course, our cave-dwelling ancestors didn't crave a Milky Way bar like you do, and most would have quickly spat out that cup of coffee because taste has evolved in humans over time as a result of technological and cultural events. For instance, the ability to preserve foods through curing (salt) and brining (acid) changed our reluctance to ingest these basic tastes. We taught ourselves to like alcohol and coffee (fermented, bitter, and astringent beverages) because we found their effects pleasurable. People brought up with a diet of highly spiced foods have a much higher tolerance for it. Much of the body's natural defense mechanisms have been thwarted in the name of flavor.

In deconstructing flavor, we divide foods into four taste groups based on the sensory capabilities of our tongue: salty, sour, sweet, and bitter. But the basic elements of flavor are classified differently from culture to culture. *Hot* is an added taste sensation in China. India adds *spicy* and *astringent*. The Japanese term *umami*, meaning "delicious flavor" and also called *savory* or *succulent*, has recently been accepted around the world as a legitimate taste element. At the University of Burgundy, researchers have isolated a taste receptor for *fat*. Some consider *metallic* a taste, especially after experiencing their tongue on the flag pole or accidentally chewing aluminum foil. There even those who identify *neutral* as a taste, as in water. The number of primary tastes is up for some debate, so let's start by identifying the obvious ones.

> **Tidbit**
>
> Inability to taste is called *ageusia*. Older people often suffer from a reduced ability to taste, called *hypoagusia*, caused by slow rejuvenation of taste receptor cells. Increased use of medications can also cause this condition.

Salty

Saltiness is mainly experienced in the presence of sodium chloride (NaCl). Sodium is necessary for physiological survival to keep the concentration of our body fluids at the correct levels. It helps our cells absorb nutrients, and it helps transmit electrical impulses to our nerves. Like sugar, it's possible that the craving for salt is a built-in survival reflex.

Sodium naturally occurs in meats, so people and animals who eat mostly plants can easily become deficient. Overconsumption of sodium is problematic, too, causing dehydration and retention of water that can lead to high blood pressure.

Salt is universally used to bring out the natural flavors of foods. When used correctly, the food should taste deliciously like itself and not a salty version of itself. One reason for this effect from salt could be the way the sensation is transmitted. The receptor for salt is an ion channel that allows sodium ions to pass directly through the cell membrane, creating the sensory perception of saltiness. Acid, another taste used to brighten the flavor of foods, penetrates the cells in the same way. Sweet and bitter substances, however, must wind through the cell membrane several times before they're perceived. This direct perception may explain the ability of salt and acid to wake up our taste buds and brighten food's flavor.

The effect that salt has on the balance of flavors is vital in the kitchen. If you've ever had a meal devoid of salt, you'll know what I mean. Bread, pasta, and meats prepared without salt are bland and nondescript. Salt vastly improves all recipes, enhancing the natural flavor of everything from lettuce to chocolate cake.

Hot Stuff

Salt absorbs moisture from the air just as it absorbs moisture from food. This can be problematic for your salt shaker if you live in a humid environment. To combat clumpy salt in your shaker, add a few grains of rice. The rice will absorb the moisture and keep the salt dry.

Salt also reduces the bitterness of foods by actually changing your perception of it. You can test this by adding a little salt to bitter tonic water. Just before it begins to taste salty, the quinine tastes sweet.

Chemically, salt plays a role in several key culinary applications. If added to water, it will raise the temperature of the boil and lower the temperature of the freeze. The use of rock salt in old-fashioned ice-cream machines is an example of this chilling effect.

In bread making, salt inhibits the growth of yeast. Without a carefully controlled amount of salt, the yeast would feed uncontrollably and produce an unpleasant, overly fermented flavor.

Salt has been used as a preservative for centuries because it draws out moisture. The process is called *salt-curing*. Fish and meat packed in salt release moisture, creating an unsuitable environment for bacterial growth. It was an early method for transporting foods on long journeys. This dehydration is the principle behind koshered meats. During the butchering process, the meat is heavily salted, releasing all body fluids. For this reason, too, meat stays juicier if it's left unsalted until cooking is complete. Salt draws the moisture out of vegetables and fruits in the same way.

Sour

Sour taste seems to be innately unpleasant. This is by design, as soured foods, like spoiled milk and rotten fruit, tend to make us ill. But as children age, there tends to be a period in which the sour taste is highly prized (which explains the popularity of sour gummy worms).

In cooking, acid is used to wake up flavor, much like salt is. It makes us salivate, which is a necessary step in moving taste to the receptors and in digestion. In our stomach, acid encourages production of hydrochloric acid for digestion. (This is why vinaigrette salads are served at the beginning of a meal.) Acid has an antifungal effect and is often referred to as the disinfectant of the intestines.

The particular health benefits of vinegar include lowering blood pressure and suppressing lactic acid build-up. In Japan, vinegar cafés are popping up in train stations, serving beverages made with vinegar, fruits, and vegetables to health-conscious commuters.

> **Tidbit**
>
> Try this experiment with salt and acid: take a bland food, like an avocado, and divide it into three portions. Sprinkle one portion with a pinch of salt, one with a drop of lemon juice, and leave the third one alone. Taste the difference in flavor the salt and acid makes, and compare it to the plain avocado.

Every cuisine utilizes the acidic pucker. Vinegar, lemon, lime, *tamarind, amchoor,* gooseberries, *tomatillos,* and *sorrel* all lend a sour edge to food and make it characteristic of the country in question. Tart beverages are common all over the world, too, like *aguas frescas* in Mexico, made with sugar and tamarind, or *citron presse* in France, which is nothing more than a glass of straight lemon juice with a side of water and sugar. The pucker is so desirable that chefs incorporate citric acid as an ingredient to up the pucker factor of their recipes.

> **Tidbit**
>
> Carnivores, like cats, are unable to recognize sweetness. In the wild, they're strictly meat eaters, so they have evolved without the sweet taste receptor. Dogs choose sugar water over plain, but not cats. Test it on your own pets.

Sweet

Human babies respond to sugar quite early. The taste is innately pleasant because the calorie-rich carbohydrates are an essential energy source for humans.

Sweetness works with other tastes in interesting ways. Acidic and bitter foods are made palatable by sugars. If you need proof, think about coffee or lemon pie. Chocolate is another great example. No one likes to eat unsweetened chocolate, but just a little sugar creates bitter-sweet and semisweet, craved by chocoholics worldwide.

But excess sweetness drastically changes the sensation of the other tastes. This is why sweet wines and desserts are best enjoyed at the end of a meal.

Conversely, sweetness is tamed by acid and bitterness. Chefs commonly use acid to cut the cloying sweetness of certain recipes, including candies, fruits, and sweet vegetables like yams.

> **Tidbit**
>
> *Miraculin* is a protein found in the small red berries of the West African *miracle fruit plant*. It has no flavor of its own, but it makes sour foods taste sweet for up to an hour. The miracle fruit has long been used to improve the flavor of sour food.

We think of sweet as being derived from sugar (sucrose), but other naturally sweet compounds are even sweeter, such as *licorice root* and *angelica*.

Bitter

Bitterness is meant to be a warning against toxicity. Sharp, disagreeable tastes occur as a natural indication of poison. Synthetic, bitter-tasting chemicals are commonly added to toxic substances like antifreeze and denatured alcohol to prevent accidental poisoning. Nail-biting remedies employ a similar tactic. But as humans evolved, we learned to ignore the bitter warnings. The so-called *acquired* or *grown-up* flavors of coffee and alcohol are essentially toxic, especially in large quantities. But because we enjoy the effects, we add sugar, acid, and other flavorings to make them palatable.

Herbivores have an altered sensitivity to bitterness as a means of survival. Their bodies have adapted to allow the ingestion of toxins that would cause adverse reaction in the rest of us. This provides them with a much wider variety of food options.

Umami

Scientists have recently isolated taste receptors that respond to glutemic acids, or glutamates. First found in seaweed, glutamates are used in the flavor enhancer *monosodium glutamate* (*MSG*). Some call it the fifth taste, while others still refer to it as more of a mouthfeel. It's taste has been described in several ways, including meaty, savory, succulent, woodsy, and earthy.

Glutamates drive our appetite for amino acids, the building block of protein, which is essential for tissue repair. It's found in meats, as well as fermented and aged foods like cheese, fish sauce, and mushrooms.

Sensing Flavor

Knowing that there are only a few basic tastes, you may have concluded by now that there's more to flavor than just your tongue.

The Nose Knows

Although the tongue can distinguish a handful of tastes, the nose can differentiate hundreds of substances in minute quantities. If you doubt the importance your sense of smell plays in flavor, think back to the last time you had a bad cold. The texture of the chicken soup was warm and soothing, but could you really taste it? For this reason, good chefs never wear cologne.

 Tidbit

Test the power of your nose. Peel and dice a potato and an apple. Mix them up, plug your nose, close your eyes, and pick a piece to eat. Can you tell which it is?

There are more than 1,000 olfactory receptors in the upper part of the nasal cavity. They can distinguish the nuances of essential oils, esters, and other aromatic compounds that make up the world around us. If you really want to taste something, chew it, close your mouth, and exhale through your nose. This forces the aromatic compounds through the pharynx, past the largest concentration of olfactory receptors, giving you the most flavor possible.

Mouthfeel

Much of how food is described is based on feel in addition to flavor. During chewing, you perceive pressure throughout your mouth. Your *somatosensory system* detects multiple sensations from the body, including touch and pressure, temperature, pain, itch, and tickle. From the mouth, this system sends impulses to the brain, which, in cases of shockingly sweet, tart, or bitter foods, may result in jaw pain, tongue thrusting, puckering, and shuddering. Crunchy, crispy, chewy, soggy, juicy, and slimy all conjure up very specific food traits. Whether these sensations are good or bad is entirely determined by your expectations. Juicy may be pleasant in an apple, but not necessarily in a cookie.

> **Hot Stuff**
>
> Take care when describing your culinary creations. Use *moist* instead of *wet*, *crisp* instead of *hard*, and *mild* instead of *bland*.

The touch and pressure of food in the mouth is typically referred to as *mouthfeel*. The Japanese call it *Kokumi*, or "thickness." Chefs strive to create dishes with pleasant mouthfeel by combining textures in an agreeable way, such as crispy cookies with creamy custards. Of course, what's pleasurable to one is not necessarily pleasurable to all. Take carbonated beverages, for example. Many find effervescence very unpleasant, even painful. Gelatin is another food with a texture folks either love or hate.

> **Tidbit**
>
> As a culinary instructor, I was constantly testing my students' palettes. My favorite examination was the blind taste test. I carefully gathered an assortment of spices and herbs and ground or chopped them to similar consistency. Each was numbered and placed in a small paper cup. Students tasted each one and tried to identify them. Try it yourself and test your *taste IQ*.

Astringency is a dryness brought about by foods that contain tannins. Derived from seeds, skins, bark, leaves, and unripened fruits, tannins constrict the tissue of any part of the mouth they come in contact with. Examples of tannic, astringent foods include aged red wines, hops, and tea. Unripened persimmons are especially known for their astringency.

The effects of astringency sound unpleasant, but consider what tannins can do when combined with other foods. Hoppy beer with fried foods, red wines with fatty meats, and tea with scones and clotted cream are all classic combinations that use astringency to cut through fats and expose more of the food's flavor.

Temperature

One of the easiest ways to alter the flavor of food is with temperature. A temperature change can alter flavor, texture, and even render some food unpalatable. Coldness tends to subdue all flavors. Cheese, beer, meats, vegetables, and fruits are always better if allowed to warm up a bit after they've come out of the fridge. As the temperature increases, more odor molecules are released and can be detected. (This is not only true for food. Consider dumpsters—and people.)

Tidbit

Test the effect temperature has on food by scooping out a dish of ice cream and letting it melt at room temperature. Then taste it side by side with frozen ice cream. The low temperature subdues the sweetness. You can test this with warm and cold soda pop, too.

Some sugar substitutes have been shown to actually change temperature on the tongue, but most temperature changes are false. Certain foods trick the tongue into thinking there has been a temperature change by activating the same nerve cells that actual temperature changes activate.

False heat, also referred to as *spicy* or *piquant*, is best exemplified by capsaicin, the compound found in chile peppers. Similar reactions occur with black pepper, cinnamon (as in red-hot candies), mustard oil (wasabi and hot mustard), eugenol (clove oil), and ethanol (distilled alcohol). *False cooling* is found in menthol, spearmint, and camphor (think vapor rub). These effects can be put to great use in the kitchen, as in cooling mint beverages and warming spiced ciders.

Eat With Your Eyes

Let us not neglect the importance of vision in our enjoyment of foods. Few things in the world are more exciting than having a beautiful plate of food set in front of you. But besides the obvious appreciation of an artistically designed presentation, what we see has a lot to do with what we taste. Our brain has specific expectations regarding color and food, and when those expectations are not met, our body reacts physically.

Take for example, a pile of soft, fluffy mashed potatoes. If it came in a lovely shade of charcoal gray, you might not enjoy it as much as if it were white. (This brings new appreciation for Sam-I-Am and his *Green Eggs and Ham*.)

Tidbit

In high school, I worked at a small ice-cream parlor after school. Every month it held a contest: anyone who could guess the secret flavor would win a free gallon. It was almost always vanilla, colored purple or green or yellow stripped with orange. We had very few winners.

Hot Stuff

Certain foods turn gray through *oxidation*, a color change that occurs in the presence of oxygen. Cut and left exposed to air, foods such as potatoes, apples, artichokes, and bananas can quickly lose their appeal. Oxidation can be prevented, or at least slowed, by application of acid. Squirt the sliced food with lemon juice, or soak it in *acidulated* water (water with acid).

Combining the Senses

By now you've probably realized that it's impossible to enjoy food to its fullest extent without combining the senses. And if you pay attention to what you eat, you'll find that tastes seldom occur alone. They are almost always in combination.

Sweet and sour is a common pair, as in Chinese sweet-and-sour pork, or candies like Jolly Ranchers and lemon drops. Bitter and sweet are heavenly in chocolate and coffee. We feed our craving for salty and sour with pickled foods. And salty and sweet make terrific snacking with combinations like popcorn and candy at the movies, caramel corn, or honey-roasted nuts.

> **Tidbit**
>
> To experience the sweet and sour combination at its best, add a little raspberry vinegar to your favorite caramel sauce.

Once we begin to recognize flavor, we are compelled to explain it. Wine connoisseurs are renowned, and frequently mocked, for their creative flavor descriptions. The more one tries to explain flavor, the more adjectives from outside the realm of the kitchen are apt to be invoked. You will be hard pressed to find a description of flavor that does not include texture, but a few purely flavor-based adjectives are commonly used in combination to describe the way food tastes.

Meaty, *earthy*, and *woodsy* are often used to explain *umami*. Vegetables and herbs are commonly described as green, *herbaceous*, *grassy*, *piney*, *freshly mown hay*, *lawnmower bags*, and *football fields*. The unique flavors of spices are expressed with words like *musty*, *musky*, *fragrant*, *perfumey*, *floral*, *smoky*, and unfortunately, *spicy*. *Toasted*, *roasted*, *nutty*, *charred*, *carbonized*, and *caramelized* are used to describe flavor as well as explain cooking techniques.

Researchers have isolated hundreds of compounds that make food taste the way it does. When these compounds are concentrated, they become what are commonly known as *natural flavors*. Once the compound is understood, it can then be reproduced for *artificial flavors*. But although the compounds are chemically made of the same stuff, a banana jelly bean tastes different from an actual banana because more than one compound makes a banana taste the way it does. In addition, the jelly bean lacks the texture and color of the real thing.

> **Hot Stuff**
>
> Artificial flavoring can be used quite successfully to enhance a food's natural quality. But use a light hand, as too much can overpower a dish and mask the natural flavors. A common culprit is almond extract, used with too heavy a hand by many pastry chefs and bakers.

The Least You Need to Know

◆ Taste buds work throughout the mouth to detect the basic elements of taste.

◆ Flavor is determined by several senses working together.

◆ Tastes work best when used in combination.

Part 2

Flavor at Your Fingertips

What is *asafetida*, or *amchoor*, or *perilla*? Why do you need any of them? How do you get them?

From A to Z, in the following pages, you'll find a global array of flavor. Spices and herbs are listed with the cook in mind; included are flavor descriptions, common usage, and historical importance. Also included are a few recipes to whct your appetite and show you how a particular spice can be used. Some are common dishes from around the world, while others are more unusual flavor pairings meant to highlight the unique qualities of the ingredients. Try them and then venture out into your own culinary experiments.

WOW. THAT'S ONE IMPRESSIVE SPICE RACK.

Chapter 4

Spices and Herbs, A to Z

Now for the fun stuff: in this chapter is everything you ever wanted to know about spices and herbs. In addition to their culinary uses, I've given some basic botanical information, which will be of interest to gardening enthusiasts and those looking to find actual specimens of these plants.

In most cases, I've listed a botanical family for each entry. If it's been a while since your last science class, botanical families are a part of *scientific classification*, a system that categorizes species of organisms into increasingly specific groups. Order of classification is as follows:

Life

Domain   plants, animals, fungi, and protists fall into the domain called *Eukaryote*

Kingdom   plants are in the kingdom *plantae*, mushrooms and other fungus are in the kingdom *fungi*, and most algae is of the kingdom *protista*

Phylum/division   plant divisions are myriad and include those that are nonvascular, vascular, and seed bearing

Class   groups plants by physical characteristics

Order   more descriptive than class

Family   large, related groups of plants, like roses, citrus, palms, etc

Genus   groups of similar plants, such as *thymus*, *cinnamomum*, and *rosmarinus*

Species   one specific variation of a plant

For the purpose of this book, I feel that the *family* is the most interesting level of classification, because it indicates the more unusual plant relationships.

Algae and seaweed classification is more difficult because these organisms fall somewhere in between plants and animals. The kingdom *protista* has been established for such plants and animals. They share the characteristic of complex cell or cells with a membrane bound nucleus.

Individual *species* are also listed throughout the text when specific plant variations are discussed. This nomenclature is useful when ordering plants from nurseries and through the Internet.

Also listed, when necessary, are pseudonyms. In some cases, I listed only the most common names because there were so many. If you're having trouble locating a certain spice or herb, try one of its aliases.

As you read through this section, I urge you to jot down the spices and herbs you find interesting. Be adventurous, and visit a specialty spice market, or go online to order something new, just for fun. There's a big world of flavor out there just waiting for you to take a bite!

Achiote

See Annatto.

Agar

A member of the botanical family *gelidiaceae*

(Algae is technically neither plant nor animal.)

Also known as *agar-agar, kanten,* and *Japanese gelatin*

Agar is a tasteless thickener made from a type of red algae (*gelidium*).
After the marine plant is harvested, it's dried and bleached in the sun.
Next it goes through a series of stages—boiling, crushing, freezing,
and thawing—all designed to eliminate impurities and extract the pure
gum.

Agar is used in much the same manner as gelatin. The product is
dissolved in hot water, added to recipes, and chilled to set. It absorbs
nearly three times its volume of water, and for that reason has its place
in the halls of fad diets, especially in Japan, where kanten tea is a hot
item for the overweight.

Agar is used in many desserts and sweets throughout Asia and in
beer brewing as a clarifying agent. The gums extracted from marine
vegetation (called *alginates*) make frequent appearances on the labels
of processed food as thickeners, emulsifiers, and stabilizers. Like agar,
the other alginates, which include carrgeenan and furcellaran, are used
widely in the food industry. Agar is the only one frequently used by
home and restaurant cooks.

Agar is available in better supermarkets and most Asian grocery
stores. It comes as sticks of dried seaweed or in powdered form.

Agave

A member of the botanical family *agavaceae*

Also known as *century plant*, *American aloe*, and *maguey*

This succulent plant (*agave americana*), a relative of yucca and aloe, is native to Mexico and grows abundantly there, as well as areas of the southwestern United States. It has large, long, thick leaves with spiny sharp edges that taper to a sharp point. The leaves sprout out from the root like a green fountain. After a decade of development, the flower majestically sprouts like a tree from the center just once during the plant's life, hence its pseudonym, century plant. The plant is poisonous if eaten raw, but sweet fruit, sap, or nectar is extracted from the stem.

Native tribes used this sap to make a ceremonial fermented drink called *pulque*. Pulque is still enjoyed in Mexico, but because it has a short shelf life, it's rarely seen outside that country. Some canned versions see limited import into the United States, but most agree that pulque is best enjoyed fresh in pulqueria cantinas.

The sap from agave is also distilled into a spirit known in Mexico as *Mescal*. Mescal is any distillation of agave that is not tequila. To be called tequila, the juice must come from the *blue agave* (*agave tequilana*) and be produced under strict guidelines in specific regions surrounding the town of Tequila in the central western state of Jalisco.

Agave nectar is used as a sweetener and sugar substitute. It is $1\frac{1}{2}$ times sweeter than cane sugar or honey, but it has a much lower glycemic index, which means it's absorbed more slowly into the bloodstream. This prevents it from raising blood sugar levels significantly, eliminating the highs and lows associated with sugar intake. For this reason, it's favored among those with diabetes and hyperglycemia.

Creative chefs use agave nectar anywhere sugar or honey will go: barbecue sauces, marinades, baked goods, etc. It adds a distinctive sweet flavor, reminiscent of—you guessed it—tequila.

Agave nectar is available through Internet sources (rawagave.com, agavenectar.com) and at health food stores.

Agave Vinaigrette

Don't limit this dressing to your salad bowl. Try it on grilled sea-food and poultry, too.

3 TB. agave nectar
1 clove garlic, minced
½ tsp. sea salt
¼ tsp. fresh ground black pepper
Zest and juice of 1 Mexican lime
2 TB. fresh cilantro, minced
¼ cup champagne vinegar
1 cup olive oil
6 cups loosely packed fresh salad greens (baby mixed greens, spinach, halved cherry tomatoes, and diced avocado)
1 cup fried flour or corn tortilla strips
½ cup crumbled cotija cheese

1. Whisk together agave nectar, garlic, sea salt, pepper, lime zest and juice, cilantro, vinegar, and olive oil in a large bowl, or combine in a jar with a tight-fitting lid and shake.

2. Pour vinaigrette over salad greens, toss, and top with tortilla strips and crumbled cotija.

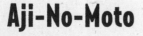

Aji-No-Moto

See MSG.

Ajowan

A member of the botanical family *umbelliferae* (parsley)

Also known as *ajwain, carum, Ethiopian cumin,* and *bishop's weed*

Native to India and North Africa, the ajowan plant (*trachyspermum ammi*) is a thin plant with leaves like carrot tops and white tufts of flowers that look like Queen Anne's lace. The tiny seeds look striped upon close inspection, much like fennel seeds, and they have a hairlike tail similar to anise.

The flavor of the ajowan seed is a little like thyme, as it contains the same aromatic compound thymol. But it's more complex, reminiscent of caraway, celery seed, and cumin.

The seed is common in Indian cuisine, often finding its way into starchy foods like breads, legumes, and vegetable dishes. It's an important flavor element in West African dishes as well, especially groundnut soup, and it is included in several of the region's traditional spice blends, including *kala masla* and *berbere* (see Appendix B).

Look for ajowan in Indian markets or online (nirmalaskitchen.com).

Aloo Paratha Bread

This stuffed Indian bread is a meal in itself.

2 cups whole-wheat flour
1 tsp. salt
½ to 1 cup cold water
½ cup ghee or vegetable oil
1 small onion, chopped
1 green chile pepper, minced
1 tsp. coriander seeds, crushed
1 tsp. ajowan seeds, crushed
5 small red new potatoes, boiled
1 tsp. cilantro, chopped

1. In a small bowl, combine flour and salt. Slowly stir in water to form a firm dough. Knead dough for 2 minutes, cover, and let rest for 30 minutes.

2. Heat 2 tablespoons ghee in a large sauté pan over high heat. Add onion, cook until golden. Add chile pepper, coriander seeds, and ajowan seeds, and fry briefly to toast. Remove from heat and stir in potatoes and cilantro. Set aside to cool.

3. Divide dough into 6 portions and form into balls. Pat each ball into a flat disc and fill with 1 or 2 tablespoons potato filling. Pinch dough closed around filling, and roll out into flat circle on a floured work surface, seam side down. Repeat with remaining dough.

4. Fry stuffed dough circles in 1 or 2 tablespoons ghee until golden brown on each side.

Allspice

A member of the botanical family *myrtaceae* (myrtle)

Also known as *Jamaican pepper* and *pimento*

This evergreen member of the myrtle family (*pimenta dioica*) grows in tropical and subtropical regions of South America and the West Indies. It has tough, thick leaves and small white clumps of tiny flowers that give way to dark purple berries. The berries are picked green and dried off the tree. Once dried, they resemble black pepper, which is why, upon discovery of this spice in Jamaica, Christopher Columbus named it *Jamaican Pepper*. Back in Europe, it was dubbed *pimento*.

The most sought-after allspice is Jamaican, but it is grown in other tropical regions as well, including Mexico, Guatemala, and Honduras.

Despite its name, allspice is not a blend of all the spices, although its flavor does closely resemble a combination of clove, cinnamon, nutmeg, and pepper.

Because of its similarity to those spices, allspice is frequently used in sweet, spicy baking. Its flavor is particularly suited to firm but mild root vegetables and squashes, like beets, parsnips, butternut, and acorn squash. It adds a nice flavor to peas and leafy greens and is commonly used much like nutmeg is in classic egg, cheese, and starch dishes. Allspice makes frequent appearances in sauces and marinades, most famously *Jerk* (see Appendix B).

Ground or powdered allspice is readily available, while whole allspice berries are available in larger supermarkets.

Almond

A member of the botanical family *rosaceae* (rose)

Although usually considered a nut, this fruit pit is a seed and an important flavoring worldwide. A native tree of Asia, almonds are now cultivated mainly in California, Spain, and Italy.

Two types of almonds are used in food production. Sweet almonds (*prunus dulcius*) can be eaten out of hand and are used in most recipes. Bitter almonds (*prunus dulcius amara*) have a specific, unique flavor used in the preparation of amaretto liqueur and almond extract. A similar flavor is extracted from apricot and peach pits and is often used in conjunction with or in place of bitter almonds.

Sweet almonds are available in multiple forms, including whole, skin on, blanched, toasted, slivered, sliced, chopped, and ground into fine almond meal and almond flour. Bitter almonds take a bit more effort to track down but are usually available at Indian or Middle Eastern Markets or online (bitteralmond.com). Bitter almonds contain a high percentage of hydrocyanic acid, which, while poisonous, is easily cooked out. Almonds contain a large amount of oil and are best refrigerated if not used right away to prevent rancidity.

Alum

Potassium aluminum sulfate

This mysterious white powder is actually powdered crystals of a salt of sulfuric acid. Alum is found in many industrial applications, including use as a dye fixative and as a fire retardant, but home cooks have relied on it for years as a crisping agent for pickling. Today, while most pickled vegetable recipes rely on refrigeration as a crisper and preservative, many pickling aficionados still add alum for the extra edge, especially during county fair time.

Alum is also an astringent and can be found in many old home remedies for relief of canker sores, to stop bleeding of small cuts, and as a deodorant. It's used in some home recipes for play dough, slowing down the growth of bacteria, and making it taste so bad that even paste-loving kids won't eat it.

Although alum is no longer a pantry staple, you can still find it in the spice aisle, as enterprising homemakers rely on it to this day.

Amaranth

A member of the botanical family *amaranthaceae* (pigweed)

Also known as *kiwicha*, *Chinese spinach*, and *bayam*

Amaranth (*amaranthus cruentis*) is a showy plant, with bushy broad leaves and a feathery fountain of tiny pink, red, and purple flowers. Several species are grown for specific uses, including the edible seeds, the edible leaves, dye extracted from the flowers, and their beauty in the garden.

The tiny tan and black amaranth seed contains complete protein, and for that reason, it was a staple food of the Incas, Aztecs, and Mayans. Its cultivation stopped when the Spanish arrived in the new world, but amaranth has experienced renewed popularity in recent years because of its nutritional value, especially among vegetarians.

The amaranth seed is used in a multitude of ways. It's ground to a flour and added to breads and pasta. The grain itself contains no gluten, but it adds an interesting nutty flavor when added to wheat flour. It can be used alone in recipes for crackers and flatbreads and makes good pancakes, similar in flavor to buckwheat. The seeds can be eaten as a porridge, boiled like rice with $1^1/_2$ times its volume in water. Add other herbs, vegetables, and nuts for an interesting pilaf.

The grains can also be popped like popcorn for a completely different flavor and texture. These tiny airy grains are commonly mixed with honey or syrup to create nutritious confections—called *alegria* in Mexico and *laddoos* in India—similar to Rice Krispy treats.

The greens are eaten like spinach throughout Asia, Mexico, and Peru. Amaranth sprouts are added to salads or sandwiches.

Amaranth seeds are available in most health food stores. For the leaves, look to local farmers' markets, or try to grow your own (naturehills.com).

Amchoor

A member of the botanical family *anacardiaceae* (cashew)

Also known as *mango powder* and *amchur*

Amchoor is a yellow-green powder made from mangos (*magifera*) that are picked green, dried in the sun, and ground to a powder. It's a common ingredient in Northern India and Nepal, used frequently in spice blends, including *Chaat Masala* (see Appendix B).

Amchoor has a very tart, sour-apple flavor and is used like lemon or lime juice to awaken flavors of a dish. It contains citric acid and proteolytic enzymes (enzymes that break down protein), which not only add flavor, but act as a meat tenderizer.

Amchoor is available whole or powdered in Indian markets and online (thespicebazaar.com).

Sweet Fruit Chutney

The sweet tanginess of this dish is the perfect antidote to fiery curry.

2 TB. amchoor powder
1 tsp. cumin
1 tsp. red chile powder
½ tsp. sea salt
¼ cup sugar
2 TB. fresh ginger, grated
2 TB. fresh cilantro, chopped
4 bananas, diced
1 mango, diced
1 papaya, diced
½ cup shredded coconut
½ cup golden raisins

1. In a large bowl, combine amchoor powder, cumin, red chile powder, sea salt, and sugar. Mix well, and add ginger and cilantro. Add bananas, mango, papaya, coconut, and raisins, and toss to coat.

2. Serve with spicy curries and warm flatbread.

Ammonia Bicarbonate

Also known as *hartshorn*, *baking ammonia*, and *carbonate of ammonia*

Ammonia bicarbonate was commonly used as a leavener before the advent of baking soda. It was used in many heavily spiced recipes because it left behind a slight ammonia flavor that's easily masked by spices.

Like baking powder, ammonia bicarbonate releases carbon dioxide when moistened and heated. The name *hartshorn* came from one early form of processing, when it was extracted from a distillation of hoofs and horns. Old Scandinavian recipes still call for hartshorn. It's not readily available, although some pharmacies may carry a crystalline version, which must be ground before using.

An equal amount of baking powder can be substituted.

Ancho

See Appendix C.

Anaheim

See Appendix C.

Angelica

A member of the botanical family *umbelliferae* (parsley)

Also known as *angel's root* and *wild celery*

Native to subarctic regions—including Russia, Northern Europe, Scandinavia, Iceland, and northern parts of North America—this giant herb (*angelica archangelica*) has large jagged-edged leaves that grow in groups of three. The tall, hollow stalk has red-tinged celerylike ridges and can grow as high as 6 feet tall. The tiny yellow-green flowers grow in pom-pom clusters.

Many cultures used angelica medicinally and spiritually throughout history. It was tacked above doorways to ward off plague, carried as defense against evil spirits and witchcraft, and smoked by Native Americans as a cure for respiratory ailments. Best of all, it's believed to be a panacea, and as such is protected by the Archangel Michael.

The subtle licorice-anise-sage flavor of angelica is enjoyed in several forms. The stalks are eaten as a vegetable in Scandinavian cuisines, and the leaves and seeds (see *Golpar*) are found in fish, meat, and stew preparations. Angelica seeds are among the many herbs used to flavor vermouth, chartreuse, and gin. The sweet root is used in jellies, fruit sauces, and potpourri. But by far the most common application of angelica is the candied stem.

The celerylike stalk is candied, often artificially colored green, and used by pastry chefs as a decorative element or incorporated into recipes with other dried and candied fruits. Angelica is naturally sweet, but candied angelica has extra sugar added, masking much of the natural herb's delicate flavor.

You can find angelica plants at better nurseries or online (mountainvalleygrowers.com). Candied angelica is imported from France; many spice companies carry it (herbies.com.au).

Angelica can be stored in syrup, or drained, coated with granulated sugar, and air dried. Store dried, sugared angelica in an airtight container at room temperature. Save the syrup for sweetening your iced tea.

Candied Angelica

Store-bought candied angelica is too sugary for me. This version lets the flavor shine through.

4 cups sugar

4 cups water

2 or 3 cups angelica stems, peeled, blanched, and cut into
   1-in. segments

1. In a large saucepan, combine sugar and water and bring to a boil. At the boil, add angelica and reduce heat to low.

2. Cook at barely a simmer for 30 to 60 minutes until stems are tender and translucent. Remove from heat and cool completely.

Anise

A member of the botanical family *umbelliferae* (parsley)

Anise refers to an annual flowering herb (*pimpinella anisum*) grown mainly for its seeds. Growing about 20 inches high, the leaves at the base of the plant look similar to cilantro, with the leaves at the top looking more like dill. White flowers produce a distinctive ridged seed with a small curly tail.

Anise was well-known to the ancient Romans, who used it to flavor hardtack carried by soldiers and sailors, a food similar to today's Italian biscotti, the twice-baked cookie, which is so hard it is meant to be dipped in *vin santo* or coffee.

The anise seed tastes like light licorice, but is sweeter and more delicate than fennel or licorice root. It's used most famously in several liqueurs, including its Italian namesake Anisette, Sambuca, Middle Eastern Arak, Greek Ouzo, and French Pastis. It also appears in many candies and chocolates. Lighter meats like fish and poultry are enhanced by its delicate but distinct flavors, and it shows up in several soups and stews throughout the Pyrenees region of France.

The anise seed is well loved in India as a digestive aid. Brightly colored, sugar-coated seeds of anise, fennel, and sesame called *mukhwas* are commonly served after meals to soothe the tongue and tummy after spicy meals—and to freshen breath.

You can find anise seed and powder at any well-stocked market. Specialty stores, especially pastry suppliers, may also carry anise extract or oil. Sometimes fennel bulb is mislabeled *sweet anise* in the produce department of your grocery store. Don't be fooled.

Annatto

A member of the botanical family *bixaceae* (annatto)

Also known as *achiote*

The achiote tree or shrub (*bixa orellana*), native to South America and the Caribbean, has heart-shape leaves and a spiny heart-shape seed pod that contains the annatto seed. The red pulp and tiny red seeds have been used historically as paint and dye. It's currently used as a colorant in many commercially prepared foods, including cheese, butter, candy, and smoked fish.

Annatto seed has a subtle bay-juniper flavor that's favored in meat dishes throughout South America and the Pacific. Philippine cuisine takes full advantage of the annatto seed, incorporating it into all kinds of stews, sauces, and fried foods.

The seeds themselves are very hard, and when ground, still tend to add a touch of grit to a recipe. The most efficient method of incorporating annatto seeds is to first cook them in oil, strain out the seeds, and use the oil. Another way to incorporate annatto is to use a commercially prepared paste, called *achiote paste*.

Both the seeds and the paste can be found easily in Latin American markets or in the ethnic aisle of better supermarkets.

Annatto Chicken

This dish can be frightening to those who don't enjoy spicy heat. But tell them to relax. It's more *spiced* than *spicy*.

1 cup olive oil
½ cup annatto seeds
4 cloves garlic, minced
1 yellow onion, diced
1 TB. fresh oregano, chopped
1 tsp. cumin seeds, crushed
1 tsp. whole allspice, crushed
2 bay leaves, crushed
1 tsp. peppercorns, crushed
Zest and juice of 1 large orange
Zest and juice of 1 lime
¼ cup white wine vinegar
1 (4- or 5-lb.) chicken, cut into serving pieces and rinsed with water

1. In a small saucepan over low heat, combine oil and annatto seeds and cook, stirring, until oil is red and aromatic, about 10 minutes. Cool and strain off and discard seeds.

2. In a large bowl, combine annatto oil with garlic, onion, oregano, cumin, allspice, bay leaves, peppercorns, orange zest and juice, lime zest and juice, and vinegar. Stir well to combine.

3. Put rinsed chicken pieces into a large plastic zipper bag. Pour in marinade and seal the bag. Massage marinade into meat and refrigerate for 4 to 6 hours. Grill or sauté chicken over low heat until the skin is crispy and the internal temperature reaches 180°F, about 10 minutes per side.

Variation: You could also roast the chicken at 400°F for 45 to 60 minutes.

Aonori

From the botanical family *ulvales*

(Algae is technically neither a plant nor an animal.)

Also known as *green nori*

Aonori is a Japanese product made from green algae (*monostroma* and *enteromorpha*). It is farmed in bays around Japan, harvested, dried, and ground into a fine, bright-green powder.

High in calcium, iron, and protein, aonori is used as a flavoring and garnish in everyday dishes such as soup, rice, noodles, and tempura.

Find powdered and traditional flaked and paper forms of aonori in Japanese markets or online (importfood.com).

Arrowroot

From the botanical family *marantaceae*

Also known as the *obedience plant*

This perennial plant (*maranta arundinaceae*), native to the West Indies, shoots stalks up as high as 5 feet. But it's the *rhizome* that contains the precious starch so important to the cuisines of Southeast Asia.

According to legend, the roots were pounded, and the starchy pulp was used to extract the toxins from poisoned-arrow wounds. Today, the flavorless white powder is a thickening agent preferred in lighter sauces that are meant to stay clear. Unlike flour or cornstarch, arrowroot requires no additional cooking or boiling time to eliminate a starchy flavor, nor does it take on an opaque, cloudy appearance.

Chefspeak

Although often confused with a root, a **rhizome** is actually a bulbous, underground stem that grows horizontally at the soil surface.

Arrowroot is not, however, an all-purpose starch replacement. Overheating arrowroot destroys its thickening power. It can also take on a slimy consistency when used with dairy products. It's best to add arrowroot to a sauce at the end of cooking, when a little more body and texture is desired.

Arrowroot is available in larger supermarkets and most health food stores.

Asafetida

A member of the botanical family *umbelliferae* (parsley)

Also known as *asefoetida* and *devil's dung*

Foetida is Latin for "foul-smelling," which makes one wonder who discovered asafetida and why they decided to put it in their mouth. Asafetida is the dried sap of a giant fennel plant (*ferula asafetida*). It has a distinct, off-putting, sulphurous smell, but once gently heated, it imparts a pleasantly distinctive garlicy essence.

Asafetida is an integral component of many forms of Indian *dal* (legumes), South Indian *Sambar Podi* (see Appendix B), and the ubiquitous Worcestershire sauce.

The dried sap or resin is very hard and, thus, difficult to grind. It must be fried in hot oil to release its flavors. For asafetida first-timers, buy it in Middle Eastern and Indian Markets in prepared powder form, which usually includes some proportion of starch. Keep asafetida powder tightly sealed, or the rest of the spices in the pantry can take on its menacing odor.

Toasted Rice Pilaf

The spices in this dish makes it special, but it's the toasting of the rice before the liquid is added that provides a deep, rich, nutty flavor.

¼ cup vegetable oil
1 yellow onion, diced
2 cloves garlic, minced
1 sweet red pepper, diced
½ tsp. mustard seed, crushed
½ tsp. cumin seed, crushed
½ tsp. coriander seed, crushed
1 tsp. fresh ginger, grated
1 tsp. asafetida powder
2 curry leaves
2 cups basmati rice
1 cup golden raisins
1 cup sliced almonds
4 cups water
¼ cup chopped cilantro

1. In a large, wide-bottomed sauté pan or soup pot, heat vegetable oil. Add onion, garlic, and sweet red pepper, and sauté until translucent.

2. Add mustard seed, cumin seed, coriander seed, ginger, asafetida powder, curry leaves, and rice, and stir to coat with oil. Toast over high heat until rice begins to turn golden brown and spices become fragrant.

3. Add raisins, almonds, and water, and bring to a boil. At the boil, turn heat down to a bare simmer, cover, and cook for 20 minutes or until water is absorbed and rice is tender.

4. Serve topped with chopped cilantro.

Baking Powder

This leavener is not technically a spice, but it does appear on every spice shelf, so it's worth a quick mention. First marketed in the 1860s, baking powder is a mixture of *bicarbonate of soda* and an acidic salt, such as cream of tartar or calcium phosphate, with some starch thrown in for easy blending.

When baking powder is mixed into a recipe, it reacts with the moisture of the batter and the heat of the oven to produce carbon dioxide. The gas builds up and raises the product. Double-acting baking powder begins this process when moistened but holds a portion of the reaction until heat is applied. The original baking powder, single-acting baking powder, releases all the carbon dioxide with moisture and must, therefore, be baked immediately upon mixing.

Baking Soda

Bicarbonate of soda

This chemical compound is created when ammonia is used to separate the sodium (Na) from the chloride (Cl) of salt (NaCl) in the presence of carbon dioxide and water. When added to acid, it releases carbon dioxide gas. (Remember the papier-mâché volcano trick from elementary school science class?) When mixed into batters with acidic ingredients like vinegar, sour cream, or buttermilk, the gas accumulates and leavens the product.

Baking soda is also used in some applications to increase alkali in highly acidic foods. This increased alkali preserves the color of some fruits vegetables.

Basil

A member of the botanical family *labiatae* (mint)

Also known as *sweet basil* and *holy basil*

A native of India, basil *(ocimum basilicum)* spread to Asia and Egypt as early as 2000 B.C.E. It moved up through Europe with the help of the Romans and came to the New World with the colonists. Basil is a sacred plant in India, a symbol of love, faithfulness, and eternal life. It is often associated with the scorpion, thought to protect against them in some cultures and attract them in others. Early Christians believe basil grew at the sight of the Crucifixion and is, therefore, found on the altar and in the Holy Water at the Greek Orthodox Church.

This short plant, which can be grown as a perennial in hot climates, is favored for its silky, shiny, juicy, fragrant leaves. There are many varieties, including those with smooth green leaves, serrated-edged leaves, curly lettuce leaves, purple-tinged leaves, and very dark purple leaves. Flowers shoot up in purple or white spikes and are as fragrant as the leaves.

Basil leaves are strong and oily when fresh, with a gingery, licorice flavor. When dried, basil takes on the minty flavor of its plant family. To preserve the fresh flavor of basil, store it frozen as blanched leaves or purées, or pack the fresh leaves in salt. Interesting hybrids are available, and the flavors can be surmised from the names, such as pineapple basil, lemon basil, and cinnamon basil.

Although most often associated with Mediterranean cuisines, basil is also a vital ingredient in foods from Thailand and Vietnam. The pungent aroma complements all kinds of food, including red meat, seafood, poultry, vegetables, eggs, cheeses, and many different berries and stone fruits.

Dried basil is readily available in most markets. Better supermarkets and most farmers' markets carry fresh basil, especially throughout the summer. Basil is also an easy plant to grow in the garden or on the kitchen windowsill.

Bay

A member of the botanical family *lauraceae* (laurel)

Also known as *bay laurel, sweet bay, roman laurel,* and *Turkish bay*

This evergreen tree (*laurus nobilis*) is native to the Mediterranean but thrives wherever the climate is similar. It was dedicated to Apollo, the god of music and poetry, and garlands of laurel were given as prizes—hence *poet laureate* and *baccalaureate*. It grows up to 30 feet high and produces creamy little flowers and blackberries. But it's the leaves that are prized above all.

About 3 inches long, thick and shiny, the leaves are used dry or fresh with meats, fish, vegetables, stews, soups, pâtés, marinades, and even fruits. The subtle pine-camphor aroma is slightly bitter when fresh but takes on a sweetness as it dries.

Indian Bay (*cinnamomum tamala*) is also known as cinnamon leaf and has a decidedly cinnamon flavor. It's used extensively in *kormas* and curries. California Bay (*umbellularia californica*) is a more potent, mentholated variety, and is best when not overcooked. Indonesian Bay (*Eugenia polyantha*) is actually in the myrtle family and has the subtle essence of anise.

Chefspeak

A **korma** is a mild meat or vegetable curry, usually made with nuts, coconut milk, yogurt, or cream.

Common bay leaves are available dried at most markets. Looking for specific Turkish or California bay may require a trip online (savoryspiceshop.com). You can find Indian Bay at Indian markets, but Indonesian is a little trickier to find—unless you live near an Indonesian community.

Hot Stuff

Many people prefer to remove the bay leaves from a dish before serving, but I like the look of them. They don't hurt and won't make anyone ill, so I leave them in for beauty and aroma. People can eat around them!

Warm Winter Compote

This recipe calls for the *bosc* variety of pear, the very pear-shape pears with brownish skin and firm flesh. They hold their shape well for prolonged cooking, which makes them ideal here. If you can't find them, any pear will do, as will, for that matter, apples.

2 pt. dried black mission figs
4 bosc pears, peeled, cored, and sliced
1 cup pomegranate seeds
1 vanilla bean, split
1 cinnamon stick, crushed
3 bay leaves, crushed
Zest and juice of 1 lemon
1 TB. honey
3 cups apple juice
1 cup water

1. Trim fig stems, cut figs in half, and place in a medium sauce-pan. Add pears, pomegranate seeds, vanilla bean, cinnamon stick, bay leaves, lemon zest and juice, honey, apple juice, and water, and set over high heat.

2. At the boil, reduce heat to a bare simmer and cook for 30 minutes. Remove from heat and cool. Spoon warm over vanilla ice cream or gingerbread.

Bear's Garlic

A member of the botanical family *alliaceae* (onion)

Also known as *ramsons* and *wood garlic*

Some believe this wild onion (*alium ursinum*) is the first food bears eat upon awaking from hibernation. It grows in swampy, shady woodlands throughout Central Europe and is used in many local cuisines. It has broad, short green leaves, and sprouts into an onion stalk with a pom-pom of white star-shaped flowers.

The young leaves of this wild onion have a delicate chive flavor and are collected before the plant flowers to flavor salads, cheese, soups, and sauces. The flowers themselves have a delicate onion flavor and can be scattered into salads. Bear's garlic is currently the hot, trendy ingredient sought by European foodies.

Bear's garlic is not cultivated in the United States, but if you have a shady, woodsy yard, and a green thumb, you can give it a shot (b-and-t-world-seeds.com).

Benne Seed

See Sesame Seed.

Bergamot

A member of the botanical family *labiatae* (mint)

Also known as *red bergamot, Oswego tea, Indian plume*, and *bee balm*

You can find several varieties of this tall perennial (*monarda didyma*), native to North America. The Oswego Indians of western New York dried and steeped the leaves into tea, and colonists drank it when English tea was politically incorrect. Early settlers used it to relieve sore throats and inhaled fumes to treat colds.

The fat, jagged leaves have a reddish tinge, and its shaggy red pom-pom flower makes it a favorite of ornamental gardeners. The leaves have a bright citrus flavor and are mixed fresh into salads, fruits, and drinks.

Bergamot is not a common market item, but it's easily grown, as many nurseries carry it or can order it (wellsweep.com).

Hot Stuff

Do not confuse bergamot with *orange bergamot* (*citrus aurantium bergamia*), a hybrid of the Seville orange and grapefruit. The distinct flavor of Earl Grey tea comes from the oil of the orange bergamot.

Bitter Almond

See Almond.

Black Cardamom

See Cardamom.

Black Mustard

See Mustard.

Black Onion Seed

See Nigella.

Blue Fenugreek

See Fenugreek.

Boldo

A member of the botanical family *monimiaceae*

Also known as *boldina leaf*

This aromatic evergreen tree (*peumus boldus*) is native to the Andes, and its leaves are used extensively in the cuisines of Chile and Argentina. It has been used by the native tribes of the Andes as an all-purpose elixir, curing everything from the common cold to gallbladder and liver disease. It's still frequently steeped into a tea to calm an upset stomach.

Similar in appearance to its cousin, bay laurel, boldo is has a similar flavor, with a hint of peppery cinnamon. Use it wherever you would bay leaf, including roasted and stewed meats, vegetables, soups, and stews.

If you live in Brazil, you'll find boldo in every market. If not, try the Internet (mountainroseherbs.com).

Borage

A member of the botanical family *boraginaceae*

Also known as *star flower*

Native of Syria, this small annual plant (*borago officinalis*) has a fuzzy stem and leaves and small blue flowers with five-pointed petals, like a star.

Like many herbs, borage made its way to Europe via the Romans, who considered it a source of courage. Early colonists brought it to North America. Besides its culinary applications, the herb was used to improve mood and drive out melancholy. It's still considered a good herbal remedy for PMS. Borage is rich in potassium and calcium and has been shown to stimulate adrenal glands.

The leaves and young buds have a cool, cucumberlike flavor that's well suited to salads and herb sauces. The flowers, which have a subtle honey essence, are often candied and used as pastry decoration, frozen in ice cubes, or steeped and pounded into refreshing beverages. Large leaves are eaten like spinach, fresh, sautéed, or added to vegetable dishes. The Germans use it in a well-known green sauce mixed with parsley, chives, chervil, sorrel, yogurt, and cream cheese, and served with boiled eggs and potatoes.

Borage is available at many farmers markets in the spring, and seeds can be found at most nurseries (snowseedco.com).

Burnet

A member of the botanical family *rosacea* (rose)

Also known as *salad burnet*

This hearty perennial is native to the Mediterranean. Its botanical name, *sanguisorba officinalis*, means "to absorb blood," and historically, its astringent properties were thought to reduce bleeding. Soldiers going into battle drank tea infused with burnet to improve their chances of survival.

Burnet was common in formal herb gardens throughout England and is used extensively as a salad green throughout Europe. Colonists brought it to North America, where its delicate foliage and tiny red blossoms are prized more as ornamental than culinary.

As its pseudonym indicates, burnet is terrific on salads. Its young tender, lacy leaves have a light, pleasant cucumber flavor. Pick the leaves young, as they tend to get bitter with age. Add them not only to salads, but to soups, cool drinks, or butter or mix into eggs and cheese.

This crop appears at trendier farmers markets, but your best bet is to grow your own, from plants (mulberrycreek.com) or seeds (greenchronicle.com).

Herb Cooler

Serve this thirst-quencher over ice, with some borage flowers floating on top.

¼ cup chopped fresh burnet
2 TB. chopped fresh peppermint
Zest and juice of 1 lemon
Zest and juice of 1 orange
2 TB. honey
1 (1-in.) chunk fresh ginger root
4 cups boiling water
6 cups cold water
1 handful borage flowers

1. In a large heatproof bowl, combine burnet, peppermint, lemon zest and juice, orange zest and juice, honey, and ginger. Pour boiling water over and steep for 30 minutes, stirring occasionally.

2. Strain into a serving pitcher, add cold water, stir, and top with borage flowers before serving.

Cajun Spice

See Appendix B.

Caper

A member of the botanical family *capparidaceae*

Also known as *caperberry*

Native of the Mediterranean, capers come from a small biennial bush (*capparis sipinosa*) with trailing prickly stems and thin, glossy leaves. If allowed to blossom, the flowers are tiny purple and white. But the olive-green buds are harvested before they bloom, dried, and pickled in a salt and vinegar brine or packed in salt.

The tangy flavor of capers is a common accompaniment to seafood. It appears in sauces, tomato dishes, eggs, as garnish, and even in cocktails. Use care when adding capers to a recipe. Because they are cured in salt, they add salt to whatever recipe they go into. Rinsing them before use reduces this effect, and lets more of the sharp, acidic caper flavor emerge.

You can find capers in the same grocery store aisle as pickles and olives.

Caraway

A member of the botanical family *umbelliferae* (parsley)

This ancient herb (*carum caravi*) has been found among Neolithic ruins of Europe, and in the Middle Ages, it was known as a useful anti-gas remedy.

The leaves of this biennial plant look like carrot leaves at the base and then become thin and feathery toward the top as it flowers in tufts of tiny white blossoms. The stems and leaves have a mild flavor similar to parsley. The roots have a sweet, parsnip flavor and can be cooked and eaten in a similar manner—boiled or fried. It's the seeds, however, that get the most attention.

In the west, caraway seeds are most associated with breads, notably rye bread. Those who find rye bread disagreeable blame the caraway. The flavor is heady, like a strong combination of thyme and dill. It's found in all kinds of foods throughout northern Europe and Scandinavia, paired often with cabbage and root vegetables, meats, cheeses, and even fruits. Caraway is also a major component of *aquavit*, a herbal Scandinavian distilled liquor.

Apples, Fennel, and Onions with Caraway

This dish make a terrific accompaniment to roasted poultry, pork, or sausage.

4 TB. butter
1 TB. caraway seed, crushed
1 yellow onion, sliced thin
1 fennel bulb, sliced thin
2 fuji apples, peeled, cored, and sliced thin
1 cup dry white wine
1 tsp. sea salt

1. In a large sauté pan, melt butter over high heat. Add caraway seed and toast until fragrant, 1 or 2 minutes. Add onion and sauté until translucent. Add fennel and apples, and continue sautéing over high heat until everything is golden brown and caramelized.

2. Deglaze with white wine, and cook until liquid is evaporated. Remove from heat, add salt, and serve warm.

Cardamom

A member of the botanical family *zingiberaceae* (ginger)

An Asian shrub in the ginger family, cardamom (*elettaria cardamomum*) grows long, pointed leaves off a large stem, similar to tulips or iris. Its tropical flower makes way for plump seed pods that contain the pungent, oil-rich cardamom seeds. The pods are picked by hand when green and dried in the sun. They're sold green, which are not processed beyond natural drying, and white, which are treated with sulfur dioxide to mute the flavors.

Black cardamom (*afromomum subulatun*) has a completely different smoky, peppery quality because it's dried over open, smoky flames. It can hold up well to, and is preferred for, heavier, spicier dishes than the green or white pods. That said, there's no need to run to the store for black if all you've got is green.

Cardamom is popular in India, where it's a common ingredient in curries and rice dishes. Scandinavian and Bavarian chefs know cardamom well and take advantage of its sweet overtones in fruits, breads, and pastries. It's also a key ingredient in strong, cloyingly sweet Turkish coffee.

Ground cardamom is widely available, and white pods can be found in better markets. Green and black may take a little more time to track down (savoryspiceshop.com).

Turkish Coffee Cookies

These cookies are sweet and exotic and make a terrific accompaniment to coffee, tea, or a tall glass of milk.

2⅓ cups all-purpose flour
¾ tsp. baking powder
¼ tsp. salt
2 sticks butter
2 tsp. freshly ground cardamom
2 TB. instant powdered espresso
3⅔ cups sugar
1 TB. vanilla extract
1 egg
1 TB. milk
2 TB. *cinnamon sugar*

1. Preheat the oven to 350°F. Line 2 baking sheets with parchment paper.

2. Sift together flour, baking powder, and salt, and set aside.

3. In a large bowl and using a sturdy spoon or an electric mixer, cream butter, cardamom, powdered espresso, and sugar until free of lumps. Add vanilla extract, egg, and milk. Slowly add sifted ingredients and mix well to fully incorporate. Chill dough for 30 minutes.

4. Roll out chilled cookie dough on a floured surface to ¼ inch thick. Cut out cookies with a floured cookie cutter and place cookies on lined baking sheets 1 inch apart. Sprinkle each cookie lightly with cinnamon sugar and bake at 350° for 10 to 12 minutes or until golden brown on the edges. Cool for 5 minutes before removing from baking sheets.

Chefspeak

Cinnamon sugar is simply a mixture of granulated sugar and ground cinnamon. I prefer mine in a 2:1 ratio (2 parts sugar to 1 part cinnamon).

Cassava

A member of the botanical family *euphorbiaceae*

Also known as *yuca* and *manioc*

A woody annual shrub in the spurge family, cassava (*manihot esculenta*) is cultivated for its root. The plant is native to South America but is now grown and eaten all over the world. It is a staple food throughout Africa, where it's grated or pounded, mixed with water, and cooked to a paste. India and Indonesia also consider it an important food, where it's eaten like a potato—boiled, fried, mashed, and added to recipes like dumplings, stews, and soups. In South and Central America, it goes by the name *yuca* and is a favorite side dish with meat and fish.

Cassava root is also ground into flour, commonly known as *tapi-oca*. Its high starch content is utilized in puddings and custards. Tapioca is also made into pearls, common in Asian desserts and drinks, including *boba*, or bubble tea.

The juice of the cassava is combined with sugar and spices to create the sweet syrup called *cassareep* (see Appendix B), used in Asian and Caribbean cuisines.

Cassava can be found in Latin American markets, usually under the name yuca, both fresh and frozen. Tapioca flour and pearls are available at better supermarkets and Asian grocers. You can probably find cassareep in stores that carry Caribbean ingredients, or try online (wifglobal.com/Caribbeanpopularitems.htm).

Cassia

See Cinnamon.

Cayenne

See Appendix C.

Celery

A member of the botanical family *umbelliferae* (parsley)

Everyone is familiar with the stalks of this plant. Celery (*apium graveolens*) finds its way into everything. It's a vital member of French *mirepoix*, its crunchy texture enhances everything from turkey stuffing to tuna salad, and its afternoon snack appeal, slathered with peanut butter, is undeniable. But we often forget the appeal of the rest of the celery plant. The entire thing is edible—and delicious.

Celery's fresh, crisp flavor runs throughout the shiny jagged leaves, white flowers, and root. The variety known as celery root or celeriac (*apium graveolens rapaceum*) is delicious when peeled and boiled or shaved thin and eaten in salads.

The firm, dark seeds have a similar but stronger flavor. They're an important ingredient in all kinds of pickling, Worcestershire sauce, ketchup, barbecue sauce, coleslaw, and spice blends like Creole, Indian, and Bay.

Celery seeds, plants, and roots are commonly available at markets and nurseries.

Century Plant

See Agave.

Chameleon Plant

A member of the botanical family *saururaceae*

Also known as *fish mint* and *diep ca* (Vietnamese)

In the United States, the yellow, red, and green heart-shape leaves of this East Asian plant (*houttuynia cordata*) are valued largely for their beauty and heartiness as a perennial ground cover. But in Vietnam, both the leaves and rhizome find their way into the kitchen.

A typical ingredient in salads and spring rolls, chameleon plant leaves and roots have an aromatic taste of coriander and citrus.

Many Asian markets carry chameleon plant greens, and if you want to grow your own, they're even easier to find (naturehills.com).

Vietnamese Herb Salad

This salad is great eaten as is, but you can also wrap it in rice paper to make spring rolls. Or roll it into tortillas for a healthful wrap sandwich.

2 cups Napa cabbage, shredded
1 cup sorrel, chopped
1 cup chameleon plant leaves, chopped
1 cup perilla leaves, chopped
1 cup cilantro leaves
½ medium purple onion, sliced
1 cucumber, peeled, seeded, and sliced
1 clove garlic, minced
1 Thai chile, minced
1 tsp. honey
Zest and juice of 1 lime
1 TB. sesame oil
¼ cup fish sauce
¼ cup rice vinegar
Salt

1. In a large salad bowl, combine cabbage, sorrel, chameleon plant, perilla, cilantro, onion, and cucumber. Set aside.

2. In a jar with a tight-fitting lid, combine garlic, chile, honey, lime zest and juice, sesame oil, fish sauce, and vinegar. Close the lid and shake well. Season with salt and then pour dressing over salad greens with light hand.

Hot Stuff

Be careful not to drown the greens in dressing when making this salad. Let the flavor of the herbs shine through. You'll be glad you did.

Chamomile

A member of the botanical family *asteraceae* (sunflower)

Also known as *mayweed*

You can find many varieties of this flowering plant, both annual and perennial, prized for both its ornamental beauty and its essential oil. But the most common culinary variety is German Chamomile (*matricaria recutita*). Like others of its species, chamomile has thin divided leaves and daisylike flowers with large cone-shape centers.

The flowers are dried and brewed into a tea that is well-known to soothe nerves. The flowers are rich in oil, and once dried, are used to flavor jams, jellies, puddings, cookies, and cakes. In addition, the Spanish use it to flavor their famous dry sherry *manzanilla*.

Dried chamomile is widely available in tea shops and health food stores.

Chervil

A member of the botanical family *umbelliferae* (parsley)

Also known as *French parsley*

Native to Eastern Europe and West Asia, chervil (*anthriscus cerefolium*) has long been a symbol of spring and is a part of many traditional Easter recipes as a symbol of renewal. In the past century, chervil has become an indispensable element of French cuisine. Its fine, lacy leaves and delicate white flowers have a slight anise flavor, which complements all sorts of foods, including fish, poultry, eggs, cheese, soups, and salads.

The beauty of this herb is all but lost when the herb is dried. It's best added fresh into recipes at the end of cooking, tossed into salads, or used as a fragrant garnish. Chopped fresh, it's a crucial ingredient in *fines herbes*, and the less-aromatic dried chervil is a component of *herbes de Provençe* (see Appendix B).

Chervil is available fresh at better supermarkets and at farmers' markets in the spring and summer. You can find or order seeds and seedlings at any nursery.

Chile Pepper

A member of the botanical family *solanaceae* (nightshade)

Known by many varietal names, such as *anaheim*, *cayenne*, *jalapeño*, and *poblano* (see Appendix C)

There are dozens of varieties of this New World native. Evidence of chile cultivation has been linked to several prehistoric tribes, from the tip of South America to the Great Plains of North America. They were known to the Aztecs, who are said to have harnessed the heat for ritualistic purposes. The Spanish brought the chile back to Europe, where it spread to the Far East. Today it's grown in all tropical regions.

All chile pepper varieties contain capsicum, a chemical compound that's perceived in the mouth as spicy heat. Capsicum heat has been measured extensively, and chiles are rated on the Scoville scale, named for Wilbur Scoville, who first rated capsicum's intensity in the early 1900s.

A pepper's heat is concentrated in the membrane found running through the center of the fruit from the interior stem. The seeds, which attach to the membrane, carry the heat, too, as does anything the membrane touches. Depending on your tolerance, you can cook chiles with or without the membrane and seeds. The flavor of the chile itself is often better appreciated without the intensity of the capsicum. Roasting, grilling, sautéing, and blanching all bring out different characteristics; dried and smoked, they take on still more personality. Dried and ground, their unique qualities are blended with other spices for specific cultural culinary applications (see Appendix B).

Hot Stuff

Capsicum is easily transferable through touch, so wear gloves and take care when cooking with chiles. One accidental touch to the eye is intensely painful, as is any contact with delicate dry or tender skin.

All varieties share similar characteristic shiny leaves and white flowers. The fruits range in size, and color varies from green through red, yellow, orange, and purple.

Chile peppers, either fresh or dried, are available at Latin American markets, many large supermarkets, and online (melissas.com). They're also very easy to grow, even for the novice gardener.

See also Appendix C.

Chili Powder

See Appendix B.

> **Hot Stuff**
>
> Chili or chile? When referring to the fruit, the word is spelled *chile*. When referring to the spicy stew, it's spelled *chili*. Chili powder is a spice blend made for use in the stew and, therefore, is spelled with an *i*. This can be confusing, because chili powder contains powdered chiles.

Chipotle

See Appendix C.

Chive

See Onion.

Cicely

A member of the botanical family *umbelliferae* (parsley)

Also known as *sweet cicely, anise fern,* and *great chervil*

The leaves of this perennial plant (*myrrhis odorata*) are like those of flat-leaf parsley or chervil, and like many in the parsley family, its flowers shoot up into flat tufts of tiny white blooms that give way to long, pointed seeds.

Cicely has a flavor similar to that of anise or licorice. The entire plant is edible, and most parts are used, although not extensively in the United States. Because of the plant's tolerance for low temperatures, it's better known in Scandinavia and Northern Europe.

The leaves are extremely sweet and are commonly combined with foods like rhubarb to reduce tartness. The seeds are very large and are added like cloves into spice mixes, cakes, and candies. They play a similar role to caraway and fennel seeds and can be found in herbal distilled spirits, including aquavit and chartreuse. The flowers are tossed into salads, and the root is boiled or sautéed and eaten as a vegetable. Tea made from the leaves is said to relieve upset stomach.

Fresh cicely is hard to find in American markets, although you might have some luck at a farmers' market in a real foodie town. You'll have better luck growing your own; look for seeds at garden centers (greenchronicle.com).

Cicely Strawberries and Cream

When sugar is tossed into fresh fruit, it pulls out the natural moisture, which creates a luscious sauce. Try it with all your fresh, ripe fruits.

2 pt. fresh, ripe strawberries, washed, trimmed, and halved
2 TB. sugar
½ cup cicely leaves, chopped
½ cup cicely blossoms
1 pt. heavy whipping cream
1 tsp. sugar
1 TB. cicely seeds, crushed

1. In a large bowl, combine strawberries, sugar, cicely leaves, and cicely blossoms. Toss to combine, cover, and set aside at room temperature for 1 or 2 hours.

2. Whip cream with sugar and cicely seeds until stiff peaks form. Set cream in the refrigerator until berries are ready.

3. To serve, spoon berries and their accumulated sweet juices in glass serving bowls and top with a dollop of whipped cicely cream. Serve with a crisp cookie.

Cilantro

See Coriander.

Cinnamon

A member of the botanical family *lauraceae* (laurel)

Both members of the laurel family, cinnamon (*cinnamomum verum*) and cassia (*cinnamomum aromaticum*) are combined into what we Americans recognize as cinnamon. The actual flavors are similar but are easily distinguishable when tasted side by side.

The spices come from the bark of Asian evergreen trees, harvested with much skill and tradition from trees 25 years or older. When the trees are still moist from seasonal rains, the inner bark is carefully stripped with special tools using techniques that have been passed down through many generations.

Cassia bark is much stronger than true cinnamon. In stick form, it's thicker and almost impossible to grind. True cinnamon bark is much finer and crumbles easily in the hand.

The buds and leaves are used in several Asian dishes and make delightful aromatic additions to candies, liqueurs, and potpourri. Cinnamon is a crucial element in many spice blends, including curries, barbecue rub, jerk rub, mulling spice, mole, and of course, pumpkin pie spice (see Appendix B).

Both cinnamon and cassia are readily available. Sticks sold whole in markets and specialty shops are usually clearly labeled as one or the other. If you happen across a bin of unmarked sticks in an ethnic market, remember that the hard ones are cassia and the brittle ones are cinnamon.

Cinnamon Basil

See Basil.

Citron

See Lemon.

Clove

A member of the botanical family *myrtaceae* (myrtle)

This incredibly tall evergreen tree (*syzygium aromaticum*) is native to the Molucca Islands (also known as the Spice Islands) in Southeast Asia. The name *clove* comes from the Latin *clavus*, which means "nail," and describes the shape and texture of the clove. The spice is a flower bud, picked when bright red, and dried. The result is a potent nugget of volatile oil, a natural anesthetic so strong it was commonly chewed to relieve toothaches. Cloves have long been appreciated for their aroma, burned as incense, smoked in cigarettes, and jabbed into citrus fruit as pomander balls.

Its popularity prompted a spice race of epic proportions, and domination of the Spice Islands jostled between the Portuguese, Spanish, British, and Dutch throughout the sixteenth and seventeenth centuries.

While the United States and much of Europe see the clove as a sweet spice, it's utilized in more savory applications in the East. Cloves easily find their way into curries, pickles, sausages, and spice mixes like *Chinese five-spice* (see Appendix B). It's an important element of classic French Béchamel sauce, where its character combines deliciously with onion and bay.

Cloves are available everywhere you find grocery carts.

Coffee

A member of the botanical family *rubiaceae* (bedstraw)

Also known by many species names, including *arabica* and *robusta*

This small tree (*coffea*), native to Ethiopia, is now grown all over the world, with major production in South and Central America. The tree bears a fruit called the coffee cherry, which, when ripe and red, are picked by hand. Each cherry holds two seeds, which are called beans. The beans are removed, dried, and exported. They are blended and roasted to bring out aromatic oils and then ground and brewed to produce, of course, the second most popular drink in the world (next to tea).

But besides the beverage, coffee is used to flavor many types of foods. Crushed or ground, these seeds can be steeped in any liquid to infuse their flavor. Try steeping beans in cream or milk for coffee custards, ices, and sauces. Grind beans to a fine powder to dust the outside of chocolate candies. Similarly, brewed coffee adds a pleasant bitterness to chocolate batters, not to mention pot roasts and barbecue sauces.

Coffee beans are widely available. Look for wide-eyed folks lingering with recycled paper cups and disposable income.

Beef Braised in Black Coffee

The deep, dark coffee flavor paired with acidic tomatoes and vinegar makes a mouthwatering combination that perfectly complements the moist, tender, slow-roasted beef.

2 or 3 lb. beef chuck roast or brisket
8 cloves garlic
4 slices bacon, diced
1 yellow onion, diced
2 stalks celery
1 (16-oz.) can crushed tomatoes
½ cup cider vinegar
4 cups strong black coffee
2 cups water
2 bay leaves
1 tsp. kosher salt
1 tsp. black pepper

1. Preheat the oven to 300°F.

2. Rinse beef and pat dry. On all sides of roast, make a total of 8 incisions with a boning knife, and insert 1 clove garlic into each one.

3. In a large roasting pan, cook bacon over high heat until brown and fat is rendered. Add onions and cook until translucent. Add roast, and brown on all sides. Add celery, tomatoes, vinegar, coffee, water, bay leaves, salt, and pepper. Bring liquid to a boil. At the boil, cover tightly with a lid or foil, and transfer to oven.

4. Roast for 6 to 8 hours or until fork tender. Slice meat thinly and serve with boiled potatoes or buttered noodles.

Coriander

A member of the botanical family *umbelliferae* (parsley)

Also known as *cilantro, Chinese parsley,* and *fresh coriander*

This annual herb (*coriandrum sativum*) was cultivated in ancient Egypt and has become an essential element in cuisines throughout Asia, India, South and Central America, Africa, and the Caribbean.

Coriander is grown for its seed as well as its leaves, known commonly as *cilantro*. The leaves are similar to and often mistaken for flat leaf parsley and chervil. To tell them apart, remember that the broad, divided leaves of cilantro are larger than chervil and have more rounded leaf tips than parsley. Of course, you can also tell them apart by taste.

Some people are put off by the flavor of cilantro at first, finding it bitter and soapy. But the unpleasant taste disappears when the herb is cooked. Fresh cilantro is used in conjunction with many spicy dishes, including chiles, salsas, curries, and soups, and it has a particular affinity for chile, garlic, and lime.

This herb's tiny pink flowers produce large pungent seeds that look like white peppercorns. Their flavor is that of strong citrus oil, and they're used whole or ground in many spice blends. They pop up in brines for vegetables and meats and are fundamental to curries and chili powders.

Cilantro and coriander are available in most large supermarkets and in Latin American markets.

Costmary

A member of the botanical family *asteraceae* (sunflower)

Also known as *Bible leaf, balsam herb*, and *alecost*

A native of Asia, costmary (*tanacetum balsamita*) is a lemony, minty, balsam-flavored leaf that was favored throughout medieval Europe and a common component of Elizabethan gardens. It was used as a bittering agent in brewing, before the common use of hops. Brought to America by colonists, costmary was steeped in wash water to discourage moths, and similarly used as a Bible bookmark, hence its name *Bible leaf.*

Its long, ovoid, jagged-edged light-green leaves add a fresh flavor to salads and stuffings and can be steamed or sautéed as a vegetable. When dried, it makes tea with a subtle bubblegum aroma.

It's not commonly available in markets, but it is a popular addition to herb gardens (richters.com).

Cream of Tartar

Tartaric acid

This is another mysterious white powder that, although not technically a spice or herb, can be found on nearly every spice shelf.

Crystals of tartaric acid accumulate on the interior walls of the barrels used to hold fermenting wine. The crystals are powdered and used in many culinary applications as an acidic ingredient. It loosens the protein of egg whites and aids in their whipping. It's added to lique-fied sugar to prevent crystallization. In candy and frosting recipes, it promotes a creamy consistency. Before the advent of baking powder, cream of tartar was added to batters and dough as an acidic ingredient to activate baking soda. Occasionally, older recipes still call for that leavening combination.

Look for cream of tartar in the spice aisle.

Cress

A member of the botanical family *brassicaceae* (mustard)

There are *several edible species in the cress family, including watercress, garden cress, and winter cress.* Watercress (*nasturtium nasturtium-aquaticum,* although not related to the nasturtium flower), a fast-growing semi-aquatic perennial, is the most commonly eaten cress today. The thick, hollow stem; tiny, deep-green divided leaves; and small white flowers have a clean, peppery flavor.

Cress is native to Europe and Asia and is one of the oldest known leaf vegetables consumed by man. The Ancient Greeks believed it made them smarter, the Romans used it to cure baldness, and the Egyptians fed watercress juice to slaves to increase productivity. It grows prolifically in Southern England, and because it's highly nutritious, it has been a staple of the English diet for centuries. Full of vitamins, iron, and calcium—and low in cost—watercress has been eaten raw, mixed into salads, or sandwiched between bread by rich and poor alike. High in vitamin C, watercress was used to prevent scurvy long before citrus was available.

The ruffled, grassy leaves of garden cress (*lepidium sativum*) are easily distinguished from watercress, but they share a similar tangy pepper flavor. Garden cress is used in the same manner, in salads, sandwiches, and soups. It has pretty, edible orange flowers and small berries similar to capers, but it's also enjoyed early, as a sprout.

Winter cress (*barbarea vulgaris*), also known as *yellow rocket*, bears more resemblance to mustard in appearance, flavor, and use than other cress. Its wide leaves are valued as a sautéed vegetable as well as a salad green, and the seeds are pungent like mustard.

Watercress is available in better supermarkets and farmers' markets. Garden cress and winter cress are more difficult to buy fully grown. Try looking for them as baby plants and raising them as your own (kitchengardenseeds.com).

Cubeb Pepper

A member of the botanical family *piperaceae* (pepper)

Also known as *tailed pepper* and *Java pepper*

Originally grown in India, cubeb (*piper cubeba*) was popular in the Middle Ages, before black pepper was widely available. Brought to Europe by Arab traders, its use was eventually discouraged to advance the use of black pepper. Today the vine is grown in Java and Sumatra.

The long stalk produces berries that look like black peppercorns with a tail. Its spicy, gingery, pepper flavor is used extensively in Middle Eastern, Indonesian, and North African cuisines. It's also a common ingredient in gin and cigarettes.

Look for cubeb at Indian markets and on the Internet (www.silk.net/sirene).

Dates Stuffed with Cubeb and Parmesan

This is one of my all-time favorite food combinations. It sounds a little risky, but once you try it, you'll be hooked! It's a sure-fire hit for your next cocktail party.

1 cup freshly grated Parmesan cheese
1 tsp. ground cubeb pepper
1 pt. pitted medjool dates

1. Preheat the oven to 350°F.

2. In a small bowl, combine cheese and pepper and blend well.

3. Open each date, fill with cheese mixture, and pinch shut. Place filled dates on a cookie sheet, and bake for 10 minutes to warm through. Serve immediately.

Cuitlucoche

A member of the fungus species *ustilago maydis*

Also known as *huitlacoche, corn smut, maize mushroom,* and *Mexican truffle*

Technically, cuitlucoche isn't an herb or spice, but it is used in the same manner. Cuitlucoche is a fungus that grows on ears of corn. The Hopi, Zuni, and Aztec tribes have long considered it a delicacy, but farmers in the United States see it as a nuisance. Infected kernels expand as they fill with spores and become dark gray and black tumors or "galls." Don't let the appearance fool you, though. The smoky-sweet flavor, similar to mushrooms, is prized throughout Central America. It adds a delicious element to chile-cheesy recipes.

Fresh cuitlucoche is available fresh at some farmers' markets in the late summer. You can probably find it canned at most Latin American markets, although it's not as good as fresh.

Cuitlucoche and Corn Casserole

This recipe is put together like a classic *chilaquile* casserole, layered like lasagna with tortillas instead of noodles and chiles and cheese instead of tomato sauce. Look for *panella* cheese in Mexican markets, or substitute jack cheese.

4 TB. butter
1 large yellow onion, diced
4 cloves garlic, minced
2 roasted Anaheim, Poblano, or Pasilla chiles, diced
¼ cup fresh cilantro, chopped
¼ cup fresh epazote, chopped
1 lb. fresh or canned cuitlucoche
1 (10-oz.) pkg. frozen corn kernels
2 cups whipping cream
1 tsp. kosher salt
1 tsp. black pepper
8 to 10 corn tortillas
1 lb. panella cheese, grated

1. Preheat the oven to 350°F.

2. In a large sauté pan over high heat, melt butter. Add onion and sauté until golden brown. Add garlic, chiles, cilantro, and epazote, and continue cooking until tender. Add cuitlucoche, corn, and whipping cream, and stir. Reduce heat and simmer 5 minutes. Remove from heat.

3. In a casserole dish, layer cuitlucoche-corn mixture with tortillas and grated cheese, as you would lasagna, finishing with sauce and then cheese on the very top.

4. Cover casserole and bake for 30 minutes or until bubbly. Remove lid and bake 5 more minutes until the top is golden brown. Serve with fresh tomato salsa and sour cream.

Cumin

A member of the botanical family *umbelliferae* (parsley)

Also known as *Shah jeera*, *zeera*, and *geerah*

Like other members of the parsley family, the leaves of the cumin plant (*cuminum cyminum*) are thin and feathery, and the flowers are tiny white or pink. The distinctive striped or ridged seed grows in clusters after flowering. Its flavor is a little bitter and grassy but intensifies into a warm, musty flavor when toasted.

Native to the Mediterranean and the rivers of Egypt, cumin is mentioned in the Bible and was well-known in ancient Greece and Rome. In the Middle Ages, it was thought to promote fidelity and was consequently carried during wedding ceremonies.

The cumin seed is a favorite flavor worldwide, making a significant contribution to many cuisines. It is a base flavor in dishes and spice blends as diverse as Indian curries, Mexican moles, Arabic *baharat*, and American chili powder (see Appendix B).

Cumin is available whole and ground in most markets.

Curry

See Appendix B.

Curry Leaf

A member of the botanical family *rutaceae* (citrus)

From India and Sri Lanka, the small curry leaf tree (*murraya koenigii*) has matte green leaves that look like they could be from any citrus tree. But rubbed to a paste or steeped into liquids, they impart a unique, orangey, peanutlike fragrance that makes them a key ingredient in so much Indian and Sri Lankan cooking.

Prolonged cooking destroys the distinctive aroma, so curry leaves are best added at the end of a recipe. You'll see them floating like bay leaves in soups and broths, and they're often used to complement to fish, coconut, *dal*, *tandoor* cuisine, *nann*, and *paneer* cheese.

Curry leaf is available at Indian markets.

Dill

A member of the botanical family *umbelliferae* (parsley)

Also known as *dill seed* and *dill weed*

The fine, threadlike leaves of this delicate annual (*anthum graveolens*) have been used since the Middle Ages as an herbal remedy to relieve upset stomachs and gas and to protect against witchcraft.

Dill greens, flowers, and seeds are common accompaniments to cured fish, potatoes, and root vegetables. Dill is also used frequently in pickling, not just for cucumbers, but other vegetables as well. The aroma of all parts resembles caraway and anise but has a somewhat more sour, vinegary essence.

Dill, dill seed, and dried dill weed are readily available in most markets.

Dry Rub

See Appendix B.

Epazote

A member of the botanical family *chenopodiaceae*

Also known as *Mexican tea*, *skunk weed*, *pigweed*, and *wormseed*

Known mainly in Mexican cuisine, epazote (*chenopodium ambrosioides*) is a critical element in traditional bean dishes. When fresh, the jagged green leaves give off a potent kerosene aroma. But simmered long in stew and broths, they impart a subtle, peppery, bitter flavor very close to that of thyme. Most important, epazote is purported to alleviate the gaseous effects of the beloved bean.

Epazote is available in Latin American markets.

Epices Fine

See Spice Parisienne in Appendix B.

Fagara

See Szechwan Pepper.

Fennel

A member of the botanical family *umbelliferae* (parsley)

Also known as *finocchio* and *sweet anise* (the bulb)

Fennel (*foeniculum vulgare*) is native to the Mediterranean and thrives in similar climates. Bulb, leaves, stem, and seed all have a sweet anise scent and flavor. This prolific perennial can grow up to 6 feet tall. Its thin feathery leaves and flat, multi-flower heads are akin to dill. Of the several varieties, the Florence fennel (*foeniculum vulgare azoricum*) is grown mainly for its bulb, while the common fennel is used primarily for its seed, which is distinctively curved and ridged.

As a vegetable, fennel bulb is delicious grilled, sautéed, braised, or shaved thin and tossed raw into a salad. The seeds are best toasted and ground but turn up whole in tomato sauces, Italian sausages, and rye breads. They are believed to aid digestion, and consequently are an integral component of *mukhwas*, the colorful, sugar-coated seeds served after Indian meals to freshen breath and assist digestion.

Fennel stalks make excellent smoking matter, lit under roasting meats and fish to impart a unique flavor. Fennel pollen is a fine powder, easily airborne, coveted by adventurous chefs for its uncommon form and price tag as much as its flavor. It has the distinct scent of fennel with a hint of curry.

Fennel bulb and seeds are available in most markets.

Fenugreek

A member of the botanical family *fabaceae* (bean)

Also known as *methi*, *Greek hay*, and *goat's horn*

An annual in the bean family, fenugreek (*trigonella foenum-graecum*) grows like peas, with a thick stem, yellow sweet-pea–like flowers, and long, horn-shape seed pods that contain square yellow seeds. The seeds must be ground to release their maple-curry-nutty flavor.

Fenugreek is used in many spice blends, breads (Ethiopoian *Injera*), confectionery (for its maple qualities), and pickling. The seed can also be ground into flour and used as a thickener.

Fenugreek sprouts and leaves have a similar, but sweeter, flavor than the seeds, are eaten as a vegetable, and mixed into dough, beans, and stews.

Blue Fenugreek (*trigonella caerulea*) is related, with a similar but subtler flavor and aroma, found in the alpine mountain regions of southeastern Europe. The leaves, seeds, flowers are used dried, and the herb is used extensively in alpine cheeses and breads of the region.

Find fenugreek in Middle Eastern, Indian, and African markets or on the Internet (penzys.com).

Filé

See Sassafras.

Fines Herbes

See Appendix B.

Finger Root

> A member of the botanical family *zingiberaceae* (ginger)
>
> Also known as *Chinese keys*

The finger root plant (*kaempferia pandurata*), native to Indonesia, is a tall, leafy biennial with beautiful pink tubular flowers shooting off from a long stalk. Its bright orange rhizome root is used throughout the cuisines of Southeast Asia. The flavor, while close to that of ginger, contains a hint of citrus and a bite of pepper.

Finger root is best used fresh and whole, as drying greatly diminishes its strength. Look for it in Asian markets.

Finger Root Ale

This homemade soda pop is a grown-up version of ginger ale. It has a small amount of alcohol, so serve it accordingly.

¼ cup freshly grated finger root
1 cup sugar
¼ tsp. active dry yeast
Zest and juice of 1 lime
Water

1. In a small bowl, combine finger root, sugar, yeast, lime zest and juice, and 2 cups water. Stir to combine.

2. Using a funnel, pour finger root mixture into a clean 2-liter plastic soda bottle. Fill the bottle with water to 2 inches below the cap. Seal the cap and place in a sunny window for 24 to 48 hours.

3. When the bottle feels very firm, chill it for 24 hours. Open chilled soda carefully, and serve, strained if desired.

 **Hot Stuff**

This ale has a small amount of alcohol. Also, soda left at room temperature for more than 48 hours, or in a location that is too hot, could explode.

Fish Boil

See Appendix B.

Fish Sauce

See Appendix B.

Five-Spice Powder, Chinese

See Appendix B.

Flax

A member of the botanical family *linaceae*

Also known as *linseed*

This tall annual plant (*linum usitatissimum*) has a thin stem, slender green leaves, and beautifully delicate pale blue flowers. Flax is grown for its oil-rich seed, as an ornamental plant, and for its stems, which when soaked and pounded provide fibers that are spun into cloth.

Flax oil was used for centuries to dry oil paint and varnish, but today it is prized for its omega-3 content. Essential fatty acids, the omega-3s have been found to reduce cholesterol, blood pressure, and plaque formation in arteries. Flax is a useful food source, especially for those with a diet low in fish, the most common source of omega-3. In addition, flax seeds are believed to reduce certain types of tumor growth and are taken as treatment of some forms of cancer.

The most common form of flax is oil, but more recently the seeds themselves have become a popular pantry addition. The nut-flavored seeds make a healthful addition to granolas, breads, and pilaf and are commonly ground as an egg replacement in vegan baking.

Flax and linseed oil are available at health food stores.

Vegan Oatmeal Cookies

This is a surprisingly good cookie, even for nonvegans.

1 TB. flax seeds
¼ cup plus 2 TB. water
½ cup vegetable oil
¼ cup soy milk
¾ cup brown sugar, packed
1 tsp. baking powder
½ tsp. cinnamon
1¾ cups rolled oats
1¼ cups all-purpose flour
1 cup raisins

1. Preheat the oven to 350°F. Line 2 baking sheets with parchment paper.

2. In a coffee grinder, grind flax seed to a fine powder.

3. In a large bowl, using a sturdy spoon, combine ground flax seed, water, oil, and soy milk, and stir well. Mix in brown sugar, baking powder, cinnamon, oats, flour, and raisins, and beat well to fully incorporate.

4. Drop cookies by the tablespoonful onto lined baking sheets 1 inch apart. Bake for 10 to 12 minutes or until golden brown on the edges. Cool cookies for 5 minutes before removing from the baking sheets.

Flower Pepper

See Szechwan Pepper.

Galangal

A member of the botanical family *zingiberaceae* (ginger)

Also known as *Laos root* and *China root*

This pale yellow-orange rhizome (*alpinia officinarum*) is striped with dark rings, and shoots out long, large leaves at the base of a thick stem topped with red and white flower buds.

Galangal was brought to Europe by Arab traders in the Middle Ages, but it fell out of favor when the more potent ginger hit the scene. Occasionally, old recipes pop up calling for galangal in mulled wines, cider, spiced meat, soups, and stews.

There are several varieties of galangal, all similar to ginger, but with a little zing of mustard heat and a floral or citrus essence. Native to Indonesia, galangal is favored in the cuisines of Vietnam (phõ soup), Thailand, and Malaysia.

Galangal is easy to find in Asian markets.

Old English Mulled Wine

This is a great recipe to warm you up on a cold-winter day.

1 cup sugar
2 cups cream
2 cinnamon sticks, crushed
1 knuckle galangal, sliced
1 tsp. fresh grated nutmeg
1 tsp. black peppercorns, crushed
4 cardamom pods, crushed
1 bottle dry red wine, such as cabernet sauvignon

1. In a small saucepan, combine sugar, cream, cinnamon sticks, galangal, nutmeg, pepper, and cardamom. Bring to a simmer over medium heat, and gently warm for 15 minutes.

2. Turn off heat, add red wine, and steep another 15 minutes. Strain and serve warm.

Gale

A member of the botanical family *myricaceae* (myrtle)

Also known as *bog myrtle* and *sweet gale*

This evergreen shrub (*myrica gale*) grows profusely in the Scottish moors and bogs and was first used in medieval brewing before hops were readily available. The leaves and berries are very oily, and when boiled, wax rose to the surface and was gathered for use in candles.

As it's abundant in northern Europe, gale is occasionally mentioned as a flavoring in local soups and broths. The berries and leaves are steeped as a bay leaf would be and removed before serving. The flavor is similar to bayberry, with a slight eucalyptus-citrus aroma.

Gale is currently making a comeback as a favorite ingredient of home brewers, and as such is now available wherever home brewing supplies and ingredients are sold.

Garam Masala

See Appendix B.

Garlic

6

A member of the botanical family *liliaceae* (lily, onion)

Garlic (*allium sativum*) comes from Asia and is one of the oldest cultivated plants known to man. It is a perennial bulb (called a head) made up of divided cloves that are covered in papery skin. The strong sulfur scent of garlic has been known to repel insects (and vampires) and was thought to protect against disease and increase strength. Roman sailors and Egyptian slaves were given daily rations of garlic to ensure productivity.

Garlic is familiar in almost every cuisine worldwide. Its effect varies according to the way it's prepared. Juice squeezed from the cloves or cloves chopped fresh and raw add a pungent quality to recipes. Sautéed slowly or roasted whole, garlic's natural sugar is released and caramelized for a sweet buttery texture. Overcooked, and its bitterness is revealed.

There are several garlic varieties, and the flavor of one variety can vary by grower. The most common garlic in grocery stores is the soft-necked *allium sativum*. Purple striped *allium ophios* have a hard neck with a stem that's hard like a twig. Their flavor is rich, but the aroma is mild. Hard to find is the beautiful rose-colored garlic, with a dozen well-defined cloves visible around the outer edge, known as creoles. Elephant garlic is a different species, *allium ampeloprasm*, and has a softer taste.

Garlic is commonly available in supermarkets fresh, dried, ground, or mixed with salt. Use processed forms with care, as the flavor is concentrated and can easily overpower a dish.

Garum

See Appendix B.

Ginger

A member of the botanical family *zingiberaceae* (ginger)

Also known as *shoga*

This rhizome (*zingiber officinale*) heads up its own botanical family. Growing wild in Southeast Asia, ginger rhizomes produce a tall perennial plant with a broad stem, fat leaf blades that grow up the stalk, and tiny purple flowers.

The rhizome is used in several forms. It can be grated or sliced fresh, dried and ground to a powder, pickled in vinegar, or candied in sugar crystals or syrup. It plays a central role in all Asian cuisines, as both a central element and as part of more complex spice and herb combinations.

Once introduced to Europe, ginger became an indispensable element of medieval cookery. Its relevance in spiced foods has not diminished, and it's still used on its own or in conjunction with other sweet spices in baking.

Ginger can be found fresh in most supermarket produce sections and dried in the spice aisle.

Ginseng

A member of the botanical family *araliaceae*

Also known as *man root*

There are several varieties of ginseng, some native to America (*panax quinquefolius*), while others are native to Asia (*panax ginseng*). The low-growing plant produces vivid red flowers, but it's the root that's prized. Like ginger, ginseng root can be used fresh, dried, and steeped, or ground to a powder.

Ginseng's restorative powers have long been known around the globe. Native American tribes used wild ginseng as a love potion, to promote female fertility, and to treat respiratory ailments. Ancient Chinese medicine used ginseng to increase blood supply, improve circulation, and regain strength after illness. Today ginseng is thought to lower cholesterol, reduce stress, and enhance strength.

Although most commonly seen in tea form, ginseng is also used to flavor soups and broths, gum and candy, toothpaste, cigarettes, and America's favorite lemon-lime soda pop, 7-Up.

Ginseng is available in Asian markets.

6

Korean Chicken Soup

Samgyetang is the Korean name for this soup, which is used not only as a cure, but as a sickness preventive as well. You might find many variations, including those with sticky rice and dried jujube fruit.

2 qt. chicken broth
4 cloves garlic, minced
¼ cup grated ginseng
1 cup rice
¼ cup fresh pitted dates, chopped
2 TB. soy sauce
1 TB. chile paste
2 cups cooked chicken, shredded
1 cup green onions, chopped
2 TB. toasted sesame seeds

1. In a large soup pot, combine broth, garlic, and ginseng, and bring to a boil. Add rice, reduce heat, and simmer, covered, for 20 minutes.

2. Add dates, soy sauce, chile paste, and chicken, and simmer another 20 minutes. Serve hot, garnished with green onions and sesame seeds.

Goma

See Sesame.

Golpar

A member of the botanical family *umbelliferae* (parsley)

Also known as *hogweed*

A giant member of the parsley family, golpar (*heracleum mantegaz-zianum*) produces seeds common to Iranian cuisine. Ground or used whole in breads and pastries, the flavor is close to that of a mustardy celery seed. You'll also find golpar accompanying fruits, and its anti-gas effects make it an obvious ingredient in slow cooked bean recipes. You can also enjoy leaves and leaf stems pickled.

The plant itself is banned in the United States, as it produces a noxious sap that's quite painful on the skin and can cause a lot of damage, especially if ingested.

You can find the seeds in Arabic markets and online.

Pomegranate Salad

Native to Iran and the Himalayas, pomegranates also thrive in the drier climates of California and Arizona. The juice—high is vitamin C, folic acid, and antioxidants—is a popular drink worldwide and is thickened and sweetened to make Grenadine syrup.

2 cups pomegranate seeds
3 mandarin oranges, sectioned and cut into small pieces
1 cup walnuts, toasted and chopped
½ tsp. golpar
½ tsp. sea salt

1. Combine pomegranate seeds, oranges, walnuts, golpar, and salt, and toss well to combine.

2. Marinate at room temperature for 1 or 2 hours before serving.

Green Onion

See Onion.

Green Peppercorn

See Pepper.

Gremolata

See Appendix B.

Grains of Paradise

> A member of the botanical family *zingiberaceae* (ginger)
>
> Also known as *Guinea pepper, ginger pepper, alligator pepper,* and *meleguenta pepper*

Grains of paradise come from a perennial reedlike plant of West Africa (*aframomum melegueta*). From swampy terrain sprout narrow bamboo-like leaves with pink-purple flowers growing at the base. The flowers are trumpet shaped, like lilies, and produce long seed pods. Each pod contains many seeds whose flavor is a cross between pepper, ginger, coriander, and cardamom.

Grains of paradise were used throughout the Middle Ages before pepper became readily available. Many medieval spice powders include grains of paradise as their base. The name was an advertisement of sorts, enticing men to come in search of the spice along the West African pepper coast. But as trade for black pepper became easier, grains of paradise fell out of favor.

Today the spice is well-known throughout Morocco and Tunisia and is used in specialty brewing, distillation, and more adventurous confectionery.

Buy grains of paradise on the Internet (thespicehouse.com) and in Middle Eastern markets.

Lemon Cake with Grains of Paradise and Rosemary

This cake is best served the day it is made. Top it with a dollop of crème fraiche (a tangy thickened cream) or lightly sweetened whipped cream. If you have any leftovers, try eating it toasted, spread with cream cheese.

2¼ cups cake flour
1 tsp. baking powder
¼ tsp. salt
2 sticks butter
1 cup sugar
Zest of 4 lemons
1 TB. grains of paradise, ground
4 eggs
2 TB. milk
1 cup confectioners' sugar, sifted
1 tsp. fresh rosemary, chopped very fine
¼ cup lemon juice

1. Preheat the oven to 325°F. Line a 9×6-inch loaf pan with butter and parchment paper.

2. In a large bowl, sift together flour, baking powder, and salt, and set aside.

3. In another large bowl, and with a sturdy spoon or electric mixer, cream together butter, sugar, lemon zest, and grains of paradise until light and fluffy. Add eggs, one by one. Add milk, and slowly add sifted ingredients.

4. Pour batter into the loaf pan and bake for 45 to 60 minutes or until a pick inserted at the center of cake comes out clean. Cool cake for 10 minutes before inverting onto a rack.

5. Make glaze by mixing confectioners' sugar, rosemary, and lemon juice. Drizzle over warm cake. Cool before slicing.

Guajillo

See Appendix C.

Gum Arabic

> A member of the botanical family *fabaceae* (bean)

Here's another example of a common ingredient that's not a spice but
nevertheless finds its way onto spice shelves. Extracted from the bark
of a deciduous acacia tree (*acacia senegal*) of sub-Saharan Africa, gum
arabic is used to thicken and emulsify foods. In confectionery, gum
arabic is useful in preventing crystallization, especially in recipes with
low moisture and high sugar, like gummy bears and marshmallows. It's
also used in brewing and soft drinks, causing the fizzy foams to stick to
the side of a glass.

Buy gum arabic in shops specializing in pastry and candy-making
supplies.

Habanero

See Appendix C.

Harissa Sauce

See Appendix B.

Herbes de Provençe

See Appendix B.

Hijiki

From the family *sargassaceae* (brown algae)

(Algae are technically neither plant nor animal.)

Found along the rocky shoreline of Japan, this algae (*hizikia fusiformes*) is a traditional element of the Japanese diet. Rich in fiber and minerals, hijiki is dried and packaged in thin strips and then prepared by either soaking or simmering. Its slightly sweet flavor is used to enhance soups, vegetables, fish, and rice.

Look for hijiki in Japanese markets.

Hoisin

See Appendix B.

Hop

From the botanical family *cannabidaceae*

The rhizome of this perennial (*humulus lupulus*) shoots off vines up to 25 feet long every year. Its flowers develop into cones that consist of layers of papery, tannic petals concealing powdery yellow aromatic resin used extensively in brewing for both its flavor and its preservative qualities. Hop has been grown in Germany since the eighth century for use as a dye and a natural sedative, and Germany is still an important producer. Hop vines can be seen throughout the German countryside climbing up poles throughout the summer.

Dried hop cones are used in brewing, and young shoots of hops are considered a delicacy, and served steamed or sautéed with vinaigrette or deep-fried like tempura.

Dried hops are available wherever home brewing supplies and ingredients are sold. Look for fresh hops online (www.essentiallyhops.co.uk).

Horehound

A member of the botanical family *labiatae* (mint)

Horehound is a dark-green perennial (*marrubium vulgare*) with clover-like white flowers that grow up the stem. The stems and leaves, which are covered in white fuzz, are steeped as a cough remedy. Turned into drops and candy for similar purpose, the grown-up flavor became popular at the turn of the twentieth century.

Horehound is available dried online (glenbrookfarm.com) or as seed (richfarmgarden.com).

Horehound Candy

My Grandpa Reed introduced this candy to me when I was a kid. He bought me some at the old-time candy shop in Roaring Camp, an old-time railroad in the Santa Cruz Mountains. The flavor still makes me think of trains.

2 cups water
½ cup horehound leaves, chopped
2 cups brown sugar
2 cups granulated sugar
½ tsp. lemon juice

1. In a small saucepan, combine water and horehound leaves. Bring to a boil, remove from heat, and steep for 1 hour. Strain out leaves.

2. In a small saucepan, combine strained horehound water, brown sugar, and granulated sugar, and bring to a boil over high heat. At the boil, add lemon juice and insert a candy thermometer. Cook until syrup reaches 300°F, or hard crack stage.

3. Spoon syrup on buttered waxed paper in nickel-size lozenges. When cool, dust with granulated sugar. Wrap pieces individually in parchment paper, waxed paper, or candy wrappers. Store in an airtight container.

Horseradish

A member of the botanical family *cruciferae* (mustard, cabbage)

Also known as *horse root* and *mountain radish*

Native to Eastern Europe, this perennial (*armoracia rusticana*) is identified by its huge leaves and loose white flowers that grow at the top of a tall stalk, not unlike mustard. The leaves, one of the Passover Seder bitter herbs, are quite tasty when cooked like spinach, steamed or sautéed with garlic and butter. But it's the root that gets most of the attention.

Peeling through the horseradish's dirty brown outer skin reveals the tender white root, full of oils similar to those found in its cousin, the mustard seed. It's spicy hot, especially near the skin, and is grated and incorporated into dressings and sauces to be served alongside meat, sausage, and fish. Once grated, the oils dissipate rapidly.

Horseradish is available fresh or prepared in most supermarkets.

H

Roasted Horseradish Beets

Beets are delicious, but they do make a mess. Many cooks wear gloves when peeling and slicing them to spare their hands from the magenta dye.

6 large beets
2 large yellow onions
1 head garlic
½ cup freshly grated horseradish
12 TB. cider vinegar
2 TB. brown sugar
2 cups sour cream
1 tsp. kosher salt

1. Preheat the oven to 450°F.

2. Wrap whole beets together in a large piece of aluminum foil. Wrap whole onions together in another large piece of aluminum foil. Wrap garlic head in another small piece of aluminum foil. Place all the foil packets on a baking sheet, and roast until tender, about 30 minutes for garlic and about 1 hour for onions and beets. Cool completely.

3. Cut roasted garlic bulb in half and squirt out soft garlic paste. Combine garlic paste in a large bowl with horseradish, vinegar, brown sugar, sour cream, and salt. Mix well to combine.

4. Unwrap beets and carefully peel off skin. (Watch out! It stains.) Slice peeled roasted beets into wedges. Peel roasted onions and cut in the same manner as beets.

5. Add beets and onions to the bowl and toss to thoroughly combine. Serve hot, warm, or cold.

Hyssop

A member of the botanical family *labiatae* (mint)

A shrubby plant with narrow leaves, hyssop (*hyssopus officinalis*) is often confused with tarragon. The flavor, however, is less like the anise hint of tarragon and more like a combination of thyme and rosemary.

Hyssop is best used fresh, and the entire plant is edible, including the tiny purple flowers, which are lovely tossed into salads and vegetable dishes. Like thyme and rosemary, hyssop melds well with many flavors as diverse as heavy meats, legumes, and even fruits. Hyssop is one of the many herbs infused into the French distilled *Chartreuse*.

Hyssop tea is available in health food stores, or you can grow your own plants from seeds (greenchronicle.com).

Jalapeño

See Appendix C.

Jerk

See Appendix B.

Juniper

A member of the botanical family *cupressaceae* (cypress)

A shrubby, spiny-needled evergreen native to southern Europe, juniper (*juniperus communis*) is prized for its deep purple berries full of aromatic oils that may be most recognized as the main flavor component of gin.

Crushed or whole, dried juniper berries are a common ingredient to pickling brines, marinades, sauerkraut, and mustards. They are a traditional seasoning of lamb and heavy game meat and poultry. Their heavy, woody flavor cuts through fatty, pungent flavors. Juniper berries, however, are quite pungent, so use them with a light hand. A little goes a long way.

Juniper berries are available in better supermarkets.

Martini Bread

Serve this with softened butter and a gin martini, shaken not stirred.

2 TB. active dry yeast
1 cup warm water
2 TB. sugar
4 TB. butter, softened
1 tsp. salt
2 tsp. juniper berries, ground
½ cup pimiento-stuffed Spanish olives, chopped
2 or 3 cups bread flour

1. In a large bowl, combine yeast and water, and stir to combine. Add sugar, butter, salt, juniper berries, and olives, and mix well. Add flour, 1 cup at a time, until a firm dough forms.

2. Turn out dough onto a table, and knead for 8 to 10 minutes until dough is smooth and elastic. Add more flour, a little at a time, as needed. Cover dough with a warm damp towel and let rise until doubled in volume, 1 or 2 hours.

3. Preheat the oven to 375°F.

4. Form dough into a smooth, long loaf shape and place on a baking sheet lined with parchment paper. Sprinkle dough lightly with flour, and bake until golden brown and firm, about 30 minutes. Cool completely before slicing.

Kaffir Lime

A member of the botanical family, *rutaceae* (citrus)

The kaffir lime tree (*citrus hystrix*) produces a fruit, but its zest and juice are nowhere near as potent or popular as its unique double lobed, figure-8 leaf. The leaf's intense aroma is an essential ingredient throughout Southeast Asia. You'll find it floating in broths, soups (*pho, tom kha gai*), and curries and combined with other herbs and spices like garlic, galangal, and chiles.

The fruit is bright green and very bumpy and is no substitute for the intense lime aroma of the leaves.

Kaffir lime leaves are available at Asian markets.

Thai Chicken Soup with Coconut

In Thailand the name of this soup is *Thom Kha Gai*. The flavor combination of kaffir leaves, coconut, lemongrass, and galangal is heavenly.

1 (5.6-oz.) can coconut milk
4 cups chicken broth
¼ cup fresh galangal, grated
2 stalks lemongrass, cut into 2-in. pieces
4 TB. fish sauce (nam pla)
6 kaffir lime leaves, crushed
2 Thai chiles, minced
3 cups cooked chicken, shredded
2 limes, cut into wedges
¼ cup fresh cilantro, chopped

1. In a large soup pot, combine coconut milk, chicken broth, galangal, and lemongrass. Bring to a boil, reduce heat, and simmer for 30 minutes. Strain and return liquid to the pot.

2. Add fish sauce, kaffir lime leaves, Thai chiles, and chicken. Simmer for 30 minutes more. Serve hot with lime wedges and chopped cilantro.

Kecap Manis

See Appendix B.

Kenchur

A member of the botanical family *zingiberaceae* (ginger)

Used in Asian curries and stir-fries, the kenchur rhizome (*kaempferia galangal*) looks like dark baby ginger. The flavor, however, is less like ginger and more like a cross between cardamom and eucalyptus. It is used in spice blends and spicy pastes to flavor vegetables, noodles, rice, and tofu.

Find Kenchur in powdered form in Asian markets.

inome

See Szechwan Pepper.

ochu Chang

See Appendix B.

Kombu

From the family *laminariaceae* (kelp)

(Kelp is technically neither a plant nor an animal.)

Also known as *konbu*

This dark brown sea vegetable (*laminaria japonica*) is widely eaten in Northeast Asia. Sun-dried, it's used to flavor sushi, vegetables, and soups and is an essential ingredient in the Japanese broth *dashi*. Cooked with beans, it's thought to relieve their gaseous effect. Kombu is available whole, shredded, powdered, and pickled.

Also from kombu come glutamic acid, an ingredient in *MSG* (monosodium glutamate), and the basis of the taste *umami*.

Kombu is available in Japanese markets.

Kosher Salt

See Salt.

Ku Chai

See Onion.

Laurel

See Bay.

Lavender

A member of the botanical family *lamiaceae* (mint)

This common perennial shrub grows in any Mediterraneanlike climate. The stem becomes very woody over the years, shooting off stiff, thin stalks. The leaves are silvery gray and bushy at the base of the stem, and at the top sits the skinny purple flowers, loaded with aromatic oil.

An ancient cure for headaches, lavender's restorative powers are still extolled by aroma therapists. The flavor is floral, although some consider it soapy. In fact, lavender has been used in wash water since ancient times. The name comes from the Latin *lavare*, meaning "to wash," and is the root of the word *lavatory* (wash room) and the Spanish *lavanderia* (laundry).

There are many varieties of lavender, including common (*lavandula officinalis*), English (*lavandula angustifolia*), French (*lavandula dentate*), and Spanish (*lavandula stoechas*).

Lavender is an integral part of the French seasoning blend *herbes de Provençe* (see Appendix B), but on its own it enhances all kinds of foods, just like its cousins rosemary, oregano, and sage. On the sweet side of the kitchen, lavender has become popular as a dessert flavor, used in combination with fruits, chocolate, and vanilla.

Look for lavender in Latin American markets, health food stores, and specialty grocers.

Purple Potatoes with Lavender

If you've never seen a purple potato, don't be afraid! They're dark gray skin conceals a beautifully vibrant purple flesh that tastes like a sweeter version of any average potato.

8 to 10 small purple Peruvian potatoes
Water
1 tsp. kosher salt
6 TB. unsalted butter
¼ cup lavender buds, crushed
1 tsp. sea salt

1. In a large saucepan, cover potatoes with water, add kosher salt, and boil until potatoes are tender. Strain water off potatoes and set aside to cool. When cool, slice potatoes into medallions.

2. In a large sauté pan, melt butter over medium heat. Add lavender and cook until butter solids turn dark brown. (Don't be alarmed if they turn a little black—that just adds to the flavor.) Add potatoes and sea salt, and toss to coat. Serve immediately.

Leek

See Onion.

Lemon

A member of the botanical family *rustaceae* (citrus)

There are about 50 varieties of lemon (*citrus limonum*), but all are derived from the Citron, a large bumpy lemon with a very thick rind and comparatively little fruit inside. The citron was first used in India, spreading to Persia, Babylonia, and finally Europe with the help of Alexander the Great. The Buddha's hand (*citrus sarcodactyla*), a Chinese variety, is unusual looking, with fingerlike lobes. Other more common varieties include the Meyer, Eureka, Lisbon, Fino, and Verna. Trees can reach 12 feet high, and most have straggly branches covered with thorns, shiny evergreen leaves, and fragrant white flowers that produce the fruit each winter.

Lemons are cultivated throughout the Mediterranean, Greece, Spain, Italy, and North Africa, but more are grown in California than in all of Europe combined.

Lemon oil, pressed from skins that remain after juicing, is becoming a popular ingredient. Lemon oil and lemon extract are available in better supermarkets.

Lemon Balm

A member of the botanical family *lamiaceae* (mint)

The fat, pointy leaves of this lush perennial (*melissa officinalis*) have a lemony, minty flavor that's a common addition to tea, mulled wine, ice cream, fruit compotes, and candies.

As a tea, lemon balm was traditionally used as a stress reliever and fever reducer. It's a favorite of bees (*melissa* is Greek for "bee") and was commonly planted around orchards to attract them for pollination.

Fresh lemon balm is occasionally available at farmers' markets. You can grow your own from seeds (greenchronicle.com) or look for it dried (mountainroseherbs.com).

Lemon Balm Sherbet

A sherbet is a frozen fruit dessert made with milk. If you replace the milk with water, juice, or fruit purée, it becomes a sorbet.

2 cups granulated sugar
2 cups water
2 cups lemon balm leaves, chopped
¼ tsp. kosher salt
2 qt. whole or nonfat milk

1. In a medium saucepan, combine sugar, water, and lemon balm leaves, and bring to a boil over high heat. At the boil, remove from heat and cool completely.

2. Strain leaves out of cooled syrup, and combine syrup with salt and milk. Process in an ice-cream machine following the manufacturer's instructions. Serve with fresh berries and crisp cookies.

Lemon Basil

See Basil.

Lemon Myrtle

A member of the botanical family *myrtaceae* (myrtle)

Also known as *sweet verbena*

This bushy tree (*backhousia citriodora*) from the rainforests of Queensland is a major producer of *citral*, the oil responsible for all things lemony. Leaves of the lemon myrtle contain as much as 95 percent citral. To put that in perspective, lemongrass contains 65 percent, and lemons have a mere 5 percent.

So what do you do with a flavor more lemony than a lemon? Seafood and poultry recipes come to mind first, but it's a good choice for dairy recipes that would ordinarily be curdled by the acid of lemon juice. Ice cream, custards, and cream sauces can all be steeped with the leaf of the lemon myrtle to impart the lemony goodness.

Ask your Australian friends to send you some lemon myrtle, or look for it on the Internet (www.thespiceshop.co.uk).

Lemon Verbena

A member of the botanical family *verbenaceae* (verbena)

Also known as *bee brush*

Native to South and Central America, lemon verbena (*aloysia triphylla*) is a perennial, deciduous shrub with long thin leaves and clusters of tiny purple flowers. The shrubs, sometimes growing upward of 30 feet, were brought to Europe by Spanish explorers, where it has thrived.

The leaves are sticky with oil that produces a sweet, lemony scent that's much loved in soaps, perfumes, jams, and jellies. It's a natural addition to simmering seafood and poultry and rice dishes, and makes great tea, fruits sorbets, and cocktails.

Verbena is available dried in tea shops and health food stores and occasionally shows up fresh at farmers' markets.

Lemongrass

A member of the botanical family *poaceae* (sugarcane, bamboo)

Also known as *citronella* and *sereh*

Originally from Asia, lemongrass (*cymbopogon citrates*) is easily grown in any mild climate. The grassy stalk is woody and fibrous, but when pounded and infused into liquid, it imparts an exotic lemon essence. Like *lemon myrtle* and *lemon verbena*, it's the essential oil *citral* that is responsible for lemongrass's flavor. The best-quality lemongrass should be fresh and still green.

Lemongrass is a major ingredient in Thai and Vietnamese cuisine, but it can be used wherever lemony flavor is welcome. Look for it in Asian markets.

Licorice

A member of the botanical family *fabaceae* (legume)

The bushy licorice plant (*glycyrrhiza glabra*) grows about 3 feet high and has delicate thin leaves, furry seedpods, and creamy pink pealike flowers. But it's the root that is prized above all. It was known by the ancient Greeks, and bits of licorice root are said to have been found in King Tut's tomb.

Naturally sweeter than table sugar, licorice root has long been chewed as a breath freshener, or sliced and added to teas, liqueurs, stews, and soups. When the roots are pounded and the juice extracted, it can be solidified into black sticks or drops. This pure licorice is eaten as candy and as a natural cough drop and expectorant. It's added as a sweetener for liqueurs and teas, too.

Most licorice candy today is highly sweetened and flavored with anise, but in some parts of Europe and Scandinavia, licorice candy is made the old-fashioned way, with lots of salt.

Although difficult to grind, licorice sticks can be steeped into stews, used as skewers for kebabs, or as smoking wood for barbecues. Licorice extract is available at stores specializing in confectionery supplies, but dried root will take a trip on the Internet (kalyx.com).

Lily Bud

A member of the botanical family *hermerocallidaceae*

Also known as *golden needles, tiger lily buds*, and *pinyin*

The dried, unopened buds of orange and yellow day lilies, (*hemerocallis fulva*) are an ancient ingredient in Chinese cooking. Their musky, earthy flavor is common in stir-fries, hot and sour soup, and moo shu pork.

Look for buds that are pale in color and flexible, not dry and brittle. Be sure to soak lily buds in warm water before adding them to recipes.

Lily buds are readily available in Asian markets.

Stir-Fried Pork with Lily Buds

This stir-fry tastes just as good with beef, chicken, or shrimp.

½ cup lily buds
2 cups hot water
1 TB. peanut oil
2 cloves garlic
1 tsp. fresh ginger, grated
¼ cup cilantro, chopped fine
1 stalk celery, chopped thinly
1 lb. pork tenderloin, sliced thin
2 tsp. fish sauce
1 tsp. honey
½ cup chopped cashews
1 TB. sesame seeds

1. Soak lily buds in hot water for 20 minutes, until soft. Slice in half and discard tough ends. Set aside.

2. Heat a wok over high heat and add peanut oil. Add garlic, ginger, cilantro, and celery, and fry, stirring, until translucent. Add pork and fry, stirring, until cooked through. Add lily buds, fish sauce, and honey, and stir until warmed through.

3. Serve over steamed rice sprinkled with cashews and sesame seeds.

Lime

A member of the botanical family *rutaceae* (citrus)

The common lime tree (*citrus acida*) is smaller than other citrus, growing only about 10 feet tall. Like many of its citrus cousins, the lime tree has prickly branches and small, fragrant white flowers.

Introduced from Persia to Europe during the crusades, lime became highly prized for its oil-rich zest and floral aroma. Because the lime is high in vitamin C, British sailors ate a daily ration of lime to prevent scurvy (that's where the nickname *Limey* originated).

Lime juice is used throughout Central and South America as an acidic ingredient to flavor foods and to cook seafood *ceviche*. Dried limes are common in Persian cuisine, and the *kaffir lime* leaf is common throughout Southeast Asia. The most common varieties include the Persian lime (*citrus latifolia*), which grows without thorns or seeds, and the Key or Mexican lime (*citrus aurantifolia*), which is much smaller and more fragrant. Both turn yellow when ripe but are usually picked green.

Most grocers stock the Persian lime, but depending on where you live you may have to go to a Latin American market or specialty grocer to find Key or Mexican limes.

Lovage

A member of the botanical family *umbelliferae* (parsley)

Also known as *alexanders*

Common throughout southern Europe, this hearty perennial (*levisticum officinale*) has a thick hollow stem that can grow quite tall. Its shiny tri-leaflets look a lot like celery leaves, and it has large flat pom-poms of small yellow flowers.

Its celerylike appearance is a clue to its flavor. The seeds are often mistaken (or substituted) for celery seed. Fresh or dried, the leaves, seeds, and stems are used in salads, breads, added to potatoes, eggs, meat, and fish. The root, too, can be boiled and eaten like celery root.

Lovage is occasionally found at fancier farmers' markets, but your best bet is to grow your own (greenchronicle.com).

Lovage-Poached Shrimp Salad

Used in poaching liquid, lovage lends it essence to the shrimp without overpowering. It's a great way to feature flavors subtly.

2 cups white wine
1 ½ cup lovage, chopped
Juice of 1 lemon
1 TB. black peppercorns, crushed
1 lb. medium shrimp, peeled and deveined
1 tsp. Dijon mustard
1 cup olive oil
1 tsp. sea salt
½ tsp. black peppercorns, ground
2 stalks celery, chopped fine
2 green onions, chopped fine
1 avocado, diced
4 cups mixed baby green lettuces, washed and dried

1. In a large pot, combine wine, 1 cup lovage, juice of ½ lemon, and crushed peppercorns. Bring to a boil and simmer 30 minutes. Remove from heat, strain liquid, and add raw shrimp. Return to heat and simmer until shrimp are pink, about 5 minutes. (Do not overcook.) Drain shrimp and cool.

2. In a large bowl, mix together mustard, remaining ½ cup lovage, remaining lemon juice, olive oil, sea salt, and ground black pepper. Add celery, onions, shrimp, avocado, and baby greens, and toss to combine.

Mace

See Nutmeg.

Maché

A member of the botanical family *valerianaceae* (valerian)

Also known as *corn salad*, *lambs lettuce*, and *field lettuce*

Native to the Mediterranean, the tangy, nutty flavor of this delicate salad green (*valerianella locusta*) is a well-kept secret. The dark green leaves have a soft velvety texture that blends well with stronger salad greens. Used mostly fresh, it can also be added successfully to eggs and other vegetable dishes.

Maché is available from specialty growers and at farmers' markets. You can also grow your own (horizonherbs.com).

Mahleb

A member of the botanical family *rosaceae* (rose)

This spice is made from the pits of a very tart black cherry (*prumus mahaleb*) that's ground into flour. The flavor is a bit fruity, with some characteristics of marzipan—which makes sense, as cherries are cousins to the almond.

Hailing from the eastern Mediterranean, mahleb is well-known in the cuisines of Greece, Lebanon, and Armenia. Ground into flour, the pits are used to thicken meat and vegetable stew and lentils, and are incorporated into breads.

Mahleb is available in Arabic markets.

Mahleb Date Bars

Dates are an ancient sweet treat. Before sugar, dates and other dried fruits were the candy of the "common folk."

1 egg
1 cup sugar
½ tsp. salt
1 TB. mahleb, finely ground
1 tsp. anise seed, finely ground
½ cup milk
2 tsp. baking powder
1 cup all-purpose flour
1½ cup dates, pitted and chopped
1 cup walnuts, chopped
2 cups confectioners' sugar, sifted

1. Preheat the oven to 350°F. Lightly butter a 9×13-inch cake pan.

2. In a large bowl, stir together egg and sugar. Add salt, mahleb, anise, and milk, and stir to combine.

3. In a separate bowl, sift together baking powder and flour. Fold in dates and walnuts.

4. Pour batter into the prepared pan, and bake for 20 to 30 minutes or until golden brown. Cool completely, cut into bars, and roll each bar in confectioners' sugar. Store in an airtight container at room temperature for 1 week, or freeze for up to 1 month.

Mango Powder

See Amchoor.

Marigold

A member of the botanical family *asteraceae* (sunflower)

These round orange and yellow flowers (*calendula officinalis*) are common in the home garden as an ornamental, but the petals have long been used in the kitchen. Their spicy flavor was common throughout the Middle Ages, added to wines, grains, cakes, and puddings.

Today, marigolds are a popular edible flower, tossed into salads and cold soups. As a colorant, marigolds are often used as a substitute for saffron, and they are commonly fed to chickens to color egg yolks and skin.

You can get marigold plants and seeds at any nursery.

Marjoram

A member of the botanical family *labiatae* (mint)

Also known as *sweet marjoram, French marjoram,* and *wild marjoram*

Marjoram is in the same family and species as oregano (*origanum*), and the flavors are very similar. In fact, they may be difficult to distinguish at first glance. But taste them side by side, and you'll find that marjoram is more delicate and the flavor more subtle. Marjoram combines a peppery hint of many related herbs, like rosemary and lavender, with no one flavor overwhelming. Perhaps this is why marjoram is a part of so many herb blends. Its long, thin, twiggy stem is sparsely dotted with tiny round green leaves and white or pink flowers.

Marjoram is a natural with many savory foods, including soups, vegetables, meat, and fish. But it can be surprisingly good with sweeter foods, too. Try steeping it with lemonade for a refreshing summer drink, or mixing it with fruit.

Look for fresh marjoram at better grocers and farmers' markets. Dried marjoram is readily available at most supermarkets.

Masala

See Appendix B.

Chefspeak

Masala is a term that describes a mixture of spices. You can find dozens of variations from every region in India.

Mint

A member of the botanical family *labiatae* (mint)

Several species, including *spearmint* and *peppermint*

M

Members of the *menthe* species all share similar characteristics. They are perennial, coming back year after year stronger than ever. If you've ever had mint growing in your yard, you know what I mean. It's spread by seed and creeping rhizomes, and it takes charge of the garden. All of the menthes have four-sided stems, paired leaves, and small cloverlike flowers. Mint leaves can be cut and dried or used fresh.

Spearmint is the most common mint used in the kitchen. Its flavor is most associated with gum or toothpaste and the leaf is used most often to dress up dessert plates. Recognize it by its thick, wrinkled leaves and clearly defined veins. Peppermint has the flavor of a candy cane and is the mint most often used in extract form. Its leaves are darker, shinier, and smoother than spearmint. Black peppermint is very dark green with purple stems, and its oil is quite strong. White peppermint has a green stem, and its flavor is more subtle.

Mint oil contains *menthol*, which induces a familiar sensation that numbs the mouth. It's a natural antiseptic and anesthetic and has been used for centuries in liqueurs, soaps, and teas. It settles an upset stomach, aids digestion, is used as a diuretic, and also serves as an insecticide.

In the West, we associate mint with sweeter foods, but it has savory application in the East. Beans, grains, and meats all get the mint treatment in the Middle East, in dishes such as *tabouleh*, lamb, yogurt, and *baharat* spice blend. In Asia, mint is mixed into curries and chutneys, rolled in to spring rolls, and floated in soups. Mint is a surprisingly pleasant accompaniment to spicy foods.

There are some interesting varieties available at garden centers and farmers' markets, with names that indicate their flavors, such as pineapple mint, licorice mint, chocolate mint, and orange mint.

Miso

See Appendix B.

MSG

Monosodium glutamate

Also known as *aji-no-moto*

This flavor-enhancing compound was discovered in the early twentieth century in kelp (*laminaria japonica*). After a large batch of *kombu* broth was evaporated, the remaining crystals had a meaty, savory taste now referred to as *umami*. The compound was isolated and identified as *glutamic acid*.

Tomatoes, cheese, and mushrooms all have high amounts of naturally occurring glutamate. It has no taste of its own, yet it somehow enhances flavor of other foods. It was shown to cause brain damage in lab mice, but theories differ on the danger to humans. Most agree that occasional use does not affect adults but may cause problems in young children.

MSG is available in supermarkets in a product called Accent and in Asian markets.

Mugwort

A member of the botanical family *asteraceae* (sunflowers)

Also known as *Saint Johns plant*

Considered a perennial weed, the silver fuzzy leaves and small yellow flowers of mugwort (*artemisia vulgaris*) were a traditional ale flavoring before hops came into common use.

The leaves and flowers have a flavor reminiscent of mint and juniper, and they work as a nice accompaniment to poultry, pork, and legumes, as well as stronger meats like lamb. Mugwort is also commonly used to flavor sweet Japanese rice cakes called *mochi*.

Find mugwort dried or in plant form on the Internet (blessedherbs.com).

Must

This is the name given to the juice of grapes which includes the seeds, skin and stems. In ancient Rome, must was boiled into a sweet syrup called *defrutum* or *sapa*, and used to preserve foods, and add a sour tannic flavor. The term must is commonly used to describe the flavor of certain spices and herbs.

Must is used in Greece (called *moustos*) for syrups and candies, but it is difficult to obtain, and typically made at home.

Mustard

A member of the botanical family *brassicaceae* (mustard, cabbage)

Mustard (*brassicaceae*) is the head of its own botanical family. Most kids know mustard as the yellow stuff in the squeeze bottle and are surprised to learn that it comes from a tiny seed.

There are several varieties of mustard that all look similar, with large green leaves and long stems topped with yellow flowers, but the long seed pods bear a variety of different seeds. White (*brassica sinapis alba*) and yellow (*brassica hirta*) produce large seeds that really pack a spicy punch. Black (*brassica nigra*) and brown (*brassica junicea*) are the most common forms and have a milder flavor.

The essential mustard oils are only released when the seeds are ground and mixed with water. (That's why mustard powder lasts so long in your pantry.) Any mixture made with ground mustard should be allowed to sit for 15 minutes to fully develop.

Major mustard production takes place in Dijon, France, where the main ingredient, besides mustard, is wine. England is known for its mustard powder. In Asia, mustard seeds are fried in oil until they pop, releasing their oil.

Leaves of the variety *brassica junicea* are grown as a vegetable. The flavor is similar to kale, with a mustard-horseradish flavor. It's a common ingredient in soul food, cooked with ham hocks, collards, and kale.

Mustard seeds are available at most supermarkets.

Homemade Herb Mustard

Once you see how easy making mustard is, you'll be hooked. Try making it with different spices and herbs, horseradish, or honey.

3 TB. yellow mustard seeds
3 TB. brown mustard seeds
½ tsp. caraway seeds
1 whole allspice berry
¼ tsp. white peppercorns
¼ tsp. salt
1 shallot, minced
½ tsp. fresh thyme, chopped
¼ cup white wine
¼ cup white wine vinegar

1. In a small coffee grinder, grind yellow mustard, brown mustard, caraway, allspice, and peppercorns to a fine powder. Transfer to a blender, and add salt, shallot, and thyme. Blend.

2. In a small bowl, combine wine and vinegar, and add to running blender very slowly. Continue to purée until mixture is a smooth paste. Store in a glass or plastic airtight container in the refrigerator.

Myrtle

A member of the botanical family *myrtaceae* (myrtle)

The head of its botanical family, the myrtle (*myrtus communis*) is a bushy evergreen shrub native to the Mediterranean region. Its pointed, shiny leaves carry a distinctive rosemary-bay fragrance. Both its leaves and its deep purple berries are used to flavor meats, similar to juniper berries.

Myrtles' long white showy flowers are a common addition to pot-pourri, and they add a peppery, floral flavor when tossed into fruit or green leaf salads. The wood makes an aromatic addition to the grill for curing, roasting, and smoking. The leaves dry well, and grinding them brings out a more peppery flavor.

Look for myrtle leaves on the Internet (silk.net/sirene).

Nam Pla

See Appendix B.

Nasturtium

A member of the botanical family *tropaeolaceae* (nasturtium)

Originally from Peru, the trailing, climbing vines of the nasturtium (*tropaeolum majus*) produce one of the most common edible flowers on the American plate. The large round flat leaves and yellow or orange flowers have a grassy, peppery taste that become popular in the 1970s, along with other organic, seasonal foods. The flowers make a lovely edible garnish and are equally at home stuffed with herbed cheese, creamed into butter, or fried in batter. The leaves can be wrapped around shrimp or filled with rice like grape leaves. Crushed with garlic and olive oil, the leaves make a nice, pestolike sauce, too. Not to leave them out, the flower buds can be picked and pickled like capers.

Nasturtiums are sometimes available at farmers' markets. They are easy to grow from seed, which are available at any nursery.

Nasturtium Salmon in Parchment

This classic cooking method is called *en papillote* in French, meaning "in paper." Parchment is sold in many supermarkets, but if you can't find it, foil works just as well.

2 shallots, minced
1 TB. fresh tarragon, minced
1 TB. fresh chervil, minced
1 TB. fresh parsley, minced
1 TB. fresh chives, minced
¼ cup nasturtium leaves and petals
Zest and juice of 1 small lemon
1 cup olive oil
4 (3-oz.) salmon fillets
1 TB. sea salt

1. Preheat the oven to 400°F.

2. In a large bowl, whisk together shallots, tarragon, chervil, parsley, chives, nasturtiums, and lemon zest and juice. Slowly add olive oil, whisking until well combined.

3. Lay each salmon fillet in the center of a large piece of parchment paper or aluminum foil. Distribute herb dressing evenly over each fillet.

4. Bring together the edges of the parchment paper up around fish and crimp together to seal tightly. Place packets on a baking sheet and bake for 15 minutes. Transfer packets to plates, and open at the table.

Natto

See Appendix B.

N

Nigella

A member of the botanical family *ranunculaceae* (buttercup)

Also known as *kalongi, black onion seed, Black cumin,* and *black caraway*

Nigella seeds (*nigella sativa*) have many confusing synonyms, but it bears no relation to any of them. Worse still, nigella seeds look a lot like black sesame seeds and are often used interchangeably. It's too bad, because the nigella seed gives off a musty, smoky flavor that none of the others have.

Swollen seed pods grow out of center of the flowers, which sit at the top of long stalks, with dill-like leaves and flowers that range from white, yellow, pink, blue, and purple. The flowers (known as love-in-the-mist) are popular with ornamental gardeners and are often seen whole as a garnish.

Nigella seeds are commonly used in Indian cuisine, in breads like *naan*, curries and korma, dahl, and in several spice blends.

Look for nigella at Indian markets.

Naan

This East Indian flat bread is used as a utensil alongside traditional curries. Made in a cylindrical clay tandoor oven, a flat circle of dough is slapped onto the side of the oven, giving it the tradional snowshoe shape.

1 pkg. active dry yeast
1 cup warm water
1 TB. sugar
¼ cup plain yogurt
1 TB. nigella
1 tsp. kosher salt
3 or 4 cups bread flour
2 to 4 TB. *ghee*

1. In a large bowl, combine yeast and warm water, and stir to dissolve. Add sugar, yogurt, nigella, and salt, and stir to combine. Add flour slowly, and stir until a firm dough forms.

2. Turn out dough onto a lightly floured surface, and knead for 8 to 10 minutes or until dough is smooth and elastic, adding more flour as needed. Cover dough with a warm, damp towel, and let rise until double in volume.

3. Divide dough into 8 portions and roll into balls. Pat balls flat into discs and elongate into ovals about ½ inch thick.

4. Preheat an iron skillet or griddle to high. Oil lightly with ghee, add dough, and cook for 2 to 4 minutes or until golden brown and puffy. Brush uncooked side with ghee, flip, and brown. Serve warm.

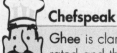

Chefspeak

Ghee is clarified butter in which all the moisture has been evaporated and the fat itself browns and takes on a nutty flavor. You can make it at home by slowly melting a pound of butter, carefully skimming off the foam, and pouring the pure fat off the sediment. This is clarified butter. Cook the clarified butter slowly until it turns a deep golden brown. Store ghee in the refrigerator for several weeks.

Nopales

A member of the botanical family *cactaceae* (cactus)

Also known as *prickly pear*

The large round flat pads, also known as stem segments, of the prickly pear cactus (*opuntia ficus-indica*) are a favorite ingredient in both Mexican and Mediterranean cuisines. Native to Mexico, the plant was brought back to Europe by Spanish explorers, where it now grows abundantly. Its prickly pear fruit is still consumed on both continents.

The spines need to be carefully removed from the stems with a knife or peeler, and the pads can be sliced thinly and used in recipes with seafood, eggs, vegetables, and salsas or eaten grilled with lime and olive oil.

Nopales are highly nutritious, with loads of vitamins, potassium, and iron. Take care when preparing, as excessive heat will create a slimy, okralike consistency.

Buy nopales at Latin American markets.

Nori

A member of the family *bangiaceae* (red algae)

(Algae is technically neither a plant nor animal.)

Also known as *kim, gim* in Korea, and *hǎitái* in Chinese

Nori is the most familiar form of seaweed in the West. It's processed in the same way as paper, and the thin sheets are used to wrap sushi and rice balls. Nori is also shredded as a garnish for soups and vegetable dishes. It's commonly toasted and often flavored with soy sauce, sugar, and spices.

Buy nori at Japanese markets.

Nutmeg

A member of the botanical family *myristicaceae*

This tall evergreen tree (*myristica fragrans*) is native to the Indonesian Banda Islands, where the Portuguese first found it in the 1500s. The Dutch soon monopolized the nutmeg trade, displacing the natives and working the plantations with indentured slaves and convicts.

Today nutmeg grows throughout Indonesia, Madagascar, Grenada, and the Caribbean. The tree has long, thin leaves and tiny yellow flowers, similar to a peach tree. The fruit itself looks like a fig as it buds and a funny round pear when it's ripe. The juicy pulp hides a pit surrounded by a red fleshy net, or *mace*. Beneath the mace is a pit with a hard exterior shell. And inside the shell is the nutmeg. The nutmeg is soft when first removed, but becomes rock hard when dried in the sun. Mace is also dried in the sun, and the two are packaged and sold separately.

Historically, nutmeg was used as a mild sedative, and it's a common belief that taking large quantities will produce a hallucinogenic effect.

Nutmeg and mace share a similar flavor when ground. Mace is a bit stronger than the sweet, spicy nutmeg. Both are available whole and ground, but the flavor of the ground versions tends to dissipate rapidly. Special nutmeg graters are available for gadget-lovers, and they greatly extend the life of nuts. A grated nut will seal itself up after use, and very little of the flavorful oil will dissipate through the wound. Mace is equally long-lasting, although a bit more difficult to grind. I find that a mortar and some muscle work best for small amounts. Grind larger amounts of mace in a coffee grinder.

Nutmeg is commonly thought of as a sweet spice, but it's used in all sorts of savory recipes, too. French cuisine especially uses nutmeg in starch, grain, egg, and cheese dishes for just the right balance.

Whole and ground nutmeg is widely available in markets across the globe.

Onion

A member of the botanical family *liliaceae* (lily, onion)

There are many varieties of onion (*allium*), including leeks, shallots, chives, and garlic. They all share a similar structure, with hollow single stems growing out of bulbs and flowering into pom-pom flowers, and every part of the plant is edible.

The ancient Egyptians worshipped the onion, its concentric rings a symbol of eternal life. Onions are still prized for their different parts. Bulb onions have a round core expanding into layers, with a papery outer skin. They include the red or purple Bermudas, sweet Vidalia and Walla Wallas, common white and yellow, as well as round and elongated shallots (*allium oschaninii*).

Some alliums are valued for their stems. They do not have a rounded bulb, but instead grow a long cylinder of tightly packed leaves. These include the leek (*allium ampeloprasum*), the scallion or green onion, the Welsh onion (*allium fistulosum*), and the smallest of the species, the chive (*allium schoenoprasum*), which grows in clumps and includes the Japanese garlic *chive Ku chai*, (*allium tuberosum*). The greens and flowers can be harvested from all onions, regardless of their variety.

The pearl onion (*allium cepa*), or *walking onion* or *tree onion*, is a peculiar form. The plant grows a mass of bulbs at the top of the stem, where a normal onion flower would appear.

Onions are used in infinite ways, but certain preparation methods bring out different characteristics. Cut onions release more of their harsh oils than onions cooked whole. If onions are to be eaten raw, you can tame the harsh oils by thoroughly soaking and rinsing in cold water. Roasting whole or chopped and sautéed over slow heat brings out an onion's natural sugars, which can be further cooked to caramelization.

In addition to fresh, onions are also commonly available in dried, flaked, powdered, or salted forms, all processed from dehydrated bulbs. Be aware that these dried forms have a more concentrated flavor.

Onions are available wherever people like to eat.

Opal Basil

See Basil.

Orange

A member of the botanical family *rustaceae* (citrus)

Originally from China, the common sweet orange (*citrus sinensis*) is probably a hybrid of ancient pomelos and tangerines that grew wild throughout Asia. Like other citrus fruits, the orange comes from a tall tree with shiny, deep-veined tapered evergreen leaves and fragrant white flowers. Citrus trees were planted along trade routes by Portuguese, Spanish, Arab, and Dutch sailors to prevent scurvy. Ponce de Leon and Columbus planted trees in the new world.

There are several varieties and hybrids of orange, including the bitter Seville orange (*citrus aurantium*); the sweet Valencia, grown for its juice; and the navel, taken from an odd mutation of a Brazilian sweet orange and planted in Riverside, California. The blood orange, grown throughout the Mediterranean and more recently in California, contains streaks of red *anthocynin* pigment not usually found in citrus but common in other vegetables and flowers. Rumor has it that the orange was cross-pollinated with a rose. The mandarin orange (*citrus reticulate*) is smaller and sweeter than an orange and has loose skin.

The tangerine is a less-sweet variety of mandarin. The tangelo is hybrid of tangerine (mandarin) and pomelo. The pomelo (*citrus maxima*), also known as the *shaddock*, is the largest and oldest citrus fruit, native to Southeast Asia, where it grows wild on riverbanks. The pomelo tastes like a sweet, mild grapefruit and has a very thick peel, which is commonly used for candies and preserves. The grapefruit is hybrid of pomelo and orange and is named for the way the fruit clusters on the branch. Kumquats, which look like tiny oranges, are a separate genus, *fortunella*.

In the spice world, the orange is valued for its peel's aroma. The essential oils, once used by Chinese women to scent their hands by simply holding the fruit, add their aroma to foods of all kinds. It can be used fresh, grated or peeled from the fruit, chopped fine, infused in chunks, or dried and pulverized to a powder.

Orange flower water is the distillation of orange blossoms and is used in cocktails and baked goods. The flavor and aroma are floral, not citrusy, and are favored both in Middle Eastern and in recipes from the Victorian era.

Oranges are available everywhere. Find orange extract and oil in better supermarkets.

Oregano

A member of the botanical family *lamiaceae* (mint)

The same species and family as marjoram, oregano (*origanum vulgare*) grows taller, bushier, and hardier. The flavor is quite a bit stronger than that of marjoram, and the herb is used throughout the Americas, Italy, and Greece more than marjoram. Originally from the Mediterranean, for centuries oregano was used as an antidote for hemlock.

Oregano is one of the more pungent herbs. If tasted carefully, you can draw out hints of pepper, mint, and fennel. Oregano dries well, and if kept whole, it will retain its fragrance longer than most dried herbs. Powdered oregano has a much shorter life. When using fresh oregano, look for woody, bushy stems, and crush or rub it before adding it to a pot to release the flavorful oils.

Mexican or Puerto Rican oregano is another plant altogether (*lippia graveolens*, of the family *verbenaceae*). It's very similar to Mediterranean oregano, but because it's from the verbena family, it has more citrus essence.

Oregano is available fresh and dried at most supermarkets. Mexican oregano can be found in Latin American markets.

Pandan Leaf

A member of the botanical family *pandanaceae*

Also known as *screwpine*

Historically, the pandan tree (*pandanus amaryllifolius*) had many uses throughout the Pacific, including building and clothing material, dyes, medicines, as well as spiritual significance. But the fruity-rose essence of the flowers and the earthy, smoky-nut flavor of the leaves have made the pandan essential in the region's cuisines, where it's used as much as vanilla is in the West. Look for it cooked with chicken in Thailand, confectionery in Vietnam, and custards and rice in Bali and Malaysia. In addition to the unique flavor, pandan leaves impart a natural green color.

The leaves are best fresh, as they lose most of their flavor when dried. Fresh leaves are hard to come by outside the Pacific Rim. However, you can find pandan essence in a liquid form in Asian markets.

Pandan Coconut Rice

You can make this luscious green rice using 2 teaspoons pandan essence if don't have pandan leaves.

1 (5.6-oz.) can coconut milk
3 cups water
3 pandan leaves, knotted
1 tsp. fresh ginger, grated
2 TB. chives, minced
1 cinnamon stick
3 star anise
2 TB. sugar
1 tsp. kosher salt
1 tsp. black pepper
2 cups rice
½ cup peanuts, chopped

1. In a large saucepan, combine coconut milk, water, pandan leaves, ginger, chives, cinnamon stick, anise, sugar, salt, and pepper. Bring to a boil over high heat. At the boil, add rice. Stir, reduce heat to low, and cover.

2. Cook for 20 minutes or until liquid is absorbed. Serve warm, topped with chopped peanuts.

P

Paprika

A member of the botanical family *solanaceae* (nightshade)

The sweet red peppers (*capsicum annum*) used in the production of paprika are native to South America, but major production of paprika takes place in Hungary and Spain. There, they have elevated spice-making to an art form. More than simply ground sweet red peppers, real paprika is sweet and complex with a touch of heat.

How the peppers got to Hungary is not entirely clear. Turkish traders traveling between Portugal and Asia probably brought them. Regardless of how or why, the Danube region has become the only European region that eats chiles as an integral part of its cuisine. This is in no small part due to the perfect combination of soil, weather, rain, and sun the Szeged region of southern Hungary enjoys.

Specific grades of paprika all come from the same chiles. The flavor and heat are controlled by the degree of ripeness and the size of the pods when they're picked, which is directly related to the proportion of pepper wall to the seeds and inner membrane. The following table lists the common grades of paprika.

Paprika Grades		
Különleges	special quality	brightest red and most mild
Édes Csemege	delicate	mild with rich pepper flavor
Csemegepaprika	exquisite delicate	slightly spicier than delicate
Csipõs Csemege, Pikáns	pungent exquisite	hotter than delicate
Rózsa	rose	strong aroma, mild pungency, the most exported
Édesnemes	noble sweet	bright red, mild flavor
Félédes	half-sweet	a blend of mild and spicy
Erõs	hot	light brown, hottest of all paprika

The color of paprika ranges from pale orange to deep dark red, the brighter being the most mild. Real Hungarian and Spanish paprika has little in common with the red powder found in most American markets. Here, it's a blend of chile powder and cayenne, and it's used less for its flavor than its color.

In Hungary, paprika is the foundation of the national dish, goulash (*gulyás*, meaning "cattleman"), which, in its traditional form, is a brothy beef stew with vegetables and plenty of paprika. The paprika must be delicately fried to bring out just the right flavors without turning bitter.

Look for good-quality paprika at gourmet stores and specialty markets, or try the Internet (thespicehouse.com).

Paracress

A member of the botanical family *asteraceae* (sunflower)

Also known as *toothache plant*

Not a member of the cress family, paracress (*spilanthes acmella*) has large dark green leaves, red stems, and big yellow-red flower heads that look like the center of a daisy with no petals.

Native to Brazil, fresh paracress has a unique quality. At first taste, they're savory, almost mushroomlike. As it sits on the tongue, a warming sensation begins, triggering salivation and then tingling into numbness before dissipating. The unique qualities are often combined with other hot and spicy flavorings like garlic, chiles, and other peppers for a layered effect.

Paracress is rare outside Brazil but can be found in some online catalogues (www.koppertcress.nl).

Paracress Salsa

Serve this salsa to all your chile-loving friends. It will knock their socks off!

1 cup cilantro, chopped
¼ cup epazote, chopped
2 paracress flower heads, chopped
5 green onions, chopped
2 cloves garlic, minced
Zest and juice of 6 Key or Mexican limes
¼ cup olive oil
4 ripe tomatoes, diced
4 tomatillos, diced
1 cucumber, peeled and diced
2 jalapeño chiles, minced
2 poblano chiles, roasted and chopped
½ tsp. sea salt
½ tsp. black pepper

1. In a large bowl, combine cilantro, epazote, paracress, onions, garlic, and lime zest and juice. Stir together and slowly add olive oil.

2. Add tomatoes, tomatillos, cucumber, jalapeño chiles, poblano chiles, salt, and pepper. Toss to combine, and marinate at room temperature for 1 hour.

3. Taste and adjust seasoning with salt or lime as needed. Serve with tortilla chips.

Parsley

A member of the botanical family *umbelliferae* (parsley)

The two most common forms of parsley are the original flat Italian (*petroselinum neapolitanum*) and curly (*petroselinum crispum*). Flat parsley, which is slightly stronger in flavor, has small, flat, leaves clumped together on thin, tender stems that grow tall and flower into tiny pale yellow blooms. Curly parsley has ruffled leaves, and is commonly used as a garnish. Both types can be used fresh and dried, although much of the essence is lost in the later form.

Parsley is an essential ingredient in *tabbouleh*, the national dish of Lebanon; the French herb sachet *bouqet garni;* and the Italian condiment *gremolata*. Parsley has a high chlorophyll content, which gives food an herby flavor without the presence of heat, spice, or floral perfumes. Chlorophyll also makes parsley a natural breath freshener.

Another form of parsley (*petroselinum tuberosum*) is cultivated for its root, which can be eaten like a carrot, either fresh or cooked.

Parsley is available everywhere.

Beurre Maître d'Hôtel (Maitre D'Butter)

Serve this classic French spread on fish, beef, poultry, vegetables, potatoes, eggs, and bread.

1 lb. unsalted butter, softened to room temperature
¼ cup parsley, chopped
2 TB. shallot, minced
3 TB. lemon juice
¼ tsp. sea salt
¼ tsp. white pepper, ground

1. In a large bowl, beat together butter, parsley, shallot, lemon juice, salt, and pepper until well combined.

2. Spoon mixture onto a sheet of parchment or waxed paper, and roll into a log. Refrigerate until firm.

Pasilla

See Appendix C.

Pepper

A member of the botanical family *piperaceae* (pepper)

The pepper vine (*piper nigrum*) grows in tropical regions, close to the equator. In its natural jungle habitat, it climbs up trees 20 feet high. It has thick, broad, dark green leaves and small white flowers that grow in clumps. The flowers mature into berries that ripen from green to orange to red.

 Tidbit

Pink peppercorns are actually a different species from white or black.

To produce black pepper, berries are harvested green and dried in the sun until wrinkled and black. White pepper is made from ripe berries that have had the skin removed before drying. Unripe green peppercorns are also sold in brine, still green and soft.

Pepper is one of the most popular spices in history. It was used in the embalming rituals of ancient Egypt, paid as taxes in ancient Rome, and the third-century cookbook *Apicius* uses pepper in nearly every entry. Let's not forget Vasco de Gama and his Portuguese mariners, who were inspired by pepper to find a route to India.

The finest pepper is produced in Southwest India, where the large berries are picked by hand off trellised vines. The flavor is more pungent than the stuff in the shaker on your table. It's higher priced, too.

Spicy and pungent, peppercorns can be added whole or ground for use in both savory and sweet dishes. They are commonly available.

Pineapple Pepper Ice Cream

The combination of spicy black pepper and sweet, acidic pineapple creates an explosion of flavor on your tongue. It's suprisingly refreshing.

½ pineapple, cut into large dice
2 TB. black peppercorns, crushed
½ cup brown sugar
1 vanilla bean, split and scraped
1½ cups heavy cream
1½ cups half-and-half
6 egg yolks
¾ cup sugar
½ tsp. kosher salt

1. Preheat the oven to 400°F.

2. In a large bowl, combine pineapple, pepper, brown sugar, and vanilla bean. Mix well, transfer to a baking sheet, and spread out into an even layer. Roast, stirring occasionally, until pineapple begins to brown, about 45 minutes. Transfer to a large bowl.

3. In a large saucepan, combine cream and half-and-half and bring to a boil.

4. In a medium bowl, whisk together egg yolks, sugar, and salt. Add ½ cup hot cream to yolk mixture, and whisk together quickly. Add yolks back to cream. Continue stirring over high heat until mixture is thick like a runny milkshake, about 2 or 3 minutes. Pour over roasted pineapple and cool completely.

5. Run cooled custard and pineapple through a blender, and strain out the chunks. Freeze in an ice-cream machine, following the manufacturer's instructions.

Pepper, Chile

See Chile Pepper.

Pepper, Pink

A member of the botanical family *anacardiaceae* (cashew)

The Peruvian (*shinus molle*) and Brazilian (*shinus terebinthifolius*) pepper trees are common ornamental trees in the warm climates of California, Florida, and the Mediterranean. The berries, while peppery in flavor initially, carry more of a sweet, juniper quality once bitten. They're commonly mixed with other peppercorns but then its flavor is lost. Try it on lighter foods, like fish and vegetables, where its subtleties can be appreciated. Add pink peppercorns at the end of the cooking, as excessive heat diminishes the flavor.

Dried pink peppercorns do not retain their flavor long. Look for the papery pink outer skin to be on the berry, and not at the bottom of the jar.

Pink peppercorns are available at better supermarkets.

Pink Peppercorn Biscotti

These twice-baked cookies were originally meant to be dipped in *vin santo*, a sweet Italian red wine. They are just as good dipped in coffee or milk, and this particular variation does well in Earl Grey tea.

2¾ cups flour
2 tsp. baking powder
¼ tsp. salt
1½ sticks butter
1 cup sugar
3 TB. pink peppercorns, crushed
Zest of 3 lemons, minced
1 egg
1 TB. milk

1. Preheat the oven to 350°F. Line 2 baking sheets with parchment paper.

2. In a medium bowl, sift together flour, baking powder, and salt, and set aside.

3. In a large bowl, using a sturdy spoon or an electric mixer, cream butter, sugar, peppercorns, and lemon zest until lump free. Add egg and milk. Slowly add sifted ingredients, and mix well to fully incorporate.

4. Roll dough into logs approximately 3 inches wide by the length of the baking sheet. Bake for 30 to 40 minutes or until golden brown and firm to the touch. Remove from the oven, and while warm, cut into ¾-inch slices using a serrated knife.

5. Return biscotti to the baking sheet and return to the oven. Bake for 5 to 10 minutes or until toasted. Flip cookies and toast other side for 5 to 10 more minutes.

P

Pepper, Sweet

See Sweet Pepper.

Pepper, White

See Pepper.

Peppermint

See Mint.

Perilla

A member of the botanical family *lamiacea* (mint)

Also known as *shiso*, *Chinese basil*, and *purple mint*

Native to Southeast Asia, this green pointed, jagged-edged leaf (*perilla crispa*) is most recognized as a sashimi and tempura garnish. A purple variety (*perilla altropurpurea*) is used for its red pigment (*anthocynin*) to dye pickled foods, including the pickled ginger on the side of your sushi. Purple perilla is sometimes mistaken for purple or opal basil.

The flavor is an interesting mix of mint, cinnamon, licorice, and citrus. The green variety sometimes tastes gingery as well.

Another perilla variety (*frutescens*) is grown for its oil and seeds, which are dried and used as a spice. The leaves lose their flavor easily when overcooked, so add them at the end of cooking or eat them fresh.

Perilla is available at Asian markets.

Mixed Berry-Perilla Compote

Use this decadent mixture to top ice cream, shortcakes, brownies, or lemon pie.

1 pt. blackberries
1 pt. raspberries
1 pt. blueberries
1 pt. strawberries, stems removed and cut in ½ or ¼
¼ cup purple perilla leaves, chopped
¼ cup sugar
Zest and juice of 1 lime
¼ tsp. kosher salt

1. Pick through, rinse, and air dry blackberries, raspberries, and blueberries.

2. In a large bowl, combine berries, strawberries, perilla, sugar, lime zest and juice, and salt, and toss to combine thoroughly.

3. Marinate at room temperature for 1 hour before serving.

Persillade

See Appendix B.

Pimiento

See Sweet Pepper.

Poblano

See Appendix C.

Ponzu

See Appendix B.

Poppy Seed

A member of the botanical family *papaveraceae* (poppy)

The same poppy from which the dangerously poisonous and addictive opium is derived (*papaver somniferum*) also produces the perfectly safe and flavorful seeds floating in your muffins, cakes, pastries, and candies. The white or pink flower gives way to a seed capsule that contains both the poisonous juice and the safe seeds.

The blue-black poppy seed is the most common, but a smaller, milder white version (*papaver somniferum album*) is sometimes seen in Indian cuisine. The poppy seed, with its nutty flavor, can be ground into a paste, and the white seeds can be ground to a flour and used as a thickener. Both seeds are used to fill pastries, including *mohn*, the filling for *hamentaschen* cookies.

Poppy seeds are high in oil and should be bought in small quantities as needed or stored in the refrigerator to prevent rancidity. Poppy seeds are very hard, and many recipes call for the seeds to be soaked in liquid to soften.

You can find poppy seeds in most supermarkets.

Poppy Seed Fruit Salad

This is a refreshing salad for hot summer days—or days you wish were hot.

½ cup orange juice
¼ cup raspberry vinegar
Zest and juice of 1 lime
3 TB. poppy seeds
¼ tsp. Szechwan pepper, ground
¼ tsp. anise seed, ground
¼ tsp. sea salt
¼ cup olive oil
1 banana, sliced into rounds
½ cantaloupe, diced
½ honeydew, diced
1 mango, diced
1 papaya, diced
2 kiwis, diced
1 pt. strawberries, rinsed, trimmed, and halved
2 cucumbers, peeled and diced

1. In a large bowl, whisk together orange juice, vinegar, lime zest and juice, poppy seeds, Szechwan pepper, anise, salt, and olive oil.

2. Add banana, cantaloupe, honeydew, mango, papaya, kiwi, strawberries, and cucumbers, and toss well to incorporate. Chill for 30 minutes before serving.

Quatre-Epice

See Appendix B.

Rakkyo, Rakyo

See Appendix B.

Ras el Hanout

See Appendix B.

Rock Salt

See Salt.

Rocket

> A member of the botanical family *brassicaceae* (mustard)
>
> Also known as *arugala*

This hearty annual (*eruca vesicaria*) thrives in hot, dry Mediterranean climates. Its large leaves and pale white flowers have a delicate, peppery flavor.

Rocket is used fresh as a vegetable in salads, chopped and added to soups and pastas, and crushed with olive oil and garlic like pesto. It's best used fresh or added to recipes at the end of cooking. Serve it on Valentine's Day, as it's a known aphrodisiac.

Rocket is available from specialty growers and at better farmers' markets.

Rose

A member of the botanical family *rosaceae* (rose)

The head of its own botanical family, the flowering rose (*rosa*) has long been used in the Middle East as a flavoring and was all the rage during the Victorian era. Roses are currently experiencing a surge in popularity. Floral additions to food, especially pastry, are popping up more and more.

The aroma come from the petals, and while the standard garden-variety roses work, the heirloom tea roses seem to provide the best flavor and most pungent aroma.

The petals can be steeped into recipes or packed in sugar to absorb their oils. Distilled rose water is an even easier way to add rose flavor to your favorite recipes.

Rose hips, classically used for jellies and teas, are the fruit of the rose plant. They appear as red, orange, or purple balls, left on the bush after the flower has died. Roses with opened-faced flowers produce the best hips, with a fruity, spicy, tart flavor, a little like rhubarb. The best hips are firm, not mushy or wrinkled. Remove the seeds and skin and dry or purée the inner pulp. Rose hips are a potent source of vitamin C.

Roses and rose hips are available from specialty growers, and rose hip tea is available at health food stores.

R

Rose Hip Applesauce

This dish is great on its own, spooned over fresh fruit and granola, or as a sweet accompaniment to roasted pork and lamb.

6 fuji apples, peeled, cored, and diced
2 cups rose hips, bud end removed
½ cup water
½ cup sugar
Zest and juice of 1 lemon
½ tsp. salt

1. In a large saucepan, combine apples, rose hips, water, sugar, lemon zest and juice, and salt. Place over medium heat and simmer, covered and stirring occasionally, until apples and rose hips are tender. Add more water during simmering if necessary.

2. Remove the pan from heat, and pass mixture through a food mill or purée in a food processor and then pass through a colander.

Rosemary

A member of the botanical family *lamiaceae* (mint)

Rosemary (*rosmariunus officinalis*) is one of the most familiar of all herbs, probably because it doesn't look like any of the others. Its evergreen leaves look just like pine needles, and its stalks, topped with tiny blue flowers, can grow quite tall. Throughout the Middle Ages, rosemary was considered an herb of fidelity and love and was worn as a wreath at weddings.

Rosemary's flavor is unmistakable. Its woody, pine-sage aroma can easily overpower a dish, so it's commonly paired with strong foods that can stand up to it, like gamey meats and winter vegetables. But in moderation, rosemary adds a delightful touch to sweet foods, too. Try it in apple pie, lemon scones, or vanilla sauce. Use the flowers for a salad garnish, or candy them as you would violets. The woody stalks make great smoke for the grill, and the twigs, peeled and soaked in water or wine, make aromatic skewers.

Rosemary is readily available in supermarkets, both fresh and dried.

Rue

> A member of the botanical family *rutaceae* (citrus)
>
> Also known as *garden rue*

Rue (*ruta graveolens*) is an evergreen shrub from the Mediterranean with a bitter citrus flavor that's used to balance flavors of foods as varied as cheese, spirits, and salads.

Its carrot top–like leaves and yellow flowers have long been believed to hold spiritual and medicinal properties, and during the Middle Ages, it was hung in doorways to keep evil spirits at bay. Some say the phrase *rue the day* comes from the Roman habit of throwing rue at an enemy.

In Ethipoia, rue is added to coffee and is an integral part of the national spice mix *berbere* (see Appendix B). The bitter flavor complements acidic foods like tomatoes, pickled vegetables, and olives, and it's a flavor component in both grappa and bitters.

Grow your own rue, or look for it on the Internet (mountainroseherbs.com).

 **Hot Stuff**

Don't confuse *rue* with *roux*, the French thickening agent made of equal parts melted butter or fat and flour.

R

Olive Spread

Spread this on slices of crusty French bread.

3 TB. fresh rue, chopped fine
1 tsp. red wine vinegar
¼ cup olive oil
¼ cup Parmesan cheese
1 cup pitted kalamata olives, minced
1 cup pitted green Spanish olives, minced
1 clove garlic, minced
1 tsp. capers, minced

1. In a large bowl, mix together rue, vinegar, olive oil, and cheese. Add kalamata olives, green olives, garlic, and capers, and stir to combine.

2. Marinate at room temperature for several hours before serving.

Safflower

A member of the botanical family *asteraceae* (sunflower)

The low-cholesterol oil of the safflower (*carthamus tinctorius*), extracted from its seeds, is the most common use of this thistlelike herb today. But historically, it was grown as a dye, both for food and textiles. Its shaggy orange flowers look a lot like saffron to the uninitiated, so beware. Disreputable vendors have been known to try and fool the consumer. If you fall victim, you'll know right away, as the flavor of safflower is practically nonexistent.

Safflower threads are sold for dye and tea on the Internet, and in health food stores (mountainroseherbs.com).

Saffron

A member of the botanical family *iridaceae* (iris)

In the center of a low-growing purple crocus (*crocus sativus*) are three orange stigma. These stigma are the most cherished of all spices, saffron. Its exorbitant price is justified when you consider that the stigma must be picked by hand, and it takes approximately 75,000 stigma to make 1 pound saffron.

Luckily, it doesn't take much saffron to color and flavor your food. One or two strands, carefully steeped in liquid, can infuse a whole pot of rice with its dry, floral aroma. Nonbelievers soon discover that too much of a good thing is bitter and unpleasant.

Saffron is used throughout Europe and the Middle East. It's grown in India, Iran, and Spain, as well as Mexico. The Spanish government oversees a grading system, but no such system exists in Iran or India. Still, the quality is high, and connoisseurs can judge the quality, country of origin, and even territory by flavor and aroma.

Often the color is simulated by the use of turmeric, safflower, or marigold, but the sweet and pungent flavor cannot be duplicated.

When buying saffron, look for a vibrant red color. The older it gets, the closer to brown it becomes. Saffron is harvested in late fall, and good suppliers will date their product. Saffron keeps well, but don't pay too much for a batch that's obviously old. Old saffron is dry and brittle, so avoid a batch with a lot of broken pieces at the bottom of the jar.

Saffron is available at most fine supermarkets.

Russian Easter Bread (*Kulich*)

This bread is a celebration of spring, but it tastes great any time of year.

1 cup golden raisins
1 cup rum
1 cup milk, at room temperature
½ cup sugar
1 pinch saffron threads
1 (.25-oz.) pkg. active dry yeast
4 eggs
Zest of 1 orange
1½ sticks butter, softened to room temperature
2 tsp. salt
4 to 6 cups bread flour
1 egg yolk
¼ cup cream

1. In a small bowl, combine raisins and rum and soak overnight, or warm together in the microwave and set aside for 1 hour.

2. In a large bowl, stir together milk, sugar, saffron threads, and yeast. Set aside for 15 minutes or until bubbles begin to appear. Stir in eggs, orange zest, butter, salt, and raisins. Add flour slowly, and stir until a firm dough forms.

3. Turn out dough onto a lightly floured surface, and knead for 8 to 10 minutes or until smooth and elastic. Add more flour as needed. Cover dough with a warm, damp towel, and let rise until double in volume, about 2 hours.

4. Preheat the oven to 350°F.

5. Divide dough into three equal pieces, and roll each into a rope about 18 inches long. Braid ropes together into one loaf, and set on a buttered baking sheet.

6. Mix egg yolk and cream, and brush over the surface of loaf. Bake for 30 to 40 minutes or until golden brown. The loaf should sound hollow when thumped. Cool completely before slicing.

Sage

A member of the botanical family *labiatae* (mint)

Many varieties of sage grow wild wherever the climate is comparable to the Mediterranean. The most common culinary species (*salvia officinalis*) has a long woody stem, with silvery-gray-green leaves that are a little fuzzy, and purple flowers. The leaves can be used both fresh and dry. Rubbed sage, named for the method by which it is removed from the stem, is full of air, and should be used in greater quantity than fresh leaves.

Historically, sage has been an important medicinal herb. Its species name, *salvia*, is the Latin root of *salvation*. The herb has been known to cure everything from digestive disorders to sore throats, and was thought to promote longevity and improve the memory of the elderly. (If I'm remembering correctly.)

Sage is a common addition to Mediterranean and Middle Eastern cuisines. Its cedarlike aroma complements meats of all kinds, cheese, vegetables, and even fruits.

Sage is available fresh and dried in most supermarkets.

Salsify

A member of the botanical family *asteraceae* (sunflower)

Also known as *goatsbeard* and *oyster plant*

The root, shoots, flowers, and sprouted seeds of this showy purple wildflower (*tragopogon porrifolius*) originally from the Mediterranean are all edible. The root, often called oyster plant because of its flavor, is eaten as a vegetable and has a flavor akin to that of sun chokes or artichokes. The shoots have a similar flavor and are often steamed or tossed in vinaigrette. The seeds are sprouted and added to salads and sandwiches.

The root is available in better supermarkets and farmers' markets in the winter. Look for seeds online (yankeegardener.com) or in your nursery to start a crop in your garden.

Salt

Sodium chloride

Easily the most important addition to any pantry, salt not only flavors food, but also plays a vital role in human existence by regulating the water content in the body. More important, salt enables us to preserve food, making us less dependent on seasonal availability and able to wander from our homes for extended periods of time. It enabled early civilizations to move about the globe, discovering one another. Salt was our ticket to ride.

Salt was historically a hot commodity, difficult to obtain and, therefore, quite expensive. It can be harvested from sea water or rock deposits left from ancient seas. From the ocean, salt water is dried by the sun in shallow pools. Mined salt (*halite*), also known as rock salt, grows in isometric crystals and is very hard.

Several types of edible salt are commonly available. Table salt is usually iodized. Potassium iodide is added as a dietary supplement to preventing iodine deficiency, a major cause of goiter and cretinism. Most table salt has a water-absorbing additive to keep it from clumping, and some countries add fluoride as well.

Many chefs prefer kosher salt, which gets its name from its use in the koshering process of meats. Koshering requires that all fluids be extracted from an animal before it is consumed. The larger crystals dissolve more slowly, extracting more fluids from the meat. Kosher salt has no additives, which gives it a cleaner, less-metallic taste.

Fleur de sel ("salt flower") is natural sea salt, hand harvested and gourmet priced. It usually comes from specific locations, most notably off the coast of Brittany, in France. Each location produces distinct flavors due to the area's naturally occurring vegetation and minerals. Sea salt removed from the top layer of water is pale and delicate in flavor, while gray sea salt, which is allowed to sink and mix with the ocean water, is more robust in flavor.

You might also find black salt, gray salt, pink salt, smoked salt, marsh salt, and even moon salt (harvested at night, not from the moon). You can spend quite a lot of money on salt, but beware: once it's mixed into foods, the unique character of these specialty salts is easily lost. Reserve their use for applications in which you'll notice it.

Get your pricey salt at gourmet markets or on the Internet (saltworks.us).

Salted Figs with Chocolate and Almonds

This dish makes an exquisite after-dinner sweet. Serve it with strong coffee or a glass of port.

2 TB. almonds, toasted and ground
1 (8-oz.) bittersweet chocolate bar, chopped or grated into fine
  chunks
16 dried black mission figs
2 tsp. fleur de sel or other coarse sea salt

1. Preheat the oven to 350°F.

2. In a small bowl, mix together almonds and chocolate.

3. Insert your thumb into the bottom of each fig (opposite the stem end), making a pocket. Stuff each fig pocket with almond-chocolate mixture, and set stuffed figs on a baking sheet. Bake at 350° for 10 minutes or until warmed through.

4. Place warm figs on a serving platter, and sprinkle each with a pinch of salt. Serve immediately.

Sambal

See Appendix B.

Sansho

See Szechuan Pepper.

Santa Fe

See Appendix C.

Sassafras

A member of the botanical family *lauraceae* (laurel)

Also known as *gumbo filé* and *filé powder*

This North American tree (*Sassafras albidum*) with mitten-shaped leaves was first appreciated for the flavor of its bark. The roots, saplings, and leaves were boiled and steeped into a root beer–flavored tea.

Native American tribes were the first to discover the thickening power of the sassafras leaf. Today the leaf is dried and powdered and available as *filé*. This thickener has a slight root beer–camphor flavor. It should be used sparingly, as it's very powerful. If too much is added too soon to a recipe, the result is a thick, gluey paste. Add it at the end of cooking, off the heat, and let the residual heat thicken and flavor your pot.

Filé powder is available at most supermarkets. Look for sassafras bark on the Internet (worldspice.com).

Savory

From the botanical family *lamiaceae* (mint)

You can find several varieties, both annual and perennial, of savory (*satureja*). Summer savory is more delicate in flavor and has a shorter growing season. Winter savory is the stronger of the two and can be used for prolonged cooking with stronger flavors.

The leaves of this short plant have a peppery flavor, similar to rosemary and thyme. It's an important ingredient in several spice blends and is commonly used to flavor legumes and meat stuffing throughout northern and eastern Europe and Canada.

You can grow your own savory, or look for it from specialty growers at your farmers' market. Seeds are available at most nurseries.

Toasted Almonds with Savory and Garlic

These nuts are as at home at a classy cocktail party as they are at a casual football party.

2 TB. olive oil
3 cloves garlic, minced
¼ cup fresh savory, minced
1 lb. almonds, whole, raw, skin-on
¼ cup kasseri cheese

1. Preheat the oven to 350°F.

2. In a small saucepan, heat olive oil and add garlic. Sauté over high heat until garlic begins to color. Remove from heat, add savory, and set aside.

3. Spread almonds out on a baking sheet and toast for 8 to 10 minutes or until fragrant. Remove nuts from the oven and toss with oil mixture and cheese. Serve warm.

Scallion

See Onion.

Scotch Bonnet

See Appendix C.

Sereh

See Lemongrass.

Serrano

See Appendix C.

Sesame Seed

A member of the botanical family *pedaliaceae*

Also known as *goma* and *benne seeds*

Originally from North Africa, the sesame seed (*sesamum indicum*) comes from an annual plant with long bushy leaves and white or purple tubular flowers.

Both white and black seeds are commonly available, and both share a rich nutty flavor that's greatly improved by toasting. The seed is full of oil, which is used extensively throughout the world. Sesame oil has a short shelf life and should be bought in small quantities or stored in the refrigerator to prevent rancidity.

A common form of sesame is *tahini*, a paste used in Arabic and Greek cuisine. It's added to recipes, served as a spread and condiment, or sweetened for candy. The Japanese have a similar sesame paste called *neri-goma*. Sesame seeds are often also combined with honey in confectionery.

Benne is the Nigerian name for the seeds, and they are considered lucky in West Africa. Slaves brought them to the United States, and sesame seeds remain a popular baking ingredient throughout the South. The rest of the country knows them more commonly as a topping for breads, either on their own or mixed with other seeds.

Sesame seeds are widely available.

Sesame Brittle

This is a sweet-spicy treat. If you're not into heat, omit the cayenne.

1 cup sesame seeds
1 ½ cups sugar
½ cup corn syrup
⅓ cup cold water
3 TB. butter
1 tsp. salt
¼ tsp. baking soda
½ tsp. vanilla extract
½ tsp. cayenne

1. Preheat the oven to 200°F. Lightly butter a large sheet of waxed or parchment paper and set aside.

2. Spread sesame seeds on a baking sheet and keep warm in the oven while sugar boils.

3. In a large saucepan, combine sugar, corn syrup, and water, and bring to a boil. At the boil add butter, and cook to 300°F on a candy thermometer (hard-crack stage). Remove from heat, and add salt, baking soda, and vanilla extract. Stir until foamy, and immediately fold in warm sesame seeds and cayenne.

4. Quickly transfer to prepared wax paper and spread out as thin as possible. Cool completely and then break into pieces. Store in an airtight container at room temperature.

Shallot

See Onion.

Shiso

See Perilla.

Shoga

See Ginger.

Sichuan

See Szechuan Pepper.

Silphium

A member of the botanical family *apiacea* (parsley)

Also known as *silphion* and *laser*

This is an ancient variety of giant fennel—or so we think, because most agree that it's now extinct.

To the ancient Greek costal city of Cyrene, in what is now Libya, silphium was a crucial source of wealth. So revered was the herb that its image was depicted on their coins. As you might imagine, it was valued as a food, eaten like fennel is today, from the root to the seed. But this alone didn't make it popular. It was silphium's medicinal properties that made it the rock star of herbs. The resin extracted from its stalk was a reliable contraceptive, strictly regulated and exported across the ancient world.

Alas, the herb was difficult to propagate, and it was soon overharvested into extinction.

Sofrito

See Appendix B.

Sorrel

A member of the family *polygonaceae* (knotweed)

Also known as *sheep's sorrel* and *field sorrel*

The leaves of this perennial plant (*rumex acetosa*) are shaped like an arrow, and its spikes of red flowers make it one of the more recognizable weeds. Its rhizome can easily take over a field. Happily for food lovers, the leaves have a fresh acidic flavor, similar to a kiwi fruit. It's a welcome ingredient in salads, soups, and sauces. The sour bite sharpens the flavor of other ingredients and stimulates the appetite, much like vinaigrette. Additionally, juice from the leaves will curdle milk and has been used historically in place of rennet for cheese-making.

Jamaican red sorrel is an unrelated hibiscus, used in jellies and teas (it's the red in *red zinger*). Its flavor is very close to that of common sorrel and has often been used as a tart substitute for cranberry juice.

Sorrel is available at better supermarkets and farmers' markets. Red sorrel is available as a dried herb in ethnic markets.

Iced Sorrel

This is zingy-er than anything you can buy.

1 cup chopped fresh sorrel
¼ cup dried Jamaican sorrel
1 cinnamon stick
2 or 3 star anise
¼ cup brown sugar
Zest and juice of 1 Mexican lime
6 cups boiling water
2 or 3 cups ice

1. In a large saucepan, combine fresh sorrel, Jamaican sorrel, cinnamon stick, star anise, brown sugar, lime zest and juice, and water. Bring to a boil, remove from heat, and steep for 15 minutes. Strain into a large pitcher and add ice.
2. Chill, and serve over ice.

Spearmint

See Mint.

Spice *Parisienne*

See Appendix B.

Star Anise

A member of the botanical family *illiciaceae*

This small evergreen tree (*illicium verum*) native to China produces small yellow flowers; large, thick leaves; and star-shape fruit. This fruit, which contains hard shiny seeds, has a potent anise flavor. The flavor of both anise seed and star anise comes from the compound anethol, but the two plants are not botanically related.

The fruit has more flavor than the seeds, although both are packaged together in bits and pieces. Higher grades of star anise can be had for a price, but the grades are based on appearance only and have no effect on flavor. Finding a star intact with all its seeds in place is considered very good luck.

Star anise is a component of *Chinese five-spice powder* and a common addition many dishes, both savory and sweet.

Star anise is available in most supermarkets and Asian grocers.

Sumac

A member of the botanical family *anacardiaceae* (cashew)

This wild shrub (*rhus coriaria*) grows throughout Sicily, southern Italy, and Iran. Its clusters of tiny red berries are prized for their sour, astringent taste. Sun-dried and shriveled, sumac is ground into a purple powder and used to flavor meat for grilling, stews, rice, and sauces. It's an important ingredient in the Arabic spice blend *za'atar* (see Appendix B).

If you're using whole berries, be sure to soak them to soften before grinding.

Look for sumac at Middle Eastern markets or online (nirmalaskitchen.com).

Sumac Lamb Kebabs

Kebab means "skewer of roasted meat," and similar dishes are found throughout Eastern Europe, the Middle East, and Asia. Both metal and wooden skewers work fine, but be sure to soak wooden ones in warm water for at least 30 minutes so they won't ignite.

3 cloves garlic, minced
1 TB. fresh ginger, grated
1 TB. dried thyme
2 tsp. dried chile powder (such as ground dried New Mexico Chiles)
¼ cup sumac, ground
½ tsp. allspice, ground
1 tsp. kosher salt
3 lb. lamb leg or loin, trimmed and diced into 2-in. cubes

1. In a large zipper bag, combine garlic, ginger, thyme, dried chile powder, sumac, allspice, salt, and lamb. Seal the bag and toss to mix ingredients. Marinate in the refrigerator for 12 to 24 hours or overnight.

2. Preheat the grill to high heat.

3. Remove meat from marinade and discard marinade. Thread meat onto skewers, and grill, turning every 4 or 5 minutes, until desired doneness, about 15 minutes for medium-rare. Serve with yogurt and rice.

S

Sweet Pepper

A member of the botanical family *solanaceae* (nightshade)

Also known as *bell pepper*

Native to the tropical regions of the Americas, sweet peppers (*capsicum annuum*, *grossum group*) are like chile peppers in most ways, except the leaves and fruits are larger and the seeds are not spicy. The annual bushes produce fruits that ripen from green to all shades of red, yellow, orange, and purple.

Sweet peppers are eaten as vegetables, adding color to dishes such as soups, stews, salads, and pasta. Their flavor changes when roasted or grilled, adding charred, smoky flavor to recipes. Pimientos are roasted sweet red peppers that have been skinned, seeded, and preserved.

Like chile peppers, sweet peppers can be dried and ground into powder or preserved in brine.

Sweet peppers are commonly available at most markets.

See also Chile Pepper and Paprika.

Szechwan Pepper

A member of the botanical family *rutaceae* (citrus)

Also known as *sichuan pepper, fagara*, and *flower pepper*

This prickly ash tree (*zanthoxylum piperitum*) native to China bears no relation to peppers or chiles. The tiny berries' red outer pods are prized in cuisines throughout Asia. The flavor is tart and citrusy with a peppery numbness, similar to that of clove. The inner black seeds are bitter and should be avoided. Szechwan pepper is an ingredient in *Chinese five-spice powder*.

A related tree, the Japanese prickly ash, *sansho* or *kinome* (*zanthoxylum sancho*) is prized for its leaves as well as its buds.

Szechwan pepper is available at Asian markets.

Szechwan Pepper Melons

Try this refreshing snack by the pool on the hottest of hot days. Dice everything either large or small, but all the same size.

1 cup lime juice
1 tsp. sea salt
2 TB. Szechwan pepper
1 cup honeydew melon, peeled and diced
1 cup cantaloupe melon, peeled and diced
1 cup watermelon, peeled and diced
1 cup jicama, peeled and diced
1 mango, peeled and diced
1 cucumber, peeled, seeded, and diced

1. In a large bowl, stir together lime juice, salt, and Szechwan pepper. Add honeydew, cantaloupe, watermelon, jicama, mango, and cucumber, and toss together.

2. Marinate in the refrigerator for 30 minutes before serving.

Hot Stuff

You can peel a mango with a peeler, but I have an easier method: cut both halves off the center pit and use an extra large spoon to scoop out, like you would an avocado. The fruit can then be easily diced or sliced.

Tabasco

See Appendix C.

Tahini

See Sesame; Appendix B.

T

Tamari

See Appendix B.

Tamarind

A member of the botanical family *fabaceae* (bean)

Also known as *tamarindo*, *sampaloc*, and *Indian date*

Tamarind is a sticky brown pulp found inside a fuzzy brown bean pod. The pods are found on a tropical evergreen tree (*tamarindus indica*) originally from East Africa and grown now throughout Sudan, Madagascar, India, and Mexico. It's a huge tree, growing easily over 50 feet tall. Its bright green leaves are feathery, and the yellow flowers look like orchids.

Sweetened for candy or salted and dried into snacks, the tart pulp is as popular worldwide as lemons are in the West. It plays a prominent role in Philippine *adobo*, Indian *sambar*, and *pad thai* from Thailand. In Mexico, it's used to make candy and sweet beverages. (*Tamarind* is the nickname given to the traffic cops of Mexico city—because of their uniform color, not their fuzzy, lumpy shape.) Tamarind is a key ingredient in Worcestershire sauce, English brown sauce, and western barbecue sauce.

Purchase tamarind pods whole at Asian or Mexican markets, or find the pulp in brick form, with or without seeds. Steep the pulp in liquid and strain out the hard seeds before using.

Refreshing Tamarind Punch

This refreshingly tart drink is common south of the border. Make it a special treat at your next pinic or barbecue.

¼ cup tamarind pulp
½ cup sugar
8 cups water
1 mango, peeled and diced
2 oranges, sliced
1 pt. strawberries, trimmed and halved

1. In a large pitcher, combine tamarind pulp and sugar. Add water, and stir to blend. Add mango, oranges, and strawberries.

2. Chill for 30 minutes before serving over ice.

Tarragon

A member of the botanical family *asteraceae* (sunflower)

A native of Central Europe, tarragon (*artemisia dracunculus*) can be identified by its smooth and narrow, pointed leaves that look like grass growing up a thin stem.

The flavor is a pleasant, peppery anise, and used fresh and young it will perfume a dish wonderfully. Tarragon is favored in French cuisine and finds its way into many of the classic spice blends, as well being the backbone of *sauce béarnaise* (tarragon-infused hollandaise).

Tarragon doesn't dry well but is commonly preserved in oils and vinegars. You can also chop and freeze it in ice cubes or zipper bags. Its tiny green flowers are too pungent for most palettes.

Mexican tarragon is a separate species (*tagetes lucida*) with the same flavor.

Fresh tarragon is available at better supermarkets.

T

Tasmanian Pepper

A member of the botanical family *winteraceae* (winters bark)

Also known as *mountain pepper*

The berries, flowers, and leaves of this tree (*tasmania lanceolata*) are used in cuisines of the Southern Hemisphere, including Australia, New Zealand, and throughout the Pacific Rim.

Unrelated to black pepper, the taste of the dried berry is at first sweet, then spicy, then numbing. The leaves are dried and used like bay, with similar heat and a hint of citrus. When ground, the leaves have a thickening power similar to sassafras.

Tasmanian pepper is an integral component of Australian cuisine, commonly found in meat marinades. It's not readily available outside the country but can be ordered online (www.atasteofthebush.com.au).

Tasmanian Marinade

This is a great marinade for red meat and game. For seafood and poultry, replace the red wine with white, omit the Worcestershire sauce, and add some lime juice.

2 tsp. Tasmanian pepper, crushed
4 cloves garlic, minced
2 bay leaves, crushed
1 TB. Worcestershire sauce
1 tsp. kosher salt
2 cups dry red wine
2 cups olive oil
4 (6-oz.) beef or lamb steaks or chops

1. In a large bowl, combine Tasmanian pepper, garlic, bay, Worcestershire sauce, salt, wine, and olive oil. Mix well, and add meat. Marinate for 6 to 12 hours.

2. Preheat the grill to high heat.

3. Remove meat from marinade and discard marinade. Grill meat to desired doneness.

Thai Chile

See Appendix C.

Thyme

A member of the botanical family *lamiaceae* (mint)

There are more than 300 species of thyme (*thymus*), a low perennial shrub with twiggy stems, tiny oval leaves, and little white or pink blossoms. Many thyme plants are grown as a fragrant ornamental ground cover, but its usefulness in the kitchen cannot be overlooked.

Thyme is a standard ingredient in all Mediterranean and Middle Eastern cuisines. It's an important ingredient in several spice blends, including *Bouquet Garni, Herbes de Provençe, Za'atar,* and *Jerk* (see Appendix B).

One reason for thyme's popularity is that its flavor is strong and long lasting. *Thymol,* the main flavor compound, can be found in many other herbs. It holds up well to prolonged cooking and drying, and it complements all foods, sweet and savory.

Several interesting varieties of thyme can be found with distinctive aromas, indicated by the names, including caraway thyme, lavender thyme, mint thyme, oregano thyme, coconut thyme, lime thyme, and lemon thyme. With the exception of lemon, which is fairly common at farmers' markets, you should be able to find these unique species through specialty growers (mountainvalleygrowers.com).

Tiger Lily Bud

See Lily Bud.

Tonka Bean

A member of the botanical family *fabaceae* (bean)

Also known as *tonquin* and *tonqua*

The bean of this South American legume tree (*dipteryx odorata*) has a distinctive vanilla flavor, with some spicy cinnamon, clove, and almond undertones. It's used frequently in perfumes, soaps, potpourri, and incense and was for years a component of pipe tobacco. Because of its spicy-nutty nature, tonka is sometimes used as a substitute for *mahlab* or *bitter almond*.

But tonka beans are rarely seen as a vanilla substitute because it contains high levels of *coumarin,* a lethal anti-coagulant, also found in woodruff. You can reduce the amount of this compound by soaking the bean in alcohol and then allowing fermentation.

The beans are produced in Venezuela and Nigeria, but the Food and Drug Administration (FDA) has banned them for use as a food product in the United States. If you're daring, you can find them through online auctions for use in witchcraft and perfumery.

Turmeric

A member of the botanical family *zingiberaceae* (ginger)

It's obvious that turmeric (*curcuma domestica*) is related to ginger. It grows in knobby rhizomes and has a similar gingery flavor with a hint of pepper heat. But once you cut into a turmeric root, it's clear you don't have ginger. The flesh inside is bright yellow-orange, and that pigment lends its color to many foods, including curry powder, cheese, butter, pickles, and hot dog mustard.

Powdered turmeric is made from the smaller offshoots of the main rhizome that are boiled, peeled, dried, and ground. Turmeric is available fresh, but its flavor is no more remarkable than the easily attained powder. Both forms will stain your skin and clothes, so take care.

Curcumin, the main flavor component and a powerful antioxidant, is being studied for its possible beneficial effects on Alzheimer's disease, cystic fibrosis, colon cancer, breast cancer, and melanoma.

Turmeric is widely available at most supermarkets.

T

Pineapple Chutney

This is a great accompaniment to spicy curries, or spread it over cream cheese for an exotic appetizer spread.

1 large pineapple, peeled, cored, and diced small
1 large purple (Bermuda) onion, minced
2 cups brown sugar
2 cups cider vinegar
1 TB. Dijon mustard
Zest and juice of 1 orange
Zest and juice of 1 lime
1 TB. ground turmeric
1 cup pitted dates, chopped fine
1 cup zante currants
1 mango, peeled and diced fine
2 bananas, peeled and diced fine

1. In a large saucepan, combine pineapple, onion, and brown sugar. Bring to a boil, stirring, reduce heat to a simmer, and add vinegar, Dijon mustard, orange zest and juice, lime zest and juice, and turmeric. Simmer, covered, for 1 hour, stirring occasionally, until thick.

2. Remove the pan from heat, add dates and currants, cool to room temperature, and chill for 2 hours or overnight.

3. Just before serving, stir in mango and bananas.

Vanilla

A member of the botanical family *orchidaceae* (orchid)

Vanilla comes from a perennial climbing orchid (*vanilla planifolia*) from South America. Its white flowers are followed by long, green pods that have been treasured for centuries. The Aztecs used it to flavor their *xocolatl* (bitter water). The Spanish brought the beans to Europe, where it became all the rage.

The French tried unsuccessfully to propagate vanilla on the Islands of Bourbon (now Reunion) and Madagascar in the Indian Ocean. As it turns out, the orchid had been naturally pollinated by bees and hummingbirds only found in Mexico. To make matters more difficult, the orchids themselves open for only a short time. But where there's a will, there's a way. Vanilla orchids grown outside of Mexico are now hand-pollinated, which, combined with their complicated processing procedure, guarantees their high price.

When the green, unripe pods are picked they have little flavor or aroma. Not until they are cured and fermented do they emit the familiar fragrance. *Vanillin* is the flavor compound that we love, and on fine beans it can be seen on the surface as white dust.

You can find three vanilla beans on the market. Madagascar beans are used mainly for extract production. Tahitian beans have a nice aroma but less flavor and are used mainly for perfumes. Mexican beans are fat and fragrant. The extract from Mexico may sometimes contain *coumarin*, a substance from the *tonka bean* that is banned in the United States.

Look for beans that are thick and tough but pliable. To use vanilla beans, pound them first before splitting them lengthwise to crush the millions of inner mini-seeds and activate as much oil as possible. Once scraped, spent pods can be stored in sugar or steeped in rum to harness as much of the oil as possible.

Most people use vanilla in its extract form. It's made by macerating the vanilla beans in alcohol. Beware of Mexican vanilla extract, as it's often made with banned *tonka beans*. Vanilla paste, which is concentrated extract with added seeds, has become popular in recent years. There's also vanilla powder, which is dried, ground pods. Imitation vanilla is much weaker than the real thing. You can make vanilla extract at home by storing beans and spent pods in rum. Or store them in granulated sugar to absorb every bit of oil and then use the sugar in recipes for a vanilla essence.

V

Vanilla extract and beans are available at most markets. Look in better stores for better-quality extracts. Beans are expensive, but several online sources offer fair prices (thespicehouse.com, vanilla.com).

Aztec Hot Chocolate

This red-hot chocolate milk will warm your insides, to say the least.

6 dried pasilla chile pods
4 cups boiling water
1 qt. half-and-half
2 cinnamon sticks, crushed
1 lb. bittersweet chocolate, chopped fine
3 vanilla beans, split and scraped

1. Preheat the oven to 400°F.

2. Spread chile pods on a baking sheet and toast for 5 minutes or until soft. Cool, remove stems, and seeds (be careful of the capsicum). Cover chile pods with boiling water, and steep for 30 minutes.

3. In a large saucepan, combine half-and-half and cinnamon sticks. Simmer over medium heat for 5 minutes and remove from heat. Add chocolate and vanilla beans, and stir to melt.

4. Transfer soaked chiles to a blender. Blend until smooth, adding chocolate mixture slowly as needed. Combine chile paste with remaining chocolate mixture, stir, strain, and re-warm before serving.

Verbena

See Lemon Verbena.

Violet

A member of the botanical family *violaceae*

Violets (*viola odorata*) are native to Europe, Asia, and North Africa. They are recognized by their heart-shape, fuzzy-bottomed leaves and five-petal purple flowers, two of which have a fuzzy yellow beard. Violets have long been treasured for their fragrance, beauty, and healing power. Violet petals are high in vitamin C and were once worn on the head in garlands to prevent headaches.

Violet leaves and petals have a fragrant, nutty flavor and make a nice addition to salads and soups. The flowers are a favorite for candying and are crystallized to decorate confections. Dried petals are infused into tea and syrup and used to make pudding and jelly.

Look for violets at farmers' markets, or grow your own (canyoncreeknursery.com).

Violet Granita

Serve this refreshing summer dessert in chilled glasses so it doesn't melt too quickly.

2 cups violet petals
4 cups water
1 cup sugar
1 TB. lemon juice
¼ tsp. kosher salt

1. In a large saucepan, combine violet petals, water, sugar, lemon juice, and salt. Bring to a boil, remove from heat, and cool completely. Strain into a shallow baking dish and place in the freezer.

2. Use a fork to mix up ice crystals every 20 minutes until the entire pan is frozen and slushy, about 2 hours. Serve over sliced peaches or berries.

V

Wasabi

A member of the botanical family *brassicaceae* (mustard)

Also known as *Japanese horseradish*

The wasabi root (*wasabia japonica*) looks like the trunk of a tiny palm tree. It grows naturally in riverbeds and cool mountain streams, but its production in Japan is pretty secretive. Consequently, unless you're eating at high-end sushi bars, most wasabi in the United States is actually horseradish dyed green.

Unlike horseradish, it's the inner core of wasabi that's the most potent. The fresh root is either shredded very fine or dried and powdered. Like mustard, the vapors of wasabi burn the nasal passage, not the tongue, a shocking revelation to wasabi newcomers.

Real wasabi paste dries and loses flavor very quickly and is, therefore, served between the fish and rice on sushi to keep it moist and prevent evaporation.

Wasabi-joyu is a combination of wasabi and soy sauce, used for dipping sushi and sashimi. Wasabi leaves are eaten in salads or batter-fried in tempura. They have a similar but milder flavor.

Look for wasabi root, powdered, paste, or fresh at Japanese markets.

Wasabi Potato Salad

This chilled salad comes with a kick. If you're not very heat-tolerant, cut the wasabi in half.

2 lb. red new potatoes
1 tsp. salt
1 tsp. wasabi, fresh grated, paste, or powder with 1 tsp. water
1 tsp. honey
1 clove garlic, minced
1 small purple (Bermuda) onion, minced
¼ cup cilantro, chopped
¼ cup rice vinegar
1 tsp. sesame oil
1 cup olive oil
2 stalks celery, chopped fine
6 to 8 red radishes, chopped fine
2 cups Napa cabbage, shredded

1. In a large pot, boil red potatoes in salted water until tender. Drain, cool, and slice into quarters. Set aside.

2. In a large bowl, whisk together wasabi, honey, garlic, onion, cilantro, rice vinegar, and sesame oil. Slowly add olive oil while whisking. Add potatoes, celery, radishes, and cabbage, and toss together to combine.

3. Chill for 30 minutes before serving.

Watercress

See Cress.

Wintergreen

A member of the botanical family *ericaceae* (heather)

Also known as *eastern teaberry* and *boxberry*

The wintergreen (*gaultheria procumbens*) is in the same family as the cranberry, blueberry, and huckleberry. The small evergreen shrub has tapered oval leaves, white bell-shaped flowers, and red berries. The leaves have a minty compound, *mentyl-salicylate*, which is the natural oil of wintergreen. Before the advent of chewing gum, wintergreen leaves were chewed as a breath freshener. The berries are also used as flavoring for desserts and beverages.

Wintergreen is also a natural source of *triboluminescence*. When dried and mixed with a hard substance like sugar, it builds up an electrical charge. When the asymmetrical crystal bonds are broken, scratched, or rubbed, an electrical charge builds and generates light. Because wintergreen oil is fluorescent, it turns ultraviolet light to blue light. If you happen to be in the dark, you'll see this as blue sparks.

Fresh and dried wintergreen is hard to find—unless it's growing in your yard—because it's currently endangered in several states and parts of Canada. Wintergreen oil is available at some health food stores.

Woodruff

A member of the botanical family *rubiaceae* (bedstraw)

Also known as *wild baby's breath* and *sweet scented bedstraw*

The white starry flowers, tall stems, and successive parasol-like leaves of woodruff (*galium odoratum*) are all dried and used for teas, liqueurs, and potpourri. Its sweet scent, a combination of mown hay and vanilla, comes from *coumarin*, the same substance found in *tonka beans* and banned in the United States for its anti-coagulant properties. Unlike the tonka bean, woodruff contains a relatively small amount of coumarin.

Woodruff grows wild in the shady woods of Germany's Black Forest region. There, it's used abundantly in sausages, preserves, and traditional May Wine.

Woodruff is available on the Internet dried (comfycountrycreations.com) and in seed form (seeds.ca).

May Wine

On May 1, celebrate spring the German way with this traditional wine punch.

1 cup fresh woodruff, roughly chopped
1 pt. strawberries, washed, trimmed, and quartered
1 pt. raspberries
¼ cup sugar
1 bottle white Moselle or Rhine wine
2 cups sparkling water

1. In a large bowl, combine woodruff, strawberries, raspberries, and sugar. Toss together, and set aside at room temperature for 30 minutes to marinate.

2. Add wine and sparkling water, and stir to combine. Serve over ice.

Wormwood

A member of the botanical family *asteraceae* (sunflower)

Also known as *absinthe wormwood* and *grand wormwood*

W

Native of Europe, Asia, and North Africa, this perennial shrub (*artemisia absiuthium*) gets quite a lot of attention. That's because the fuzzy silver stems, carrotlike leaves, and yellow bell flowers contain *thujone*, a chemical compound blamed for the supposed hallucinatory effects of *absinthe*, a highly alcoholic distilled spirit flavored with many herbs, including *anise* and wormwood.

Wormwood's flavor is fairly bitter, but it was coveted for its medicinal effects by the ancient cultures of Egypt and Greece. It's used against tapeworm, rheumatism, gout, and the common cold, as an anesthetic, and an appetite stimulant. It has a fever-reducing effect and repels moths and fleas. Pure wormwood oil is very poisonous and can cause convulsions, coma, and death.

Wormwood plants are available in nurseries throughout the spring and summer.

Yarrow

A member of the botanical family *asteraceae* (sunflower)

Also known as *milefolium* and *woundwort*

Native to Europe, yarrow (*achillea millefolium*) was believed to heal wounds and stop the flow of blood, and Achilles carried it into battle to treat his soldiers on the battlefields of Troy.

Yarrow grows in California, China, and anywhere gardeners want butterflies. Its fuzzy feathery leaves and flat pods of flower clusters spring up on a single stem from perennial rhizomes.

Yarrow's sweet, slightly bitter, sage-flavored leaves are eaten as a vegetable, fresh or cooked like spinach. Its flower heads are used to flavor wines, spirits, and tea. Medieval brewers used yarrow in an herbal mixture called *gruit*, which was used to bitter beer before hops were used.

Yarrow is available at most nurseries and on the Internet in tea form (kalyx.com).

Za'atar, Zahtar

See Appendix B.

Zedoary

A member of the botanical family *zingiberaceae* (ginger)

Also known as *white turmeric*

Native to India and Indonesia, zedoary (*curcuma zedoaria*) was known in sixth-century Europe. Its pink rhizomes have a musky, mango flavor, and are used in perfumes and spirit distillation.

Like ginger, zedoary can be grated and used fresh, or dried and used as a powder. If you chew it fresh it will turn your spit yellow. In powder form it is a common addition to pickles and curries, and the rhizome itself is often pickled as a condiment.

Look for zedoary in Indian and Asian markets and on the Internet (spiceworld.uk.com).

Zest

Exocarp

Zest is the outermost rind, or *exocarp* of citrus fruit. The outer colorful skin contains the essential oils and flavor compound that flavor the fruit itself and add strong citrus flavor to foods.

Zest from all the citrus fruits is used in sweet and savory recipes of all kinds. Additionally, zest can be cooked in sugar and eaten as candy, or peeled, dried, pulverized, and added as a spice.

Avoid the white pith underneath the zest but outside the fruit pulp. It's bitter.

Z

Glossary

absinthe   A distilled spirit flavored with herbs, most notably wormwood. Prohibited in many countries based on rumors of psychedelic and addictive properties, absinthe has recently been allowed back in to some European countries.

amaretto   An Italian liqueur with the distinctive flavor of bitter almonds.

annual   A plant that germinates, flowers, and dies within a single growing season.

anthocyanin   Red and blue pigments that occur in the plant kingdom.

aquavit   A Scandinavian distilled spirit flavored with herbs and spices, most commonly caraway.

biennial   A plant that takes up to 24 months to complete its life cycle.

boba   An Asian beverage made originally with sweetened black tea, condensed milk, and large tapioca pearls, which sit at the bottom of the cup and drinkers suck up through oversize straws. Variations include fruit flavors.

botulism   A potentially fatal foodborne illness, caused by ingestion of the nerve toxin *botulin*, most commonly occurring from improperly canned foods.

bouquet garni An aromatic sachet of herbs and spices used in all kinds of classic French stocks, stews, and soups. The classic preparation uses a wilted leek green to wrap a bay leaf, parsley stem, thyme sprig, 3 peppercorns, and a clove. Today, the ingredients are often wrapped in cheesecloth. The bundle is tied with a long piece of kitchen twine and secured to the pot handle for easy removal.

brown sauce A malt vinegar–based condiment flavored primarily with tamarind and Worcestershire sauce, popular in the United Kingdom. Elsewhere in the world, the term refers to a meat-based sauce or gravy, thickened with flour or roux.

capsaicin The compound found in chiles that gives them their fiery heat (see Appendix C).

coumarin A chemical compound found in plants, including the *tonka bean* and *woodruff*. It is commonly found as a flavorant in artificial vanilla and pipe tobacco. It has been banned as a food additive in the United States because it's considered mildly toxic to the kidneys.

dal, dahl An Indian dish made from dried beans (*pulses*), often puréed and served alongside curry.

E. coli This bacterium (*Escherichia coli*) is naturally occurring in the human intestinal tract, but certain strains can cause serious gastrointestinal distress, and in some cases, death. It is most commonly caused by undercooked meats and cross-contamination.

exocarp The botanical name for the tough outer skin of fruit.

fish sauce A liquid condiment and ingredient similar in appearance to soy sauce. Popular in Asia, fish sauce was known in ancient Rome.

foie gras A French delicacy, foie gras is the enlarged liver of a goose or duck.

frankincense This ancient aromatic resin from the *boswellia* tree is prized for its aroma and used in perfume and incense.

game meat Game meat comes from animals who are wild, or were historically wild, such as venison, rabbit, buffalo, and bear. The term *gamey* refers to the strong flavor of the meat.

ghee   A clarified butter used in Indian cuisine in which all the moisture has been evaporated and the fat itself browns and takes on a nutty flavor.

grow light   These electric lamps produce light specifically to encourage photosynthesis. Spectrums of light can be adjusted to benefit the plant throughout its lifecycle.

gruit   An herb mixture used to add bitterness and flavoring to beer before the common use of hops.

hamentaschen, hamentash, oznei haman   This Ashkenazi cookie, which is shaped like a tri-corner hat, is eaten during the Jewish holiday of Purim. It is classically filled with a sweetened poppy seeds, but it is also seen with dried fruit, jams, and chocolate.

injera   A spongy, pancakelike Ethiopian bread, used as a utensil to scoop up the traditional spicy stews.

julienne   A thin, matchstick-size knife cut, typically $^1/_8$-inch thick, used for many different foods.

legume   A plant with long seed pods containing beans or seeds, such as lentils, peanuts, and soybeans.

macerate   To soak food, usually fruit, in liquid to infuse flavor.

mirepoix   A blend of aromatic vegetables used in stocks, soups, and stew. Typically, the mix consists of carrot, onion, and celery sautéed in butter.

mortar   A bowl, usually made of ceramic or stone, into which spices, herbs, vegetables, and pharmaceuticals are put to be crushed by a pestle, a hard instrument shaped like a small baseball bat.

Moselle   Dry white wine produced along the Moselle River in Southwest Germany, made from *Riesling* and sometimes *Traminer* grape varieties.

mukhwas   Brightly colored, sugar-coated seeds, usually fennel, anise, and sesame, served in India as an after-dinner digestive aid and breath freshener.

myrrh This dried resin from the *commiphora* tree has been used for perfume and incense since ancient times and was worth as much as gold. Today, it's also used in skin ointments and some distilled spirits.

paneer This fresh, un-aged Indian cheese is similar in consistency and taste to fresh mozzarella.

panella A fresh, un-aged Mexican cheese, fairly bland and firm, similar to paneer.

perennial A plant that lives for several years, perennials may possess woody stems, bulbs, or rhizomes.

pulse The dried seeds of beans and peas, also called *legumes*.

rancidity A foul odor and taste of spoiled oil, or products containing oil, brought about by exposure to light and heat. Refrigeration prevents it.

Rhine wine Several varieties of dry white wine produced in the German Rhine River Valley.

rhizome Although often confused with a root, a rhizome is actually a bulbous, underground stem that grows horizontally at the surface of the soil.

sweet anise Another name for *fennel* bulb, although the actual herb *anise* is unrelated to fennel.

tandoor Used in Indian cuisine, this cylindrical clay charcoal oven cooks food at extremely high temperatures, retaining moisture, flavor, and nutritional benefits.

tapioca A starch extracted from the root of the cassava plant. Ground into flour or formed into pearls, it is used as a thickening agent.

thujone This chemical, found in *wormwood* and other herbs, has been blamed for supposed hallucinatory effects of the distilled spirit *absinthe*. Recently, however, it has been determined that the thujone does not induce hallucinations.

thymol This aromatic chemical compound is the main constituent in the oil of *thyme*.

tomatillos   This small, acidic green fruit with a paperlike husk is commonly mistaken for green tomatoes, but is in fact closely related to the gooseberry.

triboluminescence   This phenomenon of light generation occurs when certain hard crystal substances are broken or scratched.

vanillin   This is one of the organic compounds responsible for vanilla flavor and is the main component of vanilla extract.

zante currants   These tiny raisins are made from dried miniature seedless grapes.

Appendix B

Spice Blends and Condiments

The following list of spice blends and condiments are meant to get you started on your global culinary journey. There are thousands of other blends and condiments, for food and drink, from every country in the world. And there are hundreds of variations on most of the blends I've included here. Every region, spice vendor, family, and cook has a different interpretation of these mixes, and that's just fine. It's what makes cooking interesting.

Spice Blends

There are three basic methods of mixing spice blends: simply stirring ingredients together; stirring and then grinding; and stirring, toasting, and grinding. Stirring, you know about. There's not much expertise I can add to that.

Grinding isn't that hard either, but I have a few tips that might make it easier for you. I prefer to use a coffee grinder. It's small, which forces the spices through the blade more often than a larger food processor or blender does, producing a finer, more even grind. I recommend you get a separate grinder just for spices. I have had some mighty weird-tasting coffee after a particularly spicy kitchen escapade.

When I'm feeling historic, I enjoy grinding in a mortar. The result is rougher but more satisfying. There's also a method the French call *mignonette* in which you crush whole spices with the flat bottom of a frying pan. Don't whack the pan onto the spices like a fly swatter, but rather use the pan to knead or rub the spices into submission. This is typically done with pepper, but in a pinch, it works for everything.

Toasting is a vital stage in cooking with spices. Heat releases the spice oils, which changes their flavor, usually for the better. Use a dry pan, preferably made of iron, as it conducts heat evenly. Add the spices to the pan, and keep them moving by shaking the pan or stirring. This constant movement ensures the spices toast evenly. As soon as they become fragrant, the toasting is done. Be careful, as these tiny seeds and berries can burn very quickly. Remove them from the heat *and the pan*. Remember, the pan is still hot and it keeps cooking the spices until you remove them.

> **Hot Stuff**
>
> Cool the spices before you grind them. They are easier to handle, and they emit fewer fumes.

There are blends in the following pages that are not toasted first because the recipes they're typically used in call for the ground spices to be toasted in oil. And some blends simply do not benefit from toasting, such as the *Sweet Spices Mix* for baking.

Sometimes the toasting is done in stages, giving each ingredient in the blend the perfect cooking time to release its maximum flavor. But when we're talking about blends of 10 to 20 spices and herbs—who has that kind of time? Just keep in mind that small particles of spice cook faster than large ones. If your mixture includes a powder, either add it to the pan last, or watch that powder carefully while it cooks and use it as an indication of doneness for the rest of the mix.

Tidbit

The names of these blends can be intimidating, but don't let a lot of consonants scare you away. To get authentic flavor, you need the authentic spice blends, but you don't have to pronounce them correctly. And yes, I have called these recipes *spice* blends, even though they contain herbs. I use the term *spice* as an adjective and a verb here, because I want to help you *spice* up your life.

Baharat (North Africa)

This powder is fried to release its oils before being used in recipes. It's a common flavoring for meats in Lebanon, Syria, Jordan, and Israel.

¼ cup paprika
3 TB. black peppercorns
3 TB. coriander seed
3 TB. cumin seed
1 TB. allspice
1 TB. cardamom
1 TB. dried red chiles
1 TB. dried mint
1 tsp. clove
1 tsp. nutmeg
2 cinnamon sticks

1. In a small bowl, combine paprika, black peppercorns, coriander seed, cumin seed, allspice, cardamom, dried red chiles, dried mint, clove, nutmeg, and cinnamon sticks.

2. Grind to a fine powder using a coffee grinder.

Barbecue Rub (USA)

Rub this blend on beef, pork, or poultry and then marinate 6 to 12 hours prior to slow cooking over open fire. It can also be used as barbecue sauce seasoning.

½ cup chili powder
½ cup garlic powder
½ cup onion powder
½ cup cumin seed
½ cup dried oregano
½ cup dried thyme
¼ cup kosher salt
¼ cup celery seed
¼ cup black peppercorns
¼ cup yellow mustard seed
¼ cup paprika
2 TB. whole cloves
2 TB. cayenne

1. In a small bowl, combine chili powder, garlic powder, onion powder, cumin seed, dried oregano, dried thyme, kosher salt, celery seed, black peppercorns, yellow mustard seed, paprika, whole cloves, and cayenne.

2. Grind to a fine powder using a coffee grinder.

Variation: For Barbecue Sauce, combine 1 cup Barbecue Rub with 1 cup brown sugar, 1 cup tomato sauce, ¼ cup tamarind paste, and 3 tablespoons cider vinegar.

Berbere (Ethiopia)

This blend is essential to authentic Ethiopian food. It's used on meats and combined with onions and oil for use as a curry paste.

¼ cup ginger
¼ cup cumin
¼ cup coriander
¼ cup cardamom
¼ cup fenugreek
¼ cup paprika
2 TB. allspice berries
2 TB. red chiles
2 TB. nutmeg
2 cinnamon sticks
1 TB. kosher salt

1. In a small bowl, combine ginger, cumin, coriander, cardamom, fenugreek, paprika, allspice berries, red chiles, nutmeg, cinnamon sticks, and kosher salt.

2. Toast in a dry skillet, and grind to a fine powder using a coffee grinder.

Bouquet Garni (France)

Dangle this packet of herbs in soups and stocks to infuse the essence of France. The twine makes it easily removable and keeps spent herbs from clouding your creation.

1 sprig parsley
1 sprig thyme
1 sprig marjoram
1 bay leaf
3 peppercorns
1 whole clove

1. Wrap parsley, thyme, marjoram, bay leaf, peppercorns and clove in a wilted leek leaf or cheesecloth sachet and tie with kitchen twine.

2. Toss in your favorite soup or stock.

Cajun Spice (USA)

Use this spiced-up mix when you feel like a taste of the Big Easy.

1 cup bay leaves
1 cup paprika
¼ cup dried thyme
¼ cup dried oregano
¼ cup yellow mustard seed
¼ cup white peppercorns
¼ cup onion powder
¼ cup garlic powder
2 TB. cumin seed
2 TB. celery seed
2 TB. cayenne

1. In a small bowl, combine bay leaves, paprika, dried thyme, dried oregano, yellow mustard seed, white peppercorns, onion powder, garlic powder, cumin seed, celery seed, and cayenne.

2. Grind to a fine powder using a coffee grinder.

Chili Powder (USA)

Combine this mix with chopped or ground meat for chili. It also makes a great barbecue rub.

½ cup each paprika
½ cup dried red New Mexico chiles
½ cup cumin
¼ cup each garlic powder
¼ cup onion powder
¼ cup dried oregano
¼ cup dried thyme
2 TB. sesame seed
2 TB. allspice berries
2 TB. kosher salt
3 cinnamon sticks

1. In a small bowl, combine paprika, dried red New Mexico chiles, cumin, garlic powder, onion powder, dried oregano, dried thyme, sesame seed, allspice berries, kosher salt, and cinnamon sticks.

2. Grind to a coarse powder using a coffee grinder.

Chinese Five-Spice Powder (China)

This blend is commonly used to flavor duck, chicken, pork, and fish.

¼ cup black peppercorns
2 TB. fennel seed
8 star anise
1 tsp. whole cloves
2 cinnamon sticks

1. In a small bowl, combine black peppercorns, fennel seed, star anise, cloves, and cinnamon sticks.

2. Toast in a dry skillet before grinding to a fine powder using a coffee grinder.

Chaat Masala (India)

Chaat means "to lick," and this tangy blend makes you lick your lips, thanks to the amchoor. It's suitable as a topping for everything from curries to fruit salads.

¼ cup black peppercorns
3 TB. cumin seed, dried mint
2 TB. amchoor
2 TB. mint
2 TB. kosher salt
1 TB. cubeb pepper
1 TB. ajwain
1 TB. ginger
1 TB. asafetida
1 TB. cayenne

1. In a small bowl, combine black peppercorns, cumin seed, dried mint, amchoor, mint, kosher salt, cubeb pepper, ajwain, ginger, asafetida, and cayenne.

2. Toast in a dry skillet before grinding to a fine powder using a coffee grinder.

Char Masala (India)

This toasted blend is a common ingredient of Indian and North African rice dishes.

2 TB. cumin seed
1 TB. cardamom seed
1 tsp. allspice
1 crushed cinnamon stick

1. In a small bowl, combine cumin seed, cardamom seed, allspice, and cinnamon stick.
2. Toast in a dry skillet before grinding to a fine powder using a coffee grinder.

Corning Spice (Great Britain)

Use this blend for pickling and preserving meat or vegetables.

½ cup coriander seed
½ cup red chiles
½ cup mustard seed
½ cup bay leaves
¼ cup white peppercorns
¼ cup celery seed
¼ cup allspice berries
¼ cup grated ginger
2 cinnamon sticks, crushed

1. In a small bowl, combine coriander seed, red chiles, mustard seed, bay leaves, white peppercorns, celery seed, allspice berries, grated ginger, and cinnamon sticks.
2. Wrap mixture in a cheesecloth sachet, and use to infuse brines or vinegars.

Curry Powder (India)

Each region of India has its typical curry spice blends, and each cook within that region has his or her own interpretation of those blends. What's more, Indian spices are rarely premixed in India like they are here. This is a very generalized blend.

¼ cup coriander seed
¼ cup cumin seed
¼ cup brown mustard seed
3 TB. turmeric
3 TB. fenugreek
3 TB. black peppercorns
2 TB. ground ginger
2 TB. cardamom seed
1 TB. dried chiles
2 cinnamon sticks

1. In a small bowl, combine coriander seed, cumin seed, brown mustard seed, turmeric, fenugreek, black peppercorns, ground ginger, cardamom seed, dried chiles, and cinnamon sticks.

2. Grind to a coarse powder using a coffee grinder.

Dukka (Egyptian)

Use this spice blend when cooking meats, or mix it with olive oil as a dip for bread.

¼ cup sesame seed
¼ cup hazelnuts
¼ cup coriander seed
3 TB. cumin seed
3 TB. black pepper
3 TB. dried thyme
1 TB. kosher salt

1. In a small bowl, combine sesame seed, hazelnuts, coriander seed, cumin seed, black pepper, dried thyme, and kosher salt.
2. Toast in a dry skillet before grinding to a fine powder using a coffee grinder.

Fines Herbes (France)

Sprinkle these chopped fresh herbs onto seafood, poultry, stews, soups, vegetables, or salads.

Fresh chopped parsley
Fresh chopped chervil
Fresh chopped chives
Fresh chopped tarragon
Fresh chopped marjoram (optional)
Fresh chopped savory (optional)
Fresh chopped burnet (optional)

1. Combine equal amounts of chervil, chives, tarragon, marjoram, savory, and burnet.
2. Mix well.

Fish Boil (USA)

Use this blend to flavor boiling liquid for crab, shrimp, lobster, and crayfish. It can also be ground into a fine powder and added to soups, stews, and seafood dishes like shrimp salad or crab puffs.

1 cup sea salt
1 cup paprika
1 cup celery seed
1 cup bay leaves
3 TB. allspice berries
3 TB. white peppercorns
3 TB. yellow mustard seed
3 TB. grated ginger root
2 TB. cayenne pepper
2 TB. whole cloves
1 TB. cardamom seed
2 cinnamon sticks
1 whole nutmeg, crushed

1. In a small bowl, combine sea salt, paprika, celery seed, bay leaves, allspice berries, white peppercorns, yellow mustard seed, grated ginger root, cayenne pepper, cloves, cardamom seeds, cinnamon sticks, and nutmeg.

2. Mix well.

Garam Masala (Indian)

Garam means "warm" or "hot," but this is not a spicy hot. Rather, it makes you feel warm after you've eaten it. Also, it's toasted prior to grinding.

1 cup bay leaves
½ cup cumin seed
¼ cup coriander seed
3 TB. black pepper
3 TB. cardamom seed
3 TB. cloves
3 TB. ground nutmeg

1. In a small bowl, combine bay leaves, cumin seed, coriander seed, black pepper, cardamom seed, cloves, and nutmeg.

2. Toast in a dry skillet before grinding to a fine powder using a coffee grinder.

Gâlat Dagga (Tunisia)

This 5-spice blend is commonly used for Arabic stews.

¼ cup black peppercorns
¼ cup cloves
3 TB. grains of paradise
3 TB. grated nutmeg
1 cinnamon stick

1. In a small bowl, combine black peppercorns, cloves, grains of paradise, nutmeg, and cinnamon stick.

2. Grind to a coarse powder using a coffee grinder.

Gomashio (Japanese)

This simple combination tops Japanese rice dishes of all kinds.

¼ cup sesame seed
1 TB. sea salt

1. In a small bowl, combine sesame seed and sea salt.
2. Toast in a dry skillet.

Herbed Pepper (USA)

This is a nice change of pace for vegetables and meats.

¼ cup white pepper
¼ cup black pepper
1 TB. thyme
1 TB. savory
1 TB. oregano
1 TB. rosemary

1. In a small bowl, combine white pepper, black pepper, thyme, savory, oregano, and rosemary.
2. Mix well.

Herbes de Provençe (France)

This classic blend can be made with fresh or dried versions of these herbs.

¼ cup chervil
¼ cup marjoram
¼ cup tarragon
¼ cup basil
2 TB. thyme
2 TB. lavender

1. In a small bowl, combine chervil, marjoram, tarragon, basil, thyme, and lavender.
2. If fresh, mince all ingredients together. If dry, simply stir.

Italian Spice Mix (Italy)

Use this seasoning blend in sauces, sausages, vegetables, or as a marinade rub.

¼ cup fresh chopped oregano
¼ cup fresh chopped basil
¼ cup ground fennel seed
2 TB. fresh chopped sage
2 TB. fresh chopped rosemary
3 cloves garlic, minced

1. In a small bowl, combine oregano, basil, fennel seed, sage, rosemary, and garlic.
2. Mix well.

Jerk (Jamaica)

Use this traditional blend to marinate turkey, chicken, fish, or pork.

½ cup ground allspice
½ cup dried thyme
½ cup fresh grated ginger
½ cup fresh minced garlic
½ cup fresh minced onion
½ cup brown sugar
3 TB. ground coriander
3 TB. ground nutmeg
2 TB. ground clove
2 TB. kosher salt
2 cinnamon sticks, crushed
1 or 2 scotch bonnet peppers, minced
½ cup vegetable oil
½ cup rum

1. In a small bowl, combine allspice, dried thyme, ginger, garlic, onion, brown sugar, coriander, nutmeg, clove, kosher salt, cinnamon sticks, scotch bonnet peppers, vegetable oil, and rum.

2. Mix well.

3. Add meat and marinate 2 or 3 hours, or overnight, before cooking.

Kala Masala (India)

Kala means "black," and that's an apt description of the color and flavor after this blend has been toasted.

1 guajillo chile
¼ cup black pepper
3 TB. cardamom seed
3 TB. cumin seed
2 TB. shredded coconut
2 TB. nutmeg
2 TB. cloves
1 TB. anise seed
1 TB. poppy seed
1 TB. sesame seed
1 TB. turmeric
1 TB. amchoor
5 bay leaves
2 cinnamon sticks

1. In a small bowl, combine guajillo chile, black pepper, cardamom seed, cumin seed, coconut, nutmeg, cloves, anise seed, poppy seed, sesame seed, turmeric, amchoor, bay leaves, and cinnamon sticks.

2. Toast in a dry skillet before grinding to a fine powder using a coffee grinder.

Khmeli Suneli (Georgia)

This blend is used in Georgia and throughout the Caucuses with slow-braised stews of mutton, beef, or chicken.

¼ cup dill seed
¼ cup fenugreek
¼ cup dried marjoram
¼ cup bay leaves
3 TB. coriander seed
3 TB. dried peppermint
3 TB. celery seed
3 TB. dried parsley
2 TB. turmeric
2 TB. dried savory
2 TB. dried basil
2 TB. dried thyme
2 TB. black peppercorns

1. In a small bowl, combine dill seed, fenugreek, dried marjoram, bay leaves, coriander seed, dried peppermint, celery seed, dried parsley, turmeric, dried savory, dried basil, dried thyme, and black peppercorns.

2. Grind to a fine powder using a coffee grinder.

Mulled Wine Spice (Europe)

Steep this blend in a full-bodied red wine and simmer for 30 minutes.

2 TB. anise seed
2 TB. allspice
2 TB. cardamom
2 TB. fresh grated ginger
1 tsp. whole cloves
2 cinnamon sticks
Zest of 1 orange

1. In a small bowl, combine anise seed, allspice, cardamom, ginger, cloves, cinnamon sticks, and orange zest.

2. Mix well.

3. Wrap mixture in a cheesecloth sachet.

Panch Phoran (India)

This Bengali 5-spice powder is fried in oil to release flavors and then added to lentils, beans, potatoes, and fish.

2 TB. fenugreek
2 TB. nigella seed
2 TB. yellow mustard seed
2 TB. fennel seed
2 TB. cumin seed

1. In a small bowl, combine fenugreek, nigella seed, yellow mustard seed, fennel seed, and cumin seed.

2. Grind to a fine powder using a coffee grinder.

Quatre-Epice (France)

These four spices were traditionally combined for the ancient French spice bread, *pain d'epice*.

2 TB. white pepper
2 TB. nutmeg
2 TB. cinnamon
2 TB. ginger
Whole cloves (optional)

1. In a small bowl, combine white pepper, nutmeg, cinnamon, ginger and cloves (if using).

2. Grind to a fine powder using a coffee grinder.

Ras el Hanout (North Africa)

This is a Moroccan mix whose name means "top of the shop."
There's no specific recipe, but it's the spice merchant's best blend.

¼ cup cardamom seed
¼ cup allspice berries
¼ cup cumin seed
¼ cup coriander seed
3 TB. dried chile pods
3 TB. black peppercorns
3 TB. cubebs
3 TB. grains of paradise
2 TB. whole cloves
2 TB. grated nutmeg
2 TB. rose petals
2 TB. grated galangal
2 cinnamon sticks

1. In a small bowl, combine cardamom seeds, allspice berries, cumin seed, coriander seeds, dried chile pods, black peppercorns, cubebs, grains of paradise, cloves, nutmeg, rose petals, grated galangal, and cinnamon sticks.

2. Toast in a dry skillet before grinding to a fine powder using a coffee grinder.

Salt Substitute (USA)

This is for those who need to watch their sodium intake.

1 TB. cayenne
1 TB. onion powder
1 TB. garlic powder
1 TB. dried savory
1 TB. dried thyme
1 TB. dried oregano
1 TB. dried sage
1 TB. nutmeg
1 TB. crushed black pepper
Grated zest of 1 lemon

1. In a small bowl, combine cayenne, onion powder, garlic powder, dried savory, dried thyme, dried oregano, dried sage, nutmeg, crushed black pepper, and lemon zest.

2. Mix well.

Hot Stuff

Be sure to use garlic and onion powder, not garlic and onion salt, which would defeat the purpose of a salt substitute.

Sambar Podi (Indian)

This powder is used for *sambar,* a Southern Indian soup that's also served over rice as an accompaniment to curry.

1 cup *chana dal* (small split chickpea)
¼ cup cumin seed
¼ cup coriander seed
¼ cup black peppercorn
¼ cup crushed red chiles
1 TB. turmeric
1 TB. amchoor
1 TB. turmeric
1 tsp. asafetida
1 cinnamon stick, crushed

1. In a small bowl, combine chana dal, cumin seed, coriander seed, black peppercorn, red chiles, turmeric, amchoor, turmeric, asafetida, and cinnamon stick.

2. Toast in a dry skillet before grinding to a fine powder using a coffee grinder.

Spice *Parisienne* (France)

This is a typical French blend, used as a rub on meats or to flavor stews, soups, and vegetables. It also goes by the name *épices fines,* which means "fine spices."

2 TB. black peppercorns
2 TB. white peppercorns
2 TB. crushed bay leaves
1 TB. sea salt
1 TB. grated nutmeg
1 TB. dried thyme
1 TB. ground ginger
1 tsp. whole cloves
2 cinnamon sticks

1. In a small bowl, combine black peppercorns, white peppercorns, bay leaves, sea salt, nutmeg, dried thyme, ginger, cloves, and cinnamon sticks.

2. Grind to a coarse powder using a coffee grinder.

Spiced Salt (USA)

Use this blend on meat, fish, and root vegetables before roasting or grilling.

1 lb. kosher salt
¼ cup black pepper
¼ cup coriander seed
¼ cup bay leaves
¼ cup whole cloves
¼ cup dried basil

1. In a small bowl, combine kosher salt, black pepper, coriander seed, bay leaves, whole cloves, dried basil.

2. Mix well.

Sweet Spice Mix (USA)

This is great for pumpkin pie, gingerbread, or baked apples.

¼ cup nutmeg
2 TB. grated ginger
2 TB. allspice berries
2 TB. cardamom seed
1 tsp. black pepper
1 tsp. whole clove
3 cinnamon sticks

1. In a small bowl, combine nutmeg, ginger, allspice berries, cardamom seed, black pepper, whole clove, and cinnamon sticks.

2. Grind to a fine powder using a coffee grinder.

Za'atar (Middle East)

This blend is popular in Lebanon, Turkey, Jordon, Syria, and North Africa. It's commonly mixed with olive oil and used as a dip for bread or a marinade for olives.

¼ cup sesame seed
¼ cup thyme
¼ cup sumac
1 TB. dill seed
1 TB. anise seed
1 TB. dried oregano
1 TB. kosher salt
Zest of 2 lemons

1. In a small bowl, combine sesame seed, thyme, sumac, dill seed, anise seed, dried oregano, kosher salt, and lemon zest.

2. Grind to a fine powder using a coffee grinder.

Condiments

This list provides descriptions of condiments mentioned throughout this book. It does not provide recipes, because most are long and involved. Production often includes fermentation, long reduction, or just plain nasty ingredients. But like spices and herbs, these condiments lend flavor to foods. And they're interesting, to boot!

Amazu Shoga   Japanese pickled ginger, served with sushi.

Anchoiade   A paste from Provençe made with anchovies, olive oil, garlic, capers, and herbs, used as a spread for bread and a dip for vegetables.

Bagoong   A Philippine paste made from fermented ground shrimp, used in many curries, sauces, and as a condiment.

Beni Shoga   A Japanese pickled ginger, colored red by *perilla* leaf. It's commonly served with fried noodles and Gyūdon (beef bowl), a popular fast food that consists of a bowl of rice topped with savory beef and onions.

Bitters   A spirit distilled from aromatic herbs, bark, roots, seeds, and citrus. It is used to flavor *aperitifs* and cocktails.

Cassareep   A bitter sugar syrup from the West Indies made from cassava juice, brown sugar, and spices. It's commonly used in a Caribbean stew called pepper pot.

Fish Sauce   A condiment made from fermented raw or dried fish. There are many versions around the world made from specific fish and according to specific techniques. Many recipes include other flavorings, including spices and herbs. Although it may smell fishy, the fish flavor cooks away, adding a rich, deep flavor to recipes.

Garum   An ancient Roman fish sauce made from fish innards, vinegar, spices, and wine, Garum was considered an aphrodisiac, and as such was reserved for the upper class. It's still produced in Spain and is favored as an alternative to salt, as it contains taste-enhancing glutamates.

Gremolata An Italian condiment made from chopped lemon zest, parsley, garlic, and sometimes anchovies. It's the classic accompaniment to the braised veal dish Osso Bucco.

Harissa Sauce A Tunisian hot paste made from chiles, garlic, cumin, coriander, caraway, and olive oil. It's an important ingredient in North Africa and a typical accompaniment to couscous.

Hoisin A sweet Chinese sauce made from fermented soybeans, garlic, vinegar, sweet potato, and chiles used as a recipe ingredient, barbecue sauce, and as a condiment.

Kecap Manis A thick soy sauce from Indonesia flavored with star anise, garlic, and palm sugar. It's used in recipes as a replacement for traditional soy sauce and as a dipping sauce.

Kochu Chang/Gocgujang A Korean chile bean paste made from fermented soybeans, dried chiles, and garlic used to marinate meat, stews, and *bibimbab*, a popular dish of rice covered with vegetables, meat, and an egg.

Mirin A Japanese rice wine used as a recipe ingredient and condiment.

Miso There are many varieties of this paste made from fermented soybeans injected with a fungus derived from rice, barley, or soybeans. After aging, the result is salty, sweet, and earthy. It's used to flavor broth, sauces, dressing, dips, and as a condiment.

Nam Pla A fish sauce from Thailand, usually made from anchovies.

Natto A popular breakfast food in Japan made from steamed, fermented soybeans, mashed into a sticky, cheeselike consistency, and commonly eaten on top of rice.

Nuoc Mam A fish sauce from Vietnam made from anchovies and other small fish.

Persillade A French combination of equal parts chopped garlic and parsley. *Persil* is the French word for "parsley."

Ponzu A Japanese sauce made from mirin, rice vinegar, *konbu*, and dried flaked tuna (*katsuobushi*). It's used as a dip, marinade, and condiment.

Preserved Lemons   A North African condiment, in which lemons are sliced open and packed in salt. As they age, the salt mixes with the acidic lemon juice and softens the lemons. Sometimes spices are added, including red pepper, coriander, clove, cinnamon, and bay.

Rakkyo   A type of Japanese shallot, usually pickled in vinegar.

Sambal   A condiment made from chile peppers, sugar, and salt. There are many variations, including those from Malaysia, Indonesia, Sri Lanka, and Singapore. Some contain other ingredients such as garlic, tomato, amchoor, kaffir lime, shrimp paste, and tamarind.

Shottsuru   A fish sauce from Japan made from the sandfish.

Sofrito   A Latin American condiment used widely in Cuban cuisine. There are many variations, but most include garlic, onions, chile peppers, and cilantro.

Tabasco   A small red pepper from the Mexican state of Tabasco, grown in Louisiana specifically for use in the pepper sauce of the same name. The McIlhenny company of Avery Island, Louisiana, combines the chiles with vinegar and salt, and ages the blend in white oak barrels for 3 years.

Tahini   A Middle Eastern paste made from sesame seeds and used as a condiment and in recipes such as hummus and halva. A similar Japanese version is called *neri-goma*.

Appendix C

Chile Pepper Guide

Chile peppers can be intimidating. Not only are they hot, but there are a lot of them, and they often look alike. In this appendix, I give you some basic chile pepper information to help you navigate through spicy recipes, as well as the chile pepper section of your market.

Commonly Used Fresh and Dried Chiles

There's no standard method of naming chiles. They could be named for a guy, a town, or a characteristic of their appearance or flavor. And if that weren't confusing enough, chiles have aliases. They can have different names in different parts of the country and even different names when fresh or dried.

One common bond among chile peppers is that they all contain *capsicum*, the compound that creates the sensation of heat on the tongue. In the early 1900s, Wilbur Scoville was the first to carefully measure the amount of heat in chiles. Here's a quick breakdown of Scoville Units (SU; higher Scoville Units exist for things like police pepper spray, but you won't be cooking with that stuff, I hope!):

Temperature	Range
Mild	0 to 2,000 SU
Moderate	2,500 to 23,000 SU
Hot	12,000 to 50,000 SU
Very hot	50,000 to 325,000 SU

Scoville measured the peppers' heat by diluting chile pepper extract with sugar until the heat was no longer detectable; today, the measuring is done with more precise methods. Despite all the technology, though, the range of heat for each chile still varies tremendously. While the Scoville Unit for a cayenne chile might register 30,000 today, next week it might register 50,000 due to variations in growing conditions, including weather, soil, and neighboring crops.

> **Hot Stuff**
>
> Capsicum can create some discomfort, especially on tender, sensitive skin. To be safe, wear gloves when chopping chiles, and keep your hands away from your eyes. Hot stuff indeed!

Chiles, both fresh and dried, have varying availability depending on where you live. Throughout the west, they can be found in most big city markets. For the rest of the world, where you might not be able to find peppers in your market, there's always the Internet. Try melissas.com for fresh and dried chiles, or chileplants.com if you want to grow your own.

Let's get to the chiles!

Anaheim

> *4 to 6 inches long, tapering to a point*
>
> *Available fresh*
>
> *Mildly hot*

Also called *California* and *Chiles Verde* when green, Anaheim chiles ripen to red, at which time they can be dried, and go by the name *California Red, Colorado,* or *California Chile Pods.* These are what you'll find inside a can of green chiles. They're just barely hotter than a bell pepper.

Ancho

> *3 to 5 inches long, triangular or heart shaped*
>
> *Available dried*
>
> *Mildly hot*

These brown, dried Poblanos are commonly used for enchilada sauce.

California Red

> *4 to 6 inches long, tapering to a point*
>
> *Available fresh and dried*
>
> *Mildly hot*

These are red Anaheims. When dried, they're often decoratively strung together.

Cascabel

> *1 or 2 inches round*
>
> *Available dried*
>
> *Very hot*

You'll know this reddish-brown dried chile when you hear it. Its seeds are loose inside and can be heard when shaken, like a bell.

Cayenne

4 or 5 inches long

Available dried

Hot

These peppers ripen green to red. They're mainly seen dried and ground.

Chiles del Arbol

2 or 3 inches long, very thin

Available dried

Very hot

These bright red chiles are quite hot and are often used in sauces, oils, and vinegars. They're also known as *bird's beak chiles*.

Chipotle

2 or 3 inches long, tapering to a point

Available dried

Hot

These are jalapeño chiles that have been smoked and dried. They are available loose or canned in adobo sauce.

Colorado

> *6 to 8 inches long, tapered*
>
> *Available fresh and dried*
>
> *Mild*

These are Anaheim chiles, ripened to red. They're also available dried and used as the base of Colorado sauce.

Guajillo

> *2 or 3 inches long, tapered to a point*
>
> *Available dried*
>
> *Hot*

This dark orange-brown chile has a fairly smooth skin and a hot but also sweet and fruity flavor.

Habanero

> *2 inches long, short, and wrinkly*
>
> *Available fresh*
>
> *Very hot*

Look out for these bright orange chiles! They're cute, but they're deadly.

Hungarian Cherry

2 inches round

Available fresh

Very hot

These can be used green, but the flavor—and heat—intensifies as the chile ripens to red.

Hungarian Yellow Wax

1 or 2 inches long, tapering to a rounded point

Available fresh

Moderately hot

If left on the vine, these chiles ripen to red. They're also called *Guero* and *banana peppers*.

Jalapeño

1 or 2 inches long, tapering to a rounded point

Available fresh

Moderately hot

The most commonly used chile, jalapeños are deep, dark green, sometimes red, and are available fresh, canned, and pickled.

Mulato

3 to 5 inches long

Available dried

Mildly hot

This deep, dark brown chile has a chocolaty flavor and is often used for mole.

New Mexico

4 to 6 inches long, curved

Available fresh and dried

Moderately hot

These chiles are green when fresh and then ripen to red. They're commonly used for chile paste and powder.

Pasilla

5 to 7 inches long, tapering to a rounded end

Available fresh and dried

Moderately hot

Also called *chilaca* when fresh and *pasilla negro* when dried, pasillas ripen to a deep green-brown.

Pequin

¹/₄ to ¹/₂ inch small ovals

Available dried

Very hot

Also called *chilepequeno* and *bird peppers*, these little red peppers are petite, but potent.

Poblano

4 inches long, tapering to a rounded end

Available fresh

Moderately hot

Poblanos ripen to dark green or brown-green and are most often used in Chiles Rellenos.

Santa Fe

4 to 6 inches long, curving to a point

Available fresh

Moderately hot

Santa Fe chiles ripen from yellow to orange and red. They're also known as *Santa Fe Grande* and *Big Jims* when they reach sizes up to 12 inches.

Scotch Bonnet

1 or 2 inches, like a squat bell pepper

Available fresh

Very hot

These bright yellow torpedoes are common in Caribbean cuisines.

Serrano

> *1 or 2 inches long, thin, and pointed*
>
> *Available fresh*
>
> *Hot*

Available both green and red, serranos are often used in Asian cuisine. They're also often used as a hotter substitute for jalapeños.

Tabasco

> *1 to 1¹/₂ inches long, very thin*
>
> *Rarely seen fresh or dried*
>
> *Hot*

Tabasco chiles ripen from yellow to red. They're used specifically to make Tabasco sauce (see Appendix B).

Thai

> *1 inch long, thin*
>
> *Available fresh*
>
> *Very hot*

Available both dark green and red, Thai chiles are smaller and hotter than serranos.

Basic Chile Preparations

The more you taste chiles, the more the variety of flavors become evident. Recipes call for specific chile blends for sauces and powders, but you can, of course, experiment. Here are a couple ways you can transform chiles in your kitchen.

Chili Paste

Dried chiles are commonly made into chili paste. Here's how to do this at home with your own peppers:

1. Toast whole chiles in a 400°F oven for 5 minutes, until they're soft and fragrant. Remove chiles from the oven and let cool. (As they cool, they should become crisp.)

2. When chiles are cool, break them open, carefully shake out all the seeds and discard them, along with the stems. Cover seeded chiles with hot water, and steep for 30 to 60 minutes.

3. Strain chiles from the steeping water and add to a blender. Purée, adding some steeping water as necessary, until a smooth purée forms.

Chili paste will hold for 2 or 3 days in the refrigerator and will freeze well for several weeks.

Chili Powder

To make your own chili powder:

1. Toast whole dried chiles in a 400°F oven for 5 minutes, until they're soft and fragrant. Remove chiles from the oven and let cool. (As they cool, they should become crisp.)

2. When chiles are cool, break them open, carefully shake out all the seeds and discard them, along with the stems.

3. Pulverize chiles in a coffee grinder to the desired consistency. Store airtight in a cool dark place.